INSOLVENCY ACT 1986

with annotations

by

Ian Fletcher, *M.A., LL.M., M.C.L., Ph.D., Barrister*
Professor of Law and Acting Head of Department of Law, University College of Wales, Aberystwyth

and

Letitia Crabb, *LL.B., LL.M., Solicitor, Lecturer in Law,*
University College of Wales, Aberystwyth

LONDON
SWEET & MAXWELL
1986

Published in 1986 by
Sweet & Maxwell Limited of,
11 New Fetter Lane, London,
and printed in Great Britain
by The Eastern Press Limited
of London and Reading

Reprinted 1987

British Library Cataloguing in Publication Data

Great Britain
  [Insolvency Act 1986]. Insolvency Act 1986.
  ——(Current law statutes annotated reprints)
  1. Bankruptcy—England
  I. [Insolvency Act 1986]   II. Title
  III. Fletcher, Ian F.   IV. Crabb, Letitia
  V. Series
  344.206'78   KD2139

ISBN 0-421-36970-1

CONTENTS

Contents

TABLE OF CASES

Table of Cases

viii

INSOLVENCY ACT 1986*

(1986 c. 45)

Tables of derivations and destinations will be found at the end of the Act. The Tables have no official status.

ARRANGEMENT OF SECTIONS

THE FIRST GROUP OF PARTS

COMPANY INSOLVENCY; COMPANIES WINDING UP

PART I

COMPANY VOLUNTARY ARRANGEMENTS

The proposal

PART II

ADMINISTRATION ORDERS

Making, etc. of administration order

---

* Annotations by Ian Fletcher, M.A., LL.M., M.C.L., Ph.D., Barrister, Professor of Law and Acting Head of Department of Law, University College of Wales, Aberystwyth; and Letitia Crabb, LL.B., LL.M., Solicitor, Lecturer in Law, University College of Wales, Aberystwyth. The annotators wish to acknowledge the assistance they derived from consultation of the Current Law annotations to those sections of the Companies Act 1985 which have been consolidated within the present Act. The annotations in question were the work of John Farrar, LL.B., LL.M., Ph.D., Professor of Law, University of Canterbury (N.Z.); and David Milman, LL.B., Ph.D., Lecturer in Law, University of Manchester.

CHAPTER IX

DISSOLUTION OF COMPANIES AFTER WINDING UP

CHAPTER X

MALPRACTICE BEFORE AND DURING LIQUIDATION;

PENALISATION OF COMPANIES AND COMPANY OFFICERS;

INVESTIGATIONS AND PROSECUTIONS

Offences of fraud, deception, etc.

Penalisation of directors and officers

Investigation and prosecution of malpractice

PART V

WINDING UP OF UNREGISTERED COMPANIES

Part VI

MISCELLANEOUS PROVISIONS APPLYING TO COMPANIES WHICH ARE INSOLVENT OR IN LIQUIDATION

Office-holders

Management by administrators, liquidators, etc.

Adjustment of prior transactions (administration and liquidation)

PART VII

INTERPRETATION FOR FIRST GROUP OF PARTS

THE SECOND GROUP OF PARTS

INSOLVENCY OF INDIVIDUALS; BANKRUPTCY

PART VIII

INDIVIDUAL VOLUNTARY ARRANGEMENTS

Moratorium for insolvent debtor

Consideration and implementation of debtor's proposal

PART IX

BANKRUPTCY

CHAPTER I

BANKRUPTCY PETITIONS; BANKRUPTCY ORDERS

Preliminary

Creditor's petition

Debtor's petition

Other cases for special consideration

Commencement and duration of bankruptcy; discharge

CHAPTER II

PROTECTION OF BANKRUPT'S ESTATE AND INVESTIGATION OF HIS AFFAIRS

CHAPTER III

TRUSTEES IN BANKRUPTCY

Tenure of office as trustee

PART XI

INTERPRETATION FOR SECOND GROUP OF PARTS

THE THIRD GROUP OF PARTS

MISCELLANEOUS MATTERS BEARING ON BOTH COMPANY AND INDIVIDUAL INSOLVENCY; GENERAL INTERPRETATION; FINAL PROVISIONS

PART XII

PREFERENTIAL DEBTS IN COMPANY AND INDIVIDUAL INSOLVENCY

PART XIII

INSOLVENCY PRACTITIONERS AND THEIR QUALIFICATION

Restrictions on unqualified persons acting as liquidator, trustee in bankruptcy, etc.

The requisite qualification, and the means of obtaining it

PART XIV

PUBLIC ADMINISTRATION (ENGLAND AND WALES)

Official receivers

The Official Petitioner

An Act to consolidate the enactments relating to company insolvency and winding up (including the winding up of companies that are not insolvent, and of unregistered companies); enactments relating to the insolvency and bankruptcy of individuals; and other enactments bearing on those two subject matters, including the functions and qualification of insolvency practitioners, the public administration of insolvency, the penalisation and redress of malpractice and wrongdoing, and the avoidance of certain transactions at an undervalue.

[25th July 1986]

INTRODUCTION AND GENERAL NOTE

The Insolvency Act 1986, which received the Royal Assent on July 25, is a major landmark in the evolution of the insolvency law of England and Wales. When the Act comes into force on December 15, 1986, the principal statutory provisions relating to both corporate and individual insolvency will for the first time be contained within a single, well-structured statute. The only significant exception to that proposition concerns the provisions relating to the disqualification of directors, which have been separately consolidated in the Company Directors Disqualification Act 1986 (c.46). Thus, the process of extricating the statutory provisions governing corporate insolvency from their traditional location within the companies legislation (itself consolidated as recently as 1985), and of uniting them with the provisions governing the insolvency of individuals, has been carried to its logical conclusion by means of two successive statutes, each bearing the title "Insolvency Act", enacted in 1985 and 1986 respectively. The Insolvency Act 1985 (referred to hereafter as "the 1985 Act") was a necessary precursor to the consolidation of this area of the law, and effected numerous reforms to, as well as extensive repeals of, the wide variety of legislative provisions then in force relating to different aspects of personal and corporate insolvency. Although certain parts of the 1985 Act were brought into force during the course of 1986, the majority of the provisions of that Act will actually come into operation in their consolidated form within the Insolvency Act 1986. The commencement section of the 1986 Act, s.443, is so designed as to bring the whole of the Act into force immediately after the moment when Part III of the 1985 Act (dealing with individual insolvency and bankruptcy) comes into force for England and Wales. Thus, unusually, the commencement of the 1986 Act will be brought about through the making of a commencment order relating to a separate statute, namely the 1985 Act, the greater part of which will furthermore be repealed by virtue of Sched. 12 to the 1986 Act immediately after the moment of entering into force.

Although the 1986 Act effects a consolidation of the law of insolvency, it does not eliminate the historic distinction under English law whereby individual and corporate insolvency are respectively dealt with by means of separate codes of law. Thus, the First Group of Parts of the Act (Parts I–VII inclusive) governs the insolvency and winding-up of companies, while the Second Group of Parts (Parts VIII–XI inclusive) governs the insolvency of individuals and bankruptcy. Matters which bear upon both company and individual insolvency, and other general and final provisions, are gathered in the Third Group of Parts (Parts XII–XIX inclusive). However, one very notable aspect of the consolidation process is the achievement of an unprecedented unity and consistency in the statutory drafting of all provisions relating to insolvency. It is of course an established convention that a consolidation Act may effect drafting amendments to the law provided that these in no way alter its substance. The preparation of the Insolvency Bill 1986 was made the responsibility of a single, experienced, Parliamentary draftsman, Mr. Godfrey Carter, (also the principal draftsman of the Companies Act 1985) who has imposed a new, logical framework upon the form and sequence of the Act as a whole, while subjecting each individual section to a thorough process of recasting and redrafting with a view to enhancing the clarity of each provision while ensuring that stylistic unity is maintained throughout. The new style of drafting has the decided merits of being more straightforward, and far less ponderous, than that in which former insolvency legislation has been cast, and should prove somewhat less daunting to the non-specialist reader.

As a consolidation measure, the Insolvency Bill 1986 enjoyed an unremarkable and tranquil passage through all Parliamentary stages, commencing with its introduction in the House of Lords on May 13. There was minimal debate upon the floor of each House, and for its committee stage the Bill was referred to the Joint Committee on Consolidated Bills, and a mere handful of drafting corrections were made. The absence of controversy or contention which thus accompanied the enactment of the Insolvency Act 1986 was in marked contrast to the atmosphere attending every stage of the proceedings on the 1985 Act. The reforms first introduced by means of that earlier measure, and now serenely consolidated within the Act of 1986, were enacted under circumstances of exceptional drama and passion which were rendered all the more remarkable by reason of their association with an area of the law traditionally regarded as remote, obscure and technical, and essentially non-political in aspect. In view of the significance of the Parliamentary proceedings relating to the 1985 Act, as compared the the bland and uninformative nature of the reported proceedings on the Act of 1986, a full set of references to the Hansard reports relating to the 1985 Act is supplied at the end of this General Introduction, in addition to the references relating to the present Act itself. It is also worthwhile to recall that the reforms embodied in the 1985 Act were the product of an extended process of re-examination of the entire working of the insolvency law which began to gain in urgency in the period from 1975 onwards, as successive phases of economic recession brought about abnormally high levels of corporate and individual financial failures. At this time, the inadequacies of the legal provisions and the administrative machinery for dealing with insolvency became increasingly exposed, producing conditions conducive to the carrying out of the first thorough reform of either branch of insolvency law to have been undertaken since the second half of the 19th century, and indeed the first ever comprehensive restatement of the insolvency law in its entirety.

In 1975 a report by "Justice", the British section of the International Commission of Jurists, made numerous proposals for reform, some of which were soon afterwards adopted in the Insolvency Act 1976. The latter was, however, a short Act of limited scope, and was essentially an interim measure to alleviate some of the law's more serious shortcomings pending a wholesale review. Another line of investigation had been pursued since 1973 in consequence of the United Kingdom's accession to membership of the European Economic Community. Among the requirements of membership it became necessary to engage in negotiations with the other Member States in relation to a Draft EEC Bankruptcy Convention (concerning allocation of jurisdiction, choice of law, and international recognition in relation to all types of cross-border insolvency). To prepare for these negotiations an Advisory Committee was appointed in 1973 under the chairmanship of Mr. Kenneth Cork (as he then was). This Committee reported in August 1976 (Cmnd. 6602), at a time when Parliament was about to conclude the process of enactment of the Insolvency Act 1976, which received the Royal Assent on November 15 of that year. The Advisory Committee's Report demonstrated in a particularly cogent manner the desirability of undertaking a rigorous reform and modernisation of our domestic insolvency laws, the better to prepare our position for the conducting of serious negotiations with our EEC partners. In recognition of the fact that such a reform was already long overdue, the Secretary of State for Trade announced in October 1976 that he was to set up a Review Committee on Insolvency Law and Practice (Hansard, H.C. Vol. 918, October 1976, written answer No. 20). This Committee was established in January 1977, again under the chairmanship of Mr. (later Sir) Kenneth Cork, with the following terms of reference:

  (i) to review the law and practice relating to insolvency, bankruptcy, liquidation and receiverships in England and Wales and to consider what reforms are necessary or desirable;
 (ii) to examine the possibility of formulating a comprehensive insolvency system and the extent to which existing procedures might, with advantage, be harmonised and integrated;
(iii) to suggest possible less formal procedures as alternatives to bankruptcy and company winding up proceedings in appropriate circumstances.
 (iv) to make recommendations.

The progress of the work of the Insolvency Law Review Committee was considerably affected by the change of Government after May 1979. As part of its general programme of scrutinising the cost-effectiveness of most aspects of public administration, the incoming Government made an approach to the Committee in August 1979 to elicit an early indication of their likely recommendations, viewed especially from the standpoint of achieving a reduction in the amount of time devoted by the personnel of the Insolvency Service to the fulfilment of their duties. In consequence, the Committee submitted an Interim Report to the Minister in October 1979, subsequently published in July 1980 (Cmnd. 7968) simultaneously with a Government Green Paper (Cmnd. 7967) purporting to respond to the intimations contained in the Interim Report. The Green Paper contained unsatisfactory and unconvincing proposals for the wholesale privatisation of insolvency procedures and was unfavourably received (see *e.g. Fletcher* (1981) 44 M.L.R. 77) and in their Final Report (see especially chap. 14) the Reivew Committee went to considerable lengths to refute the arguments previously put forward by Government for a radical re-shaping of the law in a way which would have resulted in the almost entire elimination of the active participation of the Insolvency Service. It is noteworthy that in their subsequent *White Paper, A Revised Framework for Insolvency Law* (Cmnd. 9175) of February 1984 the Government tacitly abandoned the drastic model for privatisation formulated in the *Green Paper* and indicated that other ways would be sought for achieving economies in the operation of the Insolvency Service (see especially chaps. 7 and 8, and also paras. 17–18, 71–74, 76–77, 82, 90–93, 96, 102, 105–107, 117–119, 120 and 124).

Regrettably, very little time was allowed following the publication of the *White Paper* for interested parties to submit comments before the process of drafting the Insolvency Bill was embarked upon. Neither the *Cork Report* nor the *White Paper* were the subject of any formal debate in either House of Parliament, and hence no official public proceedings took place in relation to the proposed re-shaping of the law prior to the introduction of the Insolvency Bill in the House of Lords on December 10, 1984. The deficiencies in the processes of consultation and public debate in preparation for a significant, if technical, piece of legislation to effect the first major overhaul of insolvency law for over a hundred years were undoubtedly responsible for the atmosphere of controversy and confusion which developed at successive stages over certain parts of what ought to have been a non-contentious, non-party Bill. The want of proper preparation for the introduction of the Bill furthermore resulted in the quite exceptionally high number of tabled amendments— estimated to have approached 1200 by the time of Royal Assent. A high proportion of these amendments were actually tabled by the government itself during successive stages in both Houses of Parliament. In the event, the Act did not receive Royal Assent until October 30, 1985, and was in the early stages of being brought into effect in a piecemeal fashion by means of Commencement orders made between January and May 1986 (S.I. 1986 Nos. 6, 185, 463, and 840), when the measure designed to supplant it as the Insolvency Act 1986 made its first public appearance on being presented and read for the first time in the House of Lords on May 13. The 1986 Act consists of 444 sections and 14 Schedules, and effects a consolidation (and consequential repeal) of almost the whole of the Act of 1985, together with those Parts of the Companies Act 1985 which relate to the insolvency and winding up of companies, chiefly Parts XIX, XX (apart from Chapter VI) and XXI. The Insolvency Services (Accounting and Investment) Act 1970 is also consolidated in the 1986 Act. The full list of enactments repealed is contained in Sched. 12, while Sched. 13 contains consequential amendments of the Companies Act 1985, and Sched. 14 contains consequential amendments of other enactments. Most of the statutory provisions previously in force in relation to insolvency were repealed either by the Insolvency Act 1985 (see Sched. 10 to that Act) or as a consequence of the consolidation of the Companies Acts of that same year (see Companies Consolidation (Consequential Provisions) Act 1985, Schedules 1 and 2).

The First Group of Parts

Part I. Contains the new type of company voluntary arrangement, first introduced in Chapter II of Part II of the Act of 1985, whereby a debtor company may conclude a composition of debts or scheme of arrangement of its affairs with its creditors.

Part II. Contains the new insolvency procedure known as the administration order procedure, first introduced in Chapter III of Part II of the 1985 Act, whereby the management of a failed or failing company may be placed under the control of an administrator for a period of time with a view to securing the survival of as much of the company as can be saved, or alternatively the most orderly and advantageous realisation of its assets as can be achieved.

Part III. Consolidates the law of receivership.

Chapter I. Is concerned with the law of receivers and managers in England and Wales.

Chapter II. Contains the law relating to Receivers in Scotland.

Chapter III. Deals with the cross-border operation of receivership provisions.

Part IV. Contains the law on the winding up of companies registered under the Companies Acts.

Chapter I. Specifies the different modes of winding up, and contains the statutory provisions applicable to contributories.

Chapter II. Contains the introductory and general provisions relating to voluntary winding up.

Chapter III. Contains the provisions applicable to members' voluntary winding up only.

Chapter IV. Contains the provisions applicable to creditors' voluntary winding up only.

Chapter V. Contains the provisions applying to both kinds of voluntary winding up.

Chapter VI. Contains the provisions applicable to winding up by the court (otherwise known as compulsory winding up).

Chapter VII. Deals with the appointment, removal and release of liquidators, and defines their powers and duties.

Chapter VIII. Contains provisions which are of general application to every mode of winding up.

Chapter IX. Deals with the dissolution of companies after winding up.

Chapter X. Contains provisions dealing with malpractice before and during liquidation, the penalisation of companies and company officers, and investigations and prosecutions. The respective malpractices of fraudulent trading and wrongful trading are governed by provisions within this Chapter.

Part V. Deals with the winding up of unregistered companies.

Part VI. Contains miscellaneous provisions applying to companies which are insolvent or in liquidation, and includes provisions governing entitlement of persons to hold any of the various types of office associated with company insolvency proceedings, particular powers and remedies available to office holders, and provisions regulating the adjustment of prior transactions entered into by companies which have subsequently gone into liquidation or administration.

Part VII. Is exclusively concerned with matters of interpretation relating to the First Group Of Parts.

The Second Group of Parts

Part VIII. Contains the provisions relating to the new form of voluntary arrangement, first introduced in Chapter I of Part III of the 1985 Act, whereby an individual debtor may conclude a composition of debts or scheme of arrangement of his affairs with his creditors.

Part IX. Contains the new, consolidated code of bankruptcy law, corresponding in substance to the enactments within Chapters II–VI inclusive of Part III of the 1985 Act. Among the most notable aspects of the law of bankruptcy in its newly recast state are the abolition of the concept of acts of bankruptcy and of the receiving order; new rules concerned with discharge from bankruptcy so that most first-time bankrupts will be automatically discharged after three years, or even after two in cases of summary administration; alterations in the provisions for public examination of bankrupts, so that this will only take place where the official receiver applies for one to be held; and an investigative process designed to help debtors who present their own bankruptcy petitions to explore the possibility of avoiding adjudication through some alternative procedure. There have also been important revisions to the rules defining the bankrupt's estate available for distribution to creditors, and in relation to the exemption of certain property from that category. There are special provisions regarding the position of the family home in the event of the bankruptcy of either spouse. The doctrine of reputed ownership has been abolished, as has the doctrine of relation-back of the trustees title to the bankrupt's property to a date anterior to that when the bankruptcy order is made. There is now a close parallel between the rules applicable in company insolvency and in bankruptcy whereby property which has been disposed of by the debtor at an undervalue or by way of a preference may be recovered for the benefit of the creditors. Similarly, parallel sets of rules are now applicable to enable the office holder in cases of individual or corporate insolvency to bring about the re-opening of any extortionate credit transactions into which the debtor may have entered.

Chapter I. Deals with bankruptcy petitions, bankruptcy orders and the commencement and duration of bankruptcy, including provisions concerning discharge from bankruptcy.

Chapter II. Defines the bankrupt's estate available for distribution to creditors, and also deals with the protection of the bankrupt's estate and investigation of his affairs.

Chapter III. Is concerned with the appointment, removal, replacement and release of trustees in bankruptcy, and with the control to be exercised over the trustee by a committee of creditors.

Chapter IV. Contains provisions relating to the administration of the bankruptcy by the trustee, including the acquisition, control and realisation of the bankrupt's estate, the disclaimer of onerous property and the distribution of the bankrupt's estate in accordance with the prescribed schedule of priorities.

Chapter V. Deals with the effect of bankruptcy on certain rights and transactions, including rights of occupation of the family home; the adjustment of prior transactions at an undervalue; and the avoidance of preferences.

Chapter VI. Contains the modernised code of criminal offences relating to bankruptcy.

Chapter VII. Deals with the powers of the court in bankruptcy.

Part IX. Contains general provisions relating to individual insolvency, and also includes a parallel section to that operating in company insolvency, whereby utility suppliers may be prevented from exploiting their position in such a way as to circumvent the principle of *pari passu* distribution in insolvency.

Part XI. Deals with matters of interpretation relating to the Second Group of Parts.

The Third Group of Parts

Part XII. Establishes, in conjunction with Sched. 6, the categories of preferential debts which are to apply in company and individual insolvency alike.

Part XIII. Contains the new provisions, originally introduced in Part I of the 1985 Act, regulating the provisions of the services of an insolvency practitioner, as defined in s.388, makes it a criminal offence to act as an insolvency practitioner when not qualified to do so, and prescribes the criteria to be satisfied for qualification to act as an insolvency practitioner, and the procedures whereby the necessary authorisation may be obtained.

Part XIV. Contains provisions dealing with the public administration of insolvency law in England and Wales, including provisions governing the appointment, functions and status of official receivers, and the financing of the Insolvency Service and the operation of the Insolvency Services Account.

Part XV. Contains enabling provisions under which the various forms of subordinate legislation relating to all aspects of insolvency law may be made, revised and periodically amended.

Part XVI. Contains the new provision of general law, replacing s.172 of the Law of Property Act 1925, whereby transactions defrauding creditors may be avoided and ancillary and restitutional remedies granted.

Part XVII. Contains miscellaneous and general provisions.

Part XVIII. Is concerned with matters of interpretation, in relation to expressions used generally throughtout the Act. In particular the meaning of the term "associate" is defined by s.435.

Part XIX. Contains the final provisions of the Act, including transitional provisions, savings, repeals, consequential amendments, extent, citation and commencement.

Schedule 1. Sets out the powers of an administrator or administrative receiver.

Schedule 2. Sets out the powers of a Scottish receiver.

Schedule 3. Relates to the making of orders in the course of winding up announced in vacation in Scotland.

Schedule 4. Sets out the powers of a liquidator in a winding up.

Schedule 5. Sets out the powers of a trustee in bankruptcy.

Schedule 6. Sets out the categories of preferential debts applicable in both company and individual insolvency.

Schedule 7. Is concerned with the Insolvency Practitioners Tribunal which determines cases on appeal where an authorisation to practice as an insolvency practitioner has been refused or revoked.

Schedule 8. Contains general enabling powers to authorise the making of detailed rules governing company insolvency.

Schedule 9. Contains general enabling powers to authorise the making of detailed rules governing individual insolvency.

Schedule 10. Sets out the table of punishments for all criminal offences under the Act.

Schedule 11. Contains transitional provisions and savings relating to various provisions of pre-existing legislation repealed or affected by the coming into force of this Act.

Schedule 12. Specifies the enactments repealed upon the coming into force of this Act.

Schedule 13. Sets out amendments to the Companies Act 1985 which are consequential upon this Act.

Schedule 14. Sets out consequential amendments to legislation apart from the Companies Act 1985.

PARLIAMENTARY DEBATES

Hansard: H.L. Vol. 474, col. 1038; Vol. 475, cols. 711–714; Vol. 477, cols. 420–422, 758, 1036; H.C. Vol. 120, cols. 152, 153.

PARLIAMENTARY DEBATES RELATING TO THE INSOLVENCY ACT 1985

Hansard: H.L. Vol. 458, cols. 875, 894; Vol. 459, cols. 565, 833, 835, 906, 1212, 1233; Vol. 461, col. 711; Vol. 462, cols. 11, 123, 606; Vol. 467, cols. 1093, 1188; H.C. Vol. 78, col. 141; Vol. 83. col. 526; Vol. 84, col. 677.

The Bill was considered in Committee by the House of Commons in Standing Committee E on May 14, 16, 21, 23 and 4, 6, 11, 13, 18 and 20 June, 1985.

ABBREVIATIONS

The 1985 Act: The Insolvency Act 1985. (c.65).

C.A. 1985 or *The Companies Act*: The Companies Act 1985. (c.6).

C.A. 1948: The Companies Act 1948. (c.38).

C.A. 1967: The Companies Act 1967. (c.81).

C.A. 1980: The Companies Act 1980. (c.22).

C. (F.C. & R.) (S) A. 1972: The Companies (Floating charges and Receivers) (Scotland) Act 1972. (c.76).

B.(Sc.): The Bankruptcy (Scotland) Act 1985. (c.66).

Cork Report: Final Report of the Review Committee on Insolvency Law and Practice (June 1982) Cmnd. 8558.

White Paper: A Revised Framework for Insolvency Law (February 1984) Cmnd. 9175.

THE FIRST GROUP OF PARTS

COMPANY INSOLVENCY; COMPANIES WINDING UP

PART I

COMPANY VOLUNTARY ARRANGEMENTS

The proposal

Those who may propose an arrangement

1.—(1) The directors of a company (other than one for which an administration order is in force, or which is being wound up) may make a proposal under this Part to the company and to its creditors for a composition in satisfaction of its debts or a scheme of arrangement of its affairs (from here on referred to, in either case, as a "voluntary arrangement").

(2) A proposal under this Part is one which provides for some person ("the nominee") to act in relation to the voluntary arrangement either as trustee or otherwise for the purpose of supervising its implementation; and the nominee must be a person who is qualified to act as an insolvency practitioner in relation to the company.

(3) Such a proposal may also be made—

(*a*) where an administration order is in force in relation to the company, by the administrator, and

(*b*) where the company is being wound up, by the liquidator.

DEFINITIONS
"administration order": s.8(2).
"director": s.251.
"person qualified to act as an insolvency practitioner": s.390.
"the administrator": s.8(2).
"the nominee": this section, subs. (2).
"to act as an insolvency practitioner": s.388.
"voluntary arrangement": this section, subs. (1).

GENERAL NOTE
The purpose underlying Part I (ss.1–7) is to make available a suitably simple procedure whereby a company may conclude a legally effective arrangement with its creditors. It was considered that the various procedures established under the provisions of the Companies Act 1985 (ss.425–427; 582, or 601) should be supplemented or replaced by a new procedure for voluntary arrangements, since the existing ones in practice proved cumbersome and unsuitable in the context of an attempt to rationalise the affairs of a company which is nearly or actually insolvent. The matter is discussed in section 2 of chap. 7 of the *Cork Report*. The provisions now contained in Part I broadly match the recommendations of the Cork Committee. The new procedure is so designed as to be available for use at any appropriate time, whether before or after the commencement of any proceedings whereby the company is to be wound up or an administration order employed. Ss.582 and 601 of the Companies Act 1985 are repealed by Sched. 12 to this Act. This section embodies the substance of s.20 of the 1985 Act.

Subs. (2)

Person who is qualified to act as an insolvency practitioner in relation to the company
In selecting a suitable person to occupy the position of "nominee," regard must be had both to the general requirements of s.390 with regard to qualification to act as an insolvency practitioner, and also to the possible existence of any ties or relationships between the nominee and the company which, if he were in due course to act as supervisor of the proposed arrangement, would give rise to a contravention of the rules of practice of the professional body to which he belongs, or of any regulations made under s.419 of this Act or rules made under s.10(2)(*b*) of the 1985 Act. An unqualified person who acts as supervisor of an arrangement under this Part of the Act commits a criminal offence under s.389, by virtue of the provision in s.388(1)(*b*).

Procedure where nominee is not the liquidator or administrator

2.—(1) This section applies where the nominee under section 1 is not the liquidator or administrator of the company.

(2) The nominee shall, within 28 days (or such longer period as the court may allow) after he is given notice of the proposal for a voluntary arrangement, submit a report to the court stating—

(*a*) whether, in his opinion, meetings of the company and of its creditors should be summoned to consider the proposal, and

(*b*) if in his opinion such meetings should be summoned, the date on which, and time and place at which, he proposes the meetings should be held.

(3) For the purposes of enabling the nominee to prepare his report, the person intending to make the proposal shall submit to the nominee—

(*a*) a document setting out the terms of the proposed voluntary arrangement, and

(*b*) a statement of the company's affairs containing—

(i) such particulars of its creditors and of its debts and other liabilities and of its assets as may be prescribed, and

(ii) such other information as may be prescribed.

(4) The court may, on an application made by the person intending to make the proposal, in a case where the nominee has failed to submit the report required by this section, direct that the nominee be replaced as such by another person qualified to act as an insolvency practitioner in relation to the company.

<small>DEFINITIONS</small>
"person qualified to act as an insolvency practitioner": s.390.
"prescribed": s.251.
"the administrator": s.8(2).
"the court": s.251; Companies Act 1985, s.744.
"the nominee": s.1(2).
"to act as an insolvency practitioner": s.388.

<small>GENERAL NOTE</small>
The purpose of this section, which is in substance identical to s.21 of the 1985 Act, is to ensure that any proposal for a voluntary arrangement is subjected to preliminary scrutiny by a qualified insolvency practitioner, who is required to form a professional judgment as to the soundness and feasibility of the proposal. If the company is in liquidation or is the subject of an administration order, the combined effect of subss. (1) and (3) of s.1 is that any proposal for an arrangement must be initiated by the liquidator or administrator, whose own professional judgment will inevitably have been brought to bear upon the proposal he has formulated. However if the liquidator or administrator does not intend personally to become the supervisor of the arrangement, and in all other cases where the proposal emanates from the directors pursuant to s.1(1), this section requires the nominee to pronounce his own judgment upon the proposal and report to the court, in effect, as to whether it is worthwhile taking the next immediate steps which would be required to bring the proposal into effect. The requirements of subs. (3) are designed to ensure that the nominee is able to form his judgment on the basis of sufficient information, and if in his opinion the proposal is unsound, or is unlikely to command the necessary support from the meetings of the company and of the creditors required to be convened under s.3, no further progress can be taken and the expense of holding abortive or futile meetings is thereby saved.

The terms of subs. (2) require the nominee to submit his report to the court within 28 days after receiving notice of the proposal, and in case he is unable or unwilling to do so within the time allowed, provision is made in subs. (4) for application to be made to the court for the replacement of the original nominee with some other, suitably qualified person. Such an application is to be made by the person intending to make the proposal for the voluntary arrangement.

Summoning of meetings

3.—(1) Where the nominee under section 1 is not the liquidator or administrator, and it has been reported to the court that such meetings as are mentioned in section 2(2) should be summoned, the person making the report shall (unless the court otherwise directs) summon those meetings for the time, date and place proposed in the report.

(2) Where the nominee is the liquidator or administrator, he shall summon meetings of the company and of its creditors to consider the proposal for such a time, date and place as he thinks fit.

(3) The persons to be summoned to a creditors' meeting under this section are every creditor of the company of whose claim and address the person summoning the meeting is aware.

DEFINITIONS
"the administrator": s.8(2).
"the nominee": s.1(2).

GENERAL NOTE
This makes it incumbent upon the person who has submitted a report under s.2 expressing the opinion that meetings of the company and of its creditors should be summoned, to assume responsibility for the summoning of those meetings at the time and place proposed, or otherwise according to the court's directions. The meeting of the company will be convened and conducted in accordance with the provisions contained in Chap. IV of Pt. XI of the Companies Act 1985; the convening of the creditors' meeting will take place subject to the requirement of subs. (3) indicating the persons to whom notice of the meeting must be sent. This section corresponds to s.22 of the 1985 Act.

Consideration and implementation of proposal

Decisions of meetings

4.—(1) The meetings summoned under section 3 shall decide whether to approve the proposed voluntary arrangement (with or without modifications).

(2) The modifications may include one conferring the functions proposed to be conferred on the nominee on another person qualified to act as an insolvency practitioner in relation to the company.

But they shall not include any modification by virtue of which the proposal ceases to be a proposal such as is mentioned in section 1.

(3) A meeting so summoned shall not approve any proposal or modification which affects the right of a secured creditor of the company to enforce his security, except with the concurrence of the creditor concerned.

(4) Subject as follows, a meeting so summoned shall not approve any proposal or modification under which—

(*a*) any preferential debt of the company is to be paid otherwise than in priority to such of its debts as are not preferential debts, or

(*b*) a preferential creditor of the company is to be paid an amount in respect of a preferential debt that bears to that debt a smaller proportion than is borne to another preferential debt by the amount that is to be paid in respect of that other debt.

However, the meeting may approve such a proposal or modification with the concurrence of the preferential creditor concerned.

(5) Subject as above, each of the meetings shall be conducted in accordance with the rules.

(6) After the conclusion of either meeting in accordance with the rules, the chairman of the meeting shall report the result of the meeting to the court, and, immediately after reporting to the court, shall give notice of the result of the meeting to such persons as may be prescribed.

(7) References in this section to preferential debts and preferential creditors are to be read in accordance with section 386 in Part XII of this Act.

DEFINITIONS
"administration order": s.8(2).
"modifications": s.436.
"person qualified to act as an insolvency practitioner": s.390.
"preferential creditor"; "preferential debt": s.386, Sched. 6.
"prescribed": s.251.
"secured creditor": s.248.
"the nominee": s.1(2).
"the rules": ss.251, 411.
"voluntary arrangement": s.1(1).

GENERAL NOTE

This section governs the conduct and procedure of meetings held for the purpose of deciding whether to approve the proposal for a voluntary arrangement made under s.1. There is provision in subs. (2) for the substitution of some other, qualified person to serve as the supervisor of the composition or scheme in place of the original nominee, and provision also for the effecting of modifications to the original proposal, subject to the limitation that the proposal as modified must remain compatible with the terms of s.1. The section corresponds to s.23 of the 1985 Act.

Subs. (3)

This preserves the position of any secured creditor of the company by providing that no arrangement which affects such a creditor's right to enforce his security can be approved without his consent.

Subs. (4)

This preserves the position of any preferential creditor of the company, by providing that no arrangement which affects such a creditor's right to receive payment in priority to any non-preferential debts, and in a proportion equal to that received by all other preferential creditors, can be approved without his consent.

Subs. (6)

The chairman of the meeting shall report the result . . . to the court

Note that the court itself has no further role to play in relation to the approval of the proposal, and that it does not rest with the court to decide whether the scheme shall become binding, unless some qualified party seeks to challenge the approved scheme under s.6 on either of the grounds specified in subs. (1) of that section.

Effect of approval

5.—(1) This section has effect where each of the meetings summoned under section 3 approves the proposed voluntary arrangement either with the same modifications or without modifications.

(2) The approved voluntary arrangement—

(*a*) takes effect as if made by the company at the creditors' meeting, and

(*b*) binds every person who in accordance with the rules had notice of, and was entitled to vote at, that meeting (whether or not he was present or represented at the meeting) as if he were a party to the voluntary arrangement.

(3) Subject as follows, if the company is being wound up or an administration order is in force, the court may do one or both of the following, namely—

(*a*) by order stay or sist all proceedings in the winding up or discharge the administration order;

(*b*) give such directions with respect to the conduct of the winding up or the administration as it thinks appropriate for facilitating the implementation of the approved voluntary arrangement.

(4) The court shall not make an order under subsection (3)(*a*)—

(*a*) at any time before the end of the period of 28 days beginning with the first day on which each of the reports required by section 4(6) has been made to the court, or

(*b*) at any time when an application under the next section or an appeal in respect of such an application is pending, or at any time in the period within which such an appeal may be brought.

DEFINITIONS

"administration order": s.8(2).
"modifications": s.436.
"the rules": ss.251, 411.
"voluntary arrangement": s.1(1).

This section, corresponding to s.24 of the 1985 Act, specifies the requirements for, and consequences of, the approval of a proposed voluntary arrangement. In addition to the matters mentioned in this section, by virtue of s.233(1)(c) the provisions of that section apply when a composition or scheme has taken effect through having been approved by the meetings convened under s.3.

Subs. (1)

This section has effect
This subsection introduces the crucial precondition that formal approval of a proposal put forward under this Part is dependent upon the proposal's being approved in identical terms by *both* of the meetings summoned under s.3. Only then do the effects specified in subs. (2) become operative.

Subs. (2)(b)

Binds every person who in accordance with the rules had notice of, and was entitled to vote at, that meeting
This operates in accordance with the requirement of natural justice that a person should not be bound by the outcome of a meeting of which he did not have notice, so that he lacked the opportunity to participate in its deliberations and voting. On the other hand, any person who was entitled to vote at either of the meetings convened under s.3 and who did receive notice, will be bound by the outcome regardless of whether or not he was present or represented.

Subs. (4)(a)
The delay of 28 days which must occur between the receipt by the court of the reports upon the outcome of the meetings summoned under s.3 and the making of any order under subs. (3)(a) corresponds to the interval of time allowed under s.6(3) for the bringing of any challenge under that section against the approved scheme.

Challenge of decisions

6.—(1) Subject to this section, an application to the court may be made, by any of the persons specified below, on one or both of the following grounds, namely—
  (a) that a voluntary arrangement approved at the meetings summoned under section 3 unfairly prejudices the interests of a creditor, member or contributory of the company;
  (b) that there has been some material irregularity at or in relation to either of the meetings.
  (2) The persons who may apply under this section are—
  (a) a person entitled, in accordance with the rules, to vote at either of the meetings;
  (b) the nominee or any person who has replaced him under section 2(4) or 4(2); and
  (c) if the company is being wound up or an administration order is in force, the liquidator or administrator.
  (3) An application under this section shall not be made after the end of the period of 28 days beginning with the first day on which each of the reports required by section 4(6) has been made to the court.
  (4) Where on such an application the court is satisfied as to either of the grounds mentioned in subsection (1), it may do one or both of the following, namely—
  (a) revoke or suspend the approvals given by the meetings or, in a case falling within subsection (1)(b), any approval given by the meeting in question;
  (b) give a direction to any person for the summoning of further meetings to consider any revised proposal the person who made the original proposal may make or, in a case falling within subsec-

tion (1)(*b*), a further company or (as the case may be) creditors' meeting to reconsider the original proposal.

(5) Where at any time after giving a direction under subsection (4)(*b*) for the summoning of meetings to consider a revised proposal the court is satisfied that the person who made the original proposal does not intend to submit a revised proposal, the court shall revoke the direction and revoke or suspend any approval given at the previous meetings.

(6) In a case where the court, on an application under this section with respect to any meeting—

(*a*) gives a direction under subsection (4)(*b*), or

(*b*) revokes or suspends an approval under subsection (4)(*a*) or (5),

the court may give such supplemental directions as it thinks fit and, in particular, directions with respect to things done since the meeting under any voluntary arrangement approved by the meeting.

(7) Except in pursuance of the preceding provisions of this section, an approval given at a meeting summoned under section 3 is not invalidated by any irregularity at or in relation to the meeting.

DEFINITIONS

"administration order": s.8(2).
"proposal": s.1(2).
"the administrator": s.8(2).
"the nominee": s.1(2).
"the rules": ss.251, 411.
"voluntary arrangement": s.1(1).

GENERAL NOTE

This section prescribes the steps which may be taken to challenge either the approved voluntary arrangement itself or the manner by which its approval was gained. The section also indicates which persons have standing to make application to the court by way of challenge, the grounds on which such challenge may be based, and the time limit within which the right of challenge is exercisable. Finally, the powers of the court on an application of this kind are laid down. The section corresponds to s.25 of the 1985 Act.

Subs. (1)(a)

Unfairly prejudices the interests of a creditor, member or contributory

No statutory test or guideline is laid down to indicate what degree of prejudice shall be regarded as unfair for the purposes of this subsection.

Subs. (3)

The period of 28 days

This period of time, running from the first day on which each of the reports submitted in accordance with the requirements of s.4(6) is made to the court, corresponds to the period of delay specified in s.5(4)(*a*), so that no order staying the winding up or discharging the administration order will be made by the court until the period has expired during which any qualified party could initiate a challenge to the arrangement whose approval has been reported to the court.

Subs. (7)

The wide effect of this provision ensures that, unless a challenge is mounted under the foregoing provisions of this section within the limited time allowed, an arrangement which has been ostensibly approved in the requisite manner cannot otherwise be invalidated despite the fact that at either of the meetings some irregularity may have occurred which could have formed the basis of a successful challenge, had the procedure been invoked in time.

Implementation of proposal

7.—(1) This section applies where a voluntary arrangement approved by the meetings summoned under section 3 has taken effect.

(2) The person who is for the time being carrying out in relation to the voluntary arrangement the functions conferred—

(*a*) by virtue of the approval on the nominee, or

(*b*) by virtue of section 2(4) or 4(2) on a person other than the nominee,

shall be known as the supervisor of the voluntary arrangement.

(3) If any of the company's creditors or any other person is dissatisfied by any act, omission or decision of the supervisor, he may apply to the court; and on the application the court may—

(*a*) confirm, reverse or modify any act or decision of the supervisor,

(*b*) give him directions, or

(*c*) make such other order as it thinks fit.

(4) The supervisor—

(*a*) may apply to the court for directions in relation to any particular matter arising under the voluntary arrangement, and

(*b*) is included among the persons who may apply to the court for the winding up of the company or for an administration order to be made in relation to it.

(5) The court may, whenever—

(*a*) it is expedient to appoint a person to carry out the functions of the supervisor, and

(*b*) it is inexpedient, difficult or impracticable for an appointment to be made without the assistance of the court,

make an order appointing a person who is qualified to act as an insolvency practitioner in relation to the company, either in substitution for the existing supervisor or to fill a vacancy.

(6) The power conferred by subsection (5) is exercisable so as to increase the number of persons exercising the functions of supervisor or, where there is more than one person exercising those functions, so as to replace one or more of those persons.

DEFINITIONS

"administration order": s.8(2).

"person qualified to act as an insolvency practitioner": s.390.

"the court": s.251; Companies Act 1985, s.744.

"the nominee": s.1(2).

"the supervisor of the voluntary arrangement": subs. (2).

"to act as an insolvency practitioner": s.388.

"voluntary arrangement": s.1(1).

GENERAL NOTE

This deals with the ensuing phases of implementation of an arrangement which has taken effect following approval under the foregoing sections of this Part. The formal title of "supervisor" attaches for the first time to the person who has hitherto carried out his functions in the capacity of "nominee" or as substitute for the nominee. Under ss.388(1)(*b*) and 389 it is a criminal offence for a person to act as supervisor of a composition or scheme at a time when he is not qualified to do so. Provision is made for any interested party to apply to the court in the event that the supervisor's conduct in office proves unsatisfactory, and the court enjoys overriding powers in relation to anything the supervisor may have done, and can issue directions to him as to his future conduct of his responsibilities. Correspondingly, the supervisor may take the initiative in seeking directions from the court by way of an application, and is clothed with the important right to apply for the company to be wound up or for an administration order to be made. Finally, the court enjoys the right to replace any person as supervisor, and to appoint further persons to act in that capacity either instead of or in addition to any person who may previously have exercised the functions of supervisor. This section corresponds to s.26 of the 1985 Act.

PART II

ADMINISTRATION ORDERS

Making etc. of administration order

Power of court to make order

8.—(1) Subject to this section, if the court—

(*a*) is satisfied that a company is or is likely to become unable to pay its debts (within the meaning given to that expression by section 123 of this Act), and

(*b*) considers that the making of an order under this section would be likely to achieve one or more of the purposes mentioned below,

the court may make an administration order in relation to the company.

(2) An administration order is an order directing that, during the period for which the order is in force, the affairs, business and property of the company shall be managed by a person ("the administrator") appointed for the purpose by the court.

(3) The purposes for whose achievement an administration order may be made are—

(*a*) the survival of the company, and the whole or any part of its undertaking, as a going concern;

(*b*) the approval of a voluntary arrangement under Part 1;

(*c*) the sanctioning under section 425 of the Companies Act of a compromise or arrangement between the company and any such persons as are mentioned in that section; and

(*d*) a more advantageous realisation of the company's assets than would be effected on a winding up;

and the order shall specify the purpose or purposes for which it is made.

(4) An administration order shall not be made in relation to a company after it has gone into liquidation, nor where it is—

(*a*) an insurance company within the meaning of the Insurance Companies Act 1982, or

(*b*) a recognised bank or licensed institution within the meaning of the Banking Act 1979, or an institution to which sections 16 and 18 of that Act apply as if it were a licensed institution.

DEFINITIONS

"administration order": subs. (2).

"administrator": subs. (2).

"goes into liquidation": s.247(2).

"insurance company": Insurance Companies Act 1982, ss.1, 96(1); Sched. 1, 2.

"recognised bank or licensed institution": Banking Act 1975, ss.48, 50.

"the court": s.251; Companies Act 1985, s.744.

"unable to pay its debts": subs. (1)(*a*); s.123.

TRANSITIONAL PROVISION: Sched. 11, para. 1.

GENERAL NOTE

This section, together with the following provisions contained in ss.9–27 inclusive, comprising Pt. II of the Act, establishes a new, alternative procedure for dealing with the affairs of a potentially or actually insolvent company. The procedure, known as the administration order procedure, is aimed at procuring the rehabilitation and survival of the company as a going concern or, failing that, at securing a more advantageous realisation of the company's assets than would ensue from a winding up. The procedure can also be used in conjunction with an attempt to conclude an effective composition or arrangement between the company and its creditors. The proposal to establish such an institutionalised process of "company rescue" was one of the principal innovations of the *Cork Report,* chap. 9 of which bears the heading "the Administrator," after the title proposed for the insolvency practitioner whose appointment would arise from the making of an administration order but whose task it would become to carry out the order's objectives. The Government in their White Paper voiced agreement with this proposal for a new insolvency mechanism, and in two chapters (chaps. 6 and 14 respectively, headed "the Administrator" and "the Administrator Procedure") set out their own somewhat different vision of what the procedure would involve.

The inspirational model for the administrator was the receiver and manager (henceforth to be known as an administrative receiver) appointed under a floating charge: tribute was paid in para. 495 of the *Cork Report* to the successes in terms of the rescue and rehabilitation of ailing companies, which can be achieved by a combination of skill and imagination on the part of such a receiver and manager in the exercise of the powers conferred upon him by the terms of his appointment under a suitably-drafted floating charge. The powers conferred upon the administrator by virtue of the provisions within Pt. II of the Act are deliberately analogous to those of a receiver and manager which are to be found in Chap. I of Pt. III, although the basis of his appointment, and the formulation of the task with which he is entrusted, differ from those associated with the exercise of rights enjoyed by an individual creditor whose debt is secured by means of a floating charge. This section corresponds to s.27 of the 1985 Act.

Subs. (1)

This subsection indicates the circumstances in which the court is empowered to make an administration order in relation to a company.

The court may make an administration order

The terms of this subsection are permissive, not mandatory, and the court's powers in this respect are exercisable at its own discretion. The circumstances in which the court's discretion to make an administration order becomes exercisable are specified in paragraphs (*a*) and (*b*) of the subsection in the form of a compound requirement, each limb of which must be satisfied. The first precondition, expressed in para. (*a*), is that the court must be satisfied that the company is, or is likely to become, unable to pay its debts. The subsection incorporates by reference the definition of inability to pay debts which is embodied in s.123 of the Act. Thus any circumstances or facts which would render it possible for the company to be wound up by the court under s.122(1)(*f*) of the Act may in the alternative be utilised as the basis for making an administration order if application for this alternative species of order is duly made under s.9.

The second precondition to the court's being at liberty to make an administration order is contained in para. (*b*) which stipulates that the court must form the opinion that the making of such an order would be likely to promote one or more of the alternative purposes mentioned in paras. (*a*)–(*d*) inclusive of subs. (3). These grounds represent a relatively restricted approach to the operability of the administrator procedure as compared with the more open-ended vision of the authors of the *Cork Report* and are indeed more restrictively framed than the terms of the *White Paper* suggested they would be. Indeed, para. 506 of the *Cork Report* ventured the suggestion that it would be unwise to prescribe in legislative form the exact circumstances under which it would be expedient to appoint an administrator. Nevertheless, both the *Report* and the *White Paper* (para. 151) went on to declare, in almost identical terms, that a court should not consider appointing an administrator unless either of two alternative propositions was established. While the first alternative effectively corresponds to the "purpose" expressed in subs. (3)(*a*), there is no direct statutory equivalent of the second one, namely that "the interests of creditors, shareholders, employees or other interested parties would be better served by an administration order rather than some form of insolvency proceedings." The "purpose" currently expressed in subs. (3)(*d*) is at once more narrow and more specific than that.

Subs. (2)

This subsection supplies the statutory definition of the related terms "administrator" and "administration order." The subsection simply establishes an association between these two new terms of insolvency law and renders it necessary to infer that "the administrator" means "the person appointed by the court under an administration order for the purpose of managing the affairs, business and property of the company during the period for which the order is in force."

Subs. (4)

An administration order shall not be made . . .

In addition to the requirements imposed by way of precondition by the combined provisions of subs. (1) and subs. (3), the opening words of the former have the further effect that an administration order cannot be made in relation to a company if any of the three alternative propositions expressed in subs. (4) is true of it.

After the company has gone into liquidation
The unqualified terms of this proposition have the effect of precluding the making of an administration order after the company has already gone into any form of liquidation. The statutory meaning of the expression "goes into liquidation" is given in s.247(2).

(a) Where the company is an insurance company
The reason for this exclusion, given in para. 35 of the *White Paper,* is that such companies are the subject of special requirements in the Insurance Companies legislation, so that separate consideration will need to be given to the practicability of extending the administrator procedure to companies of this kind. Such a development, if it eventually takes place, will be effected by an amendment to the Insurance Companies legislation itself.

Finally, it may be noted that a further, mandatory ground on which the court's power to make an administration order is taken away arises from the provisions of s.9(3) which impose a mandatory obligation to dismiss the applications for an administration order in the circumstances there described.

Application for order

9.—(1) An application to the court for an administration order shall be by petition presented either by the company or the directors, or by a creditor or creditors (including any contingent or prospective creditor or creditors), or by all or any of those parties, together or separately.

(2) Where a petition is presented to the court—
(*a*) notice of the petition shall be given forthwith to any person who has appointed, or is or may be entitled to appoint, an administrative receiver of the company, and to such other persons as may be prescribed, and
(*b*) the petition shall not be withdrawn except with the leave of the court.

(3) Where the court is satisfied that there is an administrative receiver of the company, the court shall dismiss the petition unless it is also satisfied either—
(*a*) that the person by whom or on whose behalf the receiver was appointed has consented to the making of the order, or
(*b*) that, if an administration order were made, any security by virtue of which the receiver was appointed would—
   (i) be liable to be released or discharged under sections 238 to 240 in Part VI (transactions at an undervalue and preferences),
   (ii) be avoided under section 245 in that Part (avoidance of floating charges), or
   (iii) be challengeable under section 242 (gratuitous alienations) or 243 (unfair preferences) in that Part, or under any rule of law in Scotland.

(4) Subject to subsection (3), on hearing a petition the court may dismiss it, or adjourn the hearing conditionally or unconditionally, or make an interim order or any other order that it thinks fit.

(5) Without prejudice to the generality of subsection (4), an interim order under that subsection may restrict the exercise of any powers of the directors or of the company (whether by reference to the consent of the court or of a person qualified to act as an insolvency practitioner in relation to the company, or otherwise).

DEFINITIONS
"administration order": s.8(2).
"administrative receiver": ss.29(2), 51, 251.
"person qualified to act as an insolvency practitioner": s.390.
"prescribed": s.251.

"the court": s.251; Companies Act 1985, s.744.
"to act as an insolvency practitioner": s.388.

GENERAL NOTE
This provision describes how an administration order may be obtained, the prescribed procedure being the presentation of a petition to the court by all or any of the parties referred to in subs. (1). There is also an important safeguard in subs. (3) to ensure that the position of a creditor who has appointed an administrative receiver of the company cannot be eroded against his will, unless that creditor's security is impeachable.

As was observed in the General Note to s.8 the inspiration of the development of the administrator procedure was derived in part from the appreciation of the constructive role capable of being played by a receiver and manager (henceforth to be known as an administrative receiver) where one can be appointed. The main purpose of the new procedure is therefore to ensure that such a rehabilitative programme can be undertaken in relation to any company able to benefit therefrom, regardless of whether there happens to exist a floating charge under whose terms an administrative receiver could be appointed by the creditor in whose favour the charge was created. It is not however part of the legislative intention to undercut the position of any creditor who takes a floating charge in this way, because the right to appoint a receiver is an integral aspect of the security device itself, and its erosion would have wide and serious implications for the whole realm of credit and security. Therefore, in line with the proposal in para. 153 of the *White Paper* (with which *cf.* the notably less absolute terms of paras. 503–504 of the *Cork Report*), subs. (3) protects the position of a debenture holder who has already appointed an administrative receiver by the time that an application for an administration order is heard by the court. In such circumstances the court is required to dismiss the application unless the debenture holder is prepared to consent in the making of an administration order. However, if it can be shown that the security on which the debenture holder's position is based is in reality capable of being overturned by virtue of either ss.238–240, 242, 243 or 245 of the Act, the court remains free to proceed at its discretion to make an administration order. Thereafter by virtue of s.11(3)(*b*) the right of any holder of a floating charge to appoint an administrative receiver becomes suspended for the period during which the order is in force. Bearing in mind that the provisions contained in Pt. III of the Act have in part the effect of ensuring that the duties of the administrative receiver will in future be owed on a more generally conceived basis than hitherto, the attempt has been made to strike a balance between the interests of the various parties involved, namely the debenture holder, the general body of creditors and the company itself, its members and its employees. This section corresponds to s.28 of the 1985 Act.

Subs. (1)

Application to the court
By virtue of s.251 any expression for whose interpretation provision is made in Pt. XXVI of the Companies Act and for which no definition is supplied by s.251 of this Act, is to be construed in accordance with the provision contained in the Companies Act. Hence the expression "court" should be understood in the sense laid down by s.744 of the Companies Act, namely "the court having jurisdiction to wind up the company."

The directors of the company are included among the various parties or combinations of parties on whom this subsection confers the right to make application for an administration order. There is no requirement that the directors need first obtain the endorsement of a general meeting of members before they present an application for an administration order. However, the drafting confines the right to make such application to the board of directors acting collectively and denies an individual director the standing to do so on his own. Nevertheless, if one or more individual directors vainly seek to persuade their colleagues that an administration order should be applied for, their actions may be of some significance from the aspect of their personal position and potential liability should the company subsequently pass into liquidation. This is because in determining a director's responsibility for a company's wrongful trading the court is required by s.214(3) to have regard to the steps taken by him with a view to minimising the potential loss to creditors. The fact that any of the directors is or are on record as having advocated recourse to the administration order procedure should help to ensure that the directors concerned are absolved from the sanctions and disabilities which are inflicted upon their colleagues on the board.

It may be noted that the suggestions in the *Cork Report* (para. 500) that a petition for an administration order should also be capable of being presented by the Secretary of State for Trade, or that the court should be empowered to make such an appointment *proprio motu* in lieu of an order for winding up (para. 510), were not adopted in the *White Paper* nor incorporated into the Act.

Subs. (2)

Notice of the petition

The requirement that notice of the presentation of a petition for an administration order must be given forthwith to any debenture holder (and to any other persons to be prescribed in the rules) is a necessary counterpart to the provisions in subs. (3)(*a*) whereby such persons are effectively enabled to prevent the court from making the order by the act of withholding their consent thereto. At the hearing of the petition it will be necessary to satisfy the court that the debenture holder has positively consented to the making of the order, otherwise the court is obliged to dismiss the petition. It is made a statutory duty that the requisite notice must be given "forthwith," but no indication is given as to who is required to give the notice although it is perhaps implicit that this duty is incumbent upon the party by whom the petition is presented. More detailed provision as to the manner in which such notice is to be given to debenture holders will be embodied in the company insolvency rules. The subsection is also silent as to whether, in the event that the petition for an administration order is presented by one or more creditors, there is any formal requirement that notice of the petition be sent to the company itself, in order that it may appear and be represented at the actual hearing by the court. This elementary requirement of justice, which was expressly proposed in para. 502 of the *Cork Report,* is a matter for which provision will be made in the insolvency rules and is presaged by the concluding reference to the giving of notice to "such other persons as may be prescribed."

Subs. (2)(b)

This provision enables the court to deal in an appropriate way with any petitions which prove to be vexatious or frivolous.

Subs. (3)(a)

The person . . . has consented to the making of the order

These words render it essential that the debenture holder by or on behalf of whom an administrative receiver was appointed must actually have given his positive consent to the making of an administration order. It would not be sufficient for the petitioner to show merely that the debenture holder has not expressed his dissent to the making of an administration order. However the position of a debenture holder who is merely entitled to appoint an administrative receiver but who has not yet done so by the time the petition for an administration order is heard, is not protected by this subsection. Earlier versions of the corresponding provision in the Insolvency Bill of 1984–85, which also gave such creditors a power of veto over the making of an administration order, were modified during the successive phases of transformation undergone by the 1985 Act during its passage through Parliament, with the result that a protected position is enjoyed only by a debenture holder who has actually appointed a receiver by the time of the hearing of the petition for an administration order.

Subss. (4), (5)

These provisions indicate that, apart from those cases where by virtue of subs. (3) the court is under a mandatory obligation to dismiss the petition, it enjoys a range of discretionary powers enabling it to respond to and deal with the instant case in the light of all the various interests involved.

Effect of application

10.—(1) During the period beginning with the presentation of a petition for an administration order and ending with the making of such an order or the dismissal of the petition—

    (*a*) no resolution may be passed or order made for the winding up of the company;

    (*b*) no steps may be taken to enforce any security over the company's property, or to repossess goods in the company's possession under any hire-purchase agreement, except with the leave of the court and subject to such terms as the court may impose; and

    (*c*) no other proceedings and no execution or other legal process may be commenced or continued, and no distress may be levied, against the company or its property except with the leave of the court and subject to such terms as aforesaid.

(2) Nothing in subsection (1) requires the leave of the court—

(a) for the presentation of a petition for the winding up of the company,

(b) for the appointment of an administrative receiver of the company, or

(c) for the carrying out by such a receiver (whenever appointed) of any of his functions.

(3) Where—

(a) a petition for an administration order is presented at a time when there is an administrative receiver of the company, and

(b) the person by or on whose behalf the receiver was appointed has not consented to the making of the order,

the period mentioned in subsection (1) is deemed not to begin unless and until that person so consents.

(4) References in this section and the next to hire-purchase agreements include conditional sale agreements, chattel leasing agreements and retention of title agreements.

(5) In the application of this section and the next to Scotland, references to execution being commenced or continued include references to diligence being carried out or continued, and references to distress being levied shall be omitted.

DEFINITIONS

"administration order": s.8(2).
"administrative receiver": ss.29(2), 51, 251.
"chattel leasing agreement": s.251.
"conditional sale agreement": s.436; Consumer Credit Act 1974, s.198(1).
"hire purchase agreement": subs. (4); s.436; Consumer Credit Act 1974, s.189(1).
"property": s.436.
"retention of title agreement": s.251.

GENERAL NOTE

This section has the effect of imposing a moratorim over the company's affairs during the period between the date of presentation of a petition for an administration order and the date on which the court either makes the order sought or dismisses the petition. In particular no steps may be taken during that time to bring about the winding up of the company by means of a resolution for voluntary winding up, and no order for compulsory winding up may be made, although a winding up petition may be presented during this period. Simultaneously creditors' rights to enforce any security or charge, or to commence or continue other remedies or proceedings against the company or its property, can only be exercised with the leave of the court and subject to terms. This section corresponds to s.29 of the 1985 Act.

Subs. (1)

This provision defines the period of time during which a moratorium or "freeze" is imposed upon certain important aspects of the company's affairs, and also specifies the matters to which the "freezing" effect is applicable. As to the former, the period of time commences with the presentation (by a duly qualified party) of a petition for an administration order, and ends when the court disposes of the application by either making an administration order or dismissing the petition. As to the latter, the proceedings or steps which are forbidden to be taken during the aforesaid period are specified in paras. (a), (b) and (c) which are so drafted as to represent an exhaustive list of matters to which the "freeze" applies. Para. (a) prevents the company itself from passing a resolution for winding up (under s.84 of the Act), and also prevents any court before which proceedings for compulsory winding up of the company are already in progress from making an order for winding up. Since the paragraph contains no reference to the stage at which winding up proceedings may have arrived by the time the petition for an Administration Order is presented, it is accordingly possible for such a "stay of execution" to be attained through the taking of the requisite steps even at the very eleventh hour provided that the court before which winding up proceedings are in progress has not actually made an order for the winding up of the company. However as the petition for an Administration Order is presented to the court with jurisdiction to wind up the company it should be possible to dispose relatively speedily of any petition which is apparently presented (*e.g.* by the directors) for the purpose of delaying the making of an order for winding up.

Subs. (1)(b)

No steps may be taken

This subsubsection lists certain procedural steps which might otherwise be taken by creditors in relation to property belonging to or in the possession of the company, and which are forbidden to be taken without the leave of the court during the period for which the "freeze" is effective. These are, any steps to enforce any charge on or security over the company's property or steps to repossess any goods in the possession of the company under any retention of title agreement or under any hire purchase agreement, conditional sale agreement or chattel leasing agreement (the latter two types of agreement, and also the first type, being incorporated into the scope of this paragraph by virtue of subs. (4)).

Hire-purchase agreement

This is defined by s.189(1) of the Consumer Credit Act 1974 as "an agreement, other than a conditional sale agreement, under which (a) goods are bailed or (in Scotland), hired in return for periodical payments by the person to whom they are bailed or hired, and (b) the property in the goods will pass to the person if the terms of the agreement are complied with and one or more of the following occurs: (i) the exercise of an option to purchase by that person: (ii) the doing of any other specified act by any party to the agreement; (iii) the happening of any other specified event."

Conditional sale agreement

This is also defined by s.189(1) of the Consumer Credit Act 1984 and means "an agreement for the sale of goods or land under which the purchase price or part of it is payable by instalments, and the property in the goods or land is to remain in the seller (notwithstanding that the buyer is to be in possession of the goods or land) until such conditions as to the payment of instalments or otherwise as may be specified in the agreement are fulfilled."

Chattel leasing agreement

This is defined in s.251 as "an agreement for the bailment, or in Scotland, the hiring of goods, which is capable of subsisting for more than three months."

Retention of title agreement

This is defined in s.251 as "an agreement for the sale of goods to a company, being an agreement (*a*) which does not constitute a charge on the goods; but (*b*) under which, if the seller is not paid and the company is wound up, the seller will have priority over all other creditors of the company as respects the goods or any property representing the goods."

If the court grants the requisite leave to a creditor to whom the provisions of this paragraph apply, terms may be attached to the granting of leave, at the court's unfettered discretion.

Subs. (1)(c) No other proceedings . . .

This is so drafted as to give rise to a comprehensive prohibition against the commencement or continuation without the leave of the court of any other species of proceedings, or execution or other legal process, against the company apart from those already specifically covered by para. (*b*). However, the potential effects of this form of drafting are cut back by subs. (2), which excludes the three types of act therein described from being caught by the "freeze" imposed by subs. (1). Thus a petition for winding up the company may be presented (albeit the court may not make an order until the administration order application has been disposed of) and a debenture holder may appoint an administrative receiver of the company (by availing himself of the protection afforded by s.9(3)). It should be noted, however, that if a person entitled to appoint an administrative receiver does not avail himself of this final opportunity to do so following the presentation of a petition for an administration order, he will thereafter lose the right to resort to this remedy during the period for which the order is in force: s.11(3)(*b*).

Subs. (3)

The suspension introduced by this provision with regard to the commencement of the period of moratorium over the company's affairs is a logical counterpart to the provision in s.9(3) whereby the court is obliged to dismiss the petition at the eventual hearing if the consent of the debenture holder has not by then been obtained.

Effect of order

11.—(1) On the making of an administration order—

(*a*) any petition for the winding up of the company shall be dismissed, and

(*b*) any administrative receiver of the company shall vacate office.

(2) Where an administration order has been made, any receiver of part of the company's property shall vacate office on being required to do so by the administrator.

(3) During the period for which an administration order is in force—

(*a*) no resolution may be passed or order made for the winding up of the company;

(*b*) no administrative receiver of the company may be appointed;

(*c*) no other steps may be taken to enforce any security over the company's property, or to repossess goods in the company's possession under any hire-purchase agreement, except with the consent of the administrator or the leave of the court and subject (where the court gives leave) to such terms as the court may impose; and

(*d*) no other proceedings and no execution or other legal process may be commenced or continued, and no distress may be levied, against the company or its property except with the consent of the administrator or the leave of the court and subject (where the court gives leave) to such terms as aforesaid.

(4) Where at any time an administrative receiver of the company has vacated office under subsection (1)(*b*), or a receiver of part of the company's property has vacated office under subsection (2)—

(*a*) his remuneration and any expenses properly incurred by him, and

(*b*) any indemnity to which he is entitled out of the assets of the company,

shall be charged on and (subject to subsection (3) above) paid out of any property of the company which was in his custody or under his control at that time in priority to any security held by the person by or on whose behalf he was appointed.

(5) Neither an administrative receiver who vacates office under subsection (1)(*b*) nor a receiver who vacates office under subsection (2) is required on or after so vacating office to take any steps for the purpose of complying with any duty imposed on him by section 40 or 59 of this Act (duty to pay preferential creditors).

DEFINITIONS

"administration order": s.8(2).
"administrative receiver": ss.29(2), 51, 251.
"administrator": s.8(2).
"chattel leasing agreement": ss.10(4), 251.
"conditional sale agreement": ss.10(4), 436; Consumer Credit Act 1974, s.189(1).
"hire purchase agreement": ss.10(4), 436; Consumer Credit Act 1974, s.189(1).
"receiver": s.251.
"retention of title agreement": ss.10(4), 251.

GENERAL NOTE

The provisions of this section are applicable in most cases where the court makes an administration order in response to a petition presented under s.9. They have the effect in the first place of maintaining the general moratorium over the company's affairs which by virtue of s.10 commences with the presentation of the petition. To a certain extent therefore the provisions of s.11 simply complement those of s.10, but in certain other respects they go further. Thus under subss. (3)(*a*), (*c*) and (*d*), for the duration of the administration order remaining in force no steps may be taken to bring about the winding up of the company, and no steps to enforce any charge or security or to repossess goods may be taken, and no other proceedings or execution may be commenced or continued against the company or its property except with the consent of the administrator or the leave of the court, and subject to any terms which the court may impose. While these stipulations closely match those to be found in s.10, there is an additional stipulation in sub. (*b*) to forbid the appointment of an administrative receiver after an administration order has been made (in contrast to the position which obtains up until that moment by virtue of s.10(2)(*b*)). Moreover the sweeping provisions of subss. (1) and (2) have the effect that, once an administration order is made, other insolvency procedures are rendered inapplicable, any winding up petition must be dismissed and any administrative receiver must vacate the office, as must any receiver of part of the company's property if so required by the administrator, thus leaving the administrator himself free to embark upon his duties. This section corresponds to s.30 of the 1985 Act.

Subs. (1)(b)

Any administrative receiver of the company shall vacate office
A debenture holder who has appointed an administrative receiver before a petition for an administration order is presented, or who appoints one subsequently when still able to do so by virtue of s.10(2)(*b*), will not suffer any loss of protection because s.9(3) renders it obligatory for the court to dismiss the application for an administration order unless the consent of the debenture holder has been given to the making of the order. However, any debenture holder whose consent is sought should be aware of the consequences from his point of view, for not only must the administrative receiver whom he has appointed vacate office under this subsection, but by subs. (2)(*b*) no other appointment of an administrative receiver may be made for so long as the administration order is in force. This is the necessary corollary to the careful protection of the debenture holder's position and expectations maintained by the provisions of s.9(2)(*a*) and (3), and 10(2)(*b*): having been given due notice of the petition for an administration order, together with the opportunity to prevent the order from being made, a debenture holder who has elected instead to allow the administration order procedure to be embarked upon is not allowed to renege upon that decision until the administration order has run its course.

Subs. (3)(c)

Hire-purchase agreement
By virtue of s.10(4) this term is to be taken as referring also to conditional sale agreements, chattel leasing agreements and retention of title agreements. The statutory definitions of all four terms are reproduced above in the note to s.10(2)(*b*).

Subs. (3)(d)

No execution
By virtue of s.10(5), in relation to Scotland this term is to be construed as a reference to diligence.

Notification of order

12.—(1) Every invoice, order for goods or business letter which, at a time when an administration order is in force in relation to a company, is issued by or on behalf of the company or the administrator, being a document on or in which the company's name appears, shall also contain the administrator's name and a statement that the affairs, business and property of the company are being managed by the administrator.

(2) If default is made in complying with this section, the company and any of the following persons who without reasonable excuse authorises or permits the default, namely, the administrator and any officer of the company, is liable to a fine.

DEFINITIONS
"a fine": s.430; Sched. 10.
"administration order": s.8(2).

"administrator": s.8(2).
"business": s.436.
"officer of the company . . . in default": s.430(5).
"property": s.436.

GENERAL NOTE

This section is designed to ensure that persons dealing with the company during the period when an administration order is in force are furnished with proper notification of the fact that its affairs are being managed by an administrator, notice to that effect being required to be contained in every document bearing the company's name which is employed in business transactions. It is closely modelled upon the provision now contained in s.39 of the Act regarding notification of the appointment of a receiver and manager. The requirement of notice is especially important in that it enables any party dealing with the company to assess the implications of dealing with the company on credit terms, since it is necessary to contemplate the possibility that the administrator may not succeed in his basic objectives, and that the company may subsequently pass into an insolvent liquidation. The seriousness of the need to ensure that proper notification is given to parties dealing with the company is indicated by the fact that the sanction of criminality is employed as the means of seeking to ensure compliance with this requirement. Moreover the very fact that any default has been made constitutes an offence on the part of the company, irrespective of whether the person actually responsible for the act in question had a reasonable excuse or not. This section corresponds to s.31 of the 1985 Act.

Subs. (1)

Invoice, order for goods or business letter

The requirement concerning notification applies only in relation to three specified types of business document, and only where the company's name appears on or in the document in question. Thus a purely oral communication—or one conveyed by means of a telegram, telemessage or telex—would seem to be exempt from the requirements of this section whether the company's name is mentioned therein or not. So, too, would any business document which did not take the form of either an "invoice, order for goods or business letter", for example a receipt, a catalogue or brochure, or even a cheque. Moreover even a business document which did assume the form of an invoice, order for goods or business letter would be outside the ambit of the section, provided that the company's name itself did not appear. It will be a matter of integrity however for the person acting as administrator—mindful, naturallv, of the criteria attaching to the obtaining and retention of a licence to act as an insolvency practitioner—to ensure that during the period in which the management of the company's affairs, business and property is his responsibility nothing is done which contravenes the spirit, as well as the letter, of this section of the Act. Contrast may be made, however, with the far wider terms of s.349 of the Companies Act in relation to the requirement that the company's name must appear in legible characters on all letters, notices and other official publications of the company.

At a time when an administration order is in force

This further delimits the requirement of notification in terms of the time during which any failure in respect of notification will give rise to the commission of a criminal offence. The section requires that the offending document must be "issued" at a time when an administration order is in force. Therefore if no such order was in force at the time when the document was "issued" (a term whose legal meaning is not defined in the Act), no offence will be committed even though, quite possibly, the order may have come into force by the time that the document is received or read by a party to whom notice of the administration order would be of relevance or interest.

Being a document on or in which the company's name appears

Any attempt to evade the operation of this subsection by omitting to mention the company's name on or in a document belonging to one of the three categories to which the requirement of notification attaches would at any rate give rise to the commission of an offence under s.349 of the Companies Act, which imposes the requirement that the company's name must appear in legible characters in a wide variety of documents including all business letters of the company, all orders for money or goods, and all bills of parcels, invoices, receipts and letters of credit of the company. The maximum fines which, by virtue of this provision of the Companies Act, may be imposed upon the company, or upon any officer of the company responsible for the contravention in question, are £400 in respect of each party liable, as specified by Sched. 24 to the Companies Act.

Subs. (2)

The company . . . is liable
It is apparently not open to the company to plead, in defence to a prosecution under this section, that the person by whom the default was authorised or permitted had a reasonable excuse for the action taken, even where that excuse results in the person in question escaping from conviction in the selfsame case.

Without reasonable excuse
These words relate solely to the persons subsequently referred to specifically as being liable to commit an offence under this section, namely the administrator and any officer of the company. These persons may therefore avoid criminal liability if they are able to furnish a reasonable excuse for their actions. It further follows from the wording of this subsection that if the default occurs through the action of some other person apart from the administrator or an officer of the company, and is done without the permission of any of the persons named in subs. (2), no criminal liability is incurred by any individual.

A fine
See Sched. 10 to the Act, and the General Note thereto, for information as to the maximum amount of the fine which may be imposed in respect of this offence.

Administrators

Appointment of administrator

13.—(1) The administrator of a company shall be appointed either by the administration order or by an order under the next subsection.

(2) If a vacancy occurs by death, resignation or otherwise in the office of the administrator, the court may by order fill the vacancy.

(3) An application for an order under subsection (2) may be made—

(*a*) by any continuing administrator of the company; or

(*b*) where there is no such administrator, by a creditors' committee established under section 26 below; or

(*c*) where there is no such administrator and no such committee, by the company or the directors or by any creditor or creditors of the company.

DEFINITIONS
"administration order": s.8(2).
"administrator": s.8(2).
"creditors' committee": s.26(1).

GENERAL NOTE
This provision governs the basis and mode of appointment of an administrator, and also empowers the court to fill a vacancy in the office of administrator arising after the making of the original administration order. The section corresponds to s.32 of the 1985 Act.

General powers

14.—(1) The administrator of a company—

(*a*) may do all such things as may be necessary for the management of the affairs, business and property of the company, and

(*b*) without prejudice to the generality of paragraph (*a*), has the powers specified in Schedule 1 to this Act;

and in the application of that Schedule to the administrator of a company the words "he" and "him" refer to the administrator.

(2) The administrator also has power—

(*a*) to remove any director of the company and to appoint any person to be a director of it, whether to fill a vacancy or otherwise, and (*b*) to call any meeting of the members or creditors of the company.

(3) The administrator may apply to the court for directions in relation to any particular matter arising in connection with the carrying out of his functions.

(4) Any power conferred on the company or its officers, whether by this Act or the Companies Act or by the memorandum or articles of association, which could be exercised in such a way as to interfere with the exercise by the administrator of his powers is not exercisable except with the consent of the administrator, which may be given either generally or in relation to particular cases.

(5) In exercising his powers the administrator is deemed to act as the company's agent.

(6) A person dealing with the administrator in good faith and for value is not concerned to inquire whether the administrator is acting within his powers.

DEFINITIONS
"administrator": s.8(2).
"business": s.436.
"property": s.436.

GENERAL NOTE
The purpose of this section is to establish the scope and extent of the powers enjoyed by an administrator upon appointment. Effectively, in conjunction with s.17, it provides for the powers and duties of the directors of the company to become exclusively exercisable by the administrator during the period for which the administration order is in force. The administrator thus occupies a position in relation to the company similar to that of an administrative receiver appointed under a floating charge. Although the directors are not automatically dismissed by virtue of the making of the order, their powers are suspended and the administrator has the power, under subs. (2)(*a*), to remove any director and to appoint any person to be a director either in place of or in addition to the members of the existing management team. The sweeping terms of the general powers described in subs. (1)(*a*) are supplemented by the specific provisions of Sched. 1 to the Act, which is made applicable to administrators by virtue of subs. (1)(*b*). An overriding statutory rule is embodied in subs. (4) to prevent any provision being inserted in the company's own memorandum or articles so as to create an impediment to an administrator's freedom of action. It may be noted besides that, although the directors are deprived of their powers of management during the period for which the administration order is in force, their statutory duties—such as the requirement to make annual returns—are not suspended, so that they remain responsible for the timely performance of these matters (*cf.* H.C. Standing Committee E, June 20, 1985, Col. 497). This section corresponds to s.33 of the 1985 Act.

Subs (2)(b)

Power . . . to call any meeting of the members or creditors of the company
The purpose of this power is to enable the administrator to consult creditors and members on matters of importance, and on which their assent is felt to be desirable. One such occasion would occur if, the rehabilitation of the company having been accomplished, the administrator were to prepare the way for his own discharge from office by seeking the confirmation by a meeting of the members of the company of the board of directors he had assembled to resume responsibility for the company's affairs following his departure. At the same time, a meeting of creditors could be convened so as to inform them of the impending development, and to ensure that the new board would command the confidence of the still-unpaid creditors.

Subs. (5)
This provision places the administrator in the same legal position as an administrative receiver in that all his actions in exercise of his official powers are deemed to be performed as agent on behalf of the company, which is thus bound by all that he does and which consequently incurs liability in respect of every action taken by the administrator. However, in contrast to the provisions of s.44 which apply to an administrative receiver, there is no statutory provision to the effect that an administrator contracts with personal liability. Such

liability will therefore only arise if there is an express term to that effect in the contract entered into by the administrator as agent of the company.

Subs. (6)

A person dealing with the administrator in good faith and for value

This provision is designed to protect a third party dealing with the administrator in the manner specified, if it should transpire that the act or transaction was one which the administrator in reality had no power to perform. Thus neither the company nor the administrator are able to raise a defence that his act was *ultra vires*. No presumption is expressed to apply in relation to the aspect of good faith, nor as to the question whether value was given, and it will therefore be incumbent upon the third party claiming the protection of the subsection to establish that he did act in good faith, and that the transaction took place for value. The position can thus be contrasted with that arising under s.35 of the Companies Act (formerly s.9(1) of the European Communities Act 1972), which prevents the defence of *ultra vires* being raised against a person dealing with the company in good faith. Moreover a presumption is established by the terms of s.35(2) of the Companies Act to the effect that a person dealing with a company is to be deemed to have acted in good faith unless the contrary is proved, for the purpose of his being able to enjoy the benefit of the protection to which that section gives rise in cases where the transaction in question was one which it either lay outside the capacity of the company to enter into, or lay outside the power of the directors to bind the company thereto.

Power to deal with charged property, etc.

15.—(1) The administrator of a company may dispose of or otherwise exercise his powers in relation to any property of the company which is subject to a security to which this subsection applies as if the property were not subject to the security.

(2) Where, on an application by the administrator, the court is satisfied that the disposal (with or without other assets) of—

(*a*) any property of the company subject to a security to which this subsection applies, or

(*b*) any goods in the possession of the company under a hire-purchase agreement,

would be likely to promote the purpose or one or more of the purposes specified in the administration order, the court may by order authorise the administrator to dispose of the property as if it were not subject to the security or to dispose of the goods as if all rights of the owner under the hire-purchase agreement were vested in the company.

(3) Subsection (1) applies to any security which, as created, was a floating charge; and subsection (2) applies to any other security.

(4) Where property is disposed of under subsection (1), the holder of the security has the same priority in respect of any property of the company directly or indirectly representing the property disposed of as he would have had in respect of the property subject to the security.

(5) It shall be a condition of an order under subsection (2) that—

(*a*) the net proceeds of the disposal, and

(*b*) where those proceeds are less than such amount as may be determined by the court to be the net amount which would be realised on a sale of the property or goods in the open market by a willing vendor, such sums as may be required to make good the deficiency,

shall be applied towards discharging the sums secured by the security or payable under the hire-purchase agreement.

(6) Where a condition imposed in pursuance of subsection (5) relates to two or more securities, that condition requires the net proceeds of the disposal and, where paragraph (*b*) of that subsection applies, the sums mentioned in that paragraph to be applied towards discharging the sums secured by those securities in the order of their priorities.

(7) An office copy of an order under subsection (2) shall, within 14 days after the making of the order, be sent by the administrator to the registrar of companies.

(8) If the administrator without reasonable excuse fails to comply with subsection (7), he is liable to a fine and, for continued contravention, to a daily default fine.

(9) References in this section to hire-purchase agreements include conditional sale agreements, chattel leasing agreements and retention of title agreements.

DEFINITIONS
"administration order": s.8(2).
"administrative receiver": ss.29(2), 51, 251.
"administrator": s.8(2).
"a fine": s.430; Sched. 10.
"chattel leasing agreement": subs. (9), s.251.
"conditional sale agreement": subs. (9), s.436; Consumer Credit Act 1974, s.189(1).
"hire-purchase agreement": subs. (9); s.436; Consumer Credit Act 1974, s.189(1).
"property": s.436.
"retention of title agreement": subs. (9), s.251.

GENERAL NOTE
The function of this section, which corresponds to s.34 of the 1985 Act, is to empower the administrator to deal with and dispose of property of the company which is subject to a fixed or floating charge or to a combination of the two or of any goods in the possession of the company under a hire purchase agreement (as specially defined in subs. (9)). The advantage of such a provision is that by enabling the charged property to be disposed of as if it were not subject to any charge or security, the prospects for such a disposal are enhanced and the disposal value of the assets is maximised. The protection for the secured creditor of the company is that by virtue of subs. (5) the net proceeds of disposal, augmented out of other funds if necessary, must be applied towards discharging the debt whose security has been overreached by the application of this statutory power of disposal. During the process of enacting the 1985 Act, the technical difficulties of drafting a provision which would actually produce the desired legal effects proved to be formidable, and the counterpart of the present section was substituted for the original version as late as the Committee stage in the House of Commons (see H.C. Standing Committee E, June 20, 1985, cols. 483–4 and 537). The provision is intended to enable the administrator to deal with and dispose of property which is subject to a floating charge debenture, including the case where the debenture also contains one or more fixed charges. This purpose is achieved by means of the combined effects of subs. (1) together with subs. (3). Where the charge or security, as created, was a floating charge subss. (1) and (3) together have the effect of enabling the administrator to deal with the property without reference to the court. Where however the charge or security is of any other type, as where the property is covered by a fixed charge only or is subject to a hire-purchase or other agreement (as listed in subs. (9)), the administrator must obtain the authorisation of the court pursuant to subs. (2) before he is able to dispose of the property free from the relevant encumbrance. Since the property or goods which fall within the ambit of subs. (2) are also the subject of the moratorium arising under ss.10(1)(*b*) and 11(3)(*c*), the opportunity is established for the administrator and the owner of the property to negotiate satisfactory terms for the property's continued use or disposal. In the event however that no such agreement is forthcoming, the administrator may seek an order under subs. (2) of this section.

Subs. (5)(a)

The net proceeds of the disposal
This means net of the costs and expenses incurred in making the sale.

Subs. 5(b)

The net amount which would be realised on a sale . . . in the open market
This form of words establishes the maximum level of compensation which is payable to the person who holds a charge or security over property which is disposed of pursuant to a court order under subs. (2). The amount which is to be paid to that person towards the discharge of the debts owed to him by the company is the net amount equivalent to the open

market value of the property disposed of. If the sale fails to yield net proceeds at least equal to this notional figure, the administrator must make up the deficiency out of other proceeds from realisations of company assets.

Operation of s.15 in Scotland

16.—(1) Where property is disposed of under section 15 in its application to Scotland, the administrator shall grant to the disponee an appropriate document of transfer or conveyance of the property, and—

(*a*) that document, or

(*b*) where any recording, intimation or registration of the document is a legal requirement for completion of title to the property, that recording, intimation or registration,

has the effect of disencumbering the property of or, as the case may be, freeing the property from the security.

(2) Where goods in the possession of the company under a hire-purchase agreement, conditional sale agreement, chattel leasing agreement or retention of title agreement are disposed of under section 15 in its application to Scotland, the disposal has the effect of extinguishing, as against the disponee, all rights of the owner of the goods under the agreement.

DEFINITIONS

"administrator": s.8(2).
"chattel leasing agreement": ss.15(9), 251.
"conditional sale agreement": ss.15(9), 436; Consumer Credit Act 1974, s.189(1).
"hire purchase agreement": ss.15(9), 436; Consumer Credit Act 1974, s.189(1).
"property": s.436.
"retention of title agreement": ss.15(9), 251.

GENERAL NOTE

This section embodies the provisions formerly contained in subss. (9) and (10) of s.34 of the 1985 Act. These provisions are exclusively applicable to Scotland, and thus a greater clarity is given to the special aspects of the operation of the administrator's powers of disposal under s.15 where these are exercised in Scotland.

General duties

17.—(1) The administrator of a company shall, on his appointment, take into his custody or under his control all the property to which the company is or appears to be entitled.

(2) The administrator shall manage the affairs, business and property of the company—

(*a*) at any time before proposals have been approved (with or without modifications) under section 24 below, in accordance with any directions given by the court, and

(*b*) at any time after proposals have been so approved, in accordance with those proposals as from time to time revised, whether by him or a predecessor of his.

(3) The administrator shall summon a meeting of the company's creditors if—

(*a*) he is requested, in accordance with the rules, to do so by one-tenth, in value, of the company's creditors, or

(*b*) he is directed to do so by the court.

DEFINITIONS

"business": s.436.
"modifications": s.436.
"property": s.436.
"the administrator": s.8(2).
"the rules": ss.251, 411.

This provision completes the conceptual framework within which the administration order is to operate, by requiring the administrator to take over control of the company's affairs, business and property. Thus he displaces the directors from their functions in relation to the company albeit they remain in office. While the directors' powers are suspended, the administrator is able to fulfil his duties imposed by this section, utilising the powers conferred on him by ss.14, 15 and 16 together with Sched. 1. The administrator's scope for acting is not an unfettered one, because of the requirements in subs. (2) that he act in accordance with any directions that the court may give prior to the approval of his proposals, and thereafter in accordance with the terms of those proposals themselves. A further check on the administrator's conduct will be introduced if the creditors at a meeting summoned under s.23 decide to establish a committee of creditors in accordance with the provisions of s.26. This section corresponds to s.35 of the 1985 Act.

Subs. (1)
The terms of this provision should be compared with those of s.144(1) of the Act with regard to the duties of a liquidator or provisional liquidator upon taking office.

Subs. (2)(b)
Proposals . . . as from time to time revised
See s.25 for the procedure whereby the administrator's proposals may be revised subsequently to their approval, and for the conditions under which this procedure is required to be initiated.

Subs. (3)
If (a) he is requested, in accordance with the rules
The insolvency rules will introduce a restriction upon the number of times such meetings can be convened by use of this coercive procedure, lest a group among the creditors, representing the necessary one-tenth in value, contrive to make a nuisance of themselves and thereby render the administrator's task unduly and unnecessarily onerous.

Discharge or variation of administration order

18.—(1) The administrator of a company may at any time apply to the court for the administration order to be discharged, or to be varied so as to specify an additional purpose.

(2) The administrator shall make an application under this section if—

(*a*) it appears to him that the purpose or each of the purposes specified in the order either has been achieved or is incapable of achievement, or

(*b*) he is required to do so by a meeting of the company's creditors summoned for the purpose in accordance with the rules.

(3) On the hearing of an application under this section, the court may by order discharge or vary the administration order and make such consequential provision as it thinks fit, or adjourn the hearing conditionally or unconditionally, or make an interim order or any other order it thinks fit.

(4) Where the administration order is discharged or varied the administrator shall, within 14 days after the making of the order effecting the discharge or variation, send an office copy of that order to the registrar of companies.

(5) If the administrator without reasonable excuse fails to comply with subsection (4), he is liable to a fine and, for continued contravention, to a daily default fine.

DEFINITIONS
"administration order": s.8(2).
"a fine": s.430, Sched. 10.
"the administrator": s.8(2).
"the rules": ss.251, 411.

This provision enables the administrator to apply to the court for the administration order to be varied or discharged. Such applications may be made at his discretion in the circumstances specified in subs. (1). In the circumstances described in subs. (2) the making of an application is obligatory. The further provisions of the section specify the powers of the court upon hearing any application under subs. (1) or (2), and lay down the steps to be taken by the administrator in the event that his application is successful. This section corresponds to s.36 of the 1985 Act.

Subs. (1)

An additional purpose
The purposes for which an administration order may be made are expressed in s.8(3). By the concluding words of that subsection, the court is required to specify which of the permitted purposes forms the basis of the order. The present subsection therefore caters for the possibility that the administrator's closer acquaintance with the company may persuade him that it would be expedient to include one or more additional purposes which were not specified in the original order. The precise determination of the purposes which are specified in the order is of particular importance, not least because the administrator's proposals, which are to be submitted for approval pursuant to s.23 must be framed with reference to the purpose or purposes specified in the administration order.

Subs. (5)

A fine
See Sched. 10 to the Act, and the General Note thereto.

Vacation of office

19.—(1) The administrator of a company may at any time be removed from office by order of the court and may, in the prescribed circumstances, resign his office by giving notice of his resignation to the court.

(2) The administrator shall vacate office if—

(*a*) he ceases to be qualified to act as an insolvency practitioner in relation to the company, or

(*b*) the administration order is discharged.

(3) Where at any time a person ceases to be administrator, the next two subsections apply.

(4) His remuneration and any expenses properly incurred by him shall be charged on and paid out of any property of the company which is in his custody or under his control at that time in priority to any security to which section 15(1) then applies.

(5) Any sums payable in respect of debts or liabilities incurred, while he was administrator, under contracts entered into or contracts of employment adopted by him or a predecessor of his in the carrying out of his or the predecessor's functions shall be charged on and paid out of any such property as is mentioned in subsection (4) in priority to any charge arising under that subsection.

For this purpose, the administrator is not to be taken to have adopted a contract of employment by reason of anything done or omitted to be done within 14 days after his appointment.

DEFINITIONS
"administration order": s.8(2).
"prescribed": s.251.
"property": s.436.
"qualified to act as an insolvency practitioner": s.390.
"to act as an insolvency practitioner in relation to a company": s.388(1).

GENERAL NOTE
This section makes provision for the voluntary or involuntary vacation of his office by the administrator. Provisions are included to safeguard the entitlement of a former administrator to receive his remuneration, and reimbursement of expenses, by means of a preferential

charge over any property of the company which is in his custody or control at the time when he ceases to hold office. The terms of this section are similar in many respects to those of ss.171 and 172 (concerning removal of a liquidator in a voluntary and a compulsory winding up respectively) and to a lesser degree those of s.45 (concerning vacation of office by an administrative receiver), and s.62 (cessation of office by a receiver in Scotland). In particular the same approach is adopted with regard to the debts and liabilities of the administrator as that which applies in the case of a liquidator, namely that these form part of the costs of the administration and are payable first out of the assets (*cf.* s.156). This is in contrast with the position under a receivership, whereby the receiver incurs personal liability with a right of indemnity out of the assets (see ss.44(1), 45(3)). This section incorporates those provisions in s.37 of the 1985 Act which dealt with vacation of office by the administrator (subss. (1)–(3) inclusive).

Subs. (5)

The administrator is not to be taken to have adopted a contract of employment by reason of anything done or omitted to be done within 14 days after his appointment

This provision may be compared with that in s.44(2), which gives the same period of grace to an administrative receiver.

Release of administrator

20.—(1) A person who has ceased to be the administrator of a company has his release with effect from the following time, that is to say—
> (*a*) in the case of a person who has died, the time at which notice is given to the court in accordance with the rules that he has ceased to hold office;
> (*b*) in any other case, such time as the court may determine.

(2) Where a person has his release under this section, he is, with effect from the time specified above, discharged from all liability both in respect of acts or omissions of his in the administration and otherwise in relation to his conduct as administrator.

(3) However, nothing in this section prevents the exercise, in relation to a person who has had his release as above, of the court's powers under section 212 in Chapter X of Part IV (summary remedy against delinquent directors, liquidators, etc.).

DEFINITIONS
> "the administrator": s.8(2).
> "the rules": ss.251, 411.

GENERAL NOTE

This section incorporates those provisions in s.37 of the 1985 Act which dealt with release of the administrator following his vacation of office (subss. (4) and (5) of that section). The time when such release takes effect is indicated in subs. (1) and the legal significance of the concept of release is explained in subs. (2).

Subs. (3)

The court's powers under s.212

This saving provision in respect of the powers of the court under the section referred to ensures that, although the release of the administrator under this section has the effect of discharging him from liabilities of a contractual or tortious nature in respect of his conduct in office he shall remain amenable to the summary procedure established by s.212 which may be employed against a variety of persons who have been officers of, or who have acted as liquidator, administrator or administrative receiver of a company and in that capacity have misapplied or retained or otherwise dealt improperly with any money or other property of the company. Similar provisions to preserve the effects of s.212 are contained in ss.173(4) and 174(6) in relation to the release of the liquidator in a voluntary and in a compulsory winding up respectively.

Ascertainment and investigation of company's affairs

Information to be given by administrator

21.—(1) Where an administration order has been made, the administrator shall—

(*a*) forthwith send to the company and publish in the prescribed manner a notice of the order, and

(*b*) within 28 days after the making of the order, unless the court otherwise directs, send such a notice to all creditors of the company (so far as he is aware of their addresses).

(2) Where an administration order has been made, the administrator shall also, within 14 days after the making of the order, send an office copy of the order to the registrar of companies and to such other persons as may be prescribed.

(3) If the administrator without reasonable excuse fails to comply with this section, he is liable to a fine and, for continued contravention, to a daily default fine.

DEFINITIONS
"administration order": s.8(2).
"a fine": s.430; Sched. 10.
"prescribed": s.251.
"the administrator": s.8(2).

GENERAL NOTE
This section establishes a duty to be fulfilled by the administrator on appointment, whereby he is required to publish the order in the manner to be prescribed in the rules. He is also required to send notice of the administration order to the company itself, to all creditors of whose addresses he is aware, and finally (in the form of a sealed copy of the order of the court) to the registrar of companies. The period of time within which the administrator is required to perform each of these functions differs according to the identity of the party to whom notice is required to be given, and it is made a criminal offence for the administrator to contravene any requirement of the section without reasonable excuse. This section corresponds to s.38 of the 1985 Act.

Subs. (1)(b)

(so far as he is aware of their addresses)
It is apparently not incumbent upon the administrator to go to inordinate lengths in order to ascertain the addresses of the company's creditors: he must use his best endeavours and make reasonable enquiries and searches, but if he cannot thereby find a creditor's address he is under no obligation to search far and wide to discover it (*cf.* H.C. Standing Committee E, June 20, 1985, col. 492).

Subs. (3)

A fine
See the Note to Sched. 10 for explanation of the levels of fines which may be imposed by a court before which an administrator is convicted of a criminal offence under this section.

Statement of affairs to be submitted to administrator

22.—(1) Where an administration order has been made, the administrator shall forthwith require some or all of the persons mentioned below to make out and submit to him a statement in the prescribed form as to the affairs of the company.

(2) The statement shall be verified by affidavit by the persons required to submit it and shall show—

(*a*) particulars of the company's assets, debts and liabilities;
(*b*) the names and addresses of its creditors;
(*c*) the securities held by them respectively;
(*d*) the dates when the securities were respectively given; and

   (*e*) such further or other information as may be prescribed.

(3) The persons referred to in subsection (1) are—

   (*a*) those who are or have been officers of the company;

   (*b*) those who have taken part in the company's formation at any time within one year before the date of the administration order;

   (*c*) those who are in the company's employment or have been in its employment within that year, and are in the administrator's opinion capable of giving the information required;

   (*d*) those who are or have been within that year officers of or in the employment of a company which is, or within that year was, an officer of the company.

In this subsection "employment" includes employment under a contract for services.

(4) Where any persons are required under this section to submit a statement of affairs to the administrator, they shall do so (subject to the next subsection) before the end of the period of 21 days beginning with the day after that on which the prescribed notice of the requirement is given to them by the administrator.

(5) The administrator, if he thinks fit, may—

   (*a*) at any time release a person from an obligation imposed on him under subsection (1) or (2), or

   (*b*) either when giving notice under subsection (4) or subsequently, extend the period so mentioned;

and where the administrator has refused to exercise a power conferred by this subsection, the court, if it thinks fit, may exercise it.

(6) If a person without reasonable excuse fails to comply with any obligation imposed under this section, he is liable to a fine and, for continued contravention, to a daily default fine.

DEFINITIONS

   "administration order": s.8(2).

   "employment": subs. (3).

   "fine": s.430; Sched. 10.

   "officer of the company": s.251; Companies Act 1985, s.744.

   "prescribed": s.251.

   "the administrator": s.8(2).

GENERAL NOTE

This section governs the next step in the sequence of events which follow upon the making of an administration order. The requirement that a statement of the company's affairs be prepared in the prescribed form by one or more of the persons listed in subs. (3) is designed to harmonise as far as possible with the provisions contained in Parts III and IV of this Act, regarding the submission of a statement of the company's affairs in cases of receivership and compulsory winding up respectively (ss.47, 66 and 131). These standardised provisions obviate any question that the statement of affairs in the three kinds of insolvency procedure may somehow be on a different footing, taking one procedure as against another. The administrator—like an administrative receiver or the Official Receiver—enjoys a discretionary power to extend the period of 21 days specified in subs. (4) as the time limit for the submission of the statement of affairs, and the person involved has a right to appeal to the court if the administrator refuses to extend the time allowed. Similarly, the administrator is enabled to release someone from the obligation to supply him with information under this section, and there is again a right of appeal to the court if the administrator will not exercise his power of release. Subject to these possibilities of gaining an extended period of grace, or even a complete release from the obligation to supply information, failure to comply with the requirements of this section constitutes a criminal offence unless there is a reasonable excuse for non-compliance.

This section corresponds to s.39 of the 1985 Act.

Administrator's proposals

Statement of proposals

23.—(1) Where an administration order has been made, the administrator shall, within 3 months (or such longer period as the court may allow) after the making of the order—

(*a*) send to the registrar of companies and (so far as he is aware of their addresses) to all creditors a statement of his proposals for achieving the purpose or purposes specified in the order, and

(*b*) lay a copy of the statement before a meeting of the company's creditors summoned for the purpose on not less than 14 days' notice.

(2) The administrator shall also, within 3 months (or such longer period as the court may allow) after the making of the order, either—

(*a*) send a copy of the statement (so far as he is aware of their addresses) to all members of the company, or

(*b*) publish in the prescribed manner a notice stating an address to which members of the company should write for copies of the statement to be sent to them free of charge.

(3) If the administrator without reasonable excuse fails to comply with this section, he is liable to a fine and, for continued contravention, to a daily default fine.

DEFINITIONS

"administration order": s.8(2).

"a fine": s.430; Sched. 10.

"prescribed": s.251.

"the administrator": s.8(2).

"the purpose or purposes specified in the order": s.8(3).

GENERAL NOTE

The central element in the administration order procedure is the preparation by the administrator of a plan whereby the purposes specified in the administration order (if necessary augmented by means of the procedure established by s.18(1)) may be achieved. This will necessarily involve a considerable amount of preparation and consultation with all relevant parties, and thus a period of three months (capable of extension with the permission of the court) is allowed within which the administrator must prepare his proposals and send a statement of them to the parties indicated in subs. (1), and also publish them either in an individual manner to the members of the company, or by means of a notice as specified in subs. (2). A statement is also required to be laid before a meeting of the company's creditors convened for this purpose and conducted in accordance with the provisions of s.24. Only if approved in the manner there prescribed do the administrator's proposals become the basis on which, under s.17(2)(*b*), the administrator is subsequently required to exercise the powers which he enjoys by virtue of s.14 and Sched. 1.

This section corresponds to s.40 of the 1985 Act.

Consideration of proposals by creditors' meeting

24.—(1) A meeting of creditors summoned under section 23 shall decide whether to approve the administrator's proposals.

(2) The meeting may approve the proposals with modifications, but shall not do so unless the administrator consents to each modification.

(3) Subject as above, the meeting shall be conducted in accordance with the rules.

(4) After the conclusion of the meeting in accordance with the rules, the administrator shall report the result of the meeting to the court and shall give notice of that result to the registrar of companies and to such persons as may be prescribed.

(5) If a report is given to the court under subsection (4) that the meeting has declined to approve the administrator's proposals (with or without

modifications), the court may by order discharge the administration order and make such consequential provision as it thinks fit, or adjourn the hearing conditionally or unconditionally, or make an interim order or any other order that it thinks fit.

(6) Where the administration order is discharged, the administrator shall, within 14 days after the making of the order effecting the discharge, send an office copy of that order to the registrar of companies.

(7) If the administrator without reasonable excuse fails to comply with subsection (6), he is liable to a fine and, for continued contravention, to a daily default fine.

DEFINITIONS
"a fine": s.430; Sched. 10.
"modifications": s.436.
"prescribed": s.251.
"the administrator": s.8(2).
"the rules": ss.251, 411.

GENERAL NOTE
This section governs proceedings at the meeting of creditors convened by the administrator under s.23(1)(*b*) and also regulates the subsequent developments which must take place, depending upon the outcome of the meeting. If the creditors approve the administrator's proposals—with or without any modification effected in accordance with subs. (2)—the administrator is thereafter required to manage the affairs, business and property of the company in accordance with the approved proposals (s.17(2)(*b*)). No further authorisation is required in order to give the administrator's regime legal effect, and the requirement of subs. (4) with regard to the giving of notice to various parties, including the registrar of companies, and for the reporting of the outcome to the court, do not have the force of preconditions. Moreover, no criminal sanction is made applicable in any case of omission by the administrator to comply with the requirements of subs. (4).

If the creditors do not approve the proposals, and if no modified version can be agreed at the meeting under subs. (2), the provisions of subs. (5) become applicable following the administrator's giving his report to the court. The court enjoys a wide range of discretionary powers to enable it to make the most suitable arrangements in consequence of the collapse of the administrator's proposals. If the administration order is discharged the moratorium of the company's affairs is lifted and a winding-up petition may be presented, but the court may elect to adjourn the hearing to allow time for such a step to be prepared without any hiatus between the lifting of the moratorium imposed since the presentation of the petition for an administration order, and the reimposition of control over the company's affairs which will occur when a winding-up petition is presented.

As is also the case under ss.18(4) and 27(6), if the administration order is discharged in consequence of the non-approval of the proposals of the administrator, the latter is required to send the registrar of companies a sealed copy of the order of the court within 14 days after it is made. Non-compliance with this requirement constitutes a criminal offence under subs. (7). This section corresponds to s.41 of the 1985 Act.

Subs. (1)

Shall decide whether to approve
No indication is given within the Act of the manner in which voting is to be conducted when a meeting of creditors is taking its decision whether to approve an administrator's proposals. However, subs. (3) indicates that the meeting is to be conducted according to the rules, and it will be provided therein that decisions of the creditors' meetings shall be taken on the basis of a simple majority in value only. This accords with the main recommendation in the *Cork Report* regarding the matter of voting (paras. 920–925) that the power of a creditor's vote should be related to the value of his claim. The Government *White Paper* (para. 78) accepted this as the essential principle to be employed henceforth but rejected the collateral proposal in the *Cork Report* (para. 923) for a system of allotting each creditor one vote per £100 of debt or part thereof.

Any creditor who is dissatisfied with the majority decision at a meeting may utilise the procedure under s.27, provided the conditions specified in that section are satisfied, but he must do so within 28 days of the meeting.

Subs. (7)

A fine

See the Note to Sched. 10 for explanation of the levels of fines which may be imposed by a court before which an administrator is convicted of a criminal offence under this section.

Approval of substantial revisions

25.—(1) This section applies where—

(*a*) proposals have been approved (with or without modifications) under section 24, and

(*b*) the administrator proposes to make revisions of those proposals which appear to him substantial.

(2) The administrator shall—

(*a*) send to all creditors of the company (so far as he is aware of their addresses) a statement in the prescribed form of his proposed revisions, and

(*b*) lay a copy of the statement before a meeting of the company's creditors summoned for the purpose on not less than 14 days' notice;

and he shall not make the proposed revisions unless they are approved by the meeting.

(3) The administrator shall also either—

(*a*) send a copy of the statement (so far as he is aware of their addresses) to all members of the company, or

(*b*) publish in the prescribed manner a notice stating an address to which members of the company should write for copies of the statement to be sent to them free of charge.

(4) The meeting of creditors may approve the proposed revisions with modifications, but shall not do so unless the administrator consents to each modification.

(5) Subject as above, the meeting shall be conducted in accordance with the rules.

(6) After the conclusion of the meeting in accordance with the rules, the administrator shall give notice of the result of the meeting to the registrar of companies and to such persons as may be prescribed.

DEFINITIONS

"modifications": s.436.
"prescribed": s.251.
"the administrator": s.8(2).
"the rules": ss.251, 411.

GENERAL NOTE

This section operates in conjunction with s.17(2)(*b*), whereby the administrator is required to manage the company's affairs, business and property in accordance with the proposals which have been duly approved by the creditors at a meeting conducted under ss.23 and 24. S.17(2)(*b*) expressly contemplates the possibility of periodical revision of the proposals by means of the further process for seeking the approval of a meeting of creditors for which the present section makes provision. Subs. (1) defines the circumstances in which it becomes necessary for the administrator to obtain approval of a meeting of creditors to the revisions which he proposes to make. The provisions of subss. (2) and (3) regarding the giving of notice of the administrator's statement of his proposed revisions and for convening the meeting of creditors are essentially identical to those of s.23(1) and (2) which govern the sanctioning of the administrator's original proposals, save that there is no requirement that the registrar of companies shall receive a copy of the statement, although notice of the result of the meeting must be sent to him under subs. (6). The provisions of subss. (4) and (5) match those of s.24(2) and (3) with regard to the conduct of the meeting and the manner in which the creditors' approval is to be obtained. However, there is no requirement corresponding to that of s.24(4) whereby the result of the meeting must be reported to the court, although the drafting of subs. (6) leaves open the possibility that such a requirement could be included in the insolvency rules. This section corresponds to s.42 of the 1985 Act.

Subs. (1)(b)

Revisions . . . which appear to him substantial

This formulation is such as to make the necessity for the administrator to utilise the procedure under this section dependent upon his own subjective evaluation of the quality of the revisions he has in mind. If in his judgment any revisions which he contemplates making to the plan of action originally approved by the creditors are of a non-substantial nature, the obligation to seek fresh approval does not arise. The administrator is thus left free to make minor adjustments in his manner of going about the task entrusted to him, but his professional judgment and integrity must be brought to bear at all times with a view to respecting the requirements of the present section.

Subs. (2)

Approved by the meeting

As is the case under s.24(1) (*q.v.*) the method of voting on whether to approve the proposed revisions will be in accordance with the new principle that resolutions of creditors' meetings should be on the basis of a simple majority in value only. Any dissatisfied creditor may have recourse to the procedure under s.27, but must do so within 28 days after the meeting, in view of the provision of s.27(3)(*b*).

Miscellaneous

Creditors' committee

26.—(1) Where a meeting of creditors summoned under section 23 has approved the administrator's proposals (with or without modifications), the meeting may, if it thinks fit, establish a committee ("the creditors' committee") to exercise the functions conferred on it by or under this Act.

(2) If such a committee is established, the committee may, on giving not less than 7 days' notice, require the administrator to attend before it at any reasonable time and furnish it with such information relating to the carrying out of his functions as it may reasonably require.

DEFINITIONS

"the administrator": s.8(2).
"modifications": s.436.

GENERAL NOTE

Chap. 19 of the *Cork Report* contains numerous proposals for the law to be recast so as to give creditors a larger role in the conduct of insolvency proceedings, and also to provide them with a genuine incentive to take an active part. In particular, paras. 930–967 are devoted to a close examination of the way in which committees of creditors should function. The *White Paper* made only a lukewarm response to those proposals, devoting only two paragraphs (83–84) to the topic of creditors' committees. The present section (which is a parallel to ss.49 and 68 regarding creditors' committees in cases of receivership) leaves it to the creditors themselves to take the initiative in setting up a committee. They may do this at the meeting summoned by the administrator under s.23 to approve his proposals. The committee, if established, enjoys the right under subs. (2) to summon the administrator before it at seven days' notice and is entitled to obtain information from him regarding his performance in office. This section corresponds to s.43 of the 1985 Act.

Subs. (1)

The functions conferred on it by or on under this Act

Despite the insertion of this phrase in the subsection, there is no overt reference elsewhere in Pt. II of the Act to the functions of a creditors' committee under the administration order procedure. Apart from the specific powers conferred upon the committee by subs. (2), therefore, the committee's functions are left unspecified, although the way is left open for further provisions to be included in the rules, as provided for in para. 10 of Sched. 8. By contrast, the provisions of ss.141(1) and 142(1), and subsequent references in the Act to functions of a creditors' committee in a case of company liquidation, indicate that a more significant role is performed by a creditors' committee in that context.

Subs. (2)

At any reasonable time; . . . such information . . . as it may reasonably require
The purpose underlying the two references to reasonableness in relation to the committee's powers to summon the administrator to attend before them and to furnish them with information is to protect the administrator from unreasonable demands which might be made upon him, especially if the committee's view as to what ought to be done is at variance with his.

Protection of interests of creditors and members

27.—(1) At any time when an administration order is in force, a creditor or member of the company may apply to the court by petition for an order under this section on the ground—

(a) that the company's affairs, business and property are being or have been managed by the administrator in a manner which is unfairly prejudicial to the interests of its creditors or members generally, or of some part of its creditors or members (including at least himself), or

(b) that any actual or proposed act or omission of the administrator is or would be so prejudicial.

(2) On an application for an order under this section the court may, subject as follows, make such order as it thinks fit for giving relief in respect of the matters complained of, or adjourn the hearing conditionally or unconditionally, or make an interim order or any other order that it thinks fit.

(3) An order under this section shall not prejudice or prevent—

(a) the implementation of a voluntary arrangement approved under section 4 in Part I, or any compromise or arrangement sanctioned under section 425 of the Companies Act; or

(b) where the application for the order was made more than 28 days after the approval of any proposals or revised proposals under section 24 or 25, the implementation of those proposals or revised proposals.

(4) Subject as above, an order under this section may in particular—

(a) regulate the future management by the administrator of the company's affairs, business and property;

(b) require the administrator to refrain from doing or continuing an act complained of by the petitioner, or to do an act which the petitioner has complained he has omitted to do;

(c) require the summoning of a meeting of creditors or members for the purpose of considering such matters as the court may direct;

(d) discharge the administration order and make such consequential provision as the court thinks fit.

(5) Nothing in section 15 or 16 is to be taken as prejudicing applications to the court under this section.

(6) Where the administration order is discharged, the administration shall, within 14 days after the making of the order effecting the discharge, send an office copy of that order to the registrar of companies; and if without reasonable excuse he fails to comply with this subsection, he is liable to a fine and, for continued contravention, to a daily default fine.

DEFINITIONS
"administration order": s.8(2).
"a fine": s.430, Sched. 10.
"business": s.436.
"property": s.436.
"the administrator": s.8(2).

GENERAL NOTE

This section establishes a procedure, which may be invoked by any creditor or member of the company whose standing to complain about the administrator's conduct is founded upon actual or potential prejudice to his interest as a result of what has either been done or is proposed to be done. The court's powers are discretionary, and by virtue of subs. (3)(*a*) it is made impossible for the procedure under this section to be used to obstruct or overturn any voluntary arrangement approved under s.4 or any compromise or arrangement sanctioned under s.425 of the Companies Act 1985. Similarly, by subs. (3)(*b*) any complaint under this section concerning the effects of any of the administrator's proposals which have been approved or revised by means of the procedures laid down by ss.24 or 25 must be initiated within 28 days of the meeting by which the creditors' approval was given. This prevents any party from disrupting the administrator's work by petitioning for an order under this section when implementation of the proposals is well advanced. The expression "28 days" refers to business days, as defined in s.251. This section, apart from subs. (5) as noted below, corresponds to s.44 of the 1985 Act.

Subs. (5)

This provision is designed to ensure that the right of any interested party to make application to the court under this section is not impeded or cut down as a result of any possible construction which might be placed upon the provisions of ss.15 or 16, which enable the administrator to dispose of charged property free from encumbrance. Although this subsection has no counterpart in s.44 of the 1985 Act, its purpose and effect are clearly in accordance with the legislative intention underlying that provision, and its inclusion in the present section is seemingly *ex abundanti cautela*.

Subs. (6)

A fine

See Sched. 10 to the Act, and the General Note thereto.

PART III

RECEIVERSHIP

CHAPTER I

RECEIVERS AND MANAGERS (ENGLAND AND WALES)

Preliminary and general provisions

Extent of this Chapter

28. This Chapter does not apply to receivers appointed under Chapter II of this Part (Scotland).

GENERAL NOTE

By way of introduction this provision emphasises that Chap. 1 of the Act does not apply to Scottish receivers.

Receivership in English law is a well-established equitable remedy. It is not the product of statutory intervention, unlike the position in Scotland. Consequently, much of the law is case-orientated, subject, of course, to some statutory modification. For a general review, see *Palmer* (23rd ed.), Chap. 46 and *Buckley* on the Companies Acts (14th ed.), p.276 *et seq*. It was for the first time put upon a proper statutory basis in Chap. IV, Pt. II, I.A. 1985. It was also amended at that time to bring it more into line with the Scottish Law (see Chap. 8, *Cork Report* and Chaps. 13 and 15 of the *White Paper*). Even after these changes it remained subject, in certain respects to Pt. XIX, C.A. 1985 and therefore the law had to be sought in two statutes. Both sets of provisions have now been consolidated in Chap. I of this Part.

Scottish Law had been governed by the Companies (Floating Charges and Receivers) (Scotland) Act 1972 and now, via Pt. XVIII, C.A. 1985, appears as Chap. II of this Part.

Thus, though differences survive, the same statute now governs, in neighbouring chapters, the law relating to both England and Wales and Scotland.

The degree of statutory regulation of the law of receivership in England and Wales was substantially increased by the provisions in the I.A. 1985. Besides amending several of the provisions of the C.A. 1985 noted below, completely new statutory provisions were introduced and find their place in the present consolidation. For instance, a statutory list of powers for a receiver is provided (s.42 and Sched. 1), as is a power to sell assets subject to a fixed charge (s.43). There is statutory confirmation of the receiver's status as the company's agent (s.44) and new rules on both the appointment of and vacation of office by a receiver (ss.33, 34, 45). The rules in Pt. XIII of the Act on the qualification of insolvency practitioners should also be noted. These provisions (except ss.33 and 34), will only apply to an administrative receiver—*i.e.* a receiver who takes control of the whole or the bulk of the company's assets to enforce a floating charge or a mixed security consisting of fixed and floating charges (s.29(2)).

Definitions

29.—(1) It is hereby declared that, except where the context otherwise requires—
   (*a*) any reference in the Companies Act or this Act to a receiver or manager of the property of a company, or to a receiver of it, includes a receiver or manager, or (as the case may be) a receiver of part only of that property and a receiver only of the income arising from the property or from part of it; and
   (*b*) any reference in the Companies Act or this Act to the appointment of a receiver or manager under powers contained in an instrument includes an appointment made under powers which, by virtue of any enactment, are implied in and have effect as if contained in an instrument.
   (2) In this Chapter "administrative receiver" means—
   (*a*) a receiver or manager of the whole (or substantially the whole) of a company's property appointed by or on behalf of the holders of any debentures of the company secured by a charge which, as created, was a floating charge, or by such a charge and one or more other securities; or
   (*b*) a person who would be such a receiver or manager but for the appointment of some other person as the receiver of part of the company's property.

DEFINITIONS
   "administrative receiver": subs. (2), s.251(*a*).
   "floating charge": s.251.
   "property": s.436.
   "receiver": s.251.
   "security": s.248(*b*).

GENERAL NOTE
   This is an interpretation section which in subs. (1) makes it clear that references to receivers and managers of a company's property include (unless the contrary is intended) receivers and managers dealing with only part of a company's assets. References to receivers appointed under any instrument would include, for example, receivers appointed under s.101(i)(iii) of the Law of Property Act 1925. This interpretation provision is derived from 1948 Act, s.376 via s.500, C.A. 1985.
   Subs. (2) supplies a statutory meaning for the expression "administrative receiver" for the purposes of Chap. I of Pt. III. The separate treatment of the law of receivership for England and Wales and for Scotland respectively is reflected in the further provisions of s.251, which indicates the statutory meaning of the terms "administrative receiver" and "receiver" for the purposes of Pts. I to VII the Act ("The First Group of Parts").

Disqualification of body corporate from acting as receiver

30. A body corporate is not qualified for appointment as receiver of the property of a company, and any body corporate which acts as such a receiver is liable to a fine.

DEFINITIONS
"body corporate": s.251; C.A. 1985, s.740.
"fine": s.430, Sched. 10.

GENERAL NOTE
This provision is derived from C.A. 1985, s.489.
English law (like the law of Scotland—s.51(3)(*a*) *supra*) still retains its largely irrational disqualification of corporations acting as receivers. For a criticism of the generality of this prohibition see Gower, *Principles of Modern Company Law* (4th ed., 1979), p.488. Surprisingly the Cork Committee (Cmnd. 8558, para. 744) supported the continuance of this prohibition. Where a corporation does assume such a position the appointment is void— *Portman Building Society* v. *Gallwey* [1955] 1 All E.R. 227—and a fine may be incurred.

Note
The ban on corporate receivers is reinforced by s.390(1) but this applies only to administrative receivers.

Disqualification of undischarged bankrupt

31. If a person being an undischarged bankrupt acts as receiver or manager of the property of a company on behalf of debenture holders, he is liable to imprisonment or a fine, or both.

This does not apply to a receiver or manager acting under an appointment made by the court.

DEFINITION
"fine or imprisonment": s.430, Sched. 10.

GENERAL NOTE
This is a much more justifiable ground for disqualification. For its origin see the Cohen Report (Cmnd. 6659, para. 69), 1948 Act, s.367 and 1985 Act, s.490. The comparable disqualification in Scotland is in s.51(3)(*b*). The prohibition does not apply to court-appointed receivers, but then the court is unlikely to appoint undischarged bankrupts as receivers. Before leaving the question of the disqualification of "undesirables" as receivers note s.295, C.A. 1985 and Ch. 1 of Pt. II, I.A. 1985, preventing certain company directors from acting as receivers. These two sets of provisions have been brought together in the Company Directors Disqualification Act 1986.

Power for court to appoint official receiver

32. Where application is made to the court to appoint a receiver on behalf of the debenture holders or other creditors of a company which is being wound up by the court, the official receiver may be appointed.

DEFINITION
"court": s.251; C.A. 1985, s.744.

GENERAL NOTE
Where the company is in liquidation this does not preclude the appointment of a receiver, but here the court can appoint the official receiver to act as receiver. For the role of the official receiver on liquidation see ss.399–401 *post*. This facility reproduces C.A. 1948, s.368 and C.A. 1985, s.491.

Receivers and managers appointed out of court

Time from which appointment is effective

33.—(1) The appointment of a person as a receiver or manager of a company's property under powers contained in an instrument—

  (*a*) is of no effect unless it is accepted by that person before the end of the business day next following that on which the instrument of appointment is received by him or on his behalf, and

  (*b*) subject to this, is deemed to be made at the time at which the instrument of appointment is so received.

(2) This section applies to the appointment of two or more persons as joint receivers or managers of a company's property under powers contained in an instrument, subject to such modifications as may be prescribed by the rules.

DEFINITIONS
"business day": s.251.
"prescribed": s.251.
"property": s.436.
"receiver": s.29(1)(*a*); s.251.
"the rules": ss.251, 411.

TRANSITIONAL PROVISION:
Sched. 11, para. 2.

GENERAL NOTE
This section is intended to give effect to the recommendations of the *Cork Report* (see paras. 470–474) to the effect that the appointment of a receiver should run from the time of receipt of the instrument of appointment by the receiver or his authorised representative, provided that he actually accepts the appointment. The rule which has been embodied in this section is to this extent a confirmation of the former case law expressed in *R. A. Cripps and Son Ltd.* v. *Wickenden* [1973] 1 W.L.R. 944; 2 All E.R. 606.

It was also recommended that the receiver's acceptance should be required to be in writing within 24-hours, and that his appointment should lapse if he has not accepted it within the 24 hour period. The adoption of this rule in subs. (1)(*a*) represents a considerable shortening, as against the previous period of seven days, of the time allowed for the receiver's acceptance.

Subs. (1)(a)
No indication is given in this section as to the mode in which acceptance must be made in order to be effective. It was indicated in para. 474 of the *Cork Report* that acceptance should be in writing, and provision will presumably be made for this matter in the rules, although the latter are not directly referred to in this part of the section.

Liability for invalid appointment

34. Where the appointment of a person as the receiver or manager of a company's property under powers contained in an instrument is discovered to be invalid (whether by virtue of the invalidity of the instrument or otherwise), the court may order the person by whom or on whose behalf the appointment was made to indemnify the person appointed against any liability which arises solely by reason of the invalidity of the appointment.

DEFINITION
"receiver": ss.29(1)(*a*), 251.

GENERAL NOTE
This section deals with liability in cases where, for any reason, the appointment of a person as receiver or manager is invalid. The Court enjoys a discretion to order those on whose behalf the appointment was made to indemnify the receiver against liability which arises solely by reason of the invalidity of the appointment. Therefore a receiver whose

appointment is invalid is not entitled to any indemnity against any damages payable by him for personally mismanaging the conduct of his abortive receivership prior to the discovery of the invalidity of his appointment. In exercising its discretion under this section, the Court will seek to establish where the blame lies for the invalidity which has been discovered. For example, if a debenture comes to be held by an individual who has bought in the open market through a trustee, the Court might conclude that it would not be appropriate in the circumstances to impose liability upon the current holder in respect of a defect for which he was not personally responsible.

(Whether by virtue of the invalidity of the instrument or otherwise)
The parenthetical insertion is to allow for the fact that the invalidity of the receiver's appointment does not in all cases result from an invalidity of the instrument of appointment itself. One example of an alternative ground of invalidity would be where, in a subsequent winding up of the company, the charge on which the creditor's right to make the appointment was based is set aside under s.245 (*cf.* also *Rolled Steel Products (Holdings) Ltd.* v. *British Steel Corporation* [1982] Ch. 478, affd. [1984] B.C.L.C. 466; [1985] 3 All E.R. 52).

Application to court for directions

35.—(1) A receiver or manager of the property of a company appointed under powers contained in an instrument, or the persons by whom or on whose behalf a receiver or manager has been so appointed, may apply to the court for directions in relation to any particular matter arising in connection with the performance of the functions of the receiver or manager.

(2) On such an application, the court may give such directions, or may make such order declaring the rights of persons before the court or otherwise, as it thinks just.

DEFINITION
"court": s.251; C.A. 1985, s.744.

GENERAL NOTE
This section was based on C.A. 1948, s.369(1) which enabled a receiver appointed out of court to apply to the court for guidance where difficulties arise. This facility was a result of the recommendations of the Cohen Committee (Cmnd. 6659, para. 67) and it has now, following proposals by the Cork Committee (Cmnd. 8558, para. 828), been extended to debenture holders. For the position in Scotland—see s.63(1) *infra.* On an application for directions the court enjoys general discretion.

Court's power to fix remuneration

36.—(1) The court may, on an application made by the liquidator of a company, by order fix the amount to be paid by way of remuneration to a person who, under powers contained in an instrument, has been appointed receiver or manager of the company's property.

(2) The court's power under subsection (1), where no previous order has been made with respect thereto under the subsection—

(*a*) extends to fixing the remuneration for any period before the making of the order or the application for it,

(*b*) is exercisable notwithstanding that the receiver or manager has died or ceased to act before the making of the order or the application, and

(*c*) where the receiver or manager has been paid or has retained for his remuneration for any period before the making of the order any amount in excess of that so fixed for that period, extends to requiring him or his personal representatives to account for the excess or such part of it as may be specified in the order.

But the power conferred by paragraph (*c*) shall not be exercised as respects any period before the making of the application for the order under this section, unless in the court's opinion there are special circumstances making it proper for the power to be exercised.

(3) The court may from time to time on an application made either by the liquidator or by the receiver or manager, vary or amend an order made under subsection (1).

DEFINITION
"court": s.251; C.A. 1985, s.744.

GENERAL NOTE
It is surprising that this little-used statutory provision has been retained. The receiver will normally ensure that the terms of his appointment will govern his appointment, and the chances of a particular liquidator challenging the remuneration of a fellow insolvency practitioner are remote. For the position in Scotland see s.58 *infra*.

Subs. (1)
This subsection allows a liquidator to apply to the court to have a receiver's remuneration fixed. It is based on C.A. 1985, s.494(1).

Subs. (2)
(Based on C.A. 1985, s.494(2). (Outlines the power of the court on such an application. Note that under subs. (2)(c) any excessive remuneration paid to a receiver can be clawed back by the court, though payments prior to the application should only be recovered in special circumstances.

Subs. (3)
Any order of the court fixing a receiver's remuneration can be varied. This reproduces C.A. 1985, s.494(3).

Liability for contracts, etc.

37.—(1) A receiver or manager appointed under powers contained in an instrument (other than an administrative receiver) is, to the same extent as if he had been appointed by order of the court—
   (a) personally liable on any contract entered into by him in the performance of his functions (except in so far as the contract otherwise provides) and on any contract of employment adopted by him in the performance of those functions, and
   (b) entitled in respect of that liability to indemnity out of the assets.
(2) For the purposes of subsection (1)(a), the receiver or manager is not to be taken to have adopted a contract of employment by reason of anything done or omitted to be done within 14 days after his appointment.
(3) Subsection (1) does not limit any right to indemnity which the receiver or manager would have apart from it, nor limit his liability on contracts entered into without authority, nor confer any right to indemnity in respect of that liability.
(4) Where at any time the receiver or manager so appointed vacates office—
   (a) his remuneration and any expenses properly incurred by him, and
   (b) any indemnity to which he is entitled out of the assets of the company,
shall be charged on and paid out of any property of the company which is in his custody or under his control at that time in priority to any charge or other security held by the person by or on whose behalf he was appointed.

GENERAL NOTE
This section renders a receiver appointed out of court personally liable for the contracts which he enters into though he will be protected by his indemnity. A receiver is not personally liable for pre-receivership contracts, see Buckley On the Companies Acts (14th

ed.), p.283, though it is now debatable whether he can avoid a decree of specific performance—see *Freevale Ltd* v. *Metrostore Holdings Ltd* [1984] Ch. 199. Contractually a receiver appointed out of court is in the same position with regard to his own contracts as a court appointed receiver—*Burt, Boulton and Hayward* v. *Bull* [1895] 1 Q.B. 276. The Cork Committee (Cmnd. 8558, para. 463) refused calls to drop this personal liability but contracting out is possible. The section is derived in part from s.492(3), C.A. 1985 but the references to contracts of employment in subs. (1) and (2) are new. The effect is to give the receiver a period of grace during which he can decide whether to adopt any contracts of employment. Similar periods apply to administrative receivers (s.44) and administrators (s.19(5)). Subs. (4) is also new. In respect of his remuneration, expenses and indemnity, the receiver has the benefit of a charge which takes priority over any enjoyed by the person who appointed him. The personal liability of the receiver under this section may be contrasted with the provisions applicable to administrative receivers (s.44) and administrators (s.14(5)) both of whom are deemed additionally to act as agents of the company.

Receivership accounts to be delivered to registrar

38.—(1) Except in the case of an administrative receiver, every receiver or manager of a company's property who has been appointed under powers contained in an instrument shall deliver to the registrar of companies for registration the requisite accounts of his receipts and payments.

(2) The accounts shall be delivered within one month (or such longer period as the registrar may allow) after the expiration of 12 months from the date of his appointment and of every subsequent period of 6 months, and also within one month after he ceases to act as receiver or manager.

(3) The requisite accounts shall be an abstract in the prescribed form showing—

(a) receipts and payments during the relevant period of 12 or 6 months, or

(b) where the receiver or manager ceases to act, receipts and payments during the period from the end of the period of 12 or 6 months to which the last preceding abstract related (or, if no preceding abstract has been delivered under this section, from the date of his appointment) up to the date of his so ceasing, and the aggregate amount of receipts and payments during all preceding periods since his appointment.

(4) In this section "prescribed" means prescribed by regulations made by statutory instrument by the Secretary of State.

(5) A receiver or manager who makes default in complying with this section is liable to a fine and, for continued contravention, to a daily default fine.

DEFINITIONS
"fine", "default fine": s.430, Sched. 10.
"instrument": s.29(1)(b).
"receiver or manager": s.29(1)(a).
"registrar": s.744, C.A. 1985; s.251.
"registrar of companies": s.744, C.A. 1985; s.251.

GENERAL NOTE
The first accounts which the receiver must furnish are to be produced within 13 months of his appointment; subsequent accounts must be delivered at intervals of six months.

Provisions applicable to every receivership

Notification that receiver or manager appointed

39.—(1) When a receiver or manager of the property of a company has been appointed, every invoice, order for goods or business letter issued by or on behalf of the company or the receiver or manager or the liquidator of the company, being a document on or in which the company's name appears, shall contain a statement that a receiver or manager has been appointed.

(2) If default is made in complying with this section, the company and any of the following persons, who knowingly and wilfully authorises or permits the default, namely, any officer of the company, any liquidator of the company and any receiver or manager, is liable to a fine.

DEFINITIONS
"fine": s.430, Sched. 10.
"name": Pt. I, Chap. II, C.A. 1985.

GENERAL NOTE
Subs. (1)
(Derived from C.A. 1985, s.493). This subsection requires business communications to disclose that a receiver has been appointed. The Scottish counterpart is s.64 *infra*. This section must be linked to s.405(1), C.A. 1985 (entry of appointment in register of charges).

Subs. (2)
The sanction for non compliance is a fine, but note that contracts entered into in breach of the provision are not invalid.

Payment of debts out of assets subject to floating charge

40—(1) The following applies, in the case of a company, where a receiver is appointed on behalf of the holders of any debentures of the company secured by a charge which, as created, was a floating charge.

(2) If the company is not at the time in course of being wound up, its preferential debts (within the meaning given to that expression by section 386 in Part XII) shall be paid out of the assets coming to the hands of the receiver in priority to any claims for principal or interest in respect of the debentures.

(3) Payments made under this section shall be recouped, as far as may be, out of the assets of the company available for payment of general creditors.

DEFINITION
"preferential debts": s.386.

GENERAL NOTE
The preferential claims régime dates back to the end of the last century and, in spite of fierce criticism in the *Cork Report* (Cmnd. 8558, para. 1450), it will continue to apply in the foreseeable future though in watered down form—see Pt. XII; Sched. 6 and notes to ss.175 and 386.

Subss. (1), (2)
These state that a receiver acting to enforce a *floating* charge (not a *fixed* charge—*Re Lewis Merthyr Consolidated Collieries* [1929] 1 Ch. 498) is subject to the obligation to pay preferential claims. For derivation see C.A. 1985, s.196(2) (part).

Subs. (3)
Derivation C.A. 1985, s.196(5). This illustrates that although it is the holder of the floating charge who suffers initially as a result of the receiver's obligation to pay preferential claims it is ultimately the unsecured creditors who foot the bill.

Note
In the comparable provision in Scotland (s.59(2)) there is a useful machinery allowing the receiver to advertise for claims.

Enforcement of duty to make returns

41.—(1) If a receiver or manager of a company's property—
(*a*) having made default in filing, delivering or making any return,

account or other document, or in giving any notice, which a receiver or manager is by law required to file, deliver, make or give, fails to make good the default within 14 days after the service on him of a notice requiring him to do so, or

(*b*) having been appointed under powers contained in an instrument, has, after being required at any time by the liquidator of the company to do so, failed to render proper accounts of his receipts and payments and to vouch them and pay over to the liquidator the amount properly payable to him,

the court may, on an application made for the purpose, make an order directing the receiver or manager (as the case may be) to make good the default within such time as may be specified in the order.

(2) In the case of the default mentioned in subsection (1)(*a*), application to the court may be made by any member or creditor of the company or by the registrar of companies; and in the case of the default mentioned in subsection (1)(*b*), the application shall be made by the liquidator.

In either case the court's order may provide that all costs of and incidental to the application shall be borne by the receiver or manager, as the case may be.

(3) Nothing in this section prejudices the operation of any enactment imposing penalties on receivers in respect of any such default as is mentioned in subsection (1).

DEFINITIONS
"court": s.744, C.A. 1985; s.251.
"receiver or manager": s.29(1)(*a*).
"registrar of companies": s.744, C.A. 1985; s.251.

GENERAL NOTE
Subs. (1)
This subsection which is derived from C.A. 1985, s.499(1), relates to the enforcement of a receiver's obligation to make returns, file accounts, etc. It establishes a machinery for enforcement of these obligations by a court order.

Subs. (2)
This subsection reproduces C.A. 1985, s.499(2) and indicates that the applications to the court will vary depending on whether the company is in liquidation or not. In any case the receiver can be ordered to pay the cost of the application.

Subs. (3)
This subsection emphasises that this enforcement procedure is in addition to the criminal penalties imposed on a receiver for failure to fulfil his obligations—see s.38(5) *supra*. This provision can be traced back to C.A. 1985, s.499(3).

Administrative receivers: general

General powers

42.—(1) The powers conferred on the administrative receiver of a company by the debentures by virtue of which he was appointed are deemed to include (except in so far as they are inconsistent with any of the provisions of those debentures) the powers specified in Schedule 1 to this Act.

(2) In the application of Schedule 1 to the administrative receiver of a company—

(*a*) the words "he" and "him" refer to the administrative receiver, and
(*b*) references to the property of the company are to the property of which he is or, but for the appointment of some other person as the receiver of part of the company's property, would be the receiver or manager.

(3) A person dealing with the administrative receiver in good faith and for value is not concerned to inquire whether the receiver is acting within his powers.

DEFINITIONS
"administrative receiver": s.251(*a*); s.29(2).
"property": s.436.
"receiver": s.251.

GENERAL NOTE
This section incorporates the provisions of Sched. 1 to the Act so that they apply to an administrative receiver appointed under this Chapter. Sched. 1 lists the powers with which an administrative receiver is invested but subs. (1) makes it clear that any express terms of the debenture itself may override any provisions of Sched. 1 insofar as they may be inconsistent with them.

Subs. (2)(b)
The restriction applied to the definition of "property of the company" in relation to the receiver's powers is intended to ensure that those powers are available only in respect of the property actually covered by the charge under which the administrative receiver was appointed, and not over the whole property of the company.

But for the appointment of some other person
This further clarifies the position of the administrative receiver by indicating what is the effect of the existence of any prior charges over parts of the Company's property which are also covered by a floating charge. Unless the prior charge holder has appointed a receiver, the administrative receiver has power to deal with those parts of the property, but once the prior charge holder appoints a receiver, the property in question ceases to be within the control of the administrative receiver or subject to his power. (The same position obtains in Scotland by virtue of s.55, which sets out the rules regarding precedence among receivers more clearly and in greater detail).

Subs. (3)
This provision, which is drafted in comparable terms to s.14(6) (*q.v.*) regarding dealings with an administrator, is designed to protect persons dealing with a receiver where they have dealt in good faith and for value.

Power to dispose of charged property, etc.

43.—(1) Where, on an application by the administrative receiver, the court is satisfied that the disposal (with or without other assets) of any relevant property which is subject to a security would be likely to promote a more advantageous realisation of the company's assets than would otherwise be effected, the court may by order authorise the administrative receiver to dispose of the property as if it were not subject to the security.

(2) Subsection (1) does not apply in the case of any security held by the person by or on whose behalf the administrative receiver was appointed, or of any security to which a security so held has priority.

(3) It shall be a condition of an order under this section that—

(*a*) the net proceeds of the disposal, and

(*b*) where those proceeds are less than such amount as may be determined by the court to be the net amount which would be realised on a sale of the property in the open market by a willing vendor, such sums as may be required to make good the deficiency,

shall be applied towards discharging the sums secured by the security.

(4) Where a condition imposed in pursuance of subsection (3) relates to two or more securities, that condition shall require the net proceeds of the disposal and, where paragraph (*b*) of that subsection applies, the sums mentioned in that paragraph to be applied towards discharging the sums secured by those securities in the order of their priorities.

(5) An office copy of an order under this section shall, within 14 days of the making of the order, be sent by the administrative receiver to the registrar of companies.

(6) If the administrative receiver without reasonable excuse fails to comply with subsection (5), he is liable to a fine and, for continued contravention, to a daily default fine.

(7) In this section "relevant property", in relation to the administrative receiver, means the property of which he is or, but for the appointment of some other person as the receiver of part of the company's property, would be the receiver or manager.

DEFINITIONS
"administrative receiver": ss.29(2); 251(*a*).
"fine", "daily default fine": s.430, Sched. 10.
"receiver": ss.251, 29(1)(*a*).
"relevant property": subs. (7).
"security": s.248(*b*).

APPLICATION
This section does not apply to Scotland (s.440(2)(*a*)).

GENERAL NOTE
This section is enacted in response to recommendations in the *Cork Report* paras. 1510–1513, and is designed to enable an administrative receiver to sell property free from a subsisting mortgage, charge, lien or other security if the Court is satisfied that such a sale is likely to promote a more advantageous realisation of the assets. The provision is considerably different from that contained in s.15 empowering an administrator to deal with charged property, and in particular it may be noted that an administrative receiver requires the authorisation of the Court in every instance where it is sought to dispose of property free from the effects of the charge or security. Moreover property which is subject to any charge falling within the terms of subs. (2) cannot be disposed of in this way. On the other hand, the same protection for the secured creditor's interest is achieved by subs. (3) as is accomplished in the case of the Administration Order procedure by s.15(5), and indeed the two provisions are here closely similar save that in s.49(3) there are no references to "goods" or "hire purchase agreement". The power of disposal under this section is partly designed to strengthen the receiver's position in any negotiations he may conduct with the charge holders in the hope of persuading them to sell a charged asset as part of a rescue scheme. If a secured creditor is unwilling to participate in such a scheme upon reasonable terms, and is thus threatening to frustrate the whole purpose of the receivership, the receiver can seek an order from the Court over-reaching the security in question. The section re-enacts s.49, I.A. 1985 with minor amendments.

Subs. (3)
(a) The net proceeds of the disposal; (b) the net amount which would be realised on a sale
See the Note to s.15(5).

Subs. (7)
This subsection is designed to prevent the power of sale from being exercisable in relation to properties over which there is a fixed charge but in respect of which the person who appointed the administrative receiver has no prior or subsequent floating charge.

Agency and liability for contracts

44.—(1) The administrative receiver of a company—
(*a*) is deemed to be the company's agent, unless and until the company goes into liquidation;
(*b*) is personally liable on any contract entered into by him in the carrying out of his functions (except in so far as the contract otherwise provides) and on any contract of employment adopted by him in the carrying out of those functions; and
(*c*) is entitled in respect of that liability to an indemnity out of the assets of the company.

(2) For the purposes of subsection (1)(*b*) the administrative receiver is not to be taken to have adopted a contract of employment by reason of anything done or omitted to be done within 14 days after his appointment.

(3) This section does not limit any right to indemnity which the administrative receiver would have apart from it, nor limit his liability on contracts entered into or adopted without authority, nor confer any right to indemnity in respect of that liability.

DEFINITIONS
"administrative receiver": ss.29(2), 251(*a*).
"company goes into liquidation": s.247(2).

GENERAL NOTE
This section reaffirms the principle that a receiver contracts with personal liability subject to a right to be indemnified out of the assets of the company in respect of his actions properly conducted within the terms of his authority. This liability may be avoided by means of an express provision in the contract, but is otherwise automatic. In addition the statutory rule is established that the receiver is to be deemed to be the agent of the company unless and until it goes into liquidation, and hence the company will be the contracting party in all cases regardless of whether the receiver is also personally liable on the contract. The provisions follow from the recommendations of paras. 455–469 of the *Cork Report,* and from para. 143 of the *White Paper.* The section re-enacts s.50, I.A. 1985 with minor amendments.

Subs. (2)
The administrative receiver is not to be taken as to have adopted a contract of employment by reason of anything done or omitted to be done within 14 days after his appointment
This provision, which is identically drafted to that of the rider to s.19(5), gives the administrative receiver a period of 14 days' grace from the time of his appointment, during which time he can assess the expediency of adopting any of the contracts of employment to which the company is a party, and if so can decide which of the contracts to adopt.

Subs. (3)
This subsection clarifies the position with respect to the indemnity to which a receiver is entitled under subs. (1)(*c*), and indicates that it only applies to liability incurred by the receiver in respect of contracts entered into or adopted by him in the carrying out of his functions. On the other hand the saving expression in respect of any other right of indemnity to which the receiver is entitled to is allow for the possibility that some express right of indemnity may be conferred by the instrument of appointment, and also takes account of the possibility that the court may exercise its discretion under s.34 where the receiver's appointment is invalid, to require the person who appointed the receiver to indemnify him against liability consequentially incurred.
Finally it is noteworthy that although all the provisions of this section are also included in the equivalent provision concerning the agency and liability of receivers in Scotland (s.57) the converse is not completely achieved because there are no counterparts in the statutory provisions for England and Wales of the provisions of s.57(4) and (7) which apply in Scotland only.

Vacation of office

45.—(1) An administrative receiver of a company may at any time be removed from office by order of the court (but not otherwise) and may resign his office by giving notice of his resignation in the prescribed manner to such persons as may be prescribed.

(2) An administrative receiver shall vacate office if he ceases to be qualified to act as an insolvency practitioner in relation to the company.

(3) Where at any time an administrative receiver vacates office—
(*a*) his remuneration and any expenses properly incurred by him, and
(*b*) any indemnity to which he is entitled out of the assets of the company,

shall be charged on and paid out of any property of the company which is in his custody or under his control at that time in priority to any security held by the person by or on whose behalf he was appointed.

(4) Where an administrative receiver vacates office otherwise than by death, he shall, within 14 days after his vacation of office, send a notice to that effect to the registrar of companies.

(5) If an administrative receiver without reasonable excuse fails to comply with subsection (4), he is liable to a fine and, for continued contravention, to a daily default fine.

DEFINITIONS
"administrative receiver": ss.29(2), 251(*a*).
"fine", "daily default fine": s.430, Sched. 10.
"prescribed": s.251.
"qualified to act as an insolvency practitioner in relation to company": s.390.
"security": s.248(*b*)

GENERAL NOTE
Subs. (1)
    This subsection specifies the sole mode of removal from office of an administrative receiver, namely by order of the court. This corresponds to the recommendation of para. 492 of the *Cork Report* that the receiver's independence should be strengthened by abolishing the right of the holder of the charge to remove him without notice. No further provisions are supplied in the section to indicate by whom an application for a receiver's removal may be made, or upon what grounds and upon what basis (mandatory or discretionary) the court may remove him (*cf.* the different position regarding removal of a receiver in Scotland under s.62, *q.v.*). The section does however make provision for voluntary resignation by a receiver, subject to the requirement that he gives due notice of his resignation in a manner to be prescribed by the rules. This part of the subsection fulfils the recommendation of para. 491 of the *Cork Report,* where it was further suggested that the required period of notice should be one month, and that the receiver should be obliged to give this notice to the company or its liquidator, to the holder of the charge, to the holders of any fixed security over the property of the company, and to the receiver's committee (if any).

Subs. (2)
    This maintains consistency with the provisions of Pt. XIII of the Act and in particular those of ss.388, 389, whereby it is a criminal offence for a person to act as an insolvency practitioner in relation to a company by acting as its administrative receiver at a time when he is not qualified to do so. The requirements for being qualified to act as an insolvency practitioner are contained in the provisions of s.390. Any administrative receiver who at any time ceases to satisfy any of those requirements is accordingly obliged by the present subsection to vacate office.

Subs. (3)
    This provides protection for the receiver after the termination of his appointment, with regard to the payment of his remuneration and proper expenses, and also with regard to any indemnity to which he is entitled, by giving the receiver's entitlements priority as against any security held by the debenture holder.

Subss. (4), (5)
    The requirement that the receiver must send notice of his vacation of office to the registrar of companies within 14 days, with the accompanying sanction of criminal penalties for non-compliance, is a counterpart to that attached to the discharge of an administration order by virtue of s.18(4) and (5) and s.24(6) and (7).

Administrative receivers: ascertainment and investigation of company's affairs

Information to be given by administrative receiver

46.—(1) Where an administrative receiver is appointed, he shall—
    (*a*) forthwith send to the company and publish in the prescribed manner a notice of his appointment, and

(*b*) within 28 days after his appointment, unless the court otherwise directs, send such a notice to all the creditors of the company (so far as he is aware of their addresses).

(2) This section and the next do not apply in relation to the appointment of an administrative receiver to act—

(*a*) with an existing administrative receiver, or

(*b*) in place of an administrative receiver dying or ceasing to act,

except that, where they apply to an administrative receiver who dies or ceases to act before they have been fully complied with, the references in this section and the next to the administrative receiver include (subject to the next subsection) his successor and any continuing administrative receiver.

(3) If the company is being wound up, this section and the next apply notwithstanding that the administrative receiver and the liquidator are the same person, but with any necessary modifications arising from that fact.

(4) If the administrative receiver without reasonable excuse fails to comply with this section, he is liable to a fine and, for continued contravention, to a daily default fine.

DEFINITIONS

"administrative receiver": ss.29(2), 251(*a*).

"prescribed": s.251.

"fine", "daily default fine": s.430, Sched. 10.

GENERAL NOTE

This section replaces s.52, I.A. 1985 and places the law of England and Wales on the same footing as that of Scotland with regard to the giving of notice of appointment by the person who becomes administrative receiver of a company (see s.65).

Subs. (1)

This provision is cast in terms identical to those of s.21 (regarding the giving of notice by an administrator) and thus creates a requirement in parallel to that imposed upon a liquidator with regard to the requirement that he should within 28 days advertise his appointment and advise all known creditors of the fact that it has taken place. This adopts the recommendation of para. 476 of the *Cork Report,* where it was also suggested that, in view of the cost involved, there should be no further requirement to send individual notice to shareholders, who would perforce need to rely on the general advertisement.

Subs. (2)

This is a sensible provision to make it clear that, when the requirements of subs. (1) have been complied with, there is no need to repeat the exercise of advertisement and giving of notice when any person is subsequently appointed as an additional administrative receiver or as a replacement to one who has died or ceased to act.

Statement of affairs to be submitted

47.—(1) Where an administrative receiver is appointed, he shall forthwith require some or all of the persons mentioned below to make out and submit to him a statement in the prescribed form as to the affairs of the company.

(2) A statement submitted under this section shall be verified by affidavit by the persons required to submit it and shall show—

(*a*) particulars of the company's assets, debts and liabilities;

(*b*) the names and addresses of its creditors;

(*c*) the securities held by them respectively;

(*d*) the dates when the securities were respectively given, and

(*e*) such further or other information as may be prescribed.

(3) The persons referred to in subsection (1) are—

(*a*) those who are or have been officers of the company;

(*b*) those who have taken part in the company's formation at any time within one year before the date of the appointment of the administrative receiver;

(c) those who are in the company's employment, or have been in its employment within that year, and are in the administrative receiver's opinion capable of giving the information required;

(d) those who are or have been within that year officers of or in the employment of a company which is, or within that year was, an officer of the company.

In this subsection "employment" includes employment under a contract for services.

(4) Where any persons are required under this section to submit a statement of affairs to the administrative receiver, they shall do so (subject to the next subsection) before the end of the period of 21 days beginning with the day after that on which the prescribed notice of the requirement is given to them by the administrative receiver.

(5) The administrative receiver, if he thinks fit, may—

(a) at any time release a person from an obligation imposed on him under subsection (1) or (2), or

(b) either when giving notice under subsection (4) or subsequently, extend the period so mentioned;

and where the administrative receiver has refused to exercise a power conferred by this subsection, the court, if it thinks fit, may exercise it.

(6) If a person without reasonable excuse fails to comply with any obligation imposed under this section, he is liable to a fine and, for continued contravention, to a daily default fine.

DEFINITIONS
"administrative receiver": s.29(2), 251(a).
"officers of the company": s.251; Companies Act 1985, s.744.
"prescribed": s.251.
"securities": s.248(b).

GENERAL NOTE
This section, which replaces s.53, I.A. 1985, is parallel to s.22 (q.v.), which relates to the obtaining of a statement of the company's affairs under the administration order procedure, and also to s.131, which applies where a company is wound up by the court. The three provisions are largely identical in substance, apart from the necessary differences in the relevant nomenclature employed, but the provisions of s.131 differ from those of both s.22 and the present section in that the Official Receiver enjoys a discretion to dispense with the requirement for a statement of affairs to be prepared, whereas both an administrator and an administrative receiver are under an obligation to require such a statement to be submitted. See also the General Note to s.22.

Report by administrative receiver

48.—(1) Where an administrative receiver is appointed, he shall, within 3 months (or such longer period as the court may allow) after his appointment, send to the registrar of companies, to any trustees for secured creditors of the company and (so far as he is aware of their addresses) to all such creditors a report as to the following matters, namely—

(a) the events leading up to his appointment, so far as he is aware of them;

(b) the disposal or proposed disposal by him of any property of the company and the carrying on or proposed carrying on by him of any business of the company;

(c) the amounts of principal and interest payable to the debenture holders by whom or on whose behalf he was appointed and the amounts payable to preferential creditors; and (*d*) the amount (if any) likely to be available for the payment of other creditors.

(2) The administrative receiver shall also, within 3 months (or such longer period as the court may allow) after his appointment, either—

(*a*) send a copy of the report (so far as he is aware of their addresses) to all unsecured creditors of the company; or

(*b*) publish in the prescribed manner a notice stating an address to which unsecured creditors of the company should write for copies of the report to be sent to them free of charge,

and (in either case), unless the court otherwise directs, lay a copy of the report before a meeting of the company's unsecured creditors summoned for the purpose on not less than 14 days' notice.

(3) The court shall not give a direction under subsection (2) unless—

(*a*) the report states the intention of the administrative receiver to apply for the direction, and

(*b*) a copy of the report is sent to the persons mentioned in paragraph (*a*) of that subsection, or a notice is published as mentioned in paragraph (*b*) of that subsection, not less than 14 days before the hearing of the application.

(4) Where the company has gone or goes into liquidation, the administrative receiver—

(*a*) shall, within 7 days after his compliance with subsection (1) or, if later, the nomination or appointment of the liquidator, send a copy of the report to the liquidator, and

(*b*) where he does so within the time limited for compliance with subsection (2), is not required to comply with that subsection.

(5) A report under this section shall include a summary of the statement of affairs made out and submitted to the administrative receiver under section 47 and of his comments (if any) upon it.

(6) Nothing in this section is to be taken as requiring any such report to include any information the disclosure of which would seriously prejudice the carrying out by the administrative receiver of his functions.

(7) Section 46(2) applies for the purposes of this section also.

(8) If the administrative receiver without reasonable excuse fails to comply with this section, he is liable to a fine and, for continued contravention, to a daily default fine.

Definitions

"administrative receiver": ss.29(2), 251(*a*).
"business": s.436.
"company goes into liquidation": s.247(2).
"fine", "daily default fine": s.430, Sched. 10.
"preferential creditor": s.386, Sched. 6.
"prescribed": s.251.
"property": s.436.
"secured creditor": s.248(*a*).

General Note

This provision adopts the recommendation made in para. 480 of the *Cork Report* and accepted with augmentation in paras. 147–148 of the *White Paper,* that a receiver should be required to furnish properly prepared information to the general body of creditors, so that they may be better informed and more directly involved. The section breaks new ground by requiring that the receiver's report must be sent to both secured and unsecured creditors and that the report is also to be laid before a meeting of the unsecured creditors unless the court accedes to an application for a dispensation from this requirement. If such a meeting is convened the creditors may exercise their right under s.49 to appoint a committee of creditors to maintain contact with the receiver and to obtain further information from him on a regular basis. The section is derived from s.54, I.A. 1985 with minor amendments.

Subs. (4)

This takes care of the possibility that the receivership may be overtaken by a winding up of the company. The requirement that the receiver's report must be sent also to the liquidator within the specified time is designed to ensure that the latter enjoys the benefit of immediate availability of the fruits of the receiver's earlier investigation and appraisal of the company's circumstances, while the provision in subs. 4(*b*) allows the receiver to be released from the obligation to notify the unsecured creditors, and to convene them in a meeting, pursuant to subs. (2), where the collective procedure of winding up has commenced, and the liquidator has been duly sent a copy of the report, before the expiry of the three month time limit contained in subs. (2).

Subs. (6)

This rather mysteriously worded provision is apparently designed to permit the adminis-trative receiver to exclude from his report anything which might be considered commercially sensitive, such as sales transactions or other agreements in course of negotiation at the time when the report is issued (see H.C. Standing Committee E, June 20, 1985, col. 509). The subsection is drafted in terms which are both wide and vague, and open to a considerable amount of subjective interpretation by the administrative receiver. The fact that the receiver will henceforth in all cases be a qualified insolvency practitioner is presumably regarded as sufficient guarantee against abuse of the obvious scope in the section for substantial omissions to be made which would effectively render the report valueless.

Subs. (7)

This incorporates by reference the provisions of subs. (2) of s.46, so that a person who is appointed as a joint receiver in addition to one who is already serving, or a person appointed to replace a receiver who has died or ceased to act, shall not be placed in the absurd position of having to issue a report under this section when the task has already been performed by a person appointed previously.

Committee of creditors

49.—(1) Where a meeting of creditors is summoned under section 48, the meeting may, if it thinks fit, establish a committee ("the creditors' committee") to exercise the functions conferred on it by or under this Act.

(2) If such a committee is established, the committee may, on giving not less than 7 days' notice, require the administrative receiver to attend before it at any reasonable time and furnish it with such information relating to the carrying out by him of his functions as it may reasonably require.

DEFINITION
"administrative receiver": ss.29(2), 251(*a*).

GENERAL NOTE
This section is a parallel to ss.26 (which applies with regard to an administration order) and 68 (which applies to Scotland). More elaborate provisions concerning the appointment and functions of a creditors' committee in a winding up by the court in England or in Scotland are contained in ss.141 and 142 respectively. See also the General Note to s.26, and the discussion in paras. 442–454 of the *Cork Report* regarding the need for greater accountability of receivers, and in paras. 477–479, 481 and 930–967 of the *Report* regarding meetings of creditors and committees of creditors.

CHAPTER II

RECEIVERS (SCOTLAND)

Extent of this Chapter

50. This Chapter extends to Scotland only.

GENERAL NOTE
See annotation to s.28.

Power to appoint receiver

51.—(1) It is competent under the law of Scotland for the holder of a floating charge over all or any part of the property (including uncalled capital), which may from time to time be comprised in the property and undertaking of an incorporated company (whether a company within the meaning of the Companies Act or not) which the Court of Session has jurisdiction to wind up, to appoint a receiver of such part of the property of the company as is subject to the charge.

(2) It is competent under the law of Scotland for the court, on the application of the holder of such a floating charge, to appoint a receiver of such part of the property of the company as is subject to the charge.

(3) The following are disqualified from being appointed as receiver—

    (*a*) a body corporate;

    (*b*) an undischarged bankrupt; and

    (*c*) a firm according to the law of Scotland.

(4) A body corporate or a firm according to the law of Scotland which acts as a receiver is liable to a fine.

(5) An undischarged bankrupt who so acts is liable to imprisonment or a fine, or both.

(6) In this section, "receiver" includes joint receivers.

DEFINITIONS
"fine": s.430, Sched. 10.
"floating charge": s.462, C.A. 1985; s.251.
"holder of such a floating charge": s.70(1).

TRANSITIONAL PROVISION: Sched. 11, para. 3.

GENERAL NOTE
The concept of a floating charge was transplanted into Scottish law by the Companies (Floating Charges) (Scotland) Act 1961. However it was soon recognised that this reform would not succeed unless the idea of a receiver, an ideal mechanism for enforcing such a security, was also transplanted—see Scottish Law Commission (1970) (Cmnd. 4336, para. 38): this was a dramatic reform in Scottish law which had no notion of a receiver. There was the possibility of a judicial factor to act as a caretaker during a debilitating internal dispute as in *Fraser, Petitioner* 1971 S.L.T. 146, but this was no true receiver. These provisions on receivers have posed major problems of interpretation for the courts. The response of the Scottish courts has been to view them as a sort of inviolate code which cannot be prejudiced by the common law of Scotland. For comments on the position in Scotland see *Palmer*, (23rd ed.), Ch. 47, *Reed* 1983 S.L.T. 229, 237, 261 and also the article by *Wilson* in 1984 S.L.T. 105. The section is derived from s.11, C. (F.C. & R.) (S.) A. 1972 and s.467, C.A. 1985. See generally note to s.28.

Subs. (1)
This subsection authorises the holder of a floating charge to appoint a receiver out of court in Scotland.

Subs. (2)
This subsection authorises the court to make such an appointment.

Subs. (3)
Neither a body corporate nor a firm under Scottish law can act as a receiver. Note that there is no provision in English law imposing a similar disqualification on a partnership—this is because the English partnership as opposed to the Scottish firm (Partnership Act 1890, s.4(2)) lacks legal personality. An undischarged bankrupt is also disqualified from acting as such by subs. (3). For disqualifications in England note ss.30–31 *supra*. Unqualified persons (see ss.388, 389) are banned from acting as "administrative receivers" (defined in s.251).

Subs. (4)

This subsection imposes the sanction of a fine where either a body corporate or firm acts as a receiver.

Subs. (5)

Where an undischarged bankrupt acts as a receiver, then on conviction, whether on indictment or after summary trial, he is liable to a fine *and/or* imprisonment.

Subs. (6)

All of the above provisions apply equally to joint receivers.

Circumstances justifying appointment

52.—(1) A receiver may be appointed under section 51(1) by the holder of the floating charge on the occurrence of any event which, by the provisions of the instrument creating the charge, entitles the holder of the charge to make that appointment and, in so far as not otherwise provided for by the instrument, on the occurrence of any of the following events, namely—

   (a) the expiry of a period of 21 days after the making of a demand for payment of the whole or any part of the principal sum secured by the charge, without payment having been made;

   (b) the expiry of a period of 2 months during the whole of which interest due and payable under the charge has been in arrears;

   (c) the making of an order or the passing of a resolution to wind up the company;

   (d) the appointment of a receiver by virtue of any other floating charge created by the company.

(2) A receiver may be appointed by the court under section 51(2) on the occurrence of any event which, by the provisions of the instrument creating the floating charge, entitles the holder of the charge to make that appointment and, in so far as not otherwise provided for by the instrument, on the occurrence of any of the following events, namely—

   (a) where the court, on the application of the holder of the charge, pronounces itself satisfied that the position of the holder of the charge is likely to be prejudiced if no such appointment is made;

   (b) any of the events referred to in paragraphs (a) to (c) of subsection (1).

DEFINITIONS

"floating charge": s.744, C.A. 1985; s.251; s.70(3), (4).
"receiver": s.70(1).
"holder of the floating charge": s.70(2).

GENERAL NOTE

This section is derived from s.12, C. (F. C. & R.) (S.) A. 1972 and s.468, C.A. 1985.

Subs. (1)

Specifies four grounds (a)–(d) upon which a holder of a floating charge may appoint a receiver out of court. These grounds may be varied by provisions in the instrument of charge itself. The reasons listed are commonly found in English debentures.

Subs. (2)

This subsection states that a court appointment may also be made where the instrument of charge permits it, on grounds (a)–(c) in subs. (1), and also where the court is "satisfied that the position of the holder of the charge is likely to be prejudiced if no such appointment is made" (subs. 2(a)). This is comparable to the English concept of "jeopardy" (see *Palmer*, (23rd ed.), para. 46–06), but it must be said that any sort of court appointment of a receiver these days is a rarity.

Mode of appointment by holder of charge

53.—(1) The appointment of a receiver by the holder of the floating charge under section 51(1) shall be by means of a validly executed instrument in writing ("the instrument of appointment"), a copy (certified in the prescribed manner to be a correct copy) whereof shall be delivered by or on behalf of the person making the appointment to the registrar of companies for registration within 7 days of its execution and shall be accompanied by a notice in the prescribed form.

(2) If any person without reasonable excuse makes default in complying with the requirements of subsection (1), he is liable to a fine and, for continued contravention, to a daily default fine.

(3) The instrument of appointment is validly executed—

   (*a*) by a company, if it is executed in accordance with the provisions of section 36 of the Companies Act as if it were a contract, and

   (*b*) by any other person, if it is executed in the manner required or permitted by the law of Scotland in the case of an attested deed.

(4) The instrument may be executed on behalf of the holder of the floating charge by virtue of which the receiver is to be appointed—

   (*a*) by any person duly authorised in writing by the holder to execute the instrument, and

   (*b*) in the case of an appointment of a receiver by the holders of a series of secured debentures, by any person authorised by resolution of the debenture-holders to execute the instrument.

(5) On receipt of the certified copy of the instrument of appointment in accordance with subsection (1), the registrar shall, on payment of the prescribed fee, enter the particulars of the appointment in the register charges.

(6) The appointment of a person as a receiver by an in~
appointment in accordance with subsection (1)—

   (*a*) is of no effect unless it is accepted by that person b
   of the business day next following that on which the i
   appointment is received by him or on his behalf, and

   (*b*) subject to paragraph (*a*), is deemed to be made on the d
   at the time at which the instrument of appointment is so r
   as evidenced by a written docquet by that person or on his

and this subsection applies to the appointment of joint receivers su
to such modifications as may be prescribed.

(7) On the appointment of a receiver under this section, the floatn
charge by virtue of which he was appointed attaches to the property then subject to the charge; and such attachment has effect as if the charge was a fixed security over the property to which it has attached.

DEFINITIONS
   "fine", "daily default fine": s.430, Sched. 10.
   "fixed security": s.70(1).
   "holder of a floating charge": s.70(2).
   "receiver": s.70(1).
   "register of charges": s.70(1).
   "registrar of companies": s.774, C.A. 1985.

GENERAL NOTE
   This section specifies the procedure to be followed where a receiver is appointed out of court. Each subsection is based on the seven subsections in C. (F.C. and R.)(S.) A. 1972, s.13 and in s.469, C.A. 1985.

Subs. (1)
   A formal instrument of appointment is required and the registrar must be notified within seven days.

Subs. (2)

Failure to comply with subs. (1) may result in a fine or daily default fine.

Subss. (3), (4)

These subsections state in detail how the instrument of appointment can be properly executed by the parties or their agents.

Subs. (5)

On notification the registrar must enter the fact of the appointment in his register of charges.

Subs. (6)

The appointment in Scottish law used to run from the date of the execution of the instrument of appointment. By way of contrast in English law the appointment only commenced when the receiver accepted it—Cork Committee (Cmnd. 8558, para. 473). Subs. (6) assimilates the law of England and Scotland. The appointment must be accepted within 24 hours and, subject to that, it will run from the date of the receipt of the letter of appointment.

Subs. (7)

The effect of the appointment is to crystallise the floating charge into a fixed security.

Appointment by court

54.—(1) Application for the appointment of a receiver by the court under section 51(2) shall be by petition to the court, which shall be served on the company.

(2) On such an application, the court shall, if it thinks fit, issue an interlocutor making the appointment of the receiver.

(3) A copy (certified by the clerk of the court to be a correct copy) of the court's interlocutor making the appointment shall be delivered by or on behalf of the petitioner to the registrar of companies for registration, accompanied by a notice in the prescribed form, within 7 days of the date of the interlocutor or such longer period as the court may allow.

If any person without reasonable excuse makes default in complying with the requirements of this subsection, he is liable to a fine and, for continued contravention, to a daily default fine.

(4) On receipt of the certified copy interlocutor in accordance with subsection (3), the registrar shall, on payment of the prescribed fee, enter the particulars of the appointment in the register of charges.

(5) The receiver is to be regarded as having been appointed on the date of his being appointed by the court.

(6) On the appointment of a receiver under this section, the floating charge by virtue of which he was appointed attaches to the property then subject to the charge; and such attachment has effect as if the charge were a fixed security over the property to which it has attached.

(7) In making rules of court for the purposes of this section, the Court of Session shall have regard to the need for special provision for cases which appear to the court to require to be dealt with as a matter of urgency.

DEFINITIONS

"fine", "daily default fine": s.430, Sched. 10.
"receiver": s.70(1).
"registrar": s.744, C.A. 1985.
"register of charges": s.70(1).
"registrar of companies": s.744, C.A. 1985.

GENERAL NOTE

This section describes the procedure to be followed where a receiver is appointed by the court. It is derived from s.14 C.(F.C. and R.)(S.)A. 1972 and s.470, C.A. 1985. It no longer refers to caution but an administrative receiver (s.251) to qualify as an insolvency practitioner would have to be covered by a caution (see ss.388–90 *infra*).

Subs. (1)
Application is to be by petition to the court.

Subs. (2)
The court enjoys general discretion as to whether to grant the interlocutor (order).

Subs. (3)
The petitioner must ensure that a copy of the interlocutor is sent to the registrar of companies within seven days, or longer if the court permits. Failure to do this may result in a fine, or daily default fine.

Subs. (4)
The registrar must enter the fact of the appointment in his register of charges.

Subss. (5), (6)
The appointment runs from the date of the court interlocutor and the effect of the appointment is to crystallise the floating charge.

Subs. (7)
The Court of Session is directed to make special rules enabling it to deal with urgent cases.

Powers of receiver

55.—(1) Subject to the next subsection, a receiver has in relation to such part of the property of the company as is attached by the floating charge by virtue of which he was appointed, the powers, if any, given to him by the instrument creating that charge.

(2) In addition, the receiver has under this Chapter the powers as respects that property (in so far as these are not inconsistent with any provision contained in that instrument) which are specified in Schedule 2 to this Act.

(3) Subsections (1) and (2) apply—
    (*a*) subject to the rights of any person who has effectually executed diligence on all or any part of the property of the company prior to the appointment of the receiver, and
    (*b*) subject to the rights of any person who holds over all or any part of the property of the company a fixed security or floating charge having priority over, or ranking pari passu with, the floating charge by virtue of which the receiver was appointed.

(4) A person dealing with a receiver in good faith and for value is not concerned to enquire whether the receiver is acting within his powers.

DEFINITIONS
"fixed security": s.70(1).
"floating charge": s.744, C.A. 1985; s.251; s.70(3), (4).
"receiver": s.70(1).

GENERAL NOTE
Subs. (1)
This subsection applies irrespective of whether the appointment was by the court or out of court.

Subs. (2)
The powers of a receiver in Scotland, previously listed in s.471(1), C.A. 1985, served as a model code for the powers of administrators and administrative receivers in England and Wales. The powers of the former having undergone drafting changes, are now listed in

Sched. 2, while those of the latter appear in Sched. 1. This list can of course be modified by the instrument under which the receiver was appointed.

Subs. (3)

The receiver's powers are subject to the rights of those persons who might have a prior claim on the company's assets—*e.g.* a prior chargee or a person who has prior to his appointment "effectually executed diligence" on the company's assets—on this phrase see the annotation to s.60 *infra.*

Subs. (4)

This protects a person dealing with the receiver in good faith and for value from the consequences of lack of authority.

Precedence among receivers

56.—(1) Where there are two or more floating charges subsisting over all or any part of the property of the company, a receiver may be appointed under this Chapter by virtue of each such charge; but a receiver appointed by, or on the application of, the holder of a floating charge having priority of ranking over any other floating charge by virtue of which a receiver has been appointed has the powers given to a receiver by section 55 and Schedule 2 to the exclusion of any other receiver.

(2) Where two or more floating charges rank with one another equally, and two or more receivers have been appointed by virtue of such charges, the receivers so appointed are deemed to have been appointed as joint receivers.

(3) Receivers appointed, or deemed to have been appointed, as joint receivers shall act jointly unless the instrument of appointment or respective instruments of appointment otherwise provide.

(4) Subject to subsection (5) below, the powers of a receiver appointed by, or on the application of, the holder of a floating charge are suspended by, and as from the date of, the appointment of a receiver by, or on the application of, the holder of a floating charge having priority of ranking over that charge to such extent as may be necessary to enable the receiver second mentioned to exercise his powers under section 55 and Schedule 2; and any powers so suspended take effect again when the floating charge having priority of ranking ceases to attach to the property then subject to the charge, whether such cessation is by virtue of section 62(6) or otherwise.

(5) The suspension of the powers of a receiver under subsection (4) does not have the effect of requiring him to release any part of the property (including any letters or documents) of the company from his control until he receives from the receiver superseding him a valid indemnity (subject to the limit of the value of such part of the property of the company as is subject to the charge by virtue of which he was appointed) in respect of any expenses, charges and liabilities he may have incurred in the performance of his functions as receiver.

(6) The suspension of the powers of a receiver under subsection (4) does not cause the floating charge by virtue of which he was appointed to cease to attach to the property to which it attached by virtue of section 53(7) or 54(6).

(7) Nothing in this section prevents the same receiver being appointed by virtue of two or more floating charges.

DEFINITIONS

"floating charge": s.744, C.A. 1985, s.251.
"holder of a floating charge": s.70(1).
"instrument of appointment": s.53(1), 70(1).
"receiver": s.70(1).

GENERAL NOTE

This section governs precedence amongst receivers where the company has created several floating charges over its assets. Its seven subsections mirror exactly the seven subsections of C.(F.C. and R.)(S.)A. 1972, s.16 and C.A. 1985, s.472.

Subs. (1)

This subsection anticipates the possibility of two or more receivers being appointed over the assets of the company but only the receiver acting for the floating charge enjoying priority has the powers specified under this Act.

Subss. (2), (3)

If floating charges rank equally then those receivers are deemed to be joint receivers and they must exercise their powers jointly.

Subs. (4)

A receiver's powers may be suspended where a receiver is subsequently appointed by a person with a prior floating charge.

Subs. (5)

The receiver, however, whose powers have been suspended must not hand over the assets gathered in by him until he receives an indemnity from the receiver who is supplanting him.

Subs. (6)

Where a receiver's powers are suspended this does not cause the floating charge under which he was appointed to refloat.

Subs. (7)

This subsection offers a way out of the problem of precedence among receivers. The holders of two or more floating charges can appoint the same person as receiver—but this of course can lead to conflicts of interest.

Agency and liability of receiver for contracts

57.—(1) A receiver is deemed to be the agent of the company in relation to such property of the company as is attached by the floating charge by virtue of which he was appointed.

(2) A receiver (including a receiver whose powers are subsequently suspended under section 56) is personally liable on any contract entered into by him in the performance of his functions, except in so far as the contract otherwise provides, and on any contract of employment adopted by him in the carrying out of those functions.

(3) A receiver who is personally liable by virtue of subsection (2) is entitled to be indemnified out of the property in respect of which he was appointed.

(4) Any contract entered into by or on behalf of the company prior to the appointment of a receiver continues in force (subject to its terms) notwithstanding that appointment, but the receiver does not by virtue only of his appointment incur any personal liability on any such contract.

(5) For the purposes of subsection (2), a receiver is not to be taken to have adopted a contract of employment by reason of anything done or omitted to be done within 14 days after his appointment.

(6) This section does not limit any right to indemnity which the receiver would have apart from it, nor limit his liability on contracts entered into or adopted without authority, nor confer any right to indemnity in respect of that liability.

(7) Any contract entered into by a receiver in the performance of his functions continues in force (subject to its terms) although the powers of the receiver are subsequently suspended under section 56.

DEFINITIONS
    "floating charge": s.744, C.A. 1985; s.251.
    "receiver": s.70(1).

GENERAL NOTE
    This section is derived from s.473, C.A. 1985 as amended by s.58, I.A. 1985. The purpose of the amendment was to bring the Scottish provision into line with that applicable in England and Wales (now s.44 *supra*). The reference to contracts of employment in subs. (2) and the whole of subs. (5) and subs. (6) are new. See further the Note to s.44.

Remuneration of receiver

58.—(1) The remuneration to be paid to a receiver is to be determined by agreement between the receiver and the holder of the floating charge by virtue of which he was appointed.

(2) Where the remuneration to be paid to the receiver has not been determined under subsection (1), or where it has been so determined but is disputed by any of the persons mentioned in paragraphs (*a*) to (*d*) below, it may be fixed instead by the Auditor of the Court of Session on application made to him by—

(*a*) the receiver;

(*b*) the holder of any floating charge or fixed security over all or any part of the property of the company;

(*c*) the company; or

(*d*) the liquidator of the company.

(3) Where the receiver has been paid or has retained for his remuneration for any period before the remuneration has been fixed by the Auditor of the Court of Session under subsection (2) any amount in excess of the remuneration so fixed for that period, the receiver or his personal representatives shall account for the excess.

DEFINITIONS
    "fixed security": s.70(1).
    "holder of a floating charge": s.70(2).
    "receiver": s.70(1).

GENERAL NOTE
    This section regulates a receiver's remuneration. It is derived from s.474, C.A. 1985 (part).

Subs. (1)
    As a general rule this will be fixed by agreement with the holder of the floating charge by virtue of which the receiver was appointed.

Subs. (2)
    Where this has not been done, or where it is disputed, application to the Auditor of the Court of Session is possible for it to be determined.

Subs. (3)
    If the receiver has received remuneration in excess of the figure fixed by the Auditor of the Court of Session he is liable to remit the excess.

Priority of debts

59.—(1) Where a receiver is appointed and the company is not at the time of the appointment in course of being wound up, the debts which fall under subsection (2) of this section shall be paid out of any assets coming to the hands of the receiver in priority to any claim for principal or interest by the holder of the floating charge by virtue of which the receiver was appointed.

(2) Debts falling under this subsection are preferential debts (within the meaning given by section 386 in Part XII) which, by the end of a period of 6 months after advertisement by the receiver for claims in the Edinburgh Gazette and in a newspaper circulating in the district where the company carries on business either—

(i) have been intimated to him, or

(ii) have become known to him.

(3) Any payments made under this section shall be recouped as far as may be out of the assets of the company available for payment of ordinary creditors.

DEFINITIONS

"holder of the floating charge": s.70(2).
"preferential debts": s.386.
"receiver": s.70(1).

GENERAL NOTE

This section, which is derived from s.475(1), (2) and (5), C.A. 1985 and I.A. 1985, Sched. 6, para. 20(2), deals with the repayment of preferential debts by the receiver out of the realised assets. The English counterpart is s.40 *supra*.

Subs. (1)

This subsection imposes the basic obligation to pay preferential debts on the receiver.

Subs. (2)

Preferential debts are those listed in Pt. XII of the Act *and* which have become known to the receiver within six months of him advertising for claims in the Edinburgh Gazette. This is a useful facility which is not to be found in English law. The Cork Committee (Cmnd. 8558, para. 490 has recommended its introduction.

Subs. (3)

Any payments made by the receiver out of the monies destined for the holder of the floating charge are to be recouped from the funds available for the general creditors.

Distribution of moneys

60.—(1) Subject to the next section, and to the rights of any of the following categories of persons (which rights shall, except to the extent otherwise provided in any instrument, have the following order of priority), namely—

(*a*) the holder of any fixed security which is over property subject to the floating charge and which ranks prior to, or pari passu with, the floating charge;

(*b*) all persons who have effectually executed diligence on any part of the property of the company which is subject to the charge by virtue of which the receiver was appointed;

(*c*) creditors in respect of all liabilities, charges and expenses incurred by or on behalf of the receiver;

(*d*) the receiver in respect of his liabilities, expenses and remuneration, and any indemnity to which he is entitled out of the property of the company; and

(*e*) the preferential creditors entitled to payment under section 59,

the receiver shall pay moneys received by him to the holder of the floating charge by virtue of which the receiver was appointed in or towards satisfaction of the debt secured by the floating charge.

(2) Any balance of moneys remaining after the provisions of subsection (1) and section 61 below have been satisfied shall be paid in accordance with their respective rights and interests to the following persons, as the case may require—

(*a*) any other receiver;

(b) the holder of a fixed security which is over property subject to the floating charge;

(c) the company or its liquidator, as the case may be.

(3) Where any question arises as to the person entitled to a payment under this section, or where a receipt or a discharge of a security cannot be obtained in respect of any such payment, the receiver shall consign the amount of such payment in any joint stock bank of issue in Scotland in name of the Accountant of Court for behoof of the person or persons entitled thereto.

DEFINITIONS
"fixed security": s.70(1).
"floating charge": s.744, C.A. 1985; s.251.
"receiver": s.70(1).

GENERAL NOTE
This section maps out the general order of repayment to be adopted by the receiver. It is derived from s.476, C.A. 1985 and I.A. 1985, Sched. 6, para. 21.

Subs. (1)
This subsection specifies, in order of priority, those claimants who take priority over the floating charge holder. As to those who have effectually executed diligence (para. (b)), see *Lord Advocate* v. *Royal Bank of Scotland*, 1977 S.C. 155; *Gordon Anderson Plant Ltd.* 1977 S.L.T. 7, *Cumbernauld Development Corp.* v. *Mustone Ltd.* 1983 S.L.T. (Sh.Ct.) 55 and *Forth and Clyde Construction* v. *Trinity Timber and Plywood Co.* 1984 S.L.T. 94.

Subs. (2)
After making all necessary payments the receiver must hand over the balance of any proceeds of realisation to either the company, its liquidator, any other receiver or chargee, whichever is the most appropriate.

Subs. (3)
Where disputes arise as to payment the disputed sum must be paid by the receiver into a recognised Scottish bank in the name of the Accountant of the Court pending settlement.

Disposal of interest in property

61.—(1) Where the receiver sells or disposes, or is desirous of selling or disposing, of any property or interest in property of the company which is subject to the floating charge by virtue of which the receiver was appointed and which is—

(a) subject to any security or interest of, or burden or encumbrance in favour of, a creditor the ranking of which is prior to, or pari passu with, or postponed to the floating charge, or

(b) property or an interest in property affected or attached by effectual diligence executed by any person,

and the receiver is unable to obtain the consent of such creditor or, as the case may be, such person to such a sale or disposal, the receiver may apply to the court for authority to sell or dispose of the property or interest in property free of such security, interest, burden, encumbrance or diligence.

(2) Subject to the next subsection, on such an application the court may, if it thinks fit, authorise the sale or disposal of the property or interest in question free of such security, interest, burden, encumbrance or diligence, and such authorisation may be on such terms or conditions as the court thinks fit.

(3) In the case of an application where a fixed security over the property or interest in question which ranks prior to the floating charge has not been met or provided for in full, the court shall not authorise the sale or disposal of the property or interest in question unless it is satisfied that

the sale or disposal would be likely to provide a more advantageous realisation of the company's assets than would otherwise be effected.

(4) It shall be a condition of an authorisation to which subsection (3) applies that—

(a) the net proceeds of the disposal, and

(b) where those proceeds are less than such amount as may be determined by the court to be the net amount which would be realised on a sale of the property or interest in the open market by a willing seller, such sums as may be required to make good the deficiency,

shall be applied towards discharging the sums secured by the fixed security.

(5) Where a condition imposed in pursuance of subsection (4) relates to two or more such fixed securities, that condition shall require the net proceeds of the disposal and, where paragraph (b) of that subsection applies, the sums mentioned in that paragraph to be applied towards discharging the sums secured by those fixed securities in the order of their priorities.

(6) A copy of an authorisation under subsection (2) certified by the clerk of court shall, within 14 days of the granting of the authorisation, be sent by the receiver to the registrar of companies.

(7) If the receiver without reasonable excuse fails to comply with subsection (6), he is liable to a fine and, for continued contravention, to a daily default fine.

(8) Where any sale or disposal is effected in accordance with the authorisation of the court under subsection (2), the receiver shall grant to the purchaser or disponee an appropriate document of transfer or conveyance of the property or interest in question, and that document has the effect, or, where recording, intimation or registration of that document is a legal requirement for completion of title to the property or interest, then that recording, intimation or registration (as the case may be) has the effect, of—

(a) disencumbering the property or interest of the security, interest, burden or encumbrance affecting it, and

(b) freeing the property or interest from the diligence executed upon it.

(9) Nothing in this section prejudices the right of any creditor of the company to rank for his debt in the winding up of the company.

DEFINITIONS
"fixed security": s.70(1).
"receiver": s.70(1).

GENERAL NOTE
This section is derived from s.477, C.A. 1985 as amended by s.59, I.A. 1985. In its amended form its provisions match s.43 of the present Act which relates to administrative receivers in England and Wales, subject to certain discrepancies attributable to the technical differences between English law and Scottish law. See Note to s.43 *supra*. The protection afforded to persons with a fixed security (s.477(2), C.A. 1985) has been diminished by the more liberal terms of subs. (3) and (4). "Effectual diligence"—see Note to s.60.

Cessation of appointment of receiver

62.—(1) A receiver may be removed from office by the court under subsection (3) below and may resign his office by giving notice of his resignation in the prescribed manner to such persons as may be prescribed.

(2) A receiver shall vacate office if he ceases to be qualified to act as an insolvency practitioner in relation to the company.

(3) Subject to the next subsection, a receiver may, on application to the court by the holder of the floating charge by virtue of which he was appointed, be removed by the court on cause shown.

(4) Where at any time a receiver vacates office—

(*a*) his remuneration and any expenses properly incurred by him, and

(*b*) any indemnity to which he is entitled out of the property of the company,

shall be paid out of the property of the company which is subject to the floating charge and shall have priority as provided for in section 60(1).

(5) When a receiver ceases to act as such otherwise than by death he shall, and, when a receiver is removed by the court, the holder of the floating charge by virtue of which he was appointed shall, within 14 days of the cessation or removal (as the case may be) give the registrar of companies notice to that effect, and the registrar shall enter the notice in the register of charges.

If the receiver or the holder of the floating charge (as the case may require) makes default in complying with the requirements of this subsection, he is liable to a fine and, for continued contravention, to a daily default fine.

(6) If by the expiry of a period of one month following upon the removal of the receiver or his ceasing to act as such no other receiver has been appointed, the floating charge by virtue of which the receiver was appointed—

(*a*) thereupon ceases to attach to the property then subject to the charge, and

(*b*) again subsists as a floating charge;

and for the purposes of calculating the period of one month under this subsection no account shall be taken of any period during which an administration order under Part II of this Act is in force.

DEFINITIONS

"floating charge": s.744, C.A. 1985; s.251.

"prescribed": s.70(1).

"property": s.436.

"qualified to act as an insolvency practitioner": s.390.

"receiver": s.70(1).

GENERAL NOTE

This section derives from s.478 of the Companies Act 1985 as amended by s.60, I.A. 1985. Its provisions now correspond closely in substance to those of s.45 of this Act, which are applicable in England and Wales. However, there is no counterpart in s.45 to the provision in subs. (3) which enables a receiver to be removed by the court on cause shown on an application by the holder of the floating charge by virtue of which the receiver was appointed. S.45 fails to indicate by whom an application may be made for the removal of an administrative receiver but the terms of subss. (1) and (3) of this section could perhaps serve as an analogy on which to base the proposition that the only party with standing to make application for the dismissal of an administrative receiver in England is the holder of the floating charge by virtue of which he was appointed.

Subs. (1)

See Note to s.45(1).

Subs. (2)

See Note to s.45(2).

Subs. (3)

Any dismissal of a receiver can only be by the court on cause shown.

Subs. (4)

See Note to s.45(3).

Subs. (5)

Notice of a receiver ceasing to act shall be given by the appropriate person to the registrar of companies within fourteen days of that happening, and the registrar must record the fact in his register of charges. Failure to do this can result in the receiver or the holder of the floating charge being fined.

Subs. (6)

If no replacement receiver is installed within one month then the floating charge will "refloat". The time limit is suspended while an administration order is in force because during that period any receiver will be supplanted by the administrator.

Powers of court

63.—(1) The court on the application of—

(*a*) the holder of a floating charge by virtue of which a receiver was appointed, or

(*b*) a receiver appointed under section 51,

may give directions to the receiver in respect of any matter arising in connection with the performance by him of his functions.

(2) Where the appointment of a person as a receiver by the holder of a floating charge is discovered to be invalid (whether by virtue of the invalidity of the instrument or otherwise), the court may order the holder of the floating charge to indemnify the person appointed against any liability which arises solely by reason of the invalidity of the appointment.

DEFINITIONS

"floating charge": s.744, C.A. 1985; s.251.
"holder of a floating charge": s.70(2).
"receiver": s.70(1).

GENERAL NOTE

This section re-enacts s.61, I.A. 1985, which completely replaced the provisions of s.479 of the Companies Act 1985 as originally enacted, and substituted new provisions which parallel in substance the position under the law applicable in England and Wales. Subs. (1) parallels for Scotland subs. (1) of s.35 (receivers and managers appointed out of court in England and Wales). Subs. (2) parallels for Scotland the provisions of s.34 of this Act (*q.v.*), which are applicable in England and Wales.

Notification that receiver appointed

64.—(1) Where a receiver has been appointed, every invoice, order for goods or business letter issued by or on behalf of the company or the receiver or the liquidator of the company, being a document on or in which the name of the company appears, shall contain a statement that a receiver has been appointed.

(2) If default is made in complying with the requirements of this section, the company and any of the following persons who knowingly and wilfully authorises or permits the default, namely any officer of the company, any liquidator of the company and any receiver, is liable to a fine.

DEFINITIONS

"fines": s.430, Sched. 10.
"receiver": s.70(1).

GENERAL NOTE

The parallel provision in English Law is s.39 *supra* (*q.v.*).

Subs. (1)

Where a receiver is appointed all invoices, business letters, etc., must disclose the fact of his appointment. For its predecessor see s.480(1), C.A. 1985.

Subs. (2)

Failure to comply with subs. (1) can result in fines for company officers, the receiver and liquidator where appropriate. For its derivation see s.480(2), C.A. 1985.

Information to be given by receiver

65.—(1) Where a receiver is appointed, he shall—

(a) forthwith send to the company and publish notice of his appointment, and

(b) within 28 days after his appointment, unless the court otherwise directs, send such notice to all the creditors of the company (so far as he is aware of their addresses).

(2) This section and the next do not apply in relation to the appointment of a receiver to act—

(a) with an existing receiver, or

(b) in place of a receiver who has died or ceased to act,

except that, where they apply to a receiver who dies or ceases to act before they have been fully complied with, the references in this section and the next to the receiver include (subject to subsection (3) of this section) his successor and any continuing receiver.

(3) If the company is being wound up, this section and the next apply notwithstanding that the receiver and the liquidator are the same person, but with any necessary modifications arising from that fact.

(4) If a person without reasonable excuse fails to comply with this section, he is liable to a fine and, for continued contravention, to a daily default fine.

DEFINITIONS

"fine", default fine": s.430, Sched. 10.
"modifications": s.436.
"receiver": s.70(1).

GENERAL NOTE

This section re-enacts s.62, I.A. 1985 which completely replaced the provisions of s.481 of the Companies Act 1985 as originally enacted, and substituted new provisions which match the substance of those contained in s.46 of this Act (*q.v.*) which applies to England and Wales.

Company's statement of affairs

66.—(1) Where a receiver of a company is appointed, the receiver shall forthwith require some or all of the persons mentioned in subsection (3) below to make out and submit to him a statement in the prescribed form as to the affairs of the company.

(2) A statement submitted under this section shall be verified by affidavit by the persons required to submit it and shall show—

(a) particulars of the company's assets, debts and liabilities;

(b) the names and addresses of its creditors;

(c) the securities held by them respectively;

(d) the dates when the securities were respectively given; and

(e) such further or other information as may be prescribed.

(3) The persons referred to in subsection (1) are—

(a) those who are or have been officers of the company;

(b) those who have taken part in the company's formation at any time within one year before the date of the appointment of the receiver;

(c) those who are in the company's employment or have been in its employment within that year, and are in the receiver's opinion capable of giving the information required;

(d) those who are or have been within that year officers of or in the employment of a company which is, or within that year was, an officer of the company.

In this subsection "employment" includes employment under a contract for services.

(4) Where any persons are required under this section to submit a statement of affairs to the receiver they shall do so (subject to the next subsection) before the end of the period of 21 days beginning with the day after that on which the prescribed notice of the requirement is given to them by the receiver.

(5) The receiver, if he thinks fit, may—

(a) at any time release a person from an obligation imposed on him under subsection (1) or (2), or

(b) either when giving the notice mentioned in subsection (4) or subsequently extend the period so mentioned,

and where the receiver has refused to exercise a power conferred by this subsection, the court, if it thinks fit, may exercise it.

(6) If a person without reasonable excuse fails to comply with any obligation imposed under this section, he is liable to a fine and, for continued contravention to a daily default fine.

DEFINITIONS

"fine", "default fine": s.430, Sched. 10.
"officers of the company": s.744, C.A. 1985; s.251.
"prescribed": s.70(1).
"receiver": s.70(1).

GENERAL NOTE

This section re-enacts s.63, I.A. 1985 which completely replaced the provisions of s.482 of the Companies Act 1985 as originally enacted, and substituted new provisions which match the substance of those contained in s.47 of this Act (*q.v.*), which applies to England and Wales.

Report by receiver

67.—(1) Where a receiver is appointed under section 51, he shall within 3 months (or such longer period as the court may allow) after his appointment, send to the registrar of companies, to the holder of the floating charge by virtue of which he was appointed and to any trustees for secured creditors of the company and (so far as he is aware of their addresses) to all such creditors a report as to the following matters, namely—

(a) the events leading up to his appointment, so far as he is aware of them;

(b) the disposal or proposed disposal by him of any property of the company and the carrying on or proposed carrying on by him of any business of the company;

(c) the amounts of principal and interest payable to the holder of the floating charge by virtue of which he was appointed and the amounts payable to preferential creditors; and

(d) the amount (if any) likely to be available for the payment of other creditors.

(2) The receiver shall also, within 3 months (or such longer period as the court may allow) after his appointment, either—

(a) send a copy of the report (so far as he is aware of their addresses) to all unsecured creditors of the company, or

(b) publish in the prescribed manner a notice stating an address to which unsecured creditors of the company should write for copies of the report to be sent to them free of charge,

and (in either case), unless the court otherwise directs, lay a copy of the report before a meeting of the company's unsecured creditors summoned for the purpose on not less than 14 days' notice.

(3) The court shall not give a direction under subsection (2) unless—

(*a*) the report states the intention of the receiver to apply for the direction, and

(*b*) a copy of the report is sent to the persons mentioned in paragraph *a* of that subsection, or a notice is published as mentioned in paragraph (*b*) of that subsection, not less than 14 days before the hearing of the application.

(4) Where the company has gone or goes into liquidation, the receiver—

(*a*) shall, within 7 days after his compliance with subsection (1) or, if later, the nomination or appointment of the liquidator, send a copy of the report to the liquidator, and

(*b*) where he does so within the time limited for compliance with subsection (2), is not required to comply with that subsection.

(5) A report under this section shall include a summary of the statement of affairs made out and submitted under section 66 and of his comments (if any) on it.

(6) Nothing in this section shall be taken as requiring any such report to include any information the disclosure of which would seriously prejudice the carrying out by the receiver of his functions.

(7) Section 65(2) applies for the purposes of this section also.

(8) If a person without reasonable excuse fails to comply with this section, he is liable to a fine and, for continued contravention, to a daily default fine.

(9) In this section "secured creditor", in relation to a company, means a creditor of the company who holds in respect of his debt a security over property of the company, and "unsecured creditor" shall be construed accordingly.

DEFINITIONS
"company goes into liquidation": s.247(2).
"fine", "default fine": s.430, Sched. 10.
"floating charge": s.744, C.A. 1985; s.251.
"holder of floating charge": s.70(2).
"preferential creditor": s.386.
"prescribed": s.70(1).
"receiver": s.70(1).
"security", "secured creditor", "unsecured creditor": subs. (9); s.248.

GENERAL NOTE
This new section is derived from s.64, I.A. 1985 and s.482A, C.A. 1985 and contains provisions which are nearly identical to those which apply in England and Wales by virtue of s.48 of this Act. However, it should be noted that under subs. (1) there is an additional requirement not included in s.48 of this Act, in that a Scottish receiver is required to send a copy of his report to the holder of the floating charge under which he was appointed. The additional subs. (9) in s.67 imports into that section a definition of "secured creditor" drafted in identical terms to the definition contained in the interpretation section for the First Group of Parts (s.248(*a*)). See further the General Note to s.48.

Committee of creditors

68.—(1) Where a meeting of creditors is summoned under section 67, the meeting may, if it thinks fit, establish a committee ("the creditors' committee") to exercise the functions conferred on it by or under this Act.

(2) If such a committee is established, the committee may on giving not less than 7 days' notice require the receiver to attend before it at any reasonable time and furnish it with such information relating to the carrying out by him of his functions as it may reasonably require.

DEFINITION
"the receiver": s.70(1).

GENERAL NOTE

This new section is derived from s.65, I.A. 1985 and s.482B, C.A. 1985 and contains provisions which are in substance the same as those of s.49 of this Act (*q.v.*) which applies to England and Wales. The meeting of creditors referred to in subs. (1) is that of the unsecured creditors, which the receiver must convene under s.67(2) *supra* within three months after his appointment, unless the court otherwise directs.

Enforcement of receiver's duty to make returns, etc.

69.—(1) If any receiver—

(*a*) having made default in filing, delivering or making any return, account or other document, or in giving any notice, which a receiver is by law required to file, deliver, make or give, fails to make good the default within 14 days after the service on him of a notice requiring him to do so; or

(*b*) has, after being required at any time by the liquidator of the company so to do, failed to render proper accounts of his receipts and payments and to vouch the same and to pay over to the liquidator the amount properly payable to him,

the court may, on an application made for the purpose, make an order directing the receiver to make good the default within such time as may be specified in the order.

(2) In the case of any such default as is mentioned in subsection (1)(*a*), an application for the purposes of this section may be made by any member or creditor of the company or by the registrar of companies; and, in the case of any such default as is mentioned in subsection (1)(*b*), the application shall be made by the liquidator; and, in either case, the order may provide that all expenses of and incidental to the application shall be borne by the receiver.

(3) Nothing in this section prejudices the operation of any enactments imposing penalties on receivers in respect of any such default as is mentioned in subsection (1).

DEFINITIONS

"court": s.744, C.A. 1985; s.251.
"receiver": s.70(1).
"registrar of companies": s.744, C.A. 1985.

GENERAL NOTE

This provision, which is mirrored in English Law by s.41 *supra*, deals with the enforcement of a receiver's duty to make returns.

Subs. (1)

Failure to perform this duty after notification that performance is required can be rectified by court order. For the relevant derivation see s.483, C.A. 1985 to which the present section exactly corresponds.

Subs. (2)

This subsection identifies those persons who may invoke this enforcement procedure and enables them to make the receiver pay their costs of application.

Subs. (3)

This subsection re-enacts subs. (3) of s.483, C.A. 1985 by providing that the above provisions do not supplant any criminal sanctions which the receiver may have incurred by his failure to submit returns.

Interpretation for Chapter II

70.—(1) In this Chapter, unless the contrary intention appears, the following expressions have the following meanings respectively assigned to them—

"company" means an incorporated company (whether or not a company within the meaning of the Companies Act) which the Court of Session has jurisdiction to wind up;

"fixed security", in relation to any property of a company, means any security, other than a floating charge or a charge having the nature of a floating charge, which on the winding up of the company in Scotland would be treated as an effective security over that property, and (without prejudice to that generality) includes a security over that property, being a heritable security within the meaning of the Conveyancing and Feudal Reform (Scotland) Act 1970;

"instrument of appointment" has the meaning given by section 53(1);

"prescribed" means prescribed by regulations made under this Chapter by the Secretary of State;

"receiver" means a receiver of such part of the property of the company as is subject to the floating charge by virtue of which he has been appointed under section 51;

"register of charges" means the register kept by the registrar of companies for the purposes of Chapter II of Part XII of the Companies Act;

"secured debenture" means a bond, debenture, debenture stock or other security which, either itself or by reference to any other instrument, creates a floating charge over all or any part of the property of the company, but does not include a security which creates no charge other than a fixed security; and

"series of secured debentures" means two or more secured debentures created as a series by the company in such a manner that the holders thereof are entitled pari passu to the benefit of the floating charge.

(2) Where a floating charge, secured debenture or series of secured debentures has been created by the company, then, except where the context otherwise requires, any reference in this Chapter to the holder of the floating charge shall—

(a) where the floating charge, secured debenture or series of secured debentures provides for a receiver to be appointed by any person or body, be construed as a reference to that person or body;

(b) where, in the case of a series of secured debentures, no such provision has been made therein but—

   (i) there are trustees acting for the debenture-holders under and in accordance with a trust deed, be construed as a reference to those trustees, and

   (ii) where no such trustees are acting, be construed as a reference to—

      (aa) a majority in nominal value of those present or represented by proxy and voting at a meeting of debenture-holders at which the holders of at least one-third in nominal value of the outstanding debentures of the series are present or so represented, or

      (bb) where no such meeting is held, the holders of at least one-half in nominal value of the outstanding debentures of the series.

(3) Any reference in this Chapter to a floating charge, secured debenture, series of secured debentures or instrument creating a charge includes, except where the context otherwise requires, a reference to that floating charge, debenture, series of debentures or instrument as varied by any instrument.

(4) References in this Chapter to the instrument by which a floating charge was created are, in the case of a floating charge created by words

in a bond or other written acknowledgement, references to the bond or, as the case may be, the other written acknowledgement.

GENERAL NOTE

This is an interpretation provision which is derived from ss.462(4), 484, 486 (part), C.A. 1985.

Subs. (1)

It is clear that the term "secured debenture" has a restricted meaning in Scottish Law—it does not include a debenture that confers only a *fixed* charge. It is important to note that the term "receiver" refers only to those receivers enforcing a floating charge.

Subs. (2)

By way of contrast a wide meaning is allocated to the phrase "the holder of a floating charge"—it includes trustees for debenture holders or the majority group of the holders of debentures in a series.

Subs. (3)

References to floating charges, secured debentures or instruments of charge include such items where they have been altered under s.466 of the C.A. 1985.

Subs. (4)

This subsection clarifies the phrase "an instrument by which a floating charge is created."

Prescription of forms, etc.; regulations

71.—(1) The notice referred to in section 62(5), and the notice referred to in section 65(1)(*a*) shall be in such form as may be prescribed.

(2) Any power conferred by this Chapter on the Secretary of State to make regulations is exercisable by statutory instrument; and a statutory instrument made in the exercise of the power so conferred to prescribe a fee is subject to annulment in pursuance of a resolution of either House of Parliament.

DEFINITION

"prescribed": s.70(1).

GENERAL NOTE

This is an ancillary provision that reproduces in part the two subsections in s.485, C.A. 1985.

Subs. (1)

This subsection relates to the form of notices mentioned in ss.62(5) and 65(1) of this Act.

Subs. (2)

Regulations are to be made by the Secretary of State by statutory instrument and can be annulled by resolution of either House of Parliament.

CHAPTER III

RECEIVERS' POWERS IN GREAT BRITAIN AS A WHOLE

Cross-border operation of receivership provisions

72.—(1) A receiver appointed under the law of either part of Great Britain in respect of the whole or any part of any property or undertaking of a company and in consequence of the company having created a charge which, as created, was a floating charge may exercise his powers in the other part of Great Britain so far as their exercise is not inconsistent with the law applicable there.

(2) In subsection (1) "receiver" includes a manager and a person who is appointed both receiver and manager.

DEFINITION
"floating charge": s.251; C.A. 1985, ss.462 and 744.

GENERAL NOTE
Subs. (1)
This subsection whose origin can be traced back to a proposal from the Scottish Law Commission in 1970 (Cmnd. 4336, para. 60), and which was formerly contained in the Administration of Justice Act 1977, s.7(1), enables a receiver appointed in one part of Great Britain to exercise his powers throughout Great Britain, in so far as this is not inconsistent with local law.

Subs. (2)
This subsection is an interpretation provision based on Administration of Justice Act 1977, s.7(2).

TRANSITIONAL PROVISION
Sched. 11, para. 4.

PART IV

WINDING UP OF COMPANIES REGISTERED UNDER THE COMPANIES ACTS

CHAPTER I

PRELIMINARY

Modes of winding up

Alternative modes of winding up

73.—(1) The winding up of a company, within the meaning given to that expression by section 735 of the Companies Act, may be either voluntary (Chapters II, III, IV and V in this Part) or by the court (Chapter VI).

(2) This Chapter, and Chapters VII to X, relate to winding up generally, except where otherwise stated.

DEFINITION
"company": s.735, C.A. 1985.

GENERAL NOTE
This section is derived from s.501 of the Companies Act 1985. A registered company can only be dissolved by winding up or striking off the register under s.652, C.A. 1985.
For voluntary winding-up, see Chaps. II, III, IV, and V *post*. Voluntary winding up under supervision has been abolished (s.438, Sched. 12) following the recommendation of the Cork Committee (Cmnd. 8558), paras. 182, 3. For winding up by the court see Chap. VI.

Contributories

Liability as contributories of present and past members

74.—(1) When a company is wound up, every present and past member is liable to contribute to its assets to any amount sufficient for payment of its debts and liabilities, and the expenses of the winding up, and for the adjustment of the rights of the contributories among themselves.

(2) This is subject as follows—

(*a*) a past member is not liable to contribute if he has ceased to be a member for one year or more before the commencement of the winding up;

(*b*) a past member is not liable to contribute in respect of any debt or liability of the company contracted after he ceased to be a member;

(*c*) a past member is not liable to contribute, unless it appears to the court that the existing members are unable to satisfy the contributions required to be made by them in pursuance of the Companies Act and this Act;

(*d*) in the case of a company limited by shares, no contribution is required from any member exceeding the amount (if any) unpaid on the shares in respect of which he is liable as a present or past member;

(*e*) nothing in the Companies Act or this Act invalidates any provision contained in a policy of insurance or other contract whereby the liability of individual members on the policy or contract is restricted, or whereby the funds of the company are alone made liable in respect of the policy or contract;

(*f*) a sum due to any member of the company (in his character of a member) by way of dividends, profits or otherwise is not deemed to be a debt of the company, payable to that member in a case of competition between himself and any other creditor not a member of the company, but any such sum may be taken into account for the purpose of the final adjustment of the rights of the contributories among themselves.

(3) In the case of a company limited by guarantee, no contribution is required from any member exceeding the amount undertaken to be contributed by him to the company's assets in the event of its being wound up; but if it is a company with a share capital, every member of it is liable (in addition to the amount so undertaken to be contributed to the assets), to contribute to the extent of any sums unpaid on shares held by him.

DEFINITION
"contributory": s.79

GENERAL NOTE
This reproduces s.502, C.A. 1985.
In general every present member of the company is liable to contribute to the assets of the company on its winding up and in certain circumstances a past member is also liable. The maximum liability is limited in the case of a company limited by shares to the amount unpaid on the shares and in the case of a company limited by guarantee to the amount of the guarantee (s.74(2)(*d*) and (3)). The liability of a past member is governed by s.74(2)(*a*)–(*c*). For a discussion on contributories' petitions see *Palmer*, paras. 85–16 *et seq.*

Directors, etc., with unlimited liability

75.—(1) In the winding up of a limited company, any director or manager (whether past or present) whose liability is under the Companies Act unlimited is liable, in addition to his liability (if any) to contribute as an ordinary member, to make a further contribution as if he were at the commencement of the winding up a member of an unlimited company.

(2) However—

(*a*) a past director or manager is not liable to make such further contribution if he has ceased to hold office for a year or more before the commencement of the winding up;

(*b*) a past director or manager is not liable to make such further contribution in respect of any debt or liability of the company contracted after he ceased to hold office;

(*c*) subject to the company's articles, a director or manager is not liable to make such further contribution unless the court deems it necessary to require that contribution in order to satisfy the company's debts and liabilities, and the expense of the winding up.

GENERAL NOTE

This section which is based on s.503, C.A. 1985 deals with the effect in a winding up of the rare case where a past or present director or manager has unlimited personal liability. This applies where a special resolution has been passed to this effect and was dealt with by s.203 of the 1948 C.A. but is now dealt with in s.306, C.A. 1985. The alterations in the present section are merely minor drafting amendments.

See *Palmer*, para. 65–04 and footnote 16.

Liability of past directors and shareholders

76.—(1) This section applies where a company is being wound up and—

(*a*) it has under Chapter VII of Part V of the Companies Act (redeemable shares; purchase by a company of its own shares) made a payment out of capital in respect of the redemption or purchase of any of its own shares (the payment being referred to below as "the relevant payment"), and

(*b*) the aggregate amount of the company's assets and the amounts paid by way of contribution to its assets (apart from this section) is not sufficient for payment of its debts and liabilities, and the expenses of the winding up.

(2) If the winding up commenced within one year of the date on which the relevant payment was made, then—

(*a*) the person from whom the shares were redeemed or purchased, and

(*b*) the directors who signed the statutory declaration made in accordance with section 173(3) of the Companies Act for purposes of the redemption or purchase (except a director who shows that he had reasonable grounds for forming the opinion set out in the declaration),

are, so as to enable that insufficiency to be met, liable to contribute to the following extent to the company's assets.

(3) A person from whom any of the shares were redeemed or purchased is liable to contribute an amount not exceeding so much of the relevant payment as was made by the company in respect of his shares; and the directors are jointly and severally liable with that person to contribute that amount.

(4) A person who has contributed any amount to the assets in pursuance of this section may apply to the court for an order directing any other person jointly and severally liable in respect of that amount to pay him such amount as the court thinks just and equitable.

(5) Sections 74 and 75 do not apply in relation to liability accruing by virtue of this section.

(6) This section is deemed included in Chapter VII of Part V of the Companies Act for the purposes of the Secretary of State's power to make regulations under section 179 of that Act.

GENERAL NOTE

This section deals with the liability of past directors and shareholders for certain payments out of capital in connection with redemption or purchase by a private company of its own shares under s.171, C.A. 1985. It is based on ss.58(1)–(5) and 61, C.A. 1981 and s.504, C.A. 1985. See *Palmer*, paras. 33–23.

Limited company formerly unlimited

77.—(1) This section applies in the case of a company being wound up which was at some former time registered as unlimited but has re-registered—

   (*a*) as a public company under section 43 of the Companies Act (or the former corresponding provision, section 5 of the Companies Act 1980), or

   (*b*) as a limited company under section 51 of the Companies Act (or the former corresponding provision, section 44 of the Companies Act 1967).

(2) Notwithstanding section 74(2)(*a*), a past member of the company who was a member of it at the time of re-registration, if the winding up commences within the period of 3 years beginning with the day on which the company was re-registered, is liable to contribute to the assets of the company in respect of debts and liabilities contracted before that time.

(3) If no persons who were members of the company at that time are existing members of it, a person who at that time was a present or past member is liable to contribute as above notwithstanding that the existing members have satisfied the contributions, required to be made by them under the Companies Act and this Act.

This applies subject to section 74(2)(*a*) above and to subsection (2) of this section, but notwithstanding section 74(2)(*c*).

(4) Notwithstanding section 74(2)(*d*) and (3), there is no limit on the amount which a person who, at that time, was a past or present member of the company is liable to contribute as above.

GENERAL NOTE

This section which deals with the case of a limited liability company which was formerly unlimited is based on s.505, C.A. 1985.

See *Palmer*, paras. 85–47.

Unlimited company formerly limited

78.—(1) This section applies in the case of a company being wound up which was at some former time registered as limited but has been re-registered as unlimited under section 49 of the Companies Act (or the former corresponding provision, section 43 of the Companies Act 1967).

(2) A person who, at the time when the application for the company to be re-registered was lodged, was a past member of the company and did not after that again become a member of it is not liable to contribute to the assets of the company more than he would have been liable to contribute had the company not been re-registered.

GENERAL NOTE

This deals with the converse to s.77, namely an unlimited company which was formerly limited. It reproduces s.506, C.A. 1985.

Meaning of "contributory"

79.—(1) In this Act and the Companies Act the expression "contributory" means every person liable to contribute to the assets of a company in the event of its being wound up, and for the purposes of all proceedings for determining, and all proceedings prior to the final determination of, the persons who are to be deemed contributories, includes any person alleged to be a contributory.

(2) The reference in subsection (1) to persons liable to contribute to the assets does not include a person so liable by virtue of a declaration by the court under section 213 (imputed responsibility for company's fraudulent trading) or section 214 (wrongful trading) in Chapter X of this Part.

(3) A reference in a company's articles to a contributory does not (unless the context requires) include a person who is a contributory only by virtue of section 76.

This subsection is deemed included in Chapter VII of Part V of the Companies Act for the purposes of the Secretary of State's power to make regulations under section 179 of that Act.

GENERAL NOTE
This is based upon s.507, C.A. 1985. The generality of the definition in subs. (1) is limited by subs. (2) which originated in the I.A. 1985, Sched. 6, para. 5 and by subs. (3) which originated in the C.A. 1981, ss.58(6) and 61.

Nature of contributory's liability

80. The liability of a contributory creates a debt (in England and Wales in the nature of a specialty) accruing due from him at the time when his liability commenced, but payable at the time when calls are made for enforcing the liability.

GENERAL NOTE
This reproduces s.508, C.A. 1985 and makes the contributory's liability a specialty debt in England and Wales. The period of limitation is therefore 12 years. Wales was not expressly referred to in s.508 but was implied in the reference to England.

Contributories in case of death of a member

81.—(1) If a contributory dies either before or after he has been placed on the list of contributories, his personal representatives, and the heirs and legatees of heritage of his heritable estate in Scotland, are liable in a due course of administration to contribute to the assets of the company in discharge of his liability and are contributories accordingly.

(2) Where the personal representatives are placed on the list of contributories, the heirs or legatees of heritage need not be added, but they may be added as and when the court thinks fit.

(3) If in England and Wales the personal representatives make default in paying any money ordered to be paid by them, proceedings may be taken for administering the estate of the deceased contributory and for compelling payment out of it of the money due.

GENERAL NOTE
This reproduces s.509 C.A. 1985 and substitutes the personal representatives or heirs and legatees in Scotland for a deceased contributory.

Effect of contributory's bankruptcy

82.—(1) The following applies if a contributory becomes bankrupt, either before or after he has been placed on the list of contributories.

(2) His trustee in bankruptcy represents him for all purposes of the winding up, and is a contributory accordingly.

(3) The trustee may be called on to admit to proof against the bankrupt's estate, or otherwise allow to be paid out of the bankrupt's assets in due course of law, any money due from the bankrupt in respect of his liability to contribute to the company's assets.

(4) There may be proved against the bankrupt's estate the estimated value of his liability to future calls as well as calls already made.

GENERAL NOTE
This section which contains a similar provision to s.81 in respect of bankruptcy reproduces s.510, C.A. 1985. The trustee in bankruptcy represents the bankrupt contributory for all purposes of the winding up.

Companies registered under Companies Act, Part XXII, Chapter II

83.—(1) The following applies in the event of a company being wound up which has been registered under section 680 of the Companies Act (or previous corresponding provisions in the Companies Act 1948 or earlier Acts).

(2) Every person is a contributory, in respect of the company's debts and liabilities contracted before registration, who is liable—

 (*a*) to pay, or contribute to the payment of, any debt or liability so contracted, or

 (*b*) to pay, or contribute to the payment of, any sum for the adjustment of the rights of the members among themselves in respect of any such debt or liability, or

 (*c*) to pay, or contribute to the amount of, the expenses of winding up the company, so far as relates to the debts or liabilities above-mentioned.

(3) Every contributory is liable to contribute to the assets of the company, in the course of the winding up, all sums due from him in respect of any such liability.

(4) In the event of the death, bankruptcy or insolvency of any contributory, provisions of this Act, with respect to the personal representatives, to the heirs and legatees of heritage of the heritable estate in Scotland of deceased contributories and to the trustees of bankrupt or insolvent contributories respectively, apply.

GENERAL NOTE

This section re-enacts s.511, C.A. 1985 and deals with contributories in the case of the winding up of the companies not formed under the Companies Acts but authorised to register under the Act.

CHAPTER II

VOLUNTARY WINDING UP (INTRODUCTORY AND GENERAL)

Resolutions for, and commencement of, voluntary winding up

Circumstances in which company may be wound up voluntarily

84.—(1) A company may be wound up voluntarily—

 (*a*) when the period (if any) fixed for the duration of the company by the articles expires, or the event (if any) occurs, on the occurrence of which the articles provide that the company is to be dissolved, and the company in general meeting has passed a resolution requiring it to be wound up voluntarily;

 (*b*) if the company resolves by special resolution that it be wound up voluntarily;

 (*c*) if the company resolves by extraordinary resolution to the effect that it cannot by reason of its liabilities continue its business, and that it is advisable to wind up.

(2) In this Act the expression "a resolution for voluntary winding up" means a resolution passed under any of the paragraphs of subsection (1).

(3) A resolution passed under paragraph (*a*) of subsection (1), as well as a special resolution under paragraph (*b*) and an extraordinary resolution under paragraph (*c*), is subject to section 380 of the Companies Act (copy of resolution to be forwarded to registrar of companies within 15 days).

DEFINITION

"special", "extraordinary" resolution: s.378, C.A. 1985.

GENERAL NOTE

This section re-enacts s.572, C.A. 1985 and deals with the circumstances in which a company may be wound up voluntarily. Although this section does not clearly say so there are two species of voluntary winding up—members' and creditors' voluntary winding up. Winding up subject to supervision by the court has been abolished. See General note to s.73.

The power to wind up voluntarily cannot be excluded by the articles although it is possible to restrict voting rights at meetings (*Re Peveril Gold Mines Ltd.* [1898] 1 Ch. 122 (C.A.)). See generally *Palmer*, Chap. 86.

Notice of resolution to wind up

85.—(1) When a company has passed a resolution for voluntary winding up, it shall, within 14 days after the passing of the resolution, give notice of the resolution by advertisement in the Gazette.

(2) If default is made in complying with this section, the company and every officer of it who is in default is liable to a fine and, for continued contravention, to a daily default fine.

For purposes of this subsection the liquidator is deemed an officer of the company.

DEFINITION

"fine", "daily default fine": s.430, Sched. 10.

GENERAL NOTE

This section re-enacts s.573, C.A. 1985. It deals with the Gazetting of a notice of a resolution to wind up voluntarily. See *Palmer*, para. 86–02.

Commencement of winding up

86. A voluntary winding up is deemed to commence at the time of the passing of the resolution for voluntary winding up.

TRANSITIONAL PROVISION

Sched. 11, para. 4.

GENERAL NOTE

This re-enacts s.574, C.A. 1985 and provides for commencement of the winding up at the date of the relevant resolution. See *Palmer*, para. 86–03.

Consequences of resolution to wind up
Effect on business and status of company

87.—(1) In case of a voluntary winding up, the company shall from the commencement of the winding up cease to carry on its business, except so far as may be required for its beneficial winding up.

(2) However, the corporate state and corporate powers of the company, notwithstanding anything to the contrary in its articles, continue until the company is dissolved.

GENERAL NOTE

This section re-enacts s.575, C.A. 1985. In essence it provides that although the company's status and powers subsist until dissolution, it shall cease to carry on business except so far as may be necessary for the purposes of winding up. The property remains in the company unless a vesting order is made under s.112.

As to the carrying on of the company's business it is sufficient that the liquidator bona fide and reasonably believes that the carrying on is necessary for the beneficial winding up of the company (*Re Great Eastern Electric Co. Ltd.* [1941] 1 Ch. 241). However, a liquidator must not carry on the business with a view to its financial reconstruction (*Re Wreck Recovery & Salvage Co.* (1880) 15 Ch.D. 353. The onus of proof that a matter is not necessary for the beneficial winding up is on the party objecting to it (*The Hire Purchase Furnishing Co. Ltd.* v. *Richens* (1887) 20 Q.B.D. 387 (C.A.)). See *Palmer*, para. 86–24.

Avoidance of share transfers, etc. after winding-up resolution

88. Any transfer of shares, not being a transfer made to or with the sanction of the liquidator, and any alteration in the status of the company's members, made after the commencement of a voluntary winding up, is void.

GENERAL NOTE

This re-enacts s.576, C.A. 1985 and avoids a transfer of shares after the commencement of the winding up unless it is made to or with the consent of the liquidator. The liquidator may give his consent without the necessity of getting the court's permission. A transfer without consent is void but not illegal (*Biederman* v. *Stone* (1867) L.R. 2 C.P. 504). The section only applies to transfers of shares, not transfers of debentures (*Re Goy & Co. Ltd., Farmer* v. *Goy & Co. Ltd.* [1900] 2 Ch. 149).

Declaration of solvency

Statutory declaration of solvency

89.—(1) Where it is proposed to wind up a company voluntarily, the directors (or, in the case of a company having more than two directors, the majority of them) may at a directors' meeting make a statutory declaration to the effect that they have made a full inquiry into the company's affairs and that, having done so, they have formed the opinion that the company will be able to pay its debts in full, together with interest at the official rate (as defined in section 251), within such period, not exceeding 12 months from the commencement of the winding up, as may be specified in the declaration.

(2) Such a declaration by the directors has no effect for purposes of this Act unless—

   (*a*) it is made within the 5 weeks immediately preceding the date of the passing of the resolution for winding up, or on that date but before the passing of the resolution, and

   (*b*) it embodies a statement of the company's assets and liabilities as at the latest practicable date before the making of the declaration.

(3) The declaration shall be delivered to the registrar of companies before the expiration of 15 days immediately following the date on which the resolution for winding up is passed.

(4) A director making a declaration under this section without having reasonable grounds for the opinion that the company will be able to pay its debts in full, together with interest at the official rate, within the period specified is liable to imprisonment or a fine, or both.

(5) If the company is wound up in pursuance of a resolution passed within 5 weeks after the making of the declaration, and its debts (together with interest at the official rate) are not paid or provided for in full within the period specified, it is to be presumed (unless the contrary is shown) that the director did not have reasonable grounds for his opinion.

(6) If a declaration required by subsection (3) to be delivered to the registrar is not so delivered within the time prescribed by that subsection, the company and every officer in default is liable to a fine and, for continued contravention, to a daily default fine.

See General Note to s.90 *infra*.

Distinction between "members' " and "creditors' " voluntary winding up

90. A winding up in the case of which a directors' statutory declaration under section 89 has been made is a "members' voluntary winding up"; and a winding up in the case of which such a declaration has not been made is a "creditors' voluntary winding up".

DEFINITION
"fine", "daily default fine": s.430, Sched. 10.

GENERAL NOTE
These sections re-enact ss.577 and 578, C.A. 1985 though the reference in subs. (1) and subs. (5) of s.89 to interest at the official rate is new. Only if a statutory declaration under s.577 is made can the voluntary winding up be a members' voluntary winding up. See generally *Palmer,* para. 86–05.

CHAPTER III

MEMBERS' VOLUNTARY WINDING UP

Appointment of liquidator

91.—(1) In a members' voluntary winding up, the company in general meeting shall appoint one or more liquidators for the purpose of winding up the company's affairs and distributing its assets.

(2) On the appointment of a liquidator all the powers of the directors cease, except so far as the company in general meeting or the liquidator sanctions their continuance.

GENERAL NOTE
This derives from s.580, C.A. 1985, but, unlike that section, refers only to the company's power to appoint a liquidator (and the effect of such appointment) and not to its power to fix the remuneration of a liquidator. The equivalent provisions in the case of a creditors' voluntary winding up are to be found in ss.100 and 103. The Cork Committee (para. 883) recommended changes in the manner in which the remuneration of the liquidator, *inter alia,* was fixed. The procedure is now contained in the Rules which provide that it be fixed, initially, by the liquidation committee, or if none, the meeting of creditors with final recourse to the court.

Power to fill vacancy in office of liquidator

92.—(1) If a vacancy occurs by death, resignation or otherwise in the office of liquidator appointed by the company, the company in general meeting may, subject to any arrangement with its creditors, fill the vacancy.

(2) For that purpose a general meeting may be convened by any contributory or, if there were more liquidators than one, by the continuing liquidators.

(3) The meeting shall be held in manner provided by this Act or by the articles, or in such manner as may, on application by any contributory or by the continuing liquidators, be determined by the court.

GENERAL NOTE
This re-enacts s.581, C.A. 1985, and deals with the power of the company to fill a vacancy in the office of liquidator. See s.104 for the power of the creditors in a creditors' voluntary winding up.

General company meeting at each year's end

93.—(1) Subject to sections 96 and 102, in the event of the winding up continuing for more than one year, the liquidator shall summon a general meeting of the company at the end of the first year from the commencement of the winding up, and of each succeeding year, or at the first convenient date within 3 months from the end of the year or such longer period as the Secretary of State may allow.

(2) The liquidator shall lay before the meeting an account of his acts and dealings, and of the conduct of the winding up, during the preceding year.

(3) If the liquidator fails to comply with this section, he is liable to a fine.

    See General Note to s.94.

Final meeting prior to dissolution

    94.—(1) As soon as the company's affairs are fully wound up, the liquidator shall make up an account of the winding up, showing how it has been conducted and the company's property has been disposed of, and thereupon shall call a general meeting of the company for the purpose of laying before it the account, and giving an explanation of it.
    (2) The meeting shall be called by advertisement in the Gazette, specifying its time, place and object and published at least one month before the meeting.
    (3) Within one week after the meeting, the liquidator shall send to the registrar of companies a copy of the account, and shall make a return to him of the holding of the meeting and of its date.
    (4) If the copy is not sent or the return is not made in accordance with subsection (3), the liquidator is liable to a fine and, for continued contravention, to a daily default fine.
    (5) If a quorum is not present at the meeting, the liquidator shall, in lieu of the return mentioned above, make a return that the meeting was duly summoned and that no quorum was present; and upon such a return being made, the provisions of subsection (3) as to the making of the return are deemed complied with.
    (6) If the liquidator fails to call a general meeting of the company as required by subsection (1), he is liable to a fine.

GENERAL NOTE
    These sections re-enact ss.584 and 585 (part), C.A. 1985 with minor amendments and provide for a general meeting of the company at the end of each year or at the first convenient date within three months thereafter or such longer period as shall be allowed, and the final meeting and dissolution. The procedure for dissolution is much simpler than in the case of a compulsory winding up. No application to the Court is necessary. The company is automatically dissolved on the expiration of three months after registration of the return of the final meeting subject to an order by the court to defer dissolution (s.201). See *Palmer,* para. 86–62.

Effect of company's insolvency

    95.—(1) This section applies where the liquidator is of the opinion that the company will be unable to pay its debts in full (together with interest at the official rate) within the period stated in the directors' declaration under section 89.
    (2) The liquidator shall—
        (*a*) summon a meeting of creditors for a day not later than the 28th day after the day on which he formed that opinion;
        (*b*) send notices of the creditors' meeting to the creditors by post not less than 7 days before the day on which that meeting is to be held;
        (*c*) cause notice of the creditors' meeting to be advertised once in the Gazette and once at least in 2 newspapers circulating in the relevant locality (that is to say the locality in which the company's principal

place of business in Great Britain was situated during the relevant period); and

(*d*) during the period before the day on which the creditors' meeting is to be held, furnish creditors free of charge with such information concerning the affairs of the company as they may reasonably require;

and the notice of the creditors' meeting shall state the duty imposed by paragraph (*d*) above.

(3) The liquidator shall also—

(*a*) make out a statement in the prescribed form as to the affairs of the company;

(*b*) lay that statement before the creditors' meeting; and

(*c*) attend and preside at that meeting.

(4) The statement as to the affairs of the company shall be verified by affidavit by the liquidator and shall show—

(*a*) particulars of the company's assets, debts and liabilities;

(*b*) the names and addresses of the company's creditors;

(*c*) the securities held by them respectively;

(*d*) the dates when the securities were respectively given; and

(*e*) such further or other information as may be prescribed.

(5) Where the company's principal place of business in Great Britain was situated in different localities at different times during the relevant period, the duty imposed by subsection (2)(*c*) applies separately in relation to each of those localities.

(6) Where the company had no place of business in Great Britain during the relevant period, references in subsection (2)(*c*) and (5) to the company's principal place of business in Great Britain are replaced by references to its registered office.

(7) In this section "the relevant period" means the period of 6 months immediately preceding the day on which were sent the notices summoning the company meeting at which it was resolved that the company be wound up voluntarily.

(8) If the liquidator without reasonable excuse fails to comply with this section, he is liable to a fine.

DEFINITIONS

"fine": s.430, Sched. 10.
"interest at the official rate": s.251.
"members' voluntary winding up": s.90.
"prescribed": s.251.
"security": s.248(*b*).
"the Gazette": s.744, C.A. 1985; s.251.
"the relevant period": subs. (7).

GENERAL NOTE

This provision re-enacts (in part) s.83, I.A. 1985 and contains a series of provisions applicable in cases where a members' voluntary winding up has commenced in relation to a company which the liquidator subsequently finds or considers to be insolvent. The procedures which the liquidator is thereupon required to follow have the effect of transforming the winding up into a creditors' voluntary winding up whose commencement is deemed to have been effective since the commencement of the members' voluntary winding up.

Subs. (1)

The period stated in the directors' declaration under s.89

This refers to the statutory declaration of solvency which must be made by the directors of a company in order that it may be wound up by means of a members' voluntary winding up. Subs. (1) of that section requires the directors to declare that in their opinion the company will be able to pay its debts in full within a specified period, not exceeding 12 months from the commencement of winding up.

Subs. (2)(c)

Two newspapers circulating in the relevant locality

This can include "free" newspapers which are circulated on a local basis and posted through householders' letterboxes without charge to the recipients (H.C. Standing Committee E, June 11, 1985, cols. 277, 278).

Conversion to creditors' voluntary winding up

96. As from the day on which the creditors' meeting is held under section 95, this Act has effect as if—

(*a*) the directors' declaration under section 89 had not been made; and

(*b*) the creditors' meeting and the company meeting at which it was resolved that the company be wound up voluntarily were the meetings mentioned in section 98 in the next Chapter;

and accordingly the winding up becomes a creditors' voluntary winding up.

DEFINITION

"creditors' voluntary winding up": s.90.

GENERAL NOTE

This re-enacts s.83(7), I.A. 1985. See General Note to s.95 *supra*.

CHAPTER IV

CREDITORS' VOLUNTARY WINDING UP

Application of this Chapter

97.—(1) Subject as follows, this Chapter applies in relation to a creditors' voluntary winding up.

(2) Sections 98 and 99 do not apply where, under section 96 in Chapter III, a members' voluntary winding up has become a creditors' voluntary winding up.

GENERAL NOTE

Subs. (1) limits the application of Ch. IV to a creditors' voluntary winding up while subs. (2) exempts such a winding-up resulting from a conversion from a members' voluntary winding up (see ss.95, 96) from the operation of ss.98 and 99 in view of the equivalent steps which will already have been taken under s.95.

Meeting of creditors

98.—(1) The company shall—

(*a*) cause a meeting of its creditors to be summoned for a day not later than the 14th day after the day on which there is to be held the company meeting at which the resolution for voluntary winding up is to be proposed;

(*b*) cause the notices of the creditors' meeting to be sent by post to the creditors not less than 7 days before the day on which that meeting is to be held; and

(*c*) cause notice of the creditors' meeting to be advertised once in the Gazette and once at least in two newspapers circulating in the relevant locality (that is to say the locality in which the company's principal place of business in Great Britain was situated during the relevant period).

(2) The notice of the creditors' meeting shall state either—

(*a*) the name and address of a person qualified to act as an insolvency practitioner in relation to the company who, during the period before the day on which that meeting is to be held, will furnish creditors free of charge with such information concerning the company's affairs as they may reasonably require; or

(b) a place in the relevant locality where, on the two business days falling next before the day on which that meeting is to be held, a list of the names and addresses of the company's creditors will be available for inspection free of charge.

(3) Where the company's principal place of business in Great Britain was situated in different localities at different times during the relevant period, the duties imposed by subsections (1)(c) and (2)(b) above apply separately in relation to each of those localities.

(4) Where the company had no place of business in Great Britain during the relevant period, references in subsections (1)(c) and (3) to the company's principal place of business in Great Britain are replaced by references to its registered office.

(5) In this section "the relevant period" means the period of 6 months immediately preceding the day on which were sent the notices summoning the company meeting at which it was resolved that the company be wound up voluntarily.

(6) If the company without reasonable excuse fails to comply with subsection (1) or (2), it is guilty of an offence and liable to a fine.

DEFINITIONS
"creditors' voluntary winding up": s.90.
"fine": s.430, Sched. 10.
"person qualified to act as an insolvency practitioner": s.390.
"prescribed": s.251.
"security": s.248(b).
"the Gazette": s.744, C.A. 1985; s.251.
"the relevant period": subs. (5).
"to act as an insolvency practitioner in relation to a company": s.388.

GENERAL NOTE
This section, which is designed to operate in close connection with s.166, replaces (in part) s.85, I.A. 1985. It governs the convening of a meeting of creditors following the passing by a company meeting of a resolution under s.84 for the winding up of the company, in circumstances where the winding up will be a creditors' voluntary winding up. At that meeting, the creditors may in turn exercise their right to nominate a person to be liquidator, in accordance with the provisions of s.100 which confers upon the creditors a pre-eminent right of appointment of the liquidator; the appointment as liquidator of the person, if any, who has been nominated by the company will only take place in default of any nomination by the creditors. As a further reform in the law aimed at improving the ability of creditors' meetings to act in a decisive way, the rules will provide for voting at creditors' meetings to to be on the basis of a majority in value only (see *Cork Report*, paras. 921–925; *White Paper*, para. 78).

Subs. (1)(c)

Two newspapers circulating in the relevant locality
   Cf. General Note to s.95(2)(c).

Directors to lay statement of affairs before creditors

99.—(1) The directors of the company shall—
(a) make out a statement in the prescribed form as to the affairs of the company;
(b) cause that statement to be laid before the creditors' meeting under section 98; and
(c) appoint one of their number to preside at that meeting;
and it is the duty of the director so appointed to attend the meeting and preside over it.

(2) The statement as to the affairs of the company shall be verified by affidavit by some or all of the directors and shall show—

(*a*) particulars of the company's assets, debts and liabilities;
(*b*) the names and addresses of the company's creditors;
(*c*) the securities held by them respectively;
(*d*) the dates when the securities were respectively given; and
(*e*) such further or other information as may be prescribed.

(3) If—

(*a*) the directors without reasonable excuse fail to comply with subsection (1) or (2); or
(*b*) any director without reasonable excuse fails to comply with subsection (1), so far as requiring him to attend and preside at the creditors' meeting,

the directors are or (as the case may be) the director is guilty of an offence and liable to a fine.

GENERAL NOTE
This section replaces (in part) s.85, I.A. 1985.

Appointment of liquidator

100.—(1) The creditors and the company at their respective meetings mentioned in section 98 may nominate a person to be liquidator for the purpose of winding up the company's affairs and distributing its assets.

(2) The liquidator shall be the person nominated by the creditors or, where no person has been so nominated, the person (if any) nominated by the company.

(3) In the case of different persons being nominated, any director, member or creditor of the company may, within 7 days after the date on which the nomination was made by the creditors, apply to the court for an order either—

(*a*) directing that the person nominated as liquidator by the company shall be liquidator instead of or jointly with the person nominated by the creditors, or
(*b*) appointing some other person to be liquidator instead of the person nominated by the creditors.

GENERAL NOTE
This section is derived from s.589, C.A. 1985. See Note to s.98 and *Palmer*, paras. 86–11.

Appointment of liquidation committee

101.—(1) The creditors at the meeting to be held under section 98 or at any subsequent meeting may, if they think fit, appoint a committee ("the liquidation committee") of not more than 5 persons to exercise the functions conferred on it by or under this Act.

(2) If such a committee is appointed, the company may, either at the meeting at which the resolution for voluntary winding up is passed or at any time subsequently in general meeting, appoint such number of persons as they think fit to act as members of the committee, not exceeding 5.

(3) However, the creditors may, if they think fit, resolve that all or any of the persons so appointed by the company ought not to be members of the liquidation committee; and if the creditors so resolve—

(*a*) the persons mentioned in the resolution are not then, unless the court otherwise directs, qualified to act as members of the committee; and
(*b*) on any application to the court under this provision the court may, if it thinks fit, appoint other persons to act as such members in place of the persons mentioned in the resolution.

(4) In Scotland, the liquidation committee has, in addition to the powers and duties conferred and imposed on it by this Act, such of the powers and duties of commissioners on a bankrupt estate as may be conferred and imposed on liquidation committees by the rules.

GENERAL NOTE

This section replaces (in part) s.590, C.A. 1985, and the term "liquidation committee" replaces the term "committee of inspection". The procedure is now governed by the Rules.

Creditors' meeting where winding up converted under s.96

102. Where, in the case of a winding up which was, under section 96 in Chapter III, converted to a creditors' voluntary winding up, a creditors' meeting is held in accordance with section 95, any appointment made or committee established by that meeting is deemed to have been made or established by a meeting held in accordance with section 98 in this Chapter.

GENERAL NOTE

Where a winding up has been converted into a creditors' voluntary winding up under ss.95 and 96, no creditors' meeting under s.98 is necessary. S.102 deems the creditors' meeting which will have been held under s.95 to have been held under s.98 in order to render ss.100 and 101 applicable in such a case.

Cesser of directors' powers

103. On the appointment of a liquidator, all the powers of the directors cease, except so far as the liquidation committee (or, if there is no such committee, the creditors) sanction their continuance.

GENERAL NOTE

This replaces (in part) s.591, C.A. 1985. It is analogous to s.91(2) *supra,* which applies to a members' voluntary winding up.

Vacancy in office of liquidator

104. If a vacancy occurs, by death, resignation or otherwise, in the office of a liquidator (other than a liquidator appointed by, or by the direction of, the court) the creditors may fill the vacancy.

GENERAL NOTE

This re-enacts s.592, C.A. 1985 and deals with the creditors' power to fill a vacancy in the office of liquidator. For the procedure see the Rules.

Meetings of company and creditors at each year's end

105.—(1) If the winding up continues for more than one year, the liquidator shall summon a general meeting of the company and a meeting of the creditors at the end of the first year from the commencement of the winding up, and of each succeeding year, or at the first convenient date within 3 months from the end of the year or such longer period as the Secretary of State may allow.

(2) The liquidator shall lay before each of the meetings an account of his acts and dealings and of the conduct of the winding up during the preceding year.

(3) If the liquidator fails to comply with this section, he is liable to a fine.

(4) Where under section 96 a members' voluntary winding up has become a creditors' voluntary winding up, and the creditors' meeting under section 95 is held 3 months or less before the end of the first year

from the commencement of the winding up, the liquidator is not required by this section to summon a meeting of creditors at the end of that year.

GENERAL NOTE

This re-enacts s.594, C.A. 1985 with minor amendments and provides for general meetings of the company and meetings of the creditors at the end of each year. Subs. (4) is new and obviates the need for the first yearly meeting in the circumstances mentioned. See General Note to s.97.

Final meeting prior to dissolution

106.—(1) As soon as the company's affairs are fully wound up, the liquidator shall make up an account of the winding up, showing how it has been conducted and the company's property has been disposed of, and thereupon shall call a general meeting of the company and a meeting of the creditors for the purpose of laying the account before the meetings and giving an explanation of it.

(2) Each such meeting shall be called by advertisement in the Gazette specifying the time, place and object of the meeting, and published at least one month before it.

(3) Within one week after the date of the meetings (or, if they are not held on the same date, after the date of the later one) the liquidator shall send to the registrar of companies a copy of the account, and shall make a return to him of the holding of the meetings and of their dates.

(4) If the copy is not sent or the return is not made in accordance with subsection (3), the liquidator is liable to a fine and, for continued contravention, to a daily default fine.

(5) However, if a quorum is not present at either such meeting, the liquidator shall, in lieu of the return required by subsection (3), make a return that the meeting was duly summoned and that no quorum was present; and upon such return being made the provisions of that subsection as to the making of the return are, in respect of that meeting, deemed complied with.

(6) If the liquidator fails to call a general meeting of the company or a meeting of the creditors as required by this section, he is liable to a fine.

DEFINITION

"fine", "daily default fine": s.430, Sched. 10.

GENERAL NOTE

This re-enacts s.595(1)–(5), (8), C.A. 1985 and deals with the final meeting prior to dissolution. It is analogous to s.94 (*q.v.*). Dissolution is now dealt with in s.201.

CHAPTER V

PROVISIONS APPLYING TO BOTH KINDS OF VOLUNTARY WINDING UP

Distribution of company's property

107. Subject to the provisions of this Act as to preferential payments, the company's property in a voluntary winding up shall on the winding up be applied in satisfaction of the company's liabilities pari passu and, subject to that application, shall (unless the articles otherwise provide) be distributed among the members according to their rights and interests in the company.

GENERAL NOTE

This re-enacts s.597, C.A. 1985 and provides *inter alia* for payment of debts *pari passu*. This means of course *pari passu* within their particular class after allowing for secured creditors' rights. For preferential creditors see s.386 and Sched. 6 where the categories are now clearly stated.

For a discussion of the liquidator's duty to provide for all debts before distribution to the shareholders see *Pulsford* v. *Devenish* [1903] 2 Ch. 625.

Appointment or removal of liquidator by the court

108.—(1) If from any cause whatever there is no liquidator acting, the court may appoint a liquidator.

(2) The court may, on cause shown, remove a liquidator and appoint another.

GENERAL NOTE

This re-enacts s.599, C.A. 1985 and deals with the courts' power to appoint and remove a liquidator for cause shown. Some unfitness must be shown for removal (see *Re Sir John Moore Gold Mining Co.* (1879) 12 Ch. D. 325 (C.A.)). A liquidator may appeal against removal (*Re Adam Eyton Ltd.* (1887) 36 Ch. D. 299 (C.A.)). See *Palmer,* paras. 86–48.

Notice by liquidator of his appointment

109.—(1) The liquidator shall, within 14 days after his appointment, publish in the Gazette and deliver to the registrar of companies for registration a notice of his appointment in the form prescribed by statutory instrument made by the Secretary of State.

(2) If the liquidator fails to comply with this section, he is liable to a fine and, for continued contravention, to a daily default fine.

DEFINITION

"fine", "daily default fine": s.430, Sched. 10.

GENERAL NOTE

This re-enacts s.600, C.A. 1985 and deals with gazetting and registration of the liquidator's appointment.

Acceptance of shares, etc., as consideration for sale of company property

110.—(1) This section applies, in the case of a company proposed to be, or being, wound up voluntarily, where the whole or part of the company's business or property is proposed to be transferred or sold to another company ("the transferee company"), whether or not the latter is a company within the meaning of the Companies Act.

(2) With the requisite sanction, the liquidator of the company being, or proposed to be, wound up ("the transferor company") may receive, in compensation or part compensation for the transfer or sale, shares, policies or other like interests in the transferee company for distribution among the members of the transferor company.

(3) The sanction requisite under subsection (2) is—

(a) in the case of a members' voluntary winding up, that of a special resolution of the company, conferring either a general authority on the liquidator or an authority in respect of any particular arrangement, and

(b) in the case of a creditors' voluntary winding up, that of either the court or the liquidation committee.

(4) Alternatively to subsection (2), the liquidator may (with that sanction) enter into any other arrangement whereby the members of the transferor company may, in lieu of receiving cash, shares, policies or other like interests (or in addition thereto), participate in the profits of, or receive any other benefit from, the transferee company.

(5) A sale or arrangement in pursuance of this section is binding on members of the transferor company.

(6) A special resolution is not invalid for purposes of this section by reason that it is passed before or concurrently with a resolution for voluntary winding up or for appointing liquidators; but, if an order is made within a year for winding up the company by the court, the special resolution is not valid unless sanctioned by the court.

GENERAL NOTE

This re-enacts and re-drafts ss.582(1)–(4), (7) and 593, C.A. 1985. Subss. (5), (6) and (8) of s.582 can now be found in s.111 *infra*. S.110 deals with a reconstruction where a liquidator of a company in voluntary winding up sells its business or property and in consideration of the transfer receives shares or other choses in action for distribution among the members in the transferor company. For a discussion of this see Weinberg and Blank, *Takeovers and Mergers* (4th ed.) Chaps. 6 and 7 and Buckley, *Companies Acts* (14th ed.) Vol. 1, pp.676–684. The section applies to a members' and a creditors' voluntary winding up with the difference referred to in subs. (3). Where there is a compulsory winding up it is arguable that a sale of this kind can be effected under s.167(1)(*b*). However in *Re London and Exchange Bank* (1867) 16 L.T. 340 Lord Romilly took a contrary view. *Cf. Re Agra and Masterman's Bank* (1866) L.R. 12 Eq. 509n and see Buckley, *Companies Acts, op. cit.* p.676.

Dissent from arrangement under s.110

111.—(1) This section applies in the case of a voluntary winding up where, for the purposes of section 110(2) or (4), there has been passed a special resolution of the transferor company providing the sanction requisite for the liquidator under that section.

(2) If a member of the transferor company who did not vote in favour of the special resolution expresses his dissent from it in writing, addressed to the liquidator and left at the company's registered office within 7 days after the passing of the resolution, he may require the liquidator either to abstain from carrying the resolution into effect or to purchase his interest at a price to be determined by agreement or by arbitration under this section.

(3) If the liquidator elects to purchase the member's interest, the purchase money must be paid before the company is dissolved and be raised by the liquidator in such manner as may be determined by special resolution.

(4) For purposes of an arbitration under this section, the provisions of the Companies Clauses Consolidation Act 1845 or, in the case of a winding up in Scotland, the Companies Clauses Consolidation (Scotland) Act 1845 with respect to the settlement of disputes by arbitration are incorporated with this Act, and—

(*a*) in the construction of those provisions this Act is deemed the special Act and "the company" means the transferor company, and

(*b*) any appointment by the incorporated provisions directed to be made under the hand of the secretary or any two of the directors may be made in writing by the liquidator (or, if there is more than one liquidator, then any two or more of them).

GENERAL NOTE

This deals with the rights of dissenting members where a special resolution has been passed providing the sanction for the liquidator to effect a reconstruction under either subs. (2) or subs. (4) of s.110. Subject to subs. (2), they consist of a right to block the reconstruction or be bought out.

Reference of questions to court

112.—(1) The liquidator or any contributory or creditor may apply to the court to determine any question arising in the winding up of a company, or to exercise, as respects the enforcing of calls or any other matter, all or any of the powers which the court might exercise if the company were being wound up by the court.

(2) The court, if satisfied that the determination of the question or the required exercise of power will be just and beneficial, may accede wholly or partially to the application on such terms and conditions as it thinks fit, or may make such other order on the application as it thinks just.

(3) A copy of an order made by virtue of this section staying the proceedings in the winding up shall forthwith be forwarded by the company, or otherwise as may be prescribed, to the registrar of companies, who shall enter it in his records relating to the company.

GENERAL NOTE
This re-enacts s.602, C.A. 1985 and is a wide and useful power to apply to the court on matters arising in the course of a voluntary winding up. See *Palmer,* paras. 86–19 for a discussion of the extent of this jurisdiction.

Court's power to control proceedings (Scotland)

113. If the court, on the application of the liquidator in the winding up of a company registered in Scotland, so directs, no action or proceeding shall be proceeded with or commenced against the company except by leave of the court and subject to such terms as the court may impose.

GENERAL NOTE
This re-enacts s.603, C.A. 1985 and gives the court in Scotland power to control proceedings.

No liquidator appointed or nominated by company

114.—(1) This section applies where, in the case of a voluntary winding up, no liquidator has been appointed or nominated by the company.

(2) The powers of the directors shall not be exercised, except with the sanction of the court or (in the case of a creditors' voluntary winding up) so far as may be necessary to secure compliance with sections 98 (creditors' meeting) and 99 (statement of affairs), during the period before the appointment or nomination of a liquidator of the company.

(3) Subsection (2) does not apply in relation to the powers of the directors—

(a) to dispose of perishable goods and other goods the value of which is likely to diminish if they are not immediately disposed of, and

(b) to do all such other things as may be necessary for the protection of the company's assets.

(4) If the directors of the company without reasonable excuse fail to comply with this section, they are liable to a fine.

DEFINITIONS
"creditors' voluntary winding up": s.90.
"fine": s.430, Sched. 10.

GENERAL NOTE
The purpose of this section is to strengthen the protection of the company's assets, and of the creditors' interests therein, during the critical period between the passing of a resolution for voluntary winding up under s.84, and the appointment of a liquidator under either s.91 or s.100 of that Act, depending on whether the winding up is a members' or a creditors' voluntary winding up. Paras. 667–673 of the *Cork Report* called attention to the need for such better protection, and the validity of the case for reform was conceded in paras. 128–133 of the *White Paper*. The provisions of this section, together with those of ss.98 and 99, form a carefully-planned response to the problem. This section covers the position up to the time of appointment of a liquidator, and effectively deprives the directors of their freedom to exercise their powers without the sanction of the court, except for the purposes specified in subss. (2) and (3).

Expenses of voluntary winding up

115. All expenses properly incurred in the winding up, including the remuneration of the liquidator, are payable out of the company's assets in priority to all other claims.

GENERAL NOTE

This re-enacts s.604, C.A. 1985 and gives the liquidator's costs priority over all other claims. See *Palmer,* paras. 86–28.

Saving for certain rights

116. The voluntary winding up of a company does not bar the right of any creditor or contributory to have it wound up by the court; but in the case of an application by a contributory the court must be satisfied that the rights of the contributories will be prejudiced by a voluntary winding up.

GENERAL NOTE

This re-enacts s.605, C.A. 1985 and allows an application for a compulsory winding up order. In the case of a contributory it must be shown that the rights of the contributory will be prejudiced by a voluntary winding up. Normally in the case of a creditor's petition the court has regard to the wishes of the majority of creditors but this is not an inflexible rule (*Re Southard & Co. Ltd.* [1979] 1 W.L.R. 1198 (C.A.)). See *Palmer,* paras. 85–06—85–07.

CHAPTER VI

WINDING UP BY THE COURT

Jurisdiction (England and Wales)

High Court and county court jurisdiction

117.—(1) The High Court has jurisdiction to wind up any company registered in England and Wales.

(2) Where the amount of a company's share capital paid up or credited as paid up does not exceed £120,000, then (subject to this section) the county court of the district in which the company's registered office is situated has concurrent jurisdiction with the High Court to wind up the company.

(3) The money sum for the time being specified in subsection (2) is subject to increase or reduction by order under section 416 in Part XV.

(4) The Lord Chancellor may by order in a statutory instrument exclude a county court from having winding-up jurisdiction, and for the purposes of that jurisdiction may attach its district, or any part thereof, to any other county court, and may by statutory instrument revoke or vary any such order.

In exercising the powers of this section, the Lord Chancellor shall provide that a county court is not to have winding-up jurisdiction unless it has for the time being jurisdiction for the purposes of Parts VIII to XI of this Act (individual insolvency).

(5) Every court in England and Wales having winding-up jurisdiction has for the purposes of that jurisdiction all the powers of the High Court; and every prescribed officer of the court shall perform any duties which an officer of the High Court may discharge by order of a judge of that court or otherwise in relation to winding up.

(6) For the purposes of this section, a company's "registered office" is the place which has longest been its registered office during the 6 months immediately preceding the presentation of the petition for winding up.

GENERAL NOTE
This reproduces s.512, C.A. 1985 with minor amendments.

Proceedings taken in wrong court

118.—(1) Nothing in section 117 invalidates a proceeding by reason of its being taken in the wrong court.

(2) The winding up of a company by the court in England and Wales, or any proceedings in the winding up, may be retained in the court in which the proceedings were commenced, although it may not be the court in which they ought to have been commenced.

GENERAL NOTE

This reproduces s.513, C.A. 1985 and deals with proceedings taken in the wrong court. Transfer is dealt with in s.75A, B and C of the County Courts Act 1959. These provisions were added by Sched. 3 to the Supreme Court Act 1981.

Proceedings in county court; case stated for High Court

119.—(1) If any question arises in any winding-up proceedings in a county court which all the parties to the proceedings, or which one of them and the judge of the court, desire to have determined in the first instance in the High Court, the judge shall state the facts in the form of a special case for the opinion of the High Court.

(2) Thereupon the special case and the proceedings (or such of them as may be required) shall be transmitted to the High Court for the purposes of the determination.

GENERAL NOTE

This section, which provides for a case stated procedure from the County Court to the High Court, re-enacts s.514, C.A. 1985. For an example of such a reference see *Re Mawcon Ltd.* [1969] 1 W.L.R. 78. Pennycuick J. said that that was the first case which had been stated pursuant to that provision.

Jurisdiction (Scotland)

Court of Session and sheriff court jurisdiction

120.—(1) The Court of Session has jurisdiction to wind up any company registered in Scotland.

(2) When the Court of Session is in vacation, the jurisdiction conferred on that court by this section may (subject to the provisions of this Part) be exercised by the judge acting as vacation judge in pursuance of section 4 of the Administration of Justice (Scotland) Act 1933.

(3) Where the amount of a company's share capital paid up or credited as paid up does not exceed £120,000, the sheriff court of the sheriffdom in which the company's registered office is situated has concurrent jurisdiction with the Court of Session to wind up the company; but—

(a) the Court of Session may, if it thinks expedient having regard to the amount of the company's assets to do so—
  (i) remit to a sheriff court any petition presented to the Court of Session for winding up such a company, or
  (ii) require such a petition presented to a sheriff court to be remitted to the Court of Session; and
(b) the Court of Session may require any such petition as above-mentioned presented to one sheriff court to be remitted to another sheriff court; and
(c) in a winding up in the sheriff court the sheriff may submit a stated case for the opinion of the Court of Session on any question of law arising in that winding up.

(4) For purposes of this section, the expression "registered office" means the place which has longest been the company's registered office during the 6 months immediately preceding the presentation of the petition for winding up.

(5) The money sum for the time being specified in subsection (3) is subject to increase or reduction by order under section 416 in Part XV.

GENERAL NOTE

This reproduces with minor amendments s.515, C.A. 1985. It deals with the winding-up jurisdiction of the Court of Session and Sheriff's Court in Scotland.

See *Palmer*, para. 87–03.

Power to remit winding up to Lord Ordinary

121.—(1) The Court of Session may, by Act of Sederunt, make provision for the taking of proceedings in a winding up before one of the Lords Ordinary; and, where provision is so made, the Lord Ordinary has, for the purposes of the winding up, all the powers and jurisdiction of the court.

(2) However, the Lord Ordinary may report to the Inner House any matter which may arise in the course of a winding up.

GENERAL NOTE

This reproduces s.516, C.A. 1985. It provides for the making of rules by the Court of Session for remission of winding up to the Lord Ordinary.

Grounds and effect of winding-up petition

Circumstances in which company may be wound up by the court

122.—(1) A company may be wound up by the court if—

(a) the company has by special resolution resolved that the company be wound up by the court,

(b) being, a public company which was registered as such on its original incorporation, the company has not been issued with a certificate under section 117 of the Companies Act (public company share capital requirements) and more than a year has expired since it was so registered,

(c) it is an old public company, within the meaning of the Consequential Provisions Act,

(d) the company does not commence its business within a year from its incorporation or suspends its business for a whole year,

(e) the number of members is reduced below 2,

(f) the company is unable to pay its debts,

(g) the court is of the opinion that it is just and equitable that the company should be wound up.

(2) In Scotland, a company which the Court of Session has jurisdiction to wind up may be wound up by the Court if there is subsisting a floating charge over property comprised in the company's property and undertaking, and the court is satisfied that the security of the creditor entitled to the benefit of the floating charge is in jeopardy.

For this purpose a creditor's security is deemed to be in jeopardy if the Court is satisfied that events have occurred or are about to occur which render it unreasonable in the creditor's interests that the company should retain power to dispose of the property which is subject to the floating charge.

DEFINITIONS

"public company": s.1(3), C.A. 1985.

"special resolution": s.378, C.A. 1985.

"unable to pay its debts": s.123.

GENERAL NOTE
This originated as s.222, C.A. 1948 (as amended by Sched. 3 para. 27, C.A. 1980 and s.4 C. (F. C. and 12) (S.) Act 1972) and for a brief period became s.517, C.A. 1985. S.122(1) deals with the grounds for a compulsory winding up and s.122(2) with the winding up of a company in Scotland which has granted a floating charge which is in jeopardy. In Scotland the floating charge is a statutory creation, hence the need for this express provision. The grounds specified in s.122(1) represent the original grounds specified in the C.A. 1948 as amended by the C.A. 1980. Examples of (*a*) are rare in practice; (*b*) and (*c*) are a result of the minimum capital requirements introduced in the C.A. 1980; (*d*), like the whole of s.122, is descretionary. The court may refuse to make an order where there are good reasons for the delay and bona fides will be considered—*Re Capital Fire Insurance Association* (1882) 21 Ch.D. 209, 222. The figure in (*e*) was seven for public companies before 1980. (*f*) is the most common in practice, and the following are the general principles which emerge from the cases. An unsatisfied creditor has a prima facie right to an order but there are exceptions which arise out of the opening words of s.122. These are (1) where the petitioner's debt does not exceed £750 (originally £50) (2) where the debt is bona fide disputed by the company (3) where the company has paid or tendered payment of the petitioner's debt (4) where the winding up is opposed by other creditors and (5) where the company is in the process of being wound up voluntarily. For a full discussion of these principles see *Palmer*, paras. 85–06—85–07.

(*g*) has been the subject of considerable flux in the caselaw culminating in the House of Lord's decision in *Ebrahimi* v. *Westbourne Galleries Ltd.* [1973] A.C. 360 which established that the court's discretion under this head is not limited to circumstances *ejusdem generis* to (*a*)–(*f*) and, in particular, existed where an equitable relationship of confidence between the members had been violated. See *Palmer*, para. 85–08; D. D. Prentice (1973) 89 L.Q.R. 107; M. R. Chesterman (1973) 36 M.L.R. 129.

Definition of inability to pay debts

123.—(1) A company is deemed unable to pay its debts—

(*a*) if a creditor (by assignment or otherwise) to whom the company is indebted in a sum exceeding £750 then due has served on the company, by leaving it at the company's registered office, a written demand (in the prescribed form) requiring the company to pay the sum so due and the company has for 3 weeks thereafter neglected to pay the sum or to secure or compound for it to the reasonable satisfaction of the creditor, or

(*b*) if, in England and Wales, execution or other process issued on a judgment, decree or order of any court in favour of a creditor of the company is returned unsatisfied in whole or in part, or

(*c*) if, in Scotland, the induciae of a charge for payment on an extract decree, or an extract registered bond, or an extract registered protest, have expired without payment being made, or

(*d*) if, in Northern Ireland, a certificate of unenforceability has been granted in respect of a judgment against the company, or

(*e*) if it is proved to the satisfaction of the court that the company is unable to pay its debts as they fall due.

(2) A company is also deemed unable to pay its debts if it is proved to the satisfaction of the court that the value of the company's assets is less than the amount of its liabilities, taking into account its contingent and prospective liabilities.

(3) The money sum for the time being specified in subsection (1)(*a*) is subject to increase or reduction by order under section 416 in Part XV.

GENERAL NOTE
This section is derived from s.518, C.A. 1985 and contains the statutory definition of inability to pay debts in relation to companies. The analogous provision in relation to individuals is s.268. See *Buckley,* Vol. 1, pp.534–5; *Palmer,* paras. 85–06—85–07.

Application for winding up *Who* ?

124.—(1) Subject to the provisions of this section, an application to the court for the winding up of a company shall be by petition presented either by the company, or the directors, or by any creditor or creditors (including any contingent or prospective creditor or creditors), contributory or contributories, or by all or any of those parties, together or separately.

(2) Except as mentioned below, a contributory is not entitled to present a winding-up petition unless either—

(a) the number of members is reduced below 2, or

(b) the shares in respect of which he is a contributory, or some of them, either were originally allotted to him, or have been held by him, and registered in his name, for at least 6 months during the 18 months before the commencement c the winding up, or have devolved on him through the death of a former holder.

(3) A person who is liable under section 76 to contribute to a company's assets in the event of its being wound up may petition on either of the grounds set out in section 122(1)(f) and (g), and subsection (2) above does not then apply; but unless the person is a contributory otherwise than under section 76, he may not in his character as contributory petition on any other ground.

This subsection is deemed included in Chapter VII of Part V of the Companies Act (redeemable shares; purchase by a company of its own shares) for the purposes of the Secretary of State's power to make regulations under section 179 of that Act.

(4) A winding-up petition may be presented by the Secretary of State—

(a) if the ground of the petition is that in section 122(1)(b) or (c), or

(b) in a case falling within section 440 of the Companies Act (expedient in the public interest, following report of inspectors, etc.).

(5) Where a company is being wound up voluntarily in England and Wales, a winding-up petition may be presented by the official receiver attached to the court as well as by any other person authorised in that behalf under the other provisions of this section; but the court shall not make a winding-up order on the petition unless it is satisfied that the voluntary winding up cannot be continued with due regard to the interests of the creditors or contributories.

DEFINITION
"contributory": s.79.

GENERAL NOTE
This section is derived from s.519, C.A. 1985. Though re-modelled, its substance remains the same except that the requirement, previously embodied in s.519(5), that a contingent or prospective creditor had to provide security for costs (or caution, in Scotland) has been dropped. In practice most petitions are creditors' petitions within subs. (1). See *Palmer,* paras. 85–06; 85–12.

Subs. (3)
Where a person claims the status of contributory *solely* under s.76 *supra* (which relates to liability resulting from the redemption or purchase by a private company, out of capital, of its own shares: see s.171, C.A. 1985) he may petition only on grounds (f) and (g) of s.122. In such a case he does not have to comply with subs. (2). If he can claim the status of contributory under some other section (see *supra* ss.74, 75, 77, 78) all of the grounds are available subject to subs. (2).

Powers of court on hearing of petition

125.—(1) On hearing a winding-up petition the court may dismiss it, or adjourn the hearing conditionally or unconditionally, or make an interim order, or any other order that it thinks fit; but the court shall not refuse to make a winding-up order on the ground only that the company's assets have been mortgaged to an amount equal to or in excess of those assets, or that the company has no assets.

(2) If the petition is presented by members of the company as contributories on the ground that it is just and equitable that the company should be wound up, the court, if it is of opinion—

(*a*) that the petitioners are entitled to relief either by winding up the company or by some other means, and

(*b*) that in the absence of any other remedy it would be just and equitable that the company should be wound up,

shall make a winding-up order; but this does not apply if the court is also of the opinion both that some other remedy is available to the petitioners and that they are acting unreasonably in seeking to have the company wound up instead of pursuing that other remedy.

DEFINITION
"contributories": s.79

GENERAL NOTE
This section which deals with the court's powers on the hearing of a petition re-enacts s.520, C.A. 1985.

The court has a broad discretion and wide powers to dismiss, adjourn or make an order but it may not refuse to make an order only on the ground of insufficiency of assets. Formerly it was possible to do this. The English courts are nevertheless reluctant to allow the winding-up proceedings to be used as a collector of small claims. See, *e.g. Re Standring & Co. Ltd.* (1895) 39 S.J. 603; *Re Fancy Dress Balls Co. Ltd.* (1899) 43 S.J. 657. In Scotland the courts adopt a different attitude. See further *Palmer,* para. 85–06.

Subs. (2)
The court will only make an order that the company shall be wound up under s.122(*g*) as a last resort. It will, therefore, decline to do so where some other, less drastic remedy is available and the petitioner is being unreasonable in not pursuing it.

Power to stay or restrain proceedings against company

126.—(1) At any time after the presentation of a winding-up petition, and before a winding-up order has been made, the company, or any creditor or contributory, may—

(*a*) where any action or proceeding against the company is pending in the High Court or Court of Appeal in England and Wales or Northern Ireland, apply to the court in which the action or proceeding is pending for a stay of proceedings therein, and

(*b*) where any other action or proceeding is pending against the company, apply to the court having jurisdiction to wind up the company to restrain further proceedings in the action or proceeding;

and the court to which application is so made may (as the case may be) stay, sist or restrain the proceedings accordingly on such terms as it thinks fit.

(2) In the case of a company registered under section 680 of the Companies Act (pre-1862 companies; companies formed under legislation other than the Companies Acts) or the previous corresponding legislation, where the application to stay, sist or restrain is by a creditor, this section extends to actions and proceedings against any contributory of the company.

DEFINITION
"contributory": s.79

GENERAL NOTE
This section which gives the court power to stay proceedings against the company after a petition and before an order to wind up has been made is a re-enactment with minor amendments of s.521, C.A. 1985. Subs. (2) relates to companies not formed under the Companies Act but authorised to register. S.126 should also be read with s.128 which deals with the avoiding of attachments and s.130(2) which prohibits proceedings after an order has been made unless leave of the court is obtained. See also the wide powers of the court in the case of a voluntary winding up in s.112.

See *Palmer,* para. 85–29.

Avoidance of property dispositions, etc.

127. In a winding up by the court, any disposition of the company's property, and any transfer of shares, or alteration in the status of the company's members, made after the commencement of the winding up is, unless the court otherwise orders, void.

DEFINITIONS
  "commencement of the winding up": s.129.
  "property": s.436.

GENERAL NOTE
  This re-enacts s.522, C.A. 1985. The section avoids dispositions, etc., of property of the company made after the commencement of winding up unless the court otherwise orders. For a recent consideration of the section by the Court of Appeal see *Re Gray's Inn Construction Co. Ltd.* [1980] 1 All E.R. 814. This case deals with the operation of a company's bank account. See also the useful discussion by Oliver J. in *Re Leslie Engineers Co. Ltd.* [1976] 2 All E.R. 85, 90–96.

Avoidance of attachments, etc.

128.—(1) Where a company registered in England and Wales is being wound up by the court, any attachment, sequestration, distress or execution put in force against the estate or effects of the company after the commencement of the winding up is void.

(2) This section, so far as relates to any estate or effects of the company situated in England and Wales, applies in the case of a company registered in Scotland as it applies in the case of a company registered in England and Wales.

DEFINITION
  "commencement of the winding up": s.129.

GENERAL NOTE
  This re-enacts s.523, C.A. 1985 and avoids execution, etc., put in force after the commencement of the winding up.

  Note that there is no reference to Northern Ireland in the old s.523 or this section (and see s.441) and also that the court is not given a discretion under this particular section. However it has been held since 1864 that the section is to be read with and is controlled by ss.126 and 130(2): *Re Exhall Coal Mining Co.* (1864) 4 De G.J. & Sm. 377. Thus a creditor can apply for leave to proceed under s.130(2). It is difficult to see why s.128 should be read in this way. See further Buckley, *Companies Acts* (14th ed.), Vol. 1, p.558.

Commencement of winding up

Commencement of winding up by the court

129.—(1) If, before the presentation of a petition for the winding up of a company by the court, a resolution has been passed by the company for voluntary winding up, the winding up of the company is deemed to have commenced at the time of the passing of the resolution; and unless the court, on proof of fraud or mistake, directs otherwise, all proceedings taken in the voluntary winding up are deemed to have been validly taken.

(2) In any other case, the winding up of a company by the court is deemed to commence at the time of the presentation of the petition for winding up.

TRANSITIONAL PROVISION
Sched. 11, para. 4.

GENERAL NOTE
This re-enacts s.524, C.A. 1985 and subs. (1) dates back to the 1929 Act. The section backdates the commencement of the winding up to the presentation of the petition or an earlier resolution to wind up voluntarily. Compare s.86 which relates to voluntary winding up.

Consequences of winding-up order

130.—(1) On the making of a winding-up order, a copy of the order must forthwith be forwarded by the company (or otherwise as may be prescribed) to the registrar of companies, who shall enter it in his records relating to the company.

(2) When a winding-up order has been made or a provisional liquidator has been appointed, no action or proceeding shall be proceeded with or commenced against the company or its property, except by leave of the court and subject to such terms as the court may impose.

(3) When an order has been made for winding up a company registered under section 680 of the Companies Act, no action or proceeding shall be commenced or proceeded with against the company or its property or any contributory of the company, in respect of any debt of the company, except by leave of the court, and subject to such terms as the court may impose.

(4) An order for winding up a company operates in favour of all the creditors and of all contributories of the company as if made on the joint petition of a creditor and of a contributory.

GENERAL NOTE
This re-enacts with minor amendment s.525, C.A. 1985 and deals with some of the consequences of a winding up order. Subs. (1) provides for a copy of the order to be filed with the registrar of companies. Subs. (2) has been referred to above in connection with s.126.

This section is not exhaustive as to the effects of a winding up order. It does not for instance deal with the effect of winding up on contracts, especially contracts of employment. See *Palmer*, paras. 85–28.

Investigation procedures

Company's statement of affairs

131.—(1) Where the court has made a winding-up order or appointed a provisional liquidator, the official receiver may require some or all of the persons mentioned in subsection (3) below to make out and submit to him a statement in the prescribed form as to the affairs of the company.

(2) The statement shall be verified by affidavit by the persons required to submit it and shall show—
  (a) particulars of the company's assets, debts and liabilities;
  (b) the names and addresses of the company's creditors;
  (c) the securities held by them respectively;
  (d) the dates when the securities were respectively given; and
  (e) such further or other information as may be prescribed or as the official receiver may require.

(3) The persons referred to in subsection (1) are—
  (a) those who are or have been officers of the company;

(*b*) those who have taken part in the formation of the company at any time within one year before the relevant date;

(*c*) those who are in the company's employment, or have been in its employment within that year, and are in the official receiver's opinion capable of giving the information required;

(*d*) those who are or have been within that year officers of, or in the employment of, a company which is, or within that year was, an officer of the company.

(4) Where any persons are required under this section to submit a statement of affairs to the official receiver, they shall do so (subject to the next subsection) before the end of the period of 21 days beginning with the day after that on which the prescribed notice of the requirement is given to them by the official receiver.

(5) The official receiver, if he thinks fit, may—

(*a*) at any time release a person from an obligation imposed on him under subsection (1) or (2) above; or

(*b*) either when giving the notice mentioned in subsection (4) or subsequently, extend the period so mentioned;

and where the official receiver has refused to exercise a power conferred by this subsection, the court, if it thinks fit, may exercise it.

(6) In this section—

"employment" includes employment under a contract for services; and

"the relevant date" means—

(*a*) in a case where a provisional liquidator is appointed, the date of his appointment; and

(*b*) in a case where no such appointment is made, the date of the winding-up order.

(7) If a person without reasonable excuse fails to comply with any obligation imposed under this section, he is liable to a fine and, for continued contravention, to a daily default fine.

(8) In the application of this section to Scotland references to the official receiver are to the liquidator or, in a case where a provisional liquidator is appointed, the provisional liquidator.

TRANSITIONAL PROVISION
Sched. 11, para. 5.

DEFINITIONS
"employment": subs. (6).
"fine"; "daily default fine": s.430, Sched. 10.
"officers of the company": s.251, C.A. 1985, s.744.
"prescribed": s.251.
"security": s.248(*b*).
"the official receiver": s.399.
"the relevant date": subs. (6).

GENERAL NOTE
This section replaces s.66, I.A. 1985. Apart from necessary differences of nomenclature employed with regard to the office holder concerned, the provisions of subss. (2)–(5) inclusive are in substance identical to those in ss.22, 47 and 66 of this Act which are respectively concerned with the statement of affairs to be submitted to an administrator, to an administrative receiver, and to a Scottish receiver. The forms of statement will be prescribed in the rules, and will be closely similar for all types of insolvency proceedings. See also the General Note to s.22.

Subs. (1)
The making of a winding up order by a court takes place under ss.117 and 120, which apply to courts in England and Wales and in Scotland respectively. The appointment of a provisional liquidator in either England or Scotland may take place under the provisions of

s.135. One important distinction is to be noted in the drafting of this subsection, as against the drafting of ss.22(1), 47(1) and 66(1), in that the use of the word "may" has the effect of making it a matter for the discretion of the official receiver (or in Scotland, the liquidator or the provisional liquidator) whether to require a statement of affairs to be prepared, whereas in the case of the other insolvency proceedings the requirement is a compulsory one. The purpose underlying this variation in the case of a winding up is to maintain the previous facility for the official receiver to dispense with a statement of affairs in certain cases, such as where the directors cannot be found or where there is insufficient information to enable a statement to be prepared, or where the director concerned is incapable of performing the task because of illness.

Subs. (4)

For the purpose of calculating the period of 21 days, the effective date on which notice will be deemed to have been given by the official receiver will be the date on which the documents are dispatched.

Subs. (8)

This additional provision is necessitated by the fact that there is no office of official receiver under Scottish law. In Scotland therefore the role allocated to the official receiver in England and Wales for the purpose of this section must perforce be played by the liquidator. However, if a provisional liquidator has been appointed in Scottish winding up proceedings his position under this section is identical to that of a provisional liquidator appointed in England and Wales.

Investigation by official receiver

132.—(1) Where a winding-up order is made by the court in England and Wales, it is the duty of the official receiver to investigate—

   (*a*) if the company has failed, the causes of the failure; and

   (*b*) generally, the promotion, formation, business, dealings and affairs of the company,

and to make such report (if any) to the court as he thinks fit.

(2) The report is, in any proceedings, prima facie evidence of the facts stated in it.

DEFINITIONS

   "business": s.436.

   "the official receiver": s.399.

GENERAL NOTE

   This section replaces s.67, I.A. 1985.

Subs. (1)(a)

If the company has failed

This takes account of the possibility that a winding up order may be made by the court in circumstances where the company is not insolvent, in which case an investigation into "the causes of the company's failure" will be patently unnecessary. It may be noted however that, although the obligation to investigate is compulsory where the company is insolvent, the making of a report to the court remains a matter for the official receiver's discretion by virtue of the concluding words of this subsection.

Subs. (1)(b)

Generally . . .

This paragraph is drafted without regard to the possibility that a winding up order may be made by the court in respect of a company which is not insolvent. Hence, in all cases where a winding up order is made, and regardless of which of the grounds mentioned in s.122 has furnished the basis for the order, the official receiver must carry out an investigation into the promotion, formation, business, dealing and affairs of the company. However, as mentioned above in relation to para. (*a*) the duty to report to the court is in each case a matter for the official receiver's discretion and it is therefore to be expected that in cases where the company is not insolvent the Official Receiver will elect to report only if serious irregularities come to light.

Public examination of officers

133.—(1) Where a company is being wound up by the court, the official receiver or, in Scotland, the liquidator may at any time before the dissolution of the company apply to the court for the public examination of any person who—

(a) is or has been an officer of the company; or

(b) has acted as liquidator or administrator of the company or as receiver or manager or, in Scotland, receiver of its property; or

(c) not being a person falling within paragraph (a) or (b), is or has been concerned, or has taken part, in the promotion, formation or management of the company.

(2) Unless the court otherwise orders, the official receiver or, in Scotland, the liquidator shall make an application under subsection (1) if he is requested in accordance with the rules to do so by—

(a) one-half, in value, of the company's creditors; or

(b) three-quarters, in value, of the company's contributories.

(3) On an application under subsection (1), the court shall direct that a public examination of the person to whom the application relates shall be held on a day appointed by the court; and that person shall attend on that day and be publicly examined as to the promotion, formation or management of the company or as to the conduct of its business and affairs, or his conduct or dealings in relation to the company.

(4) The following may take part in the public examination of a person under this section and may question that person concerning the matters mentioned in subsection (3), namely—

(a) the official receiver;

(b) the liquidator of the company;

(c) any person who has been appointed as special manager of the company's property or business;

(d) any creditor of the company who has tendered a proof or, in Scotland, submitted a claim in the winding up;

(e) any contributory of the company.

DEFINITIONS
"administrator": s.8(2).
"business": s.436.
"contributory": s.79.
"officer of the company": s.251; C.A. 1985, s.744.
"prescribed": s.251.
"property": s.436.
"receiver in Scotland": s.70(1).
"receiver or manager": s.29(1)(a).
"the official receiver": s.399.
"the rules": s.251.

GENERAL NOTE
This section replaces subs. (1)–(4) of s.68, I.A. 1985 which are repealed. In Chap. 12 of the *Cork Report* a strong case was made out for a revival of the use of the public examination in cases of company insolvency, so that it should function in the same way as the public examination of individuals in cases of bankruptcy (see paras. 653–657). This proposal was accepted in the *White Paper* (paras. 91–94), and the present section duly carries it into effect. It provides for the holding of a public examination whenever a company is being wound up by the court, irrespective of whether the company is insolvent or not. Most importantly, it is no longer a pre-condition to the holding of a public examination that the official receiver should first make a report alleging fraud, as was formerly required under s.563(1) of the Companies Act 1985.

Subs. (1)(b)

Has acted as liquidator or . . .

This power to examine a former liquidator of a company may be of particular significance in cases where a voluntary liquidation is converted into a compulsory winding up under s.124(5). The official receiver, or the liquidator appointed under the compulsory winding up proceedings, may find it expedient to cause the former liquidator to undergo public examination, for example where it appears that the conduct of the voluntary liquidation was coloured by some irregularity. The power made available by this subsection is thus a component in the overall strategy aimed at eradicating the excesses and malpractices to which the decision in *Re Centrebind Ltd.* [1967] 1 W.L.R. 377; [1966] 3 All E.R. 889 subsequently gave rise. Other elements in this same strategy include the new provisions of Pt. XIII of this Act regulating the ability of persons to act as insolvency practitioners within the law, and the special provision in ss.98 and 99 (*q.v.*).

Subs. (4)(c)

Special manager of the company's property or business

Such appointments may be made under the provisions of s.177 which replaces s.90, I.A. 1985.

Enforcement of s.133

134.—(1) If a person without reasonable excuse fails at any time to attend his public examination under section 133, he is guilty of a contempt of court and liable to be punished accordingly.

(2) In a case where a person without reasonable excuse fails at any time to attend his examination under section 133 or there are reasonable grounds for believing that a person has absconded, or is about to abscond, with a view to avoiding or delaying his examination under that section, the court may cause a warrant to be issued to a constable or prescribed officer of the court—

(*a*) for the arrest of that person; and

(*b*) for the seizure of any books, papers, records, money or goods in that person's possession.

(3) In such a case the court may authorise the person arrested under the warrant to be kept in custody, and anything seized under such a warrant to be held, in accordance with the rules, until such time as the court may order.

DEFINITIONS

"prescribed": s.251.

"the rules": s.251.

GENERAL NOTE

This re-enacts subs. (5) and (6) of s.68, I.A. 1985 and deals with the enforcement of the provisions relating to public examination of officers (see Note to s.133).

Appointment of liquidator

Appointment and powers of provisional liquidator

135.—(1) Subject to the provisions of this section, the court may, at any time after the presentation of a winding-up petition, appoint a liquidator provisionally.

(2) In England and Wales, the appointment of a provisional liquidator may be made at any time before the making of a winding-up order; and either the official receiver or any other fit person may be appointed.

(3) In Scotland, such an appointment may be made at any time before the first appointment of liquidators.

(4) The provisional liquidator shall carry out such functions as the court may confer on him.

(5) When a liquidator is provisionally appointed by the court, his powers may be limited by the order appointing him.

GENERAL NOTE

This section re-enacts s.532, C.A. 1985 and s.69(3), I.A. 1985. It deals with the appointment of a provisional liquidator.

Subs. (5)

As appearing in the C.A. 1948 (s.238(4)) this enabled the order to limit or *restrict* the powers of the provisional liquidator. The present subs. simply refers to limit.

If the court imposed conditions this would arguably not limit the scope of the power itself but simply restrict the manner of its exercise *cf.* Lord Oaksey in *Tool Metal Manufacturing Co. Ltd.* v. *Tungsten Electric Co. Ltd.* [1955] 2 All E.R. 657, 671, in the context of "restrict" in the Patents and Designs Act 1907, s.28(1).

See generally *Palmer,* paras. 85–32.

Functions of official receiver in relation to office of liquidator

136.—(1) The following provisions of this section have effect, subject to section 140 below, on a winding-up order being made by the court in England and Wales.

(2) The official receiver, by virtue of his office, becomes the liquidator of the company and continues in office until another person becomes liquidator under the provisions of this Part.

(3) The official receiver is, by virtue of his office, the liquidator during any vacancy.

(4) At any time when he is the liquidator of the company, the official receiver may summon separate meetings of the company's creditors and contributories for the purpose of choosing a person to be liquidator of the company in place of the official receiver.

(5) It is the duty of the official receiver—

(*a*) as soon as practicable in the period of 12 weeks beginning with the day on which the winding-up order was made, to decide whether to exercise his power under subsection (4) to summon meetings, and

(*b*) if in pursuance of paragraph (*a*) he decides not to exercise that power, to give notice of his decision, before the end of that period, to the court and to the company's creditors and contributories, and

(*c*) (whether or not he has decided to exercise that power) to exercise his power to summon meetings under subsection (4) if he is at any time requested, in accordance with the rules, to do so by one-quarter, in value, of the company's creditors;

and accordingly, where the duty imposed by paragraph (*c*) arises before the official receiver has performed a duty imposed by paragraph (*a*) or (*b*), he is not required to perform the latter duty.

(6) A notice given under subsection (5)(*b*) to the company's creditors shall contain an explanation of the creditors' power under subsection (5)(*c*) to require the official receiver to summon meetings of the company's creditors and contributories.

DEFINITIONS

"contributory": s.79.
"the official receiver": s.399.
"the rules": s.251.

GENERAL NOTE

This section partly replaces the provisions of s.70, I.A. 1985, which are repealed. It also incorporates the provisions announced in paras. 75–77 of the *White Paper* (see also the general discussion in Chap. 19 of the *Cork Report*), that it should become a matter for the judgment of the official receiver to determine whether any useful purpose will be served by the convening of meetings of the company's creditors and contributories for the purpose of choosing a private-sector liquidator to replace the official receiver. Under the terms of subs. (4) the convening of these meetings is now a discretionary matter for the official receiver, and subs. (5) allows the official receiver a period of up to 12 weeks from the date of the winding up order within which to decide whether to summon them. However, subs. (5)(c) enables one or more creditors, if representing at least one quarter in value of the company's creditors, by means of a formal request to render it obligatory for the official receiver to convene the meetings.

Subs. (1)

Subject to s.140 below

This proviso allows for the possibility that, in the case where a winding up order is made immediately upon the discharge of an administration order, the court is empowered by s.140(1) to appoint as liquidator the person who has been acting as the administrator of the company. In such a case, the official receiver does not become liquidator by virtue of subs. (2) of this section, nor does he incur the duties imposed by subs. (5)(a) and (b), but he will nevertheless become liquidator by virtue of his office during any vacancy, as provided by subs. (3) of this section.

Subs. (6)

An explanation of the creditors' power

This is to ensure that in cases where the official receiver decides not to convene meetings under subs. (4) of this section the creditors have notification of their power to compel him to call such meetings, using the procedure specified in subs. (5)(c).

Appointment by Secretary of State

137.—(1) In a winding up by the court in England and Wales the official receiver may, at any time when he is the liquidator of the company, apply to the Secretary of State for the appointment of a person as liquidator in his place.

(2) If meetings are held in pursuance of a decision under section 136(5)(a), but no person is chosen to be liquidator as a result of those meetings, it is the duty of the official receiver to decide whether to refer the need for an appointment to the Secretary of State.

(3) On an application under subsection (1), or a reference made in pursuance of a decision under subsection (2), the Secretary of State shall either make an appointment or decline to make one.

(4) Where a liquidator has been appointed by the Secretary of State under subsection (3), the liquidator shall give notice of his appointment to the company's creditors or, if the court so allows, shall advertise his appointment in accordance with the directions of the court.

(5) In that notice or advertisement the liquidator shall—

(a) state whether he proposes to summon a general meeting of the company's creditors under section 141 below for the purpose of determining (together with any meeting of contributories) whether a liquidation committee should be established under that section, and

(b) if he does not propose to summon such a meeting, set out the power of the company's creditors under that section to require him to summon one.

TRANSITIONAL PROVISION
Sched. 11, para. 6.

GENERAL NOTE

As an alternative to the mode of appointment of a liquidator by means of specially convened meetings under s.136(4) *supra*, s.137 enables the official receiver to apply to the Secretary of State to appoint a liquidator in his place. The same possibility arises by virtue of subs. (2) of s.137 if meetings are convened that do not result in the choice of a person as liquidator, for example because of deadlock among the persons attending the respective meetings, so that no choice in accordance with the provisions of s.136 can be made. In either circumstance, the Secretary of State is left free to decline to make an appointment, in which case the official receiver continues to be the liquidator of the company *ex officio* in accordance with subs. (2) of s.136.

Appointment of liquidator in Scotland

138.—(1) Where a winding-up order is made by the court in Scotland, a liquidator shall be appointed by the court at the time when the order is made.

(2) The liquidator so appointed (here referred to as "the interim liquidator") continues in office until another person becomes liquidator in his place under this section or the next.

(3) The interim liquidator shall (subject to the next subsection) as soon as practicable in the period of 28 days beginning with the day on which the winding-up order was made or such longer period as the court may allow, summon separate meetings of the company's creditors and contributories for the purpose of choosing a person (who may be the person who is the interim liquidator) to be liquidator of the company in place of the interim liquidator.

(4) If it appears to the interim liquidator, in any case where a company is being wound up on grounds including its inability to pay its debts, that it would be inappropriate to summon under subsection (3) a meeting of the company's contributories, he may summon only a meeting of the company's creditors for the purpose mentioned in that subsection.

(5) If one or more meetings are held in pursuance of this section but no person is appointed or nominated by the meeting or meetings, the interim liquidator shall make a report to the court which shall appoint either the interim liquidator or some other person to be liquidator of the company.

(6) A person who becomes liquidator of the company in place of the interim liquidator shall, unless he is appointed by the court, forthwith notify the court of that fact.

DEFINITIONS
  "contributory": s.79.
  "the interim liquidator": subs. (2).

GENERAL NOTE
  The need for this section results from the separate arrangements for winding up in Scotland, where there is no office of official receiver. Accordingly the provisions made in s.136 with regard to England and Wales are inappropriate in Scotland, where it is the practice, following the presentation of a winding up petition, to appoint a provisional liquidator under s.135. In most cases the provisional liquidator will subsequently be appointed as liquidator in accordance with subs. (1) of the present section and become the "interim liquidator" by virtue of subs. (2). *Cf.* s.136, *supra,* which applies to England and Wales.
  One notable difference between the drafting of this section and that of s.136 is with regard to the duty to summon meetings of the company's creditors and contributories. Whereas s.136(4) allows the official receiver a discretion whether or not to summon meetings of either kind, subss. (3) and (4) of this section render it obligatory for an interim liquidator to convene a meeting of the company's creditors, albeit he is accorded a discretion whether to convene a meeting of contributories. A further difference between English law and Scots law arises if no choice of a person as liquidator results from any meetings which are held. Whereas s.137(2) allows the official receiver a discretion whether to apply to the Secretary of State for the appointment of a liquidator, subs. (5) of this section renders it obligatory for the interim liquidator to report the matter to the court, and further obliges the court to make an appointment of some person or other as liquidator of the company.

Choice of liquidator at meetings of creditors and contributories

139.—(1) This section applies where a company is being wound up by the court and separate meetings of the company's creditors and contributories are summoned for the purpose of choosing a person to be liquidator of the company.

(2) The creditors and the contributories at their respective meetings may nominate a person to be liquidator.

(3) The liquidator shall be the person nominated by the creditors or, where no person has been so nominated, the person (if any) nominated by the contributories.

(4) In the case of different persons being nominated, any contributory or creditor may, within 7 days after the date on which the nomination was made by the creditors, apply to the court for an order either—

(*a*) appointing the person nominated as liquidator by the contributories to be a liquidator instead of, or jointly with, the person nominated by the creditors; or

(*b*) appointing some other person to be liquidator instead of the person nominated by the creditors.

DEFINITION
"contributory": s.79.

GENERAL NOTE
This section is designed to lay down a clearer indication of the manner in which a liquidator is to be chosen. It is designed as an analogue to s.100, which deals with the same situation in a creditor's voluntary winding up. However, the present section differs in particular from s.100(3), since the latter section includes a right for a director to make application to the court to settle any dispute over the appointment of the liquidator, whereas subs. (4) of this section accords no such right to a director in the case of a compulsory winding up. This is a consequence of the fact that the making of an order for compulsory winding up terminates the directors' authority to act in relation to the company, and they are accordingly excluded from the category of interested persons with standing to apply to the court on the question of who is to be liquidator.

Appointment by the court following administration or voluntary arrangement

140.—(1) Where a winding-up order is made immediately upon the discharge of an administration order, the court may appoint as liquidator of the company the person who has ceased on the discharge of the administration order to be the administrator of the company.

(2) Where a winding-up order is made at a time when there is a supervisor of a voluntary arrangement approved in relation to the company under Part I, the court may appoint as liquidator of the company the person who is the supervisor at the time when the winding-up order is made.

(3) Where the court makes an appointment under this section, the official receiver does not become the liquidator as otherwise provided by section 136(2), and he has no duty under section 136(5) (*a*) or (*b*) in respect of the summoning of creditors' or contributories' meetings.

DEFINITIONS
"administration order": s.8(2).
"administrator of the company": s.8(2).
"supervisor of a composition or scheme": s.7(2).

GENERAL NOTE
This section makes provision for the expeditious transformation of an administration order procedure under Pt. II or a composition or scheme under Pt. I into a compulsory winding up in appropriate cases. It does so by enabling the court when making the winding up order to appoint as liquidator the person who has lately ceased to be administrator in consequence of the discharge of the administration order, or who is acting as supervisor of the voluntary arrangement, as the case may be. There are consequential provisions in subs. (3) to modify the application of s.136 in view of the fact that in such cases the official receiver will not be

liquidator in the first instance. Discharge of an administration order is governed by ss.18, 24(5) and 27(4)(*d*).

Liquidation committees

Liquidation committee (England and Wales)

141.—(1) Where a winding-up order has been made by the court in England and Wales and separate meetings of creditors and contributories have been summoned for the purpose of choosing a person to be liquidator, those meetings may establish a committee ("the liquidation committee") to exercise the functions conferred on it by or under this Act.

(2) The liquidator (not being the official receiver) may at any time, if he thinks fit, summon separate general meetings of the company's creditors and contributories for the purpose of determining whether such a committee should be established and, if it is so determined, of establishing it.

The liquidator (not being the official receiver) shall summon such a meeting if he is requested, in accordance with the rules, to do so by one-tenth, in value, of the company's creditors.

(3) Where meetings are summoned under this section, or for the purpose of choosing a person to be liquidator, and either the meeting of creditors or the meeting of contributories decides that a liquidation committee should be established, but the other meeting does not so decide or decides that a committee should not be established, the committee shall be established in accordance with the rules, unless the court otherwise orders.

(4) The liquidation committee is not to be able or required to carry out its functions at any time when the official receiver is liquidator; but at any such time its functions are vested in the Secretary of State except to the extent that the rules otherwise provide.

(5) Where there is for the time being no liquidation committee, and the liquidator is a person other than the official receiver, the functions of such a committee are vested in the Secretary of State except to the extent that the rules otherwise provide.

DEFINITIONS
"contributory": s.79.
"the official receiver": s.399.
"the rules": s.251.

GENERAL NOTE
This section re-enacts s.74, I.A. 1985. The committee is by implication to be composed of both creditors and contributories, although this is nowhere indicated in the drafting of the section itself. The possibility of establishing a committee consisting of creditors is also provided for elsewhere in the Act in relation to other types of company insolvency proceedings, namely the administration order procedure, administrative receivership, and receivership in Scotland. The relevant provisions of the Act are ss.26, 49 and 68 (*q.v.*). It is in relation to winding up however that the role of the committee of creditors and contributories is most fully elaborated, building as it does on the law and practice developed in relation to what were previously termed "committees of inspection."

Subs. (1)

The functions conferred on it by or under this Act
In keeping with the recommendations in Chapter 19 of the *Cork Report* the discredited concept of "creditor control," which was largely mythical, has been relinquished in favour of a policy of encouraging "creditor participation." Accordingly the title "committee of inspection" has been abandoned, and the committee, if any, which is formed by the creditors is simply charged with the task of exercising "the functions conferred on it by or under this Act." In addition to the functions arising directly under those statutory enactments, the

possibility is provided that further functions may be conferred in the rules, as authorised by para. 10 of Sched. 8 to the Act.

Subs. (2)

The liquidator (not being the official receiver) may at any time . . . summon separate general meetings

This caters for the possibility that a private sector liquidator may take up office, pursuant to ss.136, 139 or 140, without it having been resolved whether a committee of creditors is to be appointed. The liquidator is given a discretion to convene meetings of the creditors and contributories at any time for the purpose of deciding whether such a committee shall be established, and it can be rendered obligatory for him to convene such meetings if a formal request to this effect is made by one tenth in value of its creditors. This process may also be invoked following the direct appointment of a liquidator under s.137(4), since subs. (5) of that section obliges the liquidator to notify all creditors whether he intends to summon a meeting of creditors, and further obliges him to inform creditors of their power to compel him to summon such a meeting if he is not otherwise intending to do so.

Subs. (4)

Except to the extent that the rules otherwise provide

This allows the functions which are by this subsection expressed to be vested in the Secretary of State to be delegated to the official receiver himself as a matter of course, by means of a provision to that effect inserted in the rules. *Cf.* Companies (Winding Up) Rules 1949 (S.I. 1949 No. 330) Rule 214.

Liquidation committee (Scotland)

142.—(1) Where a winding-up order has been made by the court in Scotland and separate meetings of creditors and contributories have been summoned for the purpose of choosing a person to be liquidator or, under section 138(4), only a meeting of creditors has been summoned for that purpose, those meetings or (as the case may be) that meeting may establish a committee ("the liquidation committee") to exercise the functions conferred on it by or under this Act.

(2) The liquidator may at any time, if he thinks fit, summon separate general meetings of the company's creditors and contributories for the purpose of determining whether such a committee should be established and, if it is so determined, of establishing it.

(3) The liquidator, if appointed by the court otherwise than under section 139(4)(*a*), is required to summon meetings under subsection (2) if he is requested, in accordance with the rules, to do so by one-tenth, in value, of the company's creditors.

(4) Where meetings are summoned under this section, or for the purpose of choosing a person to be liquidator, and either the meeting of creditors or the meeting of contributories decides that a liquidation committee should be established, but the other meeting does not so decide or decides that a committee should not be established, the committee shall be established in accordance with the rules, unless the court otherwise orders.

(5) Where in the case of any winding up there is for the time being no liquidation committee, the functions of such a committee are vested in the court except to the extent that the rules otherwise provide.

(6) In addition to the powers and duties conferred and imposed on it by this Act, a liquidation committee has such of the powers and duties of commissioners in a sequestration as may be conferred and imposed on such committees by the rules.

DEFINITIONS
"contributory": s.79.
"the rules": s.251.

GENERAL NOTE

This section replaces s.75, I.A. 1985. The first subsection is applicable where meetings of the company's creditors and contributories, or of the creditors only, are convened by the interim liquidator under s.138(2) or (3) respectively for the purpose of choosing a liquidator. Such meetings are empowered to resolve also to appoint a committee to exercise the functions conferred on it by or under this Act and may proceed to do so. If no such course is adopted at that stage, subs. (2) confers a discretionary power on the liquidator to summon such meetings at any subsequent time, subject to the possibility that this can be rendered obligatory where one-tenth in value of the creditors formally request that meetings be summoned.

The liquidator's functions

General functions in winding up by the court

143.—(1) The functions of the liquidator of a company which is being wound up by the court are to secure that the assets of the company are got in, realised and distributed to the company's creditors and, if there is a surplus, to the persons entitled to it.

(2) It is the duty of the liquidator of a company which is being wound up by the court in England and Wales, if he is not the official receiver—

(*a*) to furnish the official receiver with such information,

(*b*) to produce to the official receiver, and permit inspection by the official receiver of, such books, papers and other records, and

(*c*) to give the official receiver such other assistance,

as the official receiver may reasonably require for the purposes of carrying out his functions in relation to the winding up.

DEFINITION

"official receiver": s.399.

GENERAL NOTE

This re-enacts s.69(1) and (2), I.A. 1985.

Custody of company's property

144.—(1) When a winding-up order has been made, or where a provisional liquidator has been appointed, the liquidator or the provisional liquidator (as the case may be) shall take into his custody or under his control all the property and things in action to which the company is or appears to be entitled.

(2) In a winding up by the court in Scotland, if and so long as there is no liquidator, all the property of the company is deemed to be in the custody of the court.

GENERAL NOTE

This re-enacts s.537, C.A. 1985 and deals with the liquidator taking control of the company's property. Unlike bankruptcy there is no automatic *cessio bonorum* to the liquidator, but see s.145 *post*. See *Palmer,* para. 85–38.

Vesting of company property in liquidator

145.—(1) When a company is being wound up by the court, the court may on the application of the liquidator by order direct that all or any part of the property of whatsoever description belonging to the company or held by trustees on its behalf shall vest in the liquidator by his official name; and thereupon the property to which the order relates vests accordingly.

(2) The liquidator may, after giving such indemnity (if any) as the court may direct, bring or defend in his official name any action or other legal proceeding which relates to that property or which it is necessary to bring

or defend for the purpose of effectually winding up the company and recovering its property.

GENERAL NOTE
This re-enacts s.538, C.A. 1985 and deals with a vesting order to vest the company's property in the liquidator. Originally this occurred by operation of law in the case of an official manager, the predecessor of the modern liquidator, but today an order is necessary. Such applications are not, however, common. See *Palmer,* para. 85–38.

Duty to summon final meeting

146.—(1) Subject to the next subsection, if it appears to the liquidator of a company which is being wound up by the court that the winding up of the company is for practical purposes complete and the liquidator is not the official receiver, the liquidator shall summon a final general meeting of the company's creditors which—

(a) shall receive the liquidator's report of the winding up, and
(b) shall determine whether the liquidator should have his release under section 174 in Chapter VII of this Part.

(2) The liquidator may, if he thinks fit, give the notice summoning the final general meeting at the same time as giving notice of any final distribution of the company's property but, if summoned for an earlier date, that meeting shall be adjourned (and, if necessary, further adjourned) until a date on which the liquidator is able to report to the meeting that the winding up of the company is for practical purposes complete.

(3) In the carrying out of his functions in the winding up it is the duty of the liquidator to retain sufficient sums from the company's property to cover the expenses of summoning and holding the meeting required by this section.

DEFINITIONS
"official receiver": s.399.
"property": s.436.

TRANSITIONAL PROVISION
Sched. 11, para. 6(3).

GENERAL NOTE
This section replaces s.78, I.A. 1985 and concerns the conclusion of the liquidator's performance of his functions. The procedure for bringing a compulsory winding up to its conclusion has undergone a considerable modification, in accordance with the proposals in paras. 102–104 of the *White Paper.* The liquidator's duty to summon a final meeting of the company's creditors as a preliminary to the gaining of his release under s.174 gives rise to a parallel procedure to those prescribed for each kind of voluntary winding up by ss.94 and 106 respectively. The provisions of this section are applicable to England and Scotland alike, and are to be followed in all cases except those where use is made of the procedure for bringing about the early dissolution of the company under s.202 or s.204, as appropriate (*q.v.*). In view of the inevitable cost of convening a final meeting of creditors, subs. (3) requires the liquidator to retain sufficient sums from the company's property to cover this expense. S.172(8) provides for the liquidator to vacate office as soon as he has given notice to the court and the registrar of companies of the holding and outcome of a meeting under this section.

General powers of court

Power to stay or sist winding up

147.—(1) The court may at any time after an order for winding up, on the application either of the liquidator or the official receiver or any creditor or contributory, and on proof to the satisfaction of the court that all proceedings in the winding up ought to be stayed or sisted, make an order staying or sisting the proceedings, either altogether or for a limited time, on such terms and conditions as the court thinks fit.

(2) The court may, before making an order, require the official receiver to furnish to it a report with respect to any facts or matters which are in his opinion relevant to the application.

(3) A copy of every order made under this section shall forthwith be forwarded by the company, or otherwise as may be prescribed, to the registrar of companies, who shall enter it in his records relating to the company.

GENERAL NOTE

This re-enacts s.549, C.A. 1985. It expressly refers to the Scots procedure of sist.

The section gives the court a general power to stay any proceedings in a winding up. An application to stay or an appeal are the only ways in which a winding up can be halted after the order has been entered—*Re Lyric Syndicate* (1900) 17 T.L.R. 162. Before then it may be rescinded in an appropriate case—see generally *Palmer,* para. 85–299.

Settlement of list of contributories and application of assets

148.—(1) As soon as may be after making a winding-up order, the court shall settle a list of contributories, with power to rectify the register of members in all cases where rectification is required in pursuance of the Companies Act or this Act, and shall cause the company's assets to be collected, and applied in discharge of its liabilities.

(2) If it appears to the court that it will not be necessary to make calls on or adjust the rights of contributories, the court may dispense with the settlement of a list of contributories.

(3) In settling the list, the court shall distinguish between persons who are contributories in their own right and persons who are contributories as being representatives of or liable for the debts of others.

GENERAL NOTE

This re-enacts s.550, C.A. 1985 with a minor amendment and deals with settlement of a list of contributories. See *Palmer,* para. 85–46.

Debts due from contributory to company

149.—(1) The court may, at any time after making a winding-up order, make an order on any contributory for the time being on the list of contributories to pay, in manner directed by the order, any money due from him (or from the estate of the person whom he represents) to the company, exclusive of any money payable by him or the estate by virtue of any call in pursuance of the Companies Act or this Act.

(2) The court in making such an order may—

(*a*) in the case of an unlimited company, allow to the contributory by way of set-off any money due to him or the estate which he represents from the company on any independent dealing or contract with the company, but not any money due to him as a member of the company in respect of any dividend or profit, and

(*b*) in the case of a limited company, make to any director or manager whose liability is unlimited or to his estate the like allowance.

(3) In the case of any company, whether limited or unlimited, when all the creditors are paid in full (together with interest at the official rate), any money due on any account whatever to a contributory from the company may be allowed to him by way of set-off against any subsequent call.

DEFINITION

"contributory": s.79.

"interest at the official rate": s.251.

GENERAL NOTE
This re-enacts s.552, C.A. 1985. The reference in subs. (3) to "interest at the official rate" is new. The liability of a contributory referred to in subs. (2)(*a*) derives from s.74(1). The liability of a director or manager referred to in subs. (2)(*b*) derives from s.75. By subs. (2) both categories of contributory are permitted to set-off any amount due to them "on any independent dealing or contract with the company." See *Palmer*, para. 85–59.

Power to make calls

150.—(1) The court may, at any time after making a winding-up order, and either before or after it has ascertained the sufficiency of the company's assets, make calls on all or any of the contributories for the time being settled on the list of the contributories to the extent of their liability, for payment of any money which the court considers necessary to satisfy the company's debts and liabilities, and the expenses of winding up, and for the adjustment of the rights of the contributories among themselves, and make an order for payment of any calls so made.

(2) In making a call the court may take into consideration the probability that some of the contributories may partly or wholly fail to pay it.

DEFINITION
"contributory": s.79.

GENERAL NOTE
This re-enacts s.553, C.A. 1985. The power to make calls exists to satisfy the company's debts and liabilities, the expenses of winding up, and in order to adjust the rights of the contributories amongst themselves. See *Palmer,* para. 85–48.

Payment into bank of money due to company

151.—(1) The court may order any contributory, purchaser or other person from whom money is due to the company to pay the amount due into the Bank of England (or any branch of it) to the account of the liquidator instead of to the liquidator, and such an order may be enforced in the same manner as if it had directed payment to the liquidator.

(2) All money and securities paid or delivered into the Bank of England (or branch) in the event of a winding up by the court are subject in all respects to the orders of the court.

GENERAL NOTE
This re-enacts s.554, C.A. 1985 and deals with an order for payment of money owed to the company directly into the Bank of England.

Order on contributory to be conclusive evidence

152.—(1) An order made by the court on a contributory is conclusive evidence that the money (if any) thereby appearing to be due or ordered to be paid is due, but subject to any right of appeal.

(2) All other pertinent matters stated in the order are to be taken as truly stated as against all persons and in all proceedings except proceedings in Scotland against the heritable estate of a deceased contributory; and in that case the order is only prima facie evidence for the purpose of charging his heritable estate, unless his heirs or legatees of heritage were on the list of contributories at the time of the order being made.

GENERAL NOTE
This re-enacts s.555, C.A. 1985 and deals with the conclusiveness of orders against contributories.

Power to exclude creditors not proving in time

153. The court may fix a time or times within which creditors are to prove their debts or claims or to be excluded from the benefit of any distribution made before those debts are proved.

GENERAL NOTE

This re-enacts s.557, C.A. 1985 and allows the court to fix time for proof of debts and to exclude creditors who fail to prove in time from distributions made before proof of their debts.

A creditor can prove at any time before dissolution but will be excluded from the benefit of distributions made before proof.

See generally *Re Kit Hill Tunnel, ex p. Williams* (1881) 16 Ch.D. 590; *Harrison* v. *Kirk* [1904] A.C. 1. See *Palmer*, paras. 85–57.

Adjustment of rights of contributories

154. The court shall adjust the rights of the contributories among themselves and distribute any surplus among the persons entitled to it.

GENERAL NOTE

This re-enacts s.558 and deals with the adjustment of the rights of contributories *inter se*. The provision is mandatory. It is also the only provision about distribution which applies to a compulsory winding up. See *Palmer*, paras. 85–49.

Inspection of books by creditors, etc.

155.—(1) The court may, at any time after making a winding-up order, make such order for inspection of the company's books and papers by creditors and contributories as the court thinks just; and any books and papers in the company's possession may be inspected by creditors and contributories accordingly, but not further or otherwise.

(2) Nothing in this section excludes or restricts any statutory rights of a government department or person acting under the authority of a government department.

GENERAL NOTE

This re-enacts s.559, C.A. 1985 and deals with the court's power to regulate access to the books and papers of the company by creditors and contributories. Normally a special case must be made out for inspection of the books (*Re Joint Stock Discount Co., ex p. Buchan* (1866) 36 L.J.Ch. 150).

Payment of expenses of winding up

156. The court may, in the event of the assets being insufficient to satisfy the liabilities, make an order as to the payment out of the assets of the expenses incurred in the winding up in such order of priority as the court thinks just.

GENERAL NOTE

This re-enacts s.560, C.A. 1985. It deals with the power of the court to make an order for payment of the expenses of winding-up out of the assets (s.560 referred to "costs, charges and expenses). Collection and distribution of the companies assets is also dealt with in the Rules.

Attendance at company meetings (Scotland)

157. In the winding up by the court of a company registered in Scotland, the court has power to require the attendance of any officer of the company at any meeting of creditors or of contributories, or of a liquidation committee, for the purpose of giving information as to the trade, dealings, affairs or property of the company.

GENERAL NOTE
This re-enacts s.562, C.A. 1985 with a minor amendment by the substitution of "liquidation committee" for "committee of inspection."

Power to arrest absconding contributory

158. The court, at any time either before or after making a winding-up order, on proof of probable cause for believing that a contributory is about to quit the United Kingdom or otherwise to abscond or to remove or conceal any of his property for the purpose of evading payment of calls, may cause the contributory to be arrested and his books and papers and moveable personal property to be seized and him and them to be kept safely until such time as the court may order.

DEFINITION
"contributory": s.79.

GENERAL NOTE
This section re-enacts s.565, C.A. 1985. It deals with the power of the court to arrest an absconding contributory about to quit the United Kingdom.

Powers of court to be cumulative

159. Powers conferred by this Act and the Companies Act on the court are in addition to, and not in restriction of, any existing powers of instituting proceedings against a contributory or debtor of the company, or the estate of any contributory or debtor, for the recovery of any call or other sums.

GENERAL NOTE
This re-enacts s.566, C.A. 1985.

Delegation of powers to liquidator (England and Wales)

160.—(1) Provision may be made by rules for enabling or requiring all or any of the powers and duties conferred and imposed on the court in England and Wales by the Companies Act and this Act in respect of the following matters—
   (a) the holding and conducting of meetings to ascertain the wishes of creditors and contributories,
   (b) the settling of lists of contributories and the rectifying of the register of members where required, and the collection and application of the assets,
   (c) the payment, delivery, conveyance, surrender or transfer of money, property, books or papers to the liquidator,
   (d) the making of calls,
   (e) the fixing of a time within which debts and claims must be proved,
to be exercised or performed by the liquidator as an officer of the court, and subject to the court's control.

(2) But the liquidator shall not, without the special leave of the court, rectify the register of members, and shall not make any call without either that special leave or the sanction of the liquidation committee.

GENERAL NOTE
This re-enacts s.567, C.A. 1985 and deals with the power to make rules concerning the delegation by the court to the liquidator of the matters listed in subs. (1)(a)–(e). All these matters are, in fact, covered by the Rules (promulgated under s.411 *infra*).

Enforcement of, and appeal from, orders

Orders for calls on contributories (Scotland)

161.—(1) In Scotland, where an order, interlocutor or decree has been made for winding up a company by the court, it is competent to the court, on production by the liquidators of a list certified by them of the names of the contributories liable in payment of any calls, and of the amount due by each contributory, and of the date when that amount became due, to pronounce forthwith a decree against those contributories for payment of the sums so certified to be due, with interest from that date until payment (at 5 per cent. per annum) in the same way and to the same effect as if they had severally consented to registration for execution, on a charge of 6 days, of a legal obligation to pay those calls and interest.

(2) The decree may be extracted immediately, and no suspension of it is competent, except on caution or consignation, unless with special leave of the court.

GENERAL NOTE

This re-enacts s.569, C.A. 1985 and deals with the power of Scots courts to make orders for calls on contributories. See *Palmer,* paras. 87–40.

Appeals from orders in Scotland

162.—(1) Subject to the provisions of this section and to rules of court, an appeal from any order or decision made or given in the winding up of a company by the court in Scotland under this Act lies in the same manner and subject to the same conditions as an appeal from an order or decision of the court in cases within its ordinary jurisdiction.

(2) In regard to orders or judgments pronounced by the judge acting as vacation judge in pursuance of section 4 of the Administration of Justice (Scotland) Act 1933—

(*a*) none of the orders specified in Part I of Schedule 3 to this Act are subject to review, reduction, suspension or stay of execution, and

(*b*) every other order or judgment (except as mentioned below) may be submitted to review by the Inner House by reclaiming motion enrolled within 14 days from the date of the order or judgment.

(3) However, an order being one of those specified in Part II of that Schedule shall, from the date of the order and notwithstanding that it has been submitted to review as above, be carried out and receive effect until the Inner House have disposed of the matter.

(4) In regard to orders or judgments pronounced in Scotland by a Lord Ordinary before whom proceedings in a winding up are being taken, any such order or judgment may be submitted to review by the Inner House by reclaiming motion enrolled within 14 days from its date; but should it not be so submitted to review during session, the provisions of this section in regard to orders or judgments pronounced by the judge acting as vacation judge apply.

(5) Nothing in this section affects provisions of the Companies Act or this Act in reference to decrees in Scotland for payment of calls in the winding up of companies, whether voluntary or by the court.

GENERAL NOTE

This re-enacts s.571, C.A. 1985 and deals with the system of appeals from orders in Scotland. See *Palmer,* paras. 87–04.

CHAPTER VII

LIQUIDATORS

Preliminary

Style and title of liquidators

163. The liquidator of a company shall be described—
(a) where a person other than the official receiver is liquidator, by the style of "the liquidator" of the particular company, or
(b) where the official receiver is liquidator, by the style of "the official receiver and liquidator" of the particular company;
and in neither case shall he be described by an individual name.

DEFINITION
"the official receiver": s.399.

GENERAL NOTE
This replaces and reproduces in substance the provisions of s.533(7), C.A. 1985. The provisions are now relocated so as to make them applicable to every mode of winding up.

Corrupt inducement affecting appointment

164. A person who gives, or agrees or offers to give, to any member or creditor of a company any valuable consideration with a view to securing his own appointment or nomination, or to securing or preventing the appointment or nomination of some person other than himself, as the company's liquidator is liable to a fine.

DEFINITION
"fine": s.430, Sched. 10.

GENERAL NOTE
This re-enacts s.635, C.A. 1985 and makes it an offence to give or offer a corrupt inducement in connection with the appointment of a liquidator.

Liquidator's powers and duties

Voluntary winding up

165.—(1) This section has effect where a company is being wound up voluntarily, but subject to section 166 below in the case of a creditors' voluntary winding up.
(2) The liquidator may—
(a) in the case of a members' voluntary winding up, with the sanction of an extraordinary resolution of the company, and
(b) in the case of a creditors' voluntary winding up, with the sanction of the court or the liquidation committee (or, if there is no such committee, a meeting of the company's creditors),
exercise any of the powers specified in Part I of Schedule 4 to this Act (payment of debts, compromise of claims, etc.).
(3) The liquidator may, without sanction, exercise either of the powers specified in Part II of that Schedule (institution and defence of proceedings; carrying on the business of the company) and any of the general powers specified in Part III of that Schedule.
(4) The liquidator may—
(a) exercise the court's power of settling a list of contributories (which list is prima facie evidence of the liability of the persons named in it to be contributories),

(*b*) exercise the court's power of making calls,

(*c*) summon general meetings of the company for the purpose of obtaining its sanction by special or extraordinary resolution or for any other purpose he may think fit.

(5) The liquidator shall pay the company's debts and adjust the rights of the contributories among themselves.

(6) Where the liquidator in exercise of the powers conferred on him by this Act disposes of any property of the company to a person who is connected with the company (within the meaning of section 249 in Part VII), he shall, if there is for the time being a liquidation committee, give notice to the committee of that exercise of his powers.

DEFINITIONS
    "connected with the company": s.249.
    "creditors' voluntary winding up": s.90.
    "extraordinary resolution": s.378, C.A. 1985.
    "members' voluntary winding up": s.90.
    "special resolution": s.378, C.A. 1985.

GENERAL NOTE
    The layout of this section follows that in s.598, C.A. 1985 which defined the powers and duties of a liquidator in a voluntary winding up by means of a cross reference to s.539 C.A. 1985. The present section is the same in substance (save for the addition of subs. (6)) as s.598 but defines the powers and duties by means of references to relevant parts of Sched. 4. Where sanction is required (see subs. (2)) it can be furnished by an extraordinary resolution of the company in the case of a members' voluntary winding up and by the court or liquidation committee or, in the absence of the latter, a meeting of the creditors' in the case of a creditors' voluntary winding up. S.166 *infra* contains further provisions governing the liquidator's powers and duties in the case of a creditors' voluntary winding up.

Subs. (6)
    This was introduced in Sched. 6, para. 41, I.A. 1985. Its purpose is to enable the liquidation committee to challenge such a disposition. See the General Note to s.314(6) *infra* which is the equivalent provision relating to individual insolvency.

Creditors' voluntary winding up

166.—(1) This section applies where, in the case of a creditors' voluntary winding up, a liquidator has been nominated by the company.

(2) The powers conferred on the liquidator by section 165 shall not be exercised, except with the sanction of the court, during the period before the holding of the creditors' meeting under section 98 in Chapter IV.

(3) Subsection (2) does not apply in relation to the power of the liquidator—

(*a*) to take into his custody or under his control all the property to which the company is or appears to be entitled;

(*b*) to dispose of perishable goods and other goods the value of which is likely to diminish if they are not immediately disposed of; and

(*c*) to do all such other things as may be necessary for the protection of the company's assets.

(4) The liquidator shall attend the creditors' meeting held under section 98 and shall report to the meeting on any exercise by him of his powers (whether or not under this section or under section 112 or 165).

(5) If default is made—

(*a*) by the company in complying with subsection (1) or (2) of section 98, or

(*b*) by the directors in complying with subsection (1) or (2) of section 99,

the liquidator shall, within 7 days of the relevant day, apply to the court for directions as to the manner in which that default is to be remedied.

(6) "The relevant day" means the day on which the liquidator was nominated by the company or the day on which he first became aware of the default, whichever is the later.

(7) If the liquidator without reasonable excuse fails to comply with this section, he is liable to a fine.

DEFINITIONS
"creditors' voluntary winding up": s.90.
"fine": s.430, Sched. 10.
"property": s.436.
"the relevant day": subs. (6).

GENERAL NOTE
This section, in conjunction with s.98 and also s.114 is aimed at eradicating certain abusive practices associated with the voluntary winding up of companies, and in particular those practices whereby the shareholders have acted at short notice to place the company in liquidation and to appoint a liquidator, whereupon a delay of several weeks may ensue before the convening of a creditors' meeting to confirm the appointment. This practice has become known as "centrebinding" after the name of the case in which it was decided that the technical offence committed by the company in failing to convene the creditors' meeting within 24 hours of the members' meeting did not have the further consequence that the liquidator's appointment, or any exercise of his powers, were rendered retrospectively invalid (*Re Centrebind Ltd.* [1967] 1 W.L.R. 377; [1966] 3 All E.R. 889). The dangerous loss of protection for the company's assets, and for the creditors' interest, attendant upon such practices was the subject of vigorous proposals in paras. 667–673 of the *Cork Report*, accepted with reservations in paras. 128–133 of the *White Paper*. This section does not have the effect of preventing the shareholders from passing an immediate resolution for winding up, and then proceeding to nominate a liquidator. But the basis upon which this is to be done is solely now for the purpose of preserving and safeguarding the assets, rather than the converse. Until a creditors' meeting is convened under s.89, therefore, subs. (2) of this section deprives the liquidator of the power to exercise the majority of the powers conferred by s.165 except with the sanction of the court. In effect the liquidator is limited to acting as a provisional liquidator for the time being, since subs. (3) allows him to take steps which ensure the preservation and protection of durable assets, and the expeditious disposal of perishable or wasting ones. In other respects however it is made the professional duty of the liquidator to prepare for the convening of the creditors' meeting under s.98, and he is charged with the duty under subs. (5) of making application to the court within seven days if the company or the directors fail to comply with the requirements of s.98. The decision in *Re Centrebind Ltd. (supra)* itself is thus overruled by this statutory provision, because any exercise of his ostensible powers by a liquidator in contravention of this section will be *ultra vires* and invalid. Moreover, any liquidator so acting will not only commit a criminal offence under subs. (7) of this section, but will be liable to civil remedy under s.212 and to further sanctions under Part XIII of the Act with regard to his authorisation to act as an insolvency practitioner.

Winding up by the court

167.—(1) Where a company is being wound up by the court, the liquidator may—

(a) with the sanction of the court or the liquidation committee, exercise any of the powers specified in Parts I and II of Schedule 4 to this Act (payment of debts; compromise of claims, etc.; institution and defence of proceedings; carrying on of the business of the company), and

(b) with or without that sanction, exercise any of the general powers specified in Part III of that Schedule.

(2) Where the liquidator (not being the official receiver), in exercise of the powers conferred on him by this Act—

(a) disposes of any property of the company to a person who is connected with the company (within the meaning of section 249 in Part VII), or

(b) employs a solicitor to assist him in the carrying out of his functions, he shall, if there is for the time being a liquidation committee, give notice to the committee of that exercise of his powers.

(3) The exercise by the liquidator in a winding up by the court of the powers conferred by this section is subject to the control of the court, and any creditor or contributory may apply to the court with respect to any exercise or proposed exercise of any of those powers.

DEFINITION
"connected with the company": s.249.

GENERAL NOTE
This reproduces and re-drafts parts of s.539 (subss. (1), (2), (2A), and (3)). The powers of the liquidator are no longer expressed in the section but are to be found in Schedule 4.

Subs. (2)
This was introduced in Sched. 6, para. 31(3), I.A. 1985. See Notes to ss.165 and 314(6).

Supplementary powers (England and Wales)

168.—(1) This section applies in the case of a company which is being wound up by the court in England and Wales.

(2) The liquidator may summon general meetings of the creditors or contributories for the purpose of ascertaining their wishes; and it is his duty to summon meetings at such times as the creditors or contributories by resolution (either at the meeting appointing the liquidator or otherwise) may direct, or whenever requested in writing to do so by one-tenth in value of the creditors or contributories (as the case may be).

(3) The liquidator may apply to the court (in the prescribed manner) for directions in relation to any particular matter arising in the winding up.

(4) Subject to the provisions of this Act, the liquidator shall use his own discretion in the management of the assets and their distribution among the creditors.

(5) If any person is aggrieved by an act or decision of the liquidator, that person may apply to the court; and the court may confirm, reverse or modify the act or decision complained of, and make such order in the case as it thinks just.

GENERAL NOTE
This re-enacts s.540(3)–(6), C.A. 1985. The section deals with the exercise and control of the liquidator's powers and supplements s.167. The liquidator is instructed to have regard to the directions of the creditors and contributories and if he fails to do so an aggrieved person may apply to the court under s.168(5). The provision is similar to s.314(7) and the same principles apply—see *Leon* v. *York-O-Matic Ltd.* [1966] 3 All E.R. 277. The liquidator himself may use these provisions where he considers that the directions of the committee of inspection are unwise—see *Re Consolidated Diesel Engine Manufacturers Ltd.* [1915] 1 Ch. 192. See *Palmer,* paras. 85–39.

Supplementary powers (Scotland)

169.—(1) In the case of a winding up in Scotland, the court may provide by order that the liquidator may, where there is no liquidation committee, exercise any of the following powers, namely—
   (*a*) to bring or defend any action or other legal proceeding in the name and on behalf of the company, or
   (*b*) to carry on the business of the company so far as may be necessary for its beneficial winding up,
without the sanction or intervention of the court.

(2) In a winding up by the court in Scotland, the liquidator has (subject to the rules) the same powers as a trustee on a bankrupt estate.

Enforcement of liquidator's duty to make returns, etc.

170.—(1) If a liquidator who has made any default—

(a) in filing, delivering or making any return, account or other document, or

(b) in giving any notice which he is by law required to file, deliver, make or give,

fails to make good the default within 14 days after the service on him of a notice requiring him to do so, the court has the following powers.

(2) On an application made by any creditor or contributory of the company, or by the registrar of companies, the court may make an order directing the liquidator to make good the default within such time as may be specified in the order.

(3) The court's order may provide that all costs of and incidental to the application shall be borne by the liquidator.

(4) Nothing in this section prejudices the operation of any enactment imposing penalties on a liquidator in respect of any such default as is mentioned above.

Removal; vacation of office

Removal, etc. (voluntary winding up)

171.—(1) This section applies with respect to the removal from office and vacation of office of the liquidator of a company which is being wound up voluntarily.

(2) Subject to the next subsection, the liquidator may be removed from office only by an order of the court or—

(a) in the case of a members' voluntary winding up, by a general meeting of the company summoned specially for that purpose, or

(b) in the case of a creditors' voluntary winding up, by a general meeting of the company's creditors summoned specially for that purpose in accordance with the rules.

(3) Where the liquidator was appointed by the court under section 108 in Chapter V, a meeting such as is mentioned in subsection (2) above shall be summoned for the purpose of replacing him only if he thinks fit or the court so directs or the meeting is requested, in accordance with the rules—

(a) in the case of a members' voluntary winding up, by members representing not less than one-half of the total voting rights of all the members having at the date of the request a right to vote at the meeting, or

(b) in the case of a creditors' voluntary winding up, by not less than one-half, in value, of the company's creditors.

(4) A liquidator shall vacate office if he ceases to be a person who is qualified to act as an insolvency practitioner in relation to the company.

(5) A liquidator may, in the prescribed circumstances, resign his office by giving notice of his resignation to the registrar of companies.

(6) Where—

(a) in the case of a members' voluntary winding up, a final meeting of the company has been held under section 94 in Chapter III, or

(b) in the case of a creditors' voluntary winding up, final meetings of

the company and of the creditors have been held under section 106
in Chapter IV,
the liquidator whose report was considered at the meeting or meetings
shall vacate office as soon as he has complied with subsection (3) of that
section and has given notice to the registrar of companies that the meeting
or meetings have been held and of the decisions (if any) of the meeting
or meetings.

DEFINITIONS
"creditors' voluntary winding up": s.90.
"members' voluntary winding up": s.90.
"person qualified to act as an insolvency practitioner": s.390.
"the rules": s.251.
"to act as an insolvency practitioner in relation to a company": s.388(1).

GENERAL NOTE
This section contains a series of provisions under which a liquidator may be removed from
office, or may resign or be required to vacate his office, in either a creditors' or a members'
voluntary winding up, and is thus the counterpart of s.172, which applies in cases of winding
up by the court. Where in a creditors' voluntary winding up a vacancy occurs in the office
of liquidator, whether by death, resignation or otherwise, the creditors have the right to fill
the vacancy under s.104. Alternatively, in a voluntary winding up of either type, the court
may appoint a liquidator under s.108(1) if from any cause there is no liquidator acting.

Subs. (2)

The liquidator may be removed from office only by an order of the court
Such an order may be sought under s.108(2), which empowers the court at its discretion
to remove a liquidator "on cause shown", and to appoint another.

Subs. (3)
This restriction upon the convening of a meeting under subs. (2) is applicable where the
court has exercised its discretionary powers under s.108 to appoint a liquidator where there
is none acting, or to remove a liquidator for cause shown and to appoint another. The fact
that such a liquidator's appointment has been made by the court, and not by either the
creditors or the members acting under s.100 is made the basis for imposing restrictions upon
the circumstances in which the members or the creditors may procure the convening of a
meeting at which the liquidator's removal may be resolved upon.

Subs. (4)

If he ceases to be a person who is qualified to act as an insolvency practitioner
See s.390 for the requirements for being qualified to act as an insolvency practitioner, and
ss.391–393 inclusive (and relevant General Notes) for authorisation to act, and withdrawal
of authorisation to act, as an insolvency practitioner.

Removal, etc. (winding up by the court)

172.—(1) This section applies with respect to the removal from office
and vacation of office of the liquidator of a company which is being wound
up by the court, or of a provisional liquidator.

(2) Subject as follows, the liquidator may be removed from office only
by an order of the court or by a general meeting of the company's
creditors summoned specially for that purpose in accordance with the
rules; and a provisional liquidator may be removed from office only by an
order of the court.

(3) Where—

(a) the official receiver is liquidator otherwise than in succession under
section 136(3) to a person who held office as a result of a
nomination by a meeting of the company's creditors or contributories, or

(b) the liquidator was appointed by the court otherwise than under

section 139(4)(*a*) or 140(1), or was appointed by the Secretary of State,
a general meeting of the company's creditors shall be summoned for the purpose of replacing him only if he thinks fit, or the court so directs, or the meeting is requested, in accordance with the rules, by not less than one-quarter, in value, of the creditors.

(4) If appointed by the Secretary of State, the liquidator may be removed from office by a direction of the Secretary of State.

(5) A liquidator or provisional liquidator, not being the official receiver, shall vacate office if he ceases to be a person who is qualified to act as an insolvency practitioner in relation to the company.

(6) A liquidator may, in the prescribed circumstances, resign his office by giving notice of his resignation to the court.

(7) Where an order is made under section 204 (early dissolution in Scotland) for the dissolution of the company, the liquidator shall vacate office when the dissolution of the company takes effect in accordance with that section.

(8) Where a final meeting has been held under section 146 (liquidator's report on completion of winding up), the liquidator whose report was considered at the meeting shall vacate office as soon as he has given notice to the court and the registrar of companies that the meeting has been held and of the decisions (if any) of the meeting.

DEFINITIONS
"person qualified to act as an insolvency practitioner in relation to the company": s.390.
"the official receiver": s.399.
"the rules": s.251.

TRANSITIONAL PROVISION
Sched. 11, para. 6(3).

GENERAL NOTE
This section re-enacts s.79, I.A. 1985. Appointments of provisional liquidators may take place under s.135.

Subs. (2)
One consequence of this provision is that it is rendered impossible in a compulsory winding up for the contributories of the Company to procure the removal of the liquidator merely by means of a meeting of their own number. (*cf.* s.171(2)(*a*), (3) in relation to a members' voluntary winding up). Therefore, although it is possible under s.139(3) or (4)(*a*) for the contributories" nominee to become the liquidator of the Company, those same persons cannot remove him at will: an Order of the Court, or a resolution carried by a general meeting of the Company's creditors, are the only ways of bringing about the removal of a liquidator from office, except in the special cases falling under subss. (3), (4) and (5).

Subs. (4)

If appointed by the Secretary of State
Such appointments may take place under s.137, in the circumstances specified in subss. (1) and (2) of that section.

Subs. (5)

. . . If he ceases to be a person who is qualified to act as an insolvency practitioner in relation to the company.
See s.390 and General Note thereto, for the requirements for being qualified to act as an insolvency practitioner, and ss.391–393 inclusive (and relevant General Notes) for authorisation to act, and withdrawal of authorisation to act, as an insolvency practitioner.

Release of liquidator

Release (voluntary winding up)

173.—(1) This section applies with respect to the release of the liquidator of a company which is being wound up voluntarily.

(2) A person who has ceased to be a liquidator shall have his release with effect from the following time, that is to say—

(*a*) in the case of a person who has been removed from office by a general meeting of the company or by a general meeting of the company's creditors that has not resolved against his release or who has died, the time at which notice is given to the registrar of companies in accordance with the rules that that person has ceased to hold office;

(*b*) in the case of a person who has been removed from office by a general meeting of the company's creditors that has resolved against his release, or by the court, or who has vacated office under section 171(4) above, such time as the Secretary of State may, on the application of that person, determine;

(*c*) in the case of a person who has resigned, such time as may be prescribed;

(*d*) in the case of a person who has vacated office under subsection (6)(*a*) of section 171, the time at which he vacated office;

(*e*) in the case of a person who has vacated office under subsection (6)(*b*) of that section—

(i) if the final meeting of the creditors referred to in that subsection has resolved against that person's release, such time as the Secretary of State may, on an application by that person, determine, and

(ii) if that meeting has not resolved against that person's release, the time at which he vacated office.

(3) In the application of subsection (2) to the winding up of a company registered in Scotland, the references to a determination by the Secretary of State as to the time from which a person who has ceased to be liquidator shall have his release are to be read as references to such a determination by the Accountant of Court.

(4) Where a liquidator has his release under subsection (2), he is, with effect from the time specified in that subsection, discharged from all liability both in respect of acts or omissions of his in the winding up and otherwise in relation to his conduct as liquidator.

But nothing in this section prevents the exercise, in relation to a person who has had his release under subsection (2), of the court's powers under section 212 of the Act (summary remedy against delinquent directors, liquidators, etc.).

DEFINITION
 "prescribed": s.251.

GENERAL NOTE
 This section is concerned with the release of a liquidator of a company in a voluntary winding up, and is therefore the counterpart of s.174 which applies in cases of winding up by the court. Specific provision is made for each of the ways in which the functions of the liquidator may come to an end in relation to a company. A time specified in each instance as that at which his release takes effect constitutes the moment from which the liquidator is discharged from all liability in respect of his conduct in office. Despite this the possibility is retained by means of the concluding *proviso* in subs. (4), of a subsequent application being made under s.212 in respect of any misconduct rendering the former liquidator liable to make restitution for any money or property, or to make payment by way of compensation.

Subs. (2)(c)

Such time as may be prescribed

The resignation of a liquidator in a voluntary liquidation may be effected under s.171(5). The provision that the release of a liquidator who has resigned shall take effect from a time to be prescribed in the rules permits a reconciliation of the need for a speedy vacation of office by the liquidator under some circumstances, such as illness, with the need to ensure that a release from liability is not accorded before there has been proper time to assess the liquidator's conduct. The provision should also be helpful in ensuring that a liquidator will not be able, through the expedient of resigning, to avoid complying with the requirements of s.94 or s.106 with regard to the summoning of final meetings when the company's affairs are fully wound up.

Release (winding up by the court)

174.—(1) This section applies with respect to the release of the liquidator of a company which is being wound up by the court, or of a provisional liquidator.

(2) Where the official receiver has ceased to be liquidator and a person becomes liquidator in his stead, the official receiver has his release with effect from the following time, that is to say—

    (*a*) in a case where that person was nominated by a general meeting of creditors or contributories, or was appointed by the Secretary of State, the time at which the official receiver gives notice to the court that he has been replaced;

    (*b*) in a case where that person is appointed by the court, such time as the court may determine.

(3) If the official receiver while he is a liquidator gives notice to the Secretary of State that the winding up is for practical purposes complete, he has his release with effect from such time as the Secretary of State may determine.

(4) A person other than the official receiver who has ceased to be a liquidator has his release with effect from the following time, that is to say—

    (*a*) in the case of a person who has been removed from office by a general meeting of creditors that has not resolved against his release or who has died, the time at which notice is given to the court in accordance with the rules that that person has ceased to hold office;

    (*b*) in the case of a person who has been removed from office by a general meeting of creditors that has resolved against his release, or by the court or the Secretary of State, or who has vacated office under section 172(5) or (7), such time as the Secretary of State may, on an application by that person, determine;

    (*c*) in the case of a person who has resigned, such time as may be prescribed;

    (*d*) in the case of a person who has vacated office under section 172(8)—

        (i) if the final meeting referred to in that subsection has resolved against that person's release, such time as the Secretary of State may, on an application by that person, determine, and

        (ii) if that meeting has not so resolved, the time at which that person vacated office.

(5) A person who has ceased to hold office as a provisional liquidator has his release with effect from such time as the court may, on an application by him, determine.

(6) Where the official receiver or a liquidator or provisional liquidator has his release under this section, he is, with effect from the time specified in the preceding provisions of this section, discharged from all liability

both in respect of acts or omissions of his in the winding up and otherwise in relation to his conduct as liquidator or provisional liquidator.

But nothing in this section prevents the exercise, in relation to a person who has had his release under this section, of the court's powers under section 212 (summary remedy against delinquent directors, liquidators, etc.).

(7) In the application of this section to a case where the order for winding up has been made by the court in Scotland, the references to a determination by the Secretary of State as to the time from which a person who has ceased to be liquidator has his release are to such a determination by the Accountant of Court.

DEFINITIONS
"contributory": s.79.
"prescribed": s.251.
"the official receiver": s.399.
"the rules": s.251.

TRANSITIONAL PROVISION
Sched. 11, para. 6(4).

GENERAL NOTE
This section replaces s.80, I.A. 1985 which is repealed. It makes specific provisions for the release of the liquidator in relation to each of the ways in which the functions of the official receiver or liquidator may come to an end in relation to a Company. The time specified in each instance as that at which his release takes effect constitutes the moment from which the liquidator is discharged from all liability in respect of his conduct in office, although it is nevertheless possible for a subsequent application to be made under s.212 in respect of any misconduct rendering him liable to make restitution of any money or property, or to make payment by way of compensation.

Subs. (4)(c)

Such time as may be prescribed
A person may resign as liquidator by virtue of s.172(6), in accordance with the procedure thereunder prescribed. The resignation procedure in the new insolvency rules will be based upon that previously contained in rule 167 of the Companies (Winding Up) Rules 1949 (S.I. 1949 No. 330) whereby the liquidator must obtain permission from the creditors or the court before he is able to resign.

In some cases, such as where the liquidator is in ill health, it may be necessary for the liquidator to be allowed to resign without delay, but on the other hand it is equally desirable that some time should be allowed for proper consideration of all the circumstances concerning his conduct in office. The facilities in this para. whereby provision may be made in the rules for the liquidator's release to be postponed for a period after he has been permitted to resign is therefore a useful safeguard. It should also ensure that a liquidator will not be able, by the expedient of resigning, to avoid complying with the requirements of s.146 with regard to the summoning of a final meeting of creditors. In ordinary cases therefore the liquidator will be obliged to make a formal request for his release on the basis of his final report presented to the final meeting of creditors.

Subs. (6)

The court's powers under s.212
The proviso in this subsection ensures that the summary remedy provided by s.212 for use against delinquent liquidators, among others, continues to be available even after the liquidator's release has become effective.

CHAPTER VIII

PROVISIONS OF GENERAL APPLICATION IN WINDING UP

Preferential debts

Preferential debts (general provision)

175.—(1) In a winding up the company's preferential debts (within the meaning given by section 386 in Part XII) shall be paid in priority to all other debts.

(2) Preferential debts—

(*a*) rank equally among themselves after the expenses of the winding up and shall be paid in full, unless the assets are insufficient to meet them, in which case they abate in equal proportions; and

(*b*) so far as the assets of the company available for payment of general creditors are insufficient to meet them, have priority over the claims of holders of debentures secured by, or holders of, any floating charge created by the company, and shall be paid accordingly out of any property comprised in or subject to that charge.

DEFINITIONS
"floating charge": s.251.
"holder of a floating charge": s.70(1).
"preferential debt": s.386, Sched. 6.
"property": s.436.

GENERAL NOTE
This section re-enacts subs. (1) and (2) of s.89, I.A. 1985 and reflects some of the arguments and recommendations in chap. 32 of the *Cork Report,* although the Government strove to resist the efforts made at successive Parliamentary stages to cut down the Crown's privileged position as a preferential creditor for unpaid tax, as advocated in paras. 1409–1444 and 1450 of the *Cork Report.* Victories over the Government were gained in divisions in both Houses (*Hansard,* H.L. Vol. 462, cols. 628–640, H.C. Standing Committee E, June 11, 1985, cols. 304–324; see also H.L., Vol. 462, cols. 172–180) whereby Sched. 6 was amended so as to eliminate Crown preference in respect of taxes assessed upon the company directly as taxpayer to the Inland Revenue, and also to eliminate the preferential status formerly accorded to local rates. A further amendment was carried which had the effect of restricting Crown preference in respect of outstanding payments of value added tax to a period of six months, as against the period of twelve months which is applicable for other debts due to Customs and Excise. These victories were not only significant in themselves, but also symbolise an important change of attitude towards the traditional categories of preferential debt, whose status can no longer be regarded as sacrosanct. A further matter of importance is that the law regarding preferential debts has been completely unified for cases of company and individual insolvency alike, since the same Sched. 6 also applies in relation to individual insolvency by virtue of s.386(1).

Subs. (2)
This provision maintains the previous legal position with regard to the application of the *pari passu* principle to the preferential debts. Para. (*b*) also maintains the existing rule that preferential debts enjoy priority over the claims of holders of a floating charge, although this is not the case with regard to any fixed charge created by the company over any of its property (*Re Lewis Merthyr Consolidated Collieries* [1929] 1 Ch. 498; *cf. Christonette International Ltd., Re* [1982] 3 All E.R. 225).

Preferential charge on goods distrained

176.—(1) This section applies where a company is being wound up by the court in England and Wales, and is without prejudice to section 128 (avoidance of attachments, etc.).

(2) Where any person (whether or not a landlord or person entitled to rent) has distrained upon the goods or effects of the company in the

period of 3 months ending with the date of the winding-up order, those goods or effects, or the proceeds of their sale, shall be charged for the benefit of the company with the preferential debts of the company to the extent that the company's property is for the time being insufficient for meeting them.

(3) Where by virtue of a charge under subsection (2) any person surrenders any goods or effects to a company or makes a payment to a company, that person ranks, in respect of the amount of the proceeds of sale of those goods or effects by the liquidator or (as the case may be) the amount of the payment, as a preferential creditor of the company, except as against so much of the company's property as is available for the payment of preferential creditors by virtue of the surrender or payment.

GENERAL NOTE
This provision re-enacts subs. (3) and (4) of s.89 of the I.A. 1985 and has the effect of rendering void any attachment, sequestration, distress or execution put into force against the estate or effects of a company after the commencement of a winding up by the court in England and Wales or in Scotland.

Special managers

Power to appoint special manager

177.—(1) Where a company has gone into liquidation or a provisional liquidator has been appointed, the court may, on an application under this section, appoint any person to be the special manager of the business or property of the company.

(2) The application may be made by the liquidator or provisional liquidator in any case where it appears to him that the nature of the business or property of the company, or the interests of the company's creditors or contributories or members generally, require the appointment of another person to manage the company's business or property.

(3) The special manager has such powers as may be entrusted to him by the court.

(4) The court's power to entrust powers to the special manager includes power to direct that any provision of this Act that has effect in relation to the provisional liquidator or liquidator of a company shall have the like effect in relation to the special manager for the purposes of the carrying out by him of any of the functions of the provisional liquidator or liquidator.

(5) The special manager shall—

(*a*) give such security or, in Scotland, caution as may be prescribed;

(*b*) prepare and keep such accounts as may be prescribed; and

(*c*) produce those accounts in accordance with the rules to the Secretary of State or to such other persons as may be prescribed.

DEFINITIONS
"business": s.436.
"company goes into liquidation": s.247(2).
"contributory": s.79.
"prescribed": s.251.
"property": s.436.
"security": s.248(*b*).
"the rules": s.251.

GENERAL NOTE
This re-enacts s.90, I.A. 1985 which allowed a considerably widened scope for the making of application to the court of a special manager to be appointed. Formerly, such applications could only be made by the Official Receiver as liquidator of the company, but there is no such restriction in the present section and application may be made by the liquidator or provisional liquidator of the company at the time in question.

Subs. (1)

Provisional liquidator . . . appointed
The appointment of a provisional liquidator in a winding up by the court may take place under s.135.

The court may . . . appoint any person
The functions of a special manager are not among the matters mentioned in s.388(1), which lists the ways in which a person acts as an insolvency practitioner in relation to a company for the purposes of that section. Hence it is not legally required that the person appointed as special manager should be a qualified insolvency practitioner, nor will an unqualified person commit a criminal offence under s.389 by accepting such an appointment and performing the role assigned to him.
This section is drafted in parallel to s.370, which applies in relation to bankruptcy.

Disclaimer (England and Wales only)

Power to disclaim onerous property

178.—(1) This and the next two sections apply to a company that is being wound up in England and Wales.

(2) Subject as follows, the liquidator may, by the giving of the prescribed notice, disclaim any onerous property and may do so notwithstanding that he has taken possession of it, endeavoured to sell it, or otherwise exercised rights of ownership in relation to it.

(3) The following is onerous property for the purposes of this section—

(*a*) any unprofitable contract, and

(*b*) any other property of the company which is unsaleable or not readily saleable or is such that it may give rise to a liability to pay money or perform any other onerous act.

(4) A disclaimer under this section—

(*a*) operates so as to determine, as from the date of the disclaimer, the rights, interests and liabilities of the company in or in respect of the property disclaimed; but

(*b*) does not, except so far as is necessary for the purpose of releasing the company from any liability, affect the rights or liabilities of any other person.

(5) A notice of disclaimer shall not be given under this section in respect of any property if—

(*a*) a person interested in the property has applied in writing to the liquidator or one of his predecessors as liquidator requiring the liquidator or that predecessor to decide whether he will disclaim or not, and

(*b*) the period of 28 days beginning with the day on which that application was made, or such longer period as the court may allow, has expired without a notice of disclaimer having been given under this section in respect of that property.

(6) Any person sustaining loss or damage in consequence of the operation of a disclaimer under this section is deemed a creditor of the company to the extent of the loss or damage and accordingly may prove for the loss or damage in the winding up.

DEFINITIONS
"onerous property": subs. (3).
"prescribed": s.251.
"property": s.436.

GENERAL NOTE
This section, in conjunction with ss.179–182 re-enacts ss.91 and 92, I.A. 1985 which changed the law in several important ways. The opportunity was taken to harmonise the

provisions on disclaimer in winding up with those applicable in bankruptcy, now contained in ss.315–321 of this Act. The topic of disclaimer is considered in Chap. 27 of the *Cork Report.*

The most important change in the law of disclaimer in winding up was that leave of the court is no longer required when the liquidator is someone other than the official receiver. The powers of a private sector liquidator were thus enhanced to match those traditionally enjoyed in such matters by the official receiver, and also by a trustee in bankruptcy (in most cases). Secondly, the types of property which can be disclaimed were widened. Formerly the power of disclaimer was exercisable in relation to land bound by onerous covenants; to shares in companies; to unprofitable contracts; and to any other property that was unsaleable, or not readily saleable by reason of its binding its possessor to the performance of any onerous act or to the payment of any sum of money. Now the power of disclaimer is expressed to be exercisable in relation to "onerous property" as defined in subs. (3), so that it suffices if property is simply unsaleable, without any necessity that it be also subject to any onerous requirement. Conversely, it now suffices if property is subject to an onerous requirement albeit this does not have the effect of rendering the property unsaleable or not readily saleable. Thirdly, there is now no time limit within which the power of disclaimer must be exercised. The twelve-month limit formerly imposed by s.618(3) of the Companies Act 1985 was excluded contrary to the recommendation in para. 1195 of the *Cork Report.*

It is hoped that these more liberally drafted powers of disclaimer will bring about a revival in their use, and consequently bring about a simplification of the liquidator's overall task. The shortcomings of the disclaimer provisions formerly in force as s.323 of the Companies Act 1948 (latterly ss.618, 619 of the Companies Act 1985), were demonstrated in *Re Potters Oil Ltd. (in liquidation)* [1985] P.C.C. 148.

Subs. (6)
' Note that s.181(5) requires that the effect of any order made under s.181 shall be taken into account in assessing the extent of a person's claim for the purposes of this subsection.

Disclaimer of leaseholds

179.—(1) The disclaimer under section 178 of any property of a leasehold nature does not take effect unless a copy of the disclaimer has been served (so far as the liquidator is aware of their addresses) on every person claiming under the company as underlessee or mortgagee and either—

(*a*) no application under section 181 below is made with respect to that property before the end of the period of 14 days beginning with the day on which the last notice served under this subsection was served; or

(*b*) where such an application has been made, the court directs that the disclaimer shall take effect.

(2) Where the court gives a direction under subsection (1)(*b*) it may also, instead of or in addition to any order it makes under section 181, make such orders with respect to fixtures, tenant's improvements and other matters arising out of the lease as it thinks fit.

GENERAL NOTE
This re-enacts subs. (5) and (6) of s.91, I.A. 1985 and provides that a disclaimer of leasehold property shall not take effect unless a copy of the disclaimer has been served upon any underlessee or mortgagee and they have made either no application or no successful application to the court under s.181. The terms upon which the court can make an order under s.181 are governed by s.182. See generally Note to s.178. The equivalent provision in relation to individual insolvency is s.317.

Land subject to rentcharge

180.—(1) The following applies where, in consequence of the disclaimer under section 178 of any land subject to a rentcharge, that land vests by operation of law in the Crown or any other person (referred to in the next subsection as "the proprietor").

(2) The proprietor and the successors in title of the proprietor are not subject to any personal liability in respect of any sums becoming due under the rentcharge except sums becoming due after the proprietor, or some person claiming under or through the proprietor, has taken possession or control of the land or has entered into occupation of it.

GENERAL NOTE

This re-enacts subs. (7) of s.91, I.A. 1985. Disclaimer does not impose upon the Crown or other person benefited an obligation under the rentcharge. The equivalent provision in relation to individual insolvency is s.319. See generally Note to s.178.

Powers of court (general)

181.—(1) This section and the next apply where the liquidator has disclaimed property under section 178.

(2) An application under this section may be made to the court by—

(a) any person who claims an interest in the disclaimed property, or

(b) any person who is under any liability in respect of the disclaimed property, not being a liability discharged by the disclaimer.

(3) Subject as follows, the court may on the application make an order, on such terms as it thinks fit, for the vesting of the disclaimed property in, or for its delivery to—

(a) a person entitled to it or a trustee for such a person, or

(b) a person subject to such a liability as is mentioned in subsection (2)(b) or a trustee for such a person.

(4) The court shall not make an order under subsection (3)(b) except where it appears to the court that it would be just to do so for the purpose of compensating the person subject to the liability in respect of the disclaimer.

(5) The effect of any order under this section shall be taken into account in assessing for the purpose of section 178(6) the extent of any loss or damage sustained by any person in consequence of the disclaimer.

(6) An order under this section vesting property in any person need not be completed by conveyance, assignment or transfer.

DEFINITION
"property": s.436.

GENERAL NOTE

This section operates in conjunction with ss.178 and 179 and empowers the court to vest the disclaimed property in the categories of person mentioned in subs. (3). The effect of such an order has to be taken into account in assessing the extent of any loss in respect of which a person is allowed to prove under s.178(6) (see subs. (5)).

Powers of court (leaseholds)

182.—(1) The court shall not make an order under section 181 vesting property of a leasehold nature in any person claiming under the company as underlessee or mortgagee except on terms making that person—

(a) subject to the same liabilities and obligations as the company was subject to under the lease at the commencement of the winding up, or

(b) if the court thinks fit, subject to the same liabilities and obligations as that person would be subject to if the lease had been assigned to him at the commencement of the winding up.

(2) For the purposes of an order under section 181 relating to only part of any property comprised in a lease, the requirements of subsection (1) apply as if the lease comprised only the property to which the order relates.

(3) Where subsection (1) applies and no person claiming under the company as underlessee or mortgagee is willing to accept an order under section 181 on the terms required by virtue of that subsection, the court may, by order under that section, vest the company's estate or interest in the property in any person who is liable (whether personally or in a representative capacity, and whether alone or jointly with the company) to perform the lessee's covenants in the lease.

The court may vest that estate and interest in such a person freed and discharged from all estates, incumbrances and interests created by the company.

(4) Where subsection (1) applies and a person claiming under the company as underlessee or mortgagee declines to accept an order under section 181, that person is excluded from all interest in the property.

GENERAL NOTE
This section re-enacts subss. (5)–(8) of s.92, I.A. 1985.

Execution, attachment and the Scottish equivalents

Effect of execution or attachment (England and Wales)

183.—(1) Where a creditor has issued execution against the goods or land of a company or has attached any debt due to it, and the company is subsequently wound up, he is not entitled to retain the benefit of the execution or attachment against the liquidator unless he has completed the execution or attachment before the commencement of the winding up.

(2) However—

(*a*) if a creditor has had notice of a meeting having been called at which a resolution for voluntary winding up is to be proposed, the date on which he had notice is substituted, for the purpose of subsection (1), for the date of commencement of the winding up;

(*b*) a person who purchases in good faith under a sale by the sheriff any goods of a company on which execution has been levied in all cases acquires a good title to them against the liquidator; and

(*c*) the rights conferred by subsection (1) on the liquidator may be set aside by the court in favour of the creditor to such extent and subject to such terms as the court thinks fit.

(3) For the purposes of this Act—

(*a*) an execution against goods is completed by seizure and sale, or by the making of a charging order under section 1 of the Charging Orders Act 1979;

(*b*) an attachment of a debt is completed by receipt of the debt; and

(*c*) an execution against land is completed by seizure, by the appointment of a receiver, or by the making of a charging order under section 1 of the Act above-mentioned.

(4) In this section, "goods" includes all chattels personal; and "the sheriff" includes any officer charged with the execution of a writ or other process.

(5) This section does not apply in the case of a winding up in Scotland.

DEFINITION
"commencement of winding up": ss.86, 129.

GENERAL NOTE
This re-enacts s.621, C.A. 1985. The section corresponds to s.346 which applies to insolvency of individuals and prevents a creditor who has issued execution or attachment from enjoying the fruits thereof unless he has completed the execution or attachment before the commencement of the winding up. S.183(2)(*b*) protects a bona fide purchaser of goods

from the sheriff and s.183(2)(*c*) gives the court a general discretion to set aside the rights of the liquidator under the section. As to the court's exercise of its discretion see *Re Grosvenor Metal Co. Ltd.* [1950] Ch. 63; *Re Suidair International Airways Ltd.* [1951] Ch. 165 and *Re Redman (Builders) Ltd.* [1964] 1 All E.R. 851. See *Palmer,* paras. 85–72.

Duties of sheriff (England and Wales)

184.—(1) The following applies where a company's goods are taken in execution and, before their sale or the completion of the execution (by the receipt or recovery of the full amount of the levy), notice is served on the sheriff that a provisional liquidator has been appointed or that a winding-up order has been made, or that a resolution for voluntary winding up has been passed.

(2) The sheriff shall, on being so required, deliver the goods and any money seized or received in part satisfaction of the execution to the liquidator; but the costs of execution are a first charge on the goods or money so delivered, and the liquidator may sell the goods, or a sufficient part of them, for the purpose of satisfying the charge.

(3) If under an execution in respect of a judgment for a sum exceeding £250 a company's goods are sold or money is paid in order to avoid sale, the sheriff shall deduct the costs of the execution from the proceeds of sale or the money paid and retain the balance for 14 days.

(4) If within that time notice is served on the sheriff of a petition for the winding up of the company having been presented, or of a meeting having been called at which there is to be proposed a resolution for voluntary winding up, and an order is made or a resolution passed (as the case may be), the sheriff shall pay the balance to the liquidator, who is entitled to retain it as against the execution creditor.

(5) The rights conferred by this section on the liquidator may be set aside by the court in favour of the creditor to such extent and subject to such terms as the court thinks fit.

(6) In this section, "goods" includes all chattels personal; and "the sheriff" includes any officer charged with the execution of a writ or other process.

(7) The money sum for the time being specified in subsection (3) is subject to increase or reduction by order under section 416 in Part XV.

(8) This section does not apply in the case of a winding up in Scotland.

General Note
   This re-enacts s.622, C.A. 1985. It deals with the duties of a sheriff where goods are seized in execution in England and Wales and before their sale or completion of the execution notice is served of winding up. The sheriff must if required deliver up the goods, etc., but the costs of execution are a first charge thereon. S.184(3) deals with goods seized in execution for a judgment for a sum exceeding £250. Here the sheriff must deduct the cost of execution and retain the balance for 14 days.

Effect of diligence (Scotland)

185.—(1) In the winding up of a company registered in Scotland, the following provisions of the Bankruptcy (Scotland) Act 1985—
   (*a*) subsections (1) to (6) of section 37 (effect of sequestration on diligence); and
   (*b*) subsections (3), (4), (7) and (8) of section 39 (realisation of estate), apply, so far as consistent with this Act, in like manner as they apply in the sequestration of a debtor's estate, with the substitutions specified below and with any other necessary modifications.

(2) The substitutions to be made in those sections of the Act of 1985 are as follows—
   (*a*) for references to the debtor, substitute references to the company;

(*b*) for references to the sequestration, substitute references to the winding up;

(*c*) for references to the date of sequestration, substitute references to the commencement of the winding up of the company; and

(*d*) for references to the permanent trustee, substitute references to the liquidator.

(3) In this section, "the commencement of the winding up of the company" means, where it is being wound up by the court, the day on which the winding-up order is made.

(4) This section, so far as relating to any estate or effects of the company situated in Scotland, applies in the case of a company registered in England and Wales as in the case of one registered in Scotland.

GENERAL NOTE

This section is derived from s.623, C.A. 1985 and Sched. 7, para. 21 of the Bankruptcy (Scotland) Act 1985. It deals with the effect of diligence (see further Note to s.60) in the case of a company registered in Scotland. It incorporates by reference the provisions (of the Bankruptcy (Scotland) Act 1985) mentioned in subs. (1) subject to the substitutions (which are necessary to render the provisions appropriate to a company) which are set out in subs. (2)

Miscellaneous matters

Rescission of contracts by the court

186.—(1) The court may, on the application of a person who is, as against the liquidator, entitled to the benefit or subject to the burden of a contract made with the company, make an order rescinding the contract on such terms as to payment by or to either party of damages for the non-performance of the contract, or otherwise as the court thinks just.

(2) Any damages payable under the order to such a person may be proved by him as a debt in the winding up.

GENERAL NOTE

This re-enacts s.619(4), C.A. 1985. Rescission of contracts by the court has been severed from the disclaimer provisions which now appear in ss.178–82 *supra*.

Power to make over assets to employees

187.—(1) On the winding up of a company (whether by the court or voluntarily), the liquidator may, subject to the following provisions of this section, make any payment which the company has, before the commencement of the winding up, decided to make under section 719 of the Companies Act (power to provide for employees or former employees on cessation or transfer of business).

(2) The power which a company may exercise by virtue only of that section may be exercised by the liquidator after the winding up has commenced if, after the company's liabilities have been fully satisfied and provision has been made for the expenses of the winding up, the exercise of that power has been sanctioned by such a resolution of the company as would be required of the company itself by section 719(3) before that commencement, if paragraph (*b*) of that subsection were omitted and any other requirement applicable to its exercise by the company had been met.

(3) Any payment which may be made by a company under this section (that is, a payment after the commencement of its winding up) may be made out of the company's assets which are available to the members on the winding up.

(4) On a winding up by the court, the exercise by the liquidator of his powers under this section is subject to the court's control, and any creditor

or contributory may apply to the court with respect to any exercise or proposed exercise of the power.

(5) Subsections (1) and (2) above have effect notwithstanding anything in any rule of law or in section 107 of this Act (property of company after satisfaction of liabilities to be distributed among members).

GENERAL NOTE
This re-enacts s.659, C.A. 1985 and deals with the liquidator's power to make over assets to employees in satisfaction of the amount decided to be provided under s.719, C.A. 1985 on cessation or transfer of business. This overrides s.107 *supra*.

Notification that company is in liquidation

188.—(1) When a company is being wound up, whether by the court or voluntarily, every invoice, order for goods or business letter issued by or on behalf of the company, or a liquidator of the company, or a receiver or manager of the company's property, being a document on or in which the name of the company appears, shall contain a statement that the company is being wound up.

(2) If default is made in complying with this section, the company and any of the following persons who knowingly and wilfully authorises or permits the default, namely, any officer of the company, any liquidator of the company and any receiver or manager, is liable to a fine.

DEFINITIONS
"fine": s.430, Sched. 10.
"officer of the company": s.251; C.A. 1985, s.740.
"receiver or manager": s.29(1)(*a*).

GENERAL NOTE
This re-enacts s.637, C.A. 1985 and deals with the publicity to be given to the winding up on commercial documents. Compare s.12 (administration orders) and s.39 (appointment of receiver or manager).

Interest on debts

189.—(1) In a winding up interest is payable in accordance with this section on any debt proved in the winding up, including so much of any such debt as represents interest on the remainder.

(2) Any surplus remaining after the payment of the debts proved in a winding up shall, before being applied for any other purpose, be applied in paying interest on those debts in respect of the periods during which they have been outstanding since the company went into liquidation.

(3) All interest under this section ranks equally, whether or not the debts on which it is payable rank equally.

(4) The rate of interest payable under this section in respect of any debt ("the official rate" for the purposes of any provision of this Act in which that expression is used) is whichever is the greater of—

(*a*) the rate specified in section 17 of the Judgments Act 1838 on the day on which the company went into liquidation, and

(*b*) the rate applicable to that debt apart from the winding up.

(5) In the application of this section to Scotland—

(*a*) references to a debt proved in a winding up have effect as references to a claim accepted in a winding up, and

(*b*) the reference to section 17 of the Judgments Act 1838 has effect as a reference to the rules.

DEFINITIONS
"company goes into liquidation": s.247(2).
"the rules": s.251.

GENERAL NOTE

This prescribes the circumstances under which interest is payable on any debt proved in a winding up. Subs. (4) also establishes the formula by which the rate of interest payable is to be determined. The provision completely changes the former law, which was rigorously criticised in chapter 31 of the *Cork Report* in terms which were accepted in paras. 85–89 of the *White Paper*. Payment of interest in a winding up was formerly held (*Re Theo Garvin Ltd.* [1969] 1 Ch. 624) to be governed by the restrictive and anachronistic provisions of s.66 of the Bankruptcy Act 1914, made applicable in winding up by virtue of s.612 of the Companies Act 1985 (the respective sections of both Acts were repealed by I.A. 1985). This section, which re-enacts s.93, I.A. 1985, provides for payment of interest, at the rate prescribed in subs. (4), in respect of the period since the company went into liquidation. Interest up to the date of insolvency, calculated at the appropriate contract rate, is included in the creditors' claim for which proof is lodged. Payment of post-insolvency interest can only occur if there is a surplus after all creditor's claims have been met in full (including claims for pre-insolvency interest). Under s.244, the liquidator can reopen a contract which constitutes an extortionate credit transaction, and the contractual rate of interest may be adjusted by the court.

Subs. (3)

All interest . . . ranks equally

This applies the *pari passu* rule to all the company's debts for the purposes of payment of interest under this section. There is no differentiation between preferential and non-preferential debts for this purpose.

Subs. (4)

The rate specified in section 17 of the Judgments Act 1838

This provision ensures that a certain statutory minimum level is payable under this section, in respect of every one of the company's debts, regardless of whether a right to interest was reserved under the contract. If, on the other hand, the contract did specify a rate of interest, that rate would be payable in respect of the post-insolvency period, provided that the rate is greater than the statutory rate applicable to judgment debts at the relevant date, and provided that the terms of the contract are not revised under s.244.

Documents exempt from stamp duty

190.—(1) In the case of a winding up by the court, or of a creditors' voluntary winding up, the following has effect as regards exemption from duties chargeable under the enactments relating to stamp duties.

(2) If the company is registered in England and Wales, the following documents are exempt from stamp duty—

(*a*) every assurance relating solely to freehold or leasehold property, or to any estate, right or interest in, any real or personal property, which forms part of the company's assets and which, after the execution of the assurance, either at law or in equity, is or remains part of those assets, and

(*b*) every writ, order, certificate, or other instrument or writing relating solely to the property of any company which is being wound up as mentioned in subsection (1), or to any proceeding under such a winding up.

"Assurance" here includes deed, conveyance, assignment and surrender.

(3) If the company is registered in Scotland, the following documents are exempt from stamp duty—

(*a*) every conveyance relating solely to property which forms part of the company's assets and which, after the execution of the conveyance, is or remains the company's property for the benefit of its creditors,

(*b*) any articles of roup or sale, submission and every other instrument and writing whatsoever relating solely to the company's property, and

(c) every deed or writing forming part of the proceedings in the winding up.

"Conveyance" here includes assignation, instrument, discharge, writing and deed.

GENERAL NOTE

This re-enacts s.638, C.A. 1985 and exempts the specified documents from stamp duty in an insolvent winding up.

Company's books to be evidence

191. Where a company is being wound up, all books and papers of the company and of the liquidators are, as between the contributories of the company, prima facie evidence of the truth of all matters purporting to be recorded in them.

GENERAL NOTE

This re-enacts s.639, C.A. 1985 and makes the company's books and papers prima facie evidence as between contributories of the company. The truth of the evidence can be rebutted (*Re Great Northern Salt and Chemical Works, ex parte Kennedy* (1890) 44 Ch.D. 472). See *Palmer,* paras. 86–16.

Information as to pending liquidations

192.—(1) If the winding up of a company is not concluded within one year after its commencement, the liquidator shall, at such intervals as may be prescribed, until the winding up is concluded, send to the registrar of companies a statement in the prescribed form and containing the prescribed particulars with respect to the proceedings in, and position of, the liquidation.

(2) If a liquidator fails to comply with this section, he is liable to a fine and, for continued contravention, to a daily default fine.

DEFINITIONS

"fine"; "daily default fine": s.430, Sched. 10.

GENERAL NOTE

This re-enacts s.641, C.A. 1985 and deals with the obligation of the liquidator to file statements about the progress of the liquidation. See Winding Up Rules.

Unclaimed dividends (Scotland)

193.—(1) The following applies where a company registered in Scotland has been wound up, and is about to be dissolved.

(2) The liquidator shall lodge in an appropriate bank or institution as defined in section 73(1) of the Bankruptcy (Scotland) Act 1985 (not being a bank or institution in or of which the liquidator is acting partner, manager, agent or cashier) in the name of the Accountant of Court the whole unclaimed dividends and unapplied or undistributable balances, and the deposit receipts shall be transmitted to the Accountant of Court.

(3) The provisions of section 58 of the Bankruptcy (Scotland) Act 1985 (so far as consistent with this Act and the Companies Act) apply with any necessary modifications to sums lodged in a bank or institution under this section as they apply to sums deposited under section 57 of the Act first mentioned.

GENERAL NOTE

This re-enacts s.643, C.A. 1985 with minor amendments and deals with unclaimed dividends and balances in Scotland. See *Palmer,* paras. 87–80.

Resolutions passed at adjourned meetings

194. Where a resolution is passed at an adjourned meeting of a company's creditors or contributories, the resolution is treated for all purposes as having been passed on the date on which it was in fact passed, and not as having been passed on any earlier date.

DEFINITION
    "contributory": s.74.

GENERAL NOTE
    This re-enacts s.644, C.A. 1985 and deals with resolutions passed at adjourned meetings of creditors or contributories.

Meetings to ascertain wishes of creditors or contributories

195.—(1) The court may—
(*a*) as to all matters relating to the winding up of a company, have regard to the wishes of the creditors or contributories (as proved to it by any sufficient evidence), and
(*b*) if it thinks fit, for the purpose of ascertaining those wishes, direct meetings of the creditors or contributories to be called, held and conducted in such manner as the court directs, and appoint a person to act as chairman of any such meeting and report the result of it to the court.

(2) In the case of creditors, regard shall be had to the value of each creditor's debt.

(3) In the case of contributories, regard shall be had to the number of votes conferred on each contributory by the Companies Act or the articles.

GENERAL NOTE
    This re-enacts s.645, C.A. 1985 and contains the useful general power of the court to convene meetings of creditors or contributories to ascertain their wishes. As to the weight given to the creditors' wishes on the making of a winding-up order see *Palmer,* paras. 85–06—85–07.

Judicial notice of court documents

196. In all proceedings under this Part, all courts, judges and persons judicially acting, and all officers, judicial or ministerial, of any court, or employed in enforcing the process of any court shall take judicial notice—
(*a*) of the signature of any officer of the High Court or of a county court in England and Wales, or of the Court of Session or a sheriff court in Scotland, or of the High Court in Northern Ireland, and also
(*b*) of the official seal or stamp of the several offices of the High Court in England and Wales or Northern Ireland, or of the Court of Session, appended to or impressed on any document made, issued or signed under the provisions of this Act or the Companies Act, or any official copy of such a document.

GENERAL NOTE
    This re-enacts s.646, C.A. 1985 and provides for judicial notice to be taken of signature of court officers in different parts of the United Kingdom.

Commission for receiving evidence

197.—(1) When a company is wound up in England and Wales or in Scotland, the court may refer the whole or any part of the examination of witnesses—

(*a*) to a specified county court in England and Wales, or
(*b*) to the sheriff principal for a specified sheriffdom in Scotland, or
(*c*) to the High Court in Northern Ireland or a specified Northern Ireland County Court,

("specified" meaning specified in the order of the winding-up court).

(2) Any person exercising jurisdiction as a judge of the court to which the reference is made (or, in Scotland, the sheriff principal to whom it is made) shall then, by virtue of this section, be a commissioner for the purpose of taking the evidence of those witnesses.

(3) The judge or sheriff principal has in the matter referred the same power of summoning and examining witnesses, of requiring the production and delivery of documents, of punishing defaults by witnesses, and of allowing costs and expenses to witnesses, as the court which made the winding-up order.

These powers are in addition to any which the judge or sheriff principal might lawfully exercise apart from this section.

(4) The examination so taken shall be returned or reported to the court which made the order in such manner as that court requests.

(5) This section extends to Northern Ireland.

GENERAL NOTE

This re-enacts s.647, C.A. 1985 and deals with special commissions for receiving evidence in a winding up in England, Wales or Scotland. Northern Ireland is not mentioned in the opening words of s.197(1) but s.197(5) provides that the section extends to Northern Ireland and Northern Ireland is referred to in s.197(1)(*c*). For a full discussion of these changes see the Report by the Law Commission and Scottish Law Commission—Amendment to the Companies Acts 1948 to 1981, p.16 *et seq.*

Court order for examination of persons in Scotland

198.—(1) The court may direct the examination in Scotland of any person for the time being in Scotland (whether a contributory of the company or not), in regard to the trade, dealings, affairs or property of any company in course of being wound up, or of any person being a contributory of the company, so far as the company may be interested by reason of his being a contributory.

(2) The order or commission to take the examination shall be directed to the sheriff principal of the sheriffdom in which the person to be examined is residing or happens to be for the time; and the sheriff principal shall summon the person to appear before him at a time and place to be specified in the summons for examination on oath as a witness or as a haver, and to produce any books or papers called for which are in his possession or power.

(3) The sheriff principal may take the examination either orally or on written interrogatories, and shall report the same in writing in the usual form to the court, and shall transmit with the report the books and papers produced, if the originals are required and specified by the order or commission, or otherwise copies or extracts authenticated by the sheriff.

(4) If a person so summoned fails to appear at the time and place specified, or refuses to be examined or to make the production required, the sheriff principal shall proceed against him as a witness or haver duly cited; and failing to appear or refusing to give evidence or make production may be proceeded against by the law of Scotland.

(5) The sheriff principal is entitled to such fees, and the witness is entitled to such allowances, as sheriffs principal when acting as commissioners under appointment from the Court of Session and as witnesses and havers are entitled to in the like cases according to the law and practice of Scotland.

(6) If any objection is stated to the sheriff principal by the witness, either on the ground of his incompetency as a witness, or as to the production required, or on any other ground, the sheriff principal may, if he thinks fit, report the objection to the court, and suspend the examination of the witness until it has been disposed of by the court.

GENERAL NOTE
This re-enacts s.648, C.A. 1985 and allows the court to direct the examination in Scotland of any person for the time being in Scotland.

Costs of application for leave to proceed (Scottish companies)

199. Where a petition or application for leave to proceed with an action or proceeding against a company which is being wound up in Scotland is unopposed and is granted by the court, the costs of the petition or application shall, unless the court otherwise directs, be added to the amount of the petitioner's or applicant's claim against the company.

GENERAL NOTE
This re-enacts s.649, C.A. 1985. The section deals with costs in connection with an application for leave to proceed with an action against a company being wound up in Scotland, which is unopposed.

Affidavits etc. in United Kingdom and overseas

200.—(1) An affidavit required to be sworn under or for the purposes of this Part may be sworn in the United Kingdom, or elsewhere in Her Majesty's dominions, before any court, judge or person lawfully authorised to take and receive affidavits, or before any of Her Majesty's consuls or vice-consuls in any place outside Her dominions.

(2) All courts, judges, justices, commissioners and persons acting judicially shall take judicial notice of the seal or stamp or signature (as the case may be) of any such court, judge, person, consul or vice-consul attached, appended or subscribed to any such affidavit, or to any other document to be used for the purposes of this Part.

GENERAL NOTE
This re-enacts s.650, C.A. 1985. The section deals with the formalities for swearing affidavits.

CHAPTER IX

DISSOLUTION OF COMPANIES AFTER WINDING UP

Dissolution (voluntary winding up)

201.—(1) This section applies, in the case of a company wound up voluntarily, where the liquidator has sent to the registrar of companies his final account and return under section 94 (members' voluntary) or section 106 (creditors' voluntary).

(2) The registrar on receiving the account and return shall forthwith register them; and on the expiration of 3 months from the registration of the return the company is deemed to be dissolved.

(3) However, the court may, on the application of the liquidator or any other person who appears to the court to be interested, make an order deferring the date at which the dissolution of the company is to take effect for such time as the court thinks fit.

(4) It is the duty of the person on whose application an order of the court under this section is made within 7 days after the making of the

order to deliver to the registrar an office copy of the order for registration; and if that person fails to do so he is liable to a fine and, for continued contravention, to a daily default fine.

DEFINITIONS
"members' voluntary winding up": s.90.
"creditors' voluntary winding up": s.90.
"fine", "daily default fine": s.430, Sched. 10.

GENERAL NOTE
This is derived from ss.585(5), (6), and 595(6), (7), C.A. 1985. It applies to both members' and creditors' voluntary winding up where the liquidator has complied with s.94 or s.106 respectively and the registrar has registered the account and return. It is now located with other provisions relating to dissolution (of companies wound up by the court) derived from the I.A. 1985. See General Note to s.202.

Early dissolution (England and Wales)

202.—(1) This section applies where an order for the winding up of a company has been made by the court in England and Wales.
(2) The official receiver, if—
(a) he is the liquidator of the company, and
(b) it appears to him—
  (i) that the realisable assets of the company are insufficient to cover the expenses of the winding up, and
  (ii) that the affairs of the company do not require any further investigation,
may at any time apply to the registrar of companies for the early dissolution of the company.
(3) Before making that application, the official receiver shall give not less than 28 days' notice of his intention to do so to the company's creditors and contributories and, if there is an administrative receiver of the company, to that receiver.
(4) With the giving of that notice the official receiver ceases (subject to any directions under the next section) to be required to perform any duties imposed on him in relation to the company, its creditors or contributories by virtue of any provision of this Act, apart from a duty to make an application under subsection (2) of this section.
(5) On the receipt of the official receiver's application under subsection (2) the registrar shall forthwith register it and, at the end of the period of 3 months beginning with the day of the registration of the application, the company shall be dissolved.
However, the Secretary of State may, on the application of the official receiver or any other person who appears to the Secretary of State to be interested, give directions under section 203 at any time before the end of that period.

DEFINITIONS
"contributory": s.79.
"the official receiver": s.399.

GENERAL NOTE
This section is designed to enable the official receiver to bring his responsibilities to an early end in cases where he, as the liquidator, discovers that the realisable assets of the company are insufficient to cover the expenses of the winding up. The further precondition to the official receiver's ability to apply to the registrar of companies for an early dissolution of the company is that the offical receiver considers that the affairs of the company do not require further investigation. Should it subsequently transpire that either of the official receiver's conclusions as to the assets of the company and as to the impeccable character of the company's affairs was incorrect, or if there is any other reason to suggest that an early

dissolution is inappropriate, the official receiver himself or other interested parties have a limited time in which to apply for directions to the Secretary of State under s.203. The effective period within which such an application may be made consists of the 28 days' period of notice specified in subs. (3), together with the period of three months specified in subs. (5).

The section which re-enacts subs. (1)–(3), (6) of s.76, I.A. 1985, reflects the recommendations in paras. 649–651 of the *Cork Report,* accepted in modified form in paras. 105–107 of the *White Paper.* Since up to a third of companies which enter compulsory liquidation have either no assets or so few as to be practically worthless, the accelerated procedure under this section should save the time of the official receiver as well as the expense of, *inter alia,* the sending out of final notice of the official receiver's intention to apply for his release. By virtue of subs. (4), the sending of notice of intention to apply for early dissolution of the company simultaneously releases the official receiver from his duties in relation to the company in question, subject to any directions which may later be issued by the Secretary of State pursuant to s.203.

Consequence of notice under s.202

203.—(1) Where a notice has been given under section 202(3), the official receiver or any creditor or contributory of the company, or the administrative receiver of the company (if there is one) may apply to the Secretary of State for directions under this section.

(2) The grounds on which that application may be made are—
> (*a*) that the realisable assets of the company are sufficient to cover the expenses of the winding up;
> (*b*) that the affairs of the company do require further investigation; or
> (*c*) that for any other reason the early dissolution of the company is inappropriate.

(3) Directions under this section—
> (*a*) are directions making such provision as the Secretary of State thinks fit for enabling the winding up of the company to proceed as if no notice had been given under section 202(3), and
> (*b*) may, in the case of an application under section 202(5), include a direction deferring the date at which the dissolution of the company is to take effect for such period as the Secretary of State thinks fit.

(4) An appeal to the court lies from any decision of the Secretary of State on an application for directions under this section.

(5) It is the duty of the person on whose application any directions are given under this section, or in whose favour an appeal with respect to an application for such directions is determined, within 7 days after the giving of the directions or the determination of the appeal, to deliver to the registrar of companies for registration such a copy of the directions or determination as is prescribed.

(6) If a person without reasonable excuse fails to deliver a copy as required by subsection (5), he is liable to a fine and, for continued contravention, to a daily default fine.

DEFINITIONS
"contributory": s.79.
"administrative receiver": ss.251, 29(2).
"fine", "daily default fine": s.430, Sched. 10.

GENERAL NOTE
This re-enacts subss. (4), (5), (7)–(10) of s.76 I.A. 1985 and allows the categories of person mentioned in subs. (1) to challenge an early dissolution of the company under s.202, by applying to the Secretary of State for directions. See also Note to s.202.

Early dissolution (Scotland)

204.—(1) This section applies where a winding-up order has been made by the court in Scotland.

(2) If after a meeting or meetings under section 138 (appointment of liquidator in Scotland) it appears to the liquidator that the realisable assets of the company are insufficient to cover the expenses of the winding up, he may apply to the court for an order that the company be dissolved.

(3) Where the liquidator makes that application, if the court is satisfied that the realisable assets of the company are insufficient to cover the expenses of the winding up and it appears to the court appropriate to do so, the court shall make an order that the company be dissolved in accordance with this section.

(4) A copy of the order shall within 14 days from its date be forwarded by the liquidator to the registrar of companies, who shall forthwith register it; and, at the end of the period of 3 months beginning with the day of the registration of the order, the company shall be dissolved.

(5) The court may, on an application by any person who appears to the court to have an interest, order that the date at which the dissolution of the company is to take effect shall be deferred for such period as the court thinks fit.

(6) It is the duty of the person on whose application an order is made under subsection (5), within 7 days after the making of the order, to deliver to the registrar of companies such a copy of the order as is prescribed.

(7) If the liquidator without reasonable excuse fails to comply with the requirements of subsection (4), he is liable to a fine and, for continued contravention, to a daily default fine.

(8) If a person without reasonable excuse fails to deliver a copy as required by subsection (6), he is liable to a fine and, for continued contravention, to a daily default fine.

DEFINITIONS
"fine", "daily default fine": s.430, Sched. 10.
"prescribed": s.251.

GENERAL NOTE
This section creates a counterpart procedure for Scotland to that established under ss.202 and 203 for England and Wales. Some of the differences between the two procedures are attributable to the fact that there is no office of Official Receiver in Scotland, so that the office holder in a winding up is invariably the liquidator. However, a liquidator may make application under this section merely upon discovering that the realisable assets of the company are insufficient to cover the expenses of the winding up. There is no further necessity for the liquidator to be satisfied as to the additional condition which applies in England and Wales under s.202(2)(b)(ii). Moreover, in contrast to the procedure under s.202, a liquidator in Scotland makes application to the court for an order of dissolution and is not required by the provisions of this section to give prior notice to the company's creditors and contributories of his intention to do so. Although the court in Scotland has jurisdiction under subs. (5) to entertain applications from interested parties seeking deferral of the taking effect of the court's order for dissolution of the company, there is no counterpart to the provisions of s.203 for the issue of directions, either by the court or by any other authority. S.172(8) provides for the liquidator to vacate office when the dissolution of the company takes effect in accordance with subs. (4) of this section. See also the General Note to s.202.

Dissolution otherwise than under ss.202–204

205.—(1) This section applies where the registrar of companies receives—
  (a) a notice served for the purposes of section 172(8) (final meeting of creditors and vacation of office by liquidator), or
  (b) a notice from the official receiver that the winding up of a company by the court is complete.

(2) The registrar shall, on receipt of the notice, forthwith register it; and, subject as follows, at the end of the period of 3 months beginning with the day of the registration of the notice, the company shall be dissolved.

(3) The Secretary of State may, on the application of the official receiver or any other person who appears to the Secretary of State to be interested, give a direction deferring the date at which the dissolution of the company is to take effect for such period as the Secretary of State thinks fit.

(4) An appeal to the court lies from any decision of the Secretary of State on an application for a direction under subsection (3).

(5) Subsection (3) does not apply in a case where the winding-up order was made by the court in Scotland, but in such a case the court may, on an application by any person appearing to the court to have an interest, order that the date at which the dissolution of the company is to take effect shall be deferred for such period as the court thinks fit.

(6) It is the duty of the person—

(*a*) on whose application a direction is given under subsection (3);

(*b*) in whose favour an appeal with respect to an application for such a direction is determined; or

(*c*) on whose application an order is made under subsection (5),

within 7 days after the giving of the direction, the determination of the appeal or the making of the order, to deliver to the registrar for registration such a copy of the direction, determination or order as is prescribed.

(7) If a person without reasonable excuse fails to deliver a copy as required by subsection (6), he is liable to a fine and, for continued contravention, to a daily default fine.

DEFINITIONS
"prescribed": s.251.
"the official receiver": s.399.
"fine", "daily default fine": s.430, Sched. 10.

GENERAL NOTE
This provision re-enacts s.81, I.A. 1985 with minor amendments. Unlike the provisions for early dissolution, which are contained in ss.202–204, the distinctive procedures for England and for Scotland are here contained in different parts of the same section. Two alternative sequences of events are envisaged under subs. (1). The first begins with the liquidator's convening of a final meeting of creditors under s.172, followed by his giving of notice of the conclusion of the meeting to the Registrar of Companies, pursuant to s.172(8). The second begins with the Official Receiver, as liquidator of the company, giving notice to the registrar that the winding up by the court is complete. In either event, the registration of the notice by the Registrar marks the commencement of the period of three months at the end of which the company will be dissolved, unless in the meantime, an interested party has succeeded in obtaining a deferral of the dissolution by means of the procedure laid down by subs. (3) for England and Wales and by subs. (5) for Scotland.

CHAPTER X

MALPRACTICE BEFORE AND DURING LIQUIDATION; PENALISATION OF COMPANIES AND COMPANY OFFICERS; INVESTIGATIONS AND PROSECUTIONS

Offences of fraud, deception, etc.

Fraud, etc. in anticipation of winding up

206.—(1) When a company is ordered to be wound up by the court, or passes a resolution for voluntary winding up, any person, being a past or present officer of the company, is deemed to have committed an offence if, within the 12 months immediately preceding the commencement of the winding up, he has—

(*a*) concealed any part of the company's property to the value of £120 or more, or concealed any debt due to or from the company, or

(*b*) fraudulently removed any part of the company's property to the value of £120 or more, or

(*c*) concealed, destroyed, mutilated or falsified any book or paper affecting or relating to the company's property or affairs, or

(*d*) made any false entry in any book or paper affecting or relating to the company's property or affairs, or

(*e*) fraudulently parted with, altered or made any omission in any document affecting or relating to the company's property or affairs, or

(*f*) pawned, pledged or disposed of any property of the company which has been obtained on credit and has not been paid for (unless the pawning, pledging or disposal was in the ordinary way of the company's business).

(2) Such a person is deemed to have committed an offence if within the period above mentioned he has been privy to the doing by others of any of the things mentioned in paragraphs (*c*), (*d*) and (*e*) of subsection (1); and he commits an offence if, at any time after the commencement of the winding up, he does any of the things mentioned in paragraphs (*a*) to (*f*) of that subsection, or is privy to the doing by others of any of the things mentioned in paragraphs (*c*) to (*e*) of it.

(3) For purposes of this section, "officer" includes a shadow director.

(4) It is a defence—

(*a*) for a person charged under paragraph (*a*) or (*f*) of subsection (1) (or under subsection (2) in respect of the things mentioned in either of those two paragraphs) to prove that he had no intent to defraud, and

(*b*) for a person charged under paragraph (*c*) or (*d*) of subsection (1) (or under subsection (2) in respect of the things mentioned in either of those two paragraphs) to prove that he had no intent to conceal the state of affairs of the company or to defeat the law.

(5) Where a person pawns, pledges or disposes of any property in circumstances which amount to an offence under subsection (1)(*f*), every person who takes in pawn or pledge, or otherwise receives, the property knowing it to be pawned, pledged or disposed of in such circumstances, is guilty of an offence.

(6) A person guilty of an offence under this section is liable to imprisonment or a fine, or both.

(7) The money sums specified in paragraphs (*a*) and (*b*) of subsection (1) are subject to increase or reduction by order under section 416 in Part XV.

DEFINITIONS
"officer": s.251; s.744, C.A. 1985; subs. (3).
"commencement of winding up": ss.86, 129.
"shadow director": s.251; s.741, C.A. 1985.
"imprisonment or fine": s.430, Sched. 10.

GENERAL NOTE
This re-enacts s.624, C.A. 1985 with minor amendment and deals with fraud and other malpractices perpetrated by past or present officers of the company in the twelve months immediately preceding the commencement of the winding up or at any time after the commencement of winding up. An offence is committed if the officer does any of the things mentioned in subs. (1)(*a*)–(*f*) or is privy to the doing by others of any of the things mentioned

in subs. (1)(*c*)–(*e*). In the circumstances set out subs. (1)(*f*) an offence may also be committed by third parties who knowingly take an interest in the property (see subs. (5)).

Transactions in fraud of creditors

207.—(1) When a company is ordered to be wound up by the court or passes a resolution for voluntary winding up, a person is deemed to have committed an offence if he, being at the time an officer of the company—

(*a*) has made or caused to be made any gift or transfer of, or charge on, or has caused or connived at the levying of any execution against, the company's property, or

(*b*) has concealed or removed any part of the company's property since, or within 2 months before, the date of any unsatisfied judgment or order for the payment of money obtained against the company.

(2) A person is not guilty of an offence under this section—

(*a*) by reason of conduct constituting an offence under subsection (1)(*a*) which occurred more than 5 years before the commencement of the winding up, or

(*b*) if he proves that, at the time of the conduct constituting the offence, he had no intent to defraud the company's creditors.

(3) A person guilty of an offence under this section is liable to imprisonment or a fine, or both.

DEFINITIONS
"commencement of the winding up": ss.86, 129.
"imprisonment or a fine": s.430, Sched. 10.
"officer": s.251; s.744, C.A. 1985.

GENERAL NOTE
This is derived from s.625, C.A. 1985 but it has been re-drafted and another defence (subs. (2)(*a*)) has been added. It creates a general offence in relation to transactions in fraud of creditors prior to the winding up.

Misconduct in course of winding up

208.—(1) When a company is being wound up, whether by the court or voluntarily, any person, being a past or present officer of the company, commits an offence if he—

(*a*) does not to the best of his knowledge and belief fully and truly discover to the liquidator all the company's property, and how and to whom and for what consideration and when the company disposed of any part of that property (except such part as has been disposed of in the ordinary way of the company's business), or

(*b*) does not deliver up to the liquidator (or as he directs) all such part of the company's property as is in his custody or under his control, and which he is required by law to deliver up, or

(*c*) does not deliver up to the liquidator (or as he directs) all books and papers in his custody or under his control belonging to the company and which he is required by law to deliver up, or

(*d*) knowing or believing that a false debt has been proved by any person in the winding up, fails to inform the liquidator as soon as practicable, or

(*e*) after the commencement of the winding up, prevents the production of any book or paper affecting or relating to the company's property or affairs.

(2) Such a person commits an offence if after the commencement of the winding up he attempts to account for any part of the company's property by fictitious losses or expenses; and he is deemed to have committed that

offence if he has so attempted at any meeting of the company's creditors within the 12 months immediately preceding the commencement of the winding up.

(3) For purposes of this section, "officer" includes a shadow director.

(4) It is a defence—

(a) for a person charged under paragraph (a), (b) or (c) of subsection (1) to prove that he had no intent to defraud, and

(b) for a person charged under paragraph (e) of that subsection to prove that he had no intent to conceal the state of affairs of the company or to defeat the law.

(5) A person guilty of an offence under this section is liable to imprisonment or a fine, or both.

DEFINITIONS
"commencement of the winding up": ss.86, 129.
"imprisonment or a fine": s.430, Sched. 10.
"officer": subs. (3), s.251; s.744, C.A. 1985.
"shadow director": s.251; s.741, C.A. 1985.

GENERAL NOTE
This re-enacts s.626, C.A. 1985 with minor amendments. It deals with misconduct in the course of winding up. In subs. (1)(a) the liquidator must now be informed "as soon as practicable" rather than, as previously, within one month (I.A. 1985, Sched. 6, para. 43).

Falsification of company's books

209.—(1) When a company is being wound up, an officer or contributory of the company commits an offence if he destroys, mutilates, alters or falsifies any books, papers or securities, or makes or is privy to the making of any false or fraudulent entry in any register, book of account or document belonging to the company with intent to defraud or deceive any person.

(2) A person guilty of an offence under this section is liable to imprisonment or a fine, or both.

DEFINITIONS
"contributory": s.79.
"imprisonment or a fine": s.430, Sched. 10.
"officer": s.251; s.744, C.A. 1985.

GENERAL NOTE
This re-enacts s.627, C.A. 1985 and deals with falsification of a company's books.

Material omissions from statement relating to company's affairs

210.—(1) When a company is being wound up, whether by the court or voluntarily, any person, being a past or present officer of the company, commits an offence if he makes any material omission in any statement relating to the company's affairs.

(2) When a company has been ordered to be wound up by the court, or has passed a resolution for voluntary winding up, any such person is deemed to have committed that offence if, prior to the winding up, he has made any material omission in any such statement.

(3) For purposes of this section, "officer" includes a shadow director.

(4) It is a defence for a person charged under this section to prove that he had no intent to defraud.

(5) A person guilty of an offence under this section is liable to imprisonment or a fine, or both.

DEFINITIONS
"imprisonment or a fine": s.430, Sched. 10.
"officer": subs. (3), s.251; s.744. C.A. 1985.
"shadow director": s.251; s.741, C.A. 1985.

GENERAL NOTE
This re-enacts s.628, C.A. 1985 and deals with material omissions from statements relating to the company's affairs made either while the company is being wound up (subs. (1)) or prior to the winding up (subs. (2)).

False representations to creditors

211.—(1) When a company is being wound up, whether by the court or voluntarily, any person, being a past or present officer of the company—
   (*a*) commits an offence if he makes any false representation or commits any other fraud for the purpose of obtaining the consent of the company's creditors or any of them to an agreement with reference to the company's affairs or to the winding up, and
   (*b*) is deemed to have committed that offence if, prior to the winding up, he has made any false representation, or committed any other fraud, for that purpose.
(2) For purposes of this section, "officer" includes a shadow director.
(3) A person guilty of an offence under this section is liable to imprisonment or a fine, or both.

DEFINITIONS
"imprisonment or a fine": s.430, Sched. 10.
"officer": subs. (2), s.251; s.744, C.A. 1985.
"shadow director": s.251; s.741, C.A. 1985.

GENERAL NOTE
This re-enacts s.629, C.A. 1985 with minor amendment and deals with false representations to creditors made either while the company is being wound up (subs. (1)(*a*)) or prior to the winding up (subs. (1)(*b*)).

Penalisation of directors and officers

Summary remedy against delinquent directors, liquidators, etc.

212.—(1) This section applies if in the course of the winding up of a company it appears that a person who—
   (*a*) is or has been an officer of the company,
   (*b*) has acted as liquidator, administrator or administrative receiver of the company, or
   (*c*) not being a person falling within paragraph (*a*) or (*b*), is or has been concerned, or has taken part, in the promotion, formation or management of the company,
has misapplied or retained, or become accountable for, any money or other property of the company, or been guilty of any misfeasance or breach of any fiduciary or other duty in relation to the company.
(2) The reference in subsection (1) to any misfeasance or breach of any fiduciary or other duty in relation to the company includes, in the case of a person who has acted as liquidator or administrator of the company, any misfeasance or breach of any fiduciary or other duty in connection with the carrying out of his functions as liquidator or administrator of the company.
(3) The court may, on the application of the official receiver or the liquidator, or of any creditor or contributory, examine into the conduct of the person falling within subsection (1) and compel him—

(*a*) to repay, restore or account for the money or property or any part of it, with interest at such rate as the court thinks just, or

(*b*) to contribute such sum to the company's assets by way of compensation in respect of the misfeasance or breach of fiduciary or other duty as the court thinks just.

(4) The power to make an application under subsection (3) in relation to a person who has acted as liquidator or administrator of the company is not exercisable, except with the leave of the court, after that person has had his release.

(5) The power of a contributory to make an application under subsection (3) is not exercisable except with the leave of the court, but is exercisable notwithstanding that he will not benefit from any order the court may make on the application.

DEFINITIONS
"administrative receiver": s.251.
"administrator": s.8.
"contributory": s.79.

GENERAL NOTE
The purpose of this section which re-enacts s.19, I.A. 1985 is to provide a summary procedure whereby any person who has at any time mishandled or appropriated property belonging to an insolvent company may be swiftly brought to account and ordered to make restitution in whatever way is appropriate. This replaces the procedure established under s.561 of the Companies Act 1985. The range of persons who may be proceeded against under this section is a wide one, and extends to those who have acted as insolvency practitioners in relation to the company, as well as to those who are or have been its officers, or who have in any way been concerned in its promotion, formation or management. Thus the so-called "cowboy-liquidator" may be brought to book under this section just as readily as may the "delinquent director".

Subs. (1)

A person who . . . (b) has acted as liquidator, administrator . . . of the company
Note the effect of subs. (4) on the power to make applications under subs. (3) in relation to such persons.

Subs. (3)

The court
In the absence of any special definition or designation regarding jurisdiction to entertain an application under this section, it is appropriate to conclude that application should be made to the court by which the company is being wound up.

On the application . . . of any . . . contributory
Such applications are subject to the qualification imposed by subs. (5) with regard to the obtaining of leave of the court, but it is notable that a contributory is not debarred from making application on the ground that he will not personally benefit from any order to which the proceedings may give rise.

Fraudulent trading[1]

213.—(1) If in the course of the winding up of a company it appears that any business of the company has been carried on with intent to defraud creditors of the company or creditors of any other person, or for any fraudulent purpose, the following has effect.

(2) The court, on the application of the liquidator may declare that any persons who were knowingly parties to the carrying on of the business in the manner above-mentioned are to be liable to make such contributions (if any) to the company's assets as the court thinks proper.

GENERAL NOTE

This is derived from s.630(1), (2) C.A. 1985 as amended by Sched. 6, para. 6(1), I.A. 1985. Subs. (1) is unchanged but subs. (2) has been amended so as to permit only the liquidator to make the application (previously the subs. referred also to the official receiver or any creditor or contributory) and to bring the form of declaration into line with that applicable in s.214(1) *infra*. Under the new form of declaration the person is merely "liable to make such contributions (if any) to the company's assets as the court thinks proper" and is not made directly liable for any of the company's debts (compare previous wording: "personally responsible, without any limitation of liability, for all or any of the debts or other liabilities of the company".).

Because of the difficulty of establishing intent to defraud (see Maugham J. in *Re William C. Leitch Brothers Ltd.* [1932] 2 Ch. 71, 77; *Re Patrick Lyon Ltd.* [1933] 2 Ch. 786, 790; *Palmer,* para. 85–84) a similar, but new, remedy encompassing, broadly, negligent trading appears in the next section ("wrongful trading"). Though broader in this respect, the new remedy is narrower in two other respects: it applies only to directors (compare "any persons who were knowingly parties") and to *insolvent* liquidations (compare "in the course of winding up".). The concept of fraudulent trading may therefore still be useful in the context of civil liability and it remains the sole basis of criminal liability (see s.458, C.A. 1985).

As to carrying on business see *Re Gerald Cooper Chemicals Ltd.* [1978] 2 All E.R. 49 and *Re Sarflax Ltd.* [1979] 1 All E.R. 529.

For the persons covered see *Re Maidstone Building Provisions Ltd.* [1971] 3 All E.R. 363 (company secretary and financial adviser not party to carrying on business by reason of omission to advise) but compare *Panorama Developments (Guildford) Ltd.* v. *Fidelis Furnishing Fabrics Ltd.* [1971] 2 All E.R. 1028. See J. H. Farrar [1980] J.B.L. 336. See also *Re Maney & Sons de Luxe Service Station Ltd.* [1968] N.Z.L.R. 624 (N.Z.C.A.).

Wrongful trading

214.—(1) Subject to subsection (3) below, if in the course of the winding up of a company it appears that subsection (2) of this section applies in relation to a person who is or has been a director of the company, the court, on the application of the liquidator, may declare that that person is to be liable to make such contribution (if any) to the company's assets as the court thinks proper.

(2) This subsection applies in relation to a person if—

(*a*) the company has gone into insolvent liquidation.

(*b*) at some time before the commencement of the winding up of the company, that person knew or ought to have concluded that there was no reasonable prospect that the company would avoid going into insolvent liquidation, and

(*c*) that person was a director of the company at that time;

but the court shall not make a declaration under this section in any case where the time mentioned in paragraph (*b*) above was before 28th April 1986.

(3) The court shall not make a declaration under this section with respect to any person if it is satisfied that after the condition specified in subsection (2)(*b*) was first satisfied in relation to him that person took every step with a view to minimising the potential loss to the company's creditors as (assuming him to have known that there was no reasonable prospect that the company would avoid going into insolvent liquidation) he ought to have taken.

(4) For the purposes of subsections (2) and (3), the facts which a director of a company ought to know or ascertain, the conclusions which he ought to reach and the steps which he ought to take are those which would be known or ascertained, or reached or taken, by a reasonably diligent person having both—

(*a*) the general knowledge, skill and experience that may reasonably be expected of a person carrying out the same functions as are carried out by that director in relation to the company, and

(*b*) the general knowledge, skill and experience that that director has.

(5) The reference in subsection (4) to the functions carried out in relation to a company by a director of the company includes any functions which he does not carry out but which have been entrusted to him.

(6) For the purposes of this section a company goes into insolvent liquidation if it goes into liquidation at a time when its assets are insufficient for the payment of its debts and other liabilities and the expenses of the winding up.

(7) In this section "director" includes a shadow director.

(8) This section is without prejudice to section 213.

DEFINITIONS
"commencement of winding up": ss.86, 129.
"director": subs. (7); s.741, C.A. 1985.
"goes into insolvent liquidation": subs. (6).
"shadow director": s.251, s.741, C.A. 1985.

GENERAL NOTE
The provisions of this section which re-enact s.15, I.A. 1985 generated much controversy and discussion both inside and outside Parliament. However, in this instance the enacted section corresponds reasonably closely to the clause first published in the Bill. The origins of the section lie in the Cork Committee's analysis, in chap. 44 of their report, of the shortcomings of the law imposing criminal and civil responsibility for fraudulent trading, formerly embodied in s.332 of the Companies Act 1948 and latterly in ss.458 and 630 of the Companies Act 1985. The Committee proposed a severing of the criminal and civil provisions (duly accomplished in the Act of 1985) and the introduction on the civil side of a new and broader concept of "wrongful trading" to overcome misconceptions as to the degree of culpability necessary to cause a director to incur the partial or total loss of the immunity resulting from limited liability. Although the Cork Committee went to the length (unusual in their Report) of including a draft statutory clause containing a proposed definition of wrongful trading (para. 1806) the Government consistently resisted and overcame all attempts to incorporate such a provision in the Act (see *Hansard* H.L. Vol. 461, cols. 742–753; Vol. 462, cols. 37–48; H.C. Standing Committee E, June 6, 1985, cols. 218–233; H.C. Vol. 83, cols. 559–570). The result has been to leave the courts with a wide discretionary power by which directors may be made liable to contribute to the assets of an insolvent company.

The circumstances in which the court may make a declaration under this section are stated in subs. (2), while the exculpatory formula whereby a director may endeavour to persuade the court not to impose such liability, is expressed in subs. (3). It is also notable that the right to apply to the court for a declaration under this section is confined to the liquidator by whom the company is being wound up.

Subs. (1)

If in the course of the winding up of a company
This condition is an important one since it restricts the availability of the remedy to be sought under this section to cases where the company is being wound up. Subs. (2)(a) imposes the further refinement that the company must have gone into insolvent liquidation. Therefore an application can only be made in the case of a creditors' voluntary winding up or of a compulsory winding up of an insolvent company. See Note to s.213.

Person who is or has been a director of the company
This expression is qualified by the provision in subs. (2)(c) which imposes the requirement that the person against whom a declaration is sought must have been a director of the company at a time when, prior to the commencement of its winding up, he knew or ought to have concluded that an insolvent liquidation was practically inevitable. Therefore no liability under this section will fall upon a person who ceases to be a director at a time when he has no knowledge that the company has no reasonable prospect of averting insolvent liquidation, provided it is also the case that there were at the time no facts which he ought to have known or ascertained and from which the company's subsequent fate might reasonably have been deduced (see subss. (2)(b) and (4)).

The court
No special indication is given as to which court or courts have jurisdiction to hear an application under this section. It may be assumed however that the application should be

made to the court by which the company is being wound up or, if the liquidation is a voluntary one, to any court which would have had jurisdiction to wind up the company (*cf.* s.744, C.A. 1985).

On the application of the liquidator

The liquidator is the only person by whom an application may be made under this section. In a compulsory winding up the official receiver acts as liquidator by virtue of s.136(2) of this Act, unless a different person is appointed by virtue of ss.139 or 140. In most cases the necessary evidence will be difficult to assemble, and the liquidator is likely to be in the best position to decide whether the requirements of this section could be established to the satisfaction of the court. All persons who have relevant knowledge or evidence should therefore transmit that information to the liquidator. No procedure is laid down whereby interested parties can take steps to compel the liquidator to apply to the court for a declaration under this section, and hence the proper recourse for those who consider that the liquidator is unreasonably declining to make such an application is to write to the Secretary of State complaining about the liquidator's conduct in office.

Such contribution (if any) to the company's assets as the court thinks proper

This indicates that the court enjoys a complete discretion as to the extent to which, if at all, it will order any director to forfeit the immunities of limited liability and make a contribution to the company's assets, thereby augmenting the amount available to be distributed in the liquidation. Individual cases will therefore be decided on their merits, and it may be some time before any clear set of principles becomes established to determine what levels of acumen and conduct will be required of directors henceforth, and with what degree of severity they will be penalised for failure to attain those levels. See also note to s.213.

Subs. (2)

(a) The company has gone into insolvent liquidation

This expression is defined by subs. (6) as meaning that the company has gone into liquidation at a time when its assets were insufficient for the payment of its debts and other liabilities and the expenses of the winding up. Since the final outcome of a liquidation may be affected by developments which take place after the technical commencement of the winding up, it will be necessary to determine the state of the company's affairs at the time when it went into liquidation within the meaning of this Part of the Act. This is fixed by s.247(2) as the date on which the company passes a resolution for voluntary winding up or, if no such resolution is passed, the date on which an order for winding up is made by the court. If at that date the company was not insolvent within the meaning of subs. (6) the provisions of this section cannot be utilised at all.

(b) At some time before the commencement of the winding up of the company

The statutory definition of the commencement of winding up is contained in s.86 (voluntary winding up) and s.129 (winding up by the court).

That person knew or ought to have concluded

The actual state of a person's knowledge at the relevant date will be a matter to be established on the basis of the evidence. However, the provisions of subs. (4) indicate that a director cannot escape from responsibility by somehow maintaining himself in a state of ignorance of the company's true situation: the facts which he ought to know or ascertain, and the conclusions which he ought to reach, must be considered by the court in relation to the hypothetical standard of conduct of the "reasonably diligent person". Therefore the court may impose responsibility if it is satisfied that a director either was unaware of facts which he ought to have known or ascertained, or did not arrive at appropriate conclusions on the basis of the facts which he did know. In effect, such a determination involves the court in the fixing of a particular date which constitutes the "moment of truth" for each individual director, utilising the test contained in subs. (4).

No reasonable prospect that the company would avoid going into insolvent liquidation

The inclusion of the notion of reasonableness in relation to the judgment to be formed as to the company's prospect of survival is designed to eliminate any scope for a director to escape responsibility on the basis of a *bona fide* belief, however misguided or unreasonable, that the company would somehow avoid insolvency. The provisions formerly contained in s.332 of the Companies Act 1984 regarding fraudulent trading (now s.213 of this Act) enable a director to escape liability if he has behaved honestly, albeit his conduct may have been reckless or unreasonable. Such a defence will not be available where responsibility for wrongful trading under the present section is concerned. See note to s.213.

Subs. (3)

The court shall not made a declaration

This mandatory form of words has the effect that if the defence established by this subsection is made out the court is completely deprived of all discretion in the determination of the case, and can make no declaration of responsibility against the director concerned.

After the condition specified in subsection (2)(b) was first satisfied

This again invokes the concept of the "moment of truth" as discussed above in the comment upon subs. (2)(*b*), and makes this the pivotal event for the purpose of evaluating the subsequent conduct of the individual director. Since, as has been explained, responsibility may in appropriate cases be imposed upon a director in respect of his failure to ascertain facts of which he ought to have known, the probability exists that such a director will also fail to satisfy the requirements of the statutory defence, which are that from that first moment onwards he must have done all that could reasonably be expected of him with a view to minimising the potential loss to the company's creditors. It is clearly intended that a director should lose the protection of this subsection if any significant interval of time has elapsed between his personal "moment of truth" and the time when he began to take the requisite action to protect creditors' interests, no matter how energetic those belated steps may have been.

Every step . . . as . . . he ought to have taken

The evaluation of a director's conduct is to be made in accordance with the test prescribed in subs. (4), which applies the criterion of the hypothetical, reasonably diligent person to determine what steps ought to be taken with a view to minimising the potential loss to the company's creditors.

Subs. (4)

A reasonably diligent person

This hypothetical figure serves as a basis for assessing the conduct of directors for the purposes of subs. (2) and (3). The court is required to arrive at a conclusion as to the appropriate conduct of such an hypothetical person assuming him to have possessed in combination the levels of general knowledge, skill and experience specified in paras. (*a*) and (*b*). It will be noticed that these two paragraphs respectively refer to objective and subjective levels of knowledge, skill and experience. Therefore a director cannot derive any advantage from the fact that his personal qualities are lower than those which may reasonably be expected of a director entrusted with the functions which actually repose in him, while at the same time a director who subjectively possesses unusually high levels of knowledge, skill or experience will fall to be judged according to a commensurately higher standard.

Proceedings under ss.213, 214

215.—(1) On the hearing of an application under section 213 or 214, the liquidator may himself give evidence or call witnesses.

(2) Where under either section the court makes a declaration, it may give such further directions as it thinks proper for giving effect to the declaration; and in particular, the court may—

   (*a*) provide for the liability of any person under the declaration to be a charge on any debt or obligation due from the company to him, or on any mortgage or charge or any interest in a mortgage or charge on assets of the company held by or vested in him, or any person on his behalf, or any person claiming as assignee from or through the person liable or any person acting on his behalf, and

   (*b*) from time to time make such further order as may be necessary for enforcing any charge imposed under this subsection.

(3) For the purposes of subsection (2), "assignee"—

   (*a*) includes a person to whom or in whose favour, by the directions of the person made liable, the debt, obligation, mortgage or charge was created, issued or transferred or the interest created, but

(*b*) does not include an assignee for valuable consideration (not including consideration by way of marriage) given in good faith and without notice of any of the matters on the ground of which the declaration is made.

(4) Where the court makes a declaration under either section in relation to a person who is a creditor of the company, it may direct that the whole or any part of any debt owed by the company to that person and any interest thereon shall rank in priority after all other debts owed by the company and after any interest on those debts.

(5) Sections 213 and 214 have effect notwithstanding that the person concerned may be criminally liable in respect of matters on the ground of which the declaration under the section is to be made.

GENERAL NOTE

This governs proceedings under ss.213 and 214 *supra* and is derived from s.630(3)–(6), C.A. 1985 and Sched. 6, paras. 6(2), (3), I.A. 1985 respectively and permits the court to make further directions to give effect to any declaration under s.213(2) or s.214(1).

Restriction on re-use of company names

216.—(1) This section applies to a person where a company ("the liquidating company") has gone into insolvent liquidation on or after the appointed day and he was a director or shadow director of the company at any time in the period of 12 months ending with the day before it went into liquidation.

(2) For the purposes of this section, a name is a prohibited name in relation to such a person if—

(*a*) it is a name by which the liquidating company was known at any time in that period of 12 months, or

(*b*) it is a name which is so similar to a name falling within paragraph (*a*) as to suggest an association with that company.

(3) Except with leave of the court or in such circumstances as may be prescribed, a person to whom this section applies shall not at any time in the period of 5 years beginning with the day on which the liquidating company went into liquidation—

(*a*) be a director of any other company that is known by a prohibited name, or

(*b*) in any way, whether directly or indirectly, be concerned or take part in the promotion, formation or management of any such company, or

(*c*) in any way, whether directly or indirectly, be concerned or take part in the carrying on of a business carried on (otherwise than by a company) under a prohibited name.

(4) If a person acts in contravention of this section, he is liable to imprisonment or a fine, or both.

(5) In subsection (3) "the court" means any court having jurisdiction to wind up companies; and on an application for leave under that subsection, the Secretary of State or the official receiver may appear and call the attention of the court to any matters which seem to him to be relevant.

(6) References in this section, in relation to any time, to a name by which a company is known are to the name of the company at that time or to any name under which the company carries on business at that time.

(7) For the purposes of this section a company goes into insolvent liquidation if it goes into liquidation at a time when its assets are insufficient for the payment of its debts and other liabilities and the expenses of the winding up.

(8) In this section "company" includes a company which may be wound up under Part V of this Act.

DEFINITIONS
"a prohibited name": subs. (2)(*a*), (*b*).
"company": subs. (8).
"goes into insolvent liquidation": subs. (7).
"goes into liquidation": s.247(2).
"imprisonment or a fine": s.430, Sched. 10.
"prescribed": s.251.
"shadow director": C.A. 1985, s.741(2); s.251.
"the court": subs. (5).
"the liquidating company": subs. (1).

GENERAL NOTE
The purpose of this clause is to provide a means of combating the so-called "Phoenix syndrome", whereby company directors may contrive to mislead the public by utilising a company name closely similar to that of a failed company in order to conduct a business virtually identical to that formerly carried on by the latter. Rather than prohibit altogether the future use of a company name which may in itself be a disposable asset from which creditors in the winding up may derive some benefit, the section seeks to curb any abusive use of the company name by those who have been directors or shadow directors of the company within the twelve months prior to the commencement of its insolvent liquidation. During the next five years after the date of commencement of liquidation such persons must not be involved in any other company which uses the same, or a very similar, name including the trading style used by the liquidated company, unless they have first obtained the leave of the court to do so. Contravention of this prohibition is made a criminal offence for the person concerned, and by virtue of s.217(1)(*a*) also leads to personal liability for any debts incurred by the new company when that director is involved in its management.

It thus remains possible for a director of a failed company to buy out the company's name and business and to re-establish the venture in a genuine way, but in order to do this it will be necessary to obtain the approval of the court; otherwise not only will the director commit a criminal offence, but he will also forfeit the protection of limited liability.

Subs. (3)(c)

A business carried on (otherwise than by a company)
This has the effect of preventing a former director of a failed company from evading the provisions of this section through the utilisation of an alternative basis, such as a partnership, under which to carry on a business under a prohibited name.

Subs. (5)

Any court having jurisdiction to wind up companies
The wide terms of the jurisdiction conferred by means of the definition ascribed to the word "court" in this context leave it open to a director who wishes to be involved with a business which uses a prohibited name to seek the leave of that court which is most conveniently situated for the purpose in hand. There is no necessity for the application to be made to the court by which the failed company was wound up, or by which that company could have been wound up, at the time it became insolvent.

Personal liability for debts, following contravention of s.216

217.—(1) A person is personally responsible for all the relevant debts of a company if at any time—
    (*a*) in contravention of section 216, he is involved in the management of the company, or
    (*b*) as a person who is involved in the management of the company, he acts or is willing to act on instructions given (without the leave of the court) by a person whom he knows at that time to be in contravention in relation to the company of section 216.
(2) Where a person is personally responsible under this section for the relevant debts of a company, he is jointly and severally liable in respect

of those debts with the company and any other person who, whether under this section or otherwise, is so liable.

(3) For the purposes of this section the relevant debts of a company are—

    (*a*) in relation to a person who is personally responsible under paragraph (*a*) of subsection (1), such debts and other liabilities of the company as are incurred at a time when that person was involved in the management of the company, and

    (*b*) in relation to a person who is personally responsible under paragraph (*b*) of that subsection, such debts and other liabilities of the company as are incurred at a time when that person was acting or was willing to act on instructions given as mentioned in that paragraph.

(4) For the purposes of this section, a person is involved in the management of a company if he is a director of the company or if he is concerned, whether directly or indirectly, or takes part, in the management of the company.

(5) For the purposes of this section a person who, as a person involved in the management of a company, has at any time acted on instructions given (without the leave of the court) by a person whom he knew at that time to be in contravention in relation to the company of section 216 is presumed, unless the contrary is shown, to have been willing at any time thereafter to act on any instructions given by that person.

(6) In this section "company" includes a company which may be wound up under Part V.

DEFINITIONS
    "company": subs. (6).
    "involved in the management of a company": subs. (4).
    "the relevant debts": subs. (3).

GENERAL NOTE

This section creates a potent sanction against various kinds of misconduct by persons in relation to company management. It does so by providing that certain individuals shall be denied the privileges normally associated with limited liability, and shall be personally liable for the relevant debts of any company in relation to which they act in a prohibited manner. The prohibited manner of acting is cast in two modes. The first mode (expressed in subs. (1)(*a*)) consists of being personally involved in the management of a company in contravention of s.216 by virtue of the fact that the name of the company constitutes a "prohibited name" with respect to the individual in question. The second mode (expressed in subs. (1)(*b*)) consist of knowingly acting or being willing to act on the instructions given (without leave of the court) by a person in contravention of s.216, thereby becoming the medium through which that person is able to assert an influence on the affairs of the company. Thus personal liability will be incurred not only by any person who, while subject to the prohibition, acts as a director or as a shadow director within the meaning of s.741(2) of the Companies Act 1985, but also by any person who, though not personally the subject of any such legal prohibition, consciously lends himself to the arrangement whereby the prohibited party contrives to circumvent the law's intentions.

Subs. (2)

Jointly and severally liable

This provision ensures that whenever two or more persons incur personal responsibility for the same debts of a company by virtue of this section, liability shall be shared on an equal basis as between those persons themselves. But by providing that their liability shall be several as well as joint, the process of recovery is greatly facilitated since proceedings can be directed against any one of them who is both traceable and solvent. The full amount of the sum which constitutes the "relevant debts" of a company (as defined in subs. (3)) may be recovered from any such person, leaving him in his turn to seek contribution from any other persons who may have incurred joint liability with him.

Subs. (5)

This subsection establishes a significant presumption with regard to the concept of a person's willingness to act on the instructions of another for the purposes of this section (see subss. (1)(*b*) and (3)(*b*)). Effectively, once it is established that a person involved in the management of a company has at any time acted on such instructions in a manner which contravenes subs. (1)(*b*), he is presumed to have been willing to act on any instructions of a similar character given by that other person at any time thereafter. Thus, having once compromised himself, anyone to whom this subsection applies will continue to incur personal liability for the company's debts unless he can prove to the court that his subsequent actions in relation to the company were not accompanied by a willingness on his part to act on the instructions given by the person who was barred from involvement in company management for the time being.

Investigation and prosecution of malpractice

Prosecution of delinquent officers and members of company

218.—(1) If it appears to the court in the course of a winding up by the court that any past or present officer, or any member, of the company has been guilty of any offence in relation to the company for which he is criminally liable, the court may (either on the application of a person interested in the winding up or of its own motion) direct the liquidator to refer the matter to the prosecuting authority.

(2) "The prosecuting authority" means—

(*a*) in the case of a winding up in England and Wales, the Director of Public Prosecutions, and

(*b*) in the case of a winding up in Scotland, the Lord Advocate.

(3) If in the case of a winding up by the court in England and Wales it appears to the liquidator, not being the official receiver, that any past or present officer of the company, or any member of it, has been guilty of an offence in relation to the company for which he is criminally liable, the liquidator shall report the matter to the official receiver.

(4) If it appears to the liquidator in the course of a voluntary winding up that any past or present officer of the company, or any member of it, has been guilty of an offence in relation to the company for which he is criminally liable, he shall—

(*a*) forthwith report the matter to the prosecuting authority, and

(*b*) furnish to that authority such information and give to him such access to and facilities for inspecting and taking copies of documents (being information or documents in the possession or under the control of the liquidator and relating to the matter in question) as the authority requires.

(5) Where a report is made to him under subsection (4), the prosecuting authority may, if he thinks fit, refer the matter to the Secretary of State for further enquiry; and the Secretary of State—

(*a*) shall thereupon investigate the matter, and

(*b*) for the purpose of his investigation may exercise any of the powers which are exercisable by inspectors appointed under section 431 or 432 of the Companies Act to investigate a company's affairs.

(6) If it appears to the court in the course of a voluntary winding up that—

(*a*) any past or present officer of the company, or any member of it, has been guilty as above-mentioned, and

(*b*) no report with respect to the matter has been made by the liquidator to the prosecuting authority under subsection (4),

the court may (on the application of any person interested in the winding up or of its own motion) direct the liquidator to make such a report.

On a report being made accordingly, this section has effect as though the report had been made in pursuance of subsection (4).

DEFINITION
"officer": s.251; s.744, C.A. 1985.

GENERAL NOTE
This re-enacts s.632, C.A. 1985 with the addition of a subsection (subs. (3), see Sched. 6, para. 44, I.A. 1985). It deals with the procedure for prosecuting delinquent officers and members of companies being wound up in England and Wales and Scotland. In England and Wales it deals with the liaison between the liquidator, the Director of Public Prosecutions, the Official Receiver and the Department of Trade and Industry. In Scotland there is no D.P.P. and the relevant officer is the Lord Advocate. In the past not many prosecutions have been brought.

Obligations arising under s.218

219.—(1) For the purpose of an investigation by the Secretary of State under section 218(5), any obligation imposed on a person by any provision of the Companies Act to produce documents or give information to, or otherwise to assist, inspectors appointed as mentioned in that subsection is to be regarded as an obligation similarly to assist the Secretary of State in his investigation.

(2) An answer given by a person to a question put to him in exercise of the powers conferred by section 218(5) may be used in evidence against him.

(3) Where criminal proceedings are instituted by the prosecuting authority or the Secretary of State following any report or reference under section 218, it is the duty of the liquidator and every officer and agent of the company past and present (other than the defendant or defender) to give to that authority or the Secretary of State (as the case may be) all assistance in connection with the prosecution which he is reasonably able to give.

For this purpose "agent" includes any banker or solicitor of the company and any person employed by the company as auditor, whether that person is or is not an officer of the company.

(4) If a person fails or neglects to give assistance in the manner required by subsection (3), the court may, on the application of the prosecuting authority or the Secretary of State (as the case may be) direct the person to comply with that subsection; and if the application is made with respect to a liquidator, the court may (unless it appears that the failure or neglect to comply was due to the liquidator not having in his hands sufficient assets of the company to enable him to do so) direct that the costs shall be borne by the liquidator personally.

DEFINITION
"officer": s.251; s.744, C.A. 1985.

GENERAL NOTE
This re-enacts s.633, C.A. 1985.

PART V

WINDING UP OF UNREGISTERED COMPANIES

Meaning of "unregistered company"

220.—(1) For the purposes of this Part, the expression "unregistered company" includes any trustee savings bank certified under the enactments relating to such banks, any association and any company, with the following exceptions—

(*a*) a railway company incorporated by Act of Parliament,

(b) a company registered in any part of the United Kingdom under the Joint Stock Companies Acts or under the legislation (past or present) relating to companies in Great Britain.

(2) On such day as the Treasury appoints by order under section 4(3) of the Trustee Savings Banks Act 1985, the words in subsection (1) from "any trustee" to "banks" cease to have effect and are hereby repealed.

GENERAL NOTE

This is derived from s.665, C.A. 1985 and defines the meaning of unregistered company. Previously the definition expressly included "any partnership (whether limited or not)" and expressly excluded specified types of partnerships. Neither the words of inclusion nor the words of exclusion are present in the section now. One can speculate that partnerships are still included by virtue of the general phrase "any association and any company" in subs. (1). The inclusion of trustee savings banks would appear to be temporary (subs. (2)).

Winding up of unregistered companies

221.—(1) Subject to the provisions of this Part, any unregistered company may be wound up under this Act; and all the provisions of this Act and the Companies Act about winding up apply to an unregistered company with the exceptions and additions mentioned in the following subsections.

(2) If an unregistered company has a principal place of business situated in Northern Ireland, it shall not be wound up under this Part unless it has a principal place of business situated in England and Wales or Scotland, or in both England and Wales and Scotland.

(3) For the purpose of determining a court's winding-up jurisdiction, an unregistered company is deemed—

(a) to be registered in England and Wales or Scotland, according as its principal place of business is situated in England and Wales or Scotland, or

(b) if it has a principal place of business situated in both countries, to be registered in both countries;

and the principal place of business situated in that part of Great Britain in which proceedings are being instituted is, for all purposes of the winding up, deemed to be the registered office of the company.

(4) No unregistered company shall be wound up under this Act voluntarily.

(5) The circumstances in which an unregistered company may be wound up are as follows—

(a) if the company is dissolved, or has ceased to carry on business, or is carrying on business only for the purpose of winding up its affairs;

(b) if the company is unable to pay its debts;

(c) if the court is of opinion that it is just and equitable that the company should be wound up.

(6) A petition for winding up a trustee savings bank may be presented by the Trustee Savings Banks Central Board or by a commissioner appointed under section 35 of the Trustee Savings Banks Act 1981 as well as by any person authorised under Part IV of this Act to present a petition for the winding up of a company.

On such day as the Treasury appoints by order under section 4(3) of the Trustee Savings Bank Act 1985, this subsection ceases to have effect and is hereby repealed.

(7) In Scotland, an unregistered company which the Court of Session has jurisdiction to wind up may be wound up by the court if there is subsisting a floating charge over property comprised in the company's property and undertaking, and the court is satisfied that the security of the creditor entitled to the benefit of the floating charge is in jeopardy.

For this purpose a creditor's security is deemed to be in jeopardy if the court is satisfied that events have occurred or are about to occur which render it unreasonable in the creditor's interests that the company should retain power to dispose of the property which is subject to the floating charge.

DEFINITION
"unregistered company": s.220.

GENERAL NOTE
This re-enacts s.666, C.A. 1985 (in part). It deals with the winding up of unregistered companies under the Act. Subss. (2) and (3) deal with companies with principal places of business in different parts of the United Kingdom. Unregistered companies can only be wound up compulsorily. They cannot be wound up voluntarily (subs. (4)). (Note *Palmer,* para. 86–01 to the effect that they can register under Chap. II of Part XXII, C.A. 1985 and then wind up voluntarily). Subs. (5) specifies the grounds—(*a*) dissolution or cesser of business (*b*) inability to pay debts (*c*) it is just and equitable to wind the company up. In Scotland such a company can be wound up if a floating charge is in jeopardy (subs. (7)). The reference, previously in subs. (7) of s.666, to limited partnerships has been dropped. See also note to s.220.

An illegal association cannot be wound up under the Act (*Re Padstow Total Loss and Collision Assurance Association* (1882) 20 Ch.D. 137); see further Buckley, *The Companies Acts, op. cit.* Vol. 1, pp.845–846.

Inability to pay debts: unpaid creditor for £750 or more

222.—(1) An unregistered company is deemed (for the purposes of section 221) unable to pay its debts if there is a creditor, by assignment or otherwise, to whom the company is indebted in a sum exceeding £750 then due and—

> (*a*) the creditor has served on the company, by leaving at its principal place of business, or by delivering to the secretary or some director, manager or principal officer of the company, or by otherwise serving in such manner as the court may approve or direct, a written demand in the prescribed form requiring the company to pay the sum due, and
>
> (*b*) the company has for 3 weeks after the service of the demand neglected to pay the sum or to secure or compound for it to the creditor's satisfaction.

(2) The money sum for the time being specified in subsection (1) is subject to increase or reduction by regulations under section 417 in Part XV; but no increase in the sum so specified affects any case in which the winding-up petition was presented before the coming into force of the increase.

DEFINITION
"unregistered company": s.220.

GENERAL NOTE
This re-enacts s.667, C.A. 1985 as slightly amended by Sched. 6, para. 50, I.A. 1985. The statutory demand referred to in subs. (1)(*a*) must be "in prescribed form". See rules. See also note to s.224.

Inability to pay debts: debt remaining unsatisfied after action brought

223. An unregistered company is deemed (for the purposes of section 221) unable to pay its debts if an action or other proceeding has been instituted against any member for any debt or demand due, or claimed to be due, from the company, or from him in his character of member, and—

> (*a*) notice in writing of the institution of the action or proceeding has

been served on the company by leaving it at the company's principal place of business (or by delivering it to the secretary, or some director, manager or principal officer of the company, or by otherwise serving it in such manner as the court may approve or direct), and

(b) the company has not within 3 weeks after service of the notice paid, secured or compounded for the debt or demand, or procured the action or proceeding to be stayed or sisted, or indemnified the defendant or defender to his reasonable satisfaction against the action or proceeding, and against all costs, damages and expenses to be incurred by him because of it.

DEFINITION
"unregistered company": s.220.

GENERAL NOTE
This re-enacts s.668, C.A. 1985 as slightly amended by Sched. 6, para. 51, I.A. 1985. In subs. (b) the company now has three weeks (cf. 19 days) to pay, etc. See also note to s.224, and s.417.

Inability to pay debts: other cases

224.—(1) An unregistered company is deemed (for purposes of section 221) unable to pay its debts—

(a) if in England and Wales execution or other process issued on a judgment, decree or order obtained in any court in favour of a creditor against the company, or any member of it as such, or any person authorised to be sued as nominal defendant on behalf of the company, is returned unsatisfied;

(b) if in Scotland the induciae of a charge for payment on an extract decree, or an extract registered bond, or an extract registered protest, have expired without payment being made;

(c) if in Northern Ireland a certificate of unenforceability has been granted in respect of any judgment, decree or order obtained as mentioned in paragraph (a);

(d) if it is otherwise proved to the satisfaction of the court that the company is unable to pay its debts as they fall due.

(2) An unregistered company is also deemed unable to pay its debts if it is proved to the satisfaction of the court that the value of the company's assets is less than the amount of its liabilities, taking into account its contingent and prospective liabilities.

DEFINITION
"unregistered company": s.220.

GENERAL NOTE
This re-enacts s.669, C.A. 1985 as amended by Sched. 6, para. 52, I.A. 1985. Subs. (1)(d) has been clarified by the addition of the words "as they fall due" and subs. (2) sets out new circumstances in which an unregistered company is deemed unable to pay its debts (presumably, for the purposes of s.221, although this is not stated) namely, where, for the moment, the company is able to meet its debts as they fall due but, in the long term, taking into account its contingent and prospective liabilities, the value of its assets will be less than the amount of its liabilities. It is in these circumstances that an administration order (see s.8) may be appropriate in the case of a registered company but is apparently unavailable to an unregistered company (see 229(2)).

Ss. 222, 223, and 224 all deal with the inability of the company to pay its debts. Ss. 222 and 224 are the equivalents to s.123(a), (b), (c), (d) and (e) which apply to registered companies. S.223 has no such equivalent, being partly based upon the supposition that a member may be liable for the company's debts, which supposition is generally inapplicable to registered companies.

Oversea company may be wound up though dissolved

225. Where a company incorporated outside Great Britain which has been carrying on business in Great Britain ceases to carry on business in Great Britain, it may be wound up as an unregistered company under this Act, notwithstanding that it has been dissolved or otherwise ceased to exist as a company under or by virtue of the laws of the country under which it was incorporated.

GENERAL NOTE

This re-enacts s.670, C.A. 1985 and provides for the winding up of an oversea company even though it has been dissolved under the law of its incorporation. This was the section used in the famous Russian Bank cases after they were dissolved by Bolshevik decrees in the Russian Revolution. See the learned articles by K. Lipstein (1952) C.L.J. 198 and M. A. Mann (1955) 18 M.L.R. 8. See also B. Mcpherson, Q.C., *The Law of Company Liquidation* (2nd ed.), p.410 *et seq.*

S.225 is expository only and does not limit the jurisdiction conferred by s.221—see the Russian bank cases cited by Buckley *op. cit.,* Vol. 1, p.852 footnote 3.

Contributories in winding up of unregistered company

226.—(1) In the event of an unregistered company being wound up, every person is deemed a contributory who is liable to pay or contribute to the payment of any debt or liability of the company, or to pay or contribute to the payment of any sum for the adjustment of the rights of members among themselves, or to pay or contribute to the payment of the expenses of winding up the company.

(2) Every contributory is liable to contribute to the company's assets all sums due from him in respect of any such liability as is mentioned above.

(3) In the case of an unregistered company engaged in or formed for working mines within the stannaries, a past member is not liable to contribute to the assets if he has ceased to be a member for 2 years or more either before the mine ceased to be worked or before the date of the winding-up order.

(4) In the event of the death, bankruptcy or insolvency of any contributory, the provisions of this Act with respect to the personal representatives, to the heirs and legatees of heritage of the heritable estate in Scotland of deceased contributories, and to the trustees of bankrupt or insolvent contributories, respectively apply.

DEFINITION

"unregistered company": s.220.

GENERAL NOTE

This re-enacts s.671, C.A. 1985 and deals with contributories in the case of a winding up of an unregistered company. The liability is as a member or partner not a mere debtor (*Re Shields Marine Insurance Association, Lee and Moor's Case* (1868) L.R. 5 Eq. 368).

Power of court to stay, sist or restrain proceedings

227. The provisions of this Part with respect to staying, sisting or restraining actions and proceedings against a company at any time after the presentation of a petition for winding up and before the making of a winding-up order extend, in the case of an unregistered company, where the application to stay, sist or restrain is presented by a creditor, to actions and proceedings against any contributory of the company.

See note to s.228.

Actions stayed on winding-up order

228. Where an order has been made for winding up an unregistered company, no action or proceeding shall be proceeded with or commenced against any contributory of the company in respect of any debt of the company, except by leave of the court, and subject to such terms as the court may impose.

DEFINITIONS
"contributory": s.226..
"unregistered company": s.220.

GENERAL NOTE
Ss.227 and 228 re-enact ss.672 and 673, C.A. 1985. These sections deal with the power of the Court to stay proceedings after a petition and before an order to wind up, and the automatic stay of proceedings on the making of a winding-up order unless leave of the Court is obtained. These are the equivalents of ss.126 and 130(2).

Provisions of this Part to be cumulative

229.—(1) The provisions of this Part with respect to unregistered companies are in addition to and not in restriction of any provisions in Part IV with respect to winding up companies by the court; and the court or liquidator may exercise any powers or do any act in the case of unregistered companies which might be exercised or done by it or him in winding up companies formed and registered under the Companies Act.

(2) However, an unregistered company is not, except in the event of its being wound up, deemed to be a company under the Companies Act, and then only to the extent provided by this Part of this Act.

GENERAL NOTE
This re-enacts s.674, C.A. 1985 and provides that these provisions are in addition to those in Pt. IV. This is except as expressly provided to the contrary (*Rudlow* v. *Great Britain Mutual Life Assurance Society* (1881) 17 Ch.D. 600, 612 (C.A.)).

PART VI

MISCELLANEOUS PROVISIONS APPLYING TO COMPANIES
WHICH ARE INSOLVENT OR IN LIQUIDATION

Office-holders

Holders of office to be qualified insolvency practitioners

230.—(1) Where an administration order is made in relation to a company, the administrator must be a person who is qualified to act as an insolvency practitioner in relation to the company.

(2) Where an administrative receiver of a company is appointed, he must be a person who is so qualified.

(3) Where a company goes into liquidation, the liquidator must be a person who is so qualified.

(4) Where a provisional liquidator is appointed, he must be a person who is so qualified.

(5) Subsections (3) and (4) are without prejudice to any enactment under which the official receiver is to be, or may be, liquidator or provisional liquidator.

DEFINITIONS
"administration order", "administrator": s.8(2).
"administrative receiver": s.251(*a*), (*b*).
"company goes into liquidation": s.247(2).
"person qualified to act as an insolvency practitioner": s.390.
"provisional liquidator": s.135.
"the official receiver": s.399(1).

"to act as an insolvency practitioner in relation to a company": s.388(1).

GENERAL NOTE

This section corresponds to ss.95(1), (2) and 96(1) of the 1985 Act. It imposes the requirement that in each of the four types of insolvency proceeding mentioned in subss. (1)–(4) respectively, the person appointed as office-holder must in each case be a qualified insolvency practitioner, within the meaning of ss.388 and 390. Therefore every administrator, administrative receiver, liquidator or provisional liquidator must, by virtue of this section, be a person qualified to act as an insolvency practitioner in relation to the company in question. If the person appointed lacks such qualification, his appointment will be invalid, albeit s.232 will apply to render valid any acts done by the office holder before either his want of qualification is cured, or he formally relinquishes office or is removed therefrom. Under s.389, (*q.v.*) any person who acts as an insolvency practitioner in relation to a company at a time when he is not qualified to do so commits a criminal offence of strict liability. The provisions of s.388(1)(*a*) indicate that a person acts as an insolvency practitioner in relation to a company by acting as any of the four types of office holder listed above. However, s.388(1)(*b*) also provides that a person acts as an insolvency practitioner in relation to a company by acting as supervisor of a voluntary arrangement approved under Pt. I of the Act, and s.389 accordingly makes it a criminal offence for an unqualified person to act in this capacity also. By an apparent oversight, no requirement to the effect that a supervisor of a voluntary arrangement must be a qualified insolvency practitioner was included in ss.95(1), (2) or 96(1) of the 1985 Act, and hence the process of consolidation in the present Act could not alter that want of provision. However, the same net effect is accomplished by the inclusion in s.1(2) of the requirement that the nominee in a proposal for a voluntary arrangement must be a person who is qualified to act as an insolvency practitioner in relation to the company, a requirement reinforced by the further provisions in ss.2(4), 4(2) and 7(5). Nevertheless, the consequence of the present statutory provisions is that, with the exception of s.233, a supervisor of a company voluntary arrangement concluded under Pt. I is unable to avail himself of the various powers and remedies enjoyed by the other types of office-holder by virtue of Pt. VI. Moreover, the supervisor of a voluntary arrangement is excluded from the list of office-holders whose acts are validated by virtue of s.232 in cases where their appointment is defective for any of the stated reasons.

Appointment to office of two or more persons

231.—(1) This section applies if an appointment or nomination of any person to the office of administrator, administrative receiver, liquidator or provisional liquidator—

(*a*) relates to more than one person, or

(*b*) has the effect that the office is to be held by more than one person.

(2) The appointment or nomination shall declare whether any act required or authorised under any enactment to be done by the administrator, administrative receiver, liquidator or provisional liquidator is to be done by all or any one or more of the persons for the time being holding the office in question.

DEFINITIONS

"administrative receiver": s.251.

"administrator": s.8(2).

"provisional liquidator": s.135.

GENERAL NOTE

This section, whose provisions correspond to ss.95(1), (2) and 96(2) of the 1985 Act, replaces s.589(5) of the Companies Act 1985, which is repealed. The drafting of the new version is a considerable improvement over the old one in terms of clarity, and has the merit of making it a positive requirement that the terms of appointment are to contain a specific indication whether the joint office holders are required to act together, or whether any one or more of them may validly perform any act which falls to be performed.

Validity of office-holder's acts

232. The acts of an individual as administrator, administrative receiver, liquidator or provisional liquidator of a company are valid notwithstanding any defect in his appointment, nomination or qualifications.

DEFINITIONS
"administrative receiver": s.251.
"administrator": s.8(2).
"provisional liquidator": s.135.

GENERAL NOTE
This provision preserves the validity of the acts of any of the four types of office holder described in s.230(1)–(4), whose appointment, nomination or qualifications turn out to be defective. Thus if it transpires that an office holder was not qualified to act as an insolvency practitioner in relation to the company, any acts performed by him in his capacity as office holder, prior to that discovery, will be valid by virtue of this provision although the office holder will have committed a criminal offence under s.389 and will also be obliged to vacate his office forthwith (under s.19(2)(a); s.45(2) or s.172(5), as the case may be). As mentioned in the Note to s.230, through an apparent legislative oversight the position of supervisor of a voluntary arrangement was omitted from the definition of "office holder" contained in s.95(1) of the 1985 Act, although it was included within the definition of "acting as an insolvency practitioner in relation to a company" by means of an amendment which now constitutes s.388(1)(b) (see H.C. Vol. 83, col. 580). S.1(2) imposes the requirement that the nominee (potentially the supervisor) in relation to a proposed voluntary arrangement must be a person who is qualified to act as an insolvency practitioner in relation to the company, and hence the appointment of any unqualified person to the position of supervisor will be defective, while if the person appointed purports to act in that capacity he will commit a criminal offence under s.389. However, no clear indication is given within the Act with regard to the validity or otherwise of any acts which may be performed by such a person prior to the time when the defective nature of his appointment as supervisor is discovered and his removal from office takes effect. This section corresponds to ss.95(1), (2) and 96(3) of the 1985 Act.

Management by administrators, liquidators, etc.

Supplies of gas, water, electricity, etc.

233.—(1) This section applies in the case of a company where—
(a) an administration order is made in relation to the company, or
(b) an administrative receiver is appointed, or
(c) a voluntary arrangement under Part I, approved by meetings summoned under section 3, has taken effect, or
(d) the company goes into liquidation, or
(e) a provisional liquidator is appointed;
and "the office-holder" means the administrator, the administrative receiver, the supervisor of the voluntary arrangement, the liquidator or the provisional liquidator, as the case may be.
(2) If a request is made by or with the concurrence of the office-holder for the giving, after the effective date, of any of the supplies mentioned in the next subsection, the supplier—
(a) may make it a condition of the giving of the supply that the office-holder personally guarantees the payment of any charges in respect of the supply, but
(b) shall not make it a condition of the giving of the supply, or do anything which has the effect of making it a condition of the giving of the supply, that any outstanding charges in respect of a supply given to the company before the effective date are paid.
(3) The supplies referred to in subsection (2) are—
(a) a public supply of gas,
(b) a supply of electricity by an Electricity Board,

(c) a supply of water by statutory water undertakers or, in Scotland, a water authority,

(d) a supply of telecommunication services by a public telecommunications operator.

(4) "The effective date" for the purposes of this section is whichever is applicable of the following dates—

(a) the date on which the administration order was made,

(b) the date on which the administrative receiver was appointed (or, if he was appointed in succession to another administrative receiver, the date on which the first of his predecessors was appointed),

(c) the date on which the voluntary arrangement was approved by the meetings summoned under section 3,

(d) the date on which the company went into liquidation,

(e) the date on which the provisional liquidator was appointed.

(5) The following applies to expressions used in subsection (3)—

(a) "public supply of gas" means a supply of gas by the British Gas Corporation or a public gas supplier within the meaning of Part I of the Gas Act 1986,

(b) "Electricity Board" means the same as in the Energy Act 1983,

(c) "water authority" means the same as in the Water (Scotland) Act 1980, and

(d) "telecommunication services" and "public telecommunications operator" mean the same as in the Telecommunications Act 1984, except that the former does not include services consisting in the conveyance of programmes included in cable programme services (within the meaning of the Cable and Broadcasting Act 1984).

DEFINITIONS

"a Water Authority": subs. (5)(c); Water (Scotland) Act 1980, ss.3, 109(1).
"administration order": s.8(2).
"administrative receiver": s.251.
"an Electricity Board": subs. (5)(b); Energy Act 1983, s.26.
"cable programme services": Cable & Broadcasting Act 1984, ss.2(1), 56(1).
"company goes into liquidation": s.247(2).
"provisional liquidator": s.135.
"public supply of gas": subs. (5)(a); Gas Act 1986, ss.7(1), 48(1), (2).
"public telecommunications operator": subs. (5)(d); Telecommunications Act 1984, ss.9(3), 106(1).
"supplies": subs. (3).
"telecommunication services": subs. (5)(d); Telecommunications Act 1984, ss.4(3), 106(1).
"the office holder": subs. (1).
"the effective date": subs. (4).
"voluntary arrangement": s.1(1).

GENERAL NOTE

In Chap. 33 of the *Cork Report* the position of public utilities is discussed in the context of creditors with special rights, with emphasis upon the use which may be made of their monopoly position by the suppliers of such commercially essential services as electricity, gas, water and the telephone. In paras. 1451–1462 of the *Report* it is made clear that public utilities as creditors have the capability, although technically they are unsecured and non-preferential, to compel the office holder in insolvency proceedings to settle the company's outstanding account in full against the threat that otherwise supplies will be discontinued. This section is enacted in response to the recommendation in para. 1462 that the public utilities should be required to treat the office holder as a new customer with statutory right to receive supplies separate and distinct from the company whose account is in arrear. Hence, the supplier may make it a condition of the giving of the supply that the office holder personally guarantees the payment of any charges in respect of subsequent supplies, but may not make it a condition that any outstanding charges in respect of previous supplies are paid. This section corresponds to ss.95 and 97 of the 1985 Act.

Subs. (2)(b)

Or do anything which has the effect of making it a condition of the giving of the supply . . .

This is designed to meet the possibility that a monopoly supplier may use indirect means to ensure full payment of charges outstanding in respect of past supplies. One example has been the imposition of a requirement that subsequent supplies are obtained via a coin-in-the-slot meter which is so calibrated that the rate at which the service is being charged for is at a premium, thereby enabling the utility effectively to recoup the arrears while ostensibly supplying the service without imposing a condition that outstanding charges in respect of a supply given before the relevant date are paid.

This section forms a parallel to s.372, which applies in relation to the insolvency of an individual.

Getting in the company's property

234.—(1) This section applies in the case of a company where—
   (*a*) an administration order is made in relation to the company, or
   (*b*) an administrative receiver is appointed, or
   (*c*) the company goes into liquidation, or
   (*d*) a provisional liquidator is appointed;
and "the office-holder" means the administrator, the administrative receiver, the liquidator or the provisional liquidator, as the case may be.

(2) Where any person has in his possession or control any property, books, papers or records to which the company appears to be entitled, the court may require that person forthwith (or within such period as the court may direct) to pay, deliver, convey, surrender or transfer the property, books, papers or records to the office-holder.

(3) Where the office-holder—
   (*a*) seizes or disposes of any property which is not property of the company, and
   (*b*) at the time of seizure or disposal believes, and has reasonable grounds for believing, that he is entitled (whether in pursuance of an order of the court or otherwise) to seize or dispose of that property,
the next subsection has effect.

(4) In that case the office-holder—
   (*a*) is not liable to any person in respect of any loss or damage resulting from the seizure or disposal except in so far as that loss or damage is caused by the office-holder's own negligence, and
   (*b*) has a lien on the property, or the proceeds of its sale, for such expenses as were incurred in connection with the seizure or disposal.

DEFINITIONS
"administration order": s.8(2).
"administrative receiver": s.251.
"company goes into liquidation": s.247(2).
"property": s.436.
"provisional liquidator": s.135.
"records": s.436.
"the court": s.251, C.A. 1985, s.744.
"the office holder": subs. (1).

GENERAL NOTE
This replaces in part the former provisions of s.551 of the Companies Act 1985, which is repealed. The new provision is more widely applicable than that which it replaces, and is drafted so as to operate in administration and receivership proceedings as well as in winding up. Also the court's order may now be made against "any person" who satisfies the criteria laid down in subs. (2). Subs. (2) has also been approximated as closely as possible to the provisions in s.312 relating to surrender of property to a trusteee in bankruptcy. In addition, subss. (3) and (4) together confer immunity upon the office holder, provided he has acted bona fide and without negligence, in respect of the wrongful seizure or disposal of property

which did not belong to the company at the relevant time. This section corresponds to ss.95(1), (2) and 98 of the 1985 Act.

Duty to co-operate with office-holder

235.—(1) This section applies as does section 234; and it also applies, in the case of a company in respect of which a winding-up order has been made by the court in England and Wales, as if references to the office-holder included the official receiver, whether or not he is the liquidator.

(2) Each of the persons mentioned in the next subsection shall—

(*a*) give to the office-holder such information concerning the company and its promotion, formation, business, dealings, affairs or property as the office-holder may at any time after the effective date reasonably require, and

(*b*) attend on the office-holder at such times as the latter may reasonably require.

(3) The persons referred to above are—

(*a*) those who are or have at any time been officers of the company,

(*b*) those who have taken part in the formation of the company at any time within one year before the effective date,

(*c*) those who are in the employment of the company, or have been in its employment (including employment under a contract for services) within that year, and are in the office-holder's opinion capable of giving information which he requires,

(*d*) those who are, or have within that year been, officers of, or in the employment (including employment under a contract for services) of, another company which is, or within that year was, an officer of the company in question, and

(*e*) in the case of a company being wound up by the court, any person who has acted as administrator, administrative receiver or liquidator of the company.

(4) For the purposes of subsections (2) and (3), "the effective date" is whichever is applicable of the following dates—

(*a*) the date on which the administration order was made,

(*b*) the date on which the administrative receiver was appointed or, if he was appointed in succession to another administrative receiver, the date on which the first of his predecessors was appointed,

(*c*) the date on which the provisional liquidator was appointed, and

(*d*) the date on which the company went into liquidation.

(5) If a person without reasonable excuse fails to comply with any obligation imposed by this section, he is liable to a fine and, for continued contravention, to a daily default fine.

DEFINITIONS
"administration order": s.8(2).
"administrative receiver": s.251.
"administrator": s.8(2).
"business": s.436.
"date company goes into liquidation": s.247(2).
"officer of the company": s.251; C.A. 1985, s.744.
"property": s.436.
"the effective date": subs. (4).
"the office holder": s.234(1).
"the official receiver": s.399(1).
"provisional liquidator": s.135.

GENERAL NOTE
The investigative powers conferred by this section are designed to assist a liquidator to carry out his task quickly and effectively. In particular, private examinations for the office holder conducted under this section will facilitate the investigation of the company's affairs

and dealings, the tracing of assets whose existence and whereabouts may be difficult to discover, and also the gaining of information about any transactions whereby the company's assets may have been disposed of in circumstances that may render them recoverable. This section corresponds to ss.95(1), (2) and 99 of the 1985 Act.

Subs. (1)

It is noteworthy that no reference is made to a supervisor of a voluntary arrangement in the list of persons who are included among those within the definition of "office-holder" for the purposes of this section, by virtue of s.234(1). Similarly, subs. (3)(*e*) omits to provide that the supervisor of a voluntary arrangement shall be one of the persons who are liable to be made to supply the liquidator with such information as he may reasonably require.

Subs. (5)

A fine

See Sched. 10 for the table of punishments which may be imposed for this offence.

Inquiry into company's dealings, etc.

236.—(1) This section applies as does section 234; and it also applies in the case of a company in respect of which a winding-up order has been made by the court in England and Wales as if references to the office-holder included the official receiver, whether or not he is the liquidator.

(2) The court may, on the application of the office-holder, summon to appear before it—

   (*a*) any officer of the company,

   (*b*) any person known or suspected to have in his possession any property of the company or supposed to be indebted to the company, or

   (*c*) any person whom the court thinks capable of giving information concerning the promotion, formation, business, dealings, affairs or property of the company.

(3) The court may require any such person as is mentioned in subsection (2)(*a*) to (*c*) to submit an affidavit to the court containing an account of his dealings with the company or to produce any books, papers or other records in his possession or under his control relating to the company or the matters mentioned in paragraph (*c*) of the subsection.

(4) The following applies in a case where—

   (*a*) a person without reasonable excuse fails to appear before the court when he is summoned to do so under this section, or

   (*b*) there are reasonable grounds for believing that a person has absconded, or is about to abscond, with a view to avoiding his appearance before the court under this section.

(5) The court may, for the purpose of bringing that person and anything in his possession before the court, cause a warrant to be issued to a constable or prescribed officer of the court—

   (*a*) for the arrest of that person, and

   (*b*) for the seizure of any books, papers, records, money or goods in that person's possession.

(6) The court may authorise a person arrested under such a warrant to be kept in custody, and anything seized under such a warrant to be held, in accordance with the rules, until that person is brought before the court under the warrant or until such other time as the court may order.

DEFINITIONS

"business": s.436.
"officer of the company": s.251; C.A. 1985, s.744.
"property": s.436.
"records": s.436.
"the court": s.251; C.A. 1985, s.744.
"the office holder": s.234(1).
"the official receiver": s.399(1).

GENERAL NOTE

This section, together with s.237, replaces the former provisions of s.561 of the Companies Act 1985, which is repealed. The drafting of the new provisions is considerably modified and clarified, and they are relocated among the provisions applying generally in company insolvency proceedings. The court's power to summon persons belonging to any of the categories mentioned in subs. (2) is thus exercisable in administration or receivership proceedings, as well as in liquidations. It is made clear that the power of summons is activated by an application made by the office holder, a matter which was not stated in s.561 of the Companies Act.

Private examinations before the court under this section will assist the office holder in his duties to recover and realise assets of the company for the benefit of creditors. The procedure will be especially helpful where the person summoned has failed to co-operate fully with the office holder in the manner required by s.235. This section corresponds to ss.95(1), (2) and 100(1), (2) and (6) of the 1985 Act.

Subs. (1)

In addition to the reference to s.234, whereby the expression "the office-holder" is declared to apply to an administrator, an administrative receiver, a liquidator or a provisional liquidator, this subsection also contains an express provision to the effect that, in the case of a compulsory winding up, references to the office-holder include the official receiver, whether or not he is the liquidator.

This complements the independent investigative role of the official receiver by enabling him to invoke the powers established by this section even though he may not be the liquidator of the company for the time being. However, the subsection confers these powers on the official receiver only in the case of a company which has gone into compulsory liquidation in England and Wales. It does not therefore apply in the case of other insolvency procedures, including a voluntary winding-up, nor does it apply where the company is being wound up by the court in Scotland.

Court's enforcement powers under s.236

237.—(1) If it appears to the court, on consideration of any evidence obtained under section 236 or this section, that any person has in his possession any property of the company, the court may, on the application of the office-holder, order that person to deliver the whole or any part of the property to the office-holder at such time, in such manner and on such terms as the court thinks fit.

(2) If it appears to the court, on consideration of any evidence so obtained, that any person is indebted to the company, the court may, on the application of the office-holder, order that person to pay to the office-holder, at such time and in such manner as the court may direct, the whole or any part of the amount due, whether in full discharge of the debt or otherwise, as the court thinks fit.

(3) The court may, if it thinks fit, order that any person who if within the jurisdiction of the court would be liable to be summoned to appear before it under section 236 or this section shall be examined in any part of the United Kingdom where he may for the time being be, or in a place outside the United Kingdom.

(4) Any person who appears or is brought before the court under section 236 or this section may be examined on oath, either orally or (except in Scotland) by interrogatories, concerning the company or the matters mentioned in section 236(2)(*c*).

DEFINITIONS

"property": s.436.
"the court": s.251; C.A. 1985, s.744.
"the office holder": ss.236(1), 234(1).

GENERAL NOTE

This section, which corresponds to subss. (3)–(5) and (7) of s.100 of the 1985 Act, confers a variety of powers upon the court which it may exercise, as appropriate, when acting in response to an application by the office-holder to summon before it any of the persons mentioned in s.236(2). The powers are widely drawn, and enable the court to make orders against other persons besides those who have been summoned under s.236 to appear and give evidence or to produce books, papers or other records. Thus, in the light of information gained by the investigative procedures established by s.236, the court may proceed under s.237 to enforce the delivery up of company property to the office holder by those persons found to be in possession of it, and likewise to order persons found to be indebted to the company to make full or partial payment to the office holder.

Adjustment of prior transactions (administration and liquidation)

Transactions at an undervalue (England and Wales)

238—(1) This section applies in the case of a company where—
  (a) an administration order is made in relation to the company, or
  (b) the company goes into liquidation;
and "the office-holder" means the administrator or the liquidator, as the case may be.

  (2) Where the company has at a relevant time (defined in section 240) entered into a transaction with any person at an undervalue, the office-holder may apply to the court for an order under this section.

  (3) Subject as follows, the court shall, on such an application, make such order as it thinks fit for restoring the position to what it would have been if the company had not entered into that transaction.

  (4) For the purposes of this section and section 241, a company enters into a transaction with a person at an undervalue if—
  (a) the company makes a gift to that person or otherwise enters into a transaction with that person on terms that provide for the company to receive no consideration, or
  (b) the company enters into a transaction with that person for a consideration the value of which, in money or money's worth, is significantly less than the value, in money or money's worth, of the consideration provided by the company.

  (5) The court shall not make an order under this section in respect of a transaction at an undervalue if it is satisfied—
  (a) that the company which entered into the transaction did so in good faith and for the purpose of carrying on its business, and
  (b) that at the time it did so there were reasonable grounds for believing that the transaction would benefit the company.

DEFINITIONS
"a relevant time": s.240.
"administration order": s.8(2).
"company goes into liquidation": s.247(2).
"the administrator": s.8(2).
"the court": s.251; C.A. 1985, s.744.
"the office holder": subs. (1).
"transaction": s.436.
"transaction at an undervalue": subs. (4).

TRANSITIONAL PROVISION
Sched. 11, para. 9.

APPLICATION
This section does not apply to Scotland (s.440(2)(a)).

GENERAL NOTE
This section, together with ss.239–243, was enacted in response to the carefully argued recommendations in Chap. 28 of the *Cork Report,* discussed in paras. 61–69 of the *White Paper.* The new provisions replace ss.614–616 of the Companies Act 1985 and s.44 of the Bankruptcy Act 1914, which are all repealed. S.172 of the Law of Property Act 1925, which

is also repealed, is replaced by s.423 of this Act. In addition to the improved clarity of the drafting of the new provisions to enable various kinds of transactions to be set aside, important changes are made in the law. The law relating to transactions at an undervalue and preferences in company insolvency is now self-contained within this Part of the Act, although the provisions are closely parallel to those applicable in bankruptcy, now to be found in Pt. IX of the Act as ss.339–342. The provisions of s.423 (*q.v.*) are applicable both to corporate and to individual insolvency.

Instead of the former terms, "fraudulent conveyance" and "fraudulent preference", with their open connotations of fraud and moral turpitude, the new provisions employ the more neutral terminology of "transactions at an undervalue" and "(voidable) preference". The two concepts are distinct, although both may well be found to apply to one and the same transaction. On the other hand, a transaction may in some circumstances be voidable as a transaction at an undervalue albeit it did not amount to a voidable preference. This section corresponds to ss.95(1)(*a*), (b) and 101(1) (part)–(3) of the 1985 Act.

Subs. (1)

Office holder

In contrast to the position under ss.230–237, the definition of the term for the purposes of ss.238–246 inclusive is cut down, so as to exclude an administrative receiver. This is further emphasised by the internal subheading standing before ss.238–246 as printed, which indicates that these provisions apply only to administration and liquidation. The remedy established in this section is therefore not available in cases of receivership. On the other hand, it is readily conceivable that in some situations an administrative receiver would find it advantageous to be able to invoke it, but in such cases it would appear that the only way in which to set about the process of recovering assets which have been disposed of at an undervalue, or by way of a preference, is for a company which is in receivership to be put into compulsory liquidation, or for an administration order to be obtained, so that a new office holder can be appointed with standing to apply to the court for an order under this section.

Subs. (2)

This has the effect of restricting the power to make an application under this section to the person who qualifies as "the office holder" in the instant case.

Subs. (3)

This indicates in a general way the court's wide discretionary powers upon an application under this section. Further, specific powers are conferred upon the court by s.241.

Subs. (4)

This supplies the statutory test for "a transaction at an undervalue" for the purposes of this section and s.239 together. However, subs. (5) deprives the court of any discretion to make an order under this section if the two conditions therein specified are met. These effectively require the court to be convinced that the undervalue transaction was a genuine business transaction carried out in good faith in the reasonable belief that it would benefit the company. Moreover, as required by subs. (2), one of the conditions contained in s.240(2) must be met in order that the time when the transaction was entered into shall count as a "relevant time" for the purposes of this section. In consequence, for a transaction to be voidable under this section it must take place at a time when the company is already insolvent, or when the company's circumstances are such that the very transaction itself has the effect of causing the company to become insolvent in the sense employed in s.123 of the Act.

Preferences (England and Wales)

239.—(1) This section applies as does section 238.

(2) Where the company has at a relevant time (defined in the next section) given a preference to any person, the office-holder may apply to the court for an order under this section.

(3) Subject as follows, the court shall, on such an application, make such order as it thinks fit for restoring the position to what it would have been if the company had not given that preference.

(4) For the purposes of this section and section 241, a company gives a preference to a person if—

    (*a*) that person is one of the company's creditors or a surety or guarantor for any of the company's debts or other liabilities, and

    (*b*) the company does anything or suffers anything to be done which (in either case) has the effect of putting that person into a position which, in the event of the company going into insolvent liquidation, will be better than the position he would have been in if that thing had not been done.

(5) The court shall not make an order under this section in respect of a preference given to any person unless the company which gave the preference was influenced in deciding to give it by a desire to produce in relation to that person the effect mentioned in subsection (4)(*b*).

(6) A company which has given a preference to a person connected with the company (otherwise than by reason only of being its employee) at the time the preference was given is presumed, unless the contrary is shown, to have been influenced in deciding to give it by such a desire as is mentioned in subsection (5).

(7) The fact that something has been done in pursuance of the order of a court does not, without more, prevent the doing or suffering of that thing from constituting the giving of a preference.

DEFINITIONS
    "company gives a preference": subs. (4).
    "person connected with the company": ss.249, 435.
    "the court": s.251; C.A. 1985, s.744.
    "the office holder": subs. (1), s.238(1).

TRANSITIONAL PROVISION
    Sched. 11, para. 9.

APPLICATION
    This section does not apply to Scotland (s.440(2)(*a*)).

GENERAL NOTE
    This section forms part of the group of provisions under which prior transactions entered into by a company may be adjusted or avoided upon application by the office holder (as defined in s.238(1)). A liquidator or administrator may therefore apply to the court under this section for an order under subs. (3) relating to any preference given to a person by the company at "a relevant time", as defined for this purpose by s.240. This section corresponds to ss.95(1)(*a*), (*b*) and 101(1) (part), (4)–(7) and (11) of the 1985 Act.

Subs. (4)
    This supplies the statutory test for the giving of a preference to any person by the company. The drafting implements the recommendation in paras. 1270–1276 of the *Cork Report* where it was argued that in the case of a voidable preference the burden of repayment should be borne by the party intended to be preferred. In the case where the party who has been preferred is the surety or guarantor of a debt owed to some other creditor, it is now possible to proceed directly against the surety or guarantor quite independently of any proceedings which may be taken against the creditor.

Subs. (5)
    This modifies the pre-existing law which required that, to be voidable, a payment should have been made with a dominant intention of preferring the creditor. What is henceforth required is that the intention to prefer should have "influenced" the company in deciding to give the preference. In accordance with the recommendations of the *Cork Report,* the task of a liquidator or administrator seeking to have a preference declared voidable is made easier in cases where the recipient of the preference is connected with the company. This is accomplished by two provisions within this section and s.240. First, a special presumption is introduced in subs. (6), whose effect is to shift the burden of proof to the receipient of the preference, who must effectively show that in giving it the company was *not* influenced by

the desire to prefer that person within the terms of subs. (4)(*b*); and secondly s.240(1)(*a*) prescribes the more extended period of two years prior to the commencement date which is to be applicable in cases where the recipient is a connected person, so that any transaction taking place within this period takes place at a "relevant time" for the purposes of this section. The meaning of "connected person" is a compound one, provided partly by s.249 and partly by s.435. The former provision indicates that "connected person" means a director or shadow director of the company or an associate of a person who is either of those things, or a person who is an associate of the company. The latter provision supplies an elaborately drafted definition of the pivotal term "associate". Thus the range of persons onto whom a burden of proof may be placed by the combined effects of subss. (5) and (6) is potentially very large. However, the statutory meaning of "connected person" is especially modified for the purposes of the present section by the words in parentheses in subs. (6), which preclude a person from being treated as a "connected person" for this purpose if the sole ground of his or her connection consists in the fact of being an employee of the company.

The majority opinion in the *Cork Report* (para. 1256) was in favour or a retention of the existing rule whereby a payment by a debtor in response to pressure from the creditor should not be treated as a voidable preference, and that a creditor who has taken active steps to obtain payment of his own debt ought in principle to be allowed to retain the fruits of his diligence. Subject to what has been said above regarding the altered burden of proof in cases of payments to connected persons, it would appear that this section has left it open to argument that a payment made by a company in response to pressure from its creditor, although amounting to a preference, is not rendered voidable under this section because the company was not influenced in deciding to give the preference by a *desire* to produce in relation to the creditor the effect mentioned in subs. (4)(*b*).

"Relevant time" under ss.238, 239

240.—(1) Subject to the next subsection, the time at which a company enters into a transaction at an undervalue or gives a preference is a relevant time if the transaction is entered into, or the preference given—

(*a*) in the case of a transaction at an undervalue or of a preference which is given to a person who is connected with the company (otherwise than by reason only of being its employee), at a time in the period of 2 years ending with the onset of insolvency (which expression is defined below),

(*b*) in the case of a preference which is not such a transaction and is not so given, at a time in the period of 6 months ending with the onset of insolvency, and

(*c*) in either case, at a time between the presentation of a petition for the making of an administration order in relation to the company and the making of such an order on that petition.

(2) Where a company enters into a transaction at an undervalue or gives a preference at a time mentioned in subsection (1)(*a*) or (*b*), that time is not a relevant time for the purposes of section 238 or 239 unless the company—

(*a*) is at that time unable to pay its debts within the meaning of section 123 in Chapter VI of Part IV, or

(*b*) becomes unable to pay its debts within the meaning of that section in consequence of the transaction or preference;

but the requirements of this subsection are presumed to be satisfied, unless the contrary is shown, in relation to any transaction at an undervalue which is entered into by a company with a person who is connected with the company.

(3) For the purposes of subsection (1), the onset of insolvency is—

(*a*) in a case where section 238 or 239 applies by reason of the making of an administration order or of a company going into liquidation immediately upon the discharge of an administration order, the date of the presentation of the petition on which the administration order was made, and

(*b*) in a case where the section applies by reason of a company going into liquidation at any other time, the date of the commencement of the winding up.

DEFINITIONS
"a relevant time": this section.
"administration order": s.8(2).
"commencement of winding up": ss.86, 129.
"company gives a preference": s.239(4).
"company goes into liquidation": s.247(2).
"company unable to pay its debts": s.123.
"person connected with the company": ss.249, 435.
"the onset of insolvency": subs. (3).
"transaction": s.436.
"transaction at an undervalue": s.238(4).

TRANSITIONAL PROVISION
Sched. 11, para. 9.

APPLICATION
This section does not apply to Scotland (s.440(2)(*a*)).

GENERAL NOTE
This section, which corresponds to subss. (8)–(11) of s.101 of the 1985 Act, establishes the meaning of the expression "relevant time" for the purposes of ss.238 and 239. This expression bears a variable meaning, according to the context in which it is used. Both s.238(2) and s.239(2) contain the requirement that a transaction must take place, or preference be given, at "a relevant time" in order that its validity may be called into question under either of those two sections. Thus, the present section has the effect of setting the outer boundaries of the period of time within which a particular act or transaction will take place at "a relevant time".

Subs. (1)(a)
This establishes the period of two years ending with the onset of insolvency (as defined in subs. (3)) as the period within which an act will take place at "a relevant time" whenever the party in whose favour a transaction at an undervalue is entered into, or a preference is given, by the company is a person who is connected with that company. The meaning of "connected person" is supplied by the combined provisions of ss.249 and 435 (*q.v.*) and, as was explained in the General Note to s.239(5), the recommendation of the *Cork Report,* duly adopted in these provisions of the Act, was that it should be made easier for a liquidator or administrator to obtain the avoidance of prior transactions operating in favour of persons connected with the company.

Subs. (1)(b)
This establishes the period of six months ending with the onset of insolvency (again, defined in subs. (3)), as the period within which an act will take place at "a relevant time" where the provisions of subs. (1)(*a*) do not apply.

Subs. (2)
This establishes a further precondition to any moment of time counting as a "relevant time" for the purposes of this section and those to which it is linked. It is necessary that it be established that, at the time when the company entered into the transaction, or gave the preference, in question the company was at that time unable to pay its debts (within the meaning of s.123) or, alternatively, that the company became unable to pay its debts (in the same, technical sense) in consequence of the transaction or preference itself. In normal cases, the burden of proving the company's inability to pay its debts will be cast upon the party seeking to avoid the transaction—namely the office holder. However, the proviso to this subsection reverses that burden of proof whenever the party in whose favour a transaction at an undervalue was entered into was a person connected with company (in the sense explained in relation to subs. (1)(*a*) *supra*). This reversal of the burden of proof in such cases is again in accordance with the recommendation of the *Cork Report,* as explained in the General Note to s.239.

Subs. (3)

This supplies the meaning of the expression "the onset of insolvency" for the purposes of subs. (1)

Orders under ss.238, 239

241.—(1) Without prejudice to the generality of sections 238(3) and 239(3), an order under either of those sections with respect to a transaction or preference entered into or given by a company may (subject to the next subsection)—

(*a*) require any property transferred as part of the transaction, or in connection with the giving of the preference, to be vested in the company,

(*b*) require any property to be so vested if it represents in any person's hands the application either of the proceeds of sale of property so transferred or of money so transferred,

(*c*) release or discharge (in whole or in part) any security given by the company,

(*d*) require any person to pay, in respect of benefits received by him from the company, such sums to the office-holder as the court may direct,

(*e*) provide for any surety or guarantor whose obligations to any person were released or discharged (in whole or in part) under the transaction, or by the giving of the preference, to be under such new or revived obligations to that person as the court thinks appropriate,

(*f*) provide for security to be provided for the discharge of any obligation imposed by or arising under the order, for such an obligation to be charged on any property and for the security or charge to have the same priority as a security or charge released or discharged (in whole or in part) under the transaction or by the giving of the preference, and

(*g*) provide for the extent to which any person whose property is vested by the order in the company, or on whom obligations are imposed by the order, is to be able to prove in the winding up of the company for debts or other liabilities which arose from, or were released or discharged (in whole or in part) under or by, the transaction or the giving of the preference.

(2) An order under section 238 or 239 may affect the property of, or impose any obligation on, any person whether or not he is the person with whom the company in question entered into the transaction or (as the case may be) the person to whom the preference was given; but such an order—

(*a*) shall not prejudice any interest in property which was acquired from a person other than the company and was acquired in good faith, for value and without notice of the relevant circumstances, or prejudice any interest deriving from such an interest, and

(*b*) shall not require a person who received a benefit from the transaction or preference in good faith, for value and without notice of the relevant circumstances to pay a sum to the office-holder, except where that person was a party to the transaction or the payment is to be in respect of a preference given to that person at a time when he was a creditor of the company.

(3) For the purposes of this section the relevant circumstances, in relation to a transaction or preference, are—

(*a*) the circumstances by virtue of which an order under section 238 or (as the case may be) 239 could be made in respect of the transaction or preference if the company were to go into liquidation, or an administration order were made in relation to the company, within a particular period after the transaction is entered into or the preference given, and

(b) if that period has expired, the fact that the company has gone into liquidation or that such an order has been made.

(4) The provisions of sections 238 to 241 apply without prejudice to the availability of any other remedy, even in relation to a transaction or preference which the company had no power to enter into or give.

DEFINITIONS

"administration order": s.8(2).

"company goes into liquidation": s.247(2).

"preference given by a company": s.239(4).

"property": s.436.

"security": s.248(b).

"the officer holder": s.238(1).

"the relevant circumstances": subs. (3).

"transaction": ss.238(4), 436.

TRANSITIONAL PROVISION

Sched. 11, para. 9.

APPLICATION

This section does not apply to Scotland (s.440(2)(a)).

GENERAL NOTE

This section indicates the various types of order which may be made by a court in the exercise of its powers under s.238 or s.239. The opening words of subs. (1) are designed to ensure that the court's powers with regard to the type of order it may make are not restricted to those described in this section. The court could therefore devise some other form of order which in the court's estimation would be more apt to attain the purposes at which ss.238(3) and 239(3) are aimed.

This section corresponds to ss.95(1) and 102 of the 1985 Act.

Gratuitous alienations (Scotland)

242.—(1) Where this subsection applies and—

(a) the winding up of a company has commenced, an alienation by the company is challengeable by—

(i) any creditor who is a creditor by virtue of a debt incurred on or before the date of such commencement, or

(ii) the liquidator;

(b) an administration order is in force in relation to a company, an alienation by the company is challengeable by the administrator.

(2) Subsection (1) applies where—

(a) by the alienation, whether before or after 1st April 1986 (the coming into force of section 75 of the Bankruptcy (Scotland) Act 1985), any part of the company's property is transferred or any claim or right of the company is discharged or renounced, and

(b) the alienation takes place on a relevant day.

(3) For the purposes of subsection (2)(b), the day on which an alienation takes place is the day on which it becomes completely effectual; and in that subsection "relevant day" means, if the alienation has the effect of favouring—

(a) a person who is an associate (within the meaning of the Bankruptcy (Scotland) Act 1985) of the company, a day not earlier than 5 years before the date on which—

(i) the winding up of the company commences, or

(ii) as the case may be, the administration order is made; or

(b) any other person, a day not earlier than 2 years before that date.

(4) On a challenge being brought under subsection (1), the court shall grant decree of reduction or for such restoration of property to the company's assets or other redress as may be appropriate; but the court shall not grant such a decree if the person seeking to uphold the alienation establishes—

(*a*) that immediately, or at any other time, after the alienation the company's assets were greater than its liabilities, or

(*b*) that the alienation was made for adequate consideration, or

(*c*) that the alienation—

(i) was a birthday, Christmas or other conventional gift, or

(ii) was a gift made, for a charitable purpose, to a person who is not an associate of the company,

which, having regard to all the circumstances, it was reasonable for the company to make:

Provided that this subsection is without prejudice to any right or interest acquired in good faith and for value from or through the transferee in the alienation.

(5) In subsection (4) above, "charitable purpose" means any charitable, benevolent or philanthropic purpose, whether or not it is charitable within the meaning of any rule of law.

(6) For the purposes of the foregoing provisions of this section, an alienation in implementation of a prior obligation is deemed to be one for which there was no consideration or no adequate consideration to the extent that the prior obligation was undertaken for no consideration or no adequate consideration.

(7) A liquidator and an administrator have the same right as a creditor has under any rule of law to challenge an alienation of a company made for no consideration or no adequate consideration.

(8) This section applies to Scotland only.

DEFINITIONS
"administration order": s.8(2).
"associate": Bankruptcy (Scotland) Act 1985, s.74.
"charitable purpose": subs. (5).
"commencement of winding up": ss.86, 129.
"property": s.436.
"relevant day": subs. (3).
"the administrator": s.8(2).

TRANSITIONAL PROVISION
Sched. 11, para. 9.

APPLICATION
This section applies to Scotland only (subs. (8)).

GENERAL NOTE
This section corresponds to s.615A of the Companies Act, as inserted by para. 20 of Sched. 7 to the Bankruptcy (Scotland) Act 1985 and now repealed. It provides for the reduction of gratuitous alienations in Scotland, and is the counterpart of s.238, under which transactions at an undervalue may be avoided in England and Wales. It is notable that the respective periods within which such transactions may be avoided are considerably longer in cases falling under the law of Scotland. Subs. (3) prescribes a period extending back five years from the date of commencement of winding up, or the making of the administration order, (as the case may be) in the case of any transaction favouring a person who is an associate of the company (as defined in s.74 of the Bankruptcy (Scotland) Act 1985), while the relevant period in the case of alienations favouring persons who are not associates of the company is two years before the commencement date. This contrasts with the period of two years specified in s.240(1) (*q.v.*) in relation to transactions at an undervalue entered into with any person, whether or not that person is connected with the company (within the combined meaning derived from ss.249 and 435).

Unfair preferences (Scotland)

243.—(1) Subject to subsection (2) below, subsection (4) below applies to a transaction entered into by a company, whether before or after 1st April 1986, which has the effect of creating a preference in favour of a creditor to the prejudice of the general body of creditors, being a preference created not earlier than 6 months before the commencement of the winding up of the company or the making of an administration order in relation to the company.

(2) Subsection (4) below does not apply to any of the following transactions—

(a) a transaction in the ordinary course of trade or business;

(b) a payment in cash for a debt which when it was paid had become payable, unless the transaction was collusive with the purpose of prejudicing the general body of creditors;

(c) a transaction whereby the parties to it undertake reciprocal obligations (whether the performance by the parties of their respective obligations occurs at the same time or at different times) unless the transaction was collusive as aforesaid;

(d) the granting of a mandate by a company authorising an arrestee to pay over the arrested funds or part thereof to the arrester where—

(i) there has been a decree for payment or a warrant for summary diligence, and

(ii) the decree or warrant has been preceded by an arrestment on the dependence of the action or followed by an arrestment in execution.

(3) For the purposes of subsection (1) above, the day on which a preference was created is the day on which the preference became completely effectual.

(4) A transaction to which this subsection applies is challengeable by—

(a) in the case of a winding up—

(i) any creditor who is a creditor by virtue of a debt incurred on or before the date of commencement of the winding up, or

(ii) the liquidator; and

(b) in the case of an administration order, the administrator.

(5) On a challenge being brought under subsection (4) above, the court, if satisfied that the transaction challenged is a transaction to which this section applies, shall grant decree of reduction or for such restoration of property to the company's assets or other redress as may be appropriate;

Provided that this subsection is without prejudice to any right or interest acquired in good faith and for value from or through the creditor in whose favour the preference was created.

(6) A liquidator and an administrator have the same right as a creditor has under any rule of law to challenge a preference created by a debtor.

(7) This section applies to Scotland only.

DEFINITIONS
"administration order": s.8(2).
"commencement of winding up": ss.86, 129.
"day on which a preference was created": subs. (3).
"property": s.436.
"the administrator": s.8(2).

TRANSITIONAL PROVISION
Sched. 11, para. 9.

APPLICATION
This section applies to Scotland only (subs. (7)).

GENERAL NOTE

This section corresponds to s.615B of the Companies Act as inserted by para. 20 of Sched. 7 to the Bankruptcy (Scotland) Act 1985 and now repealed. It provides for the reduction of unfair preferences, and for other appropriate redress including the restoration of property to the company's assets. The section applies only to Scotland, and is the counterpart under the law of that jurisdiction to the provision in s.239 for the avoidance of preferences under the law of England and Wales. It is notable that under the law of Scotland the period within which a preference is reducible is in all cases the six months prior to the commencement of winding up or the making of an administration order: any preference created within that period is reducible if it satisfies the other requirements of this section, irrespective of whether the person favoured thereby is or is not an associate of the company. By contrast, under s.240(1)(a) a preference given by a company to a person who is connected with it is voidable at English law if the onset of insolvency occurs at any time up to two years thereafter.

Another point of contrast between the English and Scottish provisions concerning preferences is that, under subs. (4)(a) of this section, an unfair preference is in a Scottish winding up challengeable by either the liquidator or by any creditor coming within the terms of sub-para. (i), whereas in an English winding up only the liquidator, as office holder, is entitled to make application under s.239(2).

Extortionate credit transactions

244.—(1) This section applies as does section 238, and where the company is, or has been, a party to a transaction for, or involving, the provision of credit to the company.

(2) The court may, on the application of the office-holder, make an order with respect to the transaction if the transaction is or was extortionate and was entered into in the period of 3 years ending with the day on which the administration order was made or (as the case may be) the company went into liquidation.

(3) For the purposes of this section a transaction is extortionate if, having regard to the risk accepted by the person providing the credit—

(a) the terms of it are or were such as to require grossly exorbitant payments to be made (whether unconditionally or in certain contingencies) in respect of the provision of the credit, or

(b) it otherwise grossly contravened ordinary principles of fair dealing; and it shall be presumed, unless the contrary is proved, that a transaction with respect to which an application is made under this section is or, as the case may be, was extortionate.

(4) An order under this section with respect to any transaction may contain such one or more of the following as the court thinks fit, that is to say—

(a) provision setting aside the whole or part of any obligation created by the transaction,

(b) provision otherwise varying the terms of the transaction or varying the terms on which any security for the purposes of the transaction is held,

(c) provision requiring any person who is or was a party to the transaction to pay to the office-holder any sums paid to that person, by virtue of the transaction, by the company,

(d) provision requiring any person to surrender to the office-holder any property held by him as security for the purposes of the transaction,

(e) provision directing accounts to be taken between any persons.

(5) The powers conferred by this section are exercisable in relation to any transaction concurrently with any powers exercisable in relation to that transaction as a transaction at an undervalue or under section 242 (gratuitous alienations in Scotland).

DEFINITIONS

"administration order": s.8(2).
"company goes into liquidation": s.247(2).

"extortionate transaction": subs. (3).
"security": s.248(*b*).
"the office holder": s.238(1).
"transaction": s.436.
"transaction at an undervalue": s.238(4).

TRANSITIONAL PROVISION
Sched. 11, para. 9.

GENERAL NOTE
The purpose of this section, which is parallel to s.343 applicable in cases of individual insolvency, is to provide a procedure whereby a liquidator or administrator may apply to the court to reopen a credit bargain which has been entered into by the company as debtor on terms which are extortionate. The overall scheme of the section, and in particular the definition of "extortionate transaction" supplied in subs. (3), is modelled on the provisions in ss.137–139 inclusive of the Consumer Credit Act 1974, which allow the reopening of extortionate credit bargains in cases falling within the ambit of that Act. The present section, which pre-supposes that the company is either in liquidation or is subject to an administration order, permits the reopening of any kind of transaction involving the provision of credit to the company. The court's powers under subs. (4) are exercisable upon a finding that the transaction was extortionate within the meaning of subs. (3). This section corresponds to ss.95(1)(*a*), (*b*) together with 103 of the 1985 Act.

Subs. (3)

It shall be presumed, unless the contrary is proved . . .
These words give rise to a rebuttable presumption that the transaction in question was extortionate. They therefore have the effect of imposing a burden of proof upon the party who occupies the role of creditor in the transaction to which the company was a party. That party must prove to the Court that the transaction was *not* extortionate within the meaning of this subsection. Although this involves the proving of a negative, it accords with the precedent set in s.171(7) of the Consumer Credit Act 1974. The latter provision also furnishes a precedent for the additional feature in the drafting of the present subsection whereby, in order to avail himself of the presumption that a bargain is extortionate, the party seeking to have the transaction re-opened is not even required to make out a prima facie case that it is or was of dubious commercial fairness. All that is required is that the office holder make application under subs. (2) in respect of a credit transaction entered by the company as debtor within three years prior to the commencement of the insolvency proceedings. Thereupon, the transaction must be presumed by the Court to be extortionate unless the contrary is proved by the creditor.

Avoidance of certain floating charges

245.—(1) This section applies as does section 238, but applies to Scotland as well as to England and Wales.

(2) Subject as follows, a floating charge on the company's undertaking or property created at a relevant time is invalid except to the extent of the aggregate of—

(*a*) the value of so much of the consideration for the creation of the charge as consists of money paid, or goods or services supplied, to the company at the same time as, or after, the creation of the charge,

(*b*) the value of so much of that consideration as consists of the discharge or reduction, at the same time as, or after, the creation of the charge, of any debt of the company, and

(*c*) the amount of such interest (if any) as is payable on the amount falling within paragraph (*a*) or (*b*) in pursuance of any agreement under which the money was so paid, the goods or services were so supplied or the debt was so discharged or reduced.

(3) Subject to the next subsection, the time at which a floating charge is created by a company is a relevant time for the purposes of this section if the charge is created—

(*a*) in the case of a charge which is created in favour of a person who is connected with the company, at a time in the period of 2 years ending with the onset of insolvency,

(*b*) in the case of a charge which is created in favour of any other person, at a time in the period of 12 months ending with the onset of insolvency, or

(*c*) in either case, at a time between the presentation of a petition for the making of an administration order in relation to the company and the making of such an order on that petition.

(4) Where a company creates a floating charge at a time mentioned in subsection (3)(*b*) and the person in favour of whom the charge is created is not connected with the company, that time is not a relevant time for the purposes of this section unless the company—

(*a*) is at that time unable to pay its debts within the meaning of section 123 in Chapter VI of Part IV, or

(*b*) becomes unable to pay its debts within the meaning of that section in consequence of the transaction under which the charge is created.

(5) For the purposes of subsection (3), the onset of insolvency is—

(*a*) in a case where this section applies by reason of the making of an administration order, the date of the presentation of the petition on which the order was made, and

(*b*) in a case where this section applies by reason of a company going into liquidation, the date of the commencement of the winding up.

(6) For the purposes of subsection (2)(*a*) the value of any goods or services supplied by way of consideration for a floating charge is the amount in money which at the time they were supplied could reasonably have been expected to be obtained for supplying the goods or services in the ordinary course of business and on the same terms (apart from the consideration) as those on which they were supplied to the company.

DEFINITIONS
"a relevant time": subs. (3).
"administration order": s.8(2).
"commencement of winding up": ss.86, 129.
"company goes into liquidation": s.247(2).
"company unable to pay its debts": s.123.
"floating charge": s.251; C.A. 1985, s.462.
"person connected with the company": ss.249, 435.
"property": s.436.
"the onset of insolvency": subs. (5).
"value of goods or services provided by way of consideration for a floating charge": subs. (6).

TRANSITIONAL PROVISION
Sched. 11, para. 9.

GENERAL NOTE
This section reforms and replaces s.617 of the Companies Act 1985, which is repealed. Reform was recommended in paras. 1551–1556 of the *Cork Report*. The new provisions strengthen the rules under which a floating charge created within twelve months prior to the commencement of the insolvency proceedings, (or, in the case of such a charge created in favour of a connected person, within two years of that date) is rendered invalid by the fact of the company's going into liquidation or becoming the subject of an administration order. Such invalidity is effective except to the extent of money paid or goods supplied to the company at the time when the charge is created or subsequently. By subs. (4) it is made a precondition to the operation of the invalidating rule that the company was either insolvent at the time of the creation of the floating charge or was rendered insolvent in consequence of the very transaction under which the floating charge was created. However, in the case where the person in whose favour the charge was created was connected with the company (as defined in s.249) together with s.435 the precondition as to the company's state of

insolvency is not applicable, and hence all such charges are rendered invalid if the company goes into liquidation or an administration order procedure within two years of the date of their creation. This is particularly aimed at preventing those who are directors or shadow directors of the company, and other persons closely involved with its management, from conferring upon themselves an enhanced priority over the unsecured creditors by means of a floating charge security in return for any finance which they may provide to the company. The invalidation of a floating charge under this section does not affect the existence of the actual debt which was previously secured thereby: the debt remains, but becomes an unsecured debt in consequence of the application of this section. This section corresponds to ss.95(1)(*a*), (*b*) together with 104 of the 1985 Act.

Subs. (2)(a)

Money paid, or goods or services supplied
These words replace the more restrictive phrase "any cash paid" which formerly were contained in s.617 of the Companies Act 1985. Although these words were held to be applicable to a case where payment was made by cheque (*Re Matthew Ellis Ltd.* [1933] Ch. 458), there was doubt as to their applicability in a case where goods or services are supplied against the giving of a floating charge security.

Subs. (2)(b)
This is intended to provide for cases such as where a company grants a floating charge in favour of a bank to secure further advances. Payments, subsequently made by the bank to creditors of the company in whose favour cheques have been drawn, will qualify for exemption from the consequences of the invalidation of the floating charge. This confirms the case-law ruling based on the previously applicable statutory provision, as applied in *Re Yeovil Glove Co. Ltd.* [1965] Ch. 148.

Unenforceability of liens on books, etc.

246.—(1) This section applies in the case of a company where—
  (*a*) an administration order is màde in relation to the company, or
  (*b*) the company goes into liquidation, or
  (*c*) a provisional liquidator is appointed;
and "the office-holder" means the administrator, the liquidator or the provisional liquidator, as the case may be.

(2) Subject as follows, a lien or other right to retain possession of any of the books, papers or other records of the company is unenforceable to the extent that its enforcement would deny possession of any books, papers or other records to the office-holder.

(3) This does not apply to a lien on documents which give a title to property and are held as such.

DEFINITIONS
  "administration order": s.8(2).
  "company goes into liquidation": s.247(2).
  "property": s.436.
  "provisional liquidator": s.135.
  "records": s.436.
  "the office holder": subs. (1).

APPLICATION
This section does not apply to Scotland (s.440(2)(*a*)).

GENERAL NOTE
This section gives the office holder an overriding right to gain possession of any of the company's books, papers or records which may be subject to a lien or other right of retention existing in favour of some other party. This is subject to the exception in favour of the holder of a lien on documents which give a title to property and which are held as such. The provision establishes a parallel provision for company insolvency to that applicable in bankruptcy by virtue of s.349. Provision will be made in the rules for the provisions of s.38(4) of the Bankruptcy (Scotland) Act 1985 to apply to winding up in Scotland, with the consequence that a consistent set of provisions will in fact apply in England and Wales and

in Scotland with regard to liens in the event of insolvency. This section corresponds to ss.95(1)(*a*), (*b*), and (2), together with 105 of the 1985 Act.

PART VII

INTERPRETATION FOR FIRST GROUP OF PARTS

"Insolvency" and "go into liquidation"

247.—(1) In this Group of Parts, except in so far as the context otherwise requires, "insolvency", in relation to a company, includes the approval of a voluntary arrangement under Part I, the making of an administration order or the appointment of an administrative receiver.

(2) For the purposes of any provision in this Group of Parts, a company goes into liquidation if it passes a resolution for voluntary winding up or an order for its winding up is made by the court at a time when it has not already gone into liquidation by passing such a resolution.

DEFINITIONS
"administration order": s.8.
"administrative receiver": s.251.
"voluntary winding up": s.84(1), 90.

GENERAL NOTE
Subs. (2) defines the time at which a company "goes into liquidation" as the moment when it passes a resolution for voluntary winding up, if it has done so. This is not affected by the fact that, at a later stage, the court may have made an order for winding up under s.124(5). The company goes into liquidation at the date of the winding up order where there has been no previous resolution for voluntary winding up. (Compare the definition of "commencement of winding-up" in ss.86, 129). See generally Note to s.251.

"Secured creditor", etc.

248. In this Group of Parts, except in so far as the context otherwise requires—
    (*a*) "secured creditor", in relation to a company, means a creditor of the company who holds in respect of his debt a security over property of the company, and "unsecured creditor" is to be read accordingly; and
    (*b*) "security" means—
        (i) in relation to England and Wales, any mortgage, charge, lien or other security, and
        (ii) in relation to Scotland, any security (whether heritable or moveable), any floating charge and any right of lien or preference and any right of retention (other than a right of compensation or set off).

GENERAL NOTE
See Note to s.251.

"Connected" with a company

249. For the purposes of any provision in this Group of Parts, a person is connected with a company if—
    (*a*) he is a director or shadow director of the company or an associate of such a director or shadow director, or
    (*b*) he is an associate of the company;
and "associate" has the meaning given by section 435 in Part XVIII of this Act.

DEFINITION
"director", "shadow director": s.741, C.A. 1985, s.251.

GENERAL NOTE
See Note to s.251.

"Member" of a company

250. For the purposes of any provision in this Group of Parts, a person who is not a member of a company but to whom shares in the company have been transferred, or transmitted by operation of law, is to be regarded as a member of the company, and references to a member or members are to be read accordingly.

GENERAL NOTE
This section gives an extended meaning to "member" of a company. For the purposes of the First Group of Parts, transferees and persons taking by operation of law are members although their names may not have been entered on the Register of Members. See Note to s.251.

Expressions used generally

251. In this Group of Parts, except in so far as the context otherwise requires—
"administrative receiver" means—
(*a*) an administrative receiver as defined by section 29(2) in Chapter I of Part III, or
(*b*) a receiver appointed under section 51 in Chapter II of that Part in a case where the whole (or substantially the whole) of the company's property is attached by the floating charge;
"business day" means any day other than a Saturday, a Sunday, Christmas Day, Good Friday or a day which is a bank holiday in any part of Great Britain;
"chattel leasing agreement" means an agreement for the bailment or, in Scotland, the hiring of goods which is capable of subsisting for more than 3 months;
"contributory" has the meaning given by section 79;
"director" includes any person occupying the position of director, by whatever name called;
"floating charge" means a charge which, as created, was a floating charge and includes a floating charge within section 462 of the Companies Act (Scottish floating charges);
"office copy", in relation to Scotland, means a copy certified by the clerk of court;
"the official rate", in relation to interest, means the rate payable under section 189(4);
"prescribed" means prescribed by the rules;
"receiver", in the expression "receiver or manager", does not include a receiver appointed under section 51 in Chapter II of Part III;
"retention of title agreement" means an agreement for the sale of goods to a company, being an agreement—
(*a*) which does not constitute a charge on the goods, but
(*b*) under which, if the seller is not paid and the company is wound up, the seller will have priority over all other creditors of the company as respects the goods or any property representing the goods;
"the rules" means rules under section 411 in Part XV; and
"shadow director", in relation to a company, means a person in accordance with whose directions or instructions the directors of the company are accustomed to act (but so that a person is

not deemed a shadow director by reason only that the directors act on advice given by him in a professional capacity);

and any expression for whose interpretation provision is made by Part XXVI of the Companies Act, other than an expression defined above in this section, is to be construed in accordance with that provision.

GENERAL NOTE

Ss.247–251 define the meaning of terms and expressions for the purposes of the First Group of Parts. Ss.247, 248 and 251 apply "except in so far as the context otherwise provides". In relation to Chapter II (Receivers (Scotland)) further definitions are contained in s.70. Construction of terms in the First Group of Parts may also be affected by ss.435 (associate) and 436 (which applies to expressions used generally in the Act). The scope of s.251 as a definition provision is enlarged by the incorporation into it of most of the definitions contained in Pt. XXVI, C.A. 1985.

Other definition sections which do not however relate to the First Group of Parts are ss.381–385 (Second Group of Parts: Individual Insolvency, Bankruptcy).

THE SECOND GROUP OF PARTS

INSOLVENCY OF INDIVIDUALS; BANKRUPTCY

GENERAL NOTE

None of the provisions of this group of Parts apply in relation to Scotland: s.440(2)(*d*). For individual insolvency in Scotland see the Bankruptcy (Scotland) Act 1985.

TRANSITIONAL PROVISIONS

Sched. 11, paras. 10–19.

PART VIII

INDIVIDUAL VOLUNTARY ARRANGEMENTS

Moratorium for insolvent debtor

Interim order of court

252.—(1) In the circumstances specified below, the court may in the case of a debtor (being an individual) make an interim order under this section.

(2) An interim order has the effect that, during the period for which it is in force—

(*a*) no bankruptcy petition relating to the debtor may be presented or proceeded with, and

(*b*) no other proceedings, and no execution or other legal process, may be commenced or continued against the debtor or his property except with the leave of the court.

DEFINITIONS

"bankruptcy petition": s.381(3).
"property": s.436.
"the debtor": s.385(1).

GENERAL NOTE

This section, which is derived from s.112(1) and (3) of the 1985 Act, makes provision for an interim order to be made where an individual intends to make a voluntary arrangement with his creditors. The purpose of the interim order is to allow time for the formulation of proposals, and hence the main effects of the order, as expressed in subs. (2), are that during the period for which the order is in force no bankruptcy petition relating to the debtor may be presented or proceeded with, and no other proceedings or execution or other legal process may be commenced or continued against the debtor's person or property except with the leave of the court. The moratorium thus imposed is of very considerable significance, and it has been necessary to provide safeguards against the possible misuse of the facility for making an application for an interim order as a means of delaying creditors' pursuit of their legitimate remedies, including bankruptcy proceedings. The court is therefore clothed by s.255(2) with discretionary powers as to the granting of an interim order in response to an application, while s.255(1) establishes several preconditions to the court's being at liberty to exercise the discretion in a positive way through the making of the order sought. Under s.255(1) the court cannot make an interim order unless satisfied as to the debtor's *bona fides* in making the application; that he has not given previous indication of a propensity to utilise the procedure as a delaying tactic through the making of a similar application within the previous twelve months; and that independent professional endorsement of the application is evidenced by the fact that a duly qualified insolvency practitioner has signified his willingness to act in relation to the debtor's proposal.

Application for interim order

253.—(1) Application to the court for an interim order may be made where the debtor intends to make a proposal to his creditors for a composition in satisfaction of his debts or a scheme of arrangement of his affairs (from here on referred to, in either case, as a "voluntary arrangement").

(2) The proposal must provide for some person ("the nominee") to act in relation to the voluntary arrangement either as trustee or otherwise for the purpose of supervising its implementation.

(3) Subject as follows, the application may be made—

(a) if the debtor is an undischarged bankrupt, by the debtor, the trustee of his estate, or the official receiver, and

(b) in any other case, by the debtor.

(4) An application shall not be made under subsection (3)(a) unless the debtor has given notice of his proposal (that is, the proposal to his creditors for a voluntary arrangement) to the official receiver and, if there is one, the trustee of his estate.

(5) An application shall not be made while a bankruptcy petition presented by the debtor is pending, if the court has, under section 273 below, appointed an insolvency practitioner to inquire into the debtor's affairs and report.

DEFINITIONS

"bankrupt": s.381(1).
"bankruptcy petition": s.381(3).
"estate": ss.283, 385(1).
"interim order": s.252.
"property": s.436.
"proposal for a composition or scheme of arrangement": subss. (1), (2).
"the court": ss.373, 385(1).
"the debtor": s.385(1).
"the nominee": subs. (2).
"the official receiver": s.399(1).
"voluntary arrangement": subs. (1).

GENERAL NOTE

This section is derived from s.110 of the 1985 Act, together with subss. (1)–(3), inclusive of s.111 of that Act. Subss. (1) and (2) indicate the scope of application of the provisions contained in Pt. VIII, concerning voluntary arrangements between a debtor and his creditors. The meanings borne by the terms "proposals" and "nominee" within this Chapter are also explained. The new procedure for voluntary arrangements, for which this Part makes provision, is additional to that for which provision is made by the Deeds of Arrangement Act 1914. Some sections of that Act are repealed by Pt. III of Sched. 10 to the 1985 Act, but most parts have been left unrepealed, contrary to the recommendations of the *Cork Report* (para. 366), Chaps. 5–7 of which contain extensive proposals for a new range of procedures and remedies as alternatives to bankruptcy or winding up. The Government consistently gave utterance to their belief that the Deeds of Arrangement Act, which has virtually ceased to be used in recent years, could undergo a revival in use as a consequence of the other changes in personal insolvency law contained in the Act (*cf.* H.C. Standing Committee E, June 13, 1985, col. 339).

The new procedure for voluntary arrangements replaces the two types of procedure formerly available under the now-repealed provisions of ss.16 and 21 of the Bankruptcy Act 1914. The new voluntary arrangement procedure is available to any debtor, whether or not he is a bankrupt, provided that he can satisfy the criteria contained in s.255(1). Where the debtor is an undischarged bankrupt subs. (3)(*a*) authorises the making of an application for an interim order, pending consideration of the proposal, to be made by the bankrupt himself or by the trustee of his estate or by the official receiver. To ensure that proper notice is given to those responsible for the administration of a bankrupt's estate, subs. (4) prohibits the making of an application for an interim order until notice thereof has been given to the Official Receiver and to the trustee in bankruptcy, if any. The latter officials are then able to report to the court any relevant facts or circumstances which should be taken into consideration in deciding whether to approve the debtor's application.

Subs. (5)

This ensures a proper interaction between the provisions concerned with the making of an application under this Part with a view to concluding a voluntary arrangement, and those governing the determination of a bankruptcy petition already presented by the debtor himself under s.272. Under the circumstances specified in s.27(1), the court at the hearing of a debtor's petition must postpone a final determination until it has obtained a report based on an inquiry into the debtor's affairs, including investigation as to whether the debtor is willing to make a proposal for a composition or scheme under Part VIII. Where a person has been appointed under s.273(2) to inquire into the debtor's affairs and to report, the court may make an interim order under s.252 by virtue of the authorisation conferred by s.274(3)(*a*). Therefore, the fact that an application for an interim order under the present section cannot be made by a debtor whose own bankruptcy petition is for the time being pending before the court does not prevent the making of such an interim order by the court itself, acting upon its own initiative in the exercise of the power conferred by ss.252 and 274(3).

Effect of application

254.—(1) At any time when an application under section 253 for an interim order is pending, the court may stay any action, execution or other legal process against the property or person of the debtor.

(2) Any court in which proceedings are pending against an individual may, on proof that an application under that section has been made in respect of that individual, either stay the proceedings or allow them to continue on such terms as it thinks fit.

DEFINITIONS
    "bankruptcy petition": s.381(3).
    "interim order": s.252.
    "property": s.436.
    "the court": ss.373, 385(1).
    "the debtor": s.385(1).

GENERAL NOTE
This section corresponds to subss. (4) and (5) of s.111 of the 1985 Act.

Subs. (1)

This introduces a discretionary power for the court to effect a moratorium with respect to legal proceedings and enforcement processes in favour of a debtor on whose behalf an application under this section is pending.

Subs. (2)

This is a complementary power to that contained in subs. (4), and enables the court before which proceedings are pending against a debtor to adopt whatever course of action it thinks fit, pending the conclusion of the procedure for effecting a voluntary arrangement.

Thus, regardless of whether a stay of action or other process is imposed by the court to which application has been made for an interim order, any other court in which proceedings are pending against the debtor may take an independent initiative under this subsection with regard to the matters over which it is exercising jurisdiction.

Cases in which interim order can be made

255.—(1) The court shall not make an interim order on an application under section 253 unless it is satisfied—

(*a*) that the debtor intends to make such a proposal as is mentioned in that section;

(*b*) that on the day of the making of the application the debtor was an undischarged bankrupt or was able to petition for his own bankruptcy;

(*c*) that no previous application has been made by the debtor for an interim order in the period of 12 months ending with that day; and

(*d*) that the nominee under the debtor's proposal to his creditors is a person who is for the time being qualified to act as an insolvency practitioner in relation to the debtor, and is willing to act in relation to the proposal.

(2) The court may make an order if it thinks that it would be appropriate to do so for the purpose of facilitating the consideration and implementation of the debtor's proposal.

(3) Where the debtor is an undischarged bankrupt, the interim order may contain provision as to the conduct of the bankruptcy, and the administration of the bankrupt's estate, during the period for which the order is in force.

(4) Subject as follows, the provision contained in an interim order by virtue of subsection (3) may include provision staying proceedings in the bankruptcy or modifying any provision in this Group of Parts, and any provision of the rules in their application to the debtor's bankruptcy.

(5) An interim order shall not, in relation to a bankrupt, make provision relaxing or removing any of the requirements of provisions in this Group of Parts, or of the rules, unless the court is satisfied that that provision is unlikely to result in any significant diminution in, or in the value of, the debtor's estate for the purposes of the bankruptcy.

(6) Subject to the following provisions of this Part, an interim order made on an application under section 253 ceases to have effect at the end of the period of 14 days beginning with the day after the making of the order.

DEFINITIONS
    "bankrupt": s.381(1).
    "bankruptcy petition": s.381(3).
    "estate": s.385(1).
    "interim order": s.252.
    "person qualified to act as an insolvency practitioner": s.390.
    "property": s.436.
    "proposal": s.253(1), (2).
    "the court": ss.373, 385(1).
    "the debtor": s.385(1).
    "the nominee": s.253(2).
    "the rules": ss.384, 412.
    "to act as an insolvency practitioner in relation to an individual": s.388(2), (3).

GENERAL NOTE
    This section comprises the provisions formerly contained in subss. (1), (2), and (4)–(7) inclusive, of s.112 of the 1985 Act.

Subs. (1)(b)

This requirement in relation to a debtor's eligibility to apply for an interim order has the effect of restricting the availability of this form of voluntary arrangement to those cases where the debtor is already either an undischarged bankrupt or in a state of insolvency. S.272(1) provides that a debtor's petition may be presented to the court only on the ground that the debtor is unable to pay his debts. Therefore if it can be shown that a debtor is able to pay his debts which are currently due, he will be unable to obtain an interim order under this section, and hence will be deprived of the possibility of thereby postponing the need to meet his obligations.

Subss. (4) and (5)

These provisions further ensure that the staying of bankruptcy proceedings in appropriate cases during the currency of an interim order does not operate at the expense of the preservation of the bankrupt's estate for the benefit of his creditors collectively. The court's power to include a staying provision in its interim order is a discretionary one, and the discretion is controlled by the terms of subs. (5) which have regard to the need to ensure that the creditor's ultimate expectations under the bankruptcy administration are not significantly jeopardised.

Subs. (6)

The period of 14 days may be extended by the court on the application of the nominee, pursuant to s.256(4).

Nominee's report on debtor's proposal

256.—(1) Where an interim order has been made on an application under section 253, the nominee shall, before the order ceases to have effect, submit a report to the court stating—

(*a*) whether, in his opinion, a meeting of the debtor's creditors should be summoned to consider the debtor's proposal, and

(*b*) if in his opinion such a meeting should be summoned, the date on which, and time and place at which, he proposes the meeting should be held.

(2) For the purpose of enabling the nominee to prepare his report the debtor shall submit to the nominee—

(*a*) a document setting out the terms of the voluntary arrangement which the debtor is proposing, and

(*b*) a statement of his affairs containing—

(i) such particulars of his creditors and of his debts and other liabilities and of his assets as may be prescribed, and

(ii) such other information as may be prescribed.

(3) The court may, on an application made by the debtor in a case where the nominee has failed to submit the report required by this section, do one or both of the following, namely—

(*a*) direct that the nominee shall be replaced as such by another person qualified to act as an insolvency practitioner in relation to the debtor;

(*b*) direct that the interim order shall continue, or (if it has ceased to have effect) be renewed, for such further period as the court may specify in the direction.

(4) The court may, on the application of the nominee, extend the period for which the interim order has effect so as to enable the nominee to have more time to prepare his report.

(5) If the court is satisfied on receiving the nominee's report that a meeting of the debtor's creditors should be summoned to consider the debtor's proposal, the court shall direct that the period for which the interim order has effect shall be extended, for such further period as it may specify in the direction, for the purpose of enabling the debtor's proposal to be considered by his creditors in accordance with the following provisions of this Part.

(6) The court may discharge the interim order if it is satisfied, on the application of the nominee—
  (*a*) that the debtor has failed to comply with his obligations under subsection (2), or
  (*b*) that for any other reason it would be inappropriate for a meeting of the debtor's creditors to be summoned to consider the debtor's proposal.

DEFINITIONS
  "affairs": s.385(2).
  "creditor": s.383(1).
  "debt": ss.382(3), 385(1).
  "interim order": s.252.
  "liability": s.382(4).
  "person qualified to act as an insolvency practitioner": s.390.
  "prescribed": s.384(1).
  "proposal": s.353(1), (2).
  "the court": ss.373, 385(1).
  "the debtor": s.385(1).
  "the nominee": s.253(2).
  "to act as an insolvency practitioner in relation to an individual": s.388(2), (3).

GENERAL NOTE
This section specifies what steps are to be taken by a person as the nominee under a proposal which is intended to be made by a debtor by whom, or on behalf of whom, an application has been made under s.253 resulting in the making of an interim order under s.252. Unless the nominee successfully applies to the court under subs. (4) for an extension of the period for which the interim order has effect, the consequence of s.255(6) is that the order will lapse at the end of 14 days from the date on which it was made. This section corresponds to s.113 of the 1985 Act.

Subs. (1)
This provision, which is analogous to that of s.2(2) relating to voluntary arrangements made by companies, requires the nominee to form a professional judgment of the terms of the proposal which the debtor is intending to put to his creditors. This opinion must be based upon an appraisal of the debtor's affairs and circumstances derived from information which the debtor himself must supply. This information is supplied in the form of a statement of affairs which the debtor is obliged to furnish pursuant to the provisions of subs. (2)(*b*). Only if the nominee concludes that it would be worthwhile to put the debtor's proposals to a meeting of creditors, and if he duly reports to the court in those terms, will the court give the necessary direction under subs. (5), which has the effect of prolonging the duration of the interim order pending the convening of a creditors' meeting under s.257.

Subs. (3)
This provides for the possibility that the nominee may fail to submit his report under subs. (1) within the limited time allowed. The debtor may take the initiative of applying to the court under this subsection with a view to having the original nominee replaced by some other, and to obtain an extension or renewal of the interim order to allow the nominee more time in which to prepare and submit his report.

Subs. (4)
This allows the nominee himself to apply for an extension of the interim order to allow him more time in which to prepare and submit his report.

Subs. (6)
This enables the court to discharge the interim order ahead of the time at which it would otherwise cease to have effect by virtue of s.255(6). The reference to the debtor's obligation under subs. (2) lends emphasis to the debtor's duty to co-operate readily and willingly with the nominee, while the alternative ground offered by para. (*b*) indicates that the nominee must act with professional integrity and independence of judgment in deciding whether or not it would be appropriate for a meeting of creditors to be summoned.

Summoning of creditors' meeting

257.—(1) Where it has been reported to the court under section 256 that a meeting of the debtor's creditors should be summoned, the nominee (or his replacement under section 256(3)(*a*)) shall, unless the court otherwise directs, summon that meeting for the time, date and place proposed in his report.

(2) The persons to be summoned to the meeting are every creditor of the debtor of whose claim and address the person summoning the meeting is aware.

(3) For this purpose the creditors of a debtor who is an undischarged bankrupt include—

(*a*) every person who is a creditor of the bankrupt in respect of a bankruptcy debt, and

(*b*) every person who would be such a creditor if the bankruptcy had commenced on the day on which notice of the meeting is given.

DEFINITIONS
"bankrupt": s.381(1).
"bankruptcy debt": s.382.
"creditor": s.383.
"debt": ss.382(3), 385(1).
"interim order": s.252.
"the court": ss.373, 385(1).
"the debtor": s.385(1).

GENERAL NOTE
This section governs the next stage following the making of a report to the court by a person responsible for doing so under s.256 or s.274, advocating the summoning of a meeting of creditors under this section. Normally the person who has submitted the report is also responsible for summoning the meeting, but the court has the power to direct otherwise. This section corresponds to s.114 of the 1985 Act.

Subs. (2)
This indicates that the summoning of creditors to the meeting is to be by personal communication to each creditor of whose claim and address the convenor of the meeting is aware. This information should be established from the debtor's statement of affairs submitted under s.256(2)(*b*). The section itself imposes no requirement that the summoning of the meeting is to be publicly advertised (see also H.C. Standing Committee E, June 13, 1985, col. 344).

Subs. (3)

Every person who would be such a creditor if the bankruptcy had commenced on the day on which notice of the meeting is given
This subsection indicates which persons qualify as "creditors" for the purpose of being entitled to be summoned to a meeting under this section. In the case of a debtor who is an undischarged bankrupt, the eligible creditors include not only those who are creditors in the existing bankruptcy but also those who have become creditors of the bankrupt since the commencement of his existing bankruptcy, and who therefore would not be qualified to lodge proof in that administration. These post-adjudication creditors are brought into the fold for the purposes of an arrangement under this Part by having regard to the position they would have occupied if the commencement of the bankruptcy had been on the date when notice of the meeting is given, rather than at the date on which the bankruptcy order was made.

Consideration and implementation of debtor's proposal

Decisions of creditors' meeting

258.—(1) A creditors' meeting summoned under section 257 shall decide whether to approve the proposed voluntary arrangement.

(2) The meeting may approve the proposed voluntary arrangement with modifications, but shall not do so unless the debtor consents to each modification.

(3) The modifications subject to which the proposed voluntary arrangement may be approved may include one conferring the functions proposed to be conferred on the nominee on another person qualified to act as an insolvency practitioner in relation to the debtor.

But they shall not include any modification by virtue of which the proposal ceases to be a proposal such as is mentioned in section 253.

(4) The meeting shall not approve any proposal or modification which affects the right of a secured creditor of the debtor to enforce his security, except with the concurrence of the creditor concerned.

(5) Subject as follows, the meeting shall not approve any proposal or modification under which—

(a) any preferential debt of the debtor is to be paid otherwise than in priority to such of his debts as are not preferential debts, or

(b) a preferential creditor of the debtor is to be paid an amount in respect of a preferential debt that bears to that debt a smaller proportion than is borne to another preferential debt by the amount that is to be paid in respect of that other debt.

However, the meeting may approve such a proposal or modification with the concurrence of the preferential creditor concerned.

(6) Subject as above, the meeting shall be conducted in accordance with the rules.

(7) In this section "preferential debt" has the meaning given by section 386 in Part XII; and "preferential creditor" is to be construed accordingly.

DEFINITIONS
"bankrupt": s.381(1).
"creditor": s.383(1).
"interim order": s.252.
"modifications": s.436.
"person qualified to act as an insolvency practitioner": s.390.
"preferential debt", "preferential creditor": subs. (7), s.386; Sched. 6.
"prescribed": s.384(1).
"proposal": s.253(1), (2).
"secured creditor", "security": s.383.
"the court": ss.373, 385(1).
"the debtor": s.385(1).
"the nominee": s.253(2).
"the rules": ss.384, 412.
"to act as an insolvency practitioner in relation to an individual": s.388(2), (3).
"voluntary arrangement": s.253(1).

GENERAL NOTE
This section contains the main provisions which are applicable where a creditors' meeting is convened under s.257 for the purpose of considering a proposal for a composition or scheme of arrangement made by a debtor. The section corresponds to subss. (1) to (6) inclusive, and subs. (9), of s.115 of the 1985 Act.

Subs. (1)
Provision will be made in the rules, which are referred to in subs. (6), to deal with the conduct of the meeting and with matters of procedure. The rules will specify that the creditors' decision whether to approve the debtor's proposals shall be taken on the basis of a majority in value only of the creditors voting in person or by proxy at the meeting.

Subs. (2)
This provision allowing the meeting to approve the debtor's proposal in modified form, provided that the debtor assents to every modification so made, is a counterpart to the provisions in ss.4(1), (2) and 24(1), (2) which respectively apply to voluntary arrangements

by companies and to an administrator's proposals for achieving the purposes of an administration order.

Subs. (3)

This enables the creditors at their meeting to approve the substitution of some other, suitably qualified, person in place of the original nominee. If such a substitution is effected the person so appointed will in due course become supervisor of the composition or scheme, within the meaning of s.263(2), and from then onwards will displace the original nominee with regard to the ensuing responsibilities imposed by this Part.

The proviso to this subsection imposes a necessary limitation upon the competence of the creditors' meeting to approve modifications to the debtor's original proposals, even with the concurrence of the debtor himself. Any modification whose effect is such that the proposal overall is no longer compatible with the basic concept laid down by s.253 is invalid and ineffectual. It would be open to any person from among those listed in s.262(2) to apply to the court under that section, challenging the validity of what has taken place.

Subss. (4), (5)

These provisions safeguard the positions of secured and preferential creditors respectively, so that it is not possible for a composition or scheme to be validly approved which adversely affects their rights and interest, for example by depriving any debt of the priority which it would enjoy in bankruptcy, unless this happens with the concurrence of the creditor affected (*cf.* also s.4(3), (4)). Any secured or preferential creditor whose rights under either of these subsections are improperly infringed may utilise the procedure for challenging the meeting's decision under s.262.

Report of decisions to court

259.—(1) After the conclusion in accordance with the rules of the meeting summoned under section 257, the chairman of the meeting shall report the result of it to the court and, immediately after so reporting, shall give notice of the result of the meeting to such persons as may be prescribed.

(2) If the report is that the meeting has declined (with or without modifications) to approve the debtor's proposal, the court may discharge any interim order which is in force in relation to the debtor.

DEFINITIONS
"interim order": s.252.
"modifications": s.436.
"prescribed": s.384(1).
"proposal": s.253(1), (2).
"the court": ss.373, 385(1).
"the debtor": s.385(1).
"the rules": ss.384, 412.

GENERAL NOTE
This section comprises subss. (7) and (8) of s.115 of the 1985 Act.

Subs. (1)

The rules for the conduct of creditors' meetings convened under s.257 and this section will provide for the appointment of a person to be Chairman of the meeting. In most cases it is likely that a nominee, or anyone whom the court may have appointed in place of the nominee pursuant to s.256(3)(*a*), will act as Chairman of the meeting. The purport of this subsection is that the duty to report the result of the meeting to the court, and to give notice of the result in the prescribed manner, is cast upon whoever served as Chairman at the meeting. If that person was the nominee, and if also the creditors have decided in accordance with s.258(3) to substitute some other person in his place, the immediate functions which are required to be performed under this subsection must nevertheless be performed by the person who served as Chairman of the meeting. The court has no further function to perform in response to the report, unless any qualified person raises a challenge to the decision of the meeting under s.262.

Subs. (2)

This provides for the possibility that the creditors may fail to approve the debtor's proposal, and authorises the court to discharge any interim order which is in force with regard to the debtor, thereby ending the moratorium enjoyed since the order was originally made under s.252.

Effect of approval

260.—(1) This section has effect where the meeting summoned under section 257 approves the proposed voluntary arrangement (with or without modifications).

(2) The approved arrangement—

(*a*) takes effect as if made by the debtor at the meeting, and

(*b*) binds every person who in accordance with the rules had notice of, and was entitled to vote at, the meeting (whether or not he was present or represented at it) as if he were a party to the arrangement.

(3) The Deeds of Arrangement Act 1914 does not apply to the approved voluntary arrangement.

(4) Any interim order in force in relation to the debtor immediately before the end of the period of 28 days beginning with the day on which the report with respect to the creditors' meeting was made to the court under section 259 ceases to have effect at the end of that period.

This subsection applies except to such extent as the court may direct for the purposes of any application under section 262 below.

(5) Where proceedings on a bankruptcy petition have been stayed by an interim order which ceases to have effect under subsection (4), that petition is deemed, unless the court otherwise orders, to have been dismissed.

DEFINITIONS

"bankrupt": s.381(1).
"bankruptcy order": s.381(2).
"bankruptcy petition": s.381(3).
"estate": ss.283, 385(1).
"interim order": s.252.
"modifications": s.436.
"the court": ss.373, 385(1).
"the debtor": s.385(1).
"the rules": ss.384, 412.
"voluntary arrangement": s.253(1).

GENERAL NOTE

This section specifies what are the legal consequences of the approval of a proposed voluntary arrangement by a meeting of creditors summoned under s.257. The principal event is that the approved composition or scheme binds every person who had notice of and was entitled to vote at the meeting, regardless of whether he in fact attended or was represented at it, and regardless of whether he voted for or against the proposal. The only courses of action open to any creditor who is dissatisfied by the terms of the arrangement as approved, or by the manner in which the meeting was conducted, are either to raise a challenge against the meeting's decision under s.262 within the time allowed by subs. (3) of that section, or to present a petition for a bankruptcy order against the debtor under s.264(1)(*c*), subject to the requirements of s.276 being met. This section comprises subss. (1)–(3), (6) and (7) of s.116 of the 1985 Act.

Subs. (3)

The exclusionary words regarding the Deeds of Arrangement Act 1914 ensure that there is no question of any right or duty to register an arrangement which has been approved under s.258 in order for it to become legally effective and binding.

Subs. (4)

This preserves the effects of the moratorium brought about by the making of an interim order under s.252, up until the end of the period of time allowed for bringing a challenge under s.262 to the decision of the creditors' meeting. The court is nevertheless empowered by s.262(6) to prolong the effects of the interim order for a further period of time in the case where a challenge is brought under s.262.

Effect where debtor an undischarged bankrupt

261.—(1) Subject as follows, where the creditors' meeting summoned under section 257 approves the proposed voluntary arrangement (with or without modifications) and the debtor is an undischarged bankrupt, the court may do one or both of the following, namely—

(a) annul the bankruptcy order by which he was adjudged bankrupt;

(b) give such directions with respect to the conduct of the bankruptcy and the administration of the bankrupt's estate as it thinks appropriate for facilitating the implementation of the approved voluntary arrangement.

(2) The court shall not annul a bankruptcy order under subsection (1)—

(a) at any time before the end of the period of 28 days beginning with the day on which the report of the creditors' meeting was made to the court under section 259, or

(b) at any time when an application under section 262 below, or an appeal in respect of such an application, is pending or at any time in the period within which such an appeal may be brought.

DEFINITIONS
"bankrupt": s.381(1).
"bankruptcy order": s.381(2).
"creditor": s.383(1).
"modifications": s.436.
"the court": ss.373, 385(1).
"voluntary arrangement": s.253(1).

GENERAL NOTE
This section comprises subss. (4) and (5) of s.116 of the 1985 Act. It makes provision for the case where approval is given by the creditors to a proposal for a voluntary arrangement made by a debtor who has already undergone adjudication.

Subs. (1)
This enables the court at its discretion to deal with any bankruptcy order which may be in force in relation to the debtor in either or both of the ways specified. However, subs. (2) prevents the court from annulling the bankruptcy order until after the elapse of the period of time within which any challenge to the meeting's decision may be brought under s.262 by a party eligible to do so, and until after the final determination of any such challenge as may be brought under that section.

Challenge of meeting's decision

262.—(1) Subject to this section, an application to the court may be made, by any of the persons specified below, on one or both of the following grounds, namely—

(a) that a voluntary arrangement approved by a creditors' meeting summoned under section 257 unfairly prejudices the interests of a creditor of the debtor;

(b) that there has been some material irregularity at or in relation to such a meeting.

(2) The persons who may apply under this section are—

(a) the debtor;

(b) a person entitled, in accordance with the rules, to vote at the creditors' meeting;

(c) the nominee (or his replacement under section 256(3)(a) or 258(3)); and (*d*) if the debtor is an undischarged bankrupt, the trustee of his estate or the official receiver.

(3) An application under this section shall not be made after the end of the period of 28 days beginning with the day on which the report of the creditors' meeting was made to the court under section 259.

(4) Where on an application under this section the court is satisfied as to either of the grounds mentioned in subsection (1), it may do one or both of the following, namely—

(*a*) revoke or suspend any approval given by the meeting;

(*b*) give a direction to any person for the summoning of a further meeting of the debtor's creditors to consider any revised proposal he may make or, in a case falling within subsection (1)(*b*), to reconsider his original proposal.

(5) Where at any time after giving a direction under subsection (4)(*b*) for the summoning of a meeting to consider a revised proposal the court is satisfied that the debtor does not intend to submit such a proposal, the court shall revoke the direction and revoke or suspend any approval given at the previous meeting.

(6) Where the court gives a direction under subsection (4)(*b*), it may also give a direction continuing or, as the case may require, renewing, for such period as may be specified in the direction, the effect in relation to the debtor of any interim order.

(7) In any case where the court, on an application made under this section with respect to a creditors' meeting, gives a direction under subsection (4)(*b*) or revokes or suspends an approval under subsection (4)(*a*) or (5), the court may give such supplemental directions as it thinks fit and, in particular, directions with respect to—

(*a*) things done since the meeting under any voluntary arrangement approved by the meeting, and

(*b*) such things done since the meeting as could not have been done if an interim order had been in force in relation to the debtor when they were done.

(8) Except in pursuance of the preceding provisions of this section, an approval given at a creditors' meeting summoned under section 257 is not invalidated by any irregularity at or in relation to the meeting.

DEFINITIONS

"a creditor": s.383(1).
"bankrupt": s.381(1).
"estate": ss.283, 385(1).
"interim order": s.252.
"proposal": s.253(1), (2).
"the court": ss.373, 385(1).
"the debtor": s.385(1).
"the nominee": s.253(2).
"the official receiver": s.399(1).
"the rules": ss.384, 412.
"voluntary arrangement": s.253(1), (2).

GENERAL NOTE

The procedure established under this section represents the sole means of bringing about a judicial scrutiny of either the terms of an approved arrangement, or of the manner in which approval was obtained at the meeting of creditors. Even if there has been irregularity at or in relation to the meeting, subs. (8) makes it clear that this does not *per se* render the creditors' approval invalid. Only if a successful application is made under this section may the result of the meeting be undone, and it is to be noted that subs. (1)(*b*) introduces the requirement that the court be satisfied that the irregularity was a material one. This section corresponds to s.117 of the 1985 Act.

Subs. (1)

Only the grounds specified in this subsection may, jointly or individually, serve as a basis for the exercise of the court's powers under subs. (4).

Subs. (2)

This indicates which persons have standing to invoke the procedure for challenge under this section.

Subs. (3)

This imposes a time limit of 28 days for the bringing of an application under this section. Time begins to run from the day on which the Chairman of the creditors' meeting reports to the court upon the result thereof, as required by s.259(1).

Subs. (4)

This sets out the powers of the court where it is satisfied that the applicant's case has been made out as required by subs. (1). The powers are discretionary, and include the possibility, where a material irregularity has taken place at or in relation to the meeting, that the meeting may be reconvened at the court's discretion by the same or by some other person as convenor to reconsider the original proposal afresh.

Subs. (6)

This enables the court to extend the moratorium consequential upon the making of an interim order under s.252, to allow the extra time required for reconvening the meeting of creditors pursuant to directions given by the court under subs. (4)(*b*).

Subs. (7)

This enables the court to give consequential or supplemental directions upon the principal order or direction which it makes in the exercise of the powers conferred by subss. (4) or (5).

Implementation and supervision of approved voluntary arrangement

263.—(1) This section applies where a voluntary arrangement approved by a creditors' meeting summoned under section 257 has taken effect.

(2) The person who is for the time being carrying out, in relation to the voluntary arrangement, the functions conferred by virtue of the approval on the nominee (or his replacement under section 256(3)(*a*) or 258(3)) shall be known as the supervisor of the voluntary arrangement.

(3) If the debtor, any of his creditors or any other person is dissatisfied by any act, omission or decision of the supervisor, he may apply to the court; and on such an application the court may—

(*a*) confirm, reverse or modify any act or decision of the supervisor,

(*b*) give him directions, or

(*c*) make such other order as it thinks fit.

(4) The supervisor may apply to the court for directions in relation to any particular matter arising under the voluntary arrangement.

(5) The court may, whenever—

(*a*) it is expedient to appoint a person to carry out the functions of the supervisor, and

(*b*) it is inexpedient, difficult or impracticable for an appointment to be made without the assistance of the court,

make an order appointing a person who is qualified to act as an insolvency practitioner in relation to the debtor, either in substitution for the existing supervisor or to fill a vacancy.

This is without prejudice to section 41(2) of the Trustee Act 1925 (power of court to appoint trustees of deeds of arrangement).

(6) The power conferred by subsection (5) is exercisable so as to increase the number of persons exercising the functions of the supervisor or, where there is more than one person exercising those functions, so as to replace one or more of those persons.

DEFINITIONS

"a creditor": s.383(1).

"person qualified to act as an insolvency practitioner": s.390.

"the court": ss.373, 385(1).

"the debtor": s.385(1).

"the nominee": s.253(2).

"the supervisor of the composition or scheme": subs. (2).

"to act as an insolvency practitioner in relation to an individual": s.388(2), (3).

"voluntary arrangement": s.253(1), (2).

GENERAL NOTE

This section governs the implementation of an approved composition or scheme which has taken effect under s.260. The person responsible for carrying out this task is known as the supervisor, and will be either the original nominee, if he is still acting, or any person who may have been substituted in place of the original nominee, either by the court under s.256(3)(*a*) or by the meeting of creditors under s.258(3). Under subs. (3) the court has both jurisdiction to entertain an application from the debtor, or any of the creditors, or any other person who is dissatisfied by the supervisor's performance of his functions, and overriding powers in relation to the implementation of the arrangement. The supervisor may also seek directions from the court under subs. (4) if need arises. Provision is also made under subss. (5) and (6) for replacement of the supervisor by some other duly qualified person. This power may be utilised to fill any vacancy which may arise, and also to increase the number of persons exercising the functions of the supervisor. This section corresponds to s.118 of the 1985 Act.

PART IX

BANKRUPTCY

CHAPTER I

BANKRUPTCY PETITIONS; BANKRUPTCY ORDERS

Preliminary

Who may present a bankruptcy petition

264.—(1) A petition for a bankruptcy order to be made against an individual may be presented to the court in accordance with the following provisions of this Part—

(*a*) by one of the individual's creditors or jointly by more than one of them,

(*b*) by the individual himself,

(*c*) by the supervisor of, or any person (other than the individual) who is for the time being bound by, a voluntary arrangement proposed by the individual and approved under Part VIII, or

(*d*) where a criminal bankruptcy order has been made against the individual, by the Official Petitioner or by any person specified in the order in pursuance of section 39(3)(*b*) of the Powers of Criminal Courts Act 1973.

(2) Subject to those provisions, the court may make a bankruptcy order on any such petition.

DEFINITIONS

"bankruptcy order": s.381(2).

"creditor": s.383(1).

"criminal bankruptcy order": s.385(1); Powers of Criminal Courts Act 1973, s.39(1).

"person bound by a composition or scheme": s.260(1)(*b*).

"the court": ss.373, 385(1).

"the Official Petitioner": s.402; Powers of Criminal Courts Act 1973, s.41(1).
"the supervisor of a voluntary arrangement": s.263(2).

GENERAL NOTE

This provision is of great importance. It specifies the persons who may, singly or jointly, present a petition for a bankruptcy order to be made against an individual. The section corresponds to s.119(1) of the 1985 Act.

Subs. (1)(a)

Creditors' petitions are governed by the provisions of ss.267–271 inclusive.

Subs. (1)(b)

Debtors' petitions are governed by the provisions of ss.272–275 inclusive.

Subs. (1)(c)

The court cannot make a bankruptcy order on a petition under this heading unless at least one of the conditions specified in s.276(1) is met.

Subs. (1)(d)

This maintains the operation of the criminal bankruptcy procedure at present established under ss.39–41 of the Powers of Criminal Courts Act 1973, together with Sched. 2 to that Act. However, it is possible that the procedure will be superseded by new legislation aimed at giving courts more effective powers to deprive convicted offenders of the proceeds of their crimes. Further provisions applicable in cases where a petition is based on a criminal bankruptcy order are contained in s.277. See also s.266(4).

Subs. (2)

The court may make a bankruptcy order on any such petition

This indicates the discretionary nature of the court's power to make a bankruptcy order, even where the prescribed legal requirements for the making of an order are fully met. Additional, broad discretionary powers to dismiss a petition under certain circumstances are conferred by s.266(3) and by s.271(3).

Conditions to be satisfied in respect of debtor

265.—(1) A bankruptcy petition shall not be presented to the court under section 264(1)(*a*) or (*b*) unless the debtor—

    (*a*) is domiciled in England and Wales,

    (*b*) is personally present in England and Wales on the day on which the petition is presented, or

    (*c*) at any time in the period of 3 years ending with that day—

        (i) has been ordinarily resident, or has had a place of residence, in England and Wales, or

        (ii) has carried on business in England and Wales.

(2) The reference in subsection (1)(*c*) to an individual carrying on business includes—

    (*a*) the carrying on of business by a firm or partnership of which the individual is a member, and

    (*b*) the carrying on of business by an agent or manager for the individual or for such a firm or partnership.

DEFINITIONS

"bankruptcy petition": s.381(3).
"business": s.436.
"the court": ss.373, 385(1).
"the debtor": s.385(1).

GENERAL NOTE

This section, comprising subss. (2) and (3) of s.119 of the 1985 Act, specifies five alternative requirements with regard to the debtor's forensic connections with the territory of England and Wales, one of which at least must be satisfied if the court in England and Wales is to be capable of exercising jurisdiction in bankruptcy with respect of that individual.

The section contains vestigial remains of the former provisions of s.4 of the Bankruptcy Act 1914, now repealed. However, many aspects of the previous law and procedure regarding the commencement of bankruptcy proceedings have been completely eliminated, in fulfilment of many of the recommendations contained in Chaps. 10 and 11 of the *Cork Report*. In particular the whole concept of the act of bankruptcy has been abolished (*cf. Cork Report,* paras. 529, 530; *White Paper* para. 18(iv)), as has the preliminary species of order formerly known as a receiving order. However, as Chap. 12 of the *White Paper* indicated, the Government did not accept the entirely new framework of insolvency proceedings for which the *Cork Report* made elaborate proposals, and which would have reserved bankruptcy proper for use only in the more serious cases where the stigma and notoriety attaching to bankruptcy could be said to be appropriate. Under Pt. IX of the Act, the bankruptcy order remains the principal species of insolvency proceeding, although the new voluntary procedure under Pt. VIII is intended to provide an acceptable alternative to bankruptcy for all the parties concerned.

Subs. (1)

This somewhat resembles the former s.4(1)(*d*) of the Bankruptcy Act 1914, but there are significant changes in the jurisdictional criteria which have been embodied in the new law. The much-criticised domiciliary connecting factor has been retained as a useful basis on which to ensure that an absconding debtor may remain amenable to the bankruptcy jurisdiction of our courts for a considerable time after leaving these shores. The grounds stated in paras. (*a*)–(*c*) represent alternative tests, and it is enough to satisfy any one of them. The ground stated in para. (*b*), whereby the court's jurisdiction is established if the debtor was personally present in England and Wales on the day on which the petition is presented, is potentially capable of being used by a foreign creditor against a foreign debtor who merely happens to be in this country temporarily. It was assumed, perhaps too readily, on behalf of the Government that English courts would not entertain a petition in such cases (H.C. Standing Committee E, June 13, 1985, col. 351), but although the court could dismiss a petition under such circumstances at its discretion, it is under no obligation to do so: *cf. Re Pascal* (1876) 1 Ch.D. 509. On the other hand, this ground of jurisdiction could readily be used to enable a domestic creditor to present a petition against a foreign debtor who makes successive visits to this country and incurs credit without paying his debts.

The three grounds contained in para. (*c*), which utilise a residential or "doing of business" basis of jurisdiction, read in conjunction with subs. (2), are comparable to the grounds included in s.4(1)(*d*) of the Bankruptcy Act 1914, but with the important difference that the specified period, within which any such contact suffices to ground the jurisdiction of the court, is now any time within three years ending with the day a petition is presented. This is a considerable enlargement over the former period of one year, and is designed to prevent persons from too easily escaping from the jurisdiction of the courts by departing abroad before effective action can be taken against them. One example would be directors who have been implicated in wrongful trading by a company some considerable time before the eventual liquidation of the company and before their transgressions come to light.

Has carried on business

This ground can operate in association with the rule, established in *Theophile* v. *Solicitor General* [1950] A.C. 186, that a person who has once carried on business here does not cease to do so until he has discharged all trading debts and liabilities, including taxes, relating to that activity. By means of this useful decision of the House of Lords, a debtor who apparently ceased to trade more than three years before the date of presentation of the petition may yet be brought within the ambit of para. (*c*)(ii).

Other preliminary conditions

266.—(1) Where a bankruptcy petition relating to an individual is presented by a person who is entitled to present a petition under two or more paragraphs of section 264(1), the petition is to be treated for the purposes of this Part as a petition under such one of those paragraphs as may be specified in the petition.

(2) A bankruptcy petition shall not be withdrawn without the leave of the court.

(3) The court has a general power, if it appears to it appropriate to do so on the grounds that there has been a contravention of the rules or for any other reason, to dismiss a bankruptcy petition or to stay proceedings on such a petition; and, where it stays proceedings on a petition, it may do so on such terms and conditions as it thinks fit.

(4) Without prejudice to subsection (3), where a petition under section 264(1)(*a*), (*b*) or (*c*) in respect of an individual is pending at a time when a criminal bankruptcy order is made against him, or is presented after such an order has been so made, the court may on the application of the Official Petitioner dismiss the petition if it appears to it appropriate to do so.

DEFINITIONS

"bankruptcy petition": s.381(3).
"criminal bankruptcy order": s.385(1); Powers of Criminal Courts Act 1973, s.39(1).
"the court": ss.373, 385(1).
"the Official Petitioner": s.402; Powers of Criminal Courts Act 1973, s.41(1).
"the rules": ss.384, 412.

GENERAL NOTE

This section comprises subss. (4)–(7) of s.119 of the 1985 Act.

Subs. (2)

This restates the rule formerly contained in s.5(7) of the Bankruptcy Act 1914 (repealed) and is a safeguard against misuse of the legal machinery of bankruptcy. This provision applies to petitions presented by a creditor or by a debtor, and hence a provision specifically concerned with the withdrawal of a debtor's petition, which was originally included in the Bill within the clause now embodied as s.272 of this Act, was deleted in Committee (H.C. Standing Committee E, June 13, 1985, col. 360).

Creditor's petition

Grounds of creditor's petition

267.—(1) A creditor's petition must be in respect of one or more debts owed by the debtor, and the petitioning creditor or each of the petitioning creditors must be a person to whom the debt or (as the case may be) at least one of the debts is owed.

(2) Subject to the next three sections, a creditor's petition may be presented to the court in respect of a debt or debts only if, at the time the petition is presented—

 (*a*) the amount of the debt, or the aggregate amount of the debts, is equal to or exceeds the bankruptcy level,

 (*b*) the debt, or each of the debts, is for a liquidated sum payable to the petitioning creditor, or one or more of the petitioning creditors, either immediately or at some certain, future time, and is unsecured,

 (*c*) the debt, or each of the debts, is a debt which the debtor appears either to be unable to pay or to have no reasonable prospect of being able to pay, and

 (*d*) there is no outstanding application to set aside a statutory demand served (under section 268 below) in respect of the debt or any of the debts.

(3) A debt is not to be regarded for the purposes of subsection (2) as a debt for a liquidated sum by reason only that the amount of the debt is specified in a criminal bankruptcy order.

(4) "The bankruptcy level" is £750; but the Secretary of State may by order in a statutory instrument substitute any amount specified in the order for that amount or (as the case may be) for the amount which by

virtue of such an order is for the time being the amount of the bankruptcy level.

(5) An order shall not be made under subsection (4) unless a draft of it has been laid before, and approved by a resolution of, each House of Parliament.

DEFINITIONS
"a creditor", "creditor's petition": ss.264(1)(a), 385(1).
"criminal bankruptcy order": s.385(1); Powers of Criminal Courts Act 1973, s.39(1).
"debt": ss.382(3), 385(1).
"secured", "unsecured": ss.383, 385(1).
"statutory demand": s.268(1)(a).
"the bankruptcy level": subs. (4).
"the court": ss.373, 385(1).
"the debtor": s.385(1).

TRANSITIONAL PROVISIONS
Sched. 11, paras. 10–12.

GENERAL NOTE
This section, to be read in conjunction with ss.268–270, sets out the conditions which must be satisfied before a creditor or creditors can present a bankruptcy petition against a debtor. In many respects the section restates the existing law formerly contained in parts of ss.4 and 5 of the Bankruptcy Act 1914 (repealed), but the drafting is considerably modified and many purely procedural matters are removed to the rules.

The main innovation in this section is to be found in subs. (2)(c) and (d), and in the subsequent provisions of this and the next following section dependent thereto. This introduces, in place of the former requirements of the Bankruptcy Act relating to acts of bankruptcy, the new single concept of the debtor's apparent inability to pay the debt on which the petition is founded (or, in the case of a petition founded on a debt which is not immediately payable, if the debtor appears to have no reasonable prospect of being able to pay the debt). This accords with the recommendation in para. 535 of the *Cork Report*. The provisions of s.268 enable the petitioning creditor to establish the debtor's present or prospective inability to pay, for the purposes of subs. (2)(c), by serving on the debtor the appropriate form of statutory demand, which thus becomes the counterpart to the procedure which has long been applicable in relation to company winding up, and is now embodied in s.123(1)(a) of the Act. The debtor's failure to comply with the terms of a statutory demand served in accordance with subss. (1)(a) or (2)(a) of s.268 has the consequence that the requirement imposed by subs. (2)(c) is duly met. Alternatively, under s.268(1)(b), in the case of a debt which is presently due an unsatisfied execution in respect of a judgment debt due to the petitioning creditor will similarly fulfil the requirement imposed by subs. (2)(c) (cf. s.123(1)(b)). S.271(1)(b) and (4) contains further provisions applicable to the court's hearing of the creditor's petition, regarding the reasonable prospect of the debtor's being able to pay his debt.

This section comprises subss. (1), (2) and (7)–(9) of s.120 of the 1985 Act.

Subs. (1)
This is so drafted as to make it a legal requirement that the debt in respect of which a creditor presents a bankruptcy petition is a debt which is actually owed to the petitioning creditor himself. This restates the existing law under s.4(1)(a) of the Bankruptcy Act 1914 (repealed).

Subs. (2)(a)

The bankruptcy level
This is specified in subs. (4) as £750, but that provision, together with subs. (5), also enables the Secretary of State to vary the level by statutory instrument at any time, subject to the obtaining of Parliamentary approval for the draft instrument by means of the "positive" procedure.

Subs. (2(b)
This largely follows the substance of s.4(1)(b) of the Bankruptcy Act 1914 (repealed) but with the important addition of the words "and is unsecured". This establishes the main

principle that a petitioning creditor's right to resort to bankruptcy proceedings arises from the fact that his debtor appears unable to pay a debt which is unsecured. However, this is subject to the exception created by s.269 which specifies the circumstances in which the petitioning creditor's debt need not be unsecured.

Subs. (2)(d)

Application to set aside a statutory demand
This form of application is alluded to in subss. (1)(*a*) and (2)(*c*) of s.268, where it is also indicated that the relevant procedural provisions for such applications will be contained in the rules.

Definition of "inability to pay", etc.; the statutory demand

268.—(1) For the purposes of section 267(2) (*c*), the debtor appears to be unable to pay a debt if, but only if, the debt is payable immediately and either—

(*a*) the petitioning creditor to whom the debt is owed has served on the debtor a demand (known as "the statutory demand") in the prescribed form requiring him to pay the debt or to secure or compound for it to the satisfaction of the creditor, at least 3 weeks have elapsed since the demand was served and the demand has been neither complied with nor set aside in accordance with the rules, or

(*b*) execution or other process issued in respect of the debt on a judgment or order of any court in favour of the petitioning creditor, or one or more of the petitioning creditors to whom the debt is owed, has been returned unsatisfied in whole or in part.

(2) For the purposes of section 267(2)(*c*) the debtor appears to have no reasonable prospect of being able to pay a debt if, but only if, the debt is not immediately payable and—

(*a*) the petitioning creditor to whom it is owed has served on the debtor a demand (also known as "the statutory demand") in the prescribed form requiring him to establish to the satisfaction of the creditor that there is a reasonable prospect that the debtor will be able to pay the debt when it falls due,

(*b*) at least 3 weeks have elapsed since the demand was served, and

(*c*) the demand has been neither complied with nor set aside in accordance with the rules.

Definitions
"creditor": s.383.
"debt": ss.382(3), 385(1).
"the debtor": s.385(1).
"the rules": ss.384, 412.
"the statutory demand": subss. (1)(*a*), (2)(*a*).

General Note
This section operates in relation to the provision in s.267(2)(*c*), whereby a creditor is enabled to present a bankruptcy petition against a debtor if the debt in respect of which the petition is presented is one which the debtor appears either to be unable to pay or to have no reasonable prospect of being able to pay. By means of the service of a statutory demand for payment in accordance with the terms of this section, or alternatively on the basis of an unsatisfied execution as provided for in subs. (1)(*a*), the petitioning creditor is provided with the means of fulfilling the condition imposed by s.267(2)(*c*).
This section comprises subss. (3) and (4) of s.120 of the 1985 Act.

Subs. (1)

If, but only if
These words are important, because they carry the effect that the provisions within s.268 itself constitute the sole means of fulfilling the condition imposed by s.267(2)(*c*).

Creditor with security

269.—(1) A debt which is the debt, or one of the debts, in respect of which a creditor's petition is presented need not be unsecured if either—

    (*a*) the petition contains a statement by the person having the right to enforce the security that he is willing, in the event of a bankruptcy order being made, to give up his security for the benefit of all the bankrupt's creditors, or

    (*b*) the petition is expressed not to be made in respect of the secured part of the debt and contains a statement by that person of the estimated value at the date of the petition of the security for the secured part of the debt.

(2) In a case falling within subsection (1)(*b*) the secured and unsecured parts of the debt are to be treated for the purposes of sections 267 to 270 as separate debts.

DEFINITIONS
    "creditor": s.383.
    "creditor's petition": ss.264(1)(*a*), 385(1).
    "debt": ss.382(3), 385(1).
    "security", "secured", "unsecured": ss.383, 385(1).
    "the bankrupt": s.381(1).

GENERAL NOTE
This section, which corresponds to subs. (5) of s.120 of the 1985 Act, specifies the circumstances under which a creditor may present a bankruptcy petition in respect of a debt which is secured. This provision therefore qualifies the concluding three words of s.267(2)(*b*), which are to the general effect that the petitioning creditor's debt must be unsecured.

Expedited petition

270. In the case of a creditor's petition presented wholly or partly in respect of a debt which is the subject of a statutory demand under section 268, the petition may be presented before the end of the 3-week period there mentioned if there is a serious possibility that the debtor's property or the value of any of his property will be significantly diminished during that period and the petition contains a statement to that effect.

DEFINITIONS
    "creditor's petition": ss.264(1)(*a*), 385(1).
    "debt": ss.382(3), 385(1).
    "property": s.436.
    "statutory demand": ss.268(1)(*a*), (2)(*a*).
    "the debtor": s.385(1).

GENERAL NOTE
This section corresponds to subs. (6) of s.120 of the 1985 Act. It establishes an exception to the normal rule in ss.268(1)(*a*) and (2)(*b*) whereby the debtor on whom a statutory demand is served is allowed a minimum period of three weeks within which to comply with the demand. If it can be shown that a delay of even this period of time before a creditor's petition can be presented would carry the risk of significant impairment to the creditors' interests, in the manner specified in the section, the creditor's petition may be presented before the end of three weeks from the date of service of the statutory demand. However, s.271(2) precludes the court from making a bankruptcy order in such cases until the three-week period has duly expired.

Proceedings on creditor's petition

271.—(1) The court shall not make a bankruptcy order on a creditor's petition unless it is satisfied that the debt, or one of the debts, in respect of which the petition was presented is either—

    (*a*) a debt which, having been payable at the date of the petition or having since become payable, has been neither paid nor secured or compounded for, or

(b) a debt which the debtor has no reasonable prospect of being able to pay when it falls due.

(2) In a case in which the petition contains such a statement as is required by section 270, the court shall not make a bankruptcy order until at least 3 weeks have elapsed since the service of any statutory demand under section 268.

(3) The court may dismiss the petition if it is satisfied that the debtor is able to pay all his debts or is satisfied—

(a) that the debtor has made an offer to secure or compound for a debt in respect of which the petition is presented,

(b) that the acceptance of that offer would have required the dismissal of the petition, and

(c) that the offer has been unreasonably refused;

and, in determining for the purposes of this subsection whether the debtor is able to pay all his debts, the court shall take into account his contingent and prospective liabilities.

(4) In determining for the purposes of this section what constitutes a reasonable prospect that a debtor will be able to pay a debt when it falls due, it is to be assumed that the prospect given by the facts and other matters known to the creditor at the time he entered into the transaction resulting in the debt was a reasonable prospect.

(5) Nothing in sections 267 to 271 prejudices the power of the court, in accordance with the rules, to authorise a creditor's petition to be amended by the omission of any creditor or debt and to be proceeded with as if things done for the purposes of those sections had been done only by or in relation to the remaining creditors or debts.

DEFINITIONS

"bankruptcy order": s.381(2).
"creditor", "creditor's petition": ss.264(1)(a), 383, 385(1).
"debt": ss.382(3), 385(1).
"liability": s.382(4).
"petition", "bankruptcy petition": s.381(3).
"secured", "unsecured": ss.383, 385(1):
"statutory demand": ss.268(1)(a), (2)(a).
"the court": ss.373, 385(1).
"the rules": ss.384, 412.
"transaction": s.436.

GENERAL NOTE

This governs the actual hearing of the creditor's petition for a bankruptcy order against the debtor, and requires the court to adopt a certain course of action in relation to a series of specified matters. The section corresponds to s.121 of the 1985 Act.

Subs. (1)

This contains important requirements as to the court's duty to satisfy itself that the petitioning creditor's debt is either one which has become due and has in no sense been satisfied, or one which though not presently due for payment is a debt which the debtor has no reasonable prospect of being able to pay when it does so fall due. This provision must be read in conjunction with subs. (4), which effectively requires the creditor whose petition is based upon a debt payable at a future time to show that circumstances have materially altered since he allowed the debtor to incur the liability, and that there was at that time a reasonable prospect, which has subsequently ceased to be operative, that the debt would be paid on time. Subs. (4) thus prevents a creditor from taking a calculated risk concerning the debtor's continuing solvency, in the anticipation that it will be possible for him to resort to bankruptcy proceedings ahead of the repayment date if that assumption proves ill founded: there is an irrebuttable presumption that the prospect of repayment given by the facts and other matters known to the creditor at the time he entered into the transaction with the debtor was a reasonable one.

Subs. (2)

Such a statement as is required by s.270

This refers to the special provision in s.270 whereby a creditor may be allowed to present a petition before the expiry of the three week period allowed for the debtor to comply with a statutory demand for payment. This rule applies where the petition contains a statement that there is a serious possibility that the debtor's estate will be significantly diminished before the expiry of the three week period, thereby reducing the prospect for creditors to receive any return by way of dividend out of the available assets.

Subs. (3)

This in an elaboration upon the previous law contained in s.5(3) of the Bankruptcy Act 1914 (repealed). The essential principle is retained that the debtor ought not to be adjudicated bankrupt if he is able to pay all his debts. The novel requirement is that the debtor must also have made an offer to secure or compound for the petitioning creditor's debt under circumstances where acceptance of that offer would have required the dismissal of the petition, and that offer has been unreasonably refused. No guidance is supplied in the Act concerning what would constitute an unreasonable refusal of an offer by a creditor, and it will therefore be for the court to determine this question in individual cases.

Debtor's petition

Grounds of debtor's petition

272.—(1) A debtor's petition may be presented to the court only on the grounds that the debtor is unable to pay his debts.

(2) The petition shall be accompanied by a statement of the debtor's affairs containing—

(*a*) such particulars of the debtor's creditors and of his debts and other liabilities and of his assets as may be prescribed, and

(*b*) such other information as may be prescribed.

DEFINITIONS

"affairs": s.385(2).

"creditor": s.383.

"debt", "liability": ss.382(4), 383, 385(1).

"debtor's petition": ss.264(1)(*b*), 385(1).

"prescribed": s.384(1).

"the court": ss.373, 385(1).

"the debtor": s.385(1).

GENERAL NOTE

This retains the right of a debtor to petition for his own adjudication as a bankrupt, as formerly provided by s.6 of the Bankruptcy Act 1914 (repealed). The law is unchanged in requiring that the debtor must demonstrate an inability to pay his debts, which is declared to be the sole ground on which the court may make a bankruptcy order under this section. The section creates new law in requiring the debtor's statement of affairs to be filed simultaneously with the presentation of his petition. A further, apparent change from past law has been effected by the omission of any provision that a debtor's petition cannot be withdrawn after presentment without leave of the court (formerly provided by s.6(2) of the Bankruptcy Act 1914). This is now covered by the provision to that effect in s.266(2), which applies in relation to all bankruptcy petitions, whether presented by the debtor himself or by a creditor. This section corresponds to s.122 of the 1985 Act.

Appointment of insolvency practitioner by the court

273.—(1) Subject to the next section, on the hearing of a debtor's petition the court shall not make a bankruptcy order if it appears to the court—

(*a*) that if a bankruptcy order were made the aggregate amount of the bankruptcy debts, so far as unsecured, would be less than the small bankruptcies level, (*b*) that if a bankruptcy order were made, the value of the bankrupt's estate would be equal to or more than the minimum amount,

(*c*) that within the period of 5 years ending with the presentation of the petition the debtor has neither been adjudged bankrupt nor made a composition with his creditors in satisfaction of his debts or a scheme of arrangement of his affairs, and

(*d*) that it would be appropriate to appoint a person to prepare a report under section 274.

"The minimum amount" and "the small bankruptcies level" mean such amounts as may for the time being be prescribed for the purposes of this section.

(2) Where on the hearing of the petition, it appears to the court as mentioned in subsection (1), the court shall appoint a person who is qualified to act as an insolvency practitioner in relation to the debtor—

(*a*) to prepare a report under the next section, and

(*b*) subject to section 258(3) in Part VIII, to act in relation to any voluntary arrangement to which the report relates either as trustee or otherwise for the purpose of supervising its implementation.

DEFINITIONS

"affairs": s.385(2).
"bankrupt": s.381(1).
"bankruptcy debt": s.382.
"bankruptcy order": s.381(2).
"debtor's petition": ss.264(1)(*b*), 385(1).
"estate": ss. 283, 385(1).
"person qualified to act as an insolvency practitioner": s.390.
"prescribed": s.384(1).
"report": s.274.
"secured", "unsecured": ss.383, 385(1).
"the court": ss.373, 385(1).
"the minimum amount": subs. (1).
"the small bankruptcies level": subs. (1).
"to act as an insolvency practitioner in relation to an individual": s.388(2), (3).
"voluntary arrangement": s.253(1)

GENERAL NOTE

This section is actually concerned with one particular line of development which is to be explored by the court at the hearing of a debtor's petition presented under s.272. Although the Act does not follow all the recommendations in Chap. 11 of the *Cork Report* to the effect that a range of some four different insolvency procedures should be available in relation to individuals, the court is now required to give active consideration to the circumstances of each debtor presenting his own petition, in order to establish whether the possibility exists for the conclusion of a voluntary arrangement between the debtor and his creditors under Part VIII. Even if this alternative process to the making of a bankruptcy order is not undertaken, the court must still have regard to the appropriateness of invoking the summary administration procedure through the issue of a summary administration certificate under s.275.

This section corresponds to subss. (1), (2) and (8) of s.123 of the 1985 Act.

Subs. (1)

The court shall not make a bankruptcy order

Despite the mandatory terms of this provision, it may be noted that para. (*d*) of this subsection involves the court in an exercise of appraisal as to the appropriateness of embarking upon the procedure specified in subs. (2) in conjunction with s.274. Therefore, even if the factual elements contained in paras. (*a*)–(*c*) are established before the court, the final decision whether to set in motion the procedure for seeking a voluntary arrangement rests with the court itself on the basis of its own assessment of the prospects for success of such an initiative.

Para. (a): The small bankruptcies level . . .; (b) the minimum amount
The concluding words of the subsection indicate that these amounts will be prescribed in the rules.

Para. (c): The period of five years
Cf. the period of twelve months specified in s.255(1)(c) in cases where a voluntary arrangement is being sought by application made under s.253.

Subs. (2)

The court shall appoint a person
The expenses of the person appointed to prepare a report under the terms of this and the next section are to be met out of the deposit lodged by the debtor when his bankruptcy petition is presented.

Action on report of insolvency practitioner

274.—(1) A person appointed under section 273 shall inquire into the debtor's affairs and, within such period as the court may direct, shall submit a report to the court stating whether the debtor is willing, for the purposes of Part VIII, to make a proposal for a voluntary arrangement.

(2) A report which states that the debtor is willing as above mentioned shall also state—

(a) whether, in the opinion of the person making the report, a meeting of the debtor's creditors should be summoned to consider the proposal, and

(b) if in that person's opinion such a meeting should be summoned, the date on which, and time and place at which, he proposes the meeting should be held.

(3) On considering a report under this section the court may—

(a) without any application, make an interim order under section 252, if it thinks that it is appropriate to do so for the purpose of facilitating the consideration and implementation of the debtor's proposal, or

(b) if it thinks it would be inappropriate to make such an order, make a bankruptcy order.

(4) An interim order made by virtue of this section ceases to have effect at the end of such period as the court may specify for the purpose of enabling the debtor's proposal to be considered by his creditors in accordance with the applicable provisions of Part VIII.

(5) Where it has been reported to the court under this section that a meeting of the debtor's creditors should be summoned, the person making the report shall, unless the court otherwise directs, summon that meeting for the time, date and place proposed in his report.

The meeting is then deemed to have been summoned under section 257 in Part VIII, and subsections (2) and (3) of that section, and sections 258 to 263 apply accordingly.

DEFINITIONS
"bankruptcy order": s.381(2).
"creditor": s.383.
"debtor": s.385(1).
"proposal": s.253(1), (2).
"the court": ss.373, 385(1).
"voluntary arrangement": s.253(1).

GENERAL NOTE
This section, which combines together provisions formerly contained within ss.111(3), 112(1), (7)(b), 114(1) and 123(3)–(5) of the 1985 Act, is applicable where the court appoints an insolvency practitioner under s.273(2) to undertake the tasks specified in that subsection. As indicated in the General Note to s.273, the purpose of this prescribed procedure, which

the court must observe in every case where a debtor's petition is presented, is to ensure that proper consideration is given to the possibility of utilising the new procedure for effecting a voluntary arrangement between the debtor and his creditors, as an alternative to the debtor undergoing adjudication as a bankrupt.

Subs. (3)

An interim order under s.252

The making of an interim order introduces a moratorium in respect of the debtor's person and property pending the determination of the process of seeking to conclude a voluntary arrangement between the debtor and his creditors. The ensuing stages of the procedure take place in accordance with the provisions contained in ss.256–263.

Summary administration

275.—(1) Where on the hearing of a debtor's petition the court makes a bankruptcy order and the case is as specified in the next subsection, the court shall, if it appears to it appropriate to do so, issue a certificate for the summary administration of the bankrupt's estate.

(2) That case is where it appears to the court—

  (*a*) that if a bankruptcy order were made the aggregate amount of the bankruptcy debts so far as unsecured would be less than the small bankruptcies level (within the meaning given by section 273), and

  (*b*) that within the period of 5 years ending with the presentation of the petition the debtor has neither been adjudged bankrupt nor made a composition with his creditors in satisfaction of his debts or a scheme of arrangement of his affairs,

whether the bankruptcy order is made because it does not appear to the court as mentioned in section 273(1)(*b*) or (*d*), or it is made because the court thinks it would be inappropriate to make an interim order under section 252.

(3) The court may at any time revoke a certificate issued under this section if it appears to it that, on any grounds existing at the time the certificate was issued, the certificate ought not to have been issued.

DEFINITIONS

"bankrupt": s.381(1).
"bankruptcy debt": s.382.
"bankruptcy order": s.381(2).
"debtor's petition": ss.264(1)(*b*), 285(1).
"interim order": s.252(2).
"secured", "unsecured": ss.383, 385(1).
"the court": ss.373, 385(1).
"the small bankruptcies level": s.273(1).

GENERAL NOTE

This section corresponds to subs. (6) and (7) of s.126 of the 1985 Act. It provides for the summary administration of a bankrupt's estate to take place pursuant to a certificate issued by the court in the exercise of its discretion upon being satisfied that the requirements of subs. (2) are fulfilled. Summary administration is a long established procedure for use in cases where the aggregate amount of a bankrupt's unsecured debts is relatively small. The monetary figure which represents the upper limit for the use of this procedure is the amount known as the "small bankruptcies level" which, as provided in s.273(1), is an amount to be prescribed in an order made with reference to that subsection under s.418(1) of the Act.

Other cases for special consideration

Default in connection with voluntary arrangement

276.—(1) The court shall not make a bankruptcy order on a petition under section 264(1)(*c*) (supervisor of, or person bound by, voluntary arrangement proposed and approved) unless it is satisfied—

(a) that the debtor has failed to comply with his obligations under the voluntary arrangement, or

(b) that information which was false or misleading in any material particular or which contained material omissions—

   (i) was contained in any statement of affairs or other document supplied by the debtor under Part VIII to any person, or

   (ii) was otherwise made available by the debtor to his creditors at or in connection with a meeting summoned under that Part, or

(c) that the debtor has failed to do all such things as may for the purposes of the voluntary arrangement have been reasonably required of him by the supervisor of the arrangement.

(2) Where a bankruptcy order is made on a petition under section 264(1)(c), any expenses properly incurred as expenses of the administration of the voluntary arrangement in question shall be a first charge on the bankrupt's estate.

DEFINITIONS
"affairs": s.385(2).
"bankruptcy order": s.381(2).
"creditor": s.383.
"estate": ss.283, 385(1).
"supervisor of a voluntary arrangement": s.263(2).
"the bankrupt": s.381(1).
"the court": ss.373, 385(1).
"the debtor": s.385(1).
"voluntary arrangement": s.253(1)

GENERAL NOTE
This section controls the operation of s.264(1)(c), under which a petition for a bankruptcy order to be made against an individual may be presented by the supervisor of, or any person (other than the individual himself) who is for the time being bound by a composition or scheme which has taken effect under Part VIII. S.260(2) indicates which persons are bound by such an arrangement. Paras. (a), (b), and (c) of subs. (1) of the present section restrict the scope for any of the persons mentioned in s.264(1)(c) to procure the arranging debtor's adjudication, by imposing alternative requirements, one of which at least must be established to the satisfaction of the court before it is empowered to make a bankruptcy order on such a petition. This section corresponds to s.124 of the 1985 Act.

Subs. (2)
This safeguards the claims for expenses of the supervisor and other persons who have been responsible for the administration of the voluntary arrangement up to the time of its discontinuation consequential upon the debtor's adjudication. These expenses become prepreferential debts in the bankruptcy.

Petition based on criminal bankruptcy order

277.—(1) Subject to section 266(3), the court shall make a bankruptcy order on a petition under section 264(1)(d) on production of a copy of the criminal bankruptcy order on which the petition is based.

This does not apply if it appears to the court that the criminal bankruptcy order has been rescinded on appeal.

(2) Subject to the provisions of this Part, the fact that an appeal is pending against any conviction by virtue of which a criminal bankruptcy order was made does not affect any proceedings on a petition under section 264(1)(d) based on that order.

(3) For the purposes of this section, an appeal against a conviction is pending—

(a) in any case, until the expiration of the period of 28 days beginning with the date of conviction;

(*b*) if notice of appeal to the Court of Appeal is given during that period and during that period the appellant notifies the official receiver of it, until the determination of the appeal and thereafter for so long as an appeal to the House of Lords is pending within the meaning of section 40(5) of the Powers of Criminal Courts Act 1973.

DEFINITIONS
"appeal to the House of Lords": Powers of Criminal Courts Act 1973, s.40(5).
"bankruptcy order": s.381(2).
"criminal bankruptcy order": s.385(1); Powers of Criminal Courts Act 1973, s.39(1).
"the court": ss.373, 385(1).
"the official receiver": s.399(1).

GENERAL NOTE
This makes provision for an adjudication of bankruptcy to take place on a petition presented under s.264(1)(*d*) by the Official Petitioner or any person specified in the criminal bankruptcy order on which the petition is based. A criminal bankruptcy order may be made under the provisions contained in ss.39–41 inclusive of the Powers of Criminal Courts Act 1973, together with Sched. 2 to that Act. The procedure is designed to facilitate the recovery of the proceeds of criminal activity, or of compensation for the victims of such activities, by making it possible for a criminal convicted before the Crown Court to undergo subsequent adjudication by the Bankruptcy Court, upon a petition presented on the basis of a criminal bankruptcy order, made at its discretion by the court of criminal jurisdiction. However, the procedure is not considered to be a satisfactory or effective way of depriving convicted offenders of the proceeds of their crimes, and may in due course be replaced under fresh legislation.

Commencement and duration of bankruptcy; discharge

Commencement and continuance

278. The bankruptcy of an individual against whom a bankruptcy order has been made—
(*a*) commences with the day on which the order is made, and
(*b*) continues until the individual is discharged under the following provisions of this Chapter.

DEFINITION
"bankruptcy order": s.381(2).

TRANSITIONAL PROVISIONS
Sched. 11, paras. 10–12.

GENERAL NOTE
This section, which comprises subs. (1) of s.126 of the 1985 Act, supplies the basic statutory authority for determining the technical dates of commencement of bankruptcy and the termination thereof. With the abolition of the former concept of the "act of bankruptcy," the doctrine of "relation back" of the commencement of bankruptcy has likewise disappeared, so that the commencement date is the day on which the bankruptcy order itself is made. The duration of bankruptcy, until either the debtor is discharged or the bankruptcy order is annulled, is controlled by the further provisions in ss.279–282.

Duration

279.—(1) Subject as follows, a bankrupt is discharged from bankruptcy—
(*a*) in the case of an individual who was adjudged bankrupt on a petition under section 264(1)(*d*) or who had been an undischarged bankrupt at any time in the period of 15 years ending with the commencement of the bankruptcy, by an order of the court under the section next following, and

(*b*) in any other case, by the expiration of the relevant period under this section.

(2) That period is as follows—

(*a*) where a certificate for the summary administration of the bankrupt's estate has been issued and is not revoked before the bankrupt's discharge, the period of 2 years beginning with the commencement of the bankruptcy, and

(*b*) in any other case, the period of 3 years beginning with the commencement of the bankruptcy.

(3) Where the court is satisfied on the application of the official receiver that an undischarged bankrupt in relation to whom subsection (1)(*b*) applies has failed or is failing to comply with any of his obligations under this Part, the court may order that the relevant period under this section shall cease to run for such period, or until the fulfilment of such conditions (including a condition requiring the court to be satisfied as to any matter), as may be specified in the order.

(4) This section is without prejudice to any power of the court to annul a bankruptcy order.

DEFINITIONS
"bankrupt": s.381(1).
"bankruptcy order": s.381(2).
"date of commencement of bankruptcy": s.278(*a*).
"the official receiver": s.399(1).
"the relevant period": subss. (2), (3).

TRANSITIONAL PROVISION:
Sched. 11, para. 13.

GENERAL NOTE
This provides the framework of rules under which a bankruptcy shall come to an end by discharge, apart from cases where discharge is granted by order of the court under s.280, or where a bankruptcy is annulled under s.261(1)(*a*) or s.282.

The provisions for discharge from bankruptcy formerly contained in s.26 of the Bankruptcy Act 1914 and ss.7 and 8 of the Insolvency Act 1976 are repealed, and those provisions are replaced with a less complex scheme of approach, as follows. Persons who are adjudicated bankrupt for the first time will obtain an automatic discharge after the elapse of three years from the commencement of bankruptcy, and in the case where the summary administration procedure is employed that period is shortened to two years. In the case where a person has previously been adjudicated bankrupt, and had the status of undischarged bankrupt at any time in the period of fifteen years prior to the date of commencement of his subsequent bankruptcy, it will be necessary for him to apply for discharge under s.280. So, too, where a person is adjudicated bankrupt on a petition under s.264(1)(*d*) based upon a criminal bankruptcy order made against the person in question. No applications for discharge by bankrupts falling into either of these categories may be entertained until after the elapse of at least five years from the commencement of bankruptcy (s.280(1)). Finally, where an undischarged bankrupt who is eligible for automatic discharge after three or two years, as the case may be, is reported to the Official Receiver as failing or as having failed to comply with the obligations to which, as an undischarged bankrupt, he is subject for the time being the court may make an order which suspends the running of time up to automatic discharge. Such an order may operate for a specified period, or until such time as the court is satisfied that the bankrupt is properly fulfilling his legal obligations and duties. The provisions for discharge under this section bear no correspondence to the relevant recommendations of the *Cork Report* (paras. 605–615), but are broadly in line with the proposals in paras. 117–119 of the *White Paper*.

Discharge by order of the court

280.—(1) An application for an order of the court discharging an individual from bankruptcy in a case falling within section 279(1)(*a*) may be made by the bankrupt at any time after the end of the period of 5 years beginning with the commencement of the bankruptcy.

(2) On an application under this section the court may—
(*a*) refuse to discharge the bankrupt from bankruptcy,
(*b*) make an order discharging him absolutely, or
(*c*) make an order discharging him subject to such conditions with respect to any income which may subsequently become due to him, or with respect to property devolving upon him, or acquired by him, after his discharge, as may be specified in the order.

(3) The court may provide for an order falling within subsection (2)(*b*) or (*c*) to have immediate effect or to have its effect suspended for such period, or until the fulfilment of such conditions (including a condition requiring the court to be satisfied as to any matter), as may be specified in the order.

DEFINITIONS
"commencement of bankruptcy": s.278(*a*).
"property": s.436.
"the bankrupt": s.381(1).
"the court": ss.373, 385(1).

GENERAL NOTE
This section becomes applicable under the circumstances stated in s.279(1)(*a*). The procedure for seeking discharge from bankruptcy through application to the court is now reserved for cases where a person undergoes adjudication within fifteen years of any time at which he was previously an undischarged bankrupt, or where a person is adjudicated as a result of the making of a criminal bankruptcy order against him. In neither case may an application be made by the bankrupt sooner than five years from the date of the making of the bankruptcy order.
The new provision effects a drastic simplification of the law previously contained in s.26 of the Bankruptcy Act 1914 (repealed). There is no longer any requirement that the court have regard to the bankrupt's conduct prior to and during bankruptcy, and the subsidiary code of so-called "bankruptcy offences" has completely disappeared. Of the former facility, which was seldom used in practice, for the court to grant the bankrupt a certificate of misfortune in conjunction with the order of discharge, there is no trace within the new provisions.
The court's powers in relation to an application for discharge are set out in subs. (2), and are fully discretionary. The court thus enjoys the option of refusing to make an order of discharge, or of granting one either on absolute or on conditional terms, and in either of those cases the court may provide for the order to have immediate effect or to be suspended for a specified or an indefinite period. The provisions of this and the previous section are aimed at striking a balance between rehabilitation and deterrence, and to provide encouragement to the bankrupt to contribute further towards the payment to creditors after his discharge (*cf.* H.L. Vol. 459, col. 1257; H.C. Standing Committee E, June 18, 1985, col. 370). The range of powers available to the court under this section, although shorn of the former accompanying detailed provisions as to their exercise, should be sufficiently familiar to enable the courts to perform their task in a manner which may prove to be not too dissimilar to their accustomed practice.
This section corresponds to s.127 of the 1985 Act.

Subs. (2)

On an application under this section
Where such an application is made, the official receiver is required by s.289(2) to make a report to the court with regard to the debtor's conduct and affairs, and the court must consider that report before determining what order, if any, to make.

Effect of discharge

281.—(1) Subject as follows, where a bankrupt is discharged, the discharge releases him from all the bankruptcy debts, but has no effect—
(*a*) on the functions (so far as they remain to be carried out) of the trustee of his estate, or

(*b*) on the operation, for the purposes of the carrying out of those functions, of the provisions of this Part;

and, in particular, discharge does not affect the right of any creditor of the bankrupt to prove in the bankruptcy for any debt from which the bankrupt is released.

(2) Discharge does not affect the right of any secured creditor of the bankrupt to enforce his security for the payment of a debt from which the bankrupt is released.

(3) Discharge does not release the bankrupt from any bankruptcy debt which he incurred in respect of, or forbearance in respect of which was secured by means of, any fraud or fraudulent breach of trust to which he was a party.

(4) Discharge does not release the bankrupt from any liability in respect of a fine imposed for an offence or from any liability under a recognisance except, in the case of a penalty imposed for an offence under an enactment relating to the public revenue or of a recognisance, with the consent of the Treasury.

(5) Discharge does not, except to such extent and on such conditions as the court may direct, release the bankrupt from any bankruptcy debt which—

(*a*) consists in a liability to pay damages for negligence, nuisance or breach of a statutory, contractual or other duty, being damages in respect of personal injuries to any person, or

(*b*) arises under any order made in family proceedings or in domestic proceedings.

(6) Discharge does not release the bankrupt from such other bankruptcy debts, not being debts provable in his bankruptcy, as are prescribed.

(7) Discharge does not release any person other than the bankrupt from any liability (whether as partner or co-trustee of the bankrupt or otherwise) from which the bankrupt is released by the discharge, or from any liability as surety for the bankrupt or as a person in the nature of such a surety.

(8) In this section—

"domestic proceedings" means domestic proceedings within the meaning of the Magistrates' Courts Act 1980 and any proceedings which would be such proceedings but for section 65(1)(ii) of that Act (proceedings for variation of order for periodical payments);

"family proceedings" means the same as in Part V of the Matrimonial and Family Proceedings Act 1984;

"fine" means the same as in the Magistrates' Courts Act 1980; and

"personal injuries" includes death and any disease or other impairment of a person's physical or mental condition.

DEFINITIONS
  "bankrupt": s.381(1).
  "bankruptcy debt": s.382.
  "creditor": s.383.
  "debt": ss.382(3), 385(1).
  "domestic proceedings": subs. (8).
  "family": s.385(1).
  "family proceedings": subs. (8).
  "fine": subs. (8).
  "liability": s.382(4).
  "personal injuries": subs. (8).
  "prescribed": s.384(1).
  "secured", "unsecured creditor": ss.383, 385(1).

GENERAL NOTE
This section defines the effects of an order of discharge from bankruptcy and also indicates the exact limits of those effects. The section also indicates clearly which kinds of debt or liability are not released as a consequence of discharge from bankruptcy. The essential principle is that discharge releases the bankrupt from all those debts known as "the bankruptcy debts." These are defined in s.382(1) and (2) as any debt or liability to which the bankrupt is subject at the commencement of bankruptcy or which, though the bankrupt did not become subject to them until after the commencement of the bankruptcy (or even until after his discharge therefrom), arise from an obligation incurred before the commencement of bankruptcy. The term "bankruptcy debt" also includes any amount specified in a criminal bankruptcy order made against the debtor before the commencement of bankruptcy, and any interest provable in accordance with s.322(2).

As a general rule, all claims which are provable in bankruptcy are also released by discharge. There are long-standing exceptions to this rule, which are re-enacted in subss. (3), (4) and (5). Certain kinds of debt or liability are not admissible to proof in the bankruptcy of the person who has incurred them. On principle, any debt or liability which is excluded from the category of provable debts is correspondingly excluded from the category of debts from which the bankrupt is released by his discharge. This effect is preserved by subs. (6). Formerly, s.30(1) of the Bankruptcy Act 1914 (repealed) expressly excluded from proof in bankruptcy any claims for damages in tort which were unliquidated at the commencement of bankruptcy. This provision was criticised and its abolition recommended in paras. 1310–1318 of the *Cork Report*. Subs. (6) of this section indicates that the category of non-provable debts will be delineated in the rules, so it remains to be seen to what extent unliquidated claims in tort will henceforth be admissible to proof. However, it is significant that subs. (5)(*a*) now provides that certain debts resulting from liability in tort or contract shall not be released by discharge from bankruptcy except to such extent and on such conditions as the court may direct. The debts in question are those which arise in respect of personal injuries to any person resulting from negligence, nuisance or breach of a statutory, contractual or other duty. A non-exhaustive meaning of the term "personal injuries" is supplied in subs. (8).

This section corresponds to s.128 of the 1985 Act.

Court's power to annul bankruptcy order

282.—(1) The court may annul a bankruptcy order if it at any time appears to the court—

    (*a*) that, on any grounds existing at the time the order was made, the order ought not to have been made, or

    (*b*) that, to the extent required by the rules, the bankruptcy debts and the expenses of the bankruptcy have all, since the making of the order, been either paid or secured for to the satisfaction of the court.

(2) The court may annul a bankruptcy order made against an individual on a petition under paragraph (*a*), (*b*) or (*c*) of section 264(1) if it at any time appears to the court, on an application by the Official Petitioner—

    (*a*) that the petition was pending at a time when a criminal bankruptcy order was made against the individual or was presented after such an order was so made, and

    (*b*) no appeal is pending (within the meaning of section 277) against the individual's conviction of any offence by virtue of which the criminal bankruptcy order was made;

and the court shall annul a bankruptcy order made on a petition under section 264(1)(*d*) if it at any time appears to the court that the criminal bankruptcy order on which the petition was based has been rescinded in consequence of an appeal.

(3) The court may annul a bankruptcy order whether or not the bankrupt has been discharged from the bankruptcy.

(4) Where the court annuls a bankruptcy order (whether under this section or under section 261 in Part VIII)—

    (*a*) any sale or other disposition of property, payment made or other thing duly done, under any provision in this Group of Parts, by or under the authority of the official receiver or a trustee of the bankrupt's estate or by the court is valid, but

(*b*) if any of the bankrupt's estate is then vested, under any such provision, in such a trustee, it shall vest in such person as the court may appoint or, in default of any such appointment, revert to the bankrupt on such terms (if any) as the court may direct;

and the court may include in its order such supplemental provisions as may be authorised by the rules.

(5) In determining for the purposes of section 279 whether 'a person was an undischarged bankrupt at any time, any time when he was a bankrupt by virtue of an order that was subsequently annulled is to be disregarded.

DEFINITIONS

"bankrupt": s.381(1).
"bankruptcy debt": s.382.
"bankruptcy order": s.381(2).
"criminal bankruptcy order": s.385(1); Powers of Criminal Courts Act 1973, s.39(1).
"estate": ss.283, 385(1).
"property": s.436.
"secured": ss.383, 385(1).
"the court": ss.373, 385(1).
"the Official Petitioner": s.402; Powers of Criminal Courts Act 1973, s.41(1).
"the official receiver": s.399(1).
"the rules": ss.384, 412.

GENERAL NOTE

This section gathers together the various circumstances in which, and the grounds upon which, the court may annul a bankruptcy order.

The section corresponds to s.129 of the 1985 Act.

Subs. (1)

This reproduces the substance of s.29(1) of the Bankruptcy Act 1914 (repealed), but with the addition of the qualifying proviso that the court's discretionary power of annulment under para. (*a*) must be exercised on the basis of grounds existing at the time the bankruptcy order was made. On the other hand, the ground for annulment contained in para. (*b*) is more liberally conceived than the former provision in that it does not require that all the debts should have actually been paid before the annulment of the bankruptcy order can take place, provided that all the debts and expenses of the bankruptcy are at least adequately secured for.

Subs. (2)

See also s.266(4), which allows the court to dismiss a petition which is pending at a time when a criminal bankruptcy order is made against the debtor, or which is presented after the making of such an order. The intention underlying that provision, as also the present subsection, is to allow the criminal bankruptcy order to furnish the basis for the petition and adjudication in order that the amount mentioned in that order may count as a bankruptcy debt within the definition of that term contained in s.382(1).

CHAPTER II

PROTECTION OF BANKRUPT'S ESTATE AND INVESTIGATION OF HIS AFFAIRS

Definition of bankrupt's estate

283.—(1) Subject as follows, a bankrupt's estate for the purposes of any of this Group of Parts comprises—

(*a*) all property belonging to or vested in the bankrupt at the commencement of the bankruptcy, and

(*b*) any property which by virtue of any of the following provisions of this Part is comprised in that estate or is treated as falling within the preceding paragraph.

(2) Subsection (1) does not apply to—

(a) such tools, books, vehicles and other items of equipment as are necessary to the bankrupt for use personally by him in his employment, business or vocation;

(b) such clothing, bedding, furniture, household equipment and provisions as are necessary for satisfying the basic domestic needs of the bankrupt and his family.

This subsection is subject to section 308 in Chapter IV (certain excluded property reclaimable by trustee).

(3) Subsection (1) does not apply to—

(a) property held by the bankrupt on trust for any other person, or

(b) the right of nomination to a vacant ecclesiastical benefice.

(4) References in any of this Group of Parts to property, in relation to a bankrupt, include references to any power exercisable by him over or in respect of property except in so far as the power is exercisable over or in respect of property not for the time being comprised in the bankrupt's estate and—

(a) is so exercisable at a time after either the official receiver has had his release in respect of that estate under section 299(2) in Chapter III or a meeting summoned by the trustee of that estate under section 331 in Chapter IV has been held, or

(b) cannot be so exercised for the benefit of the bankrupt;

and a power exercisable over or in respect of property is deemed for the purposes of any of this Group of Parts to vest in the person entitled to exercise it at the time of the transaction or event by virtue of which it is exercisable by that person (whether or not it becomes so exercisable at that time).

(5) For the purposes of any such provision in this Group of Parts, property comprised in a bankrupt's estate is so comprised subject to the rights of any person other than the bankrupt (whether as a secured creditor of the bankrupt or otherwise) in relation thereto, but disregarding—

(a) any rights in relation to which a statement such as is required by section 269(1)(a) was made in the petition on which the bankrupt was adjudged bankrupt, and

(b) any rights which have been otherwise given up in accordance with the rules.

(6) This section has effect subject to the provisions of any enactment not contained in this Act under which any property is to be excluded from a bankrupt's estate.

DEFINITIONS

    "bankrupt": s.381(1).

    "business": s.436.

    "commencement of bankruptcy": s.278(a).

    "estate": s.385(1) and this section.

    "family": s.385(1).

    "property": subs. (4), s.436.

    "the official receiver": s.399(1).

    "the rules": ss.384, 412.

    "transaction": s.436.

GENERAL NOTE

This section replaces, and considerably modifies, the former provisions concerning the bankrupt's available property which were contained in s.38 of the Bankruptcy Act 1914 (repealed). The pre-existing law was described, and in many respects criticised, in Chaps. 22–24 inclusive of the *Cork Report*.

This section corresponds to s.130 of the 1985 Act.

Subs. (1)

All property belonging to or vested in the bankrupt at the commencement of the bankruptcy

This fixes the point in time at which the "stock taking," so to speak, is to be carried out in relation to the bankrupt's estate. The property thereby discovered to belong to or be vested in the bankrupt is capable of augmentation according to the further provisions of this Part of the Act, but is diminished, on the other hand, in consequence of the exemptions contained in subss. (2)–(6) inclusive. A notable change in the rule regarding the vesting of the bankrupt's available estate in his trustee in bankruptcy (pursuant to s.306 *et seq.*) is the abolition of the doctrine of "relation back" of the trustee's title, formerly contained in s.37 of the Bankruptcy Act 1914. This doctrine in its existing form was rendered anomalous by the abolition of the concept of acts of bankruptcy. However, important provisions imposing restrictions on a debtor's powers of disposal of property in the period following the presentation of a bankruptcy petition relating to the debtor are contained in s.284. The powers of the trustee in bankruptcy to recover property disposed of by the bankrupt at any time prior to the commencement of bankruptcy, together with other provisions for the protection and enhancement of the bankrupt's available estate, are now contained in ss.339–344 inclusive. Another notable change in the law is the abolition of the "reputed ownership" doctrine, formerly enacted in s.38(c) of the Bankruptcy Act 1914 (repealed), and the subject of a separate chapter in the *Cork Report* (Chap. 23) in which its repeal was forcefully recommended.

The relevant provisions with regard to the effects of bankruptcy upon the bankrupt's interest in any matrimonial home are contained in ss.336–338. The trustee's rights in relation to the bankrupt's after-acquired property are contained in s.307.

Subs. (2)

This exempting provision replaces that formerly enacted as s.38(2) of the Bankruptcy Act 1914 (repealed), and is not only more reasonable and flexible than its predecessor, in accordance with the more enlightened policy by which the law is now meant to be infused, but is also drafted in language more suitable to the present day. The recommendations of Chap. 24 of the *Cork Report* have been closely followed, including the notable inclusion of "vehicles" and other items of equipment falling within the terms of the broad, but practical, formula which governs all cases of exemption under para. (a), namely that the exempted item should be *necessary* to the bankrupt for *personal* use in the context of his employment, business or vocation. Section 436 defines the term "business" as including a trade or profession. Most notably, there is no longer any arbitrary monetary limit imposed upon the total value of property to which this statutory exemption may attach.

The provisions of s.308 sensibly enable the trustee in bankruptcy to reclaim any item of exempted property which proves to be of intrinsically greater value than the cost of a reasonable substitute capable of performing the same functions.

Subs. (3)(a)

This restates the existing law formerly expressed in s.38(1) of the Bankruptcy Act 1914 (repealed).

Subs. (3)(b)

This restates the existing law, which was previously contained in the infelicitiously drafted s.38(b) of the Bankruptcy Act 1914. Other components of that repealed provision are now subsumed under subs. (4).

Restrictions on dispositions of property

284.—(1) Where a person is adjudged bankrupt, any disposition of property made by that person in the period to which this section applies is void except to the extent that it is or was made with the consent of the court, or is or was subsequently ratified by the court.

(2) Subsection (1) applies to a payment (whether in cash or otherwise) as it applies to a disposition of property and, accordingly, where any payment is void by virtue of that subsection, the person paid shall hold the sum paid for the bankrupt as part of his estate.

(3) This section applies to the period beginning with the day of the presentation of the petition for the bankruptcy order and ending with the vesting, under Chapter IV of this Part, of the bankrupt's estate in a trustee.

(4) The preceding provisions of this section do not give a remedy against any person—

    (*a*) in respect of any property or payment which he received before the commencement of the bankruptcy in good faith, for value and without notice that the petition had been presented, or

    (*b*) in respect of any interest in property which derives from an interest in respect of which there is, by virtue of this subsection, no remedy.

(5) Where after the commencement of his bankruptcy the bankrupt has incurred a debt to a banker or other person by reason of the making of a payment which is void under this section, that debt is deemed for the purposes of any of this Group of Parts to have been incurred before the commencement of the bankruptcy unless—

    (*a*) that banker or person had notice of the bankruptcy before the debt was incurred, or

    (*b*) it is not reasonably practicable for the amount of the payment to be recovered from the person to whom it was made.

(6) A disposition of property is void under this section notwithstanding that the property is not or, as the case may be, would not be comprised in the bankrupt's estate; but nothing in this section affects any disposition made by a person of property held by him on trust for any other person.

DEFINITIONS

"bankrupt": s.381(1).
"bankruptcy petition": s.381(3).
"commencement of bankruptcy": s.278(*a*).
"debt": ss.382(3), 385(1).
"estate": ss.283, 385(1).
"property": s.436.

GENERAL NOTE

This section applies restrictions on dispositions of property made by a bankrupt between the time of the presentation of the petition for the bankruptcy order which is subsequently made against him and the time when his estate vests in his trustee in bankruptcy under Chap. IV of Part IX. The making of a bankruptcy order has the effect of rendering void any disposition of property made by the bankrupt during the period since the presentation of the bankruptcy petition, except to the extent that the disposition was made with the consent of the court or is or has been subsequently ratified by the court.

This section corresponds to s.131 of the 1985 Act.

Subs. (2)

This extends the meaning of "disposition of property" in subs. (1) so that it applies to any payment in cash or in kind which is made by a debtor during the "suspect period" following the presentation of a bankruptcy petition against him.

Subs. (4)

This creates a protected position in favour of certain persons who are to enjoy immunity against any remedy which might otherwise result from the fact that a payment or disposition is rendered void by this section. This protection arises in favour of a person who either has received the property or payment before the day on which the bankruptcy order was made; has dealt in good faith; for value; and without notice that the bankruptcy petition had been presented, or has derived his interest in the property from an interest which is already protected on that basis.

Subs. (5)

This provides a specially enhanced degree of protection for bankers and others, and is designed as a replacement for the former protective provision contained in s.4 of the Bankruptcy (Amendment) Act 1926 (repealed). It will give protection to bankers, among others, who, after the commencement of bankruptcy, honour a cheque drawn by the bankrupt before the commencement date in effecting a payment which in the event is rendered void by this section. The debt thus incurred by the bankrupt would, but for this subsection, not be provable in the bankruptcy because it was incurred after the commencement of bankruptcy. However, provided that the banker did not have notice of the bankruptcy before the debt was incurred by, in the example chosen, the banker's honouring the cheque, and provided also that it is not reasonably practicable for the amount of the payment to be recovered from the party by whom or on whose behalf payment was collected, the payment is by virtue of this subsection deemed to have been made before the commencement of bankruptcy, with the consequence that it will count as a provable debt in the bankruptcy.

Restriction on proceedings and remedies

285.—(1) At any time when proceedings on a bankruptcy petition are pending or an individual has been adjudged bankrupt the court may stay any action, execution or other legal process against the property or person of the debtor or, as the case may be, of the bankrupt.

(2) Any court in which proceedings are pending against any individual may, on proof that a bankruptcy petition has been presented in respect of that individual or that he is an undischarged bankrupt, either stay the proceedings or allow them to continue on such terms as it thinks fit.

(3) After the making of a bankruptcy order no person who is a creditor of the bankrupt in respect of a debt provable in the bankruptcy shall—

(*a*) have any remedy against the property or person of the bankrupt in respect of that debt, or

(*b*) before the discharge of the bankrupt, commence any action or other legal proceedings against the bankrupt except with the leave of the court and on such terms as the court may impose.

This is subject to sections 346 (enforcement procedures) and 347 (limited right to distress).

(4) Subject as follows, subsection (3) does not affect the right of a secured creditor of the bankrupt to enforce his security.

(5) Where any goods of an undischarged bankrupt are held by any person by way of pledge, pawn or other security, the official receiver may, after giving notice in writing of his intention to do so, inspect the goods.

Where such a notice has been given to any person, that person is not entitled, without leave of the court, to realise his security unless he has given the trustee of the bankrupt's estate a reasonable opportunity of inspecting the goods and of exercising the bankrupt's right of redemption.

(6) References in this section to the property or goods of the bankrupt are to any of his property or goods, whether or not comprised in his estate.

DEFINITIONS
"bankrupt": s.381(1).
"bankruptcy order": s.381(2).
"bankruptcy petition": s.381(3).
"creditor": s.383.
"debt": ss.382(3), 385(1).
"goods": subs. (6).
"property": subs. (6), s.436.
"security", "unsecured creditor": ss.383, 385(1).
"the court": ss.373, 385(1).
"the debtor": s.385(1).
"the Official Receiver": s.399(1).

GENERAL NOTE
This provides for a moratorium under the control of the court in respect of all kinds of action and legal process against the person or property of a debtor or bankrupt, with effect from the moment of the presentation of a bankruptcy petition respecting him or her. The

provision essentially re-enacts the existing law under ss.7 and 9 of the Bankruptcy Act 1914 (repealed). The new provision also maintains the existing exemption from the moratorium in respect of any creditors whose debts would not be provable in the bankruptcy: such creditors remain free to commence or continue any legal proceedings against the debtor pertaining to claims of that character.

This section corresponds to s.132 of the 1985 Act.

Subs. (4)

This is the customary saving in respect of the right of a secured creditor to enforce his security notwithstanding the bankruptcy and notwithstanding the general terms of the moratorium imposed by this section.

Subs. (5)

This re-enacts, with only minor amendments of drafting, s.59 of the Bankruptcy Act 1914 (repealed).

Power to appoint interim receiver

286.—(1) The court may, if it is shown to be necessary for the protection of the debtor's property, at any time after the presentation of a bankruptcy petition and before making a bankruptcy order, appoint the official receiver to be interim receiver of the debtor's property.

(2) Where the court has, on a debtor's petition, appointed an insolvency practitioner under section 273 and it is shown to the court as mentioned in subsection (1) of this section, the court may, without making a bankruptcy order, appoint that practitioner, instead of the official receiver, to be interim receiver of the debtor's property.

(3) The court may by an order appointing any person to be an interim receiver direct that his powers shall be limited or restricted in any respect; but, save as so directed, an interim receiver has, in relation to the debtor's property, all the rights, powers, duties and immunities of a receiver and manager under the next section.

(4) An order of the court appointing any person to be an interim receiver shall require that person to take immediate possession of the debtor's property or, as the case may be, the part of it to which his powers as interim receiver are limited.

(5) Where an interim receiver has been appointed, the debtor shall give him such inventory of his property and such other information, and shall attend on the interim receiver at such times, as the latter may for the purpose of carrying out his functions under this section reasonably require.

(6) Where an interim receiver is appointed, section 285(3) applies for the period between the appointment and the making of a bankruptcy order on the petition, or the dismissal of the petition, as if the appointment were the making of such an order.

(7) A person ceases to be interim receiver of a debtor's property if the bankruptcy petition relating to the debtor is dismissed, if a bankruptcy order is made on the petition or if the court by order otherwise terminates the appointment.

(8) References in this section to the debtor's property are to all his property, whether or not it would be comprised in his estate if he were adjudged bankrupt.

DEFINITIONS

"bankruptcy order": s.381(2).
"bankruptcy petition": s.381(3).
"debtor": s.385(1).
"debtor's petition": ss.264(1)(*b*), 385(1).
"property": subs. (8), s.436.
"the court": ss.373, 385(1).
"the official receiver": s.399(1).

GENERAL NOTE

This section empowers the court after presentation of a bankruptcy petition and before a bankruptcy order is made to appoint the official receiver to be interim receiver of the debtor's estate where this is shown to be necessary for the protection of the debtor's property. This procedure replaces the stage in the former bankruptcy procedure established under the provisions of ss.3 and 6(1) of the Bankruptcy Act 1914 (repealed), whereby a receiving order was made in all cases as the court's initial order upon the hearing of a bankruptcy petition, with the official receiver being constituted as receiver for that purpose. The elimination of the receiving order from the new bankruptcy procedure has left a necessity for provision to be made for protective arrangements of the kind embodied in the present section. Usually, the official receiver will assume responsibility for the task of interim receiver unless the court utilises its power under subs. (2) to appoint some other person than the official receiver to this position. This power is exercisable where a debtor's petition is presented in circumstances where the court is required by s.273(2) to appoint a qualified insolvency practitioner to prepare a report as to the debtor's willingness to make a proposal for a voluntary arrangement. Subs. (2) authorises the court to appoint that person as interim receiver with, usually, the rights, powers and duties of a receiver and manager under s.287.

This section corresponds to s.133 of the 1985 Act.

Receivership pending appointment of trustee

287.—(1) Between the making of a bankruptcy order and the time at which the bankrupt's estate vests in a trustee under Chapter IV of this Part, the official receiver is the receiver and (subject to section 370 (special manager)) the manager of the bankrupt's estate and is under a duty to act as such.

(2) The function of the official receiver while acting as receiver or manager of the bankrupt's estate under this section is to protect the estate; and for this purpose—

(a) he has the same powers as if he were a receiver or manager appointed by the High Court, and

(b) he is entitled to sell or otherwise dispose of any perishable goods comprised in the estate and any other goods so comprised the value of which is likely to diminish if they are not disposed of.

(3) The official receiver while acting as receiver or manager of the estate under this section—

(a) shall take all such steps as he thinks fit for protecting any property which may be claimed for the estate by the trustee of that estate,

(b) is not, except in pursuance of directions given by the Secretary of State, required to do anything that involves his incurring expenditure,

(c) may, if he thinks fit (and shall, if so directed by the court) at any time summon a general meeting of the bankrupt's creditors.

(4) Where—

(a) the official receiver acting as receiver or manager of the estate under this section seizes or disposes of any property which is not comprised in the estate, and

(b) at the time of the seizure or disposal the official receiver believes, and has reasonable grounds for believing, that he is entitled (whether in pursuance of an order of the court or otherwise) to seize or dispose of that property,

the official receiver is not to be liable to any person in respect of any loss or damage resulting from the seizure or disposal except in so far as that loss or damage is caused by his negligence; and he has a lien on the property, or the proceeds of its sale, for such of the expenses of the bankruptcy as were incurred in connection with the seizure or disposal.

(5) This section does not apply where by virtue of section 297 (appointment of trustee; special cases) the bankrupt's estate vests in a trustee immediately on the making of the bankruptcy order.

"bankrupt": s.381(1).
"bankruptcy order": s.381(2).
"creditor": s.383.
"estate": ss.283, 385(1).
"property": s.436.
"the official receiver": s.399(1).

GENERAL NOTE

The streamlining of bankruptcy procedure under this Act has led to the discontinuation of the use of receiving orders. However, in most cases (apart from those governed by s.297) an interval of time will elapse between the making of the bankruptcy order and the formal appointment of a trustee in bankruptcy in whom the bankrupt's estate will then automatically vest by virtue of s.306. To safeguard and maintain the bankrupt's property during that interval of time, this section provides for the official receiver to be receiver and manager of the bankrupt's estate with the same powers as a receiver or manager appointed by the High Court. The duties of the official receiver in this capacity are defined, and provision made for the summoning of a meeting of creditors either on the initiative of the official receiver or at the court's direction. Subs. (4) provides the customary immunity for the official receiver when acting in the bona fide and reasonable belief that property which he is seizing or of which he is disposing is part of that which he is entitled to seize or dispose of in pursuance of his functions under this section. Where the circumstances are such as to render it expedient that a special manager be appointed, an application may be made to the court by the Official Receiver under s.370. If a special manager is appointed the official receiver's functions and status in relation to the bankrupt's estate, pending the appointment of a trustee in bankruptcy, are reduced to those of a receiver only.

This section corresponds to s.134 of the 1985 Act.

Statement of affairs

288.—(1) Where a bankruptcy order has been made otherwise than on a debtor's petition, the bankrupt shall submit a statement of his affairs to the official receiver before the end of the period of 21 days beginning with the commencement of the bankruptcy.

(2) The statement of affairs shall contain—

(a) such particulars of the bankrupt's creditors and of his debts and other liabilities and of his assets as may be prescribed, and

(b) such other information as may be prescribed.

(3) The official receiver may, if he thinks fit—

(a) release the bankrupt from his duty under subsection (1), or

(b) extend the period specified in that subsection;

and where the official receiver has refused to exercise a power conferred by this section, the court, if it thinks fit, may exercise it.

(4) A bankrupt who—

(a) without reasonable excuse fails to comply with the obligation imposed by this section, or

(b) without reasonable excuse submits a statement of affairs that does not comply with the prescribed requirements,

is guilty of a contempt of court and liable to be punished accordingly (in addition to any other punishment to which he may be subject).

DEFINITIONS

"bankruptcy order": s.381(2).
"commencement of bankruptcy": s.278(a).
"creditor": s.383.
"debt", "liability": ss.382(3), (4), 385(1).
"debtor's petition": ss.264(1)(b), 385(1).
"prescribed": s.384(1).
"the bankrupt": s.381(1).
"the official receiver": s.399(1).

This provision replaces the former s.14 of the Bankruptcy Act 1914 (repealed), and modifies considerably the requirements attached to the bankrupt's traditional duty to supply a statement of affairs to the official receiver. The period of time allowed for the preparation and submission of the statement is set at 21 days from the date of the bankruptcy order, and can be extended by the official receiver at his discretion. This is a far more realistic time limit than the seven days which were formerly allowed, and which moreover could only be extended by order of the court. The official receiver is also clothed with a discretion to release the bankrupt from the duty to submit a statement of affairs. This is designed to a certain extent as a parallel to the provision in s.131(1) relating to the preparation of a statement of affairs of a company in a winding up by the court, whereby the requirement is invocable at the official receiver's discretion. It is intended that the official receiver should exercise his discretion under this section to release a bankrupt who is too ill to lodge a statement of affairs, but in such cases the rules will provide that the official receiver will be subject to a duty to send out a report to all creditors explaining why no statement has been obtained.

This section corresponds to s.135 of the 1985 Act.

Subs. (1)

Bankruptcy order has been made otherwise than on a debtor's petition
This exception arises because, under s.272(2), where a debtor's petition is presented to the court it must be accompanied by a statement of the debtor's affairs in the prescribed form.

Investigatory duties of official receiver

289.—(1) Subject to subsection (5) below, it is the duty of the official receiver to investigate the conduct and affairs of every bankrupt and to make such report (if any) to the court as he thinks fit.

(2) Where an application is made by the bankrupt under section 280 for his discharge from bankruptcy, it is the duty of the official receiver to make a report to the court with respect to the prescribed matters; and the court shall consider that report before determining what order (if any) to make under that section.

(3) A report by the official receiver under this section shall, in any proceedings, be prima facie evidence of the facts stated in it.

(4) In subsection (1) the reference to the conduct and affairs of a bankrupt includes his conduct and affairs before the making of the order by which he was adjudged bankrupt.

(5) Where a certificate for the summary administration of the bankrupt's estate is for the time being in force, the official receiver shall carry out an investigation under subsection (1) only if he thinks fit.

DEFINITIONS
   "bankrupt": s.381(1).
   "estate": ss.283, 385(1).
   "prescribed": s.384(1).
   "the court": ss.373, 385(1).
   "the official receiver": s.399(1).

GENERAL NOTE
This section is of considerable importance in that it imposes a statutory duty upon the official receiver to investigate the conduct and affairs of every bankrupt, and to report to the court if he deems it appropriate to do so. The further duty established by subs. (2) in relation to an application for discharge is a restatement of the former requirement under s.26(2) of the Bankruptcy Act 1914 (repealed), and is relocated here as a logical part of the recitation of the official receiver's investigatory duties. The Act thus commits the official receiver to an active involvement in all cases of bankruptcy, even where a privately appointed trustee in bankruptcy assumes responsibility for the administration of the bankruptcy. The Government have thus conceded the validity and importance of the vigorously-argued case made out in Chap. 14 of the *Cork Report* (esp. paras. 714–731), and have relented from their previously announced intention to withdraw the official receiver completely from all

responsibility in personal bankruptcy (see the Government's Green Paper of July 1980, Cmnd. 7967; *Fletcher* (1981) 44 M.L.R. 77). The statements contained in paras. 36 and 37 of the *White Paper* indicate that the Cork Committee's arguments subsequently prevailed, and this was acknowledged during Committee proceedings in the House of Commons (see H.C. Standing Committee E, June 18, 1985, cols. 379–380).

This section corresponds to s.136 of the 1985 Act.

Public examination of bankrupt

290.—(1) Where a bankruptcy order has been made, the official receiver may at any time before the discharge of the bankrupt apply to the court for the public examination of the bankrupt.

(2) Unless the court otherwise orders, the official receiver shall make an application under subsection (1) if notice requiring him to do so is given to him, in accordance with the rules, by one of the bankrupt's creditors with the concurrence of not less than one-half, in value, of those creditors (including the creditor giving notice).

(3) On an application under subsection (1), the court shall direct that a public examination of the bankrupt shall be held on a day appointed by the court; and the bankrupt shall attend on that day and be publicly examined as to his affairs, dealings and property.

(4) The following may take part in the public examination of the bankrupt and may question him concerning his affairs, dealings and property and the causes of his failure, namely—

(*a*) the official receiver and, in the case of an individual adjudged bankrupt on a petition under section 264(1)(*d*), the Official Petitioner,

(*b*) the trustee of the bankrupt's estate, if his appointment has taken effect,

(*c*) any person who has been appointed as special manager of the bankrupt's estate or business,

(*d*) any creditor of the bankrupt who has tendered a proof in the bankruptcy.

(5) If a bankrupt without reasonable excuse fails at any time to attend his public examination under this section he is guilty of a contempt of court and liable to be punished accordingly (in addition to any other punishment to which he may be subject).

DEFINITIONS

"affairs": s.385(2).
"bankrupt": s.381(1).
"bankruptcy order": s.381(2).
"business": s.436.
"creditor": s.383(1).
"estate": ss.283, 385(1).
"property": s.436.
"the court": ss.373, 385(1).
"the Official Petitioner": s.402(1); Powers of Criminal Courts Act 1973, s.41(1).
"the official receiver": s.399(1).
"the rules": ss.384, 412.

GENERAL NOTE

This replaces the previous provisions regarding public examination of bankrupts contained in s.15 of the Bankruptcy Act 1914 as modified by s.6 of the Insolvency Act 1976 (both repealed). Under those provisions, the holding of a public examination was obligatory in all cases unless the court by order dispensed with the requirement on specified grounds in response to an application by the official receiver. The new provisions of this section reverse the position so that the holding of a public examination will only take place if the official receiver makes application to the court for this to be done, and the court accedes to his request. The initiative will come from the official receiver in most cases as a consequence of his conclusions drawn after performing his investigative functions under s.289, but subs. (2)

also enables the creditors, or at least so many of them as represent one-half in value of the bankrupt's debts, to serve notice on the official receiver requiring him to apply to the court for a direction that a public examination be held. However, in such cases the court can override the creditors' wishes and order the official receiver not to make the application. Where however the official receiver makes application upon his own initiative under subs. (1), subs. (3) leaves the court with no discretion in the matter, and a direction must be issued for a public examination to be held.

Where a public examination is held, the form and procedure to be followed are basically unchanged, save that subs. (4)(*a*) includes the right of the Official Petitioner (that is, the Director of Public Prosecutions) to participate in the public examination of a bankrupt adjudicated on a criminal bankruptcy order. Although the participation of the official receiver is no longer expressed in mandatory terms, in practice it may be taken for granted that this will occur.

This section corresponds to s.137 of the 1985 Act.

Duties of bankrupt in relation to official receiver

291.—(1) Where a bankruptcy order has been made, the bankrupt is under a duty—

(*a*) to deliver possession of his estate to the official receiver, and

(*b*) to deliver up to the official receiver all books, papers and other records of which he has possession or control and which relate to his estate and affairs (including any which would be privileged from disclosure in any proceedings).

(2) In the case of any part of the bankrupt's estate which consists of things possession of which cannot be delivered to the official receiver, and in the case of any property that may be claimed for the bankrupt's estate by the trustee, it is the bankrupt's duty to do all such things as may reasonably be required by the official receiver for the protection of those things or that property.

(3) Subsections (1) and (2) do not apply where by virtue of section 297 below the bankrupt's estate vests in a trustee immediately on the making of the bankruptcy order.

(4) The bankrupt shall give the official receiver such inventory of his estate and such other information, and shall attend on the official receiver at such times, as the official receiver may for any of the purposes of this Chapter reasonably require.

(5) Subsection (4) applies to a bankrupt after his discharge.

(6) If the bankrupt without reasonable excuse fails to comply with any obligation imposed by this section, he is guilty of a contempt of court and liable to be punished accordingly (in addition to any other punishment to which he may be subject).

DEFINITIONS
"affairs": s.385(2).
"bankruptcy order": s.381(2).
"estate": ss.283, 385(1).
"property": s.436.
"records": s.436.
"the bankrupt": s.381(1).
"the official receiver": s.399(1).

GENERAL NOTE
This section conveniently gathers together in one discrete provision a statement of the various duties under which a person is placed as a consequence of undergoing bankruptcy adjudication, and to which, with respect to the matters specified in subs. (4), he remains subject even after discharge from bankruptcy. The latter provision restates the law previously contained in s.26(9) of the Bankruptcy Act 1914 (repealed). Other parts of the section restate the law previously contained in s.22 of the Act of 1914. The duty to deliver up to the official receiver all books, papers and other records relating to the bankrupt's own estate

and affairs admits of no exception, even in the case of items which would ordinarily be protected by legal professional privilege.

This section corresponds to s.138 of the 1985 Act.

CHAPTER III

TRUSTEES IN BANKRUPTCY

Tenure of office as trustee

Power to make appointments

292.—(1) The power to appoint a person as trustee of a bankrupt's estate (whether the first such trustee or a trustee appointed to fill any vacancy) is exercisable—

(*a*) except at a time when a certificate for the summary administration of the bankrupt's estate is in force, by a general meeting of the bankrupt's creditors;

(*b*) under section 295(2), 296(2) or 300(6) below in this Chapter, by the Secretary of State; or

(*c*) under section 297, by the court.

(2) No person may be appointed as trustee of a bankrupt's estate unless he is, at the time of the appointment, qualified to act as an insolvency practitioner in relation to the bankrupt.

(3) Any power to appoint a person as trustee of a bankrupt's estate includes power to appoint two or more persons as joint trustees; but such an appointment must make provision as to the circumstances in which the trustees must act together and the circumstances in which one or more of them may act for the others.

(4) The appointment of any person as trustee takes effect only if that person accepts the appointment in accordance with the rules. Subject to this, the appointment of any person as trustee takes effect at the time specified in his certificate of appointment.

(5) This section is without prejudice to the provisions of this Chapter under which the official receiver is, in certain circumstances, to be trustee of the estate.

DEFINITIONS

"bankrupt": s.381(1).
"creditor": s.383(1).
"estate": ss.283, 385(1).
"person qualified to act as an insolvency practitioner": s.390.
"the court": ss.373, 385(1).
"the official receiver": s.399(1).
"the rules": ss.384, 412.
"to act as an insolvency practitioner in relation to an individual": s.388(2), (3).

GENERAL NOTE

This section specifies when the power to appoint a trustee in bankruptcy is exercisable, and makes provision with respect to the persons who may be appointed. In conformity with the general policy underlying the Act as manifested in the provisions of Pt. XIII, the person appointed to the position of trustee in bankruptcy must in all cases be a duly qualified insolvency practitioner within the meaning of that Part of the Act.

This section corresponds to s.139 of the 1985 Act.

Subs. (4)

Certificate of appointment

Provisions governing the form and contents of the certificate of appointment will be contained in the rules, in accordance with powers contained in para. 11 of Sched. 9.

Summoning of meeting to appoint first trustee

293.—(1) Where a bankruptcy order has been made and no certificate for the summary administration of the bankrupt's estate has been issued, it is the duty of the official receiver, as soon as practicable in the period of 12 weeks beginning with the day on which the order was made, to decide whether to summon a general meeting of the bankrupt's creditors for the purpose of appointing a trustee of the bankrupt's estate.

This section does not apply where the bankruptcy order was made on a petition under section 264(1)(*d*) (criminal bankruptcy); and it is subject to the provision made in sections 294(3) and 297(6) below.

(2) Subject to the next section, if the official receiver decides not to summon such a meeting, he shall, before the end of the period of 12 weeks above mentioned, give notice of his decision to the court and to every creditor of the bankrupt who is known to the official receiver or is identified in the bankrupt's statement of affairs.

(3) As from the giving to the court of a notice under subsection (2), the official receiver is the trustee of the bankrupt's estate.

DEFINITIONS
  "bankrupt": s.381(1).
  "bankruptcy order": s.381(2).
  "bankruptcy petition": s.381(3).
  "creditor": s.383(1).
  "estate": ss.383, 385(1).
  "the court": ss.373, 385(1).
  "the official receiver": s.399(1).

GENERAL NOTE
  This section imposes a duty on the official receiver to decide within twelve weeks of the day on which the bankruptcy order is made whether to call a meeting of creditors for the purpose of appointing a trustee in bankruptcy. If the official receiver decides not to convene such a meeting he is required to notify the court and every known creditor of the bankrupt, and will be required at the same time to send the creditors a summary of the statement of affairs and a report thereon. The combined despatch of the notice together with supporting information will save duplication of costs and expenses. Where no meeting of creditors has been summoned, or where the official receiver has decided not to summon a meeting, s.294 empowers one-quarter or more in value of the creditors to require the official receiver to call a meeting. Where the available assets are so small as to render the administration of the estate an uneconomic proposition for a privately-appointed trustee, this provision to enable the formality of the creditors' meeting to be omitted is a sensible measure to avoid needless wastage of costs. The provision accords with the proposals in paras. 75–79 of the *White Paper*, and is a parallel to that in s.136 relating to the role of the official receiver in the winding up of a company by the court.
  This section corresponds to s.140 of the 1985 Act.

Subs. (1)

No certificate for the summary administration of the bankrupt's estate has been issued
  The procedure which may result in the making of a summary administration order is prescribed in s.275. S.297(2) provides that where such a certificate is issued, the official receiver shall be trustee of the bankrupt's estate, which thus obviates the need for the summoning of a meeting of creditors. However, s.297(3) empowers the court at its discretion to appoint some other person than the official receiver as trustee of the bankrupt's estate.

Where the bankruptcy order was made on a petition under s.264(1)(d)
  This refers to the making of a bankruptcy order under the provision specified, consequential upon a criminal bankruptcy order. S.297(1) provides that in such cases the official receiver shall be trustee of the bankrupt's estate, which thus obviates the need for the summoning of a meeting of creditors at this stage of the bankruptcy administration.

Subs. (3)

This provides that where the official receiver gives the required notice to the effect that no meeting of creditors is to be held, the official receiver himself shall become trustee in bankruptcy with effect from the date of the giving of notice.

Power of creditors to requisition meeting

294.—(1) Where in the case of any bankruptcy—

    (*a*) the official receiver has not yet summoned, or has decided not to summon, a general meeting of the bankrupt's creditors for the purpose of appointing the trustee, and

    (*b*) a certificate for the summary administration of the estate is not for the time being in force,

any creditor of the bankrupt may request the official receiver to summon such a meeting for that purpose.

(2) If such a request appears to the official receiver to be made with the concurrence of not less than one-quarter, in value, of the bankrupt's creditors (including the creditor making the request), it is the duty of the official receiver to summon the requested meeting.

(3) Accordingly, where the duty imposed by subsection (2) has arisen, the official receiver is required neither to reach a decision for the purposes of section 293(1) nor (if he has reached one) to serve any notice under section 293(2).

DEFINITIONS

    "creditor": s.383(1).
    "estate": ss.283, 385(1).
    "the bankrupt": s.381(1).
    "the official receiver": s.399(1).

GENERAL NOTE

This section makes provision for the creditors to compel the official receiver to convene a creditors' meeting for the purpose of appointing a trustee in bankruptcy, provided that at least one-quarter in value of the creditors are in favour of such a proceeding. But no such requirement can be imposed by the creditors where a certificate for the summary administration of the bankrupt's estate has been made under the procedure established in s.275.

This section corresponds to s.141 of the 1985 Act.

Failure of meeting to appoint trustee

295.—(1) If a meeting summoned under section 293 or 294 is held but no appointment of a person as trustee is made, it is the duty of the official receiver to decide whether to refer the need for an appointment to the Secretary of State.

(2) On a reference made in pursuance of that decision, the Secretary of State shall either make an appointment or decline to make one.

(3) If—

    (*a*) the official receiver decides not to refer the need for an appointment to the Secretary of State, or

    (*b*) on such a reference the Secretary of State declines to make an appointment,

the official receiver shall give notice of his decision or, as the case may be, of the Secretary of State's decision to the court.

(4) As from the giving of notice under subsection (3) in a case in which no notice has been given under section 293(2), the official receiver shall be trustee of the bankrupt's estate.

DEFINITIONS

    "estate": ss.283, 385(1).
    "the bankrupt": s.381(1).
    "the court": ss.373, 385(1).
    "the official receiver": s.399(1).

This provides for the case where a general meeting of creditors is convened under either s.293 or s.294, but no appointment of a trustee in bankruptcy results therefrom. The official receiver must thereupon decide whether or not to refer the matter to the Secretary of State. If this is done, the Secretary of State may at his discretion appoint a qualified person to be the trustee in bankruptcy, but it is not obligatory that he should do so. If the official receiver decides not to refer the matter to the Secretary of State, or if the latter, upon such a reference, declines to make an appointment, subs. (4) provides that the official receiver shall be the trustee in bankruptcy with effect from the date of his giving the requisite notice to the court as required by subs. (3).

This section corresponds to s.142 of the 1985 Act.

Appointment of trustee by Secretary of State

296.—(1) At any time when the official receiver is the trustee of a bankrupt's estate by virtue of any provision of this Chapter (other than section 297(1) below) he may apply to the Secretary of State for the appointment of a person as trustee instead of the official receiver.

(2) On an application under subsection (1) the Secretary of State shall either make an appointment or decline to make one.

(3) Such an application may be made notwithstanding that the Secretary of State has declined to make an appointment either on a previous application under subsection (1) or on a reference under section 295 or under section 300(4) below.

(4) Where the trustee of a bankrupt's estate has been appointed by the Secretary of State (whether under this section or otherwise), the trustee shall give notice to the bankrupt's creditors of his appointment or, if the court so allows, shall advertise his appointment in accordance with the court's directions.

(5) In that notice or advertisement the trustee shall—

(*a*) state whether he proposes to summon a general meeting of the bankrupt's creditors for the purpose of establishing a creditors' committee under section 301, and

(*b*) if he does not propose to summon such a meeting, set out the power of the creditors under this Part to require him to summon one.

DEFINITIONS
"creditor": s.383(1).
"estate": ss.283, 385(1).
"the bankrupt": s.381(1).
"the court": ss.373, 385(1).
"the official receiver": s.399(1).

TRANSITIONAL PROVISION
Sched. 11, para. 14.

GENERAL NOTE
This provides a general permission for the official receiver to apply to the Secretary of State for the appointment of a person as trustee in bankruptcy in place of the official receiver himself. Such an application may be made at any time when the official receiver is the trustee in bankruptcy, and is exercisable regardless of whether previous applications for such an appointment have been made under this section itself, or under s.295 or s.300(4). However it is not made obligatory for the Secretary of State to make an appointment in response to such an application, and in default of any such appointment the official receiver will continue to be trustee in bankruptcy, either by virtue of the general provision contained in s.300(2), or by virtue of any other particular provision under which he came to hold that office (see ss.293(3), 295(4), 297(1), (2)).

This section corresponds to s.143 of the 1985 Act.

Subs. (4)

This provides for the case where a trustee in bankruptcy is appointed by the Secretary of State in response to an application made under subs. (1), or in response to a reference made under s.295(2). The requirement is imposed that the trustee thus appointed shall notify the creditors of his appointment, or advertise the fact if the court so allows, and give indication whether he proposes to summon a general meeting for the purpose of establishing a creditors' committee under s.301. This subsection is a parallel to the provision of s.297(7) which applies where the trustee is appointed by the court.

Special cases

297.—(1) Where a bankruptcy order is made on a petition under section 264(1)(*d*) (criminal bankruptcy), the official receiver shall be trustee of the bankrupt's estate.

(2) Subject to the next subsection, where the court issues a certificate for the summary administration of a bankrupt's estate, the official receiver shall, as from the issue of that certificate, be the trustee.

(3) Where such a certificate is issued or is in force, the court may, if it thinks fit, appoint a person other than the official receiver as trustee.

(4) Where a bankruptcy order is made in a case in which an insolvency practitioner's report has been submitted to the court under section 274 but no certificate for the summary administration of the estate is issued, the court, if it thinks fit, may on making the order appoint the person who made the report as trustee.

(5) Where a bankruptcy order is made (whether or not on a petition under section 264(1)(*c*)) at a time when there is a supervisor of a voluntary arrangement approved in relation to the bankrupt under Part VIII, the court, if it thinks fit, may on making the order appoint the supervisor of the arrangement as trustee.

(6) Where an appointment is made under subsection (4) or (5) of this section, the official receiver is not under the duty imposed by section 293(1) (to decide whether or not to summon a meeting of creditors).

(7) Where the trustee of a bankrupt's estate has been appointed by the court, the trustee shall give notice to the bankrupt's creditors of his appointment or, if the court so allows, shall advertise his appointment in accordance with the directions of the court.

(8) In that notice or advertisement he shall—

(*a*) state whether he proposes to summon a general meeting of the bankrupt's creditors for the purpose of establishing a creditors' committee under section 301 below, and

(*b*) if he does not propose to summon such a meeting, set out the power of the creditors under this Part to require him to summon one.

DEFINITIONS

"bankruptcy order": s.381(2).
"creditor": s.383(1).
"estate": ss.283, 385(1).
"the court": ss.373, 385(1).
"the official receiver": s.399(1).
"supervisor of a voluntary arrangement": s.263(2).
"voluntary arrangement": s.253(1).

GENERAL NOTE

This section determines how the appointment of the trustee in bankruptcy shall take place in certain specially defined cases. Where the operation of any of the provisions contained in subs. (3), (4) or (5) results in the appointment of a trustee in bankruptcy being made by the court, subs. (7) applies with the effect that the trustee must give notice to the creditors of his appointment, or alternatively advertise the fact if the court so allows, and also give indication whether he proposes to summon a general meeting for the purpose of establishing a creditors' committee under s.301. This provision is a parallel to that of s.296(4).

This section corresponds to s.144 of the 1985 Act.

Removal of trustee; vacation of office

298.—(1) Subject as follows, the trustee of a bankrupt's estate may be removed from office only by an order of the court or by a general meeting of the bankrupt's creditors summoned specially for that purpose in accordance with the rules.

(2) Where the official receiver is trustee by virtue of section 297(1), he shall not be removed from office under this section.

(3) A general meeting of the bankrupt's creditors shall not be held for the purpose of removing the trustee at any time when a certificate for the summary administration of the estate is in force.

(4) Where the official receiver is trustee by virtue of section 293(3) or 295(4) or a trustee is appointed by the Secretary of State or (otherwise than under section 297(5)) by the court, a general meeting of the bankrupt's creditors shall be summoned for the purpose of replacing the trustee only if—

(*a*) the trustee thinks fit, or

(*b*) the court so directs, or

(*c*) the meeting is requested by one of the bankrupt's creditors with the concurrence of not less than one-quarter, in value, of the creditors (including the creditor making the request).

(5) If the trustee was appointed by the Secretary of State, he may be removed by a direction of the Secretary of State.

(6) The trustee (not being the official receiver) shall vacate office if he ceases to be a person who is for the time being qualified to act as an insolvency practitioner in relation to the bankrupt.

(7) The trustee may, in the prescribed circumstances, resign his office by giving notice of his resignation to the court.

(8) The trustee shall vacate office on giving notice to the court that a final meeting has been held under section 331 in Chapter IV and of the decision (if any) of that meeting.

(9) The trustee shall vacate office if the bankruptcy order is annulled.

DEFINITIONS
"creditor": s.383(1).
"estate": ss.283, 385(1).
"person qualified to act as an insolvency practitioner": s.390.
"prescribed": s.384(1).
"the bankrupt": s.381(1).
"the court": ss.373, 385(1).
"the official receiver": s.399(1).
"the rules": ss.384, 412.
"to act as an insolvency practitioner in relation to an individual": s.388(2), (3).

GENERAL NOTE
This section contains provisions regulating the circumstances in which, and the procedure by which, a trustee in bankruptcy may be removed from office. The provisions of subss. (6)–(9) inclusive specify in which circumstances a trustee in bankruptcy must vacate his office, and by what means he may resign it.
The section corresponds to s.145 of the 1985 Act.

Subs. (1)
This provides that the only two ways in which a trustee may be removed from office are either by an order of the court or alternatively by a specially convened meeting of the bankrupt's creditors. This is subject to the provision in subs. (2) whereby neither of these possible methods of removal is applicable in the case where the official receiver is serving as the trustee in bankruptcy by virtue of s.297(1), which requires the official receiver to be trustee where the bankruptcy order is made in consequence of a criminal bankruptcy order.

Further restrictions on the scope for removal of a trustee by means of a general meeting of creditors are imposed by subss. (3), (4) and (5).

Subs. (6)

This follows the general policy of the act as a whole, whereby any person who acts as an insolvency practitioner within the meaning of s.388 must be qualified to do so at all relevant times. Under most circumstances a person occupying the office of trustee in bankruptcy who ceases to be qualified to act as an insolvency practitioner in relation to the bankrupt will commit a criminal offence under s.389(1) if he does not immediately vacate office. However, s.391(5) enables transitional arrangements to be included in any order made under subs. (4) of that section whereby the Secretary of State revokes an authorisation previously granted to a professional body conferring upon the members of that body the status of qualified insolvency practitioners for the purposes of this Act. Such arrangements, if made, may enable those affected by the order to conclude their involvement in any existing bankruptcies in an orderly manner, without thereby committing a criminal offence.

Subs. (9)

Annulment of a bankruptcy order may take place in accordance with the provisions of s.282.

Release of trustee

299.—(1) Where the official receiver has ceased to be the trustee of a bankrupt's estate and a person is appointed in his stead, the official receiver shall have his release with effect from the following time, that is to say—

　　(*a*)　where that person is appointed by a general meeting of the bankrupt's creditors or by the Secretary of State, the time at which the official receiver gives notice to the court that he has been replaced, and

　　(*b*)　where that person is appointed by the court, such time as the court may determine.

(2) If the official receiver while he is the trustee gives notice to the Secretary of State that the administration of the bankrupt's estate in accordance with Chapter IV of this Part is for practical purposes complete, he shall have his release with effect from such time as the Secretary of State may determine.

(3) A person other than the official receiver who has ceased to be the trustee shall have his release with effect from the following time, that is to say—

　　(*a*)　in the case of a person who has been removed from office by a general meeting of the bankrupt's creditors that has not resolved against his release or who has died, the time at which notice is given to the court in accordance with the rules that that person has ceased to hold office;

　　(*b*)　in the case of a person who has been removed from office by a general meeting of the bankrupt's creditors that has resolved against his release, or by the court, or by the Secretary of State, or who has vacated office under section 298(6), such time as the Secretary of State may, on an application by that person, determine;

　　(*c*)　in the case of a person who has resigned, such time as may be prescribed;

　　(*d*)　in the case of a person who has vacated office under section 298(8)—

　　　　(i)　if the final meeting referred to in that subsection has resolved against that person's release, such time as the Secretary of State may, on an application by that person, determine; and

　　　　(ii)　if that meeting has not so resolved, the time at which the person vacated office.

(4) Where a bankruptcy order is annulled, the trustee at the time of the annulment has his release with effect from such time as the court may determine.

(5) Where the official receiver or the trustee has his release under this section, he shall, with effect from the time specified in the preceding provisions of this section, be discharged from all liability both in respect of acts or omissions of his in the administration of the estate and otherwise in relation to his conduct as trustee.

But nothing in this section prevents the exercise, in relation to a person who has had his release under this section, of the court's powers under section 304.

DEFINITIONS
"a bankrupt": s.381(1).
"creditor": s.383(1).
"estate": ss.283, 385(1).
"prescribed": s.384(1).
"the court": ss.373, 385(1).
"the official receiver": s.399(1).
"the rules": ss.384, 412.

TRANSITIONAL PROVISION
Sched. 11, para. 14.

GENERAL NOTE
This section provides how, and to what extent, a trustee in bankruptcy is released from liability for his acts or omissions upon his ceasing to hold office. The provisions are so designed as to form a parallel to those of ss.173 and 174, regarding the release of the liquidator in voluntary and in compulsory winding up respectively. Separate provisions are made concerning the manner and timing of the release of a trustee in bankruptcy, depending upon the circumstances in which the termination of his office comes about. Subss. (1) and (2) are concerned with the release of the official receiver when acting as trustee in bankruptcy.
This section corresponds to s.146 of the 1985 Act.

Subs. (3)
This concerns the release of the trustee when some person other than the official receiver is the holder of that office. Provision is made to ensure that, where the trustee is removed from office in circumstances where his conduct has been less than satisfactory, adequate time for investigation is allowed before the trustee's release takes effect. However, provision is inserted in subs. (5) to preserve the application of s.304 even in cases where the person concerned has had his release under this section.

Subs. (5)
This specifies the extent of the release from liability accorded to the trustee with effect from the relevant date determined according to the preceding provisions of this section, with a proviso, as mentioned above, whereby the provisions of s.304 remain applicable even after that moment.

Vacancy in office of trustee

300.—(1) This section applies where the appointment of any person as trustee of a bankrupt's estate fails to take effect or, such an appointment having taken effect, there is otherwise a vacancy in the office of trustee.

(2) The official receiver shall be trustee until the vacancy is filled.

(3) The official receiver may summon a general meeting of the bankrupt's creditors for the purpose of filling the vacancy and shall summon such a meeting if required to do so in pursuance of section 314(7) (creditors' requisition).

(4) If at the end of the period of 28 days beginning with the day on which the vacancy first came to the official receiver's attention he has not

summoned, and is not proposing to summon, a general meeting of creditors for the purpose of filling the vacancy, he shall refer the need for an appointment to the Secretary of State.

(5) Where a certificate for the summary administration of the estate is for the time being in force—

(*a*) the official receiver may refer the need to fill any vacancy to the court or, if the vacancy arises because a person appointed by the Secretary of State has ceased to hold office, to the court or the Secretary of State, and

(*b*) subsections (3) and (4) of this section do not apply.

(6) On a reference to the Secretary of State under subsection (4) or (5) the Secretary of State shall either make an appointment or decline to make one.

(7) If on a reference under subsection (4) or (5) no appointment is made, the official receiver shall continue to be trustee of the bankrupt's estate, but without prejudice to his power to make a further reference.

(8) References in this section to a vacancy include a case where it is necessary, in relation to any property which is or may be comprised in a bankrupt's estate, to revive the trusteeship of that estate after the holding of a final meeting summoned under section 331 or the giving by the official receiver of notice under section 299(2).

DEFINITIONS
"a bankrupt": s.381(1).
"creditor": s.383(1).
"estate": ss.283, 385(1).
"property": s.436.
"the court": ss.373, 385(1).
"the official receiver": s.399(1).

GENERAL NOTE
This section makes provision to enable a vacancy in the office of trustee in bankruptcy to be filled, according to the circumstances in which the vacancy has arisen. However, the appointment of a replacement in office is not made mandatory, and it is possible for the vacancy to be left unfilled. In such cases, the residual provision in subs. (2) (and in subs. (5)), whereby the official receiver is statutory trustee during any vacancy, ensures that the conduct of the bankruptcy continues to its proper conclusion. When so acting as trustee during any period of vacancy, as is indicated by subs. (3), the official receiver is subject to the effects of s.314(7) whereby at least one-tenth in value of the creditors may compel the trustee to summon a general meeting of creditors. Subs. (4) also renders it obligatory for the official receiver to refer the matter to the Secretary of State within 28 days of becoming aware of the vacancy if he himself has taken no steps to convene a meeting of creditors for the purpose of filling the vacancy. However, the Secretary of State is not obliged to respond by making any appointment (subs. (6)).

This section corresponds to s.147 of the 1985 Act.

Control of trustee

Creditors' committee

301.—(1) Subject as follows, a general meeting of a bankrupt's creditors (whether summoned under the preceding provisions of this Chapter or otherwise) may, in accordance with the rules, establish a committee (known as "the creditors' committee") to exercise the functions conferred on it by or under this Act.

(2) A general meeting of the bankrupt's creditors shall not establish such a committee, or confer any functions on such a committee, at any time when the official receiver is the trustee of the bankrupt's estate, except in connection with an appointment made by that meeting of a person to be trustee instead of the official receiver.

DEFINITIONS
"creditor": s.383(1).
"estate": ss.283, 385(1).
"the bankrupt": s.381(1).
"the official receiver": s.399(1).
"the rules": ss.384, 412.

GENERAL NOTE

In Chap. 19 of the *Cork Report* there is extended discussion of the role of creditors, and of creditors' committees, in controlling and supervising the trustee's conduct of the administration of a bankrupt's estate. Paras. 83 and 84 of the *White Paper* indicated a general acceptance of the basic thrust of these recommendations, but in the course of the gestation of the 1985 Act there was a considerable re-appraisal of the relationship to be struck between the committee of creditors and the trustee in bankruptcy, having regard to the fact that the latter will in all cases henceforth be a qualified insolvency practitioner. In view of that, it was thought inappropriate to apply the nomenclature of "supervisory committee", as originally intended. The expression "creditors' committee" has been adopted by the draftsman of the present Act.

The present section completely replaces the provision under s.20 of the Bankruptcy Act 1914 (repealed) under which creditors could formerly appoint a committee of inspection. It empowers the creditors at a general meeting to appoint a committee in accordance with the rules to function for the purposes of the Act. A general meeting for this purpose may be convened by the trustee of his own initiative in accordance with the general authorisation contained is s.314(7). Ss.296(5)(*a*) and 297(8)(*a*) direct the trustee to have regard to the practicability of establishing a creditors' committee. If however the trustee elects not to convene the meeting for this purpose he can be compelled to do so under the further provisions in s.314(7) if at least one-tenth in value of the creditors concur in formally requesting him to summon one.

This section corresponds to s.148 of the 1985 Act.

Subs. (2)

This lays down a rule to the effect that no meeting of creditors may establish a committee under this section at any time when the official receiver is trustee, except where this happens in conjunction with the appointment by such a meeting of a person to replace the official receiver as trustee. This provision complements s.302(1).

Exercise by Secretary of State of functions of creditors' committee

302.—(1) The creditors' committee is not to be able or required to carry out its functions at any time when the official receiver is trustee of the bankrupt's estate; but at any such time the functions of the committee under this Act shall be vested in the Secretary of State, except to the extent that the rules otherwise provide.

(2) Where in the case of any bankruptcy there is for the time being no creditors' committee and the trustee of the bankrupt's estate is a person other than the official receiver, the functions of such a committee shall be vested in the Secretary of State, except to the extent that the rules otherwise provide.

DEFINITIONS
"creditor": s.383(1).
"estate": ss.283, 385(1).
"the bankrupt": s.381(1).
"the official receiver": s.399(1).
"the rules": ss.384, 412.

GENERAL NOTE

This provides for the functions which would otherwise be vested by the Act in a committee of creditors to be vested in the Secretary of State during any period when the official receiver is the trustee in bankruptcy, and to be likewise vested in the Secretary of State at any time when a person other than the official receiver is the trustee in bankruptcy but no committee has been established under s.301.

This section corresponds to s.149 of the 1985 Act.

General control of trustee by the court

303.—(1) If a bankrupt or any of his creditors or any other person is dissatisfied by any act, omission or decision of a trustee of the bankrupt's estate, he may apply to the court; and on such an application the court may confirm, reverse or modify any act or decision of the trustee, may give him directions or may make such other order as it thinks fit.

(2) The trustee of a bankrupt's estate may apply to the court for directions in relation to any particular matter arising under the bankruptcy.

DEFINITIONS
"a bankrupt": s.381(1).
"creditor": s.383(1).
"estate": ss.283, 385(1).
"modify", "modifications": s.436.
"the court": ss.373, 385(1).

GENERAL NOTE
Subs. (1) restates the former provisions of s.80 of the Bankruptcy Act 1914 (repealed) in establishing a general principle that the trustee's actions are ultimately subject to control by the court at the instance of any properly interested party. Subs. (2) restates the former provisions of s.79(3) of the Act of 1914 in enabling the trustee to seek directions from the court at any time.
This section corresponds to s.150 of the 1985 Act.

Liability of trustee

304.—(1) Where on an application under this section the court is satisfied—

    (*a*) that the trustee of a bankrupt's estate has misapplied or retained, or become accountable for, any money or other property comprised in the bankrupt's estate, or

    (*b*) that a bankrupt's estate has suffered any loss in consequence of any misfeasance or breach of fiduciary or other duty by a trustee of the estate in the carrying out of his functions,

the court may order the trustee, for the benefit of the estate, to repay, restore or account for money or other property (together with interest at such rate as the court thinks just) or, as the case may require, to pay such sum by way of compensation in respect of the misfeasance or breach of fiduciary or other duty as the court thinks just.

This is without prejudice to any liability arising apart from this section.

(2) An application under this section may be made by the official receiver, the Secretary of State, a creditor of the bankrupt or (whether or not there is, or is likely to be, a surplus for the purposes of section 330(5) (final distribution)) the bankrupt himself.

But the leave of the court is required for the making of an application if it is to be made by the bankrupt or if it is to be made after the trustee has had his release under section 299.

(3) Where—

    (*a*) the trustee seizes or disposes of any property which is not comprised in the bankrupt's estate, and

    (*b*) at the time of the seizure or disposal the trustee believes, and has reasonable grounds for believing, that he is entitled (whether in pursuance of an order of the court or otherwise) to seize or dispose of that property,

the trustee is not liable to any person (whether under this section or otherwise) in respect of any loss or damage resulting from the seizure or disposal except in so far as that loss or damage is caused by the negligence of the trustee; and he has a lien on the property, or the proceeds of its sale, for such of the expenses of the bankruptcy as were incurred in connection with the seizure or disposal.

DEFINITIONS
"a bankrupt": s.381(1).
"creditor": s.383(1).
"estate": ss.283, 385(1).
"property": s.436.
"the court": ss.373, 385(1).
"the official receiver": s.399(1).

GENERAL NOTE
This section establishes a summary procedure against the trustee in respect of loss to the estate caused by his misapplication or retention of property, or by his misfeasance or breach of duty. It provides a parallel procedure for bankruptcy to that established by s.212 in relation to corporate insolvency. By virtue of s.299(5) a person who has ceased to be trustee remains subject to the provisions of this section despite the fact that he may have gained his release from liability under s.299, but in such cases subs. (2) of this section requires the leave of the court before an application can be made.
This section corresponds to s.151 of the 1985 Act.

Subs. (2)
This states what persons are qualified to make application under this section for an order to be made against a trustee or former trustee in bankruptcy within the terms of subs. (1). A bankrupt is allowed to make application irrespective of whether there is or is not likely to be a surplus at the conclusion of the bankruptcy which would be returnable to him under s.330(5), but in order to prevent vexatious or obstructive applications by a bankrupt against his own trustee, the leave of the court is required for the bringing of all such applications.

Subs. (3)
This provides the trustee with a statutory defence in respect of certain kinds of liability incurred when he seizes or disposes of property not comprised in the bankrupt's estate, in the bona fide and reasonable exercise of his functions in office, unless the trustee has acted with negligence.

CHAPTER IV

ADMINISTRATION BY TRUSTEE

Preliminary

General functions of trustee

305.—(1) This Chapter applies in relation to any bankruptcy where either—
  (*a*) the appointment of a person as trustee of a bankrupt's estate takes effect, or
  (*b*) the official receiver becomes trustee of a bankrupt's estate.
(2) The function of the trustee is to get in, realise and distribute the bankrupt's estate in accordance with the following provisions of this Chapter; and in the carrying out of that function and in the management of the bankrupt's estate the trustee is entitled, subject to those provisions, to use his own discretion.
(3) It is the duty of the trustee, if he is not the official receiver—
  (*a*) to furnish the official receiver with such information,
  (*b*) to produce to the official receiver, and permit inspection by the official receiver of, such books, papers and other records, and
  (*c*) to give the official receiver such other assistance,
as the official receiver may reasonably require for the purpose of enabling him to carry out his functions in relation to the bankruptcy.

(4) The official name of the trustee shall be "the trustee of the estate of . . . , a bankrupt" (inserting the name of the bankrupt); but he may be referred to as "the trustee in bankruptcy" of the particular bankrupt.

DEFINITIONS
"a bankrupt": s.381(1).
"estate": ss.283, 385(1).
"the official receiver": s.399(1).
"records": s.436.

GENERAL NOTE
Chap. IV contains provisions governing the powers and functions of the trustee, the vesting of the bankrupt's estate in the trustee, and the realisation and distribution of the estate to those entitled. This section states the scope of application of the provisions of Chap. IV, and describes the functions of the trustee in bankruptcy with regard to the estate, and his duty with respect to the official receiver, in broad and general terms.
This section corresponds to s.152 of the 1985 Act.

Subs. (1)

The appointment of a person as trustee . . . takes effect
See s.292(4).

The official receiver becomes trustee of the bankrupt's estate
See ss.295(4), 297(1), (2), 300(1), (2), (7).

Subs. (2)

The trustee is entitled . . . to use his own discretion
This restates the provision as to the discretionary powers of the trustee in bankruptcy which was formerly contained in s.79(4) of the Bankruptcy Act 1914 (repealed).

Subs. (3)
This provision is a parallel to s.143(2) which applies in respect of the liquidator of a company in a compulsory winding up.

Acquisition, control and realisation of bankrupt's estate

Vesting of bankrupt's estate in trustee

306.—(1) The bankrupt's estate shall vest in the trustee immediately on his appointment taking effect or, in the case of the official receiver, on his becoming trustee.
(2) Where any property which is, or is to be, comprised in the bankrupt's estate vests in the trustee (whether under this section or under any other provision of this Part), it shall so vest without any conveyance, assignment or transfer.

DEFINITIONS
"estate": ss.283, 385(1).
"property": s.436.
"the bankrupt": s.381(1).
"the official receiver": s.399(1).
"the trustee": s.385(1).

GENERAL NOTE
This section provides for the vesting of the bankrupt's estate in the trustee in bankruptcy immediately upon the latter's appointment taking effect. In the case where the official receiver becomes trustee under any of the provisions of the Act, the vesting occurs simultaneously with his becoming trustee. All vesting of property by virtue of this section occurs automatically by operation of law, without the need for any conveyance, assignment or transfer. This restates with greater clarity and precision the law formerly contained in s.18(1) of the Bankruptcy Act 1914 (repealed).
This section corresponds to s.153 of the 1985 Act.

After-acquired property

307.—(1) Subject to this section and section 309, the trustee may by notice in writing claim for the bankrupt's estate any property which has been acquired by, or has devolved upon, the bankrupt since the commencement of the bankruptcy.

(2) A notice under this section shall not be served in respect of—

(*a*) any property falling within subsection (2) or (3) of section 283 in Chapter II,

(*b*) any property which by virtue of any other enactment is excluded from the bankrupt's estate, or

(*c*) without prejudice to section 280(2)(*c*) (order of court on application for discharge), any property which is acquired by, or devolves upon, the bankrupt after his discharge.

(3) Subject to the next subsection, upon the service on the bankrupt of a notice under this section the property to which the notice relates shall vest in the trustee as part of the bankrupt's estate; and the trustee's title to that property has relation back to the time at which the property was acquired by, or devolved upon, the bankrupt.

(4) Where, whether before or after service of a notice under this section—

(*a*) a person acquires property in good faith, for value and without notice of the bankruptcy, or

(*b*) a banker enters into a transaction in good faith and without such notice,

the trustee is not in respect of that property or transaction entitled by virtue of this section to any remedy against that person or banker, or any person whose title to any property derives from that person or banker.

(5) References in this section to property do not include any property which, as part of the bankrupt's income, may be the subject of an income payments order under section 310.

DEFINITIONS

"bankrupt": s.381(1).
"commencement of the bankruptcy": s.278(*a*).
"estate": ss.283, 385(1).
"property": subs. (5), s.436.
"transaction": s.436.
"the official receiver": s.399(1).
"the trustee": s.385(1).

GENERAL NOTE

This section establishes a procedure whereby any property acquired by the bankrupt after the date of the bankruptcy order may be vested in the trustee upon the latter's intervention to claim it. In Chap. 26 of the *Cork Report* the case was argued for the retention of the basic principle, formerly expressed in s.38(*a*) of the Bankruptcy Act 1914 (repealed) that a bankrupt's available property includes such property as may be acquired by or devolve upon him before his discharge—usually referred to as "after-acquired" property. However, it was recommended at paras. 1151–1157 and 1181 that the statutory rule should be modified so that after-acquired property should not vest automatically in the trustee until he intervenes to claim it. This would entail the reversal of the decision of the Court of Appeal in *Re Pascoe* [1944] Ch. 219, and a restoration of the rule formerly regarded as expressing the law on this matter, as indicated by *dicta* in *Cohen* v. *Mitchell* (1890) 25 Q.B.D. 262. Governmental acceptance of these proposals was indicated in paras. 111–114 of the *White Paper*. The present section implements these recommendations. The trustee in bankruptcy may claim the bankrupt's available, after-acquired property by means of a notice served pursuant to subs. (1), provided that notice is served within the time limit established by the provisions of s.309.

This section corresponds to subs. (1)–(4) and (7) of s.154 of the 1985 Act.

Subss. (3) and (4)

These are important provisions which together establish a rule that where the trustee duly serves notice under subs. (1), any property thereby claimed for the bankrupt's estate shall vest in the trustee with effect from the time at which the property was first acquired by, or devolved upon, the bankrupt himself. The doctrine of relation back in this context is subject to the operation of the provisions in subs. (4) which confer protection, in the cases therein mentioned in paras. (*a*) and (*b*), upon persons dealing with the bankrupt in relation to any after-acquired property which the trustee claims, or has claimed, for the estate. As recommended in para. 1145–1150 of the *Cork Report,* this maintains the position formerly established in s.47 of the Bankruptcy Act 1914 (repealed) but is drafted with greater clarity so as to leave it beyond doubt that a third party (including a banker) can only enjoy the protection of subs. (4) if he has acted without notice of the bankruptcy.

Vesting in trustee of certain items of excess value

308.—(1) Subject to the next section, where—

(*a*) property is excluded by virtue of section 283(2) (tools of trade, household effects, etc.) from the bankrupt's estate, and

(*b*) it appears to the trustee that the realisable value of the whole or any part of that property exceeds the cost of a reasonable replacement for that property or that part of it,

the trustee may by notice in writing claim that property or, as the case may be, that part of it for the bankrupt's estate.

(2) Upon the service on the bankrupt of a notice under this section, the property to which the notice relates vests in the trustee as part of the bankrupt's estate; and, except against a purchaser in good faith, for value and without notice of the bankruptcy, the trustee's title to that property has relation back to the commencement of the bankruptcy.

(3) The trustee shall apply funds comprised in the estate to the purchase by or on behalf of the bankrupt of a reasonable replacement for any property vested in the trustee under this section; and the duty imposed by this subsection has priority over the obligation of the trustee to distribute the estate.

(4) For the purposes of this section property is a reasonable replacement for other property if it is reasonably adequate for meeting the needs met by the other property.

DEFINITIONS

"bankrupt": s.381(1).
"estate": ss.283, 385(1).
"property": s.436.
"reasonable replacement": subs. (4).
"the trustee": s.385(1).

GENERAL NOTE

This section operates in conjunction with s.283, subs. (2) of which indicates what property is excluded from the bankrupt's available estate. Under the procedure established by this section, the trustee may claim by means of a notice in writing any item of the bankrupt's exempted property which appears to have a higher intrinsic value than the cost of providing a reasonable replacement for the bankrupt or his family to use. The cost of providing such a replacement is by subs. (3) made a first charge on the funds comprised in the bankrupt's estate. Such a procedure for substitution of items of exempt property was recommended in para. 1109 of the *Cork Report.*

Subs. (4)

This endeavours to provide a definition of the term "reasonable replacement" for the purposes of this section, but is somewhat tautologous in that the notion of reasonableness occurs both in the definition and in the term defined. Essentially, it will be a matter of judgment for the trustee in bankruptcy in the first instance to determine whether a proposed substitute is a "reasonable replacement", subject to the bankrupt's right to refer the matter to the court under s.303(1) if he is dissatisfied with the trustee's decision. In a case where the trustee is personally uncertain of his own assessment, he may seek directions from the court under s.303(2).

Time-limit for notice under s.307 or 308

309.—(1) Except with the leave of the court, a notice shall not be served—

   (a) under section 307, after the end of the period of 42 days beginning with the day on which it first came to the knowledge of the trustee that the property in question had been acquired by, or had devolved upon, the bankrupt;
   (b) under section 308, after the end of the period of 42 days beginning with the day on which the property in question first came to the knowledge of the trustee.

(2) For the purposes of this section—

   (a) anything which comes to the knowledge of the trustee is deemed in relation to any successor of his as trustee to have come to the knowledge of the successor at the same time; and
   (b) anything which comes (otherwise than under paragraph (a)) to the knowledge of a person before he is the trustee is deemed to come to his knowledge on his appointment taking effect or, in the case of the official receiver, on his becoming trustee.

DEFINITIONS
   "property": ss.307(5), 436.
   "the bankrupt": s.381(1).
   "the court": ss.373, 385(1).
   "the official receiver": s.399(1).
   "the trustee": s.385(1).

GENERAL NOTE
   This section prescribes the time limits for the service of notice by the trustee in the exercise of his powers under ss.307 and 308. It also provides rules for determining the moment at which a matter is deemed to come to the knowledge of the trustee for the time being, for the purpose of establishing the date from which time commences to run. The section is a combination of the provisions formerly contained in ss.154(5), (6) and 155(3) of the 1985 Act.

Income payments orders

310.—(1) The court may, on the application of the trustee, make an order ("an income payments order") claiming for the bankrupt's estate so much of the income of the bankrupt during the period for which the order is in force as may be specified in the order.

(2) The court shall not make an income payments order the effect of which would be to reduce the income of the bankrupt below what appears to the court to be necessary for meeting the reasonable domestic needs of the bankrupt and his family.

(3) An income payments order shall, in respect of any payment of income to which it is to apply, either—

   (a) require the bankrupt to pay the trustee an amount equal to so much of that payment as is claimed by the order, or
   (b) require the person making the payment to pay so much of it as is so claimed to the trustee, instead of to the bankrupt.

(4) Where the court makes an income payments order it may, if it thinks fit, discharge or vary any attachment of earnings order that is for the time being in force to secure payments by the bankrupt.

(5) Sums received by the trustee under an income payments order form part of the bankrupt's estate.

(6) An income payments order shall not be made after the discharge of the bankrupt, and if made before, shall not have effect after his discharge except—

(*a*) in the case of a discharge under section 279(1)(*a*) (order of court), by virtue of a condition imposed by the court under section 280(2)(*c*) (income, etc. after discharge), or

(*b*) in the case of a discharge under section 279(1)(*b*) (expiration of relevant period), by virtue of a provision of the order requiring it to continue in force for a period ending after the discharge but no later than 3 years after the making of the order.

(7) For the purposes of this section the income of the bankrupt comprises every payment in the nature of income which is from time to time made to him or to which he from time to time becomes entitled, including any payment in respect of the carrying on of any business or in respect of any office or employment.

DEFINITIONS

"bankrupt": s.381(1).
"business": s.436.
"court": ss.373, 385(1).
"estate": ss.283, 385(1).
"family": s.385(1).
"income of the bankrupt": subs. (7).
"income payments order": subs. (1).
"the trustee": s.385(1).

GENERAL NOTE

This enables the court on the application of the trustee to make an income payments order whereby a proportion of the income of the bankrupt is claimed for his estate and made available for distribution to creditors. It represents a completely fresh approach in place of the former provisions of s.51 of the Bankruptcy Act 1914 (repealed). Paras. 1158–1163 of the *Cork Report,* while accepting the principle that a proportion of the bankrupt's earnings (net of tax) should be retainable for the maintenance of himself and his family, advocated a more emphatic policy of seeking to maximise the contribution towards the payment of debts by contributions from the bankrupt's surplus income. The principle is re-affirmed that any income of an undischarged bankrupt constitutes after-acquired property, so that the proper approach should be to ascertain by investigation what proportion of income can be regarded as "necessary" for meeting the reasonable domestic needs of the bankrupt and his family (meaning, in this context, the persons who are living with him *and* are dependent upon him: s.385(1)). This approach was accepted in para. 114 of the *White Paper* and forms the basis of this section.

Subs. (4)

Attachment of earnings order

Such orders may be made under the provisions of the Attachment of Earnings Act 1971, ss.1(2)(*c*) and (5).

Subs. (6)

This establishes the general rule that an income payments order may not be made after the discharge of the bankrupt, nor be made so as to remain in effect after that date, subject to the saving, in paras. (*a*) and (*b*), in respect of the exercise of powers vested in the court, firstly under s.280(2)(*c*) whereby the court may make an order for discharge subject to any conditions with respect to any subsequent income or subsequently acquired property, and secondly under s.279(3) whereby the court may make an order, subject to specified conditions, suspending the running of time towards the automatic discharge of the bankrupt under subs. 1(*b*) of that section.

Acquisition by trustee of control

311.—(1) The trustee shall take possession of all books, papers and other records which relate to the bankrupt's estate or affairs and which belong to him or are in his possession or under his control (including any which would be privileged from disclosure in any proceedings).

(2) In relation to, and for the purpose of acquiring or retaining possession of, the bankrupt's estate, the trustee is in the same position as if he were a receiver of property appointed by the High Court; and the court may, on his application, enforce such acquisition or retention accordingly.

(3) Where any part of the bankrupt's estate consists of stock or shares in a company, shares in a ship or any other property transferable in the books of a company, office or person, the trustee may exercise the right to transfer the property to the same extent as the bankrupt might have exercised it if he had not become bankrupt.

(4) Where any part of the estate consists of things in action, they are deemed to have been assigned to the trustee; but notice of the deemed assignment need not be given except in so far as it is necessary, in a case where the deemed assignment is from the bankrupt himself, for protecting the priority of the trustee.

(5) Where any goods comprised in the estate are held by any person by way of pledge, pawn or other security and no notice has been served in respect of those goods by the official receiver under subsection (5) of section 285 (restriction on realising security), the trustee may serve such a notice in respect of the goods; and whether or not a notice has been served under this subsection or that subsection, the trustee may, if he thinks fit, exercise the bankrupt's right of redemption in respect of any such goods.

(6) A notice served by the trustee under subsection (5) has the same effect as a notice served by the official receiver under section 285(5).

DEFINITIONS
 "affairs": s.385(2).
 "bankrupt": s.381(1).
 "estate": ss.283, 385(1).
 "property": s.436.
 "records": s.436.
 "security", "secured creditor": ss.383, 385(1).
 "the official receiver": s.399(1).
 "the trustee": s.385(1).

GENERAL NOTE
 This section requires the trustee to take control of the bankrupt's estate and of all his papers and records relating thereto. For this purpose the trustee is clothed with the powers and right enjoyed by a receiver of property appointed by the High Court, and may invoke any appropriate remedies for the purpose of enforcing his rights of acquisition and retention. The force of this provision is augmented by those of s.333 whereby the duties of the bankrupt in relation to his trustee are laid down.

 The consequential provisions contained in subss. (3)–(6) inclusive of this section facilitate the acquisition by the trustee of such parts of the bankrupt's property as are of an incorporeal nature—choses in action—or such as are transferable only through the instrumentality of some third party, or such as are held by any person who has a security interest or right of retention over them. The section largely restates, with suitable updating in the drafting, the provisions formerly contained in s.48 of the Bankruptcy Act 1914 (repealed).

 This section corresponds to s.157 of the 1985 Act.

Subs. (1)

(including any which would be privileged from disclosure in any proceedings)
 These words in parentheses serve to eliminate all scope for argument to the effect that any document may be exempted from the trustee's power of acquisition under this section by virtue of the fact that it is covered by professional legal privilege.

Obligation to surrender control to trustee

312.—(1) The bankrupt shall deliver up to the trustee possession of any property, books, papers or other records of which he has possession or control and of which the trustee is required to take possession.

This is without prejudice to the general duties of the bankrupt under section 333 in this Chapter.

(2) If any of the following is in possession of any property, books, papers or other records of which the trustee is required to take possession, namely—

(*a*) the official receiver,

(*b*) a person who has ceased to be trustee of the bankrupt's estate, or

(*c*) a person who has been the supervisor of a voluntary arrangement approved in relation to the bankrupt under Part VIII,

the official receiver or, as the case may be, that person shall deliver up possession of the property, books, papers or records to the trustee.

(3) Any banker or agent of the bankrupt or any other person who holds any property to the account of, or for, the bankrupt shall pay or deliver to the trustee all property in his possession or under his control which forms part of the bankrupt's estate and which he is not by law entitled to retain as against the bankrupt or trustee.

(4) If any person without reasonable excuse fails to comply with any obligation imposed by this section, he is guilty of a contempt of court and liable to be punished accordingly (in addition to any other punishment to which he may be subject).

Definitions
    "bankrupt": s.381(1).
    "estate": ss.283, 385(1).
    "property": s.436.
    "records": s.436.
    "supervisor of a voluntary arrangement": s.263(2).
    "the official receiver": s.399(1).
    "the trustee": s.385(1).

General Note
    The provisions of this section are largely complementary to those of s.311, and impose a duty upon the bankrupt, and also upon the persons referred to in subs. (2), to surrender control of the bankrupt's property, papers and records to the trustee. By subs. (4), failure on the part of any person to comply with any obligation imposed by this section is punishable *per se* as a contempt of court. S.349 makes general provision regarding the unenforceability of any liens or other rights of retention of the books, papers or records of the bankrupt, in face of the right of the trustee in bankruptcy to acquire possession thereof.
    This section corresponds to s.158 of the 1985 Act.

Charge on bankrupt's home

313.—(1) Where any property consisting of an interest in a dwelling house which is occupied by the bankrupt or by his spouse or former spouse is comprised in the bankrupt's estate and the trustee is, for any reason, unable for the time being to realise that property, the trustee may apply to the court for an order imposing a charge on the property for the benefit of the bankrupt's estate.

(2) If on an application under this section the court imposes a charge on any property, the benefit of that charge shall be comprised in the bankrupt's estate and is enforceable, up to the value from time to time of the property secured, for the payment of any amount which is payable otherwise than to the bankrupt out of the estate and of interest on that amount at the prescribed rate.

(3) An order under this section made in respect of property vested in the trustee shall provide, in accordance with the rules, for the property to cease to be comprised in the bankrupt's estate and, subject to the charge (and any prior charge), to vest in the bankrupt.

(4) Subsections (1) and (2) and (4) to (6) of section 3 of the Charging Orders Act 1979 (supplemental provisions with respect to charging orders) have effect in relation to orders under this section as in relation to charging orders under that Act.

DEFINITIONS
  "bankrupt": s.381(1).
  "dwelling-house": s.385(1).
  "estate": ss.283, 385(1).
  "property": s.436.
  "prescribed": s.384.
  "the court": ss.373, 385(1).
  "the rules": ss.384, 412.
  "the trustee": s.385(1).

GENERAL NOTE
  This section makes special provision with respect to the bankrupt's interest in a dwelling-house occupied by the bankrupt or by his spouse or former spouse, in cases where the trustee is unable for the time being to realise that property. The section enables the trustee to apply to the court for a charging order to be made in respect of the property for the benefit of the bankrupt's estate. Subs. (4) incorporates by reference certain supplemental provisions of the Charging Orders Act 1979 in relation to an order made under this section.
  The procedure established by this section is of particular relevance in view of the provisions of ss.336 and 337 which give rise to the possibility that the rights of occupation of the bankrupt personally, or of the bankrupt's spouse, or former spouse, may under certain circumstances be held to outweigh for a time the interests of the bankrupt's creditors in relation to the property in question. By s.332(2), the fact that an order has been made, or has been applied for, under this section is a condition which, if fulfilled, enables the trustee in bankruptcy to summon a final meeting of creditors under s.331 despite the fact that he has been unable to realise property in the estate consisting of an interest in a dwelling-house which is occupied by the bankrupt or by his or her past or present spouse.
  This section corresponds to s.159 of the 1985 Act.

Powers of trustee

314.—(1) The trustee may—
  (*a*) with the permission of the creditors' committee or the court, exercise any of the powers specified in Part I of Schedule 5 to this Act, and
  (*b*) without that permission, exercise any of the general powers specified in Part II of that Schedule.

(2) With the permission of the creditors' committee or the court, the trustee may appoint the bankrupt—
  (*a*) to superintend the management of his estate or any part of it,
  (*b*) to carry on his business (if any) for the benefit of his creditors, or
  (*c*) in any other respect to assist in administering the estate in such manner and on such terms as the trustee may direct.

(3) A permission given for the purposes of subsection (1)(*a*) or (2) shall not be a general permission but shall relate to a particular proposed exercise of the power in question; and a person dealing with the trustee in good faith and for value is not to be concerned to enquire whether any permission required in either case has been given.

(4) Where the trustee has done anything without the permission required by subsection (1)(*a*) or (2), the court or the creditors' committee may, for the purpose of enabling him to meet his expenses out of the bankrupt's estate, ratify what the trustee has done.

But the committee shall not do so unless it is satisfied that the trustee has acted in a case of urgency and has sought its ratification without undue delay.

(5) Part III of Schedule 5 to this Act has effect with respect to the things which the trustee is able to do for the purposes of, or in connection with, the exercise of any of his powers under any of this Group of Parts.

(6) Where the trustee (not being the official receiver) in exercise of the powers conferred on him by any provision in this Group of Parts—

(a) disposes of any property comprised in the bankrupt's estate to an associate of the bankrupt, or

(b) employs a solicitor,

he shall, if there is for the time being a creditors' committee, give notice to the committee of that exercise of his powers.

(7) Without prejudice to the generality of subsection (5) and Part III of Schedule 5, the trustee may, if he thinks fit, at any time summon a general meeting of the bankrupt's creditors.

Subject to the preceding provisions in this Group of Parts, he shall summon such a meeting if he is requested to do so by a creditor of the bankrupt and the request is made with the concurrence of not less than one-tenth, in value, of the bankrupt's creditors (including the creditor making the request).

(8) Nothing in this Act is to be construed as restricting the capacity of the trustee to exercise any of his powers outside England and Wales.

DEFINITIONS
"associate": ss.435, 436.
"bankrupt": s.381(1).
"bankruptcy debt": s.382.
"business": s.436.
"creditor": s.383(1).
"debt", "liability": ss.382(3), (4), 385(1).
"estate": ss.283, 385(1).
"property": s.436.
"security", "secured": ss.383, 385(1).
"the court": ss.373, 385(1).
"the official receiver": s.399(1).
"the trustee": s.385(1).

TRANSITIONAL PROVISION
Sched. 11, para. 14(6).

GENERAL NOTE
This section, which operates in conjunction with Sched. 5 to the Act, specifies the general powers of the trustee in bankruptcy, and indicates which of them are exercisable on his own initiative without permission (subs. (1)(b)), and which are exercisable with the permission of the creditors' committee (if there is one) or otherwise of the court (subss. (1)(a), (2)). The provisions of the first two subsections, together with Sched. 5, largely restate the provisions formerly contained in ss.55, 56 and 57 of the Bankruptcy Act 1914 (repealed). However, in accordance with the recommendation in paras. 795–6 of the *Cork Report* the former requirement that the trustee must obtain the permission of the creditors' committee before employing a solicitor has been replaced by the requirement in subs. (6) that, where a trustee other than the official receiver employs a solicitor in the exercise of his powers under this Part, he must give notice of that fact to the creditors' committee if there is one in being at the time.

This section corresponds to s.160 of the 1985 Act, save that the provisions contained in subss. (1) and (2) of that section are now contained in Sched. 5 to the present Act.

Subs. (6)(a)

Disposes of any property . . . to an associate of the bankrupt

It has been assumed that the requirements under Pt. XIII of this Act, whereby all privately appointed trustees in bankruptcy are henceforth required to be qualified insolvency practitioners within the meaning of s.390, will largely ensure the discontinuation of certain notorious malpractices whereby trustees in bankruptcy have collusively disposed of assets at a low price to persons connected with the bankrupt. This subsection therefore does not deprive the trustee of the power to dispose of any property belonging to the bankrupt's estate to a person who is an associate of the bankrupt (within the meaning of s.435), but it does impose the requirement that the trustee must inform the creditors' committee (if there is one) of any transaction falling into this category. The onus then rests with the committee to determine whether the transaction was abusive or not, and if necessary to challenge the trustee's act under s.303. Furthermore the trustee remains amenable to the procedure for imposing summary liability under s.304 even after he has obtained his release under s.299. He could therefore be challenged retrospectively on account of any transaction not initially perceived to be abusive and detrimental to the creditors' interests.

Subs. (7)
This confers a wide power upon the trustee to summon a general meeting of creditors at any time at his own discretion. It also establishes a procedure whereby one or more creditors, representing at least one-tenth in value of the bankrupt's creditors, may formally compel the trustee to convene a general meeting.

Disclaimer of onerous property

Disclaimer (general power)

315.—(1) Subject as follows, the trustee may, by the giving of the prescribed notice, disclaim any onerous property and may do so notwithstanding that he has taken possession of it, endeavoured to sell it or otherwise exercised rights of ownership in relation to it.

(2) The following is onerous property for the purposes of this section, that is to say—

(*a*) any unprofitable contract, and

(*b*) any other property comprised in the bankrupt's estate which is unsaleable or not readily saleable, or is such that it may give rise to a liability to pay money or perform any other onerous act.

(3) A disclaimer under this section—

(*a*) operates so as to determine, as from the date of the disclaimer, the rights, interests and liabilities of the bankrupt and his estate in or in respect of the property disclaimed, and

(*b*) discharges the trustee from all personal liability in respect of that property as from the commencement of his trusteeship,

but does not, except so far as is necessary for the purpose of releasing the bankrupt, the bankrupt's estate and the trustee from any liability, affect the rights or liabilities of any other person.

(4) A notice of disclaimer shall not be given under this section in respect of any property that has been claimed for the estate under section 307 (after-acquired property) or 308 (personal property of bankrupt exceeding reasonable replacement value), except with the leave of the court.

(5) Any person sustaining loss or damage in consequence of the operation of a disclaimer under this section is deemed to be a creditor of the bankrupt to the extent of the loss or damage and accordingly may prove for the loss or damage as a bankruptcy debt.

DEFINITIONS
"bankrupt": s.381(1).
"bankruptcy debt": s.382.
"commencement of trusteeship": s.292(4).
"creditor": s.383(1).
"estate": ss.283, 385(1).
"liability": s.283(4).
"onerous property": subs. (2).
"prescribed": s.384.

"property": s.436.
"the court": ss.201, 211(1).
"the trustee": s.385(1).

GENERAL NOTE

This section empowers the trustee to disclaim onerous property (as defined in subs. (2)) which is comprised in the bankrupt's estate. Chap. 27 of the *Cork Report* was devoted to a consideration of the disclaimer codes formerly applicable in winding-up and in bankruptcy respectively. The former, which were embodied in ss.618 and 619 of the Companies Act 1985 together with Pt. I of Sched. 20 to that Act (repealed) are now replaced by ss.178–182 of this Act, while the latter, formerly contained in s.54 of the Bankruptcy Act 1914 (repealed) are replaced by this section. The provisions concerning disclaimer in bankruptcy are now largely harmonised with those applicable in a winding-up: see General Note to ss.178–182.

This section corresponds to subss. (1)–(4) and (10) of s.161 of the 1985 Act.

Subs. (3)(b)

As from the commencement of his trusteeship

This phrase is intended to emphasise that a disclaimer is only effective to discharge the disclaiming trustee from liability in respect of the disclaimed property from the date specified. No predecessor in the office of trustee will obtain any discharge from liability by virtue of a disclaimer effected by the incumbent office holder.

Subs. (4)

Where the trustee in bankruptcy has previously exercised his powers under s.307 to claim an item of after-acquired property, or under s.308 to claim an item of property originally exempted from passing into the bankrupt's estate, he is not allowed to disclaim any property so claimed except with the leave of the court. This provision corresponds to the recommendation in para. 1199 of the *Cork Report*.

Subs. (5)

Note that s.320(5) requires the effect of any order made under that section to be taken into account in assessing for the purposes of this subsection the extent of any loss or damage sustained in consequence of the disclaimer.

Notice requiring trustee's decision

316.—(1) Notice of disclaimer shall not be given under section 315 in respect of any property if—

(*a*) a person interested in the property has applied in writing to the trustee or one of his predecessors as trustee requiring the trustee or that predecessor to decide whether he will disclaim or not, and

(*b*) the period of 28 days beginning with the day on which that application was made has expired without a notice of disclaimer having been given under section 315 in respect of that property.

(2) The trustee is deemed to have adopted any contract which by virtue of this section he is not entitled to disclaim.

DEFINITIONS

"property": s.436.
"the trustee": s.385(1).

GENERAL NOTE

This section, which corresponds to s.161(5) of the 1985 Act, establishes a procedure whereby a person interested in property comprised in the bankrupt's estate may put an end to any uncertainty regarding the possibility of the trustee's exercising the power of disclaimer under s.315 with regard to the property in question. By making the written application referred to in subs. (1)(*a*), the person interested sets in motion a process by which the trustee must either exercise the power of disclaimer within 28 days, or lose altogether the right to disclaim the property affected.

Disclaimer of leaseholds

317.—(1) The disclaimer of any property of a leasehold nature does not take effect unless a copy of the disclaimer has been served (so far as the trustee is aware of their addresses) on every person claiming under the bankrupt as underlessee or mortgagee and either—

   (*a*) no application under section 320 below is made with respect to the property before the end of the period of 14 days beginning with the day on which the last notice served under this subsection was served, or

   (*b*) where such an application has been made, the court directs that the disclaimer is to take effect.

(2) Where the court gives a direction under subsection (1)(*b*) it may also, instead of or in addition to any order it makes under section 320, make such orders with respect to fixtures, tenant's improvements and other matters arising out of the lease as it thinks fit.

DEFINITIONS
   "property": s.436.
   "the bankrupt": s.381(1).
   "the court": ss.373, 385(1).
   "the trustee": s.385(1).

GENERAL NOTE
This section, which comprises the provisions formerly contained in subss. (6) and (7) of s.161 of the 1985 Act, contains particular rules applicable in the case where the trustee exercises the power of disclaimer under s.315 in relation to property of a leasehold nature.

Disclaimer of dwelling house

318. Without prejudice to section 317, the disclaimer of any property in a dwelling house does not take effect unless a copy of the disclaimer has been served (so far as the trustee is aware of their addresses) on every person in occupation of or claiming a right to occupy the dwelling house and either—

   (*a*) no application under section 320 is made with respect to the property before the end of the period of 14 days beginning with the day on which the last notice served under this section was served, or

   (*b*) where such an application has been made, the court directs that the disclaimer is to take effect.

DEFINITIONS
   "dwelling house": s.385(1).
   "property": s.436.
   "the court": ss.373, 385(1).

GENERAL NOTE
This section, which comprises the provision formerly contained in s.161(8) of the 1985 Act, has application in the case where the trustee exercises the power of disclaimer under s.315 in relation to a dwelling house.

Disclaimer of land subject to rentcharge

319.—(1) The following applies where, in consequence of the disclaimer under section 315 of any land subject to a rentcharge, that land vests by operation of law in the Crown or any other person (referred to in the next subsection as "the proprietor").

(2) The proprietor, and the successors in title of the proprietor, are not subject to any personal liability in respect of any sums becoming due under the rentcharge, except sums becoming due after the proprietor, or

some person claiming under or through the proprietor, has taken possession or control of the land or has entered into occupation of it.

"the proprietor": subs. (2).

GENERAL NOTE

This section, which comprises the provision formerly contained in s.161(9) of the 1985 Act, has application in the case where the trustee exercises the power of disclaimer under s.315 in relation to any land subject to a rentcharge. The section confers protection upon the Crown or any other person (here referred to as "the proprietor") in whom the land consequently vests by operation of law, and ensures that those parties are not liable for any sums becoming due under the rentcharge prior to the date when the proprietor first takes possession or control of the land, or enters into occupation of it.

Court order vesting disclaimed property

320.—(1) This section and the next apply where the trustee has disclaimed property under section 315.

(2) An application may be made to the court under this section by—

(*a*) any person who claims an interest in the disclaimed property,

(*b*) any person who is under any liability in respect of the disclaimed property, not being a liability discharged by the disclaimer, or

(*c*) where the disclaimed property is property in a dwelling house, any person who at the time when the bankruptcy petition was presented was in occupation of or entitled to occupy the dwelling house.

(3) Subject as follows in this section and the next, the court may, on an application under this section, make an order on such terms as it thinks fit for the vesting of the disclaimed property in, or for its delivery to—

(*a*) a person entitled to it or a trustee for such a person,

(*b*) a person subject to such a liability as is mentioned in subsection (2)(*b*) or a trustee for such a person, or

(*c*) where the disclaimed property is property in a dwelling house, any person who at the time when the bankruptcy petition was presented was in occupation of or entitled to occupy the dwelling house.

(4) The court shall not make an order by virtue of subsection (3)(*b*) except where it appears to the court that it would be just to do so for the purpose of compensating the person subject to the liability in respect of the disclaimer.

(5) The effect of any order under this section shall be taken into account in assessing for the purposes of section 315(5) the extent of any loss or damage sustained by any person in consequence of the disclaimer.

(6) An order under this section vesting property in any person need not be completed by any conveyance, assignment or transfer.

DEFINITIONS
"dwelling-house": s.385(1).
"liability": s.382(4).
"property": s.436.
"the court": ss.373, 385(1).
"the trustee": s.385(1).

GENERAL NOTE

The provisions of this section are complementary to those of ss.315–319, and provide for the court to make a vesting order upon the application of any of the persons mentioned in subs. (2), being a person who either has an interest in, or is subject to, a continuing liability in respect of any property disclaimed by the trustee under s.315. This section bears a general similarity to s.181, which makes comparable provisions for the court to make vesting orders in respect of property disclaimed by a liquidator under ss.178–180. The overall clarity of drafting in this new section is a considerable improvement over that of the former provisions of s.54(6) of the Bankruptcy Act 1914 (repealed).

This section corresponds to subss. (1)–(4), (9) and (10) of s.162 of the 1985 Act.

Order under s.320 in respect of leaseholds

321.—(1) The court shall not make an order under section 320 vesting property of a leasehold nature in any person, except on terms making that person—

(*a*) subject to the same liabilities and obligations as the bankrupt was subject to under the lease on the day the bankruptcy petition was presented, or

(*b*) if the court thinks fit, subject to the same liabilities and obligations as that person would be subject to if the lease had been assigned to him on that day.

(2) For the purposes of an order under section 320 relating to only part of any property comprised in a lease, the requirements of subsection (1) apply as if the lease comprised only the property to which the order relates.

(3) Where subsection (1) applies and no person is willing to accept an order under section 320 on the terms required by that subsection, the court may (by order under section 320) vest the estate or interest of the bankrupt in the property in any person who is liable (whether personally or in a representative capacity and whether alone or jointly with the bankrupt) to perform the lessee's covenants in the lease.

The court may by virtue of this subsection vest that estate and interest in such a person freed and discharged from all estates, incumbrances and interests created by the bankrupt.

(4) Where subsection (1) applies and a person declines to accept any order under section 320, that person shall be excluded from all interest in the property.

DEFINITIONS
  "property": s.436.
  "the bankrupt": s.381(1).
  "the court": ss.373, 385(1).

GENERAL NOTE
  This section, which comprises subss. (5)–(8) of s.162 of the 1985 Act, contains provisions which apply in the case where a vesting order is made under s.320 in respect of property of a leasehold nature which has been disclaimed by the trustee under s.315.

Subs. (3)
  It is to be noted that the word "estate" is twice used in this subsection, but in a sense different from that which is ascribed to the term by the combined provisions of ss.283 and 385(1), which apply in the context of any reference to the *corpus* of property of which the bankrupt is divested in consequence of his adjudication. In this subsection, the term "estate" is employed in its alternative sense, referring to "an estate or interest in property."

Distribution of bankrupt's estate

Proof of debts

322.—(1) Subject to this section and the next, the proof of any bankruptcy debt by a secured or unsecured creditor of the bankrupt and the admission or rejection of any proof shall take place in accordance with the rules.

(2) Where a bankruptcy debt bears interest, that interest is provable as part of the debt except in so far as it is payable in respect of any period after the commencement of the bankruptcy.

(3) The trustee shall estimate the value of any bankruptcy debt which, by reason of its being subject to any contingency or contingencies or for any other reason, does not bear a certain value.

(4) Where the value of a bankruptcy debt is estimated by the trustee under subsection (3) or, by virtue of section 303 in Chapter III, by the court, the amount provable in the bankruptcy in respect of the debt is the amount of the estimate.

DEFINITIONS
    "bankrupt": s.381(1).
    "bankruptcy debt": s.382.
    "commencement of the bankruptcy": s.278(*a*).
    "debt": ss.382(3), 385(1).
    "secured creditor", unsecured creditor": ss.383, 385(1).
    "the court": ss.373, 385(1).
    "the rules": ss.384, 412.
    "the trustee": s.385(1).

GENERAL NOTE
    This section provides that the proof of bankruptcy debts by all categories of creditor shall take place in accordance with provisions to be contained in the rules. These provisions replace those formerly contained in s.32 of, and the Second Sched. to, the Bankruptcy Act 1914 (repealed).
    This section corresponds to s.163 of the 1985 Act.

Subs. (2)
    This specifies that interest is provable as part of a debt for any period up to the date of the making of the bankruptcy order. Payments in respect of any interest due for the period since the commencement of bankruptcy will only be made, pursuant to s.328(4), if any surplus remains after the payment in full of the preferential and ordinary debts.

Subss. (3), (4)
    These provisions establish the principle that proof may be lodged in respect of debts whose value is uncertain by virtue of the fact that they are subject to one or more contingencies. The amount for which such a debt is admitted to proof will be the value estimated by the trustee, subject to the right of the proving creditor, or any other person who is dissatisfied by the trustee's decision, to apply to the court under s.303(1). Alternatively, under s.303(2) the trustee himself may apply to the court for directions in case of uncertainty. In either type of case, the court's estimate is then substituted for that of the trustee.

Mutual credit and set-off

    323.—(1) This section applies where before the commencement of the bankruptcy there have been mutual credits, mutual debts or other mutual dealings between the bankrupt and any creditor of the bankrupt proving or claiming to prove for a bankruptcy debt.

    (2) An account shall be taken of what is due from each party to the other in respect of the mutual dealings and the sums due from one party shall be set off against the sums due from the other.

    (3) Sums due from the bankrupt to another party shall not be included in the account taken under subsection (2) if that other party had notice at the time they became due that a bankruptcy petition relating to the bankrupt was pending.

    (4) Only the balance (if any) of the account taken under subsection (2) is provable as a bankruptcy debt or, as the case may be, to be paid to the trustee as part of the bankrupt's estate.

DEFINITIONS
    "bankruptcy debt": s.382.
    "bankruptcy petition": s.381(3).

"commencement of the bankruptcy": s.278(*a*).
"creditor": s.383(1).
"debt": ss.382(3), 385(1).
"estate": ss.283, 385(1).
"the bankrupt": s.381(1).

GENERAL NOTE
This section re-enacts the provisions formerly contained in s.31 of the Bankruptcy Act
1914 (repealed), with the drafting suitably clarified and amended to take account of the
abolition of acts of bankruptcy and receiving orders. The substance of the law is unchanged,
and thus the new section fails to respond to the recommendations in Chap. 30 of the *Cork
Report* that amendments should be made so as to permit parties to contract out of the
provisions regarding set-off, and so as to preclude, in particular, the operation of set-off
where liabilities exist in favour of and against different Departments of State operating
under the Crown (see paras. 1343–1348 and 1362). Consequently, cases decided under s.31
of the Bankruptcy Act 1914 remain good law, including those which held that it was not
possible for parties to contract out of the statutory requirement of set-off (see *National
Westminster Bank Ltd.* v. *Halesowen Presswork and Assemblies Ltd.* [1972] A.C. 785), nor
to contract for the set-off of any claims which could not be set off under the statutory
provision where to do so would violate the principle of *pari passu* distribution in an
insolvency (see *British Eagle Airlines Ltd.* v. *Compagnie Nationale Air France* [1975] 1
W.L.R. 758, H.L.). The settled law on the requirement of mutuality is confirmed by the
reiteration of the word "mutual" in subs. (1) but, through the application of the doctrine
that the Crown is one and indivisible, this will continue to operate in relation to the Crown
in a way which is one-sided and arguably unfair to the general body of creditors. Amendments
to the Involvency Bill 1985 which would have deprived the Crown of this privileged position
were unsuccessfully moved at various stages before both Houses of Parliament (H.L. Vol.
459, cols. 1268–1270; H.C. Standing Committee E, June 18, 1985, cols. 397–404; *ibid*. June
20, 1985, col. 545).
This section corresponds to s.164 of the 1985 Act.

Subs. (3)
This restates the substance of the *proviso* to s.31 of the Bankruptcy Act 1914 (repealed),
and is an important safeguard against abusive arrangements, working against the concept of
equality of treatment of creditors, which may be concluded between a debtor and his
creditor at a time when bankruptcy proceedings are pending.

Distribution by means of dividend

324.—(1) Whenever the trustee has sufficient funds in hand for the
purpose he shall, subject to the retention of such sums as may be necessary
for the expenses of the bankruptcy, declare and distribute dividends
among the creditors in respect of the bankruptcy debts which they have
respectively proved.

(2) The trustee shall give notice of his intention to declare and distribute
a dividend.

(3) Where the trustee has declared a dividend, he shall give notice of
the dividend and of how it is proposed to distribute it; and a notice given
under this subsection shall contain the prescribed particulars of the
bankrupt's estate.

(4) In the calculation and distribution of a dividend the trustee shall
make provision—

    (*a*) for any bankruptcy debts which appear to him to be due to persons
          who, by reason of the distance of their place of residence, may not
          have had sufficient time to tender and establish their proofs,
    (*b*) for any bankruptcy debts which are the subject of claims which
          have not yet been determined, and
    (*c*) for disputed proofs and claims.

DEFINITIONS
"bankrupt": s.381(1).
"bankruptcy debt": s.382.

"creditor": s.383(1).
"estate": ss.283, 385(1).
"prescribed": s.384.
"the trustee": s.385(1).

GENERAL NOTE

This section, in conjunction with ss.325–327, essentially re-enacts, the law as previously stated in ss.56(9), 62–65 and 68 of the Bankruptcy Act 1914 (repealed). However, there is no longer any provision requiring the trustee to distribute dividends at specified intervals of time.

This section corresponds to subss. (1)–(4) of s.165 of the 1985 Act.

Claims by unsatisfied creditors

325.—(1) A creditor who has not proved his debt before the declaration of any dividend is not entitled to disturb, by reason that he has not participated in it, the distribution of that dividend or any other dividend declared before his debt was proved, but—

(a) when he has proved that debt he is entitled to be paid, out of any money for the time being available for the payment of any further dividend, any dividend or dividends which he has failed to receive; and

(b) any dividend or dividends payable under paragraph (a) shall be paid before that money is applied to the payment of any such further dividend.

(2) No action lies against the trustee for a dividend, but if the trustee refuses to pay a dividend the court may, if it thinks fit, order him to pay it and also to pay, out of his own money—

(a) interest on the dividend, at the rate for the time being specified in section 17 of the Judgments Act 1838, from the time it was withheld, and

(b) the costs of the proceedings in which the order to pay is made.

DEFINITIONS

"creditor": s.383(1).
"debt": ss.382(3), 385(1).
"the court": ss.373, 385(1).
"the trustee": s.385(1).

GENERAL NOTE

This section comprises the provisions formerly contained in subss. (5) and (6) of s.165 of the 1985 Act. It specifies the conditions under which creditors who come in late to proof are eligible to receive dividends, and also prescribes the extent to which the trustee is subject to challenge or control with regard to his decision whether or not to pay a dividend at any particular time. See also the General Note to s.324.

Distribution of property in specie

326.—(1) Without prejudice to sections 315 to 319 (disclaimer), the trustee may, with the permission of the creditors' committee, divide in its existing form amongst the bankrupt's creditors, according to its estimated value, any property which from its peculiar nature or other special circumstances cannot be readily or advantageously sold.

(2) A permission given for the purposes of subsection (1) shall not be a general permission but shall relate to a particular proposed exercise of the power in question; and a person dealing with the trustee in good faith and for value is not to be concerned to enquire whether any permission required by subsection (1) has been given.

(3) Where the trustee has done anything without the permission required by subsection (1), the court or the creditors' committee may, for

the purpose of enabling him to meet his expenses out of the bankrupt's estate, ratify what the trustee has done.

But the committee shall not do so unless it is satisfied that the trustee acted in a case of urgency and has sought its ratification without undue delay.

DEFINITIONS
"creditor": s.383(1).
"creditors' committee": s.301(1).
"estate": ss.283, 385(1).
"property": s.436.
"the bankrupt": s.381(1).
"the court": ss.373, 385(1).
"the trustee": s.385(1).

GENERAL NOTE
This section, which corresponds to subss. (7) and (8) of s.165 of the 1985 Act, makes provision for the division amongst the creditors in its existing form of any of the bankrupt's property which cannot be readily or advantageously sold.

Distribution in criminal bankruptcy

327. Where the bankruptcy order was made on a petition under section 264(1)(*d*) (criminal bankruptcy), no distribution shall be made under sections 324 to 326 so long as an appeal is pending (within the meaning of section 277) against the bankrupt's conviction of any offence by virtue of which the criminal bankruptcy order on which the petition was based was made.

DEFINITIONS
"appeal pending": s.277(3); Powers of Criminal Courts Act 1973, s.40(5).
"bankruptcy order": s.381(2).
"criminal bankruptcy order": s.385(1); Powers of Criminal Courts Act 1973, s.39(1).
"the bankrupt": s.381(1).

GENERAL NOTE
This section, which corresponds to s.165(9) of the 1985 Act, embodies a special rule for the case where a bankruptcy order is made on a petition based upon a criminal bankruptcy order, as provided for by s.264(1)(*d*). Where an appeal is pending against the bankrupt's conviction of any offence by virtue of which the criminal bankruptcy order came to be made, there can be no distribution of dividend in the bankruptcy, albeit the trustee may proceed with the other stages of his administration and realisation of the bankrupt's estate, in preparation for the eventual distribution of dividends.

Priority of debts

328.—(1) In the distribution of the bankrupt's estate, his preferential debts (within the meaning given by section 386 in Part XII) shall be paid in priority to other debts.

(2) Preferential debts rank equally between themselves after the expenses of the bankruptcy and shall be paid in full unless the bankrupt's estate is insufficient for meeting them, in which case they abate in equal proportions between themselves.

(3) Debts which are neither preferential debts nor debts to which the next section applies also rank equally between themselves and, after the preferential debts, shall be paid in full unless the bankrupt's estate is insufficient for meeting them, in which case they abate in equal proportions between themselves.

(4) Any surplus remaining after the payment of the debts that are preferential or rank equally under subsection (3) shall be applied in paying interest on those debts in respect of the periods during which they have

been outstanding since the commencement of the bankruptcy; and interest on preferential debts ranks equally with interest on debts other than preferential debts.

(5) The rate of interest payable under subsection (4) in respect of any debt is whichever is the greater of the following—

(a) the rate specified in section 17 of the Judgments Act 1838 at the commencement of the bankruptcy, and

(b) the rate applicable to that debt apart from the bankruptcy.

(6) This section and the next are without prejudice to any provision of this Act or any other Act under which the payment of any debt or the making of any other payment is, in the event of bankruptcy, to have a particular priority or to be postponed.

DEFINITIONS

"bankrupt": s.381(1).
"debt": ss.382(3), 385(1).
"estate": ss.283, 385(1).
"preferential debt": s.386; Sched. 6.

GENERAL NOTE

This section, together with s.386 and Sched. 6, provides for the order of priority in which proved debts are to be paid. These provisions replace the heavily-amended provisions of s.33 and also s.36 of the Bankruptcy Act 1914 (repealed). The provisions of Sched. 6 are common to both bankruptcy and winding up, and apply in relation to the latter pursuant to the provisions of s.175. As explained in the General Note to that section, the new common code of preferential debts represents a qualified victory for those who sought to reform this aspect of insolvency law in accordance with the recommendations of the *Cork Report* (see esp. paras. 1409–1444 and 1450). The main debates and divisions on matters of principle and substance occurred in relation to the earlier section of the Act, as mentioned in the General Note to s.175. For priority of debts in a former bankruptcy in the event of a second, or subsequent, bankruptcy, see s.335(b).

This section corresponds to subss. (1)–(5) and (7) of s.166 of the 1985 Act.

Subss. (4), (5)

These provisions replace the former s.66 of the Bankruptcy Act 1914 (repealed). In view of the fact that s.322(2) now makes provable any claim for interest accrued due up to the commencement of bankruptcy, the present subsections are concerned exclusively with payment of dividend in respect of interest for the period during which the debts have been outstanding since the date of the bankruptcy order. This provision forms a parallel to s.189 which applies in winding up.

Debts to spouse

329.—(1) This section applies to bankruptcy debts owed in respect of credit provided by a person who (whether or not the bankrupt's spouse at the time the credit was provided) was the bankrupt's spouse at the commencement of the bankruptcy.

(2) Such debts—

(a) rank in priority after the debts and interest required to be paid in pursuance of section 328(3) and (4), and

(b) are payable with interest at the rate specified in section 328(5) in respect of the period during which they have been outstanding since the commencement of the bankruptcy;

and the interest payable under paragraph (b) has the same priority as the debts on which it is payable.

DEFINITIONS

"bankruptcy debt": s.382.
"commencement of the bankruptcy": s.278(a).
"the bankrupt": s.381(1).

This section, which corresponds to s.166(6) of the 1985 Act, has the effect of relegating the entitlement of the bankrupt's spouse to receive dividends in respect of credit which he or she has provided to the bankrupt. Such debts are made payable only after the preferential and the ordinary creditors have received payment in full in accordance with the provisions of subss. (2) and (3) of s.328, together with interest payable in accordance with subs. (4) of that section. The position of the bankrupt's spouse as a postponed creditor was formerly governed by the provisions of s.36 of the Bankruptcy Act 1914 (repealed). The drafting of the present section is a considerable improvement over the former provision, and its scope has been widened so as to apply in an identical manner, regardless of whether it is the husband or the wife who is the bankrupt party in any given case.

Final distribution

330.—(1) When the trustee has realised all the bankrupt's estate or so much of it as can, in the trustee's opinion, be realised without needlessly protracting the trusteeship, he shall give notice in the prescribed manner either—

(*a*) of his intention to declare a final dividend, or

(*b*) that no dividend, or further dividend, will be declared.

(2) The notice under subsection (1) shall contain the prescribed particulars and shall require claims against the bankrupt's estate to be established by a date ("the final date") specified in the notice.

(3) The court may, on the application of any person, postpone the final date.

(4) After the final date, the trustee shall—

(*a*) defray any outstanding expenses of the bankruptcy out of the bankrupt's estate, and

(*b*) if he intends to declare a final dividend, declare and distribute that dividend without regard to the claim of any person in respect of a debt not already proved in the bankruptcy.

(5) If a surplus remains after payment in full and with interest of all the bankrupt's creditors and the payment of the expenses of the bankruptcy, the bankrupt is entitled to the surplus.

DEFINITIONS
"bankrupt": s.381(1).
"creditor": s.383(1).
"debt": ss.382(3), 385(1). ·
"estate": ss.283, 385(1).
"the final date": subs. (2).
"prescribed": s.384.
"the court": ss.373, 385(1).
"the trustee": s.385(1).

GENERAL NOTE
This section provides for the final distribution of dividend, or alternatively for the giving of notification by the trustee that no dividend, or no further dividend, will be declared. It marks the beginning of the concluding phase of the trustee's responsibilities. S.331(3) authorises the trustee to adopt the cost-saving procedure of sending out the notice of the final meeting to be convened under that section at the same time as he sends out the notice required to be sent under this section.

Subss. (1)–(4) inclusive reproduce the former s.67 of the Bankruptcy Act 1914 (repealed) in restructured form, and subs. (5) restates the law formerly contained in s.69 of that Act.

This section corresponds to s.167 of the 1985 Act.

Final meeting

331.—(1) Subject as follows in this section and the next, this section applies where—

(*a*) it appears to the trustee that the administration of the bankrupt's estate in accordance with this Chapter is for practical purposes complete, and

(b) the trustee is not the official receiver.

(2) The trustee shall summon a final general meeting of the bankrupt's creditors which—

(a) shall receive the trustee's report of his administration of the bankrupt's estate, and

(b) shall determine whether the trustee should have his release under section 299 in Chapter III.

(3) The trustee may, if he thinks fit, give the notice summoning the final general meeting at the same time as giving notice under section 330(1); but, if summoned for an earlier date, that meeting shall be adjourned (and, if necessary, further adjourned) until a date on which the trustee is able to report to the meeting that the administration of the bankrupt's estate is for practical purposes complete.

(4) In the administration of the estate it is the trustee's duty to retain sufficient sums from the estate to cover the expenses of summoning and holding the meeting required by this section.

DEFINITION
"bankrupt": s.381(1).
"court": ss.373, 385(1).
"creditor": s.383(1).
"estate": ss.283, 385(1).
"release": s.299(5).
"the official receiver": s.399(1).
"the trustee": s.385(1).

GENERAL NOTE
This section provides for the convening of a final meeting of creditors when the administration of the bankrupt's estate is complete. No such requirement is imposed in cases where the official receiver is acting as trustee, which is likely to be the case whenever the assets available for distribution are small. The twin purposes of the meeting are that the trustee should deliver a report upon his administration of the bankrupt's estate, and that the creditors should determine whether the trustee is to have his release under s.299. If the meeting resolves against release of the trustee, the provisions of s.299(3)(d)(i) become applicable with effect that the trustee must apply to the Secretary of State to determine at what date his release shall become effective. If the final meeting does not resolve against his release, the trustee's release is effective, in accordance with s.299(3)(d)(ii) from the time at which he vacates office. There is no provision in s.331 itself requiring the trustee to report to the court upon the outcome of the final meeting, but s.298(8) provides that on his giving notice to the court that such a final meeting has been held, together with a report of any decisions there taken, the trustee shall vacate office. In view of the fact that final meetings of creditors are frequently ill attended, provision will be made in the rules to enable the creditors to vote by proxy.

This section corresponds to subss. (1), (2) and (4) of s.168 of the 1985 Act.

Saving for bankrupt's home

332.—(1) This section applies where—

(a) there is comprised in the bankrupt's estate property consisting of an interest in a dwelling house which is occupied by the bankrupt or by his spouse or former spouse, and

(b) the trustee has been unable for any reason to realise that property.

(2) The trustee shall not summon a meeting under section 331 unless either—

(a) the court has made an order under section 313 imposing a charge on that property for the benefit of the bankrupt's estate, or

(b) the court has declined, on an application under that section, to make such an order, or

(c) the Secretary of State has issued a certificate to the trustee stating that it would be inappropriate or inexpedient for such an application to be made in the case in question.

DEFINITIONS
"dwelling house": s.385(1).
"estate": ss.283, 385(1).
"property": s.436.
"the bankrupt": s.381(1).
"the court": ss.373, 385(1).
"the trustee": s.385(1).

GENERAL NOTE
This section provides for the possibility that the trustee may have been unable to realise property consisting of an interest in a dwelling-house because of a right of occupation by the bankrupt or his present or former spouse. Under s.336 or s.337, such rights may be held to outweigh for a time the interests of creditors in the bankruptcy, and in such circumstances it is the purpose of this subsection to prevent the bankruptcy administration being brought to its conclusion through the holding of a final meeting of creditors, unless one of the alternative conditions mentioned in paras. (*a*)–(*c*) inclusive has been fulfilled. These include the possibility that a charging order has been made by the court under s.313, or that an application for such an order has been made without success.
This section corresponds to s.168(3) of the 1985 Act.

Supplemental

Duties of bankrupt in relation to trustee

333.—(1) The bankrupt shall—
(*a*) give to the trustee such information as to his affairs,
(*b*) attend on the trustee at such times, and
(*c*) do all such other things,
as the trustee may for the purposes of carrying out his functions under any of this Group of Parts reasonably require.
(2) Where at any time after the commencement of the bankruptcy any property is acquired by, or devolves upon, the bankrupt or there is an increase of the bankrupt's income, the bankrupt shall, within the prescribed period, give the trustee notice of the property or, as the case may be, of the increase.
(3) Subsection (1) applies to a bankrupt after his discharge.
(4) If the bankrupt without reasonable excuse fails to comply with any obligation imposed by this section, he is guilty of a contempt of court and liable to be punished accordingly (in addition to any other punishment to which he may be subject).

DEFINITIONS
"affairs": s.385(2).
"bankrupt": s.381(1).
"commencement of the bankruptcy": s.278(*a*).
"court": ss.373, 385(1).
"property": s.436.
"prescribed": s.384.
"the trustee": s.385(1).

GENERAL NOTE
This section provides for a duty of co-operation with the trustee, to which the bankrupt is subject throughout the duration of the bankruptcy and also, in the case of the matters mentioned in subs. (1), after his discharge. The section re-enacts in considerably revised form the duties formerly imposed upon the debtor by s.22 of the Bankruptcy Act 1914 (repealed). A new provision is that contained in subs. (2), whereby the bankrupt must notify his trustee of any after-acquired property or increase of income which accrues to him after the commencement of bankruptcy. This is to enable the trustee to take appropriate action to claim the property, or a proportion of the income, for the estate under s.307.
This section corresponds to s.169 of the 1985 Act.

Stay of distribution in case of second bankruptcy

334.—(1) This section and the next apply where a bankruptcy order is made against an undischarged bankrupt; and in both sections—

  (*a*) "the later bankruptcy" means the bankruptcy arising from that order,

  (*b*) "the earlier bankruptcy" means the bankruptcy (or, as the case may be, most recent bankruptcy) from which the bankrupt has not been discharged at the commencement of the later bankruptcy, and

  (*c*) "the existing trustee" means the trustee (if any) of the bankrupt's estate for the purposes of the earlier bankruptcy.

(2) Where the existing trustee has been given the prescribed notice of the presentation of the petition for the later bankruptcy, any distribution or other disposition by him of anything to which the next subsection applies, if made after the giving of the notice, is void except to the extent that it was made with the consent of the court or is or was subsequently ratified by the court.

This is without prejudice to section 284 (restrictions on dispositions of property following bankruptcy order).

(3) This subsection applies to—

  (*a*) any property which is vested in the existing trustee under section 307(3) (after-acquired property);

  (*b*) any money paid to the existing trustee in pursuance of an income payments order under section 310; and

  (*c*) any property or money which is, or in the hands of the existing trustee represents, the proceeds of sale or application of property or money falling within paragraph (*a*) or (*b*) of this subsection.

DEFINITIONS

"bankrupt": s.381(1).
"bankruptcy order": s.381(2).
"bankruptcy petition": s.381(3).
"commencement of the bankruptcy": s.278(*a*).
"discharged": s.279.
"estate": ss.283, 385(1).
"prescribed": s.384.
"property": s.436.
"the court": ss.373, 385(1).
"the earlier bankruptcy": subs. (1)(*b*).
"the existing trustee": subs. (1)(*c*).
"the later bankruptcy": subs. (1)(*a*).
"the rules": ss.207, 211(1).
"the trustee": s.385(1).

TRANSITIONAL PROVISION
Sched. 11, para. 16.

GENERAL NOTE

  This section and s.335 together make special provision for cases where a bankruptcy order is made against a person who, at the time in question, is undischarged from a previous bankruptcy adjudication which he has undergone. Such situations were formerly provided for by s.39 of the Bankruptcy Act 1914, as substituted by s.3 of the Bankruptcy (Amendment) Act 1926 (repealed). Paras. 1164–1168 of the *Cork Report* endorsed the earlier proposals of the Blagden Committee (Cmnd. 221, para. 114) in advocating a change in the law, so that while the trustee of a former bankruptcy should continue to be admitted as a creditor in any subsequent bankruptcy in respect of any unsatisfied balance of debts provable in the former bankruptcy, he should not, as hitherto, be entitled to any dividend as such creditor until the other creditors in the later bankruptcy have been paid in full, including the payment of interest on those other debts. These recommendations are adopted in ss.334 and 335 and are enacted by subss. (5) and (6) of s.335 in particular.

This section corresponds to subss. (1)–(3) of s.170 of the 1985 Act.

Adjustment between earlier and later bankruptcy estates

335.—(1) With effect from the commencement of the later bankruptcy anything to which section 334(3) applies which, immediately before the commencement of that bankruptcy, is comprised in the bankrupt's estate for the purposes of the earlier bankruptcy is to be treated as comprised in the bankrupt's estate for the purposes of the later bankruptcy and, until there is a trustee of that estate, is to be dealt with by the existing trustee in accordance with the rules.

(2) Any sums which in pursuance of an income payments order under section 310 are payable after the commencement of the later bankruptcy to the existing trustee shall form part of the bankrupt's estate for the purposes of the later bankruptcy; and the court may give such consequential directions for the modification of the order as it thinks fit.

(3) Anything comprised in a bankrupt's estate by virtue of subsection (1) or (2) is so comprised subject to a first charge in favour of the existing trustee for any bankruptcy expenses incurred by him in relation thereto.

(4) Except as provided above and in section 334, property which is, or by virtue of section 308 (personal property of bankrupt exceeding reasonable replacement value) is capable of being, comprised in the bankrupt's estate for the purposes of the earlier bankruptcy, or of any bankruptcy prior to it, shall not be comprised in his estate for the purposes of the later bankruptcy.

(5) The creditors of the bankrupt in the earlier bankruptcy and the creditors of the bankrupt in any bankruptcy prior to the earlier one, are not to be creditors of his in the later bankruptcy in respect of the same debts; but the existing trustee may prove in the later bankruptcy for—

(a) the unsatisfied balance of the debts (including any debt under this subsection) provable against the bankrupt's estate in the earlier bankruptcy;

(b) any interest payable on that balance; and

(c) any unpaid expenses of the earlier bankruptcy.

(6) Any amount provable under subsection (5) ranks in priority after all the other debts provable in the later bankruptcy and after interest on those debts and, accordingly, shall not be paid unless those debts and that interest have first been paid in full.

DEFINITIONS

"commencement of the bankruptcy": s.278(a).
"creditor": s.383(1).
"debt": ss.382(3), 385(1).
"estate": ss.283, 385(1).
"modification": s.436.
"property": s.436.
"the bankrupt": s.381(1).
"the court": ss.373, 385(1).
"the earlier bankruptcy": s.334(1)(b).
"the existing trustee": s.334(1)(c).
"the later bankruptcy": s.334(1)(a).
"trustee": s.385(1).

GENERAL NOTE

This section corresponds to subss. (4)–(9) of s.170 of the 1985 Act. The section operates in conjunction with s.334, and applies in the case where an undischarged bankrupt undergoes a second or subsequent adjudication. See also the General Note to s.334.

Subs. (4)

Property which is, . . . or by virtue of s.308 . . . is capable of being, comprised in the
bankrupt's estate

These words have the effect of excluding from the bankrupt's estate for the purpose of the later bankruptcy property which the bankrupt actually owned at the date of commencement of the earlier bankruptcy, but which was at that time exempted from his estate by virtue of s.283(2). Such property, however, remains subject to the right of the trustee under s.308 to claim the exempted item for the estate in exchange for the provision of a less expensive replacement.

CHAPTER V

EFFECT OF BANKRUPTCY ON CERTAIN RIGHTS,

TRANSACTIONS, ETC.

Rights of occupation

Rights of occupation etc. of bankrupt's spouse

336.—(1) Nothing occurring in the initial period of the bankruptcy (that is to say, the period beginning with the day of the presentation of the petition for the bankruptcy order and ending with the vesting of the bankrupt's estate in a trustee) is to be taken as having given rise to any rights of occupation under the Matrimonial Homes Act 1983 in relation to a dwelling house comprised in the bankrupt's estate.

(2) Where a spouse's rights of occupation under the Act of 1983 are a charge on the estate or interest of the other spouse, or of trustees for the other spouse, and the other spouse is adjudged bankrupt—

(a) the charge continues to subsist notwithstanding the bankruptcy and, subject to the provisions of that Act, binds the trustee of the bankrupt's estate and persons deriving title under that trustee, and

(b) any application for an order under section 1 of that Act shall be made to the court having jurisdiction in relation to the bankruptcy.

(3) Where a person and his spouse or former spouse are trustees for sale of a dwelling house and that person is adjudged bankrupt, any application by the trustee of the bankrupt's estate for any order under section 30 of the Law of Property Act 1925 (powers of court where trustees for sale refuse to act) shall be made to the court having jurisdiction in relation to the bankruptcy.

(4) On such an application as is mentioned in subsection (2) or (3) the court shall make such order under section 1 of the Act of 1983 or section 30 of the Act of 1925 as it thinks just and reasonable having regard to—

(a) the interests of the bankrupt's creditors,

(b) the conduct of the spouse or former spouse, so far as contributing to the bankruptcy,

(c) the needs and financial resources of the spouse or former spouse,

(d) the needs of any children, and

(e) all the circumstances of the case other than the needs of the bankrupt.

(5) Where such an application is made after the end of the period of one year beginning with the first vesting under Chapter IV of this Part of the bankrupt's estate in a trustee, the court shall assume, unless the circumstances of the case are exceptional, that the interests of the bankrupt's creditors outweigh all other considerations.

DEFINITIONS
  "bankrupt": s.381(1).
  "creditor": s.383(1).
  "dwelling house": s.385(1).
  "estate": ss.283, 385(1).
  "the court": ss.373, 385(1).

GENERAL NOTE
  The provisions of this section, and those of s.337, represent a compromise position reached at a late stage in the process of enactment. During the enactment of the Insolvency Bill 1985, a series of vigorous debates took place in both Houses regarding the issues of principle and policy associated with the treatment of the matrimonial home in the case of bankruptcy of either spouse (see esp. *Hansard*, H.L. Vol. 459, cols. 1262–1267; H.L. Vol. 462, cols. 160–171; H.L. Vol. 467, cols 1265–1270; H.C. Standing Committee E, June 18, 1985, cols. 372–376 and 394–395; H.C. Vol. 83, cols. 545–549 and 601–602). These debates took as their starting point the arguments and recommendations contained in paras. 1114–1131 of the *Cork Report* with regard to the family home. The use of the term "family home" is appropriate, since it serves to indicate the principal argument for the making of some provision for postponement of the ability of the trustee in bankruptcy to realise the bankrupt's interest in this particular item of property, namely the claims of the bankrupt's spouse, children and other dependents to a roof over their heads. In very few cases decided under the law prior to the enactment of this Act have the competing claims of the bankrupt's spouse and children been accorded sufficient significance so as to outweigh those of the creditors. The *Cork Report* therefore proposed a new approach which would delay, but not cancel, enforcement of the creditors' rights. The liberal terms in which the Report's recommendations were cast, although enthusiastically supported in some speeches delivered in both Houses, have not been completely embodied in the provisions ultimately enacted in this and the following section, but they at least afford the possibility for the court to strike an appropriate balance in any given case. Much will also depend upon the attitude adopted by trustees in bankruptcy in selecting the point in time at which to press for a realisation of the bankrupt's interest in the family home (*cf. Cork Report*, para. 1119).
  One important innovation which is included in the section is the facilitation of a consolidation of the hearing of applications relating to the family home before the court having jurisdiction in bankruptcy. Provision is thus made in subs. (2)(*b*) for any application for an order under s.1 of the Matrimonial Homes Act 1983 to be heard by the bankruptcy court, and the same court likewise enjoys, by virtue of subs. (3), an exclusive jurisdiction to entertain an application by the trustee in bankruptcy for an order under s.30 of the Law of Property Act 1925. The same consolidation is effected in subs. (4) of s.337.
  This section corresponds to s.171 of the 1985 Act.

Subs. (2)
  Subs. 1 of the Matrimonial Homes Act 1983 confers on a spouse without any beneficial interest in the matrimonial home, rights of occupation as against the other spouse. Hitherto, where the spouse with a beneficial estate became bankrupt the spouse without any such interest lost his or her rights of occupation as against the trustee in bankruptcy. This subsection reverses that former position so that the spouse who has no beneficial interest in the property is placed in a similar position to a spouse with a beneficial interest.

Subs. (3)
  This provides for the case where the spouse of the bankrupt already has a beneficial interest in the matrimonial home. No change is effected to the pre-existing law, whereby the trustee in bankruptcy must obtain an order of the court under s.30 of the Law of Property Act 1925 before being able to sell the property concerned.

Subs. (4)
  This sets out the powers of the court in relation to any application made under subss. (2) of (3). The court's discretion to make "such order as it thinks just and reasonable" must be exercised with regard to the various interests therein listed, which are based on those already contained in s.1(3) of the Matrimonial Homes Act 1983. Notably, the personal needs of the bankrupt are expressly excluded from consideration. Only the spouse and children of the bankrupt are expressly mentioned as persons whose needs the court is required to consider, and it is debatable whether the court may properly have regard, under the general heading of "all the circumstances of the case" to the needs of any other dependents, including any

"ailing or elderly or adult members of the family" as mentioned in paras. 1120–1121 of the *Cork Report.*

Subs. (5)

Unless the circumstances of the case are exceptional

This provision redresses the balance between the competing interests of the creditors and the bankrupt's spouse and children in favour of the former, in any case where application is not brought until a year has elapsed since the bankrupt's property first vested in a trustee under the provisions of Chap. IV of this Part (see s.303 and also ss.295(4) and 297). However, the way has been left open for argument on behalf of the spouse and children to be advanced on a basis such as exceptional hardship or inconvenience which would be occasioned by the sale of the family home at the time the application is made. In such instances the cases decided under the law prior to the coming into force of this Act are likely to be of at least a persuasive authority in the judicial determination of the expression italicised above (see *e.g. Re Turner* [1975] 1 All E.R. 5; *Re Bailey* [1977] 2 All E.R. 26; *Re Holliday* [1981] 1 Ch. 405; *Re Lowrie* [1981] 3 All E.R. 353).

Rights of occupation of bankrupt

337.—(1) This section applies where—

(*a*) a person who is entitled to occupy a dwelling house by virtue of a beneficial estate or interest is adjudged bankrupt, and

(*b*) any persons under the age of 18 with whom that person had at some time occupied that dwelling house had their home with that person at the time when the bankruptcy petition was presented and at the commencement of the bankruptcy.

(2) Whether or not the bankrupt's spouse (if any) has rights of occupation under the Matrimonial Homes Act 1983—

(*a*) the bankrupt has the following rights as against the trustee of his estate—

(i) if in occupation, a right not to be evicted or excluded from the dwelling house or any part of it, except with the leave of the court,

(ii) if not in occupation, a right with the leave of the court to enter into and occupy the dwelling house, and

(*b*) the bankrupt's rights are a charge, having the like priority as an equitable interest created immediately before the commencement of the bankruptcy, on so much of his estate or interest in the dwelling house as vests in the trustee.

(3) The Act of 1983 has effect, with the necessary modifications, as if—

(*a*) the rights conferred by paragraph (*a*) of subsection (2) were rights of occupation under that Act,

(*b*) any application for leave such as is mentioned in that paragraph were an application for an order under section 1 of that Act, and

(*c*) any charge under paragraph (*b*) of that subsection on the estate or interest of the trustee were a charge under that Act on the estate or interest of a spouse.

(4) Any application for leave such as is mentioned in subsection (2) (*a*) or otherwise by virtue of this section for an order under section 1 of the Act of 1983 shall be made to the court having jurisdiction in relation to the bankruptcy.

(5) On such an application the court shall make such order under section 1 of the Act of 1983 as it thinks just and reasonable having regard to the interests of the creditors, to the bankrupt's financial resources, to the needs of the children and to all the circumstances of the case other than the needs of the bankrupt.

(6) Where such an application is made after the end of the period of one year beginning with the first vesting (under Chapter IV of this Part)

of the bankrupt's estate in a trustee, the court shall assume, unless the circumstances of the case are exceptional, that the interests of the bankrupt's creditors outweigh all other considerations.

DEFINITIONS
  "bankrupt": s.381(1).
  "bankruptcy petition": s.381(3).
  "commencement of the bankruptcy": s.278(*a*).
  "creditor": s.383(1).
  "dwelling house": s.385(1).
  "estate": ss.283, 385(1).
  "modifications": s.436.
  "the court": ss.373, 385(1).
  "the trustee": s.385(1).

GENERAL NOTE
  This section applies the principles of s.336, in a more limited manner, to the case where a bankrupt has actual custody of children. This provides for cases where the bankrupt has no spouse with occupational rights or, because of divorce, no spouse at all, but nevertheless has children to bring up. Subs. (1)(*b*) expressly provides that only persons under the age of 18 are to be taken into account by the court. Subs. (5) further provides that the needs of such children are to be taken into account by the court, but not the needs of the bankrupt himself. As is the case under s.336(5), the court is required to assume, unless the circumstances are exceptional, that in a case where application is made by the trustee for an order under s.1 of the Matrimonial Homes Act 1983 more than one year after the date when the bankrupt's estate first vested in a trustee, the interests of the creditors are of paramount consideration.
  This section corresponds to s.172 of the 1985 Act.

Payments in respect of premises occupied by bankrupt

338. Where any premises comprised in a bankrupt's estate are occupied by him (whether by virtue of the preceding section or otherwise) on condition that he makes payments towards satisfying any liability arising under a mortgage of the premises or otherwise towards the outgoings of the premises, the bankrupt does not, by virtue of those payments, acquire any interest in the premises.

DEFINITIONS
  "bankrupt": s.381(1).
  "estate": ss.283, 385(1).
  "liability": s.382(4).

GENERAL NOTE
  This section preserves the pre-existing legal position where a bankrupt is able, for whatever reason, to continue to occupy premises comprised in his estate and makes mortgage payments or pays other outgoings in relation to the property. If such payments give rise to the acquisition by the bankrupt, after the commencement of his bankruptcy, of an interest in the property, the former prohibitions of s.38 of the Bankruptcy Act 1914 (repealed) had the effect of causing that interest to vest automatically in his trustee as after-acquired property. The present section perpetuates the rule whereby the bankrupt does not personally acquire an interest in the premises despite the fact that he may have made the payments required of him.
  This section corresponds to s.173 of the 1985 Act.

Adjustment of prior transactions, etc.

Transactions at an undervalue

339.—(1) Subject as follows in this section and sections 341 and 342, where an individual is adjudged bankrupt and he has at a relevant time (defined in section 341) entered into a transaction with any person at an undervalue, the trustee of the bankrupt's estate may apply to the court for an order under this section.

(2) The court shall, on such an application, make such order as it thinks fit for restoring the position to what it would have been if that individual had not entered into that transaction.

(3) For the purposes of this section and sections 341 and 342, an individual enters into a transaction with a person at an undervalue if—

(*a*) he makes a gift to that person or he otherwise enters into a transaction with that person on terms that provide for him to receive no consideration,

(*b*) he enters into a transaction with that person in consideration of marriage, or

(*c*) he enters into a transaction with that person for a consideration the value of which, in money or money's worth, is significantly less than the value, in money or money's worth, of the consideration provided by the individual.

DEFINITIONS
"a relevant time": s.341.
"bankrupt": s.381(1).
"bankruptcy petition": s.381(3).
"estate": ss.283, 385(1).
"the court": ss.373, 385(1).
"transaction": s.436.
"transaction at an undervalue": subs. (3).
"trustee": s.385(1).

TRANSITIONAL PROVISION
Sched. 11, para. 17.

GENERAL NOTE
This section, together with ss.340–342, forms a parallel set of provisions to those of ss.238–241 which apply in cases of company insolvency. The two sets of provisions are in most respects identical in substance, but differ in matters of detail and terminology reflecting the differences between the respective legal frameworks within which the two branches of insolvency law traditionally operate. For comment upon the general operation of the section, and of the underlying policy thereto, see the General Note to s.238. The following comments indicate the principal respects in which ss.238–241 and ss.339–342 differ from each other in substance.

(i) There is no equivalent provision in s.238 to that contained in subs. (3)(*b*) of s.339, which refers to transactions entered into in consideration of marriage. In consequence the counterpart of s.339(3)(*c*) is s.238(4)(*b*).

(ii) There is no counterpart in s.339 to s.238(5).

(iii) S.340(5) speaks of the giving of a preference by an individual to a person who at the time was an "associate" of his; s.239(6) on the other hand speaks of the giving of a preference by a company to a person who at the time was "connected with" the company. However, the latter expression is defined by s.249 as comprising those persons who are "associates" of the company, and also those who are directors or shadow directors of the company, or associates of such persons. Thus the concept of the "associated person", as defined in s.435, comes to be applicable in both situations albeit in the case of company insolvency it does so alongside other forms of involvement with the company.

(iv) There are important differences of detail as between s.341(1) and s.240(1), both of which contain rules for fixing the periods within which the act of giving a preference or entering into a transaction at an undervalue will take place "at a relevant time" for the purposes of the respective groups of sections. The cumulative effect of the differences between these two key subsections is to create a major distinction between preferences or transactions at an undervalue which are given or entered into by a company on the one hand, and those which are given or entered into by an individual on the other.

(v) The statutory definition of "insolvency" for the purposes of s.240(2) is supplied by reference to the concept of "inability to pay debts" within the meaning of s.123 of the Act, where six alternative criteria are stated; the definition of "insolvency" for the purposes of the equivalent subsection of s.341 (subs. (2)), is supplied by s.341(3) which states only two alternative criteria for establishing individual insolvency.

(vi) There is no equivalent in s.341 to s.240(3).

(vii) There are no equivalents in ss.238–241 to the provisions of subss. (4) and (5) of s.341, which are concerned with cases where a bankruptcy order is made upon a petition based on a criminal bankruptcy order against an individual who has been convicted of a criminal offence.

Ss.339–342 replace the provisions formerly contained in ss.42 and 44 of the Bankruptcy Act 1914 (repealed), and do so in a manner broadly in line with the proposals contained in Chap. 28 of the *Cork Report*.

S.339 corresponds to subss. (1) and (2) of s.173 of the 1985 Act.

Preferences

340.—(1) Subject as follows in this and the next two sections, where an individual is adjudged bankrupt and he has at a relevant time (defined in section 341) given a preference to any person, the trustee of the bankrupt's estate may apply to the court for an order under this section.

(2) The court shall, on such an application, make such order as it thinks fit for restoring the position to what it would have been if that individual had not given that preference.

(3) For the purposes of this and the next two sections, an individual gives a preference to a person if—

(a) that person is one of the individual's creditors or a surety or guarantor for any of his debts or other liabilities, and

(b) the individual does anything or suffers anything to be done which (in either case) has the effect of putting that person into a position which, in the event of the individual's bankruptcy, will be better than the position he would have been in if that thing had not been done.

(4) The court shall not make an order under this section in respect of a preference given to any person unless the individual who gave the preference was influenced in deciding to give it by a desire to produce in relation to that person the effect mentioned in subsection (3)(*b*) above.

(5) An individual who has given a preference to a person who, at the time the preference was given, was an associate of his (otherwise than by reason only of being his employee) is presumed, unless the contrary is shown, to have been influenced in deciding to give it by such a desire as is mentioned in subsection (4).

(6) The fact that something has been done in pursuance of the order of a court does not, without more, prevent the doing or suffering of that thing from constituting the giving of a preference.

DEFINITIONS

"a relevant time": s.341(1), (2).

"associate": s.435.

"bankrupt": s.381(1).

"creditor": s.383(1).

"debt": ss.382(3), 385(1).

"estate": ss.283, 385(1).

"gives a preference": subs. (3).

"the court": s.373, 385(1).

"the trustee": s.385(1).

GENERAL NOTE

This section forms part of the group of sections (ss.339–342) concerned with the adjustment of antecedent transactions which were either concluded at an undervalue or constituted preferences within the meaning of this section.

This section corresponds to subss. (1) (part), (3)–(6) and (12) (part) of s.174 of the 1985 Act. For further information, see the General Note to s.339.

"Relevant time" under ss. 339, 340

341.—(1) Subject as follows, the time at which an individual enters into a transaction at an undervalue or gives a preference is a relevant time if the transaction is entered into or the preference given—

    (*a*) in the case of a transaction at an undervalue, at a time in the period of 5 years ending with the day of the presentation of the bankruptcy petition on which the individual is adjudged bankrupt,

    (*b*) in the case of a preference which is not a transaction at an undervalue and is given to a person who is an associate of the individual (otherwise than by reason only of being his employee), at a time in the period of 2 years ending with that day, and

    (*c*) in any other case of a preference which is not a transaction at an undervalue, at a time in the period of 6 months ending with that day.

(2) Where an individual enters into a transaction at an undervalue or gives a preference at a time mentioned in paragraph (*a*), (*b*) or (*c*) of subsection (1) (not being, in the case of a transaction at an undervalue, a time less than 2 years before the end of the period mentioned in paragraph (*a*)), that time is not a relevant time for the purposes of sections 339 and 340 unless the individual—

    (*a*) is insolvent at that time, or

    (*b*) becomes insolvent in consequence of the transaction or preference;

but the requirements of this subsection are presumed to be satisfied, unless the contrary is shown, in relation to any transaction at an undervalue which is entered into by an individual with a person who is an associate of his (otherwise than by reason only of being his employee).

(3) For the purposes of subsection (2), an individual is insolvent if—

    (*a*) he is unable to pay his debts as they fall due, or

    (*b*) the value of his assets is less than the amount of his liabilities, taking into account his contingent and prospective liabilities.

(4) A transaction entered into or preference given by a person who is subsequently adjudged bankrupt on a petition under section 264(1)(*d*) (criminal bankruptcy) is to be treated as having been entered into or given at a relevant time for the purposes of sections 339 and 340 if it was entered into or given at any time on or after the date specified for the purposes of this subsection in the criminal bankruptcy order on which the petition was based.

(5) No order shall be made under section 339 or 340 by virtue of subsection (4) of this section where an appeal is pending (within the meaning of section 277) against the individual's conviction of any offence by virtue of which the criminal bankruptcy order was made.

DEFINITIONS
    "appeal pending": s.277(3); Powers of Criminal Courts Act 1973, s.40(5).
    "a relevant time": subss. (1), (2).
    "associate": s.435.
    "bankrupt": s.381(1).
    "bankruptcy petition": s.381(3).
    "criminal bankruptcy order": s.385(1); Powers of Criminal Courts Act 1973, s.39(1).
    "debt": ss.382(3), 385(1).
    "gives a preference": s.340(3).
    "insolvent": subs. (3).
    "transaction": s.436.
    "transaction at an undervalue": s.339(3).

GENERAL NOTE
    This section forms part of the group of sections (ss.339–342) concerned with the adjustment of antecedent transactions. This section supplies the meaning of the expression "a relevant

time", where it appears in ss.339 and 340. The section corresponds to subss. (7)–(11) and (12) (part) of s.174 of the 1985 Act. See also the General Note to s.339.

Orders under ss.339, 340

342.—(1) Without prejudice to the generality of section 339(2) or 340(2), an order under either of those sections with respect to a transaction or preference entered into or given by an individual who is subsequently adjudged bankrupt may (subject as follows)—

(a) require any property transferred as part of the transaction, or in connection with the giving of the preference, to be vested in the trustee of the bankrupt's estate as part of that estate;

(b) require any property to be so vested if it represents in any person's hands the application either of the proceeds of sale of property so transferred or of money so transferred;

(c) release or discharge (in whole or in part) any security given by the individual;

(d) require any person to pay, in respect of benefits received by him from the individual, such sums to the trustee of his estate as the court may direct;

(e) provide for any surety or guarantor whose obligations to any person were released or discharged (in whole or in part) under the transaction or by the giving of the preference to be under such new or revived obligations to that person as the court thinks appropriate;

(f) provide for security to be provided for the discharge of any obligation imposed by or arising under the order, for such an obligation to be charged on any property and for the security or charge to have the same priority as a security or charge released or discharged (in whole or in part) under the transaction or by the giving of the preference; and

(g) provide for the extent to which any person whose property is vested by the order in the trustee of the bankrupt's estate, or on whom obligations are imposed by the order, is to be able to prove in the bankruptcy for debts or other liabilities which arose from, or were released or discharged (in whole or in part) under or by, the transaction or the giving of the preference.

(2) An order under section 339 or 340 may affect the property of, or impose any obligation on, any person whether or not he is the person with whom the individual in question entered into the transaction or, as the case may be, the person to whom the preference was given; but such an order—

(a) shall not prejudice any interest in property which was acquired from a person other than that individual and was acquired in good faith, for value and without notice of the relevant circumstances, or prejudice any interest deriving from such an interest, and

(b) shall not require a person who received a benefit from the transaction or preference in good faith, for value and without notice of the relevant circumstances to pay a sum to the trustee of the bankrupt's estate, except where he was a party to the transaction or the payment is to be in respect of a preference given to that person at a time when he was a creditor of that individual.

(3) Any sums required to be paid to the trustee in accordance with an order under section 339 or 340 shall be comprised in the bankrupt's estate.

(4) For the purposes of this section the relevant circumstances, in relation to a transaction or preference, are—

(a) the circumstances by virtue of which an order under section 339 or 340 could be made in respect of the transaction or preference if the individual in question were adjudged bankrupt within a particular period after the transaction is entered into or the preference given, and

(*b*) if that period has expired, the fact that that individual has been adjudged bankrupt within that period.

DEFINITIONS
"bankrupt": s.381(1).
"creditor": s.383(1).
"debt": ss.382(3), 385(1).
"estate": ss.283, 385(1).
"preference": s.340(3).
"property": s.436.
"security": ss.383, 385(1).
"the court": ss.373, 385(1).
"the relevant circumstances": subs. (4).
"the trustee": s.385(1).
"transaction": s.436.

TRANSITIONAL PROVISION
Sched. 11, para. 17.

GENERAL NOTE

This section forms part of the group of sections (ss.339–342) concerned with the adjustment of antecedent transactions. This section prescribes the powers of the court with regard to the making of orders in response to applications made under s.339 or s.340. The section is an almost exact parallel to s.241, which is applicable in cases of company insolvency. The divergences in matters of substance between the two sections are that there is no counterpart in s.241 to subs. (3) of this section, while there is no counterpart in this section to s.241(4). This section corresponds to s.175 of the 1985 Act. See also General Note to s.241.

Extortionate credit transactions

343.—(1) This section applies where a person is adjudged bankrupt who is or has been a party to a transaction for, or involving, the provision to him of credit.

(2) The court may, on the application of the trustee of the bankrupt's estate, make an order with respect to the transaction if the transaction is or was extortionate and was not entered into more than 3 years before the commencement of the bankruptcy.

(3) For the purposes of this section a transaction is extortionate if, having regard to the risk accepted by the person providing the credit—

(*a*) the terms of it are or were such as to require grossly exorbitant payments to be made (whether unconditionally or in certain contingencies) in respect of the provision of the credit, or

(*b*) it otherwise grossly contravened ordinary principles of fair dealing;

and it shall be presumed, unless the contrary is proved, that a transaction with respect to which an application is made under this section is or, as the case may be, was extortionate.

(4) An order under this section with respect to any transaction may contain such one or more of the following as the court thinks fit, that is to say—

(*a*) provision setting aside the whole or part of any obligation created by the transaction;

(*b*) provision otherwise varying the terms of the transaction or varying the terms on which any security for the purposes of the transaction is held;

(*c*) provision requiring any person who is or was party to the transaction to pay to the trustee any sums paid to that person, by virtue of the transaction, by the bankrupt;

(*d*) provision requiring any person to surrender to the trustee any property held by him as security for the purposes of the transaction;

(*e*) provision directing accounts to be taken between any persons.

(5) Any sums or property required to be paid or surrendered to the trustee in accordance with an order under this section shall be comprised in the bankrupt's estate.

(6) Neither the trustee of a bankrupt's estate nor an undischarged bankrupt is entitled to make an application under section 139(1)(*a*) of the Consumer Credit Act 1974 (re-opening of extortionate credit agreements) for any agreement by which credit is or has been provided to the bankrupt to be re-opened.

But the powers conferred by this section are exercisable in relation to any transaction concurrently with any powers exercisable under this Act in relation to that transaction as a transaction at an undervalue.

DEFINITIONS
"bankrupt": s.381(1).
"estate": ss.283, 385(1).
"extortionate": subs. (3).
"property": s.436.
"security": ss.383, 385(1).
"the court": ss.373, 385(1).
"the trustee": s.385(1).
"transaction": s.436.
"transaction at an undervalue": s.339(3).

TRANSITIONAL PROVISION
Sched. 11, para. 17.

GENERAL NOTE
This section enables the court, on the application of the trustee in bankruptcy, to vary or set aside any extortionate credit transaction between the bankrupt and a creditor. The section is a parallel to s.244, which applies in relation to companies in liquidation or subject to an administration order. In almost every respect the two sections are identical in substance, with differences in drafting attributable to the different legal frameworks within which company insolvency and individual bankruptcy respectively operate. Thus, subs. (2) of s.244 provides that an application to the court may be made by the office holder, whereas subs. (2) of this section provides that the right of application is exercisable by the trustee in bankruptcy. The two points of difference in matters of substance between the two sections are found, first in subs. (5) of this section, which has no counterpart in s.244, and secondly in the opening part of subs. (6) of this section, which precludes the making of any application under s.139(1)(*a*) of the Consumer Credit Act 1984 by the trustee in bankruptcy or the bankrupt, to which there is necessarily no counterpart in subs. (5) of s.244. See also General Note to s.244.

This section corresponds to s.176 of the 1985 Act.

Avoidance of general assignment of book debts

344.—(1) The following applies where a person engaged in any business makes a general assignment to another person of his existing or future book debts, or any class of them, and is subsequently adjudged bankrupt.

(2) The assignment is void against the trustee of the bankrupt's estate as regards book debts which were not paid before the presentation of the bankruptcy petition, unless the assignment has been registered under the Bills of Sale Act 1878.

(3) For the purposes of subsections (1) and (2)—

(*a*) "assignment" includes an assignment by way of security or charge on book debts, and

(*b*) "general assignment" does not include—

(i) an assignment of book debts due at the date of the assignment from specified debtors or of debts becoming due under specified contracts, or

(ii) an assignment of book debts included either in a transfer of a business made in good faith and for value or in an assignment of assets for the benefit of creditors generally.

(4) For the purposes of registration under the Act of 1878 an assignment of book debts is to be treated as if it were a bill of sale given otherwise than by way of security for the payment of a sum of money; and the provisions of that Act with respect to the registration of bills of sale apply accordingly with such necessary modifications as may be made by rules under that Act.

DEFINITIONS
"assignment", "general assignment": subs. (3).
"bankrupt": s.381(1).
"bankruptcy petition": s.381(3).
"business": s.436.
"creditor": s.383(1).
"debt": ss.382(3), 385(1).
"estate": ss.283, 385(1).
"modification": s.436.
"security": ss.383, 385(1).

TRANSITIONAL PROVISION
Sched. 11, para. 17.

GENERAL NOTE
This section makes void as against the trustee in bankruptcy certain assignments of book debts not registered under the Bills of Sale Act 1878. It re-enacts the substance of s.43 of the Bankruptcy Act 1914 (repealed), with suitably modernised drafting.
The section corresponds to s.177 of the 1985 Act.

Contracts to which bankrupt is a party

345.—(1) The following applies where a contract has been made with a person who is subsequently adjudged bankrupt.

(2) The court may, on the application of any other party to the contract, make an order discharging obligations under the contract on such terms as to payment by the applicant or the bankrupt of damages for non-performance or otherwise as appear to the court to be equitable.

(3) Any damages payable by the bankrupt by virtue of an order of the court under this section are provable as a bankruptcy debt.

(4) Where an undischarged bankrupt is a contractor in respect of any contract jointly with any person, that person may sue or be sued in respect of the contract without the joinder of the bankrupt.

DEFINITIONS
"bankrupt": s.381(1).
"bankruptcy debt": s.382.
"the court": ss.373, 385(1).

GENERAL NOTE
This section enables the court to discharge a contract between the bankrupt and another person, on the latter's application, upon such terms as the court thinks equitable.
This section corresponds to s.178 of the 1985 Act.

Enforcement procedures

346.—(1) Subject to section 285 in Chapter II (restrictions on proceedings and remedies) and to the following provisions of this section, where the creditor of any person who is adjudged bankrupt has, before the commencement of the bankruptcy—

(*a*) issued execution against the goods or land of that person, or

(*b*) attached a debt due to that person from another person,

that creditor is not entitled, as against the official receiver or trustee of the bankrupt's estate, to retain the benefit of the execution or attachment, or any sums paid to avoid it, unless the execution or attachment was completed, or the sums were paid, before the commencement of the bankruptcy.

(2) Subject as follows, where any goods of a person have been taken in execution, then, if before the completion of the execution notice is given to the sheriff or other officer charged with the execution that that person has been adjudged bankrupt—

(*a*) the sheriff or other officer shall on request deliver to the official receiver or trustee of the bankrupt's estate the goods and any money seized or recovered in part satisfaction of the execution, but

(*b*) the costs of the execution are a first charge on the goods or money so delivered and the official receiver or trustee may sell the goods or a sufficient part of them for the purpose of satisfying the charge.

(3) Subject to subsection (6) below, where—

(*a*) under an execution in respect of a judgment for a sum exceeding such sum as may be prescribed for the purposes of this subsection, the goods of any person are sold or money is paid in order to avoid a sale, and

(*b*) before the end of the period of 14 days beginning with the day of the sale or payment the sheriff or other officer charged with the execution is given notice that a bankruptcy petition has been presented in relation to that person, and

(*c*) a bankruptcy order is or has been made on that petition,

the balance of the proceeds of sale or money paid, after deducting the costs of execution, shall (in priority to the claim of the execution creditor) be comprised in the bankrupt's estate.

(4) Accordingly, in the case of an execution in respect of a judgment for a sum exceeding the sum prescribed for the purposes of subsection (3), the sheriff or other officer charged with the execution—

(*a*) shall not dispose of the balance mentioned in subsection (3) at any time within the period of 14 days so mentioned or while there is pending a bankruptcy petition of which he has been given notice under that subsection, and

(*b*) shall pay that balance, where by virtue of that subsection it is comprised in the bankrupt's estate, to the official receiver or (if there is one) to the trustee of that estate.

(5) For the purposes of this section—

(*a*) an execution against goods is completed by seizure and sale or by the making of a charging order under section 1 of the Charging Orders Act 1979;

(*b*) an execution against land is completed by seizure, by the appointment of a receiver or by the making of a charging order under that section;

(*c*) an attachment of a debt is completed by the receipt of the debt.

(6) The rights conferred by subsections (1) to (3) on the official receiver or the trustee may, to such extent and on such terms as it thinks fit, be set aside by the court in favour of the creditor who has issued the execution or attached the debt.

(7) Nothing in this section entitles the trustee of a bankrupt's estate to claim goods from a person who has acquired them in good faith under a sale by a sheriff or other officer charged with an execution.

(8) Neither subsection (2) nor subsection (3) applies in relation to any execution against property which has been acquired by or has devolved upon the bankrupt since the commencement of the bankruptcy, unless, at the time the execution is issued or before it is completed—

(*a*) the property has been or is claimed for the bankrupt's estate under section 307 (after-acquired property), and

(*b*) a copy of the notice given under that section has been or is served on the sheriff or other officer charged with the execution.

<small>DEFINITIONS</small>
"bankrupt": s.381(1).
"bankruptcy order": s.381(2).
"bankruptcy petition": s.381(3).
"commencement of the bankruptcy": s.278(*a*).
"creditor": s.383(1).
"debt": ss.382(3), 385(1).
"estate": ss.283, 385(1).
"execution or attachment completed": subs. (5).
"prescribed": s.384.
"the court": ss.373, 385(1).
"the official receiver": s.399(1).
"the trustee": s.385(1).

<small>GENERAL NOTE</small>
This section regulates the effects of bankruptcy upon procedures for executing judgment against the property of the bankrupt. The provisions of the section restate, in an expanded and generally clearer form, the provisions formerly contained in ss.40 and 41 of the Bankruptcy Act 1914 (repealed).
This section corresponds to s.179 of the 1985 Act.

Subs. (1)

Subject to section 285
The saving for the effects of s.285 allows for the possibility that the court may exercise its powers under that section to stay any action, execution or other legal process at any time when proceedings on a bankruptcy petition are pending, or after an adjudication of bankruptcy has taken place.

Distress, etc.

347.—(1) The right of any landlord or other person to whom rent is payable to distrain upon the goods and effects of an undischarged bankrupt for rent due to him from the bankrupt is available (subject to subsection (5) below) against goods and effects comprised in the bankrupt's estate, but only for 6 months' rent accrued due before the commencement of the bankruptcy.

(2) Where a landlord or other person to whom rent is payable has distrained for rent upon the goods and effects of an individual to whom a bankruptcy petition relates and a bankruptcy order is subsequently made on that petition, any amount recovered by way of that distress which—

(*a*) is in excess of the amount which by virtue of subsection (1) would have been recoverable after the commencement of the bankruptcy, or

(*b*) is in respect of rent for a period or part of a period after the distress was levied,

shall be held for the bankrupt as part of his estate.

(3) Where any person (whether or not a landlord or person entitled to rent) has distrained upon the goods or effects of an individual who is adjudged bankrupt before the end of the period of 3 months beginning with the distraint, so much of those goods or effects, or of the proceeds of their sale, as is not held for the bankrupt under subsection (2) shall be

charged for the benefit of the bankrupt's estate with the preferential debts of the bankrupt to the extent that the bankrupt's estate is for the time being insufficient for meeting those debts.

(4) Where by virtue of any charge under subsection (3) any person surrenders any goods or effects to the trustee of a bankrupt's estate or makes a payment to such a trustee, that person ranks, in respect of the amount of the proceeds of the sale of those goods or effects by the trustee or, as the case may be, the amount of the payment, as a preferential creditor of the bankrupt, except as against so much of the bankrupt's estate as is available for the payment of preferential creditors by virtue of the surrender or payment.

(5) A landlord or other person to whom rent is payable is not at any time after the discharge of a bankrupt entitled to distrain upon any goods or effects comprised in the bankrupt's estate.

(6) Where in the case of any execution—

    (*a*) a landlord is (apart from this section) entitled under section 1 of the Landlord and Tenant Act 1709 or section 102 of the County Courts Act 1984 (claims for rent where goods seized in execution) to claim for an amount not exceeding one year's rent, and

    (*b*) the person against whom the execution is levied is adjudged bankrupt before the notice of claim is served on the sheriff or other officer charged with the execution,

the right of the landlord to claim under that section is restricted to a right to claim for an amount not exceeding 6 months' rent and does not extend to any rent payable in respect of a period after the notice of claim is so served.

(7) Nothing in subsection (6) imposes any liability on a sheriff or other officer charged with an execution to account to the official receiver or the trustee of a bankrupt's estate for any sums paid by him to a landlord at any time before the sheriff or other officer was served with notice of the bankruptcy order in question.

But this subsection is without prejudice to the liability of the landlord.

(8) Nothing in this Group of Parts affects any right to distrain otherwise than for rent; and any such right is at any time exercisable without restriction against property comprised in a bankrupt's estate, even if that right is expressed by any enactment to be exercisable in like manner as a right to distrain for rent.

(9) Any right to distrain against property comprised in a bankrupt's estate is exercisable notwithstanding that the property has vested in the trustee.

(10) The provisions of this section are without prejudice to a landlord's right in a bankruptcy to prove for any bankruptcy debt in respect of rent.

DEFINITIONS
    "bankrupt": s.381(1).
    "bankruptcy order": s.381(2).
    "bankruptcy petition": s.381(3).
    "commencement of the bankruptcy": s.278(*a*).
    "creditor": s.383(1).
    "estate": ss.283, 385(1).
    "preferential debt": s.386; Sched. 6.
    "property": s.436.
    "the official receiver": s.399(1).
    "the trustee": s.385(1).

GENERAL NOTE
    This section regulates the levying of distress by a landlord and by other persons on the property of the bankrupt. It restates the law formerly contained in s.35 of the Bankruptcy Act 1914 (repealed), with suitable improvements to, and modernisation of, the drafting.
    This section corresponds to s.180 of the 1985 Act.

Apprenticeships, etc.

348.—(1) This section applies where—

(a) a bankruptcy order is made in respect of an individual to whom another individual was an apprentice or articled clerk at the time when the petition on which the order was made was presented, and

(b) the bankrupt or the apprentice or clerk gives notice to the trustee terminating the apprenticeship or articles.

(2) Subject to subsection (6) below, the indenture of apprenticeship or, as the case may be, the articles of agreement shall be discharged with effect from the commencement of the bankruptcy.

(3) If any money has been paid by or on behalf of the apprentice or clerk to the bankrupt as a fee, the trustee may, on an application made by or on behalf of the apprentice or clerk, pay such sum to the apprentice or clerk as the trustee thinks reasonable, having regard to—

(a) the amount of the fee,

(b) the proportion of the period in respect of which the fee was paid that has been served by the apprentice or clerk before the commencement of the bankruptcy, and

(c) the other circumstances of the case.

(4) The power of the trustee to make a payment under subsection (3) has priority over his obligation to distribute the bankrupt's estate.

(5) Instead of making a payment under subsection (3), the trustee may, if it appears to him expedient to do so on an application made by or on behalf of the apprentice or clerk, transfer the indenture or articles to a person other than the bankrupt.

(6) Where a transfer is made under subsection (5), subsection (2) has effect only as between the apprentice or clerk and the bankrupt.

DEFINITIONS

"bankrupt": s.381(1).
"bankruptcy order": s.381(2).
"bankruptcy petition": s.381(3).
"commencement of the bankruptcy": s.278(a).
"estate": ss.283, 385(1).
"trustee": s.385(1).

GENERAL NOTE

This restates, with necessary modifications in the drafting, the law previously contained in s.34 of the Bankruptcy Act 1914 (repealed), whereby special provisions regulate the effect of the bankruptcy on the apprentices or articled clerks of the bankrupt.

This section corresponds to s.181 of the 1985 Act.

Unenforceability of liens on books, etc.

349.—(1) Subject as follows, a lien or other right to retain possession of any of the books, papers or other records of a bankrupt is unenforceable to the extent that its enforcement would deny possession of any books, papers or other records to the official receiver or the trustee of the bankrupt's estate.

(2) Subsection (1) does not apply to a lien on documents which give a title to property and are held as such.

DEFINITIONS

"bankrupt": s.381(1).
"estate": ss.283, 385(1).
"property": s.436.
"records": s.436.
"the official receiver": s.399(1).

This section renders certain liens on the books, papers and records of the bankrupt unenforceable against the trustee. The extent of the unenforceability of such liens is limited to the matter of the right of the official receiver or the trustee to gain possession of the items of property to which any lien is applicable. Moreover, subs. (2) expressly preserves the right of any lienholder to retain possession of documents which give title to property and which are held as such, as where a mortgage is effected by a deposit of title deeds. However, the section does effectively modify the principle long established in the case law whereby the trustee in bankruptcy was held to take "subject to equities", and hence to be affected by any pre-existing lien or other possessory right existing in favour of a third party before the commencement of bankruptcy.

This section corresponds to s.182 of the 1985 Act.

CHAPTER VI

BANKRUPTCY OFFENCES

Preliminary

GENERAL NOTE

This chapter restates in modern terms the offences contained in Pt. VII of the Bankruptcy Act 1914 (repealed), and revises the penalties for those offences. The offences are grouped in a more logical way than under the provisions of the former legislation. Offences associated with insolvency are discussed in Chap. 48 of the *Cork Report*.

TRANSITIONAL PROVISION

Sched 11, para. 18.

Scheme of this Chapter

350.—(1) Subject to section 360(3) below, this Chapter applies where the court has made a bankruptcy order on a bankruptcy petition.

(2) This Chapter applies whether or not the bankruptcy order is annulled, but proceedings for an offence under this Chapter shall not be instituted after the annulment.

(3) Without prejudice to his liability in respect of a subsequent bankruptcy, the bankrupt is not guilty of an offence under this Chapter in respect of anything done after his discharge; but nothing in this Group of Parts prevents the institution of proceedings against a discharged bankrupt for an offence committed before his discharge.

(4) It is not a defence in proceedings for an offence under this Chapter that anything relied on, in whole or in part, as constituting that offence was done outside England and Wales.

(5) Proceedings for an offence under this Chapter or under the rules shall not be instituted except by the Secretary of State or by or with the consent of the Director of Public Prosecutions.

(6) A person guilty of any offence under this Chapter is liable to imprisonment or a fine, or both.

DEFINITIONS

"affairs": s.385(2).
"annulment": s.282.
"bankrupt": s.381(1).
"bankruptcy order": s.381(2).
"bankruptcy petition": s.381(3).
"discharge": ss.279, 280, 281.
"the court": ss.373, 385(1).

This section corresponds to subss. (1)–(3), (5) and (6), together with s.192, of the 1985 Act.

Subs. (5)
This imposes a general rule that no prosecution may be brought for an offence under this Chapter or under the rules except by the Secretary of State or by or with the consent of the Director of Public Prosecutions. This accords with the reommendation made in paras. 1892–1894 of the *Cork Report.*

Subs. (6)
Sched. 10 contains the list of punishments which may be imposed for offences under this Chapter.

Definitions

351. In the following provisions of this Chapter—

(*a*) references to property comprised in the bankrupt's estate or to property possession of which is required to be delivered up to the official receiver or the trustee of the bankrupt's estate include any property which would be such property if a notice in respect of it were given under section 307 (after-acquired property) or 308 (personal property and effects of bankrupt having more than replacement value);

(*b*) "the initial period" means the period between the presentation of the bankruptcy petition and the commencement of the bankruptcy; and

(*c*) a reference to a number of months or years before petition is to that period ending with the presentation of the bankruptcy petition.

DEFINITIONS
"bankrupt": s.381(1).
"bankruptcy petition": s.381(3).
"commencement of the bankruptcy": s.278(*a*).
"estate": ss.283, 385(1).
"months before petition": para. (*c*).
"property": para. (*a*); s.436.
"the initial period": para. (*b*).
"the official receiver": s.399(1).
"the trustee": s.385(1).
"years before petition": para. (*c*).

GENERAL NOTE
This section contains special definitions of terms in relation to their use within Chapter VI of Part IX.
This section corresponds to ss.184(5) and 187(3)(*a*) of the 1985 Act.

Defence of innocent intention

352. Where in the case of an offence under any provision of this Chapter it is stated that this section applies, a person is not guilty of the offence if he proves that, at the time of the conduct constituting the offence, he had no intent to defraud or to conceal the state of his affairs.

GENERAL NOTE
This provision has the effect that a burden of proof is cast upon the bankrupt in respect of any charges brought against him under the provisions to which this section applies. Thus, although the offences in question are cast as offences of strict liability, the bankrupt can escape conviction if he effectively proves that he lacked the relevant *mens rea,* namely an intention to defraud or to conceal the state of his affairs. The presence of this section also serves as a general aid to judicial construction of the subsequent sections in which the

specific criminal offences are prescribed, since it is evidence of a legislative intention to create offences of strict liability in respect of all those provisions which contain no internal reference to the intention or state of mind of the accused person (*cf. Sweet* v. *Parsley* [1969] 1 All E.R. 347; [1970] A.C. 132).

This section corresponds to s.183(4) of the 1985 Act.

Wrongdoing by the bankrupt before and after bankruptcy

Non-disclosure

353.—(1) The bankrupt is guilty of an offence if—
   (*a*) he does not to the best of his knowledge and belief disclose all the property comprised in his estate to the official receiver or the trustee, or
   (*b*) he does not inform the official receiver or the trustee of any disposal of any property which but for the disposal would be so comprised, stating how, when, to whom and for what consideration the property was disposed of.

(2) Subsection (1)(*b*) does not apply to any disposal in the ordinary course of a business carried on by the bankrupt or to any payment of the ordinary expenses of the bankrupt or his family.

(3) Section 352 applies to this offence.

DEFINITIONS
   "business": s.436.
   "estate": ss.283, 385(1).
   "family": s.385(1).
   "property": ss.351(*a*), 436.
   "the bankrupt": s.381(1).
   "the official receiver": s.399(1).
   "trustee": s.385(1).

GENERAL NOTE
   This section deals with offences relating to the failure by the bankrupt to disclose property to the official receiver or trustee in bankruptcy as required by law, and to supply other relevant information regarding dealings with his available property.
   This section corresponds to ss.183(4) and 184(1) of the 1985 Act.

Subs. (3)
   See s.352 and General Note thereto.

Concealment of property

354.—(1) The bankrupt is guilty of an offence if—
   (*a*) he does not deliver up possession to the official receiver or trustee, or as the official receiver or trustee may direct, of such part of the property comprised in his estate as is in his possession or under his control and possession of which he is required by law so to deliver up,
   (*b*) he conceals any debt due to or from him or conceals any property the value of which is not less than the prescribed amount and possession of which he is required to deliver up to the official receiver or trustee, or
   (*c*) in the 12 months before petition, or in the initial period, he did anything which would have been an offence under paragraph (*b*) above if the bankruptcy order had been made immediately before he did it.
Section 352 applies to this offence.

(2) The bankrupt is guilty of an offence if he removes, or in the initial period removed, any property the value of which was not less than the

prescribed amount and possession of which he has or would have been required to deliver up to the official receiver or the trustee.

Section 352 applies to this offence.

(3) The bankrupt is guilty of an offence if he without reasonable excuse fails, on being required to do so by the official receiver or the court—

(*a*) to account for the loss of any substantial part of his property incurred in the 12 months before petition or in the initial period, or

(*b*) to give a satisfactory explanation of the manner in which such a loss was incurred.

DEFINITIONS
"bankrupt": s.381(1).
"bankruptcy order": s.381(2).
"debt": ss.382(3), 385(1).
"estate": ss.283, 385(1).
"months before petition": s.351(*c*).
"prescribed": s.384.
"property": ss.351(*a*), 436.
"the initial period": s.351(*b*).
"the official receiver": s.399(1).
"the trustee": s.385(1).

GENERAL NOTE
This section establishes criminal offences in relation to various acts of concealment of property, or of failure to deliver up possession of property as required by law.
This section corresponds to ss.183(4) and 184(2)–(4) of the 1985 Act.

Subss. (1) and (2)
See General Note to s.352.

Subs. (1)(c)
This provision is so worded as to give rise to criminal liability if a person is subsequently adjudicated on a bankruptcy petition presented within twelve months after he does any of the acts referred to.

Concealment of books and papers; falsification

355.—(1) The bankrupt is guilty of an offence if he does not deliver up possession to the official receiver or the trustee, or as the official receiver or trustee may direct, of all books, papers and other records of which he has possession or control and which relate to his estate or his affairs.

Section 352 applies to this offence.

(2) The bankrupt is guilty of an offence if—

(*a*) he prevents, or in the initial period prevented, the production of any books, papers or records relating to his estate or affairs;

(*b*) he conceals, destroys, mutilates or falsifies, or causes or permits the concealment, destruction, mutilation or falsification of, any books, papers or other records relating to his estate or affairs;

(*c*) he makes, or causes or permits the making of, any false entries in any book, document or record relating to his estate or affairs; or

(*d*) in the 12 months before petition, or in the initial period, he did anything which would have been an offence, under paragraph (*b*) or (*c*) above if the bankruptcy order had been made before he did it.

Section 352 applies to this offence.

(3) The bankrupt is guilty of an offence if—

(*a*) he disposes of, or alters or makes any omission in, or causes or permits the disposal, altering or making of any omission in, any book, document or record relating to his estate or affairs, or (*b*) in the 12 months before petition, or in the initial period, he did anything which would have been an offence under paragraph (*a*) if the bankruptcy order had been made before he did it.

Section 352 applies to this offence.

DEFINITIONS
  "affairs": s.385(2).
  "bankrupt": s.381(1).
  "bankruptcy order": s.381(2).
  "commencement of the bankruptcy": s.278(*a*).
  "estate": ss.283, 385(1).
  "months before petition": s.351(*c*).
  "petition", "bankruptcy petition": s.381(3).
  "records": s.436.
  "the initial period": s.351(*b*).
  "the official receiver": s.399(1).
  "the trustee": s.385(1).

GENERAL NOTE
  This section sets out the offences which may be committed by a bankrupt in relation to his books, papers and other records. The prohibited acts include concealment, non-delivery, falsification, mutilation or destruction of any of the items in question.
  This section corresponds to ss.183(4) and 185 of the 1985 Act.

Subss. (1), (2) and (3)
  See General Note to s.352.

Subss. (2)(d) , (3)(b)
  These provisions are so worded as to give rise to criminal liability if a person is subsequently adjudicated on a bankruptcy petition presented within twelve months after he does any of the acts referred to. Where the bankrupt has been engaged in business, references to certain types of "records" within this section apply with the substitution of two years for 12 months: s.361(4).

False statements

356.—(1) The bankrupt is guilty of an offence if he makes or has made any material omission in any statement made under any provision in this Group of Parts and relating to his affairs.

Section 352 applies to this offence.

(2) The bankrupt is guilty of an offence if—

(*a*) knowing or believing that a false debt has been proved by any person under the bankruptcy, he fails to inform the trustee as soon as practicable; or

(*b*) he attempts to account for any part of his property by fictitious losses or expenses; or

(*c*) at any meeting of his creditors in the 12 months before petition or (whether or not at such a meeting) at any time in the initial period, he did anything which would have been an offence under paragraph (*b*) if the bankruptcy order had been made before he did it; or

(*d*) he is, or at any time has been, guilty of any false representation or other fraud for the purpose of obtaining the consent of his creditors, or any of them, to an agreement with reference to his affairs or to his bankruptcy.

DEFINITIONS
  "affairs": s.385(2).
  "bankrupt": s.381(1).
  "commencement of the bankruptcy": s.278(*a*).
  "creditor": s.383(1).
  "debt": ss.382(3), 385(1).

"estate": ss.283, 385(1).
"months before petition": s.351(*c*).
"petition", "bankruptcy petition": s.381(3).
"property": s.436.
"the initial period": s.351(*b*).
"trustee": s.385(1).

GENERAL NOTE
This section establishes criminal offences committed through the making of false statements by the bankrupt.
This section corresponds to ss.183(4) and 186 of the 1985 Act.

Subs. (1)
See General Note to s.352.

Subs. (2)(c)
This provision is so worded as to give rise to criminal liability if a person is subsequently adjudicated bankrupt on a petition presented within 12 months after the creditors' meeting at which the act referred to was done.

Fraudulent disposal of property

357.—(1) The bankrupt is guilty of an offence if he makes or causes to be made, or has in the period of 5 years ending with the commencement of the bankruptcy made or caused to be made, any gift or transfer of, or any charge on, his property.
Section 352 applies to this offence.
(2) The reference to making a transfer of or charge on any property includes causing or conniving at the levying of any execution against that property.
(3) The bankrupt is guilty of an offence if he conceals or removes, or has at any time before the commencement of the bankruptcy concealed or removed, any part of his property after, or within 2 months before, the date on which a judgment or order for the payment of money has been obtained against him, being a judgment or order which was not satisfied before the commencement of the bankruptcy.
Section 352 applies to this offence.

DEFINITIONS
"bankrupt": s.381(1).
"commencement of the bankruptcy": s.278(*a*).
"estate": ss.283, 385(1).
"property": ss.351(*a*), 436.
"the official receiver": s.399(1).

GENERAL NOTE
This section establishes criminal offences committed through the fraudulent disposal of property by the bankrupt. There is one change of a substantive nature regarding the offence created by subs. (1), as against that previously created by s.156(*b*) of the Bankruptcy Act 1914 (repealed). In the former provision, the offence of fraudulent disposal of property could be committed through any act of disposal at any time before the commencement of bankruptcy, without limitation as to the period of time involved. The period of five years before the commencement of bankruptcy has now been introduced in subs. (1) as enacted, and is commensurate with the period of time allowed under s.339 whereby gifts and undervalued transactions can be challenged if the bankrupt was insolvent at the time of the transaction (see s.341(1)(*a*)).
This section corresponds to ss.183(4) and 187(1) and (3)(*b*) of the 1985 Act.

Subss. (1) and (3)
See General Note to s.352.

Absconding

358. The bankrupt is guilty of an offence if—

(a) he leaves, or attempts or makes preparations to leave, England and Wales with any property the value of which is not less than the prescribed amount and possession of which he is required to deliver up to the official receiver or the trustee, or

(b) in the 6 months before petition, or in the initial period, he did anything which would have been an offence under paragraph (a) if the bankruptcy order had been made immediately before he did it.

Section 352 applies to this offence.

DEFINITIONS
"bankrupt": s.381(1).
"months before petition": s.351(c).
"prescribed": s.384.
"property": ss.351(a), 436.
"the initial period": s.351(b).
"the official receiver": s.399(1).
"trustee": s.385(1).

GENERAL NOTE
This offence was formerly contained in s.159 of the Bankruptcy Act 1914 (repealed). In para. 1889 of the *Cork Report* there was criticism of the inclusion of a prescribed monetary figure (latterly £250) employed in conjunction with the commission of this offence, and it was recommended that there should be no financial limit as to amount or value of property, the proposed test being simply whether the property with which the bankrupt absconds belongs to that part of his estate which is divisible among his creditors. The inclusion in the present subsection of a reference to "prescribed amount" of value therefore constitutes a rejection of the Cork Committee's recommendation and a retention of the former rule, with the facility for effecting its upward revision periodically by means of a statutory instrument.

This section corresponds to ss.183(4) and 187(2) of the 1985 Act. See also the General Note to s.352.

Fraudulent dealing with property obtained on credit

359.—(1) The bankrupt is guilty of an offence if, in the 12 months before petition, or in the initial period, he disposed of any property which he had obtained on credit and, at the time he disposed of it, had not paid for.

Section 352 applies to this offence.

(2) A person is guilty of an offence if, in the 12 months before petition or in the initial period, he acquired or received property from the bankrupt knowing or believing—

(a) that the bankrupt owed money in respect of the property, and

(b) that the bankrupt did not intend, or was unlikely to be able, to pay the money he so owed.

(3) A person is not guilty of an offence under subsection (1) or (2) if the disposal, acquisition or receipt of the property was in the ordinary course of a business carried on by the bankrupt at the time of the disposal, acquisition or receipt.

(4) In determining for the purposes of this section whether any property is disposed of, acquired or received in the ordinary course of a business carried on by the bankrupt, regard may be had, in particular, to the price paid for the property.

(5) In this section references to disposing of property include pawning or pledging it; and references to acquiring or receiving property shall be read accordingly.

DEFINITIONS
"bankrupt": s.381(1).
"business": s.436.

"dispose of property": subs. (5).
"months before petition": s.351(*c*).
"petition", "bankruptcy petition": s.381(3).
"property": ss.351(*a*), 436.
"the initial period": s.351(*b*).

GENERAL NOTE
This section establishes criminal offences which may be committed by the bankrupt or by other persons fraudulently dealing with property obtained on credit.
This section corresponds to ss.183(4) and 188 of the 1985 Act.

Subs. (1)
See General Note to s.352.

Obtaining credit; engaging in business

360.—(1) The bankrupt is guilty of an offence if—
   (*a*) either alone or jointly with any other person, he obtains credit to the extent of the prescribed amount or more without giving the person from whom he obtains it the relevant information about his status; or
   (*b*) he engages (whether directly or indirectly) in any business under a name other than that in which he was adjudged bankrupt without disclosing to all persons with whom he enters into any business transaction the name in which he was so adjudged.
   (2) The reference to the bankrupt obtaining credit includes the following cases—
   (*a*) where goods are bailed to him under a hire-purchase agreement, or agreed to be sold to him under a conditional sale agreement, and
   (*b*) where he is paid in advance (whether in money or otherwise) for the supply of goods or services.
   (3) A person whose estate has been sequestrated in Scotland, or who has been adjudged bankrupt in Northern Ireland, is guilty of an offence if, before his discharge, he does anything in England and Wales which would be an offence under subsection (1) if he were an undischarged bankrupt and the sequestration of his estate or the adjudication in Northern Ireland were an adjudication under this Part.
   (4) For the purposes of subsection (1)(*a*), the relevant information about the status of the person in question is the information that he is an undischarged bankrupt or, as the case may be, that his estate has been sequestrated in Scotland and that he has not been discharged.

DEFINITIONS
   "bankrupt": s.381(1).
   "business": s.436.
   "estate": ss.283, 385(1).
   "obtaining credit": subs. (2).
   "prescribed": s.384.
   "the relevant information": subs. (4).
   "transaction": s.436.

GENERAL NOTE
This section deals with offences committed by an undischarged bankrupt through the obtaining of credit without revealing his status or through his engaging in business under a name other than that in which he was adjudged bankrupt, without disclosing his other identity in any business transaction entered into. This section re-enacts, with some modifications and with up-to-date drafting, the provisions formerly contained in s.155 of the Bankruptcy Act 1914 (repealed).
This section corresponds to s.189 of the 1985 Act.

Subss. (1)(a), (3), (4)

These subsections together establish an improved provision by comparison to that of the former s.155(a) of the Bankruptcy Act 1914 (repealed), since they create throughout the whole of the United Kingdom an integrated regime to control one of the most important, and best known, disabilities attaching to the status of an undischarged bankrupt. A person who has incurred equivalent personal disabilities under the laws of either of the other two parts of the United Kingdom will commit a criminal offence if he fails to make the requisite disclosure when obtaining credit from any person in England and Wales. *Cf.* Bankruptcy (Scotland) Act 1985, s.67(9), (10).

The use of the drafting device of referring to the "prescribed amount" has the effect of ensuring that the monetary amount applicable to the commission of an offence under this section can be revised periodically by statutory instrument. This offence has traditionally been one of strict liability, its purpose being to protect members of the public from risk of loss by dealing with a person presumed to be creditworthy. The maintenance of this characteristic of strict liability under the present section accords with the recommendation of the *Cork Report* (paras. 132, 1840–1845; and 1882).

Subss. (1)(b), (3)

These subsections also effect a sensible integration of the provisions regarding the offence formerly specified in s.155(b) of the Bankruptcy Act 1914 (repealed), so that a sequestration in Scotland or an adjudication in Northern Ireland are equated with adjudication in England and Wales for the purposes of rendering the person concerned subject to criminal liability for engaging in business transactions in England and Wales under an *alias*. A further refinement in the drafting consists in the insertion of the words "(whether directly or indirectly)" in relation to engagement in business, so that an undischarged bankrupt who utilises an agent to perform business on his behalf, or who otherwise contrives to control a business from behind the scenes, can also be convicted if the other ingredients of this offence are made out. (*Cf.* The drafting of the parallel provision in s.302(1) of the Companies Act 1985 whereby an undischarged bankrupt is prohibited from acting in the management of companies either directly or indirectly.)

Subs. (2)(b)

The purpose of this provision, which is an alteration to the former law, is to reverse the anomaly resulting from the decision of the House of Lords in *Fisher* v. *Raven* [1964] A.C. 210, in which an undischarged bankrupt who obtained payment in advance to carry out work which he then failed to perform was held not to have committed an offence under s.155(a) of the Bankruptcy Act 1914 because he did not obtain "credit" within the meaning of that section. A strict interpretation of the term "credit" was adopted by the House of Lords whereby the offence could only be committed if a bankrupt obtained "credit in respect of the payment or repayment of money." That ruling is now reversed by the present provision, which expressly renders it an offence for an undischarged bankrupt to receive advanced payments—whether in money or in another form—for the supply of goods or services without informing those concerned of his current status.

Failure to keep proper accounts of business

361.—(1) Where the bankrupt has been engaged in any business for any of the period of 2 years before petition, he is guilty of an offence if he—

    (a) has not kept proper accounting records throughout that period and throughout any part of the initial period in which he was so engaged, or

    (b) has not preserved all the accounting records which he has kept.

(2) The bankrupt is not guilty of an offence under subsection (1)—

    (a) if his unsecured liabilities at the commencement of the bankruptcy did not exceed the prescribed amount, or

    (b) if he proves that in the circumstances in which he carried on business the omission was honest and excusable.

(3) For the purposes of this section a person is deemed not to have kept proper accounting records if he has not kept such records as are necessary to show or explain his transactions and financial position in his business, including—

(*a*) records containing entries from day to day, in sufficient detail, of all cash paid and received,

(*b*) where the business involved dealings in goods, statements of annual stock-takings, and

(*c*) except in the case of goods sold by way of retail trade to the actual customer, records of all goods sold and purchased showing the buyers and sellers in sufficient detail to enable the goods and the buyers and sellers to be identified.

(4) In relation to any such records as are mentioned in subsection (3), subsections (2)(*d*) and (3)(*b*) of section 355 apply with the substitution of 2 years for 12 months.

DEFINITIONS

"bankrupt": s.381(1).
"business": s.436.
"commencement of the bankruptcy": s.278(*a*).
"petition", "bankruptcy petition": s.381(3).
"prescribed": s.384.
"proper accounting records": subs. (3).
"records": s.436.
"transaction": s.436.
"unsecured", "secured": ss.383, 385(1).

GENERAL NOTE

This section deals with the failure of the bankrupt to keep proper accounts. The section restates the former provisions of s.158 of the Bankruptcy Act 1914 (repealed), by comparison to which the drafting of the present section is improved and modernised. As recommended in para. 1887 of the *Cork Report* there is no longer any requirement that a special order of the bankruptcy court must be made as a precondition for the bringing of a prosecution under this section.

This section corresponds to s.190 of the 1985 Act.

Gambling

362.—(1) The bankrupt is guilty of an offence if he has—

(*a*) in the 2 years before petition, materially contributed to, or increased the extent of, his insolvency by gambling or by rash and hazardous speculations, or

(*b*) in the initial period, lost any part of his property by gambling or by rash and hazardous speculations.

(2) In determining for the purposes of this section whether any speculations were rash and hazardous, the financial position of the bankrupt at the time when he entered into them shall be taken into consideration.

DEFINITIONS

"bankrupt": s.381(1).
"petition", "bankruptcy petition": s.381(3).
"property": ss.351(*a*), 436.
"rash and hazardous speculations": see subs. (2).
"the initial period": s.251(*b*).
"years before petition": s.251(*c*).

GENERAL NOTE

This section creates two related offences which may be committed by a person who has contributed to his bankruptcy by gambling or by rash and hazardous speculations. This largely restates the law formerly contained in s.157(1)(*a*), (*b*) of the Bankruptcy Act 1914 (repealed), but in addition to the appropriate modernisation of drafting the present section broadens the scope of the offence through the omission of any references to the bankrupt's having been engaged in any trade or business, and to the existence of outstanding trade or business debts. Any bankrupt can now be convicted of these offences if the necessary ingredients are proved, regardless of whether he is or has been engaged in any trade or business. It was at one stage (H.C. Standing Committee E, June 18, 1985, cols. 414–415) declared to be intended that this section would reverse the decision in *R.* v. *Vaccari* [1958] 1 All E.R. 468 in which it was held that income or profits tax was not a debt "contracted in the course and for the purposes of" a trade or business for the purposes of the commission of an offence under s.157(1) of the Bankruptcy Act 1914. The elimination of all reference to a trading context for the commission of an offence under the present action has had the consequence of rendering this former nice distinction irrelevant.

As recommended in para. 1887 of the *Cork Report* there is no longer any requirement that a special order be made by the bankruptcy court in order that a prosecution may be brought under this section.

This section corresponds to s.191 of the 1985 Act.

CHAPTER VII

POWERS OF COURT IN BANKRUPTCY

General control of court

363.—(1) Every bankruptcy is under the general control of the court and, subject to the provisions in this Group of Parts, the court has full power to decide all questions of priorities and all other questions, whether of law or fact, arising in any bankruptcy.

(2) Without prejudice to any other provision in this Group of Parts, an undischarged bankrupt or a discharged bankrupt whose estate is still being administered under Chapter IV of this Part shall do all such things as he may be directed to do by the court for the purposes of his bankruptcy or, as the case may be, the administration of that estate.

(3) The official receiver or the trustee of a bankrupt's estate may at any time apply to the court for a direction under subsection (2).

(4) If any person without reasonable excuse fails to comply with any obligation imposed on him by subsection (2), he is guilty of a contempt of court and liable to be punished accordingly (in addition to any other punishment to which he may be subject).

DEFINITIONS
"bankrupt": s.381(1).
"estate": ss.283, 385(1).
"the court": ss.373, 385(1).
"the official receiver": s.399(1).
"trustee": s.385(1).

GENERAL NOTE
This section places every bankruptcy under the general control of the relevant court, empowers the court to direct the bankrupt to do things for the purposes of the bankruptcy and for the realisation of the estate both before and, in certain cases, after he obtains his discharge, and provides for the official receiver and the trustee in bankruptcy to apply at any time to the court for the issue of such a direction in relation to the bankrupt.

This section corresponds to s.193 of the 1985 Act.

Power of arrest

364.—(1) In the cases specified in the next subsection the court may cause a warrant to be issued to a constable or prescribed officer of the court—

(*a*) for the arrest of a debtor to whom a bankruptcy petition relates or of an undischarged bankrupt, or of a discharged bankrupt whose estate is still being administered under Chapter IV of this Part, and

(*b*) for the seizure of any books, papers, records, money or goods in the possession of a person arrested under the warrant, and may authorise a person arrested under such a warrant to be kept in custody, and anything seized under such a warrant to be held, in accordance with the rules, until such time as the court may order.

(2) The powers conferred by subsection (1) are exercisable in relation to a debtor or undischarged or discharged bankrupt if, at any time after the presentation of the bankruptcy petition relating to him or the making of the bankruptcy order against him, it appears to the court—

 (*a*) that there are reasonable grounds for believing that he has absconded, or is about to abscond, with a view to avoiding or delaying the payment of any of his debts or his appearance to a bankruptcy petition or to avoiding, delaying or disrupting any proceedings in bankruptcy against him or any examination of his affairs, or

 (*b*) that he is about to remove his goods with a view to preventing or delaying possession being taken of them by the official receiver or the trustee of his estate, or

 (*c*) that there are reasonable grounds for believing that he has concealed or destroyed, or is about to conceal or destroy, any of his goods or any books, papers or records which might be of use to his creditors in the course of his bankruptcy or in connection with the administration of his estate, or

 (*d*) that he has, without the leave of the official receiver or the trustee of his estate, removed any goods in his possession which exceed in value such sum as may be prescribed for the purposes of this paragraph, or

 (*e*) that he has failed, without reasonable excuse, to attend any examination ordered by the court.

DEFINITIONS

 "affairs": s.385(2).
 "bankrupt": s.381(1).
 "bankruptcy order": s.381(2).
 "bankruptcy petition": s.381(3).
 "creditor": s.383(1).
 "debt": ss.382(3), 385(1).
 "debtor": s.385(1).
 "estate": ss.283, 385(1).
 "prescribed": s.384.
 "records": s.436.
 "the court": ss.373, 385(1).
 "the official receiver": s.399(1).
 "the rules": ss.384, 412.

GENERAL NOTE

 This section sets out the circumstances in which the court may authorise the arrest of a debtor or bankrupt, and the seizure of documents, money or goods in his possession. This section restates, with suitable modifications and modernisation in the drafting, the former provisions of s.23 of the Bankruptcy Act 1914 (repealed).

 This section corresponds to s.194 of the 1985 Act.

Subs. (2)

 It may be noted that the wide terms of application of the powers of arrest and seizure under this section apply against a debtor even after he has obtained his discharge from bankruptcy under the provisions of ss.279–281 of the Act.

Seizure of bankrupt's property

365.—(1) At any time after a bankruptcy order has been made, the court may, on the application of the official receiver or the trustee of the bankrupt's estate, issue a warrant authorising the person to whom it is directed to seize any property comprised in the bankrupt's estate which is, or any books, papers or records relating to the bankrupt's estate or affairs which are, in the possession or under the control of the bankrupt or any other person who is required to deliver the property, books, papers or records to the official receiver or trustee.

(2) Any person executing a warrant under this section may, for the purpose of seizing any property comprised in the bankrupt's estate or any books, papers or records relating to the bankrupt's estate or affairs, break open any premises where the bankrupt or anything that may be seized under the warrant is or is believed to be and any receptacle of the bankrupt which contains or is believed to contain anything that may be so seized.

(3) If, after a bankruptcy order has been made, the court is satisfied that any property comprised in the bankrupt's estate is, or any books, papers or records relating to the bankrupt's estate or affairs are, concealed in any premises not belonging to him, it may issue a warrant authorising any constable or prescribed officer of the court to search those premises for the property, books, papers or records.

(4) A warrant under subsection (3) shall not be executed except in the prescribed manner and in accordance with its terms.

DEFINITIONS
"affairs": s.385(2).
"bankrupt": s.381(1).
"bankruptcy order": s.381(2).
"estate": ss.283, 385(1).
"prescribed": s.384.
"property": s.436.
"records": s.436.
"the court": ss.373, 385(1).
"the official receiver": s.399(1).
"trustee": s.385(1).

GENERAL NOTE
This section empowers the court to authorise the seizure of property comprised in the bankrupt's estate, and to issue warrants for the purpose of enabling authorised persons to enter premises belonging to the bankrupt or to others, and to search for and seize any relevant property or documents to be found there. The section restates in updated form the provisions formerly contained in s.49 of the Bankruptcy Act 1914 (repealed).
This section corresponds to s.195 of the 1985 Act.

Inquiry into bankrupt's dealings and property

366.—(1) At any time after a bankruptcy order has been made the court may, on the application of the official receiver or the trustee of the bankrupt's estate, summon to appear before it—
 (a) the bankrupt or the bankrupt's spouse or former spouse,
 (b) any person known or believed to have any property comprised in the bankrupt's estate in his possession or to be indebted to the bankrupt,
 (c) any person appearing to the court to be able to give information concerning the bankrupt or the bankrupt's dealings, affairs or property.
The court may require any such person as is mentioned in paragraph (b) or (c) to submit an affidavit to the court containing an account of his dealings with the bankrupt or to produce any documents in his possession or under his control relating to the bankrupt or the bankrupt's dealings, affairs or property.

(2) Without prejudice to section 364, the following applies in a case where—

(*a*) a person without reasonable excuse fails to appear before the court when he is summoned to do so under this section, or

(*b*) there are reasonable grounds for believing that a person has absconded, or is about to abscond, with a view to avoiding his appearance before the court under this section.

(3) The court may, for the purpose of bringing that person and anything in his possession before the court, cause a warrant to be issued to a constable or prescribed officer of the court—

(*a*) for the arrest of that person, and

(*b*) for the seizure of any books, papers, records, money or goods in that person's possession.

(4) The court may authorise a person arrested under such a warrant to be kept in custody, and anything seized under such a warrant to be held, in accordance with the rules, until that person is brought before the court under the warrant or until such other time as the court may order.

DEFINITIONS

"bankrupt": s.381(1).
"bankruptcy order": s.381(2).
"estate": ss.283, 385(1).
"prescribed": s.384.
"property": s.436.
"records": s.436.
"the court": ss.373, 385(1).
"the official receiver": s.399(1).
"the rules": ss.384, 412.
"trustee": s.385(1).

GENERAL NOTE

This section empowers the court to examine the bankrupt and other persons as to his affairs, dealings or property. The law is restated, with suitable modifications and modernisation in drafting, from the provision formerly contained in s.25 of the Bankruptcy Act 1914 (repealed). The provisions of s.369 apply for the purposes of any examination under this section.

This section corresponds to subss. (1) and (2) of s.196 of the 1985 Act.

Court's enforcement powers under s.366

367.—(1) If it appears to the court, on consideration of any evidence obtained under section 366 or this section, that any person has in his possession any property comprised in the bankrupt's estate, the court may, on the application of the official receiver or the trustee of the bankrupt's estate, order that person to deliver the whole or any part of the property to the official receiver or the trustee at such time, in such manner and on such terms as the court thinks fit.

(2) If it appears to the court, on consideration of any evidence obtained under section 366 or this section, that any person is indebted to the bankrupt, the court may, on the application of the official receiver or the trustee of the bankrupt's estate, order that person to pay to the official receiver or trustee, at such time and in such manner as the court may direct, the whole or part of the amount due, whether in full discharge of the debt or otherwise as the court thinks fit.

(3) The court may, if it thinks fit, order that any person who if within the jurisdiction of the court would be liable to be summoned to appear before it under section 366 shall be examined in any part of the United Kingdom where he may be for the time being, or in any place outside the United Kingdom.

(4) Any person who appears or is brought before the court under section 366 or this section may be examined on oath, either orally or by

interrogatories, concerning the bankrupt or the bankrupt's dealings, affairs and property.

"affairs": s.385(2).
"bankrupt": s.381(1).
"debt": ss.382(3), 385(1).
"estate": ss.283, 385(1).
"property": s.436.
"the court": ss.373, 385(1).
"the official receiver": s.399(1).
"trustee": s.385(1).

GENERAL NOTE
This section operates in conjunction with s.366, and empowers the court to make orders, consequential upon the examination of a person under s.366, to require the delivery up of property or the making of any payment to the official receiver or trustee, as appropriate.
This section corresponds to subss. (3)–(6) of s.196 of the 1985 Act.

Provision corresponding to s.366, where interim receiver appointed

368. Sections 366 and 367 apply where an interim receiver has been appointed under section 286 as they apply where a bankruptcy order has been made, as if—
    (*a*) references to the official receiver or the trustee were to the interim receiver, and
    (*b*) references to the bankrupt and to his estate were (respectively) to the debtor and his property.

DEFINITIONS
"bankrupt": s.381(1).
"bankruptcy order": s.381(2).
"debtor": s.385(1).
"estate": ss.283, 385(1).
"property": s.436.
"the official receiver": s.399(1).
"trustee": s.385(1).

GENERAL NOTE
This section, which corresponds to s.196(7) of the 1985 Act, embodies the modifications which are necessarily applicable to the operation of s.366 during any period when an interim receiver of a debtor's property has been appointed under s.286. The adjustments in terminology arise from the fact that no bankruptcy order will at that stage have been made, so that references to "the bankrupt" and to his "estate" are inappropriate, and technically incorrect. By virtue of s.369(7), the provisions of that section do not apply for the purposes of an examination which takes place under ss.366 and 367 during the period when an interim receiver has been appointed.

Order for production of documents by inland revenue

369.—(1) For the purposes of an examination under section 290 (public examination of bankrupt) or proceedings under sections 366 to 368, the court may, on the application of the official receiver or the trustee of the bankrupt's estate, order an inland revenue official to produce to the court—
    (*a*) any return, account or accounts submitted (whether before or after the commencement of the bankruptcy) by the bankrupt to any inland revenue official,
    (*b*) any assessment or determination made (whether before or after the commencement of the bankruptcy) in relation to the bankrupt by any inland revenue official, or
    (*c*) any correspondence (whether before or after the commencement

of the bankruptcy) between the bankrupt and any inland revenue official.

(2) Where the court has made an order under subsection (1) for the purposes of any examination or proceedings, the court may, at any time after the document to which the order relates is produced to it, by order authorise the disclosure of the document, or of any part of its contents, to the official receiver, the trustee of the bankrupt's estate or the bankrupt's creditors.

(3) The court shall not address an order under subsection (1) to an inland revenue official unless it is satisfied that that official is dealing, or has dealt, with the affairs of the bankrupt.

(4) Where any document to which an order under subsection (1) relates is not in the possession of the official to whom the order is addressed, it is the duty of that official to take all reasonable steps to secure possession of it and, if he fails to do so, to report the reasons for his failure to the court.

(5) Where any document to which an order under subsection (1) relates is in the possession of an inland revenue official other than the one to whom the order is addressed, it is the duty of the official in possession of the document, at the request of the official to whom the order is addressed, to deliver it to the official making the request.

(6) In this section "inland revenue official" means any inspector or collector of taxes appointed by the Commissioners of Inland Revenue or any person appointed by the Commissioners to serve in any other capacity.

(7) This section does not apply for the purposes of an examination under sections 366 and 367 which takes place by virtue of section 368 (interim receiver).

Definitions
  "affairs": s.385(2).
  "bankrupt": s.381(1).
  "commencement of the bankruptcy": s.278(*a*).
  "creditor": s.383(1).
  "estate": ss.283, 385(1).
  "Inland Revenue official": subs. (6).
  "the official receiver": s.399(1).
  "the court": ss.373, 385(1).
  "trustee": s.385(1).

General Note
  This section empowers the court to order the Inland Revenue to produce tax records relating to the bankrupt for the purpose of a public examination under s.290 or an examination under ss.366–368.
  This section corresponds to s.197 of the 1985 Act.

Power to appoint special manager

370.—(1) The court may, on an application under this section, appoint any person to be the special manager—

(*a*) of a bankrupt's estate, or

(*b*) of the business of an undischarged bankrupt, or

(*c*) of the property or business of a debtor in whose case the official receiver has been appointed interim receiver under section 286.

(2) An application under this section may be made by the official receiver or the trustee of the bankrupt's estate in any case where it appears to the official receiver or trustee that the nature of the estate, property or business, or the interests of the creditors generally, require the appointment of another person to manage the estate, property or business.

(3) A special manager appointed under this section has such powers as may be entrusted to him by the court.

(4) The power of the court under subsection (3) to entrust powers to a special manager includes power to direct that any provision in this Group of Parts that has effect in relation to the official receiver, interim receiver or trustee shall have the like effect in relation to the special manager for the purposes of the carrying out by the special manager of any of the functions of the official receiver, interim receiver or trustee.

(5) A special manager appointed under this section shall—
(a) give such security as may be prescribed,
(b) prepare and keep such accounts as may be prescribed, and
(c) produce those accounts in accordance with the rules to the Secretary of State or to such other persons as may be prescribed.

DEFINITIONS
"bankrupt": s.381(1).
"business": s.436.
"creditor": s.383(1).
"debtor": s.385(1).
"estate": ss.283, 385(1).
"interim receiver": s.286.
"prescribed": s.384.
"property": s.436.
"the court": ss.373, 385(1).
"the official receiver": s.399(1).
"the rules": ss.384, 412.
"trustee": s.385(1).

GENERAL NOTE
This section enables the court to appoint a special manager of the bankrupt's estate or business, or of the estate or business of a debtor in respect of whom an interim receiver has been appointed under s.286. An appointment under this section may also be made if expedient between the date of the bankruptcy order and the time at which the bankrupt's estate vests in a trustee in bankruptcy. In such cases it is indicated in s.287(1) that the appointment of a special manager has the effect of reducing the role of the official receiver in relation to the estate to that of a receiver only.

This section effects a considerable change in the law compared with the provisions formerly embodied in s.10 of the Bankruptcy Act 1914 (repealed). The official receiver no longer has the authority personally to appoint a special manager, but must apply to the court for such an appointment. On the other hand it is also competent now for the trustee in bankruptcy to apply to the court. There is no longer any requirement that one or more of the creditors should initiate the process whereby the appointment of a special manager is sought: the official receiver or trustee, as the case may be, can act on his own initiative.

The equivalent provision to this section in the winding up of companies is s.177 and the two sections are drafted in parallel.

This section corresponds to s.198 of the 1985 Act.

Re-direction of bankrupt's letters, etc.

371.—(1) Where a bankruptcy order has been made, the court may from time to time, on the application of the official receiver or the trustee of the bankrupt's estate, order the Post Office to re-direct and send or deliver to the official receiver or trustee or otherwise any postal packet (within the meaning of the Post Office Act 1953) which would otherwise be sent or delivered by them to the bankrupt at such place or places as may be specified in the order.

(2) An order under this section has effect for such period, not exceeding 3 months, as may be specified in the order.

DEFINITIONS
"bankrupt": s.381(1).
"bankruptcy order": s.381(2).

"postal packet": Post Office Act 1953, s.87(1).
"the court": ss.373, 385(1).
"the official receiver": s.399(1).
"trustee": s.385(1).

GENERAL NOTE

This section, which restates in substance the provisions formerly contained in s.24 of the Bankruptcy Act 1914 (repealed), permits the court to order the redirection of the bankrupt's post. The definition of "postal packet" contained in s.87(1) of the Post Office Act 1953 makes the term applicable to letters, postcards, parcels and telegrams. This section corresponds to s.199 of the 1985 Act.

PART X

INDIVIDUAL INSOLVENCY: GENERAL PROVISIONS

Supplies of gas, water, electricity, etc.

372.—(1) This section applies where on any day ("the relevant day")—

(a) a bankruptcy order is made against an individual or an interim receiver of an individual's property is appointed, or

(b) a voluntary arrangement proposed by an individual is approved under Part VIII, or

(c) a deed of arrangement is made for the benefit of an individual's creditors;

and in this section "the office-holder" means the official receiver, the trustee in bankruptcy, the interim receiver, the supervisor of the voluntary arrangement or the trustee under the deed of arrangement, as the case may be.

(2) If a request falling within the next subsection is made for the giving after the relevant day of any of the supplies mentioned in subsection (4), the supplier—

(a) may make it a condition of the giving of the supply that the office-holder personally guarantees the payment of any charges in respect of the supply, but

(b) shall not make it a condition of the giving of the supply, or do anything which has the effect of making it a condition of the giving of the supply, that any outstanding charges in respect of a supply given to the individual before the relevant day are paid.

(3) A request falls within this subsection if it is made—

(a) by or with the concurrence of the office-holder, and

(b) for the purposes of any business which is or has been carried on by the individual, by a firm or partnership of which the individual is or was a member, or by an agent or manager for the individual or for such a firm or partnership.

(4) The supplies referred to in subsection (2) are—

(a) a public supply of gas,

(b) a supply of electricity by an Electricity Board,

(c) a supply of water by statutory water undertakers,

(d) a supply of telecommunication services by a public telecommunications operator.

(5) The following applies to expressions used in subsection (4)—

(a) "public supply of gas" means a supply of gas by the British Gas Corporation or a public gas supplier within the meaning of Part I of the Gas Act 1986;

(b) "Electricity Board" means the same as in the Energy Act 1983; and

(c) "telecommunication services" and "public telecommunications operator" mean the same as in the Telecommunications Act 1984, except that the former does not include services consisting in the conveyance of programmes included in cable programme services (within the meaning of the Cable and Broadcasting Act 1984).

DEFINITIONS
"bankruptcy order": s.381(1).
"business": s.436.
"cable programme services": Cable and Broadcasting Act 1984, ss.2(1), 56(1).
"trustee": s.385(1).
"creditor": s.383(1).
"deed of arrangement": Deeds of Arrangement Act 1914, s.1.
"Electricity Board": Energy Act 1983, s.26.
"interim receiver": s.286.
"property": s.436.
"public supply of gas": subs. (5)(a); Gas Act 1986, ss.7(1), 48(1), (2).
"public telecommunications operator": subs. (5)(c); Telecommunications Act 1984, ss.9(3), 106(1).
"supervisor": s.263(2).
"telecommunication services": subs. (5)(c); Telecommunications Act 1984, ss.4(3), 106(1).
"the office holder": subs. (1).
"the official receiver": s.399(1).
"the relevant day": subs. (1).
"voluntary arrangement": s.253(1).

GENERAL NOTE
This section forms a parallel to s.233, which applies in relation to companies. Although the drafting and structure of the two sections differ in places, the substantial content is the same. The effects of the provisions, and the purposes underlying their enactment, are discussed in the General Note to s.233 (*q.v.*).
This section corresponds to s.200 of the 1985 Act.

Jurisdiction in relation to insolvent individuals

373.—(1) The High Court and the county courts have jurisdiction throughout England and Wales for the purposes of the Parts in this Group.
(2) For the purposes of those Parts, a county court has, in addition to its ordinary jurisdiction, all the powers and jurisdiction of the High Court; and the orders of the court may be enforced accordingly in the prescribed manner.
(3) Jurisdiction for the purposes of those Parts is exercised—
(a) by the High Court in relation to the proceedings which, in accordance with the rules, are allocated to the London insolvency district, and
(b) by each county court in relation to the proceedings which are so allocated to the insolvency district of that court.
(4) Subsection (3) is without prejudice to the transfer of proceedings from one court to another in the manner prescribed by the rules; and nothing in that subsection invalidates any proceedings on the grounds that they were initiated or continued in the wrong court.

DEFINITIONS
"insolvency district of a county court": s.374(4)(b).
"London insolvency district": s.374(4)(a).
"prescribed": s.384.
"the court": s.385(1) and this section.
"the rules": ss.384, 412.

GENERAL NOTE
This section makes provision for the exercise of individual insolvency jurisdiction to be performed by the High Court and by those county courts upon which jurisdiction in

insolvency matters is conferred under s.374(1) and (4). The division of jurisdiction as between the High Court and the county court respectively is indicated by subs. (3). The provisions of subs. (2) are of considerable significance in that they confer upon a county court, when exercising insolvency jurisdiction under this Part of the Act, all the powers and jurisdiction of the High Court, and further provide that the orders of the county court in such cases are to be enforceable like orders of the High Court. This restates the former provisions of s.103 of the Bankruptcy Act 1914 (repealed). Other matters pertaining to jurisdiction, and to transfers of proceedings, will be contained in the insolvency rules.

The jurisdictional arrangements for individual insolvency enacted by this section are thus substantially the same as those formerly contained in s.96 of the Bankruptcy Act 1914 (repealed). The arguments in Chap. 20 of the *Cork Report* in favour of the creation of a new and separate system of specialised insolvency courts to exercise jurisdiction over all insolvency matters relating to companies and individuals alike have thus been rejected, despite an attempt to introduce amendments to the 1985 Insolvency Bill which would have provided for an Insolvency Court to be established (see H.C. Standing Committee E, June 18, 1985, cols. 418–423). This is one of the most prominent examples of the non-adoption of one of the principal recommendations of the *Cork Report.*

This section corresponds to s.201 of the 1985 Act.

Insolvency districts

374.—(1) The Lord Chancellor may by order designate the areas which are for the time being to be comprised, for the purposes of the Parts in this Group, in the London insolvency district and the insolvency district of each county court; and an order under this section may—

(*a*) exclude any county court from having jurisdiction for the purposes of those Parts, or

(*b*) confer jurisdiction for those purposes on any county court which has not previously had that jurisdiction.

(2) An order under this section may contain such incidental, supplemental and transitional provisions as may appear to the Lord Chancellor necessary or expedient.

(3) An order under this section shall be made by statutory instrument and, after being made, shall be laid before each House of Parliament.

(4) Subject to any order under this section—

(*a*) the district which, immediately before the appointed day, is the London bankruptcy district becomes, on that day, the London insolvency district;

(*b*) any district which immediately before that day is the bankruptcy district of a county court becomes, on that day, the insolvency district of that court, and

(*c*) any county court which immediately before that day is excluded from having jurisdiction in bankruptcy is excluded, on and after that day, from having jurisdiction for the purposes of the Parts in this Group.

DEFINITIONS

"court": ss.373, 385(1).
"insolvency district of a county court": subs. (4)(*b*).
"London insolvency district": subs. (4)(*a*).

GENERAL NOTE

This section provides for the Lord Chancellor to designate by order the areas that are to be comprised within the London bankruptcy district and within the insolvency district of each county court having individual insolvency jurisdiction. The Lord Chancellor is also empowered to exclude any county court from having jurisdiction under this Part, and to make alterations in the jurisdictional allocations from time to time. Such arrangements, and changes, may be effected by statutory instrument subject only to the "notice" requirement in relation to Parliament.

This section corresponds to s.202 of the 1985 Act.

Subs. (4)

The London bankruptcy district
The district comprising the London bankruptcy district immediately prior to the coming into force of this Act, and which thereby becomes the London insolvency district, is the district defined in s.99 of the Bankruptcy Act 1914 together with Sched. 3 thereto, as amended subsequently by statutory instrument. See Sched. 3 to the Civil Courts Order 1983, S.I. 1983 No. 713, amended by S.I. 1984 No. 1075; S.I. 1984 No. 297; S.I. 1985 No. 511. The list of metropolitan county courts whose county court districts together comprised the London bankruptcy district was latterly as follows: Barnet; Bloomsbury; Bow; Brentford; Brompton (now known as the West London County Court); Clerkenwell; Edmonton; Ilford; Lambeth; Marylebone; Shoreditch (amalgamated with the Whitechapel County Court); Southwark; Wandsworth; Westminster; Willesden; and the Mayor's and City of London Court.

Subs. (4)(b)

District which . . . is the bankruptcy district of a county court
Prior to the enactment of this Act the arrangements for allocation of bankruptcy jurisdiction to county courts were contained in Sched. 3 to the Civil Courts Order 1983, S.I. 1983 No. 713, amended by the subsequently made statutory instruments which are listed above.

Appeals etc. from courts exercising insolvency jurisdiction

375.—(1) Every court having jurisdiction for the purposes of the Parts in this Group may review, rescind or vary any order made by it in the exercise of that jurisdiction.

(2) An appeal from a decision made in the exercise of jurisdiction for the purposes of those Parts by a county court or by a registrar in bankruptcy of the High Court lies to a single judge of the High Court; and an appeal from a decision of that judge on such an appeal lies, with the leave of the judge or of the Court of Appeal, to the Court of Appeal.

(3) A county court is not, in the exercise of its jurisdiction for the purposes of those Parts, to be subject to be restrained by the order of any other court, and no appeal lies from its decision in the exercise of that jurisdiction except as provided by this section.

DEFINITION
"court": ss.373, 385(1).

GENERAL NOTE
This section provides for courts exercising individual insolvency jurisdiction to have powers to review, rescind or vary orders made by them, and further provides for the manner in which appeals are to be made. While the provisions of subs. (1) restate those formerly embodied in s.108(1) of the Bankruptcy Act 1914 (repealed), the provisions in subs. (2) effect a considerable alteration to the arrangement for repeals in bankruptcy matters. All appeals from a first instance decision, whether made by a county court or by a Registrar of the High Court, now lie to a single judge of the High Court and any appeal from the decision of that judge lies with leave in the final instance to the Court of Appeal. There is no longer any provision for a final appeal, subject to the granting of leave, to be made to the House of Lords as was formerly possible under s.108(2)(b) of the Bankruptcy Act 1914 (repealed) in cases where proceedings originated in the High Court.
This section corresponds to s.203 of the 1985 Act.

Time-limits

376. Where by any provision in this Group of Parts or by the rules the time for doing anything is limited, the court may extend the time, either before or after it has expired, on such terms, if any, as it thinks fit.

DEFINITIONS
"the court": ss.373, 385(1).
"the rules": ss.384, 412.

GENERAL NOTE
This confers upon courts which exercise jurisdiction under this Group of Parts of the Act a discretionary power to extend time limits in insolvency proceedings, either prospectively or retrospectively, in particular cases.

This section corresponds to s.204 of the 1985 Act.

Formal defects

377. The acts of a person as the trustee of a bankrupt's estate or as a special manager, and the acts of the creditors' committee established for any bankruptcy, are valid notwithstanding any defect in the appointment, election or qualifications of the trustee or manager or, as the case may be, of any member of the committee.

DEFINITIONS
"creditors' committee": s.301(1).
"estate": ss.283, 385(1).
"special manager": s.198.
"trustee": s.385(1).

GENERAL NOTE
This section validates the acts of persons who have been purportedly appointed to any of the positions mentioned, despite the fact that their appointment, election or qualifications may be defective. There appears to be a *casus omissus* within the section with respect to persons who have been appointed to the position of supervisor of a voluntary arrangement under Part VIII, and whose appointments are defective. The provisions of this section as enacted make no reference to the validation of the acts of such persons, the defective nature of whose appointments may not come to light until some time has elapsed. The present section differs considerably from the former s.147 of the Bankruptcy Act 1914 (repealed), under which the validity of any act done by a person whose appointment was defective or irregular was made dependent upon whether that person had done the act in good faith.

This section corresponds to s.205 of the 1985 Act.

Exemption from stamp duty

378. Stamp duty shall not be charged on—
(*a*) any document, being a deed, conveyance, assignment, surrender, admission or other assurance relating solely to property which is comprised in a bankrupt's estate and which, after the execution of that document, is or remains at law or in equity the property of the bankrupt or of the trustee of that estate,
(*b*) any writ, order, certificate or other instrument relating solely to the property of a bankrupt or to any bankruptcy proceedings.

DEFINITIONS
"bankrupt": s.381(1).
"estate": ss.283, 385(1).
"property": s.436.

GENERAL NOTE
This provides for exemption from stamp duty for certain documents involved in bankruptcy proceedings. The section restates the former provisions of s.148 of the Bankruptcy Act 1914 (repealed).

This section corresponds to s.206 of the 1985 Act.

Annual report

379. As soon as practicable after the end of 1986 and each subsequent calendar year, the Secretary of State shall prepare and lay before each House of Parliament a report about the operation during that year of so much of this Act as is comprised in this Group of Parts, and about proceedings in the course of that year under the Deeds of Arrangement Act 1914.

GENERAL NOTE
    This section, which corresponds to s.210 of the 1985 Act, requires the Secretary of State for Trade to lay an annual report before Parliament on individual insolvency and about proceedings under the Deeds of Arrangement Act 1914.

PART XI

INTERPRETATION FOR SECOND GROUP OF PARTS

Introductory

380. The next five sections have effect for the interpretation of the provisions of this Act which are comprised in this Group of Parts; and where a definition is provided for a particular expression, it applies except so far as the context otherwise requires.

GENERAL NOTE
    This section, which has no counterpart in the 1985 Act, has the function of introducing the group of five sections, namely ss.381–385, which supply the definitions of various terms used within Parts VIII–XI of the Act. Although these definitions are to apply wherever the expression to which they relate is used within the second Group of Parts, this is subject to the proviso that an expression may have a divergent meaning where this is required by the particular context in which the expression is used. See also Part XVIII, which supplies the interpretation of expressions used in a particular sense throughout the Act as a whole.

"Bankrupt" and associated terminology

381.—(1) "Bankrupt" means an individual who has been adjudged bankrupt and, in relation to a bankruptcy order, it means the individual adjudged bankrupt by that order.
    (2) "Bankruptcy order" means an order adjudging an individual bankrupt.
    (3) "Bankruptcy petition" means a petition to the court for a bankruptcy order.

DEFINITIONS
    "bankrupt": subs. (1).
    "bankruptcy order": subs. (2).
    "bankruptcy petition": subs. (3).
    "the court": ss.373, 385(1).

GENERAL NOTE
    This definition section supplies the meaning of the expressions "bankrupt", "bankruptcy order" and "bankruptcy petition" for the purposes of Parts VIII–XI.

"Bankruptcy debt", etc.

382.—(1) "Bankruptcy debt", in relation to a bankrupt, means (subject to the next subsection) any of the following—
    (a) any debt or liability to which he is subject at the commencement of the bankruptcy,
    (b) any debt or liability to which he may become subject after the commencement of the bankruptcy (including after his discharge from bankruptcy) by reason of any obligation incurred before the commencement of the bankruptcy,
    (c) any amount specified in pursuance of section 39(3)(c) of the Powers of Criminal Courts Act 1973 in any criminal bankruptcy order

made against him before the commencement of the bankruptcy, and

(*d*) any interest provable as mentioned in section 322(2) in Chapter IV of Part IX.

(2) In determining for the purposes of any provision in this Group of Parts whether any liability in tort is a bankruptcy debt, the bankrupt is deemed to become subject to that liability by reason of an obligation incurred at the time when the cause of action accrued.

(3) For the purposes of references in this Group of Parts to a debt or liability, it is immaterial whether the debt or liability is present or future, whether it is certain or contingent or whether its amount is fixed or liquidated, or is capable of being ascertained by fixed rules or as a matter of opinion; and references in this Group of Parts to owing a debt are to be read accordingly.

(4) In this Group of Parts, except in so far as the context otherwise requires, "liability" means (subject to subsection (3) above) a liability to pay money or money's worth, including any liability under an enactment, any liability for breach of trust, any liability in contract, tort or bailment and any liability arising out of an obligation to make restitution.

DEFINITIONS
"bankrupt": s.381(1).
"bankruptcy debt": subs. (1).
"commencement of the bankruptcy": s.278(*a*).
"criminal bankruptcy order": s.385(1); Powers of Criminal Courts Act 1973, s.39(1).
"debt": subs. (3), s.385(1).
"discharge": s.281.
"liability": subs. (4).

GENERAL NOTE
This section supplies the meaning of the expression "bankruptcy debt," and of the related expressions "debt" and "liability" for the purposes of Parts VIII–XI. This section corresponds to subss. (1) (part), (2) and (3) of s.211 of the 1985 Act.

"Creditor", "security", etc.

383.—(1) "Creditor"—

(*a*) in relation to a bankrupt, means a person to whom any of the bankruptcy debts is owed (being, in the case of an amount falling within paragraph (*c*) of the definition in section 382(1) of "bankruptcy debt", the person in respect of whom that amount is specified in the criminal bankruptcy order in question), and

(*b*) in relation to an individual to whom a bankruptcy petition relates, means a person who would be a creditor in the bankruptcy if a bankruptcy order were made on that petition.

(2) Subject to the next two subsections and any provision of the rules requiring a creditor to give up his security for the purposes of proving a debt, a debt is secured for the purposes of this Group of Parts to the extent that the person to whom the debt is owed holds any security for the debt (whether a mortgage, charge, lien or other security) over any property of the person by whom the debt is owed.

(3) Where a statement such as is mentioned in section 269(1)(*a*) in Chapter I of Part IX has been made by a secured creditor for the purposes of any bankruptcy petition and a bankruptcy order is subsequently made on that petition, the creditor is deemed for the purposes of the Parts in this Group to have given up the security specified in the statement.

(4) In subsection (2) the reference to a security does not include a lien on books, papers or other records, except to the extent that they consist of documents which give a title to property and are held as such.

Definitions
Definitions
"bankrupt": s.381(1).
"bankruptcy debt": s.382.
"bankruptcy order": s.381(2).
"bankruptcy petition": s.381(3).
"creditor": subs. (1).
"criminal bankruptcy order": s.385(1); Powers of Criminal Courts Act 1973, s.39(1).
"property": s.436.
"records": s.436.
"security": subss. (2), (3), (4).

General Note
  This section supplies the meaning of the expressions "creditor" and "security," and hence of related expressions such as "secured" and "secured creditor." This section corresponds to subss. (1) (part), and (5)–(7) of s.211 of the 1985 Act.

"Prescribed" and "the rules"

384.—(1) Subject to the next subsection, "prescribed" means prescribed by the rules; and "the rules" means rules made under section 412 in Part XV.

(2) References in this Group of Parts to the amount prescribed for the purposes of any of the following provisions—
  section 273;
  section 346(3);
  section 354(1) and (2);
  section 358;
  section 360(1);
  section 361(2); and
  section 364(2)(*d*),
and references in those provisions to the prescribed amount are to be read in accordance with section 418 in Part XV and orders made under that section.

General Note
  This section supplies the meaning of the expressions "prescribed" and "the rules" where used throughout Parts VIII–XI. This section corresponds to parts of ss.209(1) and 211(1) of the 1985 Act.

Miscellaneous definitions

385.—(1) The following definitions have effect—
  "the court", in relation to any matter, means the court to which, in accordance with section 373 in Part X and the rules, proceedings with respect to that matter are allocated or transferred;
  "creditor's petition" means a bankruptcy petition under section 264(1)(*a*);
  "criminal bankruptcy order" means an order under section 39(1) of the Powers of Criminal Courts Act 1973;
  "debt" is to be construed in accordance with section 382(3);
  "the debtor"—
  (*a*) in relation to a proposal for the purposes of Part VIII, means the individual making or intending to make that proposal, and
  (*b*) in relation to a bankruptcy petition, means the individual to whom the petition relates;
  "debtor's petition" means a bankruptcy petition presented by the debtor himself under section 264(1)(*b*);
  "dwelling house" includes any building or part of a building which is occupied as a dwelling and any yard, garden, garage or outhouse belonging to the dwelling house and occupied with it;

"estate", in relation to a bankrupt is to be construed in accordance with section 283 in Chapter II of Part IX;

"family", in relation to a bankrupt, means the persons (if any) who are living with him and are dependent on him;

"secured" and related expressions are to be construed in accordance with section 383; and

"the trustee", in relation to a bankruptcy and the bankrupt, means the trustee of the bankrupt's estate.

(2) References in this Group of Parts to a person's affairs include his business, if any.

GENERAL NOTE

This is the miscellaneous definition section covering a variety of expressions which are used in a particular sense throughout Parts VIII–XI. The section corresponds to subss. (1) (part) and (4) of s.211 of the 1985 Act.

THE THIRD GROUP OF PARTS

MISCELLANEOUS MATTERS BEARING ON BOTH COMPANY AND INDIVIDUAL INSOLVENCY; GENERAL INTERPRETATION; FINAL PROVISIONS

PART XII

PREFERENTIAL DEBTS IN COMPANY AND INDIVIDUAL INSOLVENCY

Categories of preferential debts

386.—(1) A reference in this Act to the preferential debts of a company or an individual is to the debts listed in Schedule 6 to this Act (money owed to the Inland Revenue for income tax deducted at source; VAT, car tax, betting and gaming duties; social security and pension scheme contributions; remuneration etc. of employees); and references to preferential creditors are to be read accordingly.

(2) In that Schedule "the debtor" means the company or the individual concerned.

(3) Schedule 6 is to be read with Schedule 3 to the Social Security Pensions Act 1975 (occupational pension scheme contributions).

DEFINITIONS

"preferential creditors": subs. (1); Sched. 6.
"preferential debts": subs. (1); Sched. 6.
"the debtor": subs. (2); Sched. 6.

GENERAL NOTE

This section completes the process of establishing a single set of provisions regarding the categories of preferential debts applicable to both company and individual insolvency. This process was begun in the 1985 Act, Sched. 4 to which furnished a common set of provisions regarding preferential debts applicable to the two types of insolvency by virtue of the provisions of ss.89 and 166 of that Act. The present section is a single provision whose own terms cause it to be applicable to both types of insolvency, and provide a common point of reference—namely to the provisions of Sched. 6—for all occasions when the expressions "preferential debts" or "preferential creditors" are used anywhere in the Act. Consequently, subs. (2) provides for the expression "the debtor" to bear a flexible meaning where it appears in Sched. 6, so that it can denote a company or an individual, according to the context of any particular case to which the provisions fall to be applied.

"The relevant date"

387.—(1) This section explains references in Schedule 6 to the relevant date (being the date which determines the existence and amount of a preferential debt).

(2) For the purposes of section 4 in Part I (meetings to consider company voluntary arrangement), the relevant date in relation to a company which is not being wound up is—

(*a*) where an administration order is in force in relation to the company, the date of the making of that order, and

(*b*) where no such order has been made, the date of the approval of the voluntary arrangement.

(3) In relation to a company which is being wound up, the following applies—

(*a*) if the winding up is by the court, and the winding-up order was made immediately upon the discharge of an administration order, the relevant date is the date of the making of the administration order;

(*b*) if the case does not fall within paragraph (*a*) and the company—

(i) is being wound up by the court, and

(ii) had not commenced to be wound up voluntarily before the date of the making of the winding-up order,

the relevant date is the date of the appointment (or first appointment) of a provisional liquidator or, if no such appointment has been made, the date of the winding-up order;

(*c*) if the case does not fall within either paragraph (*a*) or (*b*), the relevant date is the date of the passing of the resolution for the winding up of the company.

(4) In relation to a company in receivership (where section 40 or, as the case may be, section 59 applies), the relevant date is—

(*a*) in England and Wales, the date of the appointment of the receiver by debenture-holders, and

(*b*) in Scotland, the date of the appointment of the receiver under section 53(6) or (as the case may be) 54(5).

(5) For the purposes of section 258 in Part VIII (individual voluntary arrangements), the relevant date is, in relation to a debtor who is not an undischarged bankrupt, the date of the interim order made under section 252 with respect to his proposal.

(6) In relation to a bankrupt, the following applies—

(*a*) where at the time the bankruptcy order was made there was an interim receiver appointed under section 286, the relevant date is the date on which the interim receiver was first appointed after the presentation of the bankruptcy petition;

(*b*) otherwise, the relevant date is the date of the making of the bankruptcy order.

DEFINITIONS

"administration order": s.8(2).

"bankrupt": s.281(1).

"bankruptcy order": s.281(2).

"bankruptcy petition": s.281(3).

"commencement of winding up by the court": s.129.

"company voluntary arrangement": s.1(1).

"date of appointment of receiver": s.33 (England and Wales); ss.53(6), 54(5) (Scotland).

"date of approval of voluntary arrangement": s.5(2)(*a*).

"discharged"; "undischarged": ss.278(*b*), 279–281.

"individual voluntary arrangement": s.253(1).

"interim order": s.252(2).

"interim receiver": s.286.

"preferential debt": s.386(1); Sched. 6.

"proposal": s.253(1), (2).
"the relevant date": subs. (1) and remainder of this section.

GENERAL NOTE
The purpose of this section is to make comprehensive provision with regard to the meaning
to be ascribed to the expression "the relevant date" in the various contexts in which it is
used throughout Sched. 6 and in different sections within the main body of the Act. The
provisions collected within this section originate from ss.196(2)–(4) and 475(3), (4) of the
Companies Act, and from ss.23(8), 115(10), Sched. 4, Pt. II para. 1(2), (3) and Sched. 6
paras. 15(4) and 20(3) of the 1985 Act.

PART XIII

INSOLVENCY PRACTITIONERS AND THEIR QUALIFICATION

*Restrictions on unqualified persons acting as liquidator, trustee in
bankruptcy, etc.*

Meaning of "act as insolvency practitioner"

388.—(1) A person acts as an insolvency practitioner in relation to a
company by acting—
  (*a*) as its liquidator, provisional liquidator, administrator or adminis-
      trative receiver, or
  (*b*) as supervisor of a voluntary arrangement approved by it under
      Part I.
(2) A person acts as an insolvency practitioner in relation to an
individual by acting—
  (*a*) as his trustee in bankruptcy or interim receiver of his property or
      as permanent or interim trustee in the sequestration of his estate;
      or
  (*b*) as trustee under a deed which is a deed of arrangement made for
      the benefit of his creditors or, in Scotland, a trust deed for his
      creditors; or
  (*c*) as supervisor of a voluntary arrangement proposed by him and
      approved under Part VIII; or
  (*d*) in the case of a deceased individual to the administration of whose
      estate this section applies by virtue of an order under section 421
      (application of provisions of this Act to insolvent estates of
      deceased persons), as administrator of that estate.
(3) References in this section to an individual include, except in so far
as the context otherwise requires, references to a partnership and to any
debtor within the meaning of the Bankruptcy (Scotland) Act 1985.
(4) In this section—
    "administrative receiver" has the meaning given by section 251 in
        Part VII;
    "company" means a company within the meaning given by section
        735(1) of the Companies Act or a company which may be
        wound up under Part V of this Act (unregistered companies);
        and
    "interim trustee" and "permanent trustee" mean the same as in the
        Bankruptcy (Scotland) Act 1985.
(5) Nothing in this section applies to anything done by the official
receiver.

DEFINITIONS
  "acts as an insolvency practitioner": subss. (1), (2), (3).
  "administrative receiver": subs. (4); s.251.

"administrator": s.8(2).
"company": subs. (4), ss.220, 221; Companies Act 1985, s.735(1).
"individual": subs. (3).
"interim receiver": s.286.
"interim trustee": subs. (4); Bankruptcy (Scotland) Act 1985, s.2.
"partnership": subs. (3).
"permanent trustee": subs. (4); Bankruptcy (Scotland) Act 1985, s.3.
"property": s.436.
"provisional liquidator": s.135.
"supervisor of a voluntary arrangement": ss.7(2) (companies), 263(2) (individuals).
"the official receiver": s.399(1).
"voluntary arrangement": ss.1(1) (companies), 253(1) (individuals).

TRANSITIONAL PROVISION
Sched. 11, para. 21.

GENERAL NOTE
This section defines the various ways in which a person may act as an insolvency practitioner for the purposes of Part XIII. The *Cork Report* made cogent recommendations for the introduction of legal regulations applicable to insolvency practitioners (see Chaps. 15, 16 and 17), partly aimed at ensuring a generally high level of competence and skill on the part of those so acting, but partly also to combat certain abusive practices, particularly in relation to voluntary liquidations, by ensuring that all those who serve in any capacity such as liquidator, trustee in bankruptcy, administrator, or administrative receiver are personally subject to the disciplinary control of a recognised professional organisation. The *White Paper* (Chapter 1) duly endorsed the proposal that exacting professional standards should be made applicable to insolvency practitioners, and the provisions of Pt. XIII, together with Sched. 7 and further rules and regulations to be made pursuant to the powers conferred by s.419, are designed to bring this about.
This section corresponds to subss. (2)–(6) of s.1 of the 1985 Act.

Subs. (1)
This subsection defines the concept of acting as an insolvency practitioner in relation to a company. The four ways in which a person may so act in relation to a company are by acting as its liquidator, administrator, or administrative receiver, or as the supervisor of a voluntary arrangement concluded under Part I.

Para. (a)
Liquidator: under Part IV of the Act, a person other than the official receiver may be appointed as liquidator of a company in the course of a compulsory winding up, while in the case of either of the forms of voluntary winding up (members' or creditors' voluntary winding up) a private liquidator is always appointed. The respective modes of appointment of a private liquidator in the three different types of winding up are specified in ss.135–140, 91–92 and 100 of the Act. The powers, duties and responsibilities of a liquidator are defined in ss.165–170 of the Act. The extensiveness and complexity of the liquidator's powers in themselves make it desirable that the person undertaking to serve in this capacity possesses a degree of professional competence and experience as well as being of unquestioned integrity. In recent years it had become a matter of considerable notoriety that, while the majority of those accustomed to function as liquidators of companies undoubtedly satisfied all three of the foregoing criteria, there were others who did not. Greatest concern centred around those instances where the initiative in nominating and appointing the liquidator rests with members of the company themselves, particularly where these are virtually synonymous with the active members of the board of directors (see *Cork Report*, paras. 772–774). The wording of subs. (1) ensures that in every type of winding up the only person lawfully eligible to serve as liquidator (apart from the Official Receiver himself where this is possible) is one who at the time of acting possesses the requisite qualification, according to s.390, authorising him so to act. An amendment to the Insolvency Bill 1985, tabled before the House of Lords in Committee, which was designed to limit the application of what is now subs. (1) to those cases where the company is insolvent, was withdrawn (*Hansard* H.L. Vol. 459, cols. 565–568). The provision therefore applies to every type of winding up in which a liquidator is appointed, and regardless of whether the company is actually insolvent at the time. The deletion from the terms of the 1985 Bill as originally published of any additional ground of disqualification based upon any personal association between an insolvency practitioner and the company in relation to which he acts means that the delicate and

complicated matter of potential conflict of interest or want of impartiality on the part of the liquidator will be regulated by the ethical code and practical guidelines subscribed to by the professional body to which the liquidator will in most instances belong. For the purposes of criminal liability under s.389, only the grounds of non-qualification specified in s.390 are relevant.

Administrator: The new procedure for making an administration order in respect of a company which is actually or nearly insolvent is created by Part II of the Act (ss.8–27 inclusive). The term "administrator" is defined in s.8(2), which makes it apparent that the administrator is a person appointed under the terms of an administration order made by the court, whereby for the duration of the period for which the order is in force the affairs, business and property of the company are to be managed by the person appointed. Further provisions concerning the powers and duties of an administrator, and the mode of his appointment to and vacation of office, are contained in ss.13–25 inclusive. As envisaged in Chap. 9 of the *Cork Report,* and subsequently affirmed by Chap. 14 of the *White Paper,* the administrator will need to possess special skills and aptitudes in order to be capable of fulfilling his responsibilities, and this office is accordingly included among the list of those which can only be undertaken by a person who is duly qualified to act as an insolvency practitioner in accordance with the provisions of s.390.

Administrative receiver: This new term is given statutory meaning by s.251 and means, in relation to a company registered in England and Wales, either (i) a receiver or manager of the whole (or substantially the whole) of the company's property appointed by or on behalf of the holders of any debentures of the company secured by a charge which, as created, was a floating charge, or by a floating charge and one or more fixed charges; or (ii) a person who would be such a receiver or manager but for the appointment of some other person as a receiver of part of the company's property. In relation to a company registered in Scotland, the use of the established term "receiver" has been retained. However, by virtue of s.251 the expression "administrative receiver," whenever it is used in the Second Group Parts, includes a receiver appointed under s.51 of the Act. Moreover, subs. (4), below, confers upon the expression "administrative receiver" the same meaning as it bears in Part II of the Act, and hence the provisions of Part XIII are equally applicable to a person appointed as a receiver of a company in Scotland as they are to a person appointed as administrative receiver of a company in England and Wales.

It is a part of the policy of the Act to place the law of receivers and managers of companies upon a clear, statutory basis and thereby to define their powers and duties, and to impose an appropriate degree of control and accountability which has hitherto been wanting under the law of England and Wales at least. Clear and comprehensive recommendations to this effect were contained in Chap. 8 of the *Cork Report,* and accepted (with certain reservations) in Chap. 5 of the *White Paper.* The provisions which accomplished this purpose are contained in Chapter I of Part III (ss.28–49) in relation to England and Wales, and by Chapter II of Part III (ss.50–71) in relation to Scotland. All the arguments concerning the attributes of skill, experience and integrity which have been deployed with regard to liquidators and administrators of companies are equally applicable in the case of administrative receivers, and hence all persons acting in this latter capacity henceforth will be required to be qualified insolvency practitioners within the meaning of this Part of the Act.

Para. (b)

Supervisor of a voluntary arrangement: Pt. I of the Act (ss.1–7) contains provisions regulating voluntary arrangements between a company and its creditors. Such arrangements, which may take the form of either a composition or a scheme of arrangement, must be administered by a person who is qualified to act as an insolvency practitioner in relation to the company. The person nominated for the purpose, who may be the liquidator or administrator of the company or some other person, will in due course become the supervisor of the composition or scheme if it is duly approved in accordance with the relevant provisions of that Part of the Act. In accordance with the overall policy of the Act, a person occupying the position of supervisor must be a qualified insolvency practitioner, and hence it is made a criminal offence for an unqualified person to serve in this capacity in relation to a company.

Subs. (2)

This subsection defines the concept of acting as an insolvency practitioner in relation to an individual. In England and Wales a person can so act in any of the following five ways, namely by acting as the individual's trustee in bankruptcy; as interim receiver of his property; as administrator of his estate; as trustee under a deed of arrangement made for the benefit of his creditors; or as supervisor of a voluntary arrangement proposed by the individual and approved under Pt. VIII of the Act. In Scotland, a person can act as an insolvency practitioner in relation to an individual in any of the following three ways, namely by acting as permanent or interim trustee in the sequestration of his estate, or as trustee under a trust deed for his creditors.

Para. (a)

Trustee in bankruptcy: This is the title conferred upon the person in whom, by virtue of s.306, the bankrupt's estate vests and by whom the property thus made available is administered and distributed among the creditors in accordance with the provisions of Chapter IV of Part IX of the Act (ss.305–335). Depending upon the circumstances the power to appoint a person as trustee of a bankrupt's estate is exercisable by a general meeting of the bankrupt's creditors, by the Secretary of State, or by the court: s.292.

Interim receiver: In certain cases, following the presentation of a bankruptcy petition but before the making of any bankruptcy order it may be necessary for the protection of the debtor's property that it be placed in the hands of a person clothed with the powers of a receiver and manager. S.286 duly empowers the court to make the necessary appointment upon cause shown, and to appoint either the official receiver or some other person to be interim receiver. A particularly apt occasion for the appointment of some person other than the Official Receiver to serve in this capacity will arise when, pursuant to s.273(2), the court has had occasion on the hearing of a debtor's petition to appoint a qualified insolvency practitioner to prepare a report based upon an enquiry into the debtor's affairs and to investigate whether the debtor is able and willing to make a proposal for a composition or scheme of arrangement. S.286(2) specifically contemplates the possibility that the person so appointed may at the court's discretion be subsequently appointed to be interim receiver of the debtor's property where the need for such an appointment is established.

Permanent trustee: In Scots law, the sequestration of the estate of a living or deceased debtor is conducted, as required by the Bankruptcy (Scotland) Act 1985, by a permanent trustee elected in accordance with s.24 of that Act. Since there is no office in Scotland equivalent to that of official receiver under the law of England and Wales, the permanent trustee in a Scottish sequestration will inevitably be a private individual. In view of this, Scottish law has traditionally taken care to specify those categories of person who are ineligible for election as permanent trustee, either on general grounds or on grounds referable to the circumstances of the instant case. S.24(2) of the Bankruptcy (Scotland) Act 1985 is the current enactment embodying the grounds of ineligibility, and it is noteworthy that para. (*b*) of that subs. refers to "a person who is not qualified to act as an insolvency practitioner or who, though qualified to act as an insolvency practitioner, is not qualified to act as such in relation to the debtor." The provisions of ss.388(2)(*a*) and 389 of the Insolvency Act therefore complement those of the Scottish legislation by rendering it a criminal offence for a person who is unqualified in the meaning of Part XIII of the Insolvency Act to act as a permanent trustee in a Scottish sequestration.

Interim trustee: S.2 of the Bankruptcy (Scotland) Act 1985 requires that in every sequestration there is to be appointed an interim trustee whose functions, as prescribed in that section, are to safeguard the debtor's estate pending the appointment of a permanent trustee, and to conduct the preliminary stages of the sequestration prior to, and indeed preparatory to, the election of a permanent trustee. The provisions of s.1(1)(*b*) of the same Act require the Accountant of Court (to be known for this purpose as "the Accountant in Bankruptcy") to maintain a list of persons from which interim trustees are to be appointed, and it will become part of the responsibilities of the Accountant in Bankruptcy to ensure that all persons whose names appear on his list are properly qualified in terms of Part XIII of the Insolvency Act 1986, with particular reference to the provisions of s.390 thereof. Nevertheless, the offence of acting as an insolvency practitioner when unqualified to do so is so formulated as to make it evident that a person may commit the offence, under certain circumstances, despite the fact that his name may for the time being be included upon the list maintained by the Accountant in Bankruptcy. If the person in question is in reality unqualified to act as an insolvency practitioner an offence will be committed by virtue of his commencing to act pursuant to his appointment as interim trustee. It is to be noted that s.2(3)(*a*) of the Bankruptcy (Scotland) Act makes provision for a person's name to be removed from the list of potential interim trustees at his own request, and it is thus incumbent upon a person who lacks, or who loses, the requisite qualification to take the necessary steps to procure the removal of his name from the list, or at the very least to decline to accept or to act upon any appointment resulting from the fact that his name still appears on the list.

Para. (b)

Trustee under a deed of arrangment: Contrary to the recommendation contained in Chap. 7 of the *Cork Report* whereby its repeal and replacement were advocated, the majority of the provisions of the Deeds of Arrangement Act 1914 remain in force (see *White Paper*, paras. 22–23). Pt. III of Sched. 10 to the Insolvency Act 1985 effects the repeal only of ss.19(2) and 27, together with parts of s.24 of the Act of 1914. It will therefore continue to be possible for a debtor to utilise the procedure established by the Deeds of Arrangement Act although in practice it is unlikely that many will choose to do so. In such cases, however, it will be necessary for a person to serve as trustee of the Deed of Arrangement in accordance with the requirements of the extant provisions of the Act of 1914. Henceforth it will be incumbent upon any person who is invited to serve as trustee of a Deed of Arrangement to ensure that he fulfils the requirements for being a qualified insolvency practitioner for the purpose in contemplation.

Trustee under a trust deed for creditors: In Scotland the statutory provisions governing voluntary trust deeds for creditors are, by virtue of s.59 of the Bankruptcy (Scotland) Act 1985, contained in Sched. 5 to that Act. The voluntary trust deed for creditors constitutes an alternative to sequestration, and is allowed to operate with minimal formal regulation (see Scottish Law Commission Report on Bankruptcy, Chap. 24). As in the case of deeds of arrangement under the law of England and Wales, the making of a voluntary trust deed usually takes the form of a conveyance by the debtor of his whole property to a trustee for the benefit of the debtor's creditors generally. The same considerations as are stated above in relation to prospective trustees under a deed of arrangement will henceforth attach also to any person who is invited to serve as trustee under a voluntary trust deed, and it will thus be incumbent upon that person to consider whether he fulfils the requirements for being a qualified insolvency practitioner for this purpose.

Para. (c)

Supervisor of a voluntary arrangement: The provisions of Pt. VIII of the Act (ss.252–263) introduce a new procedure for the conclusion of voluntary arrangements between a debtor and his creditors within the overall framework of the Insolvency Act itself. This procedure, which may be utilised either before or after the making of a bankruptcy order against the debtor, is devised in accordance with the strategy disclosed in the *White Paper* (paras. 21–23, 135–139) whereby the increased use of voluntary procedures is to be encouraged. The procedure involves the making of an application to the court for an interim order whose effect is to suspend all other proceedings against the debtor or his property. This moratorium will normally operate for a period of fourteen days, during which time the feasibility of the making of a voluntary arrangement is to be explored and reported upon by a person named in the application (and hence known as "the nominee") who is for the time being qualified to act as an insolvency practitioner in relation to the debtor (ss.253–256). If the nominee's report indicates that further progress is practicable and worthwhile, the proposal may subsequently be submitted to a creditor's meeting summoned for this purpose, and if there approved, the arrangement becomes effective and binding upon all creditors to whom notice of the meeting had been given (ss.257–261). In that event the implementation and supervision of the arrangement are functions which are automatically conferred upon the person who is known as "the supervisor of the voluntary arrangement" (s.263(2)). The supervisor will either be the person originally identified as the nominee in the initial application to the court, or some other person qualified to act as an insolvency practitioner in relation to the debtor, who has been substituted for the nominee in accordance with the provisions of s.256(3) or s.258(3). In every instance therefore the supervisor of a composition or scheme governed by the provisions of Pt. VIII must fulfil the requirements for qualification described in Pt. XIII of the Act, and any person who acts as supervisor of an arrangement when he is unqualified to do so will thereby commit a criminal offence under s.390.

Para. (d)

Administrator of that estate: Where a deceased individual's estate is insolvent, the estate may be administered under the law of bankruptcy in a specially modified form. The modifications in question will be specified in an Order made pursuant to s.421. The term "administrator" means in this context the person by whom that estate is administered in accordance with the modified procedure. The person appointed to be administrator of such an estate therefore assumes the equivalent functions, powers and duties in relation to the estate of the deceased insolvent as are assumed by the trustee in bankruptcy in normal cases where the bankrupt is alive.

Subs. (3)

This subsection extends the application of the provisions of subs. (2) in two ways, first by specifying that any reference to an individual in the earlier subs. shall include a reference to a partnership, and secondly by providing that in Scotland the reference to an individual shall include a reference to any debtor within the meaning of the Bankruptcy (Scotland) Act 1985. S.420 of the Act empowers the Lord Chancellor to make an order specially modifying the statutory regime to be applicable in relation to insolvent partnerships. Since a partnership in England and Wales is an unincorporated association with no separate legal personality of its own, proceedings resulting from insolvency of a partnership necessarily involve all those persons who are partners in the firm. The established approach is that while bankruptcy proceedings may commence and take place in the name of the firm, the making of a bankruptcy order against the firm takes effect in law as an order made against each person who is a partner of the firm at the date of the order (see the former provisions of the Bankruptcy Act 1914, s.119, Bankruptcy Rules 1952, S.I. 1952, No. 2113 (L.14), r.285), so that each partner becomes individually bankrupt. At the point of adjudication therefore the apparent entity of the firm effectively disappears, although special rules must be applied in the administration of the bankruptcy of each partner so as to distinguish between his separate affairs and his partnership affairs. Accordingly, in various situations the firm or partnership may constitute the entity in relation to which insolvency procedures, or a certain stage of them, are taking place and it follows that a person may be called upon to act as an insolvency practitioner in relation to the partnership. By virtue of subs. (3) such a person will need to fulfil all the requirements of Pt. XIII with regard to qualification as an insolvency practitioner when acting in relation to a partnership, just as when acting in relation to any individual.

In relation to Scottish law, s.73(1) of the Bankruptcy (Scotland) Act 1985 indicates that the term "debtor" includes a deceased debtor or, as the context requires, an executor or person entitled to be appointed as executor. Moreover under Scots law the process of sequestration is applicable to a variety of other entities besides living and deceased individuals, since it may take place in relation to trust estates, partnerships, limited partnerships, un-incorporated bodies and bodies corporate other than those which, being incorporated under the Companies Act, are consequently required to be wound up under the provisions of this Act (see Bankruptcy (Scotland) Act 1985, s.6). The extension of meaning thus conferred by subs. (3) upon the word "debtor" as arising within the context of Scots law ensures that in any insolvency proceedings in Scotland relating to an entity for which sequestration is a competent proceeding, the requirements of Pt. XIII with regard to qualification to act as an insolvency practitioner must be fulfilled by any person who acts in any of the capacities referred to in subs. (2)

Subs. (4)

Administrative receiver: This term is discussed in the note to subs. (1) above.

Company: Section 735 of the Companies Act 1985 defines this term as meaning a company formed and registered under that Act, or an existing company, which is further defined as a company formed and registered under the former Companies Acts of 1856–1983 (with the exception of companies registered under former companies legislation in what was then Ireland prior to the creation of the Republic of Ireland).

Interim trustee; Permanent trustee: The meanings of these terms, as defined in the Bankruptcy (Scotland) Act 1985, are discussed in the note to subs. (2) above.

Subs. (5)

This subsection ensures that no action undertaken by the official receiver shall give rise to criminal liability on his part, even though it might transpire that for some reason he did not at the relevant time fulfil the requirements of being a "qualified person" within the meaning of Pt. XIII. Hence, whenever it occurs that the official receiver, in performance of the duties of his office and in particular of those which arise by virtue of the provisions of the Insolvency Act itself, acts as an insolvency practitioner in relation to either a company or an individual within the meaning of this section, he enjoys immunity from criminal liability which he might otherwise incur by virtue of this Part of the Act. In Chap. 7 of their *White Paper,* the Government effectively conceded the validity of the case made out in Chap. 14 of the *Cork Report* in favour of maintaining the active involvement of the Insolvency Service in all aspects of corporate and individual insolvency. The statutory provisions pertaining to the appointment, status and functions of official receivers are contained in ss.399–401, and will be further augmented by rules to be made subsequently in accordance with the provisions of ss.411, 412 and 413.

Acting without qualification an offence

389.—(1) A person who acts as an insolvency practitioner in relation to a company or an individual at a time when he is not qualified to do so is liable to imprisonment or a fine, or to both.

(2) This section does not apply to the official receiver.

DEFINITIONS
  "acts as an insolvency practitioner": s.388.
  "fine": s.430, Sched. 10.
  "imprisonment": s.430, Sched. 10.
  "qualified to act as an insolvency practitioner": s.390.
  "the official receiver": s.399(1).

Transitional Provision
  Sched. 11, para. 21.

GENERAL NOTE
  This section introduces a new criminal offence into the law, whereby a person may be criminally liable if he acts as an insolvency practitioner when he is not qualified to do so. The offence is one of strict liability, and it will afford no defence to any person charged therewith that he either was without all knowledge of his lack of qualification, or reasonably believed himself to be qualified to act. The purpose underlying Pt. XIII of the Act (ss.388–397 inclusive) is to bring about the proper regulation of all those aspects of insolvency proceedings whose administration is capable of being conducted wholly or partly by someone other than the official receiver. The various capacities in which a person may act as an insolvency practitioner for the purposes of Pt. XIII of the Act are specified in subss. (1), (2) and (3) of s.388.
  This section corresponds to s.1(1) of the 1985 Act.

Subs. (1)
  Acts as an insolvency practitioner . . . when he is not qualified: The ingredients of this new criminal offence are indicated, and the possible penalties are prescribed. The offence is committed by any person who acts as an insolvency practitioner (as defined in subss. (1), (2) and (3) of s.388) at a time when he is not qualified to do so. The offence was converted into one of strict liability by means of a government amendment made in Committee of the House of Commons, which removed from the 1985 Insolvency Bill all reference to the state of knowledge of the accused person at the time of committing the offence. The requirements which are to be met in order for an individual to be qualified to act as an insolvency practitioner are laid down in s.390, and the procedure relating to the issue and revocation of certificates of authorisation is specified in and controlled by ss.391–398 inclusive.
  Imprisonment or a fine: See s.430 and Sched. 10 with regard to the levels of punishment which may be imposed for offences committed under this section.

The requisite qualification, and the means of obtaining it

Persons not qualified to act as insolvency practitioners

390.—(1) A person who is not an individual is not qualified to act as an insolvency practitioner.

(2) A person is not qualified to act as an insolvency practitioner at any time unless at that time—

  (*a*) he is authorised so to act by virtue of membership of a professional body recognised under section 391 below, being permitted so to act by or under the rules of that body, or

  (*b*) he holds an authorisation granted by a competent authority under section 393.

(3) A person is not qualified to act as an insolvency practitioner in relation to another person at any time unless—

  (*a*) there is in force at that time security or, in Scotland, caution for the proper performance of his functions, and

(b) that security or caution meets the prescribed requirements with respect to his so acting in relation to that other person.

(4) A person is not qualified to act as an insolvency practitioner at any time if at that time—

(a) he has been adjudged bankrupt or sequestration of his estate has been awarded and (in either case) he has not been discharged,

(b) he is subject to a disqualification order made under the Company Directors Disqualification Act 1986, or

(c) he is a patient within the meaning of Part VII of the Mental Health Act 1983 or section 125(1) of the Mental Health (Scotland) Act 1984.

DEFINITIONS

"a competent authority": s.392(2).

"bankrupt": s.381(1).

"discharged": ss.279–281.

"patient": Mental Health Act 1983, ss.94, 112; Mental Health (Scotland) Act 1984, s.125(1).

"to act as an insolvency practitioner": s.388.

TRANSITIONAL PROVISION

Sched. 11, para. 21.

GENERAL NOTE

This section establishes the meaning of the expression "qualified insolvency practitioner" for the purposes of the Act. It does so by prescribing a series of requirements which must be met in relation to a person in order that he or she may lawfully act as an insolvency practitioner in relation to a company or an individual. The section is drafted in negative terms throughout; that is to say the various propositions of which it is composed are so formulated as to specify in what circumstances, or upon what ground, a person is *not* qualified to act as an insolvency practitioner. Converting these propositions into positive terms, it transpires that in order to be a qualified insolvency practitioner a person (i) must be an individual; (ii) must be currently authorised to act as an insolvency practitioner by virtue of the provisions of either para. (a) or (b) of subs. (2); and (iii) must have furnished the requisite security or caution for the proper performance of his functions (subs. (3)). Furthermore, paras. (a), (b) and (c) of subs. (4) specify three separate grounds, each of which in itself is sufficient to disqualify a person from acting as an insolvency practitioner during any period for which he or she is subject to the disqualifying ground in question. As mentioned above in the notes to s.388(1) the original provisions of the Bill were modified during the course of its progress through Parliament so as to remove any grounds of disqualification of an *ad hoc* character based upon personal links between the insolvency practitioner and the party in relation to which he acts. Such matters, which raise intricate problems of actual or potential conflict of interest or want of impartiality, have been left to be regulated by the ethical and disciplinary codes established by the professional bodies to which insolvency practitioners are expected to belong, and should be covered in practical guidelines issued by those bodies to their members.

This section corresponds to ss.2 and 3(1) of the 1985 Act.

Subs. (1)

The effect of this provision is to allow only natural persons (*i.e.* individuals) to act as insolvency practitioners within the meaning of the Act. Accordingly no corporate or quasi-corporate entity may act as an insolvency practitioner within the meaning of s.388, irrespective of whether the entity in question enjoys fully or partially the attributes of legal personality which enable it to undertake other kinds of activity. On the other hand, provisions elsewhere in the Act indicate that it is possible for more than one person to act jointly as insolvency practitioners in the same case (see ss.13(3), 139(4)(a), 231(1)). Such an arrangement is clearly not precluded by the terms of s.390(1), which merely impose the requirement that each of the persons who are the subject of such a joint appointment must be an individual, and must be fully qualified in his own right to act in the instant case.

Subs. (2)

This subsection establishes the main basis of eligibility to act as an insolvency practitioner. It is made a *sine qua non* that a person must be duly authorised to act in this capacity. Such authorisation may be gained either as a consequence of membership of a recognised professional body, whose rules permit the individual in question to act as an insolvency practitioner (s.391), or as a consequence of the grant of such authorisation in response to an application submitted to the relevant authority created for this purpose (ss.392–398 inclusive).

Subs. (3)

This lays down the second main condition of eligibility to act as an insolvency practitioner. The individual in question must maintain in force at all relevant times such security (or, in Scotland, caution) for the proper performance of his functions as may be prescribed. Moreover, the security must satisfy the prescribed requirements with regard to the actual person in relation to whom the insolvency practitioner acts. The determination of the appropriate nature and extent of the security or bonding to be furnished will be administered by the Department of Trade in accordance with already established practice. An important new feature is that the requirement of furnishing security will be applicable to all cases where a person is to act as an insolvency practitioner and not merely, as formerly, to those cases where a receiver or liquidator is appointed by the court, or where a trustee in bankruptcy is appointed. This standardised requirement of compulsory bonding is in accordance with the recommendations of the *Cork Report* (paras. 763–767). In Chap. 9 of the *White Paper* it is indicated that intending insolvency practitioners will be able to provide either special or general security, the latter form being especially suitable in cases where the individual wishes to be at liberty to act in numerous cases, often at short notice (see para. 44).

Subs. (4)

The three paras. of this subsection establish three alternative grounds, any of which will furnish the basis of disqualification from acting as an insolvency practitioner during any period for which it is applicable to the individual in question. The status of "undischarged bankrupt" (para. (*a*)) attaches to a person with effect from the day on which a bankruptcy order is made against him (s.278(*a*)) and continues until such time as his discharge from bankruptcy becomes effective by virtue of the provisions of either s.279 or 280, or until the bankruptcy order is annulled pursuant to s.282. In Scotland, the sequestration of a debtor's estate is effective from the date of the making of the order of sequestration (see Bankruptcy (Scotland) Act 1985, ss.12, 31).

An order disqualifying a person from company management may be made under the Company Directors Disqualification Act 1986. The maximum and minimum duration of such orders, and the date of their commencement in force, varies depending upon the circumstances in which they are made and upon the statutory provision upon which they are based. However, the maximum periods which may be specified in the order of the court which makes it are fixed by ss.2(3), 3(5), 4(3), 5(5), 6(4), 8(4) or 10(2) of the Disqualification Act, and are five years in the case of an order made under s. 3 or s.5 of that Act, or made by a court of summary jurisdiction, and 15 years in any other case. The only statutory provision which imposes a minimum period which may be specified as the period of disqualification is s.6(4) of the Disqualification Act, which applies exclusively to orders made under that section and imposes a minimum period of disqualification of two years, and a maximum of 15 years.

A person who has been judicially assessed to be incapable, by reason of mental disorder, of managing and administering his affairs is classified as a "patient" for the purposes of Pt. VII of the Mental Health Act 1983. While such a person remains subject to the jurisdiction of the Court of Protection, he will incur the disqualification from acting as an insolvency practitioner established by para. (*c*). A similar definition of "patient" is employed in the Mental Health (Scotland) Act 1984 (s.125(1)), and an identical disqualification, from the aspect of acting as an insolvency practitioner, arises out of para. (*c*) with respect to any person who is a patient within the meaning of either the English or the Scottish Mental Health legislation.

Recognised professional bodies

391.—(1) The Secretary of State may by order declare a body which appears to him to fall within subsection (2) below to be a recognised professional body for the purposes of this section.

(2) A body may be recognised if it regulates the practice of a profession and maintains and enforces rules for securing that such of its members as are permitted by or under the rules to act as insolvency practitioners—

(*a*) are fit and proper persons so to act, and

(*b*) meet acceptable requirements as to education and practical training and experience.

(3) References to members of a recognised professional body are to persons who, whether members of that body or not, are subject to its rules in the practice of the profession in question.

The reference in section 390(2) above to membership of a professional body recognised under this section is to be read accordingly.

(4) An order made under subsection (1) in relation to a professional body may be revoked by a further order if it appears to the Secretary of State that the body no longer falls within subsection (2).

(5) An order of the Secretary of State under this section has effect from such date as is specified in the order; and any such order revoking a previous order may make provision whereby members of the body in question continue to be treated as authorised to act as insolvency practitioners for a specified period after the revocation takes effect.

DEFINITIONS

"member of recognised professional body": subs. (3).

"recognised professional body": subss. (1), (2).

"to act as an insolvency practitioner": s.388(1), (2), (3).

GENERAL NOTE

This section provides the basis upon which most persons will acquire an authorisation to act as an insolvency practitioner, as required by s.390(2), whereby it is provided that a member of a recognised professional body is authorised to act as an insolvency practitioner if he is permitted so to act by the rules of that body. The function of determining who, in the main, are to be authorised to act as insolvency practitioners has been delegated to a number of accounting and legal bodies whose precise identity will be revealed when the Secretary of State exercises the power conferred by subs. (1) to make one or more orders declaring which are to be the recognised professional bodies for the purposes of this section. The provision as enacted represents a radical recasting of the provisions of the 1985 Insolvency Bill as originally published, whereby entitlement to practice as an insolvency practitioner would have been in all cases based upon the possession of a certificate obtainable only by individual application to the Secretary of State. For those persons who are not members of recognised bodies, a modified form of the latter mode of application still furnishes the means by which the requisite authorisation to practice may be sought (see ss.392–398 inclusive). The enacted provisions represent an abandonment of one of the principal recommendations of the *Cork Report* (see Chaps. 15, 16 and 17) that all insolvency practitioners should not only be required to be members of a recognised professional body but should also be required to hold a practising certificate issued by the Secretary of State on an individual basis. It may be questioned whether the sanction of withdrawal of recognition from a professional body will prove to be as potent an incentive to the maintenance of high standards in practice, as would have been the case under the original terms of the Bill whereby the Secretary of State would have been empowered directly to withhold or revoke the licence of any person whose conduct showed him or her to be unfit to act as an insolvency practitioner.

This section corresponds to subss. (2)–(5) of s.3 of the 1985 Act.

Subs. (1)

This provision has the effect of enabling the Secretary of State in effect to delegate to those professional bodies recognised for this purpose, by means of the procedure laid down in subss. (2)–(5) inclusive, the function of determining which of their members shall be authorised to act as insolvency practitioners. It will be ultimately left for each of the bodies in question to determine what rules and procedures to adopt for this purpose, but the provisions of subss. (2) and (4) clearly indicate that these matters will be appraised by the Secretary of State in the course of deciding whether to recognise any given professional body for the purposes of this section. Moreover, efforts will be made to try to achieve the maximum amount of equivalence of treatment between the individual bodies with regard to the standards to be applied, and with regard to the qualifications, education, training and experience to be required of those acting as insolvency practitioners (H.C. Vol. 83, cols. 527–528).

Subs. (2)

This prescribes the criteria which must be satisfied in order for the discretionary power contained in subs. (1) to become exerciseable. While the actual application of their own rules is quite naturally left to the professional bodies themselves, the Secretary of State must first be satisfied that the rules in question are adequate to ensure that those who thereby gain authorisation to practice as insolvency practitioners are both "fit and proper persons so to act" and also "meet acceptable requirements as to education, practical training and experience". While the latter requirement may be capable of quite exact and objective definition, the former one will inevitably entail a degree of subjectivity of judgment on the part of those ultimately responsible for assessing whether a person is "fit and proper". In neither case however does the subsection make provision for these matters to be regulated by means of a uniform set of rules ministerially prescribed.

Subs. (3)

The second part of this subsection is designed to ensure that the provisions of s.390(2) are applicable to all persons who are subject to the rules of a particular body in the practice of their profession, whether or not those persons are actually members of that body.

Subs. (5)

This provision controls the timing and duration of the effectiveness of any recognition conferred upon a professional body under subs. (1). It also enables transitional provisions to be included in any order revoking such recognition, thereby ensuring that the members of any professional body whose recognition is revoked may, if appropriate, be authorised to complete any items of regulated insolvency business upon which they are already engaged at the date on which their professional body ceases to be recognised for the purposes of s.390(2)(*a*).

Authorisation by competent authority

392.—(1) Application may be made to a competent authority for authorisation to act as an insolvency practitioner.

(2) The competent authorities for this purpose are—

(*a*) in relation to a case of any description specified in directions given by the Secretary of State, the body or person so specified in relation to cases of that description, and

(*b*) in relation to a case not falling within paragraph (*a*), the Secretary of State.

(3) The application—

(*a*) shall be made in such manner as the competent authority may direct,

(*b*) shall contain or be accompanied by such information as that authority may reasonably require for the purpose of determining the application, and

(*c*) shall be accompanied by the prescribed fee;

and the authority may direct that notice of the making of the application shall be published in such manner as may be specified in the direction.

(4) At any time after receiving the application and before determining it the authority may require the applicant to furnish additional information.

(5) Directions and requirements given or imposed under subsection (3) or (4) may differ as between different applications.

(6) Any information to be furnished to the competent authority under this section shall, if it so requires, be in such form or verified in such manner as it may specify.

(7) An application may be withdrawn before it is granted or refused.

(8) Any sums received under this section by a competent authority other than the Secretary of State may be retained by the authority; and any sums so received by the Secretary of State shall be paid into the Consolidated Fund.

DEFINITIONS
  "prescribed": s.384.
  "the competent authority": subs. (2).
  "to act as an insolvency practitioner": s.388(1), (2), (3).

GENERAL NOTE
  This section, which operates in conjunction with ss.393–398 inclusive, is applicable in those cases where a person who wishes to obtain authorisation to act as an insolvency practitioner is not a member of any professional body which has been recognised by the Secretary of State for the purposes of s.390(2)(*a*). Such persons may seek authorisation to practice as insolvency practitioners by making an application under this section to the body or person to be specified in directions given by the Secretary of State and referred to hereafter as "the competent body". Similar applications may also be made by any persons who, despite being members of a recognised professional body, have for some reason failed to obtain, or have been deprived of, authorisation to practise conferred by the body in question. Application under s.392 could thus constitute a species of appeal from a decision of a professional body acting under s.390(2), but it is clear that both the competent body and the Insolvency Practitioners Tribunal will take into account the reasons why the applicant has been excluded from practice by the decision of his own professional body. Moreover, it is declared ministerial policy to achieve as close an equivalence of treatment as possible between the professional bodies on the one hand and the way authorisation is carried out by the Department of Trade on the other (H.C. Vol. 83, cols. 527, 528).
  This section corresponds to ss.4 and 11 (part) of the 1985 Act.

Subss. (1), (3)
  These control the manner in which applications for authorisation under s.393 are to be made, and includes powers enabling the competent authority to issue directions as to the form and contents of the application. The fees to be charged to applicants will be separately prescribed by regulations made by the Secretary of State. The nature and amount of the information which an applicant may lawfully be required to supply is limited only by the qualification, in para. (*b*) of subs. (3), that it must be such as the authority may reasonably require for the purpose in hand. In practice this is likely to prove to be a very broad power of inquiry, especially in cases where it transpires that the applicant might be expected to have obtained authorisation under s.390(2)(*a*) by virtue of his past or present membership of a recognised professional body.
  The further power enabling the authority to arrange for the publication of notice of the making of any application under s.392 provides additional and important possibilities for information to be supplied by third parties.

Subss. (2)–(8)
  The provisions are concerned with ordinary matters of detail associated with subs. (1) and are self explanatory.

Grant, refusal and withdrawal of authorisation

393.—(1) The competent authority may, on an application duly made in accordance with section 392 and after being furnished with all such information as it may require under that section, grant or refuse the application.
  (2) The authority shall grant the application if it appears to it from the information furnished by the applicant and having regard to such other information, if any, as it may have—
  (*a*) that the applicant is a fit and proper person to act as an insolvency practitioner, and
  (*b*) that the applicant meets the prescribed requirements with respect to education and practical training and experience.
  (3) An authorisation granted under this section, if not previously withdrawn, continues in force for such period not exceeding the prescribed maximum as may be specified in the authorisation.
  (4) An authorisation so granted may be withdrawn by the competent authority if it appears to it—

(*a*) that the holder of the authorisation is no longer a fit and proper person to act as an insolvency practitioner, or

(*b*) without prejudice to paragraph (a), that the holder—

    (i) has failed to comply with any provision of this Part or of any regulations made under this Part or Part XV, or

    (ii) in purported compliance with any such provision, has furnished the competent authority with false, inaccurate or misleading information.

(5) An authorisation granted under this section may be withdrawn by the competent authority at the request or with the consent of the holder of the authorisation.

DEFINITIONS

    "prescribed": s.384.
    "the competent authority": s.392(2).
    "to act as an insolvency practitioner": s.388(1), (2), (3).

GENERAL NOTE

This section makes provision for the granting of authorisation to act as insolvency practitioners to those applicants who are unable to gain an authorisation by virtue of s.390(2)(*a*). The power to grant such authorisation is expressed to be conferred upon "the competent authority", which will be a body of person specified in directions given by the Secretary of State. In the absence of such directions, the Secretary of State himself constitutes "the relevant authority" for this purpose (s.392(2)(*b*)). The section also prescribes the criteria to be applied in deciding whether to grant or refuse an authorisation. These are nearly identical to those required by s.391(2) to be applied by professional bodies in granting authorisations under that section, save that in the case of authorisations sought under s.393 the requirements with respect to education and practical training and experience will be prescribed by regulations.

This section corresponds to s.5 of the 1985 Act.

Subs. (1)

This expresses the power to grant or refuse authorisation in response to an application made under s.392.

Subs. (2)

This subsection provides that if the criteria specified in paras. (*a*) and (*b*) are satisfied, the relevant authority must grant the application. However, as is also true with regard to applications falling under s.391(2), the requirement in para. (*a*) that the applicant must be considered to be a fit and proper person to act as an insolvency practitioner involves the exercise of a subjective judgment on the part of the authority which is deciding the case. On the other hand it is a purely objective question whether the applicant also meets the prescribed requirements referred to in para. (*b*). The subsection also expressly sanctions the consideration of other information besides that supplied by the applicant personally. Thus, for example, the authority may have regard to any information supplied by third parties who receive notice of the application as a result of directions for publication made under s.392(3).

Subs. (3)

This provision indicates that a maximum duration for each grant of authorisation will be prescribed in regulations. It was originally proposed that all insolvency practitioners would be required to apply annually for the renewal of their authorisation to practise, but the administrative burden which would result from such a short-term validity of authorisation has clearly militated in favour of a more extended period, yet to be specified. However, the authority is empowered to specify a lesser period than the prescribed maximum, and it is furthermore possible for an authorisation to be withdrawn pursuant to subs. (4) or (5).

Subs. (4)

This important provision empowers the relevant authority to withdraw an authorisation which it has previously granted, if either of the grounds specified in para. (*a*) or para. (*b*) is found to be met. In view of the declared ministerial intention to procure a co-ordination of the standards of treatment in cases falling under ss.391 and 395 respectively, it may be anticipated that, in order to gain the necessary recognition for the purposes of s.391, professional bodies will need to show that their own disciplinary procedures include provisions comparable to those in s.393(4).

Notices

394.—(1) Where a competent authority grants an authorisation under section 393, it shall give written notice of that fact to the applicant, specifying the date on which the authorisation takes effect.

(2) Where the authority proposes to refuse an application, or to withdraw an authorisation under section 393(4), it shall give the applicant or holder of the authorisation written notice of its intention to do so, setting out particulars of the grounds on which it proposes to act.

(3) In the case of a proposed withdrawal the notice shall state the date on which it is proposed that the withdrawal should take effect.

(4) A notice under subsection (2) shall give particulars of the rights exercisable under the next two sections by a person on whom the notice is served.

DEFINITION
"the competent authority": s.392(2).

GENERAL NOTE
This section ensures fulfilment of the essential requirements, including those of natural justice, that a person be informed in writing of decisions affecting his or her legal rights and interests. In cases where the relevant authority is proposing to refuse or to withdraw an authorisation it is especially important that the person affected should be given adequate notice of what is impending, and of the grounds upon which the authority is proposing to act, in order that the rights of appeal under ss.395 and 396 may be exercised in a timely and effective manner.

This section corresponds to s.6 of the 1985 Act.

Subs. (1)
This provision applies to cases where an authorisation is to be granted, and is virtually self explanatory. The requirement that written notice must be given to the applicant, including a specification of the date on which the authorisation takes effect, is important especially in view of the criminal consequences ensuing from any infraction of the provisions of s.389. Since that section creates an offence of strict liability, it would be particularly unfortunate if a person to whom an authorisation had actually been granted were to incur criminal liability (with the possible result that authorisation would on that account be subsequently withdrawn), merely by virtue of the fact that he undertook some action as an insolvency practitioner before the date on which the authorisation came into effect, thus infringing s.389 in conjunction with s.390(2).

Subs. (2)
The important aspect of this provision is that in addition to the requirement that an applicant or holder must be informed in writing of any proposed refusal or withdrawal of authorisation, it is made obligatory for the relevant authority to state in writing the grounds on which the decision would be taken. By virtue of subs. (4) the notice must also inform the person to whom it is addressed of the rights exerciseable under ss.395 and 396.

Subs. (3)
This provision is essentially complementary to that contained in subs. (1), being designed to ensure that in cases where an authorisation is withdrawn the person who is thereby to be deprived of his qualification to act as an insolvency practitioner is given written notification of the date upon which the withdrawal is to take effect. This is particularly important in view of the criminal consequences which will ensue if the person in question thereafter performs any of the acts mentioned in s.388(1), (2) and (3).

Right to make representations

395.—(1) A person on whom a notice is served under section 394(2) may within 14 days after the date of service make written representations to the competent authority.

(2) The competent authority shall have regard to any representations so made in determining whether to refuse the application or withdraw the authorisation, as the case may be.

DEFINITION
"the competent authority": s.392(2).

GENERAL NOTE
    This provision creates the first mode of recourse which is available to a person on whom a notice of a proposed refusal or withdrawal of authorisation is served pursuant to s.394(2). In the first instance the person affected has the right to make written representations to the authority within 14 days after the date of service of the notice, and the authority is required to have regard to any such representations in reaching its final decision.
    This section corresponds to s.7 of the 1985 Act.

Reference to Tribunal

396.—(1) The Insolvency Practitioners Tribunal ("the Tribunal") continues in being; and the provisions of Schedule 7 apply to it.
    (2) Where a person is served with a notice under section 394(2), he may—
    (*a*) at any time within 28 days after the date of service of the notice, or
    (*b*) at any time after the making by him of representations under section 395 and before the end of the period of 28 days after the date of the service on him of a notice by the competent authority that the authority does not propose to alter its decision in consequence of the representations,
give written notice to the authority requiring the case to be referred to the Tribunal.
    (3) Where a requirement is made under subsection (2), then, unless the competent authority—
    (*a*) has decided or decides to grant the application or, as the case may be, not to withdraw the authorisation, and
    (*b*) within 7 days after the date of the making of the requirement, gives written notice of that decision to the person by whom the requirement was made,
it shall refer the case to the Tribunal.

DEFINITIONS
    "the competent authority": s.392(2).
    "the Tribunal": subs. (1), Sched. 7.

GENERAL NOTE
    This provision in conjunction with s.397 lays down the main procedure for appeal in cases where the relevant authority proposes not to grant, or proposes to withdraw, an authorisation to act as an insolvency practitioner. Following the service on him of the notice required by s.394(2), the person concerned may in the first instance elect to make representations to the competent authority under s.395. Alternatively (or subsequently, if any representations made under s.395 are ineffectual) the person on whom service of notice has originally taken place under s.394(2) may within 28 days thereof give written notice to the authority in question, invoking his right to have the matter determined by the Insolvency Practitioners Tribunal, which is maintained in existence by subs. (1) of this section together with the provisions of Sched. 7. Thereupon, unless before the expiry of the same 28 day period the authority relents from its former proposal and duly notifies the person concerned to that effect, a reference to the Tribunal becomes mandatory. The latter body is required by s.397 to formulate a reasoned opinion which essentially determines the way in which the case will be finally decided by the relevant authority, with whom the final duty of decision nevertheless reposes. Appeal from the Tribunal's decision lies, either directly or by way of case stated, to the High Court or the Court of Session, pursuant to s.13 of the Tribunals and Inquiries Act 1971, as amended by Sched. 14 to this Act and by para. 5 of Sched. 1 to the 1985 Act.
    This section corresponds to ss.8(1), (2) and (6) and 11 (part) of the 1985 Act.

Action of Tribunal on reference

397.—(1) On a reference under section 396 the Tribunal shall—

(*a*) investigate the case, and

(*b*) make a report to the competent authority stating what would in their opinion be the appropriate decision in the matter and the reasons for that opinion,

and it is the duty of the competent authority to decide the matter accordingly.

(2) The Tribunal shall send a copy of the report to the applicant or, as the case may be, the holder of the authorisation; and the competent authority shall serve him with a written notice of the decision made by it in accordance with the report.

(3) The competent authority may, if he thinks fit, publish the report of the Tribunal.

DEFINITIONS
"the competent authority": s.392(2).
"the Tribunal": s.396(1).

GENERAL NOTE
This section prescribes the procedure to be followed by the Insolvency Practitioners Tribunal when a case is referred to it under s.396.
This section corresponds to subss. (3)–(5) of s.8 of the 1985 Act.

Subs. (1)
This specifies the twofold duties of the Insolvency Practitioners Tribunal in every case referred to it under s.396(3). In its investigation the Tribunal must comply with the requirements of Sched. 7 to the Act, notably those of para. 4 thereof, which make it obligatory that a reasonable opportunity be afforded for representations to be made by or on behalf of the person whose case is the subject of the investigation. In other respects the Tribunal is left with considerable latitude as to the approach to be adopted in conducting its investigation of the case, as required by para. (a) of this subsection, but is required in its subsequent report to the competent authority to state not only its opinion as to the appropriate decision in the matter but also the reasons for that opinion. The purport of that opinion is effectively determinative of the matter, since it is stated to be the duty of the competent authority to "decide the matter accordingly".

Subs. (2)
This provision gives rise to a requirement that the person whose case has been referred to the Insolvency Practitioners Tribunal must receive both a copy of the Tribunal's report and, in due course, a written notice from the authority of its decision made in accordance with that report. Although no further right of appeal against this final decision is embodied in the Act, the information thus required to be furnished to the person concerned should serve to indicate whether any possible grounds exist for seeking to challenge the Tribunal's opinion, and the decision based thereon, by way of an application for judicial review.

Subs. (3)
The power to bring about publication of the Tribunal's report in any given case is a discretionary one, vested in the competent authority.

Refusal or withdrawal without reference to Tribunal

398. Where in the case of any proposed refusal or withdrawal of an authorisation either—

(*a*) the period mentioned in section 396(2)(*a*) has expired without the making of any requirement under that subsection or of any representations under section 395, or

(*b*) the competent authority has given a notice such as is mentioned in section 396(2)(*b*) and the period so mentioned has expired without the making of any such requirement, the competent authority may give written notice of the refusal or withdrawal to the person concerned in accordance with the proposal in the notice given under section 394(2).

DEFINITION
"the competent authority": s.392(2).

GENERAL NOTE

This section completes the sequence of procedures consequential upon the formation by the competent authority, acting under s.393(1) or (4), of a proposal to refuse or to withdraw an authorisation to act as an insolvency practitioner. If, following the service of notice of that proposal under s.394(2), the person concerned does not within the 28 days allowed avail himself of the right to require that his case be referred to the Insolvency Practitioners Tribunal, the competent authority is empowered to render its own decision final by serving written notice upon him of the refusal or withdrawal of his authorisation. This provision does not however oblige the authority to decide the matter in the manner initially indicated by the terms of the earlier notice.

This section corresponds to s.9 of the 1985 Act.

PART XIV

PUBLIC ADMINISTRATION (ENGLAND AND WALES)

Official Receivers

Appointment, etc. of official receivers

399.—(1) For the purposes of this Act the official receiver, in relation to any bankruptcy or winding up, is any person who by virtue of the following provisions of this section or section 401 below is authorised to act as the official receiver in relation to that bankruptcy or winding up.

(2) The Secretary of State may (subject to the approval of the Treasury as to numbers) appoint persons to the office of official receiver, and a person appointed to that office (whether under this section or section 70 of the Bankruptcy Act 1914)—

    (*a*) shall be paid out of money provided by Parliament such salary as the Secretary of State may with the concurrence of the Treasury direct,

    (*b*) shall hold office on such other terms and conditions as the Secretary of State may with the concurrence of the Treasury direct, and

    (*c*) may be removed from office by a direction of the Secretary of State.

(3) Where a person holds the office of official receiver, the Secretary of State shall from time to time attach him either to the High Court or to a county court having jurisdiction for the purposes of the second Group of Parts of this Act.

(4) Subject to any directions under subsection (6) below, an official receiver attached to a particular court is the person authorised to act as the official receiver in relation to every bankruptcy or winding up falling within the jurisdiction of that court.

(5) The Secretary of State shall ensure that there is, at all times, at least one official receiver attached to the High Court and at least one attached to each county court having jurisdiction for the purposes of the second Group of Parts; but he may attach the same official receiver to two or more different courts.

(6) The Secretary of State may give directions with respect to the disposal of the business of official receivers, and such directions may, in particular—

(a) authorise an official receiver attached to one court to act as the official receiver in relation to any case or description of cases falling within the jurisdiction of another court;

(b) provide, where there is more than one official receiver authorised to act as the official receiver in relation to cases falling within the jurisdiction of any court, for the distribution of their business between or among themselves.

(7) A person who at the coming into force of section 222 of the Insolvency Act 1985 (replaced by this section) is an official receiver attached to a court shall continue in office after the coming into force of that section as an official receiver attached to that court under this section.

DEFINITION
"the official receiver": subs. (1).

APPLICATION
This section does not apply to Scotland (ss.410, 440(2)(c).

GENERAL NOTE
This section provides for the office of the official receiver to be constituted and organised under the direction of the Secretary of State for Trade. The manner of appointing persons to the office, and the allocation of official receivers to the insolvency courts, are also specified. The provisions replace, and greatly expand upon, part of the former provisions of s.70 of the Bankruptcy Act 1914 (repealed). The principle of the continued involvement of the official receiver in all types of individual and incorporate insolvency proceedings, as powerfully advocated in Chap. 14 of the *Cork Report,* was accepted in Chap. 7 of the *White Paper,* and duly embodied throughout the provisions of this Act (see H.C. Standing Committee E, June 18, 1984, cols. 379–382).
This section corresponds to s.222 of the 1985 Act.

Functions and status of official receivers

400.—(1) In addition to any functions conferred on him by this Act, a person holding the office of official receiver shall carry out such other functions as may from time to time be conferred on him by the Secretary of State.

(2) In the exercise of the functions of his office a person holding the office of official receiver shall act under the general directions of the Secretary of State and shall also be an officer of the court in relation to which he exercises those functions.

(3) Any property vested in his official capacity in a person holding the office of official receiver shall, on his dying, ceasing to hold office or being otherwise succeeded in relation to the bankruptcy or winding up in question by another official receiver, vest in his successor without any conveyance, assignment or transfer.

DEFINITIONS
"the official receiver": s.399(1).
"property": s.436.

APPLICATION
This section does not apply to Scotland or to Northern Ireland (ss.410, 440(2)(c), 441).

GENERAL NOTE
This section makes further provision with regard to the official receiver and indicates the status and functions which attach to that office. This section, which replaces in part the former provisions of ss.70 and 72 of the Bankruptcy Act 1914 (repealed), corresponds to s.223 of the 1985 Act.

Subs. (3)

This makes provision of the transfer of property vested in an official receiver in his official capacity, upon his dying or ceasing to hold office.

Deputy official receivers and staff

401.—(1) The Secretary of State may, if he thinks it expedient to do so in order to facilitate the disposal of the business of the official receiver attached to any court, appoint an officer of his department to act as deputy to that official receiver.

(2) Subject to any directions given by the Secretary of State under section 399 or 400, a person appointed to act as deputy to an official receiver has, on such conditions and for such period as may be specified in the terms of his appointment, the same status and functions as the official receiver to whom he is appointed deputy.

Accordingly, references in this Act (except section 399(1) to (5)) to an official receiver include a person appointed to act as his deputy.

(3) An appointment made under subsection (1) may be terminated at any time by the Secretary of State.

(4) The Secretary of State may, subject to the approval of the Treasury as to numbers and remuneration and as to the other terms and conditions of the appointments, appoint officers of his department to assist official receivers in the carrying out of their functions.

DEFINITION

"the official receiver": s.399(1).

APPLICATION

This section does not apply to Scotland (s.440(2)(*c*)).

GENERAL NOTE

This section authorises the Secretary of State to appoint deputy official receivers and other supporting staff, as circumstances require, to assist official receivers in the carrying out of their functions. This section, which replaces the former provisions of ss.71 and 75 of the Bankruptcy Act 1914 (repealed), corresponds to s.224 of the 1985 Act.

The Official Petitioner

Official Petitioner

402.—(1) There continues to be an officer known as the Official Petitioner for the purpose of discharging, in relation to cases in which a criminal bankruptcy order is made, the functions assigned to him by or under this Act; and the Director of Public Prosecutions continues, by virtue of his office, to be the Official Petitioner.

(2) The functions of the Official Petitioner include the following—

(*a*) to consider whether, in a case in which a criminal bankruptcy order is made, it is in the public interest that he should himself present a petition under section 264(1)(*d*) of this Act;

(*b*) to present such a petition in any case where he determines that it is in the public interest for him to do so;

(*c*) to make payments, in such cases as he may determine, towards expenses incurred by other persons in connection with proceedings in pursuance of such a petition; and

(*d*) to exercise, so far as he considers it in the public interest to do so, any of the powers conferred on him by or under this Act.

(3) Any functions of the Official Petitioner may be discharged on his behalf by any person acting with his authority.

(4) Neither the Official Petitioner nor any person acting with his authority is liable to any action or proceeding in respect of anything done

or omitted to be done in the discharge, or purported discharge, of the functions of the Official Petitioner.

(5) In this section "criminal bankruptcy order" means an order under section 39(1) of the Powers of Criminal Courts Act 1973.

DEFINITIONS
"criminal bankruptcy order": subs. (5); Powers of Criminal Courts Act 1973, s.39(1).
"the Official Petitioner": subs. (1); Powers of Criminal Courts Act 1973, s.41(1).

APPLICATION
This section does not apply to Scotland (ss.410, 440(2)(*c*)).

GENERAL NOTE
This section makes provision for the continued existence of the office of Official Petitioner, which is a position occupied by the Director of Public Prosecutions *ex officio*. This office exists in relation to the procedure for making an order or adjudication against an individual following the making of a criminal bankruptcy order against him. A petition based upon such an order may be presented under s.264(1)(*d*); related provisions are contained in ss.266(4), 277, 282(2), 290(4)(*a*), 297(1), 327, and 341(4): see the General Notes to the respective provisions.

Insolvency Service finance, accounting and investment

Insolvency Services Account

403.—(1) All money received by the Secretary of State in respect of proceedings under this Act as it applies to England and Wales shall be paid into the Insolvency Services Account kept by the Secretary of State with the Bank of England; and all payments out of money standing to the credit of the Secretary of State in that account shall be made by the Bank of England in such manner as he may direct.

(2) Whenever the cash balance standing to the credit of the Insolvency Services Account is in excess of the amount which in the opinion of the Secretary of State is required for the time being to answer demands in respect of bankrupts' estates or companies' estates, the Secretary of State shall—

(*a*) notify the excess to the National Debt Commissioners, and
(*b*) pay into the Insolvency Services Investment Account ("the Investment Account") kept by the Commissioners with the Bank of England the whole or any part of the excess as the Commissioners may require for investment in accordance with the following provisions of this Part.

(3) Whenever any part of the money so invested is, in the opinion of the Secretary of State, required to answer any demand in respect of bankrupts' estates or companies' estates, he shall notify to the National Debt Commissioners the amount so required and the Commissioners—

(*a*) shall thereupon repay to the Secretary of State such sum as may be required to the credit of the Insolvency Services Account, and
(*b*) for that purpose may direct the sale of such part of the securities in which the money has been invested as may be necessary.

DEFINITIONS
"bankrupt": s.381(1).
"bankrupts' estates": ss.283, 385(1).
"the Investment Account": subs. (2)(*b*).

APPLICATION
This section does not apply to Scotland (s.410).

GENERAL NOTE
In Chap. 17 of the *Cork Report* a number of criticisms were expressed of the established rules under which liquidators and trustees in bankruptcy are severely restricted in their handling and investment of funds received by them in the course of acting in office. In particular, the obligation to pay money immediately into the Insolvency Services Account at the Bank of England, instead of into a local account specially opened for the purpose, was seen as both cumbersome and costly, in that the return of interest paid on moneys initially deposited in the Insolvency Services Account is well below currently obtainable commercial rates. It was thus observed (*C.R.* paras. 847–854) that this shortfall in receipts of interest has a direct and adverse effect upon the creditors' eventual returns in respect of the amounts owed to them. The *Cork Committee* recommendations for a change in the rules, so that trustees and liquidators would have greater control over the placement of funds on deposit pending their distribution to creditors, were not accepted in Chap. 8 of the *White Paper* and have not been carried into the new insolvency legislation. Ss.403–409 accordingly consolidate the existing law formerly contained in the Insolvency Services (Accounting and Investment) Act 1970 (hereafter referred to as "INS 1970") as amended by the provisions of the Insolvency Act 1976 (hereafter referred to as "INS 1976").

This section corresponds to s.1 of INS 1970 and s.3 of INS 1976, as amended by para. 28 of Sched. 8 to the 1985 Act.

Investment Account

404. Any money standing to the credit of the Investment Account (including any money received by the National Debt Commissioners by way of interest on or proceeds of any investment under this section) may be invested by the Commissioners, in accordance with such directions as may be given by the Treasury, in any manner for the time being specified in Part II of Schedule 1 to the Trustee Investments Act 1961.

DEFINITION
"the Investment Account": s.403(2)(*b*).

APPLICATION
This section does not apply to Scotland (s.410).

GENERAL NOTE
This section corresponds to s.2 of INS 1970.

Application of income in Investment Account; adjustment of balances

405.—(1) Where the annual account to be kept by the National Debt Commissioners under section 409 below shows that in the year for which it is made up the gross amount of the interest accrued from the securities standing to the credit of the Investment Account exceeded the aggregate of—

(*a*) a sum, to be determined by the Treasury, to provide against the depreciation in the value of the securities, and

(*b*) the sums paid into the Insolvency Services Account in pursuance of the next section together with the sums paid in pursuance of that section to the Commissioners of Inland Revenue,

the National Debt Commissioners shall, within 3 months after the account is laid before Parliament, cause the amount of the excess to be paid out of the Investment Account into the Consolidated Fund in such manner as may from time to time be agreed between the Treasury and the Commissioners.

(2) Where the said annual account shows that in the year for which it is made up the gross amount of interest accrued from the securities standing to the credit of the Investment Account was less than the aggregate mentioned in subsection (1), an amount equal to the deficiency shall, at such times as the Treasury direct, be paid out of the Consolidated Fund into the Investment Account.

(3) If the Investment Account is insufficient to meet its liabilities the Treasury may, on being informed of the insufficiency by the National Debt Commissioners, issue the amount of the deficiency out of the Consolidated Fund and the Treasury shall certify the deficiency to Parliament.

DEFINITIONS
"the Insolvency Services Account": s.403(1).
"the Investment Account": s.403(2)(*b*).

APPLICATION
This section does not apply to Scotland (s.410).

GENERAL NOTE
This section corresponds to s.3 of INS 1970 as amended by para. 5 of Sched. 2 to INS 1976.

Interest on money received by liquidators and invested

406. Where under rules made by virtue of paragraph 16 of Schedule 8 to this Act (investment of money received by company liquidators) a company has become entitled to any sum by way of interest, the Secretary of State shall certify that sum and the amount of tax payable on it to the National Debt Commissioners; and the Commissioners shall pay, out of the Investment Account—

(*a*) into the Insolvency Services Account, the sum so certified less the amount of tax so certified, and

(*b*) to the Commissioners of Inland Revenue, the amount of tax so certified.

DEFINITIONS
"the Insolvency Services Account": s.403(1).
"the Investment Account": s.403(2)(*b*).

APPLICATION
This section does not apply to Scotland (s.410).

GENERAL NOTE
This section corresponds to s.4 of INS 1970, as amended by para. 6 of Sched. 2 to INS 1976 and by para. 17 of Sched. 8 to the 1985 Act.

Unclaimed dividends and undistributed balances

407.—(1) The Secretary of State shall from time to time pay into the Consolidated Fund out of the Insolvency Services Account so much of the sums standing to the credit of that Account as represents—

(*a*) dividends which were declared before such date as the Treasury may from time to time determine and have not been claimed, and

(*b*) balances ascertained before that date which are too small to be divided among the persons entitled to them.

(2) For the purposes of this section the sums standing to the credit of the Insolvency Services Account are deemed to include any sums paid out of that Account and represented by any sums or securities standing to the credit of the Investment Account.

(3) The Secretary of State may require the National Debt Commissioners to pay out of the Investment Account into the Insolvency Services Account the whole or part of any sum which he is required to pay out of that account under subsection (1); and the Commissioners may direct the sale of such securities standing to the credit of the Investment Account as may be necessary for that purpose.

DEFINITIONS
"the Insolvency Services Account": s.403(1).
"the Investment Account": s.403(2)(*b*).

APPLICATION
This section does not apply to Scotland (s.410).

GENERAL NOTE
This section corresponds to s.5 of INS 1970, as amended by para. 7 of Sched. 2 to INS 1976.

Recourse to Consolidated Fund

408. If, after any repayment due to it from the Investment Account, the Insolvency Services Account is insufficient to meet its liabilities, the Treasury may, on being informed of it by the Secretary of State, issue the amount of the deficiency out of the Consolidated Fund, and the Treasury shall certify the deficiency to Parliament.

DEFINITIONS
"the Insolvency Services Account": s.403(1).
"the Investment Account": s.403(2)(*b*).

APPLICATION
This section does not apply to Scotland (s.410).

GENERAL NOTE
This section corresponds to s.6 of INS 1970, as amended by para. 8 of Sched. 2 to INS 1976.

Annual financial statement and audit

409.—(1) The National Debt Commissioners shall for each year ending on 31st March prepare a statement of the sums credited and debited to the Investment Account in such form and manner as the Treasury may direct and shall transmit it to the Comptroller and Auditor General before the end of November next following the year.

(2) The Secretary of State shall for each year ending 31st March prepare a statement of the sums received or paid by him under section 403 above in such form and manner as the Treasury may direct and shall transmit each statement to the Comptroller and Auditor General before the end of November next following the year.

(3) Every such statement shall include such additional information as the Treasury may direct.

(4) The Comptroller and Auditor General shall examine, certify and report on every such statement and shall lay copies of it, and of his report, before Parliament.

DEFINITION
"the Investment Account": s.403(2)(*b*).

APPLICATION
This section does not apply to Scotland (s.410).

GENERAL NOTE
This section corresponds to s.7 of INS 1970, as amended by para. 9 of Sched. 2 to INS 1976.

Supplementary

Extent of this Part

410. This Part of this Act extends to England and Wales only.

GENERAL NOTE
This section has the effect of limiting the application of all the provisions in Part XIV to England and Wales only. There is a partial overlap between the effect of this section, which applies to ss.399–410 as a block, and the effect of s.440(2)(*c*), which specifically excludes ss.399–402 from extending to Scotland. Moreover, s.441 is so drafted that only the provisions of the Act which are therein mentioned extend to Northern Ireland: none of the sections within Part XIV is mentioned in s.441 at all.

This section corresponds to s.9(3) of INS 1970 in conjunction with s.14(6) of INS 1976. The effect of s.236(3)(i) of the 1985 Act is also maintained in relation to provisions now contained in Part XIV of this Act which correspond to ss.222–225 of the 1985 Act, so that the extent of those provisions continues to be confined to England and Wales only.

PART XV

SUBORDINATE LEGISLATION

General insolvency rules

Company insolvency rules

411.—(1) Rules may be made—
  (*a*) in relation to England and Wales, by the Lord Chancellor with the concurrence of the Secretary of State, or
  (*b*) in relation to Scotland, by the Secretary of State,
for the purpose of giving effect to Parts I to VII of this Act.
  (2) Without prejudice to the generality of subsection (1), or to any provision of those Parts by virtue of which rules under this section may be made with respect to any matter, rules under this section may contain—
  (*a*) any such provision as is specified in Schedule 8 to this Act or corresponds to provision contained immediately before the coming into force of section 106 of the Insolvency Act 1985 in rules made, or having effect as if made, under section 663(1) or (2) of the Companies Act (old winding-up rules), and
  (*b*) such incidental, supplemental and transitional provisions as may appear to the Lord Chancellor or, as the case may be, the Secretary of State necessary or expedient.
  (3) In Schedule 8 to this Act "liquidator" includes a provisional liquidator; and references above in this section to Parts I to VII of this Act are to be read as including the Companies Act so far as relating to, and to matters connected with or arising out of, the insolvency or winding up of companies.
  (4) Rules under this section shall be made by statutory instrument subject to annulment in pursuance of a resolution of either House of Parliament.
  (5) Regulations made by the Secretary of State under a power conferred by rules under this section shall be made by statutory instrument and, after being made, shall be laid before each House of Parliament.
  (6) Nothing in this section prejudices any power to make rules of court.

DEFINITIONS
  "liquidator": subs. (3), Sched. 8.
  "rules": s.251 and this section.

GENERAL NOTE

This is an enabling section which confers a rule-making power upon the persons designated in subs. (1). The matters mentioned in Sched. 8 are expressly incorporated into the rule-making authority conferred by this section, but subs. (2) is so drafted as to avoid cutting down the more general language of subs. (1), which effectively confers an unfettered discretion with regard to the rules which may be made, provided these are ultimately reconcilable with the authorised purpose of giving effect to Pts. I–VII of the Act.

This section corresponds to s.106 of the 1985 Act.

Subs. (4)

This provides for the "negative" procedure to be applicable in relation to any statutory instrument whereby rules are made under this section. The rules will therefore come into force unless a resolution of either House is passed in opposition.

Individual insolvency rules (England and Wales)

412.—(1) The Lord Chancellor may, with the concurrence of the Secretary of State, make rules for the purpose of giving effect to Parts VIII to XI of this Act.

(2) Without prejudice to the generality of subsection (1), or to any provision of those Parts by virtue of which rules under this section may be made with respect to any matter, rules under this section may contain—

(*a*) any such provision as is specified in Schedule 9 to this Act or corresponds to provision contained immediately before the appointed day in rules made under section 132 of the Bankruptcy Act 1914; and

(*b*) such incidental, supplemental and transitional provisions as may appear to the Lord Chancellor necessary or expedient.

(3) Rules under this section shall be made by statutory instrument subject to annulment in pursuance of a resolution of either House of Parliament.

(4) Regulations made by the Secretary of State under a power conferred by rules under this section shall be made by statutory instrument and, after being made, shall be laid before each House of Parliament.

(5) Nothing in this section prejudices any power to make rules of court.

DEFINITION

"rules": s.384 and this section.

APPLICATION

This section does not apply to Scotland (s.440(2)(*c*)).

TRANSITIONAL PROVISION
Sched. 11, para. 19.

GENERAL NOTE

This section, together with Sched. 9, defines the scope and extent of the power to make subordinate legislation in respect of individual insolvency. Subs. (1) provides that this power is exercisable by the Lord Chancellor with the concurrence of the Secretary of State for Trade, while subs. (3) indicates that rules made under this section are to be made by statutory instrument, subject to the "negative" procedure for annulment by resolution of either House of Parliament. Subs. (4) indicates that regulations made by the Secretary of State pursuant to any power conferred by the rules is simply subject to the "notice" requirement in relation to Parliament.

This section corresponds to s.207 of the 1985 Act.

Insolvency Rules Committee

413.—(1) The committee established under section 10 of the Insolvency Act 1976 (advisory committee on bankruptcy and winding-up rules) continues to exist for the purpose of being consulted under this section.

(2) The Lord Chancellor shall consult the committee before making any rules under section 411 or 412.

(3) Subject to the next subsection, the committee shall consist of—

(a) a judge of the High Court attached to the Chancery Division;
(b) a circuit judge;
(c) a registrar in bankruptcy of the High Court;
(d) the registrar of a county court;
(e) a practising barrister;
(f) a practising solicitor; and
(g) a practising accountant;

and the appointment of any person as a member of the committee shall be made by the Lord Chancellor.

(4) The Lord Chancellor may appoint as additional members of the committee any persons appearing to him to have qualifications or experience that would be of value to the committee in considering any matter with which it is concerned.

DEFINITION

"the committee," "the insolvency rules committee"; "advisory committee on bankruptcy and winding up rules": subs. (1).

APPLICATION

This section does not apply to Scotland (s.440(2)(c)).

GENERAL NOTE

This section perpetuates the existence of the Committee, formerly known as the Advisory Committee on Bankruptcy and Winding Up Rules, which was established by s.10 of the Insolvency Act 1976 (repealed) and is henceforth known as the Insolvency Rules Committee. The section specifies the composition of the Committee and the mode of appointment of those who are to be its members. The Lord Chancellor is required to consult the Committee before making any rules under s.411 or s.412 of this Act (subs. (2)).

This section corresponds to s.226 of the 1985 Act.

Fees orders

Fees orders (company insolvency proceedings)

414.—(1) There shall be paid in respect of—

(a) proceedings under any of Parts I to VII of this Act, and
(b) the performance by the official receiver or the Secretary of State of functions under those Parts,

such fees as the competent authority may with the sanction of the Treasury by order direct.

(2) That authority is—

(a) in relation to England and Wales, the Lord Chancellor, and
(b) in relation to Scotland, the Secretary of State.

(3) The Treasury may by order direct by whom and in what manner the fees are to be collected and accounted for.

(4) The Lord Chancellor may, with the sanction of the Treasury, by order provide for sums to be deposited, by such persons, in such manner and in such circumstances as may be specified in the order, by way of security for fees payable by virtue of this section.

(5) An order under this section may contain such incidental, supplemental and transitional provisions as may appear to the Lord Chancellor,

the Secretary of State or (as the case may be) the Treasury necessary or expedient.

(6) An order under this section shall be made by statutory instrument and, after being made, shall be laid before each House of Parliament.

(7) Fees payable by virtue of this section shall be paid into the Consolidated Fund.

(8) References in subsection (1) to Parts I to VII of this Act are to be read as including the Companies Act so far as relating to, and to matters connected with or arising out of, the insolvency or winding up of companies.

(9) Nothing in this section prejudices any power to make rules of court; and the application of this section to Scotland is without prejudice to section 2 of the Courts of Law Fees (Scotland) Act 1895.

DEFINITION

"the official receiver": s.399(1).

GENERAL NOTE

Subss. (1), (2)

This section, which corresponds to ss.106(5) and 107 of the 1985 Act, makes provision for the levying of fees in respect of proceedings relating to company insolvency falling within this Part of the Act or under the Companies Act 1985. The power of determination regarding the levels of fees in England and Wales is vested exclusively in the Lord Chancellor in England and Wales, whereas the rule-making powers under s.411 are exercisable by the Lord Chancellor with the concurrence of the Secretary of State for Trade. In the case of Scotland, the relevant powers under both this section and s.411 are vested in the Secretary of State for Scotland.

Subs. (4)

This provides for the levying of deposits as security for fees payable under this section.

Subs. (6)

This prescribes the mode of enactment, with a requirement merely that any order made under this section be laid before each House of Parliament. No procedure is prescribed for opposing or modifying any Order so laid before Parliament.

Fees orders (individual insolvency proceedings in England and Wales)

415.—(1) There shall be paid in respect of—

(*a*) proceedings under Parts VIII to XI of this Act, and

(*b*) the performance by the official receiver or the Secretary of State of functions under those Parts,

such fees as the Lord Chancellor may with the sanction of the Treasury by order direct.

(2) The Treasury may by order direct by whom and in what manner the fees are to be collected and accounted for.

(3) The Lord Chancellor may, with the sanction of the Treasury, by order provide for sums to be deposited, by such persons, in such manner and in such circumstances as may be specified in the order, by way of security for—

(*a*) fees payable by virtue of this section, and

(*b*) fees payable to any person who has prepared an insolvency practitioner's report under section 274 in Chapter I of Part IX.

(4) An order under this section may contain such incidental, supplemental and transitional provisions as may appear to the Lord Chancellor or, as the case may be, the Treasury, necessary or expedient.

(5) An order under this section shall be made by statutory instrument and, after being made, shall be laid before each House of Parliament.

(6) Fees payable by virtue of this section shall be paid into the Consolidated Fund.

(7) Nothing in this section prejudices any power to make rules of court.

DEFINITIONS
"insolvency practitioner": ss.388, 390.
"the official receiver": s.399(1).

APPLICATION
This section does not apply to Scotland (s.440(2)(c)).

GENERAL NOTE
This section confers powers to require the payment of fees in individual insolvency proceedings. These powers are exercisable by the Lord Chancellor with the sanction of the Treasury. Subs. (5) indicates that fees orders made pursuant to this enabling provision are to be made by statutory instrument, subject to the "notice" requirement in relation to Parliament.
This section corresponds to ss.207(5) and 208(1)–(3) and (5) of the 1985 Act.

Subs. (3)(b)

Person who has prepared an insolvency practitioner's report under section 274
This provision enables the deposit made by a debtor when presenting his own petition for a bankruptcy order under s.272 to be used to meet the fees of any insolvency practitioner whom the court may appoint under s.273(2) to give advice and assistance to the debtor, and to prepare a report under s.274, with a view to the debtor's avoiding bankruptcy if possible and proposing instead a scheme or composition under Part VIII of the Act. This is intended to enable as many small debtors as possible to avoid bankruptcy altogether and to opt instead for the new voluntary procedure established by the Act.

Specification, increase and reduction of money sums relevant in the operation of this Act

Monetary limits (companies winding up)

416.—(1) The Secretary of State may by order in a statutory instrument increase or reduce any of the money sums for the time being specified in the following provisions in the first Group of Parts—
    section 117(2) (amount of company's share capital determining whether county court has jurisdiction to wind it up);
    section 120(3) (the equivalent as respects sheriff court jurisdiction in Scotland);
    section 123(1)(*a*) (minimum debt for service of demand on company by unpaid creditor);
    section 184(3) (minimum value of judgment, affecting sheriff's duties on levying execution);
    section 206(1)(*a*) and (*b*) (minimum value of company property concealed or fraudulently removed, affecting criminal liability of company's officer).
(2) An order under this section may contain such transitional provisions as may appear to the Secretary of State necessary or expedient.
(3) No order under this section increasing or reducing any of the money sums for the time being specified in section 117(2), 120(3) or 123(1)(*a*) shall be made unless a draft of the order has been laid before and approved by a resolution of each House of Parliament.
(4) A statutory instrument containing an order under this section, other than an order to which subsection (3) applies, is subject to annulment in pursuance of a resolution of either House of Parliament.

DEFINITION
"property": s.346.

GENERAL NOTE
This section corresponds to s.664 of the Companies Act, as amended by para. 49 of Sched. 6 to the 1985 Act. The section empowers the Secretary of State to amend the monetary limits applicable under the sections specified in subs. (1). Two different procedures are specified for the adoption of orders made under this section. Any order made in relation to the sums specified in ss.117(2), 120(3) or 123(1)(*a*) is by subs. (3) required to undergo the "positive" procedure for adoption by each House of Parliament. Orders other than those to which subs. (3) applies are by subs. (4) made subject to the "negative" procedure only.

Money sum in s.222

417. The Secretary of State may by regulations in a statutory instrument increase or reduce the money sum for the time being specified in section 222(1) (minimum debt for service of demand on unregistered company by unpaid creditor); but such regulations shall not be made unless a draft of the statutory instrument containing them has been approved by resolution of each House of Parliament.

DEFINITION
"unregistered company": s.220(1).

GENERAL NOTE
This section corresponds to part of s.667(2) of the Companies Act, and enables the Secretary of State to amend the monetary limit applicable under s.222(1) for service of a statutory demand by an unpaid creditor in relation to an unregistered company. The adjustment of the equivalent limit, specified in s.123(1)(*a*), in relation to companies which qualify as registered companies for the purposes of the Act will take place under the provisions of s.416. In each case, the making of the relevant order requires a "positive" resolution by each House of Parliament (see General Note to s.416).

Monetary limits (bankruptcy)

418.—(1) The Secretary of State may by order prescribe amounts for the purposes of the following provisions in the second Group of Parts—

section 273 (minimum value of debtor's estate determining whether immediate bankruptcy order should be made; small bankruptcies level);

section 346(3) (minimum amount of judgment, determining whether amount recovered on sale of debtor's goods is to be treated as part of his estate in bankruptcy);

section 354(1) and (2) (minimum amount of concealed debt, or value of property concealed or removed, determining criminal liability under the section);

section 358 (minimum value of property taken by a bankrupt out of England and Wales, determining his criminal liability);

section 360(1) (maximum amount of credit which bankrupt may obtain without disclosure of his status);

section 361(2) (exemption of bankrupt from criminal liability for failure to keep proper accounts, if unsecured debts not more than the prescribed minimum);

section 364(2)(*d*) (minimum value of goods removed by the bankrupt, determining his liability to arrest);

and references in the second Group of Parts to the amount prescribed for the purposes of any of those provisions, and references in those provisions to the prescribed amount, are to be construed accordingly.

(2) An order under this section may contain such transitional provisions as may appear to the Secretary of State necessary or expedient.

(3) An order under this section shall be made by statutory instrument subject to annulment in pursuance of a resolution of either House of Parliament.

DEFINITION
   "prescribed": s.384 and this section.

APPLICATION
   This section does not apply to Scotland (s.440(2)(*c*)).

GENERAL NOTE
   This section confers power upon the Secretary of State to prescribe monetary limits for
the purposes of the specified sections of the Act. Any order made under this section is by
subs. (3) made subject to the "negative" procedure for annulment by either House of
Parliament.
   This section corresponds to subss. (1) (part), (2) and (3) of s.209 of the 1985 Act.

Insolvency practice

Regulations for purposes of Part XIII

   419.—(1) The Secretary of State may make regulations for the purpose
of giving effect to Part XIII of this Act; and "prescribed" in that Part
means prescribed by regulations made by the Secretary of State.
   (2) Without prejudice to the generality of subsection (1) or to any
provision of that Part by virtue of which regulations may be made with
respect to any matter, regulations under this section may contain—
   (*a*) provision as to the matters to be taken into account in determining
         whether a person is a fit and proper person to act as an insolvency
         practitioner;
   (*b*) provision prohibiting a person from so acting in prescribed cases,
         being cases in which a conflict of interest will or may arise;
   (*c*) provision imposing requirements with respect to—
            (i) the preparation and keeping by a person who acts as an
         insolvency practitioner of prescribed books, accounts and other
         records, and
            (ii) the production of those books, accounts and records to
         prescribed persons;
   (*d*) provision conferring power on prescribed persons—
            (i) to require any person who acts or has acted as an insolvency
         practitioner to answer any inquiry in relation to a case in which
         he is so acting or has so acted, and
            (ii) to apply to a court to examine such a person or any other
         person on oath concerning such a case;
   (*e*) provision making non-compliance with any of the regulations a
         criminal offence; and
   (*f*) such incidental, supplemental and transitional provisions as may
         appear to the Secretary of State necessary or expedient.
   (3) Any power conferred by Part XIII or this Part to make regulations,
rules or orders is exercisable by statutory instrument subject to annulment
by resolution of either House of Parliament.
   (4) Any rule or regulation under Part XIII or this Part may make
different provi..ion with respect to different cases or descriptions of cases,
including different provision for different areas.

DEFINITIONS
   "prescribed": subs. (1).
   "records": s.436.
   "to act as an insolvency practitioner": s.488.

GENERAL NOTE
   This section authorises the making of rules and regulations for the purposes of any of the
matters falling within Pt. XIII. It thus governs all references concerning the making of
regulations and "prescribed" matters contained in ss.390(3)(*b*), 392(3)(*c*), 393(2)(*b*) and (3),

and 5(3), and also any rules made under para. 4(4) of Sched. 7. Subs. (2)(*e*) confers an important power on the Secretary of State to create further criminal offences for non-compliance with any of the regulations to be made in the exercise of his powers under Pt. XIII.

This section corresponds to ss.10, and 11 (part) of the 1985 Act.

Subs. (2)

This subsection indicates a number of particular matters in relation to which the Secretary of State is empowered to make regulations in addition to the more general power conferred on him by the terms of subs. (1). Some of these matters, such as that referred to in para. (*b*) concerning cases of conflict of interest, were originally intended to be governed by provisions of the Act itself. However the complexity of the issues raised by the originally published draft of these provisions was demonstrated on several occasions during the debates to the 1985 Bill on both Houses of Parliament, and it was subsequently decided to leave these matters to be regulated by statutory instrument. Where an insolvency practitioner is a member of a recognised professional body the rules and practices of that body will be directly applicable to determine, for example, whether he or she is a "fit and proper person" as required by s.391(2)(*a*). Similarly, professional bodies generally issue their own guidelines to their members regarding matters where a conflict of interest may arise. However, since it is intended that as far as possible uniform standards should be applicable to all insolvency practitioners, the regulations to be made under paras. (*a*) and (*b*) could become norms in relation to which the rules and practices of each separate professional body will have to be aligned. Alternatively any professional body whose rules and practices fail to match the norms established by the regulations could be denied, or be deprived of, recognition under s.391(1).

Subs. (3)

This prescribes the manner in which regulations, rules or orders are to be made by the Secretary of State in the exercise of the power conferred by Pt. XIII of the Act. The mode of enactment is to be by statutory instrument which is subject to annulment on the adoption of a resolution to that effect by either House of Parliament. This "negative" procedure for enactment of rules and regulations has the effect of requiring a positive, and successful, Parliamentary initiative to be undertaken in order to prevent the instrument from becoming legally effective.

Subs. (4)

This provision effectively widens the scope of the rule making power conferred by subs. (1), so as to authorise the Secretary of State to make separate and different provisions for cases described or classified in different ways. It also confers an authority to treat different areas of the country in accordance with different provisions. The most prominent occasions for the use of this latter power of differentiation will arise in relation to the need to make distinctive provisions with regard to Scotland on the one hand and England and Wales on the other, but the subsection contains no specific limitation in this respect and hence it would be permissible to establish further categories of distinction with reference to area or location, for example as between the London metropolitan area and the rest of the country.

Other order-making powers

Insolvent partnerships

420.—(1) The Lord Chancellor may, by order made with the concurrence of the Secretary of State, provide that such provisions of this Act as may be specified in the order shall apply in relation to insolvent partnerships with such modifications as may be so specified.

(2) An order under this section may make different provision for different cases and may contain such incidental, supplemental and transitional provisions as may appear to the Lord Chancellor necessary or expedient.

(3) An order under this section shall be made by statutory instrument subject to annulment in pursuance of a resolution of either House of Parliament.

APPLICATION
This section does not apply to Scotland (s.440(2)(*c*)).

GENERAL NOTE
This section confers power upon the Lord Chancellor to apply the provisions of the Act with modifications to the winding up of insolvent partnerships. This power is exercisable by means of statutory instrument subject to the "negative" procedure for annulment by either House of Parliament. This provision removes to the realm of delegated legislation a specialised topic formerly covered by the provisions of ss.33(6), 63(1), 114, 116, 117, 119 and 127 of the Bankruptcy Act 1914 (repealed). The problems associated with this subject are discussed in Chap. 39 of the *Cork Report*.
This section corresponds to s.227 of the 1985 Act.

Insolvent estates of deceased persons

421.—(1) The Lord Chancellor may, by order made with the concurrence of the Secretary of State, provide that such provisions of this Act as may be specified in the order shall apply to the administration of the insolvent estates of deceased persons with such modifications as may be so specified.

(2) An order under this section may make different provision for different cases and may contain such incidental, supplemental and transitional provisions as may appear to the Lord Chancellor necessary or expedient.

(3) An order under this section shall be made by statutory instrument subject to annulment in pursuance of a resolution of either House of Parliament.

(4) For the purposes of this section the estate of a deceased person is insolvent if, when realised, it will be insufficient to meet in full all the debts and other liabilities to which it is subject.

DEFINITIONS
"insolvent estate of deceased person": subs. (4).
"modifications": s.436.

APPLICATION
This section does not apply to Scotland (s.440(2)(*c*)).

GENERAL NOTE
This section confers power upon the Lord Chancellor to apply the provisions of the Act with modifications to the insolvent estates of deceased persons. This power is exercisable by means of statutory instrument subject to the "negative" procedure for annulment by either House of Parliament. This provision removes to the realm of delegated legislation the provisions with regard to the administration of the estates of deceased insolvents which were formerly contained in s.130 of the Bankruptcy Act 1914 (repealed). Recommendations for improving the legal provisions applicable to such cases were made in Chap. 40 of the *Cork Report*.
This section corresponds to s.228 of the 1985 Act.

Recognised banks, etc.

422.—(1) The Secretary of State may, by order made with the concurrence of the Treasury and after consultation with the Bank of England, provide that such provisions in the first Group of Parts as may be specified in the order shall apply in relation to—

    (*a*) recognised banks and licensed institutions within the meaning of the Banking Act 1979, and

    (*b*) institutions to which sections 16 and 18 of that Act apply as if they were licensed institutions, with such modifications as may be so specified.

(2) An order under this section may make different provision for different cases and may contain such incidental, supplemental and transitional provisions as may appear to the Secretary of State necessary or expedient.

(3) An order under this section shall be made by statutory instrument subject to annulment in pursuance of a resolution of either House of Parliament.

DEFINITIONS
"modifications": s.436.
"recognised bank or licensed institution": Banking Act 1979, ss.48, 50.

GENERAL NOTE
This section confers power upon the Secretary of State to apply any provisions of the first Group of Parts of the Act to recognised banks and licensed institutions within the meaning of the Banking Act 1979, and to other institutions to which the provisions of that Act apply. This power is exercisable by means of statutory instrument subject to the "negative" procedure for annulment by either House of Parliament. The provision paves the way, following consultation with the Bank of England, for provisions to be made to enable banks and other lending institutions to be wound up, and to become subject to other insolvency procedures, including the Administration Order procedure, using a modified form of the procedures established under this Act. Pending the making of any order under this section, s.8(4)(*b*) prevents the Administration Order procedure from applying to recognised banks and licensed institutions.

This section corresponds to s.229 of the 1985 Act.

PART XVI

PROVISIONS AGAINST DEBT AVOIDANCE (ENGLAND AND WALES ONLY)

Transactions defrauding creditors

423.—(1) This section relates to transactions entered into at an undervalue; and a person enters into such a transaction with another person if—

    (*a*) he makes a gift to the other person or he otherwise enters into a transaction with the other on terms that provide for him to receive no consideration;

    (*b*) he enters into a transaction with the other in consideration of marriage; or

    (*c*) he enters into a transaction with the other for a consideration the value of which, in money or money's worth, is significantly less than the value, in money or money's worth, of the consideration provided by himself.

(2) Where a person has entered into such a transaction, the court may, if satisfied under the next subsection, make such order as it thinks fit for—

    (*a*) restoring the position to what it would have been if the transaction had not been entered into, and

    (*b*) protecting the interests of persons who are victims of the transaction.

(3) In the case of a person entering into such a transaction, an order shall only be made if the court is satisfied that it was entered into by him for the purpose—

    (*a*) of putting assets beyond the reach of a person who is making, or may at some time make, a claim against him, or

    (*b*) of otherwise prejudicing the interests of such a person in relation to the claim which he is making or may make.

(4) In this section "the court" means the High Court or—

(*a*) if the person entering into the transaction is an individual, any other court which would have jurisdiction in relation to a bankruptcy petition relating to him;

(*b*) if that person is a body capable of being wound up under Part IV or V of this Act, any other court having jurisdiction to wind it up.

(5) In relation to a transaction at an undervalue, references here and below to a victim of the transaction are to a person who is, or is capable of being, prejudiced by it; and in the following two sections the person entering into the transaction is referred to as "the debtor".

DEFINITIONS

"bankruptcy petition": s.381(3).
"the court": subs. (4).
"the debtor": subs. (5).
"transaction": s.436.
"transaction entered into at an undervalue": subs. (1).
"victim of a transaction at an undervalue": subs. (5).

APPLICATION

This section does not apply to Scotland (s.440(2)(*c*)).

TRANSITIONAL PROVISION

Sched. 11, para. 20.

GENERAL NOTE

This section, together with ss.424 and 425, replaces s.172 of the Law of Property Act 1925, which is repealed. The new provisions enable the court, where a person has entered into a transaction at an undervalue with the purpose of defeating the claims of creditors, to make orders restoring the *status quo ante* and protecting the position of persons prejudiced. The case for the repeal and replacement of s.172 of the Law of Property Act 1925 was convincingly argued in Chap. 28 of the *Cork Report* (see paras. 1210–1220, and 1283–1284). The sections now enacted are designed to operate in harmony with the provisions regarding transactions at an undervalue and preferences contained in ss.238–241 and 339–342, which apply in cases of corporate and of individual insolvency respectively. The definition supplied in each group of sections for the key expression "transaction at an undervalue" is identical for all three, save that, for obvious and logical reasons, there is no counterpart in s.238(4) to the references in ss.339(3)(*b*) and 423(1)(*b*) to entering into a transaction with another person in consideration of marriage.

Ss.423–425 correspond to s.212 of the 1985 Act.

Those who may apply for an order under s.423

424.—(1) An application for an order under section 423 shall not be made in relation to a transaction except—

(*a*) in a case where the debtor has been adjudged bankrupt or is a body corporate which is being wound up or in relation to which an administration order is in force, by the official receiver, by the trustee of the bankrupt's estate or the liquidator or administrator of the body corporate or (with the leave of the court) by a victim of the transaction;

(*b*) in a case where a victim of the transaction is bound by a voluntary arrangement approved under Part I or Part VIII of this Act, by the supervisor of the voluntary arrangement or by any person who (whether or not so bound) is such a victim; or

(*c*) in any other case, by a victim of the transaction.

(2) An application made under any of the paragraphs of subsection (1) is to be treated as made on behalf of every victim of the transaction.

DEFINITIONS

"administration order": s.8(2).
"bankrupt": s.381(1).

"estate": ss.283, 385(1).
"supervisor of the voluntary arrangement": ss.7(2) (companies); 263(2) (individuals).
"the administrator": s.8(2).
"the debtor": s.433(5).
"the official receiver": s.399(1).
"transaction": ss.423(1), 436.
"victim of the transaction": s.423(5).
"voluntary arrangement": ss.1(2) (companies); 253(1) (individuals).

APPLICATION
This section does not apply to Scotland (s.440(2)(c)).

TRANSITIONAL PROVISION
Sched. 11, para. 20.

GENERAL NOTE
This section, which operates in conjunction with ss.423 and 425, prescribes which persons are allowed to apply for an order under s.423 in respect of a transaction in fraud of creditors, within the meaning of that section. See the General Note to s.423.

Provision which may be made by order under s.423

425.—(1) Without prejudice to the generality of section 423, an order made under that section with respect to a transaction may (subject as follows)—
(a) require any property transferred as part of the transaction to be vested in any person, either absolutely or for the benefit of all the persons on whose behalf the application for the order is treated as made;
(b) require any property to be so vested if it represents, in any person's hands, the application either of the proceeds of sale of property so transferred or of money so transferred;
(c) release or discharge (in whole or in part) any security given by the debtor;
(d) require any person to pay to any other person in respect of benefits received from the debtor such sums as the court may direct;
(e) provide for any surety or guarantor whose obligations to any person were released or discharged (in whole or in part) under the transaction to be under such new and revived obligations as the court thinks appropriate;
(f) provide for security to be provided for the discharge of any obligation imposed by or arising under the order, for such an obligation to be charged on any property and for such security or charge to have the same priority as a security or charge released or discharged (in whole or in part) under the transaction.

(2) An order under section 423 may affect the property of, or impose any obligation on, any person whether or not he is the person with whom the debtor entered into the transaction; but such an order—
(a) shall not prejudice any interest in property which was acquired from a person other than the debtor and was acquired in good faith, for value and without notice of the relevant circumstances, or prejudice any interest deriving from such an interest, and
(b) shall not require a person who received a benefit from the transaction in good faith, for value and without notice of the relevant circumstances to pay any sum unless he was a party to the transaction.

(3) For the purposes of this section the relevant circumstances in relation to a transaction are the circumstances by virtue of which an order under section 423 may be made in respect of the transaction.

(4) In this section "security" means any mortgage, charge, lien or other security.

DEFINITIONS
"property": s.436.
"security": subs. (4).
"the court": s.423(4).
"the debtor": s.423(5).
"the relevant circumstances": subs. (3).
"transaction": ss.423(1), 436.

APPLICATION
This section does not apply to Scotland (s.440(2)(c)).

TRANSITIONAL PROVISION
Sched. 11, para. 20.

GENERAL NOTE
This section, which operates in conjunction with ss.423 and 424, prescribes what matters may be included in an order made by the court in the exercise of its jurisdiction under s.423. See the General Note to s.423.

PART XVII

MISCELLANEOUS AND GENERAL

Co-operation between courts exercising jurisdiction in relation to insolvency

426.—(1) An order made by a court in any part of the United Kingdom in the exercise of jurisdiction in relation to insolvency law shall be enforced in any other part of the United Kingdom as if it were made by a court exercising the corresponding jurisdiction in that other part.

(2) However, without prejudice to the following provisions of this section, nothing in subsection (1) requires a court in any part of the United Kingdom to enforce, in relation to property situated in that part, any order made by a court in any other part of the United Kingdom.

(3) The Secretary of State, with the concurrence in relation to property situated in England and Wales of the Lord Chancellor, may by order make provision for securing that a trustee or assignee under the insolvency law of any part of the United Kingdom has, with such modifications as may be specified in the order, the same rights in relation to any property situated in another part of the United Kingdom as he would have in the corresponding circumstances if he were a trustee or assignee under the insolvency law of that other part.

(4) The courts having jurisdiction in relation to insolvency law in any part of the United Kingdom shall assist the courts having the corresponding jurisdiction in any other part of the United Kingdom or any relevant country or territory.

(5) For the purposes of subsection (4) a request made to a court in any part of the United Kingdom by a court in any other part of the United Kingdom or in a relevant country or territory is authority for the court to which the request is made to apply, in relation to any matters specified in the request, the insolvency law which is applicable by either court in relation to comparable matters falling within its jurisdiction.

In exercising its discretion under this subsection, a court shall have regard in particular to the rules of private international law.

(6) Where a person who is a trustee or assignee under the insolvency law of any part of the United Kingdom claims property situated in any other part of the United Kingdom (whether by virtue of an order under

subsection (3) or otherwise), the submission of that claim to the court exercising jurisdiction in relation to insolvency law in that other part shall be treated in the same manner as a request made by a court for the purpose of subsection (4).

(7) Section 38 of the Criminal Law Act 1977 (execution of warrant of arrest throughout the United Kingdom) applies to a warrant which, in exercise of any jurisdiction in relation to insolvency law, is issued in any part of the United Kingdom for the arrest of a person as it applies to a warrant issued in that part of the United Kingdom for the arrest of a person charged with an offence.

(8) Without prejudice to any power to make rules of court, any power to make provision by subordinate legislation for the purpose of giving effect in relation to companies or individuals to the insolvency law of any part of the United Kingdom includes power to make provision for the purpose of giving effect in that part to any provision made by or under the preceding provisions of this section.

(9) An order under subsection (3) shall be made by statutory instrument subject to annulment in pursuance of a resolution of either House of Parliament.

(10) In this section "insolvency law" means—

(a) in relation to England and Wales, provision made by or under this Act or sections 6 to 10, 12, 15, 19(c) and 20 (with Schedule 1) of the Company Directors Disqualification Act 1986 and extending to England and Wales;

(b) in relation to Scotland, provision extending to Scotland and made by or under this Act, sections 6 to 10, 12, 15, 19(c) and 20 (with Schedule 1) of the Company Directors Disqualification Act 1986, Part XVIII of the Companies Act or the Bankruptcy (Scotland) Act 1985;

(c) in relation to Northern Ireland, provision made by or under the Bankruptcy Acts (Northern Ireland) 1857 to 1980, Part V, VI or IX of the Companies Act (Northern Ireland) 1960 or Part IV of the Companies (Northern Ireland) Order 1978;

(d) in relation to any relevant country or territory, so much of the law of that country or territory as corresponds to provisions falling within any of the foregoing paragraphs;

and references in this subsection to any enactment include, in relation to any time before the coming into force of that enactment the corresponding enactment in force at that time.

(11) In this section "relevant country or territory" means—

(a) any of the Channel Islands or the Isle of Man, or

(b) any country or territory designated for the purposes of this section by the Secretary of State by order made by statutory instrument.

DEFINITIONS
"insolvency law": subs. (10).
"property": s.436.
"relevant country or territory": subs. (11).

APPLICATION
This section applies to Northern Ireland (s.441(1)(a)).

GENERAL NOTE
This section was introduced into the 1985 Insolvency Bill as late as the Report Stage in the House of Commons (H.C. Vol. 83, col. 550), in place of the original, far less extensive clause. It has the effect of replacing the former provisions of ss.121–123 inclusive of the Bankruptcy Act 1914 (repealed) with an extensive and potentially far-reaching provision for inter-jurisdictional co-operation and enforcement of insolvency orders of all kinds, relating

to both individual and corporate insolvency. The enactment of such a provision was advocated in Chap. 49 of the *Cork Report* (see esp. paras. 1909–1913).

In the first instance, the effect of the provisions contained in subss. (1)–(10) inclusive is that courts in the United Kingdom are required to enforce orders made by the courts of other United Kingdom jurisdictions in the exercise of jurisdiction in relation to insolvency law. Thus a complete intra-United Kingdom system of reciprocal enforcement is established in respect of bankruptcy, winding up, receivership and the administration order and voluntary arrangement procedures. Similarly, extended effect is given to orders made under the Company Directors Disqualification Act 1986. The provisions ensure that, where property exists in one jurisdiction of the United Kingdom but the insolvency proceedings are taking place in another, all such property can be protected and claimed for the benefit of the insolvent estate's creditors. Care has been taken in the drafting of the provisions however to avoid the anomalous and inelegant provision for automatic vesting of property in another jurisdiction, which was latterly a much-criticised aspect of the terms in which the Bankruptcy Act 1914 was drafted.

This section corresponds to s.213 of the 1985 Act.

Relevant country or territory

A further aspect of the provisions within this section is that they are so designed as to lend themselves to the creation of a framework for international legal co-operation in insolvency matters. This extension results from the inclusion in subs. (5) of reference to a request made to a court in any part of the United Kingdom by a court in "a relevant country or territory" as being a basis of authority for the requested court to provide the assistance referred to in subs. (4), and to apply, in relation to any matters specified in the request, the insolvency law which is applicable by *either* the requested court *or* the requesting court in relation to comparable matters falling within its jurisdiction. Express direction is also given to the requested court to have regard in particular to the rules of private international law. In the definition of "relevant country or territory" supplied by subs. (11) the possibility is established for the Secretary of State by statutory instrument to designate for the purposes of this section any country or territory with which satisfactory arrangements either already exist, or may be concluded in the future, for trans-jurisdictional co-operation in insolvency matters. Thus, not only should it be possible for designations to be accorded to those Commonwealth countries, and remaining colonial territories, with which arrangements have hitherto existed under s.122 of the Bankruptcy Act 1914 (repealed), but in due course an arrangement could be put into effect among the member states of the EEC, and with other states with which the United Kingdom has an established tradition of legal co-operation.

Parliamentary disqualification

427.—(1) Where a court in England and Wales or Northern Ireland adjudges an individual bankrupt or a court in Scotland awards sequestration of an individual's estate, the individual is disqualified—

   (*a*) for sitting or voting in the House of Lords,
   (*b*) for being elected to, or sitting or voting in, the House of Commons, and
   (*c*) for sitting or voting in a committee of either House.

(2) Where an individual is disqualified under this section, the disqualification ceases—

   (*a*) except where the adjudication is annulled or the award recalled or reduced without the individual having been first discharged, on the discharge of the individual, and
   (*b*) in the excepted case, on the annulment, recall or reduction, as the case may be.

(3) No writ of summons shall be issued to any lord of Parliament who is for the time being disqualified under this section for sitting and voting in the House of Lords.

(4) Where a member of the House of Commons who is disqualified under this section continues to be so disqualified until the end of the period of 6 months beginning with the day of the adjudication or award, his seat shall be vacated at the end of that period.

(5) A court which makes an adjudication or award such as is mentioned in subsection (1) in relation to any lord of Parliament or member of the

House of Commons shall forthwith certify the adjudication or award to the Speaker of the House of Lords or, as the case may be, to the Speaker of the House of Commons.

(6) Where a court has certified an adjudication or award to the Speaker of the House of Commons under subsection (5), then immediately after it becomes apparent which of the following certificates is applicable, the court shall certify to the Speaker of the House of Commons—

(*a*) that the period of 6 months beginning with the day of the adjudication or award has expired without the adjudication or award having been annulled, recalled or reduced, or

(*b*) that the adjudication or award has been annulled, recalled or reduced before the end of that period.

(7) Subject to the preceding provisions of this section, so much of this Act and any other enactment (whenever passed) and of any subordinate legislation (whenever made) as—

(*a*) makes provision for or in connection with bankruptcy in one or more parts of the United Kingdom, or

(*b*) makes provision conferring a power of arrest in connection with the winding up or insolvency of companies in one or more parts of the United Kingdom,

applies in relation to persons having privilege of Parliament or peerage as it applies in relation to persons not having such privilege.

DEFINITIONS
"annulled": s.282.
"bankrupt": s.381(1).
"discharge": ss.279–281 inclusive.

APPLICATION
This section applies to Northern Ireland (s.441(1)(*a*)).

GENERAL NOTE
This section provides for the disqualification of individuals made bankrupt in any part of the United Kingdom for sitting or voting in either House of Parliament and for being elected to the House of Commons; the disqualification continues until the bankruptcy is discharged or annulled. The section further provides for the notification of the bankruptcy of any Member of the House of Commons or Lord of Parliament to the Speaker of the relevant House, and also provides that parliamentary privilege shall not be invokable anywhere in the United Kingdom against the inception of personal insolvency proceedings or against the exercise of any powers of arrest conferred by the Act.

One notable alteration to the law effected by this provision is the removal of the long-standing discrepancy between Scots law and that of England and Wales with regard to the disqualification periods imposed where a Member of Parliament or Peer undergoes sequestration of his estate or is adjudicated bankrupt, as the case may be. In the case of bankruptcy declared in Scotland, a Peer or Member has long been eligible to be elected to, or to sit and vote in the House immediately upon discharge from bankruptcy. In England and Wales and in Northern Ireland a further period of five years' disqualification after the discharge from bankruptcy was formerly imposed upon all Members of either House, and also upon holders of other public offices, by virtue of the extant provisions of bankruptcy statutes of 1871, 1883 and 1890, all of which are repealed by Pt. IV of Sched. 10 to the 1985 Act. This accords with the recommendations in paras. 1849 and 1850 of the *Cork Report* where it is argued that civil rehabilitation of a bankrupt should be made fully effective from the date when his discharge from bankruptcy becomes effective.

This section corresponds to s.214 of the 1985 Act.

Exemptions from Restrictive Trade Practices Act

428.—(1) No restriction in respect of any of the matters specified in the next subsection shall, on or after the appointed day, be regarded as a restriction by virtue of which the Restrictive Trade Practices Act 1976 applies to any agreement (whenever made).

(2) Those matters are—
(*a*) the charges to be made, quoted or paid for insolvency services supplied, offered or obtained;
(*b*) the terms or conditions on or subject to which insolvency services are to be supplied or obtained;
(*c*) the extent (if any) to which, or the scale (if any) on which, insolvency services are to be made available, supplied or obtained;
(*d*) the form or manner in which insolvency services are to be made available, supplied or obtained;
(*e*) the persons or classes of persons for whom or from whom, or the areas or places in or from which, insolvency services are to be made available or supplied or are to be obtained.

(3) In this section "insolvency services" means the services of persons acting as insolvency practitioners or carrying out under the law of Northern Ireland functions corresponding to those mentioned in section 388(1) or (2) in Part XIII, in their capacity as such; and expressions which are also used in the Act of 1976 have the same meaning here as in that Act.

DEFINITIONS
"insolvency services": subs. (3).
"person acting as an insolvency practitioner": s.388.

APPLICATION
This section applies to Northern Ireland (s.441(1)(*a*)).

GENERAL NOTE
This section operates in relation to an amendment inserted in Sched. 1 to the Restrictive Trade Practices Act 1976 by s.217(4) of the 1985 Act, so that the provisions of the Restrictive Trade Practices Act do not apply to the provision of insolvency services under this Act.
This section corresponds to subss. (1)–(3) of s.217 of the 1985 Act.

Disabilities on revocation of administration order against an individual

429.—(1) The following applies where a person fails to make any payment which he is required to make by virtue of an administration order under Part VI of the County Courts Act 1984.
(2) The court which is administering that person's estate under the order may, if it thinks fit—
(*a*) revoke the administration order, and
(*b*) make an order directing that this section and section 12 of the Company Directors Disqualification Act 1986 shall apply to the person for such period, not exceeding 2 years, as may be specified in the order.
(3) A person to whom this section so applies shall not—
(*a*) either alone or jointly with another person, obtain credit to the extent of the amount prescribed for the purposes of section 360(1)(*a*) or more, or
(*b*) enter into any transaction in the course of or for the purposes of any business in which he is directly or indirectly engaged.
without disclosing to the person from whom he obtains the credit, or (as the case may be) with whom the transaction is entered into, the fact that this section applies to him.
(4) The reference in subsection (3) to a person obtaining credit includes—
(*a*) a case where goods are bailed or hired to him under a hire-purchase agreement or agreed to be sold to him under a conditional sale agreement, and
(*b*) a case where he is paid in advance (whether in money or otherwise) for the supply of goods or services.

(5) A person who contravenes this section is guilty of an offence and liable to imprisonment or a fine, or both.

DEFINITIONS
"administration order": County Courts Act 1984, s.112(2).
"business": s.436.
"obtaining credit": subs. (4).
"transaction": s.436.

APPLICATION
Subss. (1) and (2) of this section do not apply to Scotland (s.440(2)(c)).

GENERAL NOTE
This section makes provision for the imposition of several of the principal disabilities and disqualifications which apply to an undischarged bankrupt to be made applicable by order to a person who has been the subject of an administration order under the County Courts Act 1984 (Pt. VI). The order whereby these consequences are imposed upon an individual may be made by the court which has been administering the administration order if the court at its discretion decides to revoke that order. The provision is designed to counteract any attempt by a debtor to use the administration order procedure as a delaying tactic against creditors. This section replaces the provisions formerly contained in s.11 of the Insolvency Act 1976 (repealed).
This section corresponds to subss. (1) and (3)–(5) of s.221 of the 1985 Act.

Subss. (3), (4)
These provisions are drafted in terms substantially identical to those of s.360(1), (2) (*q.v.*).

Subs. (5)

Imprisonment or a fine
See Sched. 10 for the levels of punishment which may be imposed in respect of any offences committed under this section.

Provision introducing Schedule of punishments

430.—(1) Schedule 10 to this Act has effect with respect to the way in which offences under this Act are punishable on conviction.

(2) In relation to an offence under a provision of this Act specified in the first column of the Schedule (the general nature of the offence being described in the second column), the third column shows whether the offence is punishable on conviction on indictment, or on summary conviction, or either in the one way or the other.

(3) The fourth column of the Schedule shows, in relation to an offence, the maximum punishment by way of fine or imprisonment under this Act which may be imposed on a person convicted of the offence in the way specified in relation to it in the third column (that is to say, on indictment or summarily), a reference to a period of years or months being to a term of imprisonment of that duration.

(4) The fifth column shows (in relation to an offence for which there is an entry in that column) that a person convicted of the offence after continued contravention is liable to a daily default fine; that is to say, he is liable on a second or subsequent conviction of the offence to the fine specified in that column for each day on which the contravention is continued (instead of the penalty specified for the offence in the fourth column of the Schedule).

(5) For the purpose of any enactment in this Act whereby an officer of a company who is in default is liable to a fine or penalty, the expression "officer who is in default" means any officer of the company who knowingly and wilfully authorises or permits the default, refusal or contravention mentioned in the enactment.

DEFINITIONS
"daily default fine": subs. (4).
"officer of a company": s.251; Companies Act 1985, s.744.
"officer who is in default": subs. (5).

GENERAL NOTE
This section has the effect of causing the Schedule of punishments contained in Sched. 10 to be applicable to offences made punishable by the other provisions of the Act. The section further supplies guidance as to the manner in which the information contained in Sched. 10 is to be interpreted and applied.

This section corresponds to s.730 of the Companies Act and to the general purport of provisions throughout the Act of 1985 relating to offences and punishments.

Subs. (1)
This subsection states that the penalties for the various offences under this Act now are set out in table form in Sched. 10.

Subss. (2)–(4)
These subsections instruct the reader in the use of the table in Sched. 10. Basically it contains five columns which in order across the page state: (1) the section number creating the offence; (2) the general nature of the offence so created; (3) the mode of prosecution; (4) the maximum punishment corresponding with each mode of prosecution; and (5) the daily default fine (where it is applicable). The latter is explained further in subs. (4).

Subs. (4)
This subsection re-enacts what was s.730(4) of the Companies Act. It explains the term "default fine" wherever it appears throughout the Act and particularly in the fifth column of the table in Sched. 10. It is important because it establishes that for continuing offences under the Act a second or subsequent conviction makes the company (and officers when specified—see in particular s.432) liable to the default fine specified in the fifth column of Sched. 10 for each day the contravention continues and *not* for the penalty specified for the offence in column 4. The company and officers in default are not liable to both fines in those instances.

Subs. (5)
This subsection re-enacts what was s.440(2) of the Companies Act 1948. It defines the term "officer in default" wherever that appears in the Companies Acts as any officer who "knowingly and wilfully" authorises or permits what is prohibited by those provisions of the Acts. In criminal law terms the highest form of *mens rea* or guilty mind must be proved (*i.e.* intention as to consequence and knowledge as to circumstances) if a conviction is to be obtained. Proof of any lesser "state of mind" such as recklessness or negligence or inadvertence should not be sufficient.

See *Palmer*, para. 4–21.

Summary proceedings

431.—(1) Summary proceedings for any offence under any of Parts I to VII of this Act may (without prejudice to any jurisdiction exercisable apart from this subsection) be taken against a body corporate at any place at which the body has a place of business, and against any other person at any place at which he is for the time being.

(2) Notwithstanding anything in section 127(1) of the Magistrates' Courts Act 1980, an information relating to such an offence which is triable by a magistrates' court in England and Wales may be so tried if it is laid at any time within 3 years after the commission of the offence and within 12 months after the date on which evidence sufficient in the opinion of the Director of Public Prosecutions or the Secretary of State (as the case may be) to justify the proceedings comes to his knowledge.

(3) Summary proceedings in Scotland for such an offence shall not be commenced after the expiration of 3 years from the commission of the offence.

Subject to this (and notwithstanding anything in section 331 of the Criminal Procedure (Scotland) Act 1975), such proceedings may (in Scotland) be commenced at any time within 12 months after the date on which evidence sufficient in the Lord Advocate's opinion to justify the proceedings came to his knowledge or, where such evidence was reported to him by the Secretary of State, within 12 months after the date on which it came to the knowledge of the latter; and subsection (3) of that section applies for the purpose of this subsection as it applies for the purpose of that section.

(4) For purposes of this section, a certificate of the Director of Public Prosecutions, the Lord Advocate or the Secretary of State (as the case may be) as to the date on which such evidence as is referred to above came to his knowledge is conclusive evidence.

DEFINITIONS
"body corporate": s.251; Companies Act 1985, s.740.
"other person": s.432(2), (3).
"place of business": s.251; Companies Act 1985, s.744.

GENERAL NOTE
This section makes provision for the taking of summary proceedings for any offence committed under the provisions of Parts I–VII of the Act, and also prescribes how and where such proceedings are to take place.
This section corresponds to s.731 of the Companies Act and s.108(1) of the 1985 Act.

Subs. (1)
This subsection was s.49(2) of the Companies Act 1967. It states where summary proceedings may be taken against companies and other persons.

Subs. (2)
This subsection was s.49(3) of the 1967 Act. It states the time within which such proceedings must be commenced.

Subs. (3)
This subsection was s.49(4) of the 1967 Act. It states the position relating to the time for commencing such proceedings in Scotland.

Subs. (4)
This subsection was s.49(4) (1967) with the substitution therein of the Secretary of State in place of the Board of Trade as one of the certifying authorities. Note, from an administrative law point of view this subsection is of interest in that it purports to oust the jurisdiction of the court by declaring that the certificate of any of those three authorities is conclusive for purposes of ascertaining when the limitation period commenced to run.

Offences by bodies corporate

432.—(1) This section applies to offences under this Act other than those excepted by subsection (4).

(2) Where a body corporate is guilty of an offence to which this section applies and the offence is proved to have been committed with the consent or connivance of, or to be attributable to any neglect on the part of, any director, manager, secretary or other similar officer of the body corporate or any person who was purporting to act in any such capacity he, as well as the body corporate, is guilty of the offence and liable to be proceeded against and punished accordingly.

(3) Where the affairs of a body corporate are managed by its members, subsection (2) applies in relation to the acts and defaults of a member in connection with his functions of management as if he were a director of the body corporate.

(4) The offences excepted from this section are those under sections 30, 39, 51, 53, 54, 62, 64, 66, 85, 89, 164, 188, 201, 206, 207, 208, 209, 210 and 211.

DEFINITIONS
"body corporate": s.251; Companies Act 1985, s.740.
"director": s.251; Companies Act 1985, s.741.

GENERAL NOTE
This section makes provision for certain persons to be guilty of an offence under this Act, with the exception of offences under the sections listed in subs. (4), where a body corporate commits the offence with their consent or connivance or through their neglect.
This section corresponds to s.230 of the 1985 Act.

Admissibility in evidence of statements of affairs, etc.

433. In any proceedings (whether or not under this Act)—
   (*a*) a statement of affairs prepared for the purposes of any provision of this Act which is derived from the Insolvency Act 1985, and
   (*b*) any other statement made in pursuance of a requirement imposed by or under any such provision or by or under rules made under this Act,
may be used in evidence against any person making or concurring in making the statement.

GENERAL NOTE
This section makes provision for the admissibility in evidence of statements of affairs prepared for the purpose of any provision of the Act which is derived from the 1985 Act, and of any other statement made under a requirement imposed by the Act or by any subsidiary rules. This section largely re-enacts the provisions of s.663(3) of the Companies Act 1985 (repealed) and of the decision in *R.* v. *Pike* [1902] 1 K.B. 552, decided under the Bankruptcy Acts 1883–1890. The making of a statement of affairs may take place under the provisions of ss.22, 47, 66, 131 or 288.
This section corresponds to s.231 of the 1985 Act.

Crown application

434. For the avoidance of doubt it is hereby declared that provisions of this Act which derive from the Insolvency Act 1985 bind the Crown so far as affecting or relating to the following matters, namely—
   (*a*) remedies against, or against the property of, companies or individuals;
   (*b*) priorities of debts;
   (*c*) transactions at an undervalue or preferences;
   (*d*) voluntary arrangements approved under Part I or Part VIII, and
   (*e*) discharge from bankruptcy.

DEFINITIONS
"discharge from bankruptcy": ss.279–281.
"preference": ss.239(4) and 340(3).
"property": s.436.
"transaction at an undervalue": ss.238(4), 339(3), 423(1).
"voluntary arrangement": ss.1(2) (companies); 253(1) (individuals).

GENERAL NOTE
This contains the customary declaration, for the avoidance of doubt, that certain provisions of the Act bind the Crown. The provisions in question are those which derive from the Insolvency Act 1985. Provisions which derive from other legislation consolidated into the present Act will have been previously subject to the Crown application provisions of the statutes from which they are respectively derived.
This section corresponds to s.234 of the 1985 Act.

Part XVIII

Interpretation

Meaning of "associate"

435.—(1) For the purposes of this Act any question whether a person is an associate of another person is to be determined in accordance with the following provisions of this section (any provision that a person is an associate of another person being taken to mean that they are associates of each other).

(2) A person is an associate of an individual if that person is the individual's husband or wife, or is a relative, or the husband or wife of a relative, of the individual or of the individual's husband or wife.

(3) A person is an associate of any person with whom he is in partnership, and of the husband or wife or a relative of any individual with whom he is in partnership; and a Scottish firm is an associate of any person who is a member of the firm.

(4) A person is an associate of any person whom he employs or by whom he is employed.

(5) A person in his capacity as trustee of a trust other than—

(a) a trust arising under any of the second Group of Parts or the Bankruptcy (Scotland) Act 1985, or

(b) a pension scheme or an employees' share scheme (within the meaning of the Companies Act),

is an associate of another person if the beneficiaries of the trust include, or the terms of the trust confer a power that may be exercised for the benefit of, that other person or an associate of that other person.

(6) A company is an associate of another company—

(a) if the same person has control of both, or a person has control of one and persons who are his associates, or he and persons who are his associates, have control of the other, or

(b) if a group of two or more persons has control of each company, and the groups either consist of the same persons or could be regarded as consisting of the same persons by treating (in one or more cases) a member of either group as replaced by a person of whom he is an associate.

(7) A company is an associate of another person if that person has control of it or if that person and persons who are his associates together have control of it.

(8) For the purposes of this section a person is a relative of an individual if he is that individual's brother, sister, uncle, aunt, nephew, niece, lineal ancestor or lineal descendant, treating—

(a) any relationship of the half blood as a relationship of the whole blood and the stepchild or adopted child of any person as his child, and

(b) an illegitimate child as the legitimate child of his mother and reputed father;

and references in this section to a husband or wife include a former husband or wife and a reputed husband or wife.

(9) For the purposes of this section any director or other officer of a company is to be treated as employed by that company.

(10) For the purposes of this section a person is to be taken as having control of a company if—

(a) the directors of the company or of another company which has control of it (or any of them) are accustomed to act in accordance with his directions or instructions, or

(b) he is entitled to exercise, or control the exercise of, one third or

more of the voting power at any general meeting of the company
or of another company which has control of it;
and where two or more persons together satisfy either of the above
conditions, they are to be taken as having control of the company.

(11) In this section "company" includes any body corporate (whether
incorporated in Great Britain or elsewhere); and references to directors
and other officers of a company and to voting power at any general
meeting of a company have effect with any necessary modifications.

DEFINITIONS
"associate": this section.
"body corporate": s.251; Companies Act 1985, s.740.
"company": subs. (11).
"director": s.251; Companies Act 1985, s.741.
"modifications": s.436.
"officer": s.251; Companies Act 1985, s.744.

GENERAL NOTE
This elaborately drafted section supplies the statutory meaning of the word "associate"
where used in this Act. The section applies to Scotland, but doubts were expressed during
debate to the Insolvency Bill 1985 in the House of Lords whether the concept of "associate"
now embodied in this Act would cover all the cases formerly caught under Scots law by the
expression "conjunct or confident person" (*Hansard,* H.L. Vol. 459, cols. 1271–1272). *Cf.*
Chap. 21 of the *Cork Report,* entitled "Connected Persons."
This section corresponds to s.233 of the 1985 Act.

Expressions used generally

436. In this Act, except in so far as the context otherwise requires (and
subject to Parts VII and XI)—
"the appointed day" means the day on which this Act comes into
force under section 443;
"associate" has the meaning given by section 435;
"business" includes a trade or profession;
"the Companies Act" means the Companies Act 1985;
"conditional sale agreement" and "hire-purchase agreement" have
the same meanings as in the Consumer Credit Act 1974;
"modifications" includes additions, alterations and omissions and
cognate expressions shall be construed accordingly;
"property" includes money, goods, things in action, land and every
description of property wherever situated and also obligations
and every description of interest whether present or future or
vested or contingent, arising out of, or incidental to, property;
"records" includes computer records and other non-documentary
records;
"subordinate legislation" has the same meaning as in the Interpretation Act 1978; and
"transaction" includes a gift, agreement or arrangement, and references to entering into a transaction shall be construed
accordingly.

GENERAL NOTE
This is the definition section with respect to the entire Act, and supplies the statutory
meaning of terms and expressions which are used in a consistent sense throughout the Act.
Other definition sections, whose provisions are applicable only to a specific part of the Act,
are found at ss.247–251 and 380–385.
This section corresponds in part to s.232 of the 1985 Act.

Part XIX

Final Provisions

Transitional provisions and savings

437. The transitional provisions and savings set out in Schedule 11 to this Act shall have effect, the Schedule comprising the following Parts—

Part I: company insolvency and winding up (matters arising before appointed day, and continuance of proceedings in certain cases as before that day);

Part II: individual insolvency (matters so arising, and continuance of bankruptcy proceedings in certain cases as before that day);

Part III: transactions entered into before the appointed day and capable of being affected by orders of the court under Part XVI of this Act;

Part IV: insolvency practitioners acting as such before the appointed day; and

Part V: general transitional provisions and savings required consequentially on, and in connection with, the repeal and replacement by this Act and the Company Directors Disqualification Act 1986 of provisions of the Companies Act, the greater part of the Insolvency Act 1985 and other enactments.

Definitions
"appointed day": s.443.
"insolvency practitioners": s.288.

General Note
This section, which has no identical counterpart in either the 1985 Act or the Companies Act, gives effect to the transitional provisions and savings set out in Sched. 11. It also explains the general structure of that Schedule, which is subdivided into five parts.

Repeals

438. The enactments specified in the second column of Schedule 12 to this Act are repealed to the extent specified in the third column of that Schedule.

General Note
This section, which has no idential counterpart in either the 1985 Act or the Companies Act, gives effect to the repeals listed in Sched. 12. In addition to effecting the repeal of most of the provisions of the 1985 Act (apart from those provisions which are to be repealed by the separate provisions of the Company Directors Disqualification Act 1986), this section together with Sched. 12 effects the repeal of s.235(3) of, and Sched. 10 to, the 1985 Act. However, before the present Act, and its repealing provisions, enter into force by virtue of s.443, the repeals of other legislation which take place under Sched. 10 to the 1985 Act will already have been accomplished through the bringing into force of that Schedule by means of commencement orders made under s.236(2) of the 1985 Act.

Amendments of enactments

439.—(1) The Companies Act is amended as shown in Parts I and II of Schedule 13 to this Act, being amendments consequential on this Act and the Company Directors Disqualification Act 1986.

(2) The enactments specified in the first column of Schedule 14 to this Act (being enactments which refer, or otherwise relate, to those which are repealed and replaced by this Act or the Company Directors Disqualification Act 1986) are amended as shown in the second column of that Schedule.

(3) The Lord Chancellor may by order make such consequential
modifications of any provision contained in any subordinate legislation
made before the appointed day and such transitional provisions in connection with those modifications as appear to him necessary or expedient
in respect of—

(a) any reference in that subordinate legislation to the Bankruptcy Act
   1914;

(b) any reference in that subordinate legislation to any enactment
   repealed by Part III or IV of Schedule 10 to the Insolvency Act
   1985; or

(c) any reference in that subordinate legislation to any matter provided
   for under the Act of 1914 or under any enactment so repealed.

(4) An order under this section shall be made by statutory instrument
subject to annulment in pursuance of a resolution of either House of
Parliament.

DEFINITIONS
   "appointed day": s.443.
   "modification": s.436.

GENERAL NOTE
   This section, which has no identical counterpart in either the 1985 Act or the Companies
Act, gives effect to the amendments to the Companies Act which are contained in Sched.
13. These amendments are consequential on the provisions of this Act and those of the
Company Directors Disqualification Act 1986. Power is also conferred upon the Lord
Chancellor, under subs. (3), to make consequential modifications of any subordinate
legislation made before the day on which this Act enters into force. Any order so made by
the Lord Chancellor is, by virtue of subs. (4), subject to the "negative" procedure for
annulment by resolution of either House of Parliament.

Extent (Scotland)

440.—(1) Subject to the next subsection, provisions of this Act contained in the first Group of Parts extend to Scotland except where
otherwise stated.

(2) The following provisions of this Act do not extend to Scotland—

(a) in the first Group of Parts—
      section 43;
      sections 238 to 241; and
      section 246;

(b) the second Group of Parts;

(c) in the third Group of Parts—
      sections 399 to 402,
      sections 412, 413, 415, 418, 420 and 421,
      sections 423 to 425, and
      section 429(1) and (2); and

(d) in the Schedules—
      Parts II and III of Schedule 11; and
      Schedules 12 and 14 so far as they repeal or amend enactments
      which extend to England and Wales only.

GENERAL NOTE
   This section indicates which sections or Parts of this Act do, and which do not, extend to
Scotland. The section corresponds to s.236(3) of the 1985 Act.

Subss. (1), (2)(a)
   These provide that all provisions in Parts I–VII apply to Scotland, with the exception of
the provisions contained in ss.43, 238–241 and 246. However, in s.28 it is provided that
Chap. I of Pt. III does not apply to receivers appointed under Chap. II of the same Part.

Subs. (2)(b)

This provides that none of the provisions in Parts VIII–XI extend to Scotland.

Subs. (2)(c), (d)

These provide that the specified sections within Parts XII–XIX and the specified Parts or provisions of Scheds. 11 and 12 do not extend to Scotland.

Extent (Northern Ireland)

441.—(1) The following provisions of this Act extend to Northern Ireland—

(*a*) sections 197, 426, 427 and 428; and

(*b*) so much of section 439 and Schedule 14 as relates to enactments which extend to Northern Ireland.

(2) Subject as above, and to any provision expressly relating to companies incorporated elsewhere than in Great Britain, nothing in this Act extends to Northern Ireland or applies to or in relation to companies registered or incorporated in Northern Ireland.

GENERAL NOTE

This section has the effect that nothing in the Act, with the exception of the provisions mentioned in subs. (1), extends to Northern Ireland or applies to or in relation to companies registered or incorporated there. The section corresponds to s.236(4) of the 1985 Act and s.745 of the Companies Act.

Extent (other territories)

442. Her Majesty may, by Order in Council, direct that such of the provisions of this Act as are specified in the Order, being provisions formerly contained in the Insolvency Act 1985, shall extend to any of the Channel Islands or any colony with such modifications as may be so specified.

DEFINITION

"modifications": s.436.

GENERAL NOTE

This section makes provision for the extended application of certain provisions of this Act to any of the Channel Islands or any colony. This power is exercisable by the Queen by means of an Order in Council, and may be made in respect of any provisions now contained in this Act which were formerly contained in the 1985 Act.

Commencement

443. This Act comes into force on the day appointed under section 236(2) of the Insolvency Act 1985 for the coming into force of Part III of that Act (individual insolvency and bankruptcy), immediately after that Part of that Act comes into force for England and Wales.

GENERAL NOTE

This section, which has no exact counterpart in the 1985 Act, provides for the commencement of the Act. The provision is somewhat unusual in that it provides for the Act as a whole to come into force on a day to be appointed in relation to the commencement of a specified Part of another Act, namely Part III of the 1985 Act. The technique thus employed will ensure that this Act enters into force at the earliest practicable date, which is a matter essentially dependent upon the completion of the entire range of subordinate legislation which will operate in conjunction with the new insolvency law provisions contained in this Act. The 1985 Act has served as an indispensable adjunct to the process of preparation of the various new Rules, Orders and Regulations, but for the most part their actual operation will take place under the aegis of the Insolvency Act 1986. Accordingly, the setting of an appointed day under s.236(2) of the 1985 Act with regard to Part III of that Act will enable the 1985 Act itself to come fully into force, albeit briefly, whereupon the 1986 Act will displace it by virtue of the provisions in this section, in conjunction with the repealing provisions within s.438 and Sched. 12 (*q.v.*).

Citation

444. This Act may be cited as the Insolvency Act 1986.

GENERAL NOTE

This section provides for the citation of the Act.

SCHEDULES

SCHEDULE 1

POWERS OF ADMINISTRATOR OR ADMINISTRATIVE RECEIVER

1. Power to take possession of, collect and get in the property of the company and, for that purpose, to take such proceedings as may seem to him expedient.
2. Power to sell or otherwise dispose of the property of the company by public auction or private contract or, in Scotland, to sell, feu, hire out or otherwise dispose of the property of the company by public roup or private bargain.
3. Power to raise or borrow money and grant security therefor over the property of the company.
4. Power to appoint a solicitor or accountant or other professionally qualified person to assist him in the performance of his functions.
5. Power to bring or defend any action or other legal proceedings in the name and on behalf of the company.
6. Power to refer to arbitration any question affecting the company.
7. Power to effect and maintain insurances in respect of the business and property of the company.
8. Power to use the company's seal.
9. Power to do all acts and to execute in the name and on behalf of the company any deed, receipt or other document.
10. Power to draw, accept, make and endorse any bill of exchange or promissory note in the name and on behalf of the company.
11. Power to appoint any agent to do any business which he is unable to do himself or which can more conveniently be done by an agent and power to employ and dismiss employees.
12. Power to do all such things (including the carrying out of works) as may be necessary for the realisation of the property of the company.
13. Power to make any payment which is necessary or incidental to the performance of his functions.
14. Power to carry on the business of the company.
15. Power to establish subsidiaries of the company.
16. Power to transfer to subsidiaries of the company the whole or any part of the business and property of the company.
17. Power to grant or accept a surrender of a lease or tenancy of any of the property of the company, and to take a lease or tenancy of any property required or convenient for the business of the company.
18. Power to make any arrangement or compromise on behalf of the company.
19. Power to call up any uncalled capital of the company.
20. Power to rank and claim in the bankruptcy, insolvency, sequestration or liquidation of any person indebted to the company and to receive dividends, and to accede to trust deeds for the creditors of any such person.
21. Power to present or defend a petition for the winding up of the company.
22. Power to change the situation of the company's registered office.
23. Power to do all other things incidental to the exercise of the foregoing powers.

GENERAL NOTE

This Schedule is linked to ss.14 and 42, which are respectively concerned with the powers of administrators and administrative receivers. A common table of provisions is thus enacted to define the powers which are conferred upon persons holding either of these offices under this Act. This is an appropriate, and a somewhat symbolic, way of acknowledging the fact that the office of administrator has been inspired by, and created as an analogy to, that of the administrative receiver when operated in an enlightened and even an altruistic manner.

This Schedule corresponds to Sched 3 to the 1985 Act.

Section 55   SCHEDULE 2

Powers of a Scottish Receiver (Additional to Those Conferred on him by the Instrument of Charge)

1. Power to take possession of, collect and get in the property from the company or a liquidator thereof or any other person, and for that purpose, to take such proceedings as may seem to him expedient.

2. Power to sell, feu, hire out or otherwise dispose of the property by public roup or private bargain and with or without advertisement.

3. Power to raise or borrow money and grant security therefor over the property.

4. Power to appoint a solicitor or accountant or other professionally qualified person to assist him in the performance of his functions.

5. Power to bring or defend any action or other legal proceedings in the name and on behalf of the company.

6. Power to refer to arbitration all questions affecting the company.

7. Power to effect and maintain insurances in respect of the business and property of the company.

8. Power to use the company's seal.

9. Power to do all acts and to execute in the name and on behalf of the company any deed, receipt or other document.

10. Power to draw, accept, make and endorse any bill of exchange or promissory note in the name and on behalf of the company.

11. Power to appoint any agent to do any business which he is unable to do himself or which can more conveniently be done by an agent, and power to employ and dismiss employees.

12. Power to do all such things (including the carrying out of works), as may be necessary for the realisation of the property.

13. Power to make any payment which is necessary or incidental to the performance of his functions.

14. Power to carry on the business of the company or any part of it.

15. Power to grant or accept a surrender of a lease or tenancy of any of the property, and to take a lease or tenancy of any property required or convenient for the business of the company.

16. Power to make any arrangement or compromise on behalf of the company.

17. Power to call up any uncalled capital of the company.

18. Power to establish subsidiaries of the company.

19. Power to transfer to subsidiaries of the company the business of the company or any part of it and any of the property.

20. Power to rank and claim in the bankruptcy, insolvency, sequestration or liquidation of any person or company indebted to the company and to receive dividends, and to accede to trust deeds for creditors of any such person.

21. Power to present or defend a petition for the winding up of the company.

22. Power to change the situation of the company's registered office.

23. Power to do all other things incidental to the exercise of the powers mentioned in section 55(1) of this Act or above in this Schedule.

General Note

This Schedule is linked to s.55, which is concerned with the powers of a receiver appointed under a floating charge in Scotland. The list of powers corresponds to that formerly contained in s.471(1) of the Companies Act, as amended by s.57 of the 1985 Act.

SCHEDULE 3

ORDERS IN COURSE OF WINDING UP PRONOUNCED IN VACATION (SCOTLAND)

PART I

ORDERS WHICH ARE TO BE FINAL

Orders under section 153, as to the time for proving debts and claims.

Orders under section 195 as to meetings for ascertaining wishes of creditors or contributories.

Orders under section 198, as to the examination of witnesses in regard to the property or affairs of a company.

Part II

ORDERS WHICH ARE TO TAKE EFFECT UNTIL MATTER DISPOSED OF BY INNER HOUSE

Orders under section 126(1), 130(2) or (3) 147, 227 or 228, restraining or permitting the commencement or the continuance of legal proceedings.

Orders under section 135(5), limiting the powers of provisional liquidators.

Orders under section 108, appointing a liquidator to fill a vacancy.

Orders under section 167 or 169, sanctioning the exercise of any powers by a liquidator, other than the powers specified in paragraphs 1, 2 and 3 of Schedule 4 to this Act.

Orders under section 158, as to the arrest and detention of an absconding contributory and his property.

GENERAL NOTE

This Schedule corresponds to Sched. 16 to the Companies Act. It operates in conjunction with s.162, which governs appeals from orders in Scotland, and has the effect of indicating which orders of the vacation judge are to be final, and which are to take effect until the matter has been submitted to review by the Inner House and the matter there disposed of.

SCHEDULE 4

POWERS OF LIQUIDATOR IN A WINDING UP

PART I

POWERS EXERCISABLE WITH SANCTION

1. Power to pay any class of creditors in full.

2. Power to make any compromise or arrangement with creditors or persons claiming to be creditors, or having or alleging themselves to have any claim (present or future, certain or contingent, ascertained or sounding only in damages) against the company, or whereby the company may be rendered liable.

3. Power to compromise, on such terms as may be agreed—
   (a) all calls and liabilities to calls, all debts and liabilities capable of resulting in debts, and all claims (present or future, certain or contingent, ascertained or sounding only in damages) subsisting or supposed to subsist between the company and a contributory or alleged contributory or other debtor or person apprehending liability to the company, and
   (b) all questions in any way relating to or affecting the assets or the winding up of the company,
and take any security for the discharge of any such call, debt, liability or claim and give a complete discharge in respect of it.

Part II

Powers Exercisable Without Sanction in Voluntary Winding Up, with Sanction in Winding Up by the Court

4. Power to bring or defend any action or other legal proceeding in the name and on behalf of the company.

5. Power to carry on the business of the company so far as may be necessary for its beneficial winding up.

Part III

Powers Exercisable Without Sanction in any Winding Up

6. Power to sell any of the company's property by public auction or private contract, with power to transfer the whole of it to any person or to sell the same in parcels.

7. Power to do all acts and execute, in the name and on behalf of the company, all deeds, receipts and other documents and for that purpose to use, when necessary, the company's seal.

8. Power to prove, rank and claim in the bankruptcy, insolvency or sequestration of any contributory for any balance against his estate, and to receive dividends in the bankruptcy, insolvency or sequestration in respect of that balance, as a separate debt due from the bankrupt or insolvent, and rateably with the other separate creditors.

9. Power to draw, accept, make and indorse any bill of exchange or promissory note in the name and on behalf of the company, with the same effect with respect to the company's liability as if the bill or note had been drawn, accepted, made or indorsed by or on behalf of the company in the course of its business.

10. Power to raise on the security of the assets of the company any money requisite.

11. Power to take out in his official name letters of administration to any deceased contributory, and to do in his official name any other act necessary for obtaining payment of any money due from a contributory or his estate which cannot conveniently be done in the name of the company.

In all such cases the money due is deemed, for the purpose of enabling the liquidator to take out the letters of administration or recover the money, to be due to the liquidator himself.

12. Power to appoint an agent to do any business which the liquidator is unable to do himself.

13. Power to do all such other things as may be necessary for winding up the company's affairs and distributing its assets.

General Note

This Schedule operates in conjunction with ss.165 and 167, which refer to the powers of a liquidator in a voluntary and in a compulsory winding up respectively. Pt. I of the Schedule assimilates the provisions formerly contained in ss.539(*d*)–(*f*) and 598(1); Pt. II those formerly contained in ss.539(1)(*a*),(*b*) and 598(2); and Pt. III those formerly contained in ss.539(2) and 598(2) of the Companies Act. The three Parts of the Schedule now set out in a convenient form, and with greatly improved clarity, the powers exercisable by a liquidator with or without sanction (as defined in ss.165, 166 and 167 respectively) under the different forms of winding up.

Section 314   SCHEDULE 5

Powers of Trustee in Bankruptcy

Part I

Powers Exercisable with Sanction

1. Power to carry on any business of the bankrupt so far as may be necessary for winding it up beneficially and so far as the trustee is able to do so without contravening any requirement imposed by or under any enactment.

2. Power to bring, institute or defend any action or legal proceedings relating to the property comprised in the bankrupt's estate.

3. Power to accept as the consideration for the sale of any property comprised in the bankrupt's estate a sum of money payable at a future time subject to such stipulations as to security or otherwise as the creditors' committee or the court thinks fit.

4. Power to mortgage or pledge any part of the property comprised in the bankrupt's estate for the purpose of raising money for the payment of his debts.

5. Power, where any right, option or other power forms part of the bankrupt's estate, to make payments or incur liabilities with a view to obtaining, for the benefit of the creditors, any property which is the subject of the right, option or power.

6. Power to refer to arbitration, or compromise on such terms as may be agreed on, any debts, claims or liabilities subsisting or supposed to subsist between the bankrupt and any person who may have incurred any liability to the bankrupt.

7. Power to make such compromise or other arrangement as may be thought expedient with creditors, or persons claiming to be creditors, in respect of bankruptcy debts.

8. Power to make such compromise or other arrangement as may be thought expedient with respect to any claim arising out of or incidental to the bankrupt's estate made or capable of being made on the trustee by any person or by the trustee on any person.

PART II

GENERAL POWERS

9. Power to sell any part of the property for the time being comprised in the bankrupt's estate, including the goodwill and book debts of any business.

10. Power to give receipts for any money received by him, being receipts which effectually discharge the person paying the money from all responsibility in respect of its application.

11. Power to prove, rank, claim and draw a dividend in respect of such debts due to the bankrupt as are comprised in his estate.

12. Power to exercise in relation to any property comprised in the bankrupt's estate any powers the capacity to exercise which is vested in him under Parts VIII to XI of this Act.

13. Power to deal with any property comprised in the estate to which the bankrupt is beneficially entitled as tenant in tail in the same manner as the bankrupt might have dealt with it.

PART III

ANCILLARY POWERS

14. For the purposes of, or in connection with, the exercise of any of his powers under Parts VIII to XI of this Act, the trustee may, by his official name—
(a) hold property of every description,
(b) make contracts,
(c) sue and be sued,
(d) enter into engagements binding on himself and, in respect of the bankrupt's estate, on his successors in office,
(e) employ an agent,
(f) execute any power of attorney, deed or other instrument;
and he may do any other act which is necessary or expedient for the purposes of or in connection with the exercise of those powers.

GENERAL NOTE
This Schedule operates in conjunction with s.314, which refers to the powers of a trustee in bankruptcy. Pt. I of the Schedule assimilates the provisions of s.160(2), Pt. II those of s.160(1), and Pt. III those of s.160(6) of the 1985 Act. The three Parts together indicate which powers are exercisable by the trustee with sanction (*i.e.* with the permission of the creditors' committee if there is one, or otherwise with the permission of the court: s.314(1)(*a*)) and which are exercisable on the trustee's own initiative without that permission (s.314(1)(*b*)).

SCHEDULE 6

THE CATEGORIES OF PREFERENTIAL DEBTS

Category 1: Debts due to Inland Revenue

1. Sums due at the relevant date from the debtor on account of deductions of income tax from emoluments paid during the period of 12 months next before that date.

The deductions here referred to are those which the debtor was liable to make under section 204 of the Income and Corporation Taxes Act 1970 (pay as you earn), less the amount of the repayments of income tax which the debtor was liable to make during that period.

2. Sums due at the relevant date from the debtor in respect of such deductions as are required to be made by the debtor for that period under section 69 of the Finance (No. 2) Act 1975 (sub-contractors in the construction industry).

Category 2: Debts due to Customs and Excise

3. Any value added tax which is referable to the period of 6 months next before the relevant date (which period is referred to below as "the 6-month period").

For the purposes of this paragraph—

(*a*) where the whole of the prescribed accounting period to which any value added tax is attributable falls within the 6-month period, the whole amount of that tax is referable to that period; and

(*b*) in any other case the amount of any value added tax which is referable to the 6-month period is the proportion of the tax which is equal to such proportion (if any) of the accounting reference period in question as falls within the 6-month period;

and in sub-paragraph (*a*) "prescribed" means prescribed by regulations under the Value Added Tax Act 1983.

4. The amount of any car tax which is due at the relevant date from the debtor and which became due within a period of 12 months next before that date.

5. Any amount which is due—

(*a*) by way of general betting duty or bingo duty, or

(*b*) under section 12(1) of the Betting and Gaming Duties Act 1981 (general betting duty and pool betting duty recoverable from agent collecting stakes), or

(*c*) under section 14 of, or Schedule 2 to, that Act (gaming licence duty),

from the debtor at the relevant date and which became due within the period of 12 months next before that date.

Category 3: Social security contributions

6. All sums which on the relevant date are due from the debtor on account of Class 1 or Class 2 contributions under the Social Security Act 1975 or the Social Security (Northern Ireland) Act 1975 and which became due from the debtor in the 12 months next before the relevant date.

7. All sums which on the relevant date have been assessed on and are due from the debtor on account of Class 4 contributions under either of those Acts of 1975, being sums which—

(*a*) are due to the Commissioners of Inland Revenue (rather than to the Secretary of State or a Northern Ireland department), and

(*b*) are assessed on the debtor up to 5th April next before the relevant date,

but not exceeding, in the whole, any one year's assessment.

Category 4: Contributions to occupational pension schemes, etc.

8. Any sum which is owed by the debtor and is a sum to which Schedule 3 to the Social Security Pensions Act 1975 applies (contributions to occupational pension schemes and state scheme premiums).

Category 5: Remuneration, etc., of employees

9. So much of any amount which—

(a) is owed by the debtor to a person who is or has been an employee of the debtor, and

(b) is payable by way of remuneration in respect of the whole or any part of the period of 4 months next before the relevant date,

as does not exceed so much as may be prescribed by order made by the Secretary of State.

10. An amount owed by way of accrued holiday remuneration, in respect of any period of employment before the relevant date, to a person whose employment by the debtor has been terminated, whether before, on or after that date.

11. So much of any sum owed in respect of money advanced for the purpose as has been applied for the payment of a debt which, if it had not been paid, would have been a debt falling within paragraph 9 or 10.

12. So much of any amount which—

(a) is ordered (whether before or after the relevant date) to be paid by the debtor under the Reserve Forces (Safeguard of Employment) Act 1985, and

(b) is so ordered in respect of a default made by the debtor before that date in the discharge of his obligations under that Act,

as does not exceed such amount as may be prescribed by order made by the Secretary of State.

Interpretation for Category 5

13.—(1) For the purposes of paragraphs 9 to 12, a sum is payable by the debtor to a person by way of remuneration in respect of any period if—

(a) it is paid as wages or salary (whether payable for time or for piece work or earned wholly or partly by way of commission) in respect of services rendered to the debtor in that period, or

(b) it is an amount falling within the following sub-paragraph and is payable by the debtor in respect of that period.

(2) An amount falls within this sub-paragraph if it is—

(a) a guarantee payment under section 12(1) of the Employment Protection (Consolidation) Act 1978 (employee without work to do for a day or part of a day);

(b) remuneration on suspension on medical grounds under section 19 of that Act;

(c) any payment for time off under section 27(3) (trade union duties), 31(3) (looking for work, etc.) or 31A(4) (ante-natal care) of that Act; or

(d) remuneration under a protective award made by an industrial tribunal under section 101 of the Employment Protection Act 1975 (redundancy dismissal with compensation).

14.—(1) This paragraph relates to a case in which a person's employment has been terminated by or in consequence of his employer going into liquidation or being adjudged bankrupt or (his employer being a company not in liquidation) by or in consequence of—

(a) a receiver being appointed as mentioned in section 40 of this Act (debenture-holders secured by floating charge), or

(b) the appointment of a receiver under section 53(6) or 54(5) of this Act (Scottish company with property subject to floating charge), or

(c) the taking of possession by debenture-holders (so secured), as mentioned in section 196 of the Companies Act.

(2) For the purposes of paragraphs 9 to 12, holiday remuneration is deemed to have accrued to that person in respect of any period of employment if, by virtue of his contract of employment or of any enactment that remuneration would have accrued in respect of that period if his employment had continued until he became entitled to be allowed the holiday.

(3) The reference in sub-paragraph (2) to any enactment includes an order or direction made under an enactment.

15. Without prejudice to paragraphs 13 and 14—

(a) any remuneration payable by the debtor to a person in respect of a period of holiday or of absence from work through sickness or other good cause is deemed to be wages or (as the case may be) salary in respect of services rendered to the debtor in that period, and

(b) references here and in those paragraphs to remuneration in respect of a period of holiday include any sums which, if they had been paid, would have been treated for the purposes of the enactments relating to social security as earnings in respect of that period.

Orders

16. An order under paragraph 9 or 12—
   (*a*) may contain such transitional provisions as may appear to the Secretary of State necessary or expedient;
   (*b*) shall be made by statutory instrument subject to annulment in pursuance of a resolution of either House of Parliament.

DEFINITIONS

"accrued holiday remuneration": para. 14.
"preferential debt","preferential creditor": s.386(1).
"prescribed": paras. 3, 9, 12.
"remuneration in respect of a period of holiday": para. 15.
"the debtor": s.386(2).
"the relevant date": s.387.
"sum payable by way of remuneration in respect of a period": para. 13.

GENERAL NOTE

This Schedule, which operates in conjunction with s.386, provides a list of preferential debts applicable on a common basis in winding up and in bankruptcy, and incorporated into the workings of Pts. IV and IX of the Act respectively by means of the provisions of ss.175 and 328. For details of the significant changes in the categories of debts which now are accorded preferential status in insolvency proceedings, see the General Notes to the two sections referred to, especially the former. Paras. 13–15 supply the definitions of various words or expressions for the purposes of the Schedule.

This Schedule corresponds to Pt. I, and paras. 2–4 of Pt. II, of Sched. 4 to the 1985 Act.

Section 396   SCHEDULE 7

INSOLVENCY PRACTITIONERS TRIBUNAL

Panels of members

1.—(1) The Secretary of State shall draw up and from time to time revise—
   (*a*) a panel of persons who are barristers, advocates or solicitors, in each case of not less than 7 years' standing, and are nominated for the purpose by the Lord Chancellor or the Lord President of the Court of Session, and
   (*b*) a panel of persons who are experienced in insolvency matters;
and the members of the Tribunal shall be selected from those panels in accordance with this Schedule.

(2) The power to revise the panels includes power to terminate a person's membership of either of them, and is accordingly to that extent subject to section 8 of the Tribunals and Inquiries Act 1971 (which makes it necessary to obtain the concurrence of the Lord Chancellor and the Lord President of the Court of Session to dismissals in certain cases).

Remuneration of members

2. The Secretary of State may out of money provided by Parliament pay to members of the Tribunal such remuneration as he may with the approval of the Treasury determine; and such expenses of the Tribunal as the Secretary of State and the Treasury may approve shall be defrayed by the Secretary of State out of money so provided.

Sittings of Tribunal

3.—(1) For the purposes of carrying out their functions in relation to any cases referred to them, the Tribunal may sit either as a single tribunal or in two or more divisions.

(2) The functions of the Tribunal in relation to any case referred to them shall be exercised by three members consisting of—

(*a*) a chairman selected by the Secretary of State from the panel drawn up under paragraph 1(1)(*a*) above, and

(*b*) two other members selected by the Secretary of State from the panel drawn up under paragraph 1(1)(*b*).

Procedure of Tribunal

4.—(1) Any investigation by the Tribunal shall be so conducted as to afford a reasonable opportunity for representations to be made to the Tribunal by or on behalf of the person whose case is the subject of the investigation.

(2) For the purposes of any such investigation, the Tribunal—

(*a*) may by summons require any person to attend, at such time and place as is specified in the summons, to give evidence or to produce any books, papers and other records in his possession or under his control which the Tribunal consider it necessary for the purposes of the investigation to examine, and

(*b*) may take evidence on oath, and for the purpose administer oaths, or may, instead of administering an oath, require the person examined to make and subscribe a declaration of the truth of the matter respecting which he is examined;

but no person shall be required, in obedience to such a summons, to go more than ten miles from his place of residence, unless the necessary expenses of his attendance are paid or tendered to him.

(3) Every person who—

(*a*) without reasonable excuse fails to attend in obedience to a summons issued under this paragraph, or refuses to give evidence, or

(*b*) intentionally alters, suppresses, conceals or destroys or refuses to produce any document which he may be required to produce for the purpose of an investigation by the Tribunal,

is liable to a fine.

(4) Subject to the provisions of this paragraph, the Secretary of State may make rules for regulating the procedure on any investigation by the Tribunal.

(5) In their application to Scotland, sub-paragraphs (2) and (3) above have effect as if for any reference to a summons there were substituted a reference to a notice in writing.

GENERAL NOTE

This Schedule, which operates in conjunction with s.396, deals with the composition, functions and procedures of the Insolvency Practitioners Tribunal, whose purpose is to consider and determine appeals which are referred to it under s.396 in cases where an applicant for, or holder of, an authorisation to practice as an insolvency practitioner has been notified that the relevant authority proposes to refuse the application, or to withdraw the authorisation, as the case may be.

Although the Schedule contains rules which govern the procedure of the Tribunal in performing its investigative function, provision is made in para. 4(4) for the Secretary of State to make additional rules for regulating this procedure.

This Schedule corresponds to paras. 1–4 of Sched. 1 to the 1985 Act.

Section 411 SCHEDULE 8

PROVISIONS CAPABLE OF INCLUSION IN COMPANY INSOLVENCY RULES

Courts

1. Provision for supplementing, in relation to the insolvency or winding up of companies, any provision made by or under section 117 of this Act (jurisdiction in relation to winding up).

2. Provision for regulating the practice and procedure of any court exercising jurisdiction for the purposes of Parts I to VII of this Act or the Companies Act so far as relating to, and to matters connected with or arising out of, the insolvency or winding up of companies, being any provision that could be made by rules of court.

Notices, etc.

3. Provision requiring notice of any proceedings in connection with or arising out of the insolvency or winding up of a company to be given or published in the manner prescribed by the rules.

4. Provision with respect to the form, manner of serving, contents and proof of any petition, application, order, notice, statement or other document required to be presented, made, given, published or prepared under any enactment or subordinate legislation relating to, or to matters connected with or arising out of, the insolvency or winding up of companies.

5. Provision specifying the persons to whom any notice is to be given.

Registration of voluntary arrangements

6. Provision for the registration of voluntary arrangements approved under Part I of this Act, including provision for the keeping and inspection of a register.

Provisional liquidator

7. Provision as to the manner in which a provisional liquidator appointed under section 135 is to carry out his functions.

Conduct of insolvency

8. Provision with respect to the certification of any person as, and as to the proof that a person is, the liquidator, administrator or administrative receiver of a company.

9. The following provisions with respect to meetings of a company's creditors, contributories or members—

(*a*) provision as to the manner of summoning a meeting (including provision as to how any power to require a meeting is to be exercised, provision as to the manner of determining the value of any debt or contribution for the purposes of any such power and provision making the exercise of any such power subject to the deposit of a sum sufficient to cover the expenses likely to be incurred in summoning and holding a meeting);

(*b*) provision specifying the time and place at which a meeting may be held and the period of notice required for a meeting;

(*c*) provision as to the procedure to be followed at a meeting (including the manner in which decisions may be reached by a meeting and the manner in which the value of any vote at a meeting is to be determined);

(*d*) provision for requiring a person who is or has been an officer of the company to attend a meeting;

(*e*) provision creating, in the prescribed circumstances, a presumption that a meeting has been duly summoned and held;

(*f*) provision as to the manner of proving the decisions of a meeting.

10.—(1) Provision as to the functions, membership and proceedings of a committee established under section 26, 49, 68, 101, 141 or 142 of this Act.

(2) The following provisions with respect to the establishment of a committee under section 101, 141 or 142 of this Act, that is to say—

(*a*) provision for resolving differences between a meeting of the company's creditors and a meeting of its contributories or members;

(*b*) provision authorising the establishment of the committee without a meeting of contributories in a case where a company is being wound up on grounds including its inability to pay its debts; and

(*c*) provision modifying the requirements of this Act with respect to the establishment of the committee in a case where a winding-up order has been made immediately upon the discharge of an administration order.

11. Provision as to the manner in which any requirement that may be imposed on a person under any of Parts I to VII of this Act by the official receiver, the liquidator, administrator or administrative receiver of a company or a special manager appointed under section 177 is to be so imposed.

12. Provision as to the debts that may be proved in a winding up, as to the manner and conditions of proving a debt and as to the manner and expenses of establishing the value of any debt or security.

13. Provision with respect to the manner of the distribution of the property of a company that is being wound up, including provision with respect to unclaimed funds and dividends.

14. Provision which, with or without modifications, applies in relation to the winding up of companies any enactment contained in Parts VIII to XI of this Act or in the Bankruptcy (Scotland) Act 1985.

Financial provisions

15. Provision as to the amount, or manner of determining the amount, payable to the liquidator, administrator or administrative receiver of a company or a special manager appointed under section 177, by way of remuneration for the carrying out of functions in connection with or arising out of the insolvency or winding up of a company.

16. Provision with respect to the manner in which moneys received by the liquidator of a company in the course of carrying out his functions as such are to be invested or otherwise handled and with respect to the payment of interest on sums which, in pursuance of rules made by virtue of this paragraph, have been paid into the Insolvency Services Account.

17. Provision as to the fees, costs, charges and other expenses that may be treated as the expenses of a winding up.

18. Provision as to the fees, costs, charges and other expenses that may be treated as properly incurred by the administrator or administrative receiver of a company.

19. Provision as to the fees, costs, charges and other expenses that may be incurred for any of the purposes of Part I of this Act or in the administration of any voluntary arrangement approved under that Part.

Information and records

20. Provision requiring registrars and other officers of courts having jurisdiction in England and Wales in relation to, or to matters connected with or arising out of, the insolvency or winding up of companies—

(a) to keep books and other records with respect to the exercise of that jurisdiction, and

(b) to make returns to the Secretary of State of the business of those courts.

21. Provision requiring a creditor, member or contributory, or such a committee as is mentioned in paragraph 10 above, to be supplied (on payment in prescribed cases of the prescribed fee) with such information and with copies of such documents as may be prescribed.

22. Provision as to the manner in which public examinations under sections 133 and 134 of this Act and proceedings under sections 236 and 237 are to be conducted, as to the circumstances in which records of such examinations or proceedings are to be made available to prescribed persons and as to the costs of such examinations and proceedings.

23. Provision imposing requirements with respect to—

(a) the preparation and keeping by the liquidator, administrator or administrative receiver of a company, or by the supervisor of a voluntary arrangement approved under Part I of this Act, of prescribed books, accounts and other records;

(b) the production of those books, accounts and records for inspection by prescribed persons;

(c) the auditing of accounts kept by the liquidator, administrator or administrative receiver of a company, or the supervisor of such a voluntary arrangement; and

(d) the issue by the administrator or administrative receiver of a company of such a certificate as is mentioned in section 22(3)(b) of the Value Added Tax Act 1983 (refund of tax in cases of bad debts) and the supply of copies of the certificate to creditors of the company.

24. Provision requiring the person who is the supervisor of a voluntary arrangement approved under Part I, when it appears to him that the voluntary arrangement has been fully implemented and that nothing remains to be done by him under the arrangement—

(a) to give notice of that fact to persons bound by the voluntary arrangement, and

(b) to report to those persons on the carrying out of the functions conferred on the supervisor of the arrangement.

25. Provision as to the manner in which the liquidator of a company is to act in relation to the books, papers and other records of the company, including provision authorising their disposal.

26. Provision imposing requirements in connection with the carrying out of functions under section 7(3) of the Company Directors Disqualification Act 1986 (including, in particular, requirements with respect to the making of periodic returns).

General

27. Provision conferring power on the Secretary of State to make regulations with respect to so much of any matter that may be provided for in the rules as relates to the carrying out of the functions of the liquidator, administrator or administrative receiver of a company.

28. Provision conferring a discretion on the court.

29. Provision conferring power on the court to make orders for the purpose of securing compliance with obligations imposed by or under section 22, 47, 66, 131, 143(2) or 235 of this Act or section 7(4) of the Company Directors Disqualification Act 1986.

30. Provision making non-compliance with any of the rules a criminal offence.

31. Provision making different provision for different cases or descriptions of cases, including different provisions for different areas.

DEFINITION

"liquidator": s.411(3).

GENERAL NOTE

This is a general enabling Schedule to authorise the making of secondary legislation in the form of company insolvency rules, to be made by statutory instrument under s.411(4). The various matters in respect of which such rules may make provision are indicated in the various paragraphs. Para. 27 authorises the inclusion within the Rules of subsidiary enabling provisions to authorise the Secretary of State to make regulations with respect to further matters to be specified. Such regulations will also be made by statutory instrument, pursuant to the authority conferred by s.411(5).

This Schedule corresponds to Sched. 5 to the 1985 Act.

Section 412   SCHEDULE 9

PROVISIONS CAPABLE OF INCLUSION IN INDIVIDUAL INSOLVENCY RULES

Courts

1. Provision with respect to the arrangement and disposition of the business under Parts VIII to XI of this Act of courts having jurisdiction for the purpose of those Parts, including provision for the allocation of proceedings under those Parts to particular courts and for the transfer of such proceedings from one court to another.

2. Provision for enabling a registrar in bankruptcy of the High Court or a registrar of a county court having jurisdiction for the purposes of those Parts to exercise such of the jurisdiction conferred for those purposes on the High Court or, as the case may be, that county court as may be prescribed.

3. Provision for regulating the practice and procedure of any court exercising jurisdiction for the purposes of those Parts, being any provision that could be made by rules of court.

4. Provision conferring rights of audience, in courts exercising jurisdiction for the purposes of those Parts, on the official receiver and on solicitors.

Notices, etc.

5. Provision requiring notice of any proceedings under Parts VIII to XI of this Act or of any matter relating to or arising out of a proposal under Part VIII or a bankruptcy to be given or published in the prescribed manner.

6. Provision with respect to the form, manner of serving, contents and proof of any petition, application, order, notice, statement or other document required to be presented, made, given, published or prepared under any enactment contained in Parts VIII to XI or subordinate legislation under those Parts or Part XV (including provision requiring prescribed matters to be verified by affidavit).

7. Provision specifying the persons to whom any notice under Parts VIII to XI is to be given.

Registration of voluntary arrangements

8. Provision for the registration of voluntary arrangements approved under Part VIII of this Act, including provision for the keeping and inspection of a register.

Interim receiver

9. Provision as to the manner in which an interim receiver appointed under section 286 is to carry out his functions, including any such provision as is specified in relation to the trustee of a bankrupt's estate in paragraph 21 or 27 below.

Receiver or manager

10. Provision as to the manner in which the official receiver is to carry out his functions as receiver or manager of a bankrupt's estate under section 287, including any such provision as is specified in relation to the trustee of a bankrupt's estate in paragraph 21 or 27 below.

Administration of individual insolvency

11. Provision with respect to the certification of the appointment of any person as trustee of a bankrupt's estate and as to the proof of that appointment.

12. The following provision with respect to meetings of creditors—
   (*a*) provision as to the manner of summoning a meeting (including provision as to how any power to require a meeting is to be exercised, provision as to the manner of determining the value of any debt for the purposes of any such power and provision making the exercise of any such power subject to the deposit of a sum sufficient to cover the expenses likely to be incurred in summoning and holding a meeting);
   (*b*) provision specifying the time and place at which a meeting may be held and the period of notice required for a meeting;
   (*c*) provision as to the procedure to be followed at such a meeting (including the manner in which decisions may be reached by a meeting and the manner in which the value of any vote at a meeting is to be determined);
   (*d*) provision for requiring a bankrupt or debtor to attend a meeting;
   (*e*) provision creating, in the prescribed circumstances, a presumption that a meeting has been duly summoned and held; and
   (*f*) provision as to the manner of proving the decisions of a meeting.

13. Provision as to the functions, membership and proceedings of a creditors' committee established under section 301.

14. Provision as to the manner in which any requirement that may be imposed on a person under Parts VIII to XI of this Act by the official receiver, the trustee of a bankrupt's estate or a special manager appointed under section 370 is to be so imposed and, in the case of any requirement imposed under section 305(3) (information etc. to be given by the trustee to the official receiver), provision conferring power on the court to make orders for the purpose of securing compliance with that requirement.

15. Provision as to the manner in which any requirement imposed by virtue of section 310(3) (compliance with income payments order) is to take effect.

16. Provision as to the terms and conditions that may be included in a charge under section 313 (dwelling house forming part of bankrupt's estate).

17. Provision as to the debts that may be proved in any bankruptcy, as to the manner and conditions of proving a debt and as to the manner and expenses of establishing the value of any debt or security.

18. Provision with respect to the manner of the distribution of a bankrupt's estate, including provision with respect to unclaimed funds and dividends.

19. Provision modifying the application of Parts VIII to XI of this Act in relation to a debtor or bankrupt who has died.

Financial provisions

20. Provision as to the amount, or manner of determining the amount, payable to an interim receiver, the trustee of a bankrupt's estate or a special manager appointed under section 370 by way of remuneration for the performance of functions in connection with or arising out of the bankruptcy of any person.

21. Provision with respect to the manner in which moneys received by the trustee of a bankrupt's estate in the course of carrying out his functions as such are to be handled.

22. Provision as to the fees, costs, charges and other expenses that may be treated as the expenses of a bankruptcy.

23. Provision as to the fees, costs, charges and other expenses that may be incurred for any of the purposes of Part VIII of this Act or in the administration of any voluntary arrangement approved under that Part.

Information and records

24. Provision requiring registrars and other officers of courts having jurisdiction for the purposes of Parts VIII to XI—
   (*a*) to keep books and other records with respect to the exercise of that jurisdiction and of jurisdiction under the Deeds of Arrangement Act 1914, and
   (*b*) to make returns to the Secretary of State of the business of those courts.

25. Provision requiring a creditor or a committee established under section 301 to be supplied (on payment in prescribed cases of the prescribed fee) with such information and with copies of such documents as may be prescribed.

26. Provision as to the manner in which public examinations under section 290 and proceedings under sections 366 to 368 are to be conducted, as to the circumstances in which records of such examinations and proceedings are to be made available to prescribed persons and as to the costs of such examinations and proceedings.

27. Provision imposing requirements with respect to—
   (*a*) the preparation and keeping by the trustee of a bankrupt's estate, or the supervisor of a voluntary arrangement approved under Part VIII, of prescribed books, accounts and other records;
   (*b*) the production of those books, accounts and records for inspection by prescribed persons; and
   (*c*) the auditing of accounts kept by the trustee of a bankrupt's estate or the supervisor of such a voluntary arrangement.

28. Provision requiring the person who is the supervisor of a voluntary arrangement approved under Part VIII, when it appears to him that the voluntary arrangement has been fully implemented and that nothing remains to be done by him under it—
   (*a*) to give notice of that fact to persons bound by the voluntary arrangement, and
   (*b*) to report to those persons on the carrying out of the functions conferred on the supervisor of it.

29. Provision as to the manner in which the trustee of a bankrupt's estate is to act in relation to the books, papers and other records of the bankrupt, including provision authorising their disposal.

General

30. Provision conferring power on the Secretary of State to make regulations with respect to so much of any matter that may be provided for in the rules as relates to the carrying out of the functions of an interim receiver appointed under section 286, of the official receiver while acting as a receiver or manager under section 287 or of a trustee of a bankrupt's estate.

31. Provision conferring a discretion on the court.

32. Provision making non-compliance with any of the rules a criminal offence.

33. Provision making different provision for different cases, including different provision for different areas.

GENERAL NOTE

This is a general enabling Schedule to authorise the making of secondary legislation in the form of individual insolvency rules, to be made by statutory instrument under s.412. The various matters in respect of which such rules may make provision are indicated in the various paragraphs. Para. 30 authorises the inclusion within the Rules of subsidiary enabling provisions to authorise the Secretary of State to make regulations with respect to further matters to be specified. Such regulations will also be made by statutory instrument pursuant to the authority conferred by s.412(4).

This Schedule corresponds to Sched. 7 to the 1985 Act.

Section 430

SCHEDULE 10

PUNISHMENT OF OFFENCES UNDER THIS ACT

Note: In the fourth and fifth columns of this Schedule, "the statutory maximum" means—
(a) in England and Wales, the prescribed sum under section 32 of the Magistrates' Courts Act 1980 (c. 43), and
(b) in Scotland, the prescribed sum under section 289B of the Criminal Procedure (Scotland) Act 1975 (c. 21).

Section of Act creating offence	General nature of offence	Mode of prosecution	Punishment	Daily default fine (where applicable)
12(2)	Company and others failing to state in correspondence etc. that administrator appointed.	Summary.	One-fifth of the statutory maximum.	
15(8)	Failure of administrator to register office copy of court order permitting disposal of charged property.	Summary.	One-fifth of the statutory maximum.	One-fiftieth of the statutory maximum.
18(5)	Failure of administrator to register office copy of court order varying or discharging administration order.	Summary.	One-fifth of the statutory maximum.	One-fiftieth of the statutory maximum.
21(3)	Administrator failing to register administration order and give notice of appointment.	Summary.	One-fifth of the statutory maximum.	One-fiftieth of the statutory maximum.
22(6)	Failure to comply with provisions relating to statement of affairs, where administrator appointed.	1. On indictment. 2. Summary.	A fine. The statutory maximum	One-tenth of the statutory maximum.
23(3)	Administrator failing to send out, register and lay before creditors statement of his proposals.	Summary.	One-fifth of the statutory maximum.	One-fiftieth of the statutory maximum.
24(7)	Administrator failing to file court order discharging administration order under s.24.	Summary.	One-fifth of the statutory maximum.	One-fiftieth of the statutory maximum.
27(6)	Administrator failing to file court order discharging administration order under s.27.	Summary.	One-fifth of the statutory maximum.	One-fiftieth of the statutory maximum.
30	Body corporate acting as receiver.	1. On indictment. 2. Summary.	A fine. The statutory maximum.	

Section of Act creating offence	General nature of offence	Mode of prosecution	Punishment	Daily default fine (where applicable)
31	Undischarged bankrupt acting as receiver or manager.	1. On indictment. 2. Summary.	2 years or a fine, or both. 6 months or the statutory maximum, or both.	
38(5)	Receiver failing to deliver accounts to registrar.	Summary.	One-fifth of the statutory maximum.	One-fiftieth of the statutory maximum.
39(2)	Company and others failing to state in correspondence that receiver appointed.	Summary.	One-fifth of the statutory maximum.	
43(6)	Administrative receiver failing to file office copy of order permitting disposal of charged property.	Summary.	One-fifth of the statutory maximum.	One-fiftieth of the statutory maximum.
45(5)	Administrative receiver failing to file notice of vacation of office.	Summary.	One-fifth of the statutory maximum.	One-fiftieth of the statutory maximum.
46(4)	Administrative receiver failing to give notice of his appointment.	Summary.	One-fifth of the statutory maximum.	One-fiftieth of the statutory maximum.
47(6)	Failing to comply with provisions relating to statement of affairs where administrative receiver appointed.	1. On indictment. 2. Summary.	A fine. The statutory maximum.	One-tenth of the statutory maximum.
48(8)	Administrative receiver failing to comply with requirements as to his report.	Summary.	One-fifth of the statutory maximum.	One-fiftieth of the statutory maximum.
51(4)	Body corporate or Scottish firm acting as receiver.	1. On indictment. 2. Summary.	A fine. The statutory maximum.	
51(5)	Undischarged bankrupt acting as receiver (Scotland).	1. On indictment. 2. Summary.	2 years or a fine, or both. 6 months or the statutory maximum, or both.	
53(2)	Failing to deliver to registrar copy of instrument of appointment of receiver.	Summary.	One-fifth of the statutory maximum.	One-fiftieth of the statutory maximum.
54(3)	Failing to deliver to registrar the court's interlocutor appointing receiver.	Summary.	One-fifth of the statutory maximum.	One-fiftieth of the statutory maximum.

Section of Act creating offence	General nature of offence	Mode of prosecution	Punishment	Daily default fine (where applicable)
61(7)	Receiver failing to send to registrar certified copy of court order authorising disposal of charged property.	Summary.	One-fifth of the statutory maximum.	One-fiftieth of the statutory maximum.
62(5)	Failing to give notice to registrar of cessation or removal of receiver.	Summary.	One-fifth of the statutory maximum.	One-fiftieth of the statutory maximum.
64(2)	Company and others failing to state on correspondence etc. that receiver appointed.	Summary.	One-fifth of the statutory maximum.	
65(4)	Receiver failing to send or publish notice of his appointment.	Summary.	One-fifth of the statutory maximum.	One-fiftieth of the statutory maximum.
66(6)	Failing to comply with provisions concerning statement of affairs, where receiver appointed.	1. On indictment. 2. Summary.	A fine. The statutory maximum.	One-tenth of the statutory maximum.
67(8)	Receiver failing to comply with requirements as to his report.	Summary.	One-fifth of the statutory maximum.	One-fiftieth of the statutory maximum.
85(2)	Company failing to give notice in Gazette of resolution for voluntary winding up.	Summary.	One-fifth of the statutory maximum.	One-fiftieth of the statutory maximum.
89(4)	Director making statutory declaration of company's solvency without reasonable grounds for his opinion.	1. On indictment. 2. Summary.	2 years or a fine, or both. 6 months or the statutory maximum, or both.	
89(6)	Declaration under section 89 not delivered to registrar within prescribed time.	Summary.	One-fifth of the statutory maximum.	One-fiftieth of the statutory maximum.
93(3)	Liquidator failing to summon general meeting of company at each year's end.	Summary.	One-fifth of the statutory maximum.	One-fiftieth of the statutory maximum.
94(4)	Liquidator failing to send to registrar a copy of account of winding up and return of final meeting.	Summary.	One-fifth of the statutory maximum.	One-fiftieth of the statutory maximum.
94(6)	Liquidator failing to call final meeting.	Summary.	One-fifth of the statutory maximum.	
95(8)	Liquidator failing to comply with s.95, where company insolvent.	Summary.	The statutory maximum.	

Section of Act creating offence	General nature of offence	Mode of prosecution	Punishment	Daily default fine (where applicable)
98(6)	Company failing to comply with s.98 in respect of summoning and giving notice of creditors' meeting.	1. On indictment. 2. Summary.	A fine. The statutory maximum.	
99(3)	Directors failing to attend and lay statement in prescribed form before creditors' meeting.	1. On indictment. 2. Summary.	A fine. The statutory maximum.	
105(3)	Liquidator failing to summon company general meeting and creditors' meeting at each year's end.	Summary.	One-fifth of the statutory maximum.	
106(4)	Liquidator failing to send to registrar account of winding up and return of final meetings.	Summary.	One-fifth of the statutory maximum.	One-fiftieth of the statutory maximum.
106(6)	Liquidator failing to call final meeting of company or creditors.	Summary.	One-fifth of the statutory maximum.	
109(2)	Liquidator failing to publish notice of his appointment.	Summary.	One-fifth of the statutory maximum.	One-fiftieth of the statutory maximum.
114(4)	Directors exercising powers in breach of s.114, where no liquidator.	Summary.	The statutory maximum.	
131(7)	Failing to comply with requirements as to statement of affairs, where liquidator appointed.	1. On indictment. 2. Summary.	A fine. The statutory maximum.	One-tenth of the statutory maximum.
164	Giving, offering etc. corrupt inducement affecting appointment of liquidator.	1. On indictment. 2. Summary.	A fine. The statutory maximum.	
166(7)	Liquidator failing to comply with requirements of s.166 in creditors' voluntary winding up.	Summary.	The statutory maximum.	
188(2)	Default in compliance with s.188 as to notification that company being wound up.	Summary.	One-fifth of the statutory maximum.	One-fiftieth of the statutory maximum.
192(2)	Liquidator failing to notify registrar as to progress of winding up.	Summary.	One-fifth of the statutory maximum.	One-fiftieth of the statutory maximum.
201(4)	Failing to deliver to registrar office copy of court order deferring dissolution.	Summary.	One-fifth of the statutory maximum.	One-fiftieth of the statutory maximum.
203(6)	Failing to deliver to registrar copy of directions or result of appeal under s.203.	Summary.	One-fifth of the statutory maximum.	One-fiftieth of the statutory maximum.

Section of Act creating offence	General nature of offence	Mode of prosecution	Punishment	Daily default fine (where applicable)
204(7)	Liquidator failing to deliver to registrar copy of court order for early dissolution.	Summary.	One-fifth of the statutory maximum.	One-fiftieth of the statutory maximum.
204(8)	Failing to deliver to registrar copy of court order deferring early dissolution.	Summary.	One-fifth of the statutory maximum.	One-fiftieth of the statutory maximum.
205(7)	Failing to deliver to registrar copy of Secretary of State's directions or court order deferring dissolution.	Summary.	One-fifth of the statutory maximum.	One-fiftieth of the statutory maximum.
206(1)	Fraud etc. in anticipation of winding up.	1. On indictment. 2. Summary.	7 years or a fine, or both. 6 months or the statutory maximum, or both.	
206(2)	Privity to fraud in anticipation of winding up; fraud, or privity to fraud, after commencement of winding up.	1. On indictment. 2. Summary.	7 years or a fine, or both. 6 months or the statutory maximum, or both.	
206(5)	Knowingly taking in pawn or pledge, or otherwise receiving, company property.	1. On indictment. 2. Summary.	7 years or a fine, or both. 6 months or the statutory maximum, or both.	
207	Officer of company entering into transaction in fraud of company's creditors.	1. On indictment. 2. Summary.	2 years or a fine, or both. 6 months or the statutory maximum, or both.	
208	Officer of company misconducting himself in course of winding up.	1. On indictment. 2. Summary.	7 years or a fine, or both. 6 months or the statutory maximum, or both.	
209	Officer or contributory destroying, falsifying, etc. company's books.	1. On indictment. 2. Summary.	7 years or a fine, or both. 6 months or the statutory maximum, or both.	
210	Officer of company making material omission from statement relating to company's affairs.	1. On indictment. 2. Summary.	7 years or a fine, or both. 6 months or the statutory maximum, or both.	
211	False representation or fraud for purpose of obtaining creditors' consent to an agreement in connecton with winding up.	1. On indictment. 2. Summary.	7 years or a fine, or both. 6 months or the statutory maximum, or both.	

Section of Act creating offence	General nature of offence	Mode of prosecution	Punishment	Daily default fine (where applicable)
216(4)	Contravening restrictions on re-use of name of company in insolvent liquidation.	1. On indictment. 2. Summary.	2 years or a fine, or both. 6 months or the statutory maximum, or both.	
235(5)	Failing to co-operate with office-holder.	1. On indictment. 2. Summary.	A fine. The statutory maximum.	One-tenth of the statutory maximum.
353(1)	Bankrupt failing to disclose property or disposals to official receiver or trustee.	1. On indictment. 2. Summary.	7 years or a fine, or both. 6 months or the statutory maximum, or both.	
354(1)	Bankrupt failing to deliver property to, or concealing property from, official receiver or trustee.	1. On indictment. 2. Summary.	7 years or a fine, or both. 6 months or the statutory maximum, or both.	
354(2)	Bankrupt removing property which he is required to deliver to official receiver or trustee.	1. On indictment. 2. Summary.	7 years or a fine, or both. 6 months or the statutory maximum, or both.	
354(3)	Bankrupt failing to account for loss of substantial part of property.	1. On indictment. 2. Summary.	2 years or a fine, or both. 6 months or the statutory maximum, or both.	
355(1)	Bankrupt failing to deliver books, papers and records to official receiver or trustee.	1. On indictment. 2. Summary.	7 years or a fine, or both. 6 months or the statutory maximum, or both.	
355(2)	Bankrupt concealing, destroying etc. books, papers or records, or making false entries in them.	1. On indictment. 2. Summary.	7 years or a fine, or both. 6 months or the statutory maximum, or both.	
355(3)	Bankrupt disposing of, or altering, books, papers or records relating to his estate or affairs.	1. On indictment. 2. Summary.	7 years or a fine, or both. 6 months or the statutory maximum, or both.	
356(1)	Bankrupt making material omission in statement relating to his affairs.	1. On indictment. 2. Summary.	7 years or a fine, or both. 6 months or the statutory maximum, or both.	

Section of Act creating offence	General nature of offence	Mode of prosecution	Punishment	Daily default fine (where applicable)
356(2)	Bankrupt making false statement, or failing to inform trustee, where false debt proved.	1. On indictment. 2. Summary.	7 years or a fine, or both. 6 months or the statutory maximum, or both.	
357	Bankrupt fraudulently disposing of property.	1. On indictment. 2. Summary.	2 years or a fine, or both. 6 months or the statutory maximum, or both.	
358	Bankrupt absconding with property he is required to deliver to official receiver or trustee.	1. On indictment. 2. Summary.	2 years or a fine, or both. 6 months or the statutory maximum, or both.	
359(1)	Bankrupt disposing of property obtained on credit and not paid for.	1. On indictment. 2. Summary.	7 years or a fine, or both. 6 months or the statutory maximum, or both.	
359(2)	Obtaining property in respect of which money is owed by a bankrupt.	1. On indictment. 2. Summary.	7 years or a fine, or both. 6 months or the statutory maximum, or both.	
360(1)	Bankrupt obtaining credit or engaging in business without disclosing his status or name in which he was made bankrupt.	1. On indictment. 2. Summary.	2 years or a fine, or both. 6 months or the statutory maximum, or both.	
360(3)	Person made bankrupt in Scotland or Northern Ireland obtaining credit, etc. in England and Wales.	1. On indictment. 2. Summary.	2 years or a fine, or both. 6 months or the statutory maximum, or both.	
361(1)	Bankrupt failing to keep proper accounting records.	1. On indictment. 2. Summary.	2 years or a fine, or both. 6 months or the statutory maximum, or both.	
362	Bankrupt increasing extent of insolvency by gambling.	1. On indictment. 2. Summary.	2 years or a fine, or both. 6 months or the statutory maximum, or both.	
389	Acting as insolvency practitioner when not qualified.	1. On indictment. 2. Summary.	2 years or a fine, or both. 6 months or the statutory maximum, or both.	

Section of Act creating offence	General nature of offence	Mode of prosecution	Punishment	Daily default fine (where applicable)
429(5)	Contravening s.429 in respect of disabilities imposed by county court on revocation of administration order.	1. On indictment. 2. Summary.	2 years or a fine, or both. 6 months or the statutory maximum, or both.	
Sch. 7, para. 4(3)	Failure to attend and give evidence to Insolvency Practitioners Tribunal; suppressing, concealing, etc. relevant documents.	Summary.	Level 3 on the standard scale within the meaning given by section 75 of the Criminal Justice Act 1982.	

"officer who is in default": s.430(5).
"period of months": s.430(3).
"period of years": s.430(3).
"the statutory maximum": *Note* at head of this Schedule.

GENERAL NOTE
This Schedule, which operates in conjunction with s.430, constitutes a complete table of the punishments which may be imposed for conviction of any offence under any provision of this Act. The Schedule collects together provisions regarding levels of punishment which were previously dispersed throughout the provisions of the 1985 Act and the Companies Act, and in Part of Sched. 24 to the latter.

It is indicated in s.430 that the first column of this Schedule specifies the respective sections of the Act, totalling 78 in all, under which criminal offences are created. The general nature of each offence is described, alongside the section number, in the second column. The third column shows whether the offence is triable by either or both of the two modes of trial (summary or on indictment), while the fourth column shows the maximum punishment by way of a fine or imprisonment which may be imposed upon conviction, according to the mode of trial employed. The fifth column shows (where relevant) the level of the daily default fine which may be imposed upon a person convicted of the offence after continued contravention. (See also the General Note to s.430, esp. to subs. (4) thereof.)

Where the prescribed penalty consists of, or may include, a fine, the amount of the fine is expressed in columns four and five in terms of a specified percentage of "the statutory maximum." As is explained in the *Note* placed at the beginning of the Schedule, this expression means, in England and Wales, the prescribed sum under s.32 of the Magistrates' Courts Act 1980 (c.43), and in Scotland, the prescribed sum under s.289B of the Criminal Procedure (Scotland) Act 1975 (c.21). These two sections authorise the Secretary of State at his discretion to substitute by order such other sum as appears to him to be justified by the change in the value of money since the last occasion when the prescribed sum was fixed. Currently, the prescribed statutory maximum in each jurisdiction is £2,000: see Criminal Penalties, etc. (Increase) Order 1984 (S.I. 1984 No. 447) and Increase of Criminal Penalties etc. (Scotland) Order 1984 (S.I. 1984 No. 526).

Section 437

SCHEDULE 11

TRANSITIONAL PROVISIONS AND SAVINGS

PART I

COMPANY INSOLVENCY AND WINDING UP

Administration orders

1.—(1) Where any right to appoint an administrative receiver of a company is conferred by any debentures or floating charge created before the appointed day, the conditions precedent to the exercise of that right are deemed to include the presentation of a petition applying for an administration order to be made in relation to the company.

(2) "Administrative receiver" here has the meaning assigned by section 251.

Receivers and managers (England and Wales)

2.—(1) In relation to any receiver or manager of a company's property who was appointed before the appointed day, the new law does not apply; and the relevant provisions of the former law continue to have effect.

(2) "The new law" here means Chapter I of Part III, and Part VI, of this Act; and "the former law" means the Companies Act and so much of this Act as replaces provisions of that Act (without the amendments in paragraphs 15 to 17 of Schedule 6 to the Insolvency Act 1985, or the associated repeals made by that Act), and any provision of the Insolvency Act 1985 which was in force before the appointed day.

(3) This paragraph is without prejudice to the power conferred by this Act under which rules under section 411 may make transitional provision in connection with the coming into

force of those rules; and such provision may apply those rules in relation to the receiver or manager of a company's property notwithstanding that he was appointed before the coming into force of the rules or section 411.

Receivers (Scotland)

3.—(1) In relation to any receiver appointed under section 467 of the Companies Act before the appointed day, the new law does not apply and the relevant provisions of the former law continue to have effect.

(2) "The new law" here means Chapter II of Part III, and Part VI, of this Act; and "the former law" means the Companies Act and so much of this Act as replaces provisions of that Act (without the amendments in paragraphs 18 to 22 of Schedule 6 to the Insolvency Act 1985 or the associated repeals made by that Act), and any provision of the Insolvency Act 1985 which was in force before the appointed day.

(3) This paragraph is without prejudice to the power conferred by this Act under which rules under section 411 may make transitional provision in connection with the coming into force of those rules; and such provision may apply those rules in relation to a receiver appointed under section 467 notwithstanding that he was appointed before the coming into force of the rules or section 411.

Winding up already in progress

4.—(1) In relation to any winding up which has commenced, or is treated as having commenced, before the appointed day, the new law does not apply, and the former law continues to have effect, subject to the following paragraphs.

(2) "The new law" here means any provisions in the first Group of Parts of this Act which replace sections 66 to 87 and 89 to 105 of the Insolvency Act 1985; and "the former law" means Parts XX and XXI of the Companies Act (without the amendments in paragraphs 23 to 52 of Schedule 6 to the Insolvency Act 1985, or the associated repeals made by that Act).

Statement of affairs

5.—(1) Where a winding up by the court in England and Wales has commenced, or is treated as having commenced, before the appointed day, the official receiver or (on appeal from a refusal by him) the court may, at any time on or after that day—

(*a*) release a person from an obligation imposed on him by or under section 528 of the Companies Act (statement of affairs), or

(*b*) extend the period specified in subsection (6) of that section.

(2) Accordingly, on and after the appointed day, section 528(6) has effect in relation to a winding up to which this paragraph applies with the omission of the words from "or within" onwards.

Provisions relating to liquidator

6.—(1) This paragraph applies as regards the liquidator in the case of a winding up by the court in England and Wales commenced, or treated as having commenced, before the appointed day.

(2) The official receiver may, at any time when he is liquidator of the company, apply to the Secretary of State for the appointment of a liquidator in his (the official receiver's) place; and on any such application the Secretary of State shall either make an appointment or decline to make one.

(3) Where immediately before the appointed day the liquidator of the company has not made an application under section 545 of the Companies Act (release of liquidators), then—

(*a*) except where the Secretary of State otherwise directs, sections 146(1) and (2) and 172(8) of this Act apply, and section 545 does not apply, in relation to any liquidator of that company who holds office on or at any time after the appointed day and is not the official receiver;

(*b*) section 146(3) applies in relation to the carrying out at any time after that day by any liquidator of the company of any of his functions; and (*c*) a liquidator in relation to whom section 172(8) has effect by virtue of this paragraph has his release with effect from the time specified in section 174(4)(*d*) of this Act.

(4) Subsection (6) of section 174 of this Act has effect for the purposes of sub-paragraph (3)(*c*) above as it has for the purposes of that section, but as if the reference to section 212 were to section 631 of the Companies Act.

(5) The liquidator may employ a solicitor to assist him in the carrying out of his functions without the permission of the committee of inspection; but if he does so employ a solicitor he shall inform the committee of inspection that he has done so.

Winding up under supervision of the court

7. The repeals in Part II of Schedule 10 to the Insolvency Act 1985 of references (in the Companies Act and elsewhere) to a winding up under the supervision of the court do not affect the operation of the enactments in which the references are contained in relation to any case in which an order under section 606 of the Companies Act (power to order winding up under supervision) was made before the appointed day.

Saving for power to make rules

8.—(1) Paragraphs 4 to 7 are without prejudice to the power conferred by this Act under which rules made under section 411 may make transitional provision in connection with the coming into force of those rules.

(2) Such provision may apply those rules in relation to a winding up notwithstanding that the winding up commenced, or is treated as having commenced, before the coming into force of the rules or section 411.

Setting aside of preferences and other transactions

9.—(1) Where a provision in Part VI of this Act applies in relation to a winding up or in relation to a case in which an administration order has been made, a preference given, floating charge created or other transaction entered into before the appointed day shall not be set aside under that provision except to the extent that it could have been set aside under the law in force immediately before that day, assuming for this purpose that any relevant administration order had been a winding-up order.

(2) The references above to setting aside a preference, floating charge or other transaction include the making of an order which varies or reverses any effect of a preference, floating charge or other transaction.

Part II

Individual Insolvency

Bankruptcy (general)

10.—(1) Subject to the following provisions of this Part of this Schedule, so much of this Act as replaces Part III of the Insolvency Act 1985 does not apply in relation to any case in which a petition in bankruptcy was presented, or a receiving order or adjudication in bankruptcy was made, before the appointed day.

(2) In relation to any such case as is mentioned above, the enactments specified in Schedule 8 to that Act, so far as they relate to bankruptcy, and those specified in Parts III and IV of Schedule 10 to that Act, so far as they so relate, have effect without the amendments and repeals specified in those Schedules.

(3) Where any subordinate legislation made under an enactment referred to in sub-paragraph (2) is in force immediately before the appointed day, that subordinate legislation continues to have effect on and after that day in relation to any such case as is mentioned in sub-paragraph (1).

11.—(1) In relation to any such case as is mentioned in paragraph 10(1) the references in any enactment or subordinate legislation to a petition, order or other matter which is provided for under the Bankruptcy Act 1914 and corresponds to a petition, order or other matter provided for under provisions of this Act replacing Part III of the Insolvency Act 1985 continue on and after the appointed day to have effect as references to the petition, order or matter provided for by the Act of 1914; but otherwise those references have effect on and after that day as references to the petition, order or matter provided for by those provisions of this Act.

(2) Without prejudice to sub-paragraph (1), in determining for the purposes of section 279 of this Act (period of bankruptcy) or paragraph 13 below whether any person was an undischarged bankrupt at a time before the appointed day, an adjudication in bankruptcy and an annulment of a bankruptcy under the Act of 1914 are to be taken into account in the same way, respectively, as a bankruptcy order under the provisions of this Act replacing Part III of the Insolvency Act 1985 and the annulment under section 282 of this Act of such an order.

12. Transactions entered into before the appointed day have effect on and after that day as if references to acts of bankruptcy in the provisions for giving effect to those transactions continued to be references to acts of bankruptcy within the meaning of the Bankruptcy Act 1914, but as if such acts included failure to comply with a statutory demand served under section 268 of this Act.

Discharge from old bankruptcy

13.—(1) Where a person—
  (*a*) was adjudged bankrupt before the appointed day or is adjudged bankrupt on or after that day on a petition presented before that day, and
  (*b*) that person was not an undischarged bankrupt at any time in the period of 15 years ending with the adjudication,
that person is deemed (if not previously discharged) to be discharged from his bankruptcy for the purposes of the Bankruptcy Act 1914 at the end of the discharge period.

(2) Subject to sub-paragraph (3) below, the discharge period for the purposes of this paragraph is—
  (*a*) in the case of a person adjudged bankrupt before the appointed day, the period of 3 years beginning with that day, and
  (*b*) in the case of a person who is adjudged bankrupt on or after that day on a petition presented before that day, the period of 3 years beginning with the date of the adjudication.

(3) Where the court exercising jurisdiction in relation to a bankruptcy to which this paragraph applies is satisfied, on the application of the official receiver, that the bankrupt has failed, or is failing, to comply with any of his obligations under the Bankruptcy Act 1914, any rules made under that Act or any such rules as are mentioned in paragraph 19(1) below, the court may order that the discharge period shall cease to run for such period, or until the fulfilment of such conditions (including a condition requiring the court to be satisfied as to any matter) as may be specified in the order.

Provisions relating to trustee

14.—(1) This paragraph applies as regards the trustee in the case of a person adjudged bankrupt before the appointed day, or adjudged bankrupt on or after that day on a petition presented before that day.

(2) The official receiver may at any time when he is the trustee of the bankrupt's estate apply to the Secretary of State for the appointment of a person as trustee instead of the official receiver; and on any such application the Secretary of State shall either make an appointment or decline to make one.

(3) Where on the appointed day the trustee of a bankrupt's estate has not made an application under section 93 of the Bankruptcy Act 1914 (release of trustee), then—
  (*a*) except where the Secretary of State otherwise directs, sections 298(8), 304 and 331(1) to (3) of this Act apply, and section 93 of the Act of 1914 does not apply, in relation to any trustee of the bankrupt's estate who holds office on or at any time after the appointed day and is not the official receiver;
  (*b*) section 331(4) of this Act applies in relation to the carrying out at any time on or after the appointed day by the trustee of the bankrupt's estate of any of his functions; and
  (*c*) a trustee in relation to whom section 298(8) of this Act has effect by virtue of this paragraph has his release with effect from the time specified in section 299(3)(*d*).

(4) Subsection (5) of section 299 has effect for the purposes of sub-paragraph (3)(*c*) as it has for the purposes of that section.

(5) In the application of subsection (3) of section 331 in relation to a case by virtue of this paragraph, the reference in that subsection to section 330(1) has effect as a reference to section 67 of the Bankruptcy Act 1914.

(6) The trustee of the bankrupt's estate may employ a solicitor to assist him in the carrying out of his functions without the permission of the committee of inspection; but if he does so employ a solicitor, he shall inform the committee of inspection that he has done so.

Copyright

15. Where a person who is adjudged bankrupt on a petition presented on or after the appointed day is liable, by virtue of a transaction entered into before that day, to pay royalties or a share of the profits to any person in respect of any copyright or interest in copyright comprised in the bankrupt's estate, section 60 of the Bankruptcy Act 1914 (limitation on trustee's powers in relation to copyright) applies in relation to the trustee of that estate as it applies in relation to a trustee in bankruptcy under the Act of 1914.

Second bankruptcy

16.—(1) Sections 334 and 335 of this Act apply with the following modifications where the earlier bankruptcy (within the meaning of section 334) is a bankruptcy in relation to which the Act of 1914 applies instead of the second Group of Parts in this Act, that is to say—

(a) references to property vested in the existing trustee under section 307(3) of this Act have effect as references to such property vested in that trustee as was acquired by or devolved on the bankrupt after the commencement (within the meaning of the Act of 1914) of the earlier bankruptcy; and

(b) references to an order under section 310 of this Act have effect as references to an order under section 51 of the Act of 1914.

(2) Section 39 of the Act of 1914 (second bankruptcy) does not apply where a person who is an undischarged bankrupt under that Act is adjudged bankrupt under this Act.

Setting aside of preferences and other transactions

17.—(1) A preference given, assignment made or other transaction entered into before the appointed day shall not be set aside under any of sections 339 to 344 of this Act except to the extent that it could have been set aside under the law in force immediately before that day.

(2) References in sub-paragraph (1) to setting aside a preference, assignment or other transaction include the making of any order which varies or reverses any effect of a preference, assignment or other transaction.

Bankruptcy offences

18.—(1) Where a bankruptcy order is made under this Act on or after the appointed day, a person is not guilty of an offence under Chapter VI of Part IX in respect of anything done before that day; but, notwithstanding the repeal by the Insolvency Act 1985 of the Bankruptcy Act 1914, is guilty of an offence under the Act of 1914 in respect of anything done before the appointed day which would have been an offence under that Act if the making of the bankruptcy order had been the making of a receiving order under that Act.

(2) Subsection (5) of section 350 of this Act applies (instead of sections 157(2), 158(2), 161 and 165 of the Act of 1914) in relation to proceedings for an offence under that Act which are instituted (whether by virtue of sub-paragraph (1) or otherwise) after the appointed day.

Power to make rules

19.—(1) The preceding provisions of this Part of this Schedule are without prejudice to the power conferred by this Act under which rules under section 412 may make transitional provision in connection with the coming into force of those rules; and such provision may apply those rules in relation to a bankruptcy notwithstanding that it arose from a petition presented before either the coming into force of the rules or the appointed day.

(2) Rules under section 412 may provide for such notices served before the appointed day as may be prescribed to be treated for the purposes of this Act as statutory demands served under section 268.

Part III

Transitional Effect of Part XVI

20.—(1) A transaction entered into before the appointed day shall not be set aside under Part XVI of this Act except to the extent that it could have been set aside under the law in force immediately before that day.

(2) References above to setting aside a transaction include the making of any order which varies or reverses any effect of a transaction.

Part IV

Insolvency Practitioners

21. Where an individual began to act as an insolvency practitioner in relation to any person before the appointed day, nothing in section 390(2) or (3) prevents that individual from being qualified to act as an insolvency practitioner in relation to that person.

Part V

General Transitional Provisions and Savings

Interpretation for this Part

22. In this Part of this Schedule, "the former enactments" means so much of the Companies Act as is repealed and replaced by this Act, the Insolvency Act 1985 and the other enactments repealed by this Act.

General saving for past acts and events

23. So far as anything done or treated as done under or for the purposes of any provision of the former enactments could have been done under or for the purposes of the corresponding provision of this Act, it is not invalidated by the repeal of that provision but has effect as if done under or for the purposes of the corresponding provision; and any order, regulation, rule or other instrument made or having effect under any provision of the former enactments shall, insofar as its effect is preserved by this paragraph, be treated for all purposes as made and having effect under the corresponding provision.

Periods of time

24. Where any period of time specified in a provision of the former enactments is current immediately before the appointed day, this Act has effect as if the corresponding provision had been in force when the period began to run; and (without prejudice to the foregoing) any period of time so specified and current is deemed for the purposes of this Act—

(a) to run from the date or event from which it was running immediately before the appointed day, and

(b) to expire (subject to any provision of this Act for its extension) whenever it would have expired if this Act had not been passed;

and any rights, priorities, liabilities, reliefs, obligations, requirements, powers, duties or exemptions dependent on the beginning, duration or end of such a period as above mentioned shall be under this Act as they were or would have been under the former enactments.

Internal cross-references in this Act

25. Where in any provision of this Act there is a reference to another such provision, and the first-mentioned provision operates, or is capable of operating, in relation to things done or omitted, or events occurring or not occurring, in the past (including in particular past acts of compliance with any enactment, failures of compliance, contraventions, offences and convictions of offences), the reference to the other provision is to be read as including a reference to the corresponding provision of the former enactments.

Punishment of offences

26.—(1) Offences committed before the appointed day under any provision of the former enactments may, notwithstanding any repeal by this Act, be prosecuted and punished after that day as if this Act had not passed.

(2) A contravention of any provision of the former enactments committed before the appointed day shall not be visited with any severer punishment under or by virtue of this Act than would have been applicable under that provision at the time of the contravention; but where an offence for the continuance of which a penalty was provided has been committed under any provision of the former enactments, proceedings may be taken under this Act in respect of the continuance of the offence on and after the appointed day in the like manner as if the offence had been committed under the corresponding provision of this Act.

References elsewhere to the former enactments

27.—(1) A reference in any enactment, instrument or document (whether express or implied, and in whatever phraseology) to a provision of the former enactments (including the corresponding provision of any yet earlier enactment) is to be read, where necessary to retain for the enactment, instrument or document the same force and effect as it would have had but for the passing of this Act, as, or as including, a reference to the corresponding provision by which it is replaced in this Act.

(2) The generality of the preceding sub-paragraph is not affected by any specific conversion of references made by this Act, nor by the inclusion in any provision of this Act of a reference (whether express or implied, and in whatever phraseology) to the provision of the former enactments corresponding to that provision, or to a provision of the former enactments which is replaced by a corresponding provision of this Act.

Saving for power to repeal provisions in section 51

28. The Secretary of State may by order in a statutory instrument repeal subsections (3) to (5) of section 51 of this Act and the entries in Schedule 10 relating to subsections (4) and (5) of that section.

Saving for Interpretation Act 1978 ss.16, 17

29. Nothing in this Schedule is to be taken as prejudicing sections 16 and 17 of the Interpretation Act 1978 (savings from, and effect of, repeals); and for the purposes of section 17(2) of that Act (construction of references to enactments repealed and replaced, etc.), so much of section 18 of the Insolvency Act 1985 as is replaced by a provision of this Act is deemed to have been repealed by this Act and not by the Company Directors Disqualification Act 1986.

DEFINITIONS
"the former enactments": para. 22.
"the former law": paras. 2(2), 3(2), 4(2).
"the new law": para. 2(2), 3(2), 4(2).

GENERAL NOTE
This Schedule contains transitional provisions and savings in respect of the bringing into force of this Act. The various paragraphs indicate what particular transitional arrangement is to apply to the specified sections of the Act as they come into force. Throughout the foregoing annotations, references to the relevant paragraph of this Schedule are included alongside the General Note for every section of the Act to which transitional provisions apply. The first 21 paras. of this Schedule correspond to various paras. in Sched. 9 to the 1985 Act (for the full list of correspondences, see the Tables of Derivations and of Destinations). Paras. 22–29 are without any counterparts in the 1985 Act.

Section 438   SCHEDULE 12

ENACTMENTS REPEALED

Chapter	Short title	Extent of repeal
1970 c.8.	The Insolvency Services (Accounting and Investment) Act 1970.	The whole Act.
1976 c.60.	The Insolvency Act 1976.	Section 3.
1985 c.6.	The Companies Act 1985.	In section 463(4), the words "Subject to section 617".
		Sections 467 to 485.
		In section 486, in the definition of "company" the words "other than in Chapter II of this Part"; and the definitions of "instrument of appointment", "prescribed", "receiver" and "register of charges".
		Sections 488 to 650.
		Sections 659 to 664.
		Sections 665 to 674.
		Section 709(4).
		Section 710(4).
		Section 724.
		Schedule 16.
		In Schedule 24, the entries relating to section 467; all entries thereafter up to and including section 641(2); and the entry relating to section 710(4).
1985 c.65.	The Insolvency Act 1985.	Sections 1 to 11.
		Section 15.
		Section 17.
		Section 19.
		Sections 20 to 107.
		Section 108(1) and (3) to (7).
		Sections 109 to 211.
		Sections 212 to 214.
		Section 216.
		Section 217(1) to (3).
		Sections 221 to 234.
		In section 235, subsections (2) to (5).
		In section 236, subsections (3) to (5).
		In Schedule 1, paragraphs 1 to 4, and sub-paragraph (4) of paragraph 5.
		Schedules 3 to 5.
		In Schedule 6, paragraphs 5, 6, 9, 15 to 17, 20 to 22, 25 to 44 and 48 to 52.
		Schedule 7.
		In Schedule 9, paragraphs 1 and 4 to 24.
		Schedule 10.
1985 c.66.	The Bankruptcy (Scotland) Act 1985.	In Schedule 7, paragraphs 19 to 22.
1986 c.44.	The Gas Act 1986.	In Schedule 7, paragraph 31.

GENERAL NOTE

This Schedule, in conjunction with s.438, effects the repeal, in whole or in part, of the various enactments listed within columns one and two, to the extent specified in column three. The enactments thereby repealed are those whose provisions are consolidated in the present Act.

         SCHEDULE 13

CONSEQUENTIAL AMENDMENTS OF COMPANIES ACT 1985

PART I

INTERNAL AND OTHER SECTION REFERENCES AMENDED OR RE-AMENDED

Section of Act	Consequential amendment or re-amendment
Section 13(4)	After "this Act", add "and the Insolvency Act".
Section 44(7)	In paragraph (*a*), for "section 582" substitute "section 110 of the Insolvency Act".
Section 103(7)	In paragraph (*a*), the same amendment.
Section 131(7)	The same amendment.
Section 140(2)	In paragraph (*b*), for "section 518" substitute "section 123 of the Insolvency Act".
Section 153(3)	In paragraph (*f*), for "section 582" substitute "section 110 of the Insolvency Act".
	In paragraph (*g*), for "Chapter II of Part II of the Insolvency Act 1985" substitute "Part I of the Insolvency Act".
Section 156(3)	For "section 517" substitute "section 122 of the Insolvency Act".
Section 173(4)	The same amendment.
Section 196	For this section substitute—
	"**196.**—(1) The following applies in the case of a company registered in England and Wales, where debentures of the company are secured by a charge which, as created, was a floating charge.
	(2) If possession is taken, by or on behalf of the holders of any of the debentures, of any property comprised in or subject to the charge, and the company is not at that time in course of being wound up, the company's preferential debts shall be paid out of assets coming into the hands of the person taking possession in priority to any claims for principal or interest in respect of the debentures.
	(3) "Preferential debts" means the categories of debts listed in Schedule 6 to the Insolvency Act; and for the purposes of that Schedule "the relevant date" is the date of possession being taken as above mentioned.
	(4) Payments made under this section shall be recouped, as far as may be, out of the assets of the company available for payment of general creditors."
Section 222(4)	For "section 106 of the Insolvency Act 1985" substitute "section 411 of the Insolvency Act".
Section 225	At the end of the section add—
	"(8) At any time when an administration order under Part II of the Insolvency Act is in force, this section has effect as if subsections (3) and (5) to (7) were omitted".
Section 380(4)	In paragraph (*j*), for "section 572(1)(*a*)" substitute "section 84(1)(*a*) of the Insolvency Act".
Section 441(1)	For "section 13 of the Insolvency Act 1985" substitute "section 8 of the Company Directors Disqualification Act 1986".
Section 449(1)	In paragraph (*ba*), for "section 12 or 13 of the Insolvency Act 1985" substitute "section 6, 7 or 8 of the Company Directors Disqualification Act 1986".
Section 461(6)	For "section 106 of the Insolvency Act 1985" substitute "section 411 of the Insolvency Act".
Section 462(5)	After "this Part" insert "and Part III of the Insolvency Act 1986".
Section 463(2)	For "Part XX (except section 623(4))" substitute "Part IV of the Insolvency Act (except section 185)".

Section of Act	Consequential amendment or re-amendment
Section 463(3)	For this subsection substitute— "(3) Nothing in this section derogates from the provisions of sections 53(7) and 54(6) of the Insolvency Act (attachment of floating charge on appointment of receiver), or prejudices the operation of sections 175 and 176 of that Act (payment of preferential debts in winding up)".
Section 464(6)	For "section 89 of the Insolvency Act 1985" substitute "sections 175 and 176 of the Insolvency Act".
Section 657(2)	For "subsections (3) and (5) to (7) of section 91 of the Insolvency Act 1985 and section 92 of that Act" substitute "section 178(4) and sections 179 to 182 of the Insolvency Act".
Section 658(1)	For "Subsection (7) of section 91 of the Insolvency Act 1985" substitute "Section 180 of the Insolvency Act".
Section 711(2)	In paragraph (*b*), for "section 600" substitute "section 109 of the Insolvency Act".
Section 733	In subsection (1), omit "295(7)". In subsection (3), for "216(3) or 295(7)" substitute "or 216(3)".

PART II

AMENDMENT OF PART XXVI (INTERPRETATION)

In Part XXVI of the Companies Act, after section 735, insert the following section—

"Relationship of this Act to Insolvency Act

735A.—(1) In this Act "the Insolvency Act" means the Insolvency Act 1986; and in the following provisions of this Act, namely, sections 375(1)(*b*), 425(6)(*a*), 440, 449(1)(*a*) and (*d*), 460(2), 675, 676, 677, 699(1), 728 and Schedule 21, paragraph 6(1), the words "this Act" are to be read as including Parts I to VII of that Act, sections 411, 413, 414, 416 and 417 in Part XV of that Act, and also the Company Directors Disqualification Act 1986.

(2) In sections 704(5), 706(1), 707(1), 708(1)(*a*) and (4), 710(5), 713(1), 729 and 732(3) references to the Companies Acts include Parts I to VII of the Insolvency Act, sections 411, 413, 414, 416 and 417 in Part XV of that Act, and also the Company Directors Disqualification Act 1986.

(3) Subsections (1) and (2) apply unless the contrary intention appears."

GENERAL NOTE

This Schedule, in conjunction with s.439(1), effects consequential amendments to the Companies Act. These are all drafting amendments consequential on this Act and the Company Directors Disqualification Act 1986. Pt. II of the Schedule makes an important addition to Pt. XXVI of the Companies Act, concerned with interpretation of that Act: a new s.735A is added to supply a definition of the expression "The Insolvency Act" for the purposes of the Companies Act.

CONSEQUENTIAL AMENDMENTS OF OTHER ENACTMENTS

Enactment	Amendment
Deeds of Arrangement Act 1914 (c.47):	
Section 3(1)	For "Part III of the Insolvency Act 1985" substitute "Parts VIII to XI of the Insolvency Act 1986".
Section 3(4)	The same amendment.
Section 11(1) and (2)	In each subsection, the same amendment.
Section 15(1)	For "section 207 of the Insolvency Act 1985" substitute "section 412 of the Insolvency Act 1986".
Section 16	The same amendment as of section 3(1).
Section 23	The same amendment.
Section 30(1)	For the definition of "property" substitute— " 'property' has the meaning given by section 436 of the Insolvency Act 1986".
Law of Property Act 1925 (c.20):	
Section 52(2)(*b*)	For "section 91 or 161 of the Insolvency Act 1985" substitute "sections 178 to 180 or sections 315 to 319 of the Insolvency Act 1986".
Land Registration Act 1925 (c.21):	
Section 42(2)	For "section 161 of the Insolvency Act 1985" substitute "sections 315 to 319 of the Insolvency Act 1986".
Section 112AA(3)(*a*)	For "the Insolvency Act 1985 or the Companies Act 1985" substitute "the Insolvency Act 1986".
Third Parties (Rights against Insurers) Act 1930 (c.25):	
Section 1	In subsection (1)(*b*), for the words from "a composition" to "that Chapter" substitute "a voluntary arrangement proposed for the purposes of Part I of the Insolvency Act 1986 being approved under that Part". In subsection (2), for "228 of the Insolvency Act 1985" substitute "421 of the Insolvency Act 1986". In subsection (3), the same amendment.
Section 2	In subsection (1), the same amendment as of section 1(2). In subsection (1A), for the words from "composition or scheme" to the end of the subsection substitute "voluntary arrangement proposed for the purposes of, and approved under, Part I or Part VIII of the Insolvency Act 1986".
Section 4	In paragraph (*b*), the same amendment as of section 1(2).
Exchange Control Act 1947 (c.14):	
Schedule 4	In paragraphs 6 and 8(4), for "section 120 of the Insolvency Act 1985" substitute "sections 267 to 270 of the Insolvency Act 1986".
Arbitration Act 1950 (c.27):	
Section 3(2)	For "committee established under section 148 of the Insolvency Act 1985" substitute "creditors' committee established under section 301 of the Insolvency Act 1986".

Enactment	Amendment

Agricultural Marketing Act 1958 (c.47):
Schedule 2 ....
	For paragraph 4 substitute—
	    "4.—(1) A scheme shall provide for the winding up of the board, and for that purpose may apply Part V of the Insolvency Act 1986 (winding up of unregistered companies), subject to the following modifications.
	    (2) For the purposes of sections 221, 222 and 224 of the Act of 1986, the principal place of business of the board is deemed to be the office of the board the address of which is registered by the Minister under paragraph 3 above.
	    (3) Section 223 does not apply.
	    (4) Section 224 applies as if the words "or any member of it as such" were omitted.
	    (5) A petition for winding up the board may be presented by the Minister as well as by any person authorised under Part IV of the Insolvency Act 1986 to present a petition for winding up a company".

Charities Act 1960 (c.58): Section 30(1)	For "Companies Act 1985" substitute "Insolvency Act 1986".
Licensing Act 1964 (c.26): Section 8(1)	In paragraph (*c*), for the words from "composition or scheme" to "Act 1985" substitute "voluntary arrangement proposed by the holder of the licence has been approved under Part VIII of the Insolvency Act 1986"; and for "composition or scheme" substitute "voluntary arrangement".
Section 10(5)	For the words from "composition or scheme" to "Act 1985" substitute "voluntary arrangement proposed by the holder of a justices' licence has been approved under Part VIII of the Insolvency Act 1986"; and for "composition or scheme" substitute "voluntary arrangement".
Industrial and Provident Societies Act 1965 (c.12): Section 55	For "Companies Act 1985" substitute "Insolvency Act 1986".
Medicines Act 1968 (c.67): Section 72(4)	For the words from "composition or scheme" to the end of the subsection substitute "voluntary arrangement proposed for the purposes of, and approved under, Part VIII of the Insolvency Act 1986".
Income and Corporation Taxes Act 1970 (c.10): Section 247(7)	For "Companies Act 1985" substitute "Insolvency Act 1986".
Section 265(5)	For "538 of the Companies Act 1985" substitute "145 of the Insolvency Act 1986".
Conveyancing and Feudal Reform (Scotland) Act 1970 (c.35): Schedule 3	In Standard Condition 9(2)(*b*), for "228 of the Insolvency Act 1985" substitute "421 of the Insolvency Act 1986".

Enactment	Amendment
Tribunals and Inquiries Act 1971 (c.62): Schedule 1	For paragraph 10A substitute— "10A. The Insolvency Practitioners Tribunal referred to in section 396 of the Insolvency Act 1986".
Superannuation Act 1972 (c.11): Section 5(2)	For "156 of the Insolvency Act 1985" substitute "310 of the Insolvency Act 1986"; and for "the said section 156" substitute "the said section 310".
Road Traffic Act 1972 (c.20): Section 150	In subsection (1)(*b*), for "228 of the Insolvency Act 1985" substitute "421 of the Insolvency Act 1986". In subsection (2), the same amendment.
Finance Act 1972 (c.41): Schedule 16	In paragraph 13(5), for "Companies Act 1985" substitute "Insolvency Act 1986".
Land Charges Act 1972 (c.61): Section 16(2)	For "207 of the Insolvency Act 1985" substitute "412 of the Insolvency Act 1986"; and for "Part III" substitute "Parts VIII to XI".
Matrimonial Causes Act 1973 (c.18): Section 39	For "section 174 of the Insolvency Act 1985" substitute "section 339 or 340 of the Insolvency Act 1986".
Powers of Criminal Courts Act 1973 (c.62): Section 39(3)	In paragraph (*d*), for "174(10) of the Insolvency Act 1985" substitute "341(4) of the Insolvency Act 1986".
Friendly Societies Act 1974 (c.46): Section 87(2)	For "Companies Act 1985" substitute "Insolvency Act 1986".
Social Security Pensions Act 1975 (c.60): Section 58	The section is to have effect as orginally enacted, and without the amendment made by paragraph 26(1) of Schedule 8 to the Insolvency Act 1985.
Schedule 3	At the end of paragraph 3(1) add— "or (in the case of a company not in liquidation)— (*a*) the appointment of a receiver as mentioned in section 40 of the Insolvency Act 1986 (debenture-holders secured by floating charge), or (*b*) the appointment of a receiver under section 53(6) or 54(5) of that Act (Scottish company with property subject to floating charge), or (*c*) the taking of possession by debenture-holders (so secured) as mentioned in section 196 of the Companies Act 1985". In paragraph 4, for the words from the beginning to "Act 1985" substitute "Section 196(3) of the Companies Act 1985 and section 387 of the Insolvency Act 1986 apply as regards the meaning in this Schedule of the expression 'the relevant date'.".

Enactment	Amendment
Recess Elections Act 1975 (c.66): Section 1(2)	In the definition of "certificate of vacancy", for "214(6)(*a*) of the Insolvency Act 1985" substitute "427(6)(*a*) of the Insolvency Act 1986".
Policyholders Protection Act 1975 (c.75): Section 5(1)(*a*)	For "Companies Act 1985" substitute "Insolvency Act 1986".
Section 15(1)	For "532 of the Companies Act 1985" substitute "135 of the Insolvency Act 1986".
Section 16(1)(*b*)	The same amendment as of section 5(1)(*a*).
Development Land Tax Act 1976 (c.24): Section 33(1)	For "538 of the Companies Act 1985" substitute "145 of the Insolvency Act 1986".

Restrictive Trade Practices Act 1976 (c.34):
    Schedule 1 ....
	For paragraph 9A (inserted by Insolvency Act 1985, section 217(4)) substitute—
	    "9A. Insolvency services within the meaning of section 428 of the Insolvency Act 1986".

Employment Protection (Consolidation) Act 1978 (c.44): Section 106(5)	In paragraph (*b*), for "228 of the Insolvency Act 1985" substitute "421 of the Insolvency Act 1986". In paragraph (*c*), for the words from "a composition or" to the end of the paragraph substitute "a voluntary arrangement proposed for the purposes of Part I of the Insolvency Act 1986 is approved under that Part".
Section 106(6)	The same amendment as of section 106(5)(*c*).
Section 122	In subsection (7), for "181 of the Insolvency Act 1985" substitute "348 of the Insolvency Act 1986"; and for "section 106" substitute "section 411". In subsection (9), for the words from "composition or scheme" to "Act 1985" substitute "voluntary arrangement proposed for the purposes of, and approved under, Part I or VIII of the Insolvency Act 1986".
Section 123(6)	For the words from "composition or scheme" to "Act 1985" substitute "voluntary arrangement proposed for the purposes of, and approved under, Part I or VIII of the Insolvency Act 1986".

Section 125(2)	For paragraph (*a*) substitute—
	    "(*a*) the following provisions of the Insolvency Act 1986—
	            (i) sections 175 and 176, 328 and 329, 348 and Schedule 6, and
	            (ii) any rules under that Act applying section 348 of it to the winding up of a company; and"

Section 127(1)	In paragraph (*b*), for "228 of the Insolvency Act 1985" substitute "421 of the Insolvency Act 1986". In paragraph (*c*), for the words from "composition or" to the end of the paragraph substitute "voluntary arrangement proposed for the purposes of Part I of the Insolvency Act 1986 is approved under that Part".
Section 127(2)	In paragraph (*c*), the same amendment as of section 127(1)(*c*).

Enactment	Amendment
Credit Unions Act 1979 (c.34): Section 6(1)	For "517(1)(*e*) of the Companies Act 1985" substitute "122(1)(*e*) of the Insolvency Act 1986"; and for "517(1)(*e*) of the Act of 1985" substitute "122(1)(*e*) of the Act of 1986".
Banking Act 1979 (c.37): Section 6(3)	In paragraph (*b*), for "Part XXI of the Companies Act 1985" substitute "Part V of the Insolvency Act 1986".

Section 18	In subsection (1), for "Companies Act 1985" substitute "Insolvency Act 1986"; and in paragraph (*a*) of the subsection for "518" substitute "123".
	In subsection (2), for "Companies Act 1985" substitute "Insolvency Act 1986"; and for "Part XXI" substitute "Part V".
	In subsection (4)—
	    in paragraph (*a*), for "Companies Act 1985" substitute "Insolvency Act 1986";
	    in paragraph (*b*), for "518 of the said Act of 1985" substitute "123 of the said Act of 1986"; and
	    in paragraph (*c*), for "Part XXI of the said Act of 1985" substitute "Part V of the said Act of 1986".

Section 19	In subsection (2), for paragraph (*ba*) substitute—
	    "(*ba*) in connection with any proceedings under any provision of—
	        (i) Part XVIII or XX of the Companies Act 1985, or
	        (ii) Parts I to VII of the Insolvency Act 1986 (other than sections 236 and 237)".
	In subsection (8), for paragraphs (*a*) and (*aa*) substitute—
	    "(*a*) for the references in subsection (2) to Part XVIII or XX of the Companies Act 1985 and Parts I to VII of the Insolvency Act 1986, there shall be substituted references to Parts V, VI and IX of the Companies Act (Northern Ireland) 1960 (the reference to sections 236 and 237 of the Act of 1986 being disregarded)".

Section 28	In subsection (3), in paragraph (*c*), for "83 of the Insolvency Act 1985" substitute "95 of the Insolvency Act 1986".
	In subsection (4), in paragraph (*a*), for "Part XXI of the Companies Act 1985" substitute "Part V of the Insolvency Act 1986".
	In subsection (6)(*b*), for sub-paragraphs (ii) to (iv) substitute—
	    "(ii) to be a member of a liquidation committee established under Part IV or V of the Insolvency Act 1986;
	    (iii) to be a member of a creditors committee appointed under section 301 of that Act; and
	    (iv) to be a commissioner under section 30 of the Bankruptcy (Scotland) Act 1985";
	    (v) to be a member of a committee of inspection appointed for the purposes of Part V or Part IX of the Companies Act (Northern Ireland)1960;
	and (in the passage following sub-paragraph (iv)) for "such a committee as is mentioned in paragraph (*b*)(ii) or (iv) above" substitute "a liquidation committee, creditors' committee or committee of inspection".

Enactment	Amendment
Section 28—*cont.*	In subsection (7), in paragraph (*b*), for the words from "section 116(4)" to the end of the paragraph substitute "section 261(1) of the Insolvency Act 1986 to any person in whom the property of the firm is vested under section 282(4) of that Act"
Section 31(7)	For paragraph (*a*) substitute— "(*a*) for England and Wales, under sections 411 and 412 of the Insolvency Act 1986"; and in paragraph (*b*) for "the said section 106" substitute "section 411 of that Act".
British Aerospace Act 1980 (c.26): Section 9(1)	In paragraph (*a*), for "Companies Act 1985" substitute "Insolvency Act 1986".
Public Passenger Vehicles Act 1981 (c.14): Section 19(3)	In paragraph (*a*), for "Chapter III of Part II of the Insolvency Act 1985" substitute "Part II of the Insolvency Act 1986".
Finance Act 1981 (c. 35): Section 55(4)	For "Companies Act 1985" substitute "Insolvency Act 1986".
Supreme Court Act 1981 (c.54): Section 40A(2)	For "section 179 of the Insolvency Act 1985" substitute "section 346 of the Insolvency Act 1986"; and for "621 of the Companies Act 1985" substitute "183 of the Insolvency Act 1986".
Trustee Savings Banks Act 1981(c.65): Section 31	In paragraph (*b*), for "666 to 669 of the Companies Act 1985" substitute "221 to 224 of the Insolvency Act 1986".
Section 54(2)	For "666(6) of the Companies Act 1985" substitute "221(6) of the Insolvency Act 1986".
Iron and Steel Act 1982 (c.25): Schedule 4	In paragraph 3(3) after "Companies Act 1985" insert "or the Insolvency Act 1986".
Civil Jurisdiction and Judgments Act 1982 (c.27): Section 18(3)	In paragraph (*ba*), for "213 of the Insolvency Act 1985" substitute "426 of the Insolvency Act 1986".
Schedule 5	In paragraph (1), for "Companies Act 1985" substitute "Insolvency Act 1986".

Enactment	Amendment
Insurance Companies Act 1982 (c.50):	
Section 53	For "Companies Act" (the first time) substitute "Insolvency Act 1986"; and for "Companies Act" (the second time) substitute "that Act of 1986".
Section 54	In subsection (1), for "the Companies Act" (the first time) substitute "Part IV or V of the Insolvency Act 1986"; and in paragraph (*a*), for "518 or sections 667 to 669" substitute "123 or sections 222 to 224".
	In subsection (4) for "Companies Act" (the first time) substitute "Insolvency Act 1986".
Section 55	In subsection (5), for "subsection (3) of section 540 of the Companies Act" substitute "section 168(2) of the Insolvency Act 1986".
	In subsection (6), for "631 of the Companies Act" substitute "212 of the Insolvency Act 1986".
Section 56	In subsection (4), for "Section 90(5) of the Insolvency Act 1985" substitute "Section 177(5) of the Insolvency Act 1986"; and for "section 90 of the said Act of 1985" substitute "section 177 of the said Act of 1986".
	In subsection (7), for "section 539(1) of the Companies Act" substitute "section 167 of, and Schedule 4 to, the Insolvency Act 1986".
Section 59	In subsection (1), for "106 of the Insolvency Act 1985" substitute "411 of the Insolvency Act 1986".
	In subsection (2), for "106 of the Insolvency Act 1985" substitute "411 of the Insolvency Act 1986"; and for "section 89 of, and Schedule 4 to, the Insolvency Act 1985" substitute "sections 175 and 176 of, and Schedule 6 to, the Insolvency Act 1986".
Section 96(1)	In the definition of "insolvent", for "517 and 518 or section 666 of the Companies Act" substitute "122 and 123 or section 221 of the Insolvency Act 1986".
Finance Act 1983 (c.28):	
Schedule 5	In paragraph 5(4), for "Companies Act 1985" substitute "Insolvency Act 1986".
Telecommunications Act 1984 (c.12):	
Section 68(1)	In paragraph (*a*), for "Companies Act 1985" substitute "Insolvency Act 1986".
County Courts Act 1984 (c.28):	
Section 98	For subsection (3) substitute— "(3) The provisions of this section have effect subject to those of sections 183, 184 and 346 of the Insolvency Act 1986".
Section 102	For subsection (8) substitute— "(8) Nothing in this section affects section 346 of the Insolvency Act 1986".
Section 109(2)	For "179 of the Insolvency Act 1985" substitute "346 of the Insolvency Act 1986".

Enactment	Amendment
Finance Act 1985 (c.54):	
Section 79	Omit the word "altogether"; and after "Companies Act 1985" insert "sections 110 and 111 of the Insolvency Act 1986".
Housing Act 1985 (c.68):	
Schedule 18	In paragraphs 3(4) and 5(3), for "228 of the Insolvency Act 1985" substitute "421 of the Insolvency Act 1986".

GENERAL NOTE

This Schedule in conjunction with s.439(2), effects consequential amendments to the enactments listed in column one, which are enactments which refer, or otherwise relate to those which are repealed and replaced by this Act or the Company Directors Disqualification Act 1986. The extent of each amendment is shown in column two.

TABLE OF DERIVATIONS

Note: The following abbreviations are used in this Table:—

"INS 1970"	=	The Insolvency Services (Accounting and Investment) Act 1970 (c.8).
"INS 1976"	=	The Insolvency Act 1976 (c.60)
"CA"	=	The Companies Act 1985 (c.6)
"IA"	=	The Insolvency Act 1985 (c.65).
"B(Sc)"	=	The Bankruptcy (Scotland) Act 1985 (c.66)

Provision	Derivation
1	IA s.20.
2	IA s.21.
3	IA s.22.
4	IA s.23(1)–(6), (7) (part).
5	IA s.24.
6	IA s.25.
7	IA s.26.
8	IA s.27.
9	IA s.28.
10	IA s.29.
11	IA s.30.
12	IA s.31.
13	IA s.32.
14	IA s.33.
15	IA s.34(1)–(8), (12).
16	IA s.34(9), (10).
17	IA s.35.
18	IA s.36.
19	IA s.37(1)–(3).
20	IA s.37(4), (5).
21	IA s.38.
22	IA s.39.
23	IA s.40.
24	IA s.41.
25	IA s.42.
26	IA s.43.
27	IA ss.34(11), 44.
28	CA s.488; IA s.45(1)
29	CA s.500; IA s.45(2).
30	CA s.489.
31	CA s.490.
32	CA s.491.
33	IA s.46.
34	IA s.47.
35	CA s.492(1), (2); IA Sch. 6 para. 16(2).
36	CA s.494.
37	CA s.492(3); IA Sch. 6 para. 16(3), (4).
38	CA s.498; IA Sch. 6 para. 17.
39	CA s.493.
40	CA s.196 (part); IA Sch. 6 para. 15(2), (3).
41	CA s.499.
42	IA s.48.
43	IA s.49.
44	IA s.50.
45	IA s.51.
46	IA s.52.
47	IA s.53.
48	IA s.54.
49	IA s.55.
50	CA s.487.
51	CA s.467.

Provision	Derivation
52	CA s.468.
53	CA s.469; IA s.56 (part).
54	CA s.470.
55	CA s.471; IA s.57.
56	CA s.472.
57	CA s.473; IA s.58.
58	CA s.474.
59	CA s.475; IA Sch. 6 para. 20(2).
60	CA s.476; IA Sch. 6 para. 21.
61	CA s.477; IA s.59.
62	CA s.478; IA s.60, Sch. 6 para. 13.
63	CA s.479; IA s.61.
64	CA s.480.
65	CA s.481; IA s.62.
66	CA s.482; IA s.63.
67	CA s.482A; IA s.64.
68	CA s.482B; IA s.65.
69	CA s.483.
70	CA ss.462(4), 484, 486 (part).
71	CA s.485.
72	CA s.724.
73	CA s.501.
74	CA s.502.
75	CA s.503.
76	CA s.504.
77	CA s.505.
78	CA s.506.
79	CA s.507; IA Sch. 6 para. 5.
80	CA s.508.
81	CA s.509.
82	CA s.510.
83	CA s.511.
84	CA s.572.
85	CA s.573.
86	CA s.574.
87	CA s.575.
88	CA s.576.
89	CA s.577; IA Sch. 6 para. 35.
90	CA s.578.
91	CA s.580.
92	CA s.581.
93	CA s.584; IA Sch. 6 para. 36.
94	CA s.585(1)–(4), (7).
95	IA s.83(1)–(6), (9), (10).
96	IA s.83(7) (part).
97	CA s.587; IA s.85(1).
98	IA s.85(2), (3), (6)–(8), (9)(*a*), (10).
99	IA s.85(4), (5), (9)(*b*), (*c*), (10).
100	CA s.589; IA Sch. 6 para. 37(1), (2).
101	CA s.590; IA Sch. 6 para. 38(2)–(4).
102	IA s.83(7) (part).
103	CA s.591; IA Sch. 6 para. 39.
104	CA s.592.
105	CA s.594; IA s.83(8).
106	CA s.595(1)–(5), (8).
107	CA s.597.
108	CA s.599.
109	CA s.600.
110	CA ss.582(1)–(4), (7), 593; IA Sch. 6 para. 40.
111	CA s.582(5), (6), (8).

Provision	Derivation
112	CA s.602.
113	CA s.603.
114	IA s.82.
115	CA s.604.
116	CA s.605.
117	CA s.512; IA Sch. 6 paras. 25, 26.
118	CA s.513.
119	CA s.514.
120	CA s.515; IA Sch. 6 para. 25.
121	CA s.516.
122	CA s.517.
123	CA s.518; IA Sch. 6 paras. 25, 27.
124	CA s.519; IA Sch. 6 para. 28.
125	CA s.520.
126	CA s.521.
127	CA s.522.
128	CA s.523.
129	CA s.574.
130	CA s.525; IA Sch. 6 para. 29.
131	IA s.66.
132	IA s.67.
133	IA s.68(1)–(4).
134	IA s.68(5), (6).
135	CA s.532; IA s.69(3).
136	IA s.70(1)–(3), (4)(*a*), (5), (6).
137	IA s.70(4)(*b*), (7)–(9).
138	CA s.535; IA s.71, Sch. 6 para. 30.
139	IA s.72.
140	IA s.73.
141	IA s.74.
142	IA s.75.
143	IA s.69(1), (2).
144	CA s.537.
145	CA s.538.
146	IA s.78.
147	CA s.549.
148	CA s.550.
149	CA s.552; IA Sch. 6 para. 32.
150	CA s.553.
151	CA s.554.
152	CA s.555.
153	CA s.557.
154	CA s.558.
155	CA s.559.
156	CA s.560.
157	CA s.562; IA Sch. 6 para. 33.
158	CA s.565.
159	CA s.566.
160	CA s.567; IA Sch. 6 para. 34.
161	CA s.569.
162	CA s.571.
163	IA s.94.
164	CA s.635.
165	CA ss.539(1)(*d*), (*e*), (*f*), 598; IA s.84(1), Sch. 6 para. 41.
166	IA s.84.
167	CA ss.539(1), (2), (2A), (3); IA Sch. 6 para. 31(2), (3).
168	CA s.540(3)–(6).
169	CA s.539(4), (5); IA Sch. 6 para. 31(4).
170	CA s.636.
171	IA s.86.

Provision	Derivation
172	IA s.79.
173	IA s.87.
174	IA s.80.
175	IA s.89(1), (2).
176	IA s.89(3), (4).
177	IA s.90.
178	IA s.91(1)–(4), (8).
179	IA s.91(5), (6).
180	IA s.91(7).
181	IA s.92(1)–(4), (9), (10).
182	IA s.92(5)–(8).
183	CA s.621.
184	CA s.622; IA Sch. 6 para. 25.
185	CA s.623; B(Sc) Sch. 7 para. 21.
186	CA s.619(4).
187	CA s.659; IA Sch. 6 para. 48.
188	CA s.637.
189	IA s.93.
190	CA s.638.
191	CA s.639.
192	CA s.641.
193	CA s.643; B(Sc) Sch. 7 para. 22.
194	CA s.644.
195	CA s.645.
196	CA s.646.
197	CA s.647.
198	CA s.648.
199	CA s.649.
200	CA s.650.
201	CA ss.585(5), (6), 595(6), (7).
202	IA s.76(1)–(3), (6).
203	IA s.76(4), (5), (7)–(10).
204	IA s.77.
205	IA s.81.
206	CA s.624; IA Sch. 6 para. 25.
207	CA s.625; IA Sch. 6 para. 42.
208	CA s.626; IA Sch. 6 para. 43.
209	CA s.627.
210	CA s.628.
211	CA s.629.
212	IA s.19.
213	CA s.630(1), (2); IA Sch. 6 para. 6(1).
214	IA ss.12(9), 15(1)–(5), (7), Sch. 9 para. 4.
215	CA s.630(3)–(6); IA s.15(6), Sch. 6 para. 6(2), (3).
216	IA s.17, Sch. 9 para. 5.
217	IA s.18(1) (part), (2)–(6).
218	CA s.632; IA Sch. 6 para. 44.
219	CA s.633.
220	CA s.665.
221	CA s.666.
222	CA s.667; IA Sch. 6 para. 50.
223	CA s.668; IA Sch. 6 para. 51.
224	CA s.669; IA Sch. 6 para. 52.
225	CA s.670.
226	CA s.671.
227	CA s.672.
228	CA s.673.
229	CA s.674.
230	IA ss.95(1), (2), 96(1).
231	IA ss.95(1), (2), 96(2).

Provision	Derivation
232	IA ss.95(1), (2), 96(3).
233	IA ss.95, 97.
234	IA ss.95(1), (2), 98.
235	IA ss.95(1), (2), 99.
236	IA ss.95(1), (2), 100(1), (2), (6).
237	IA s.100(3)–(5), (7).
238	IA ss.95(1)(*a*), (*b*), 101(1) (part)–(3).
239	IA ss.95(1)(*a*), (*b*), 101(1) (part), (4)–(7), (11).
240	IA s.101(8)–(11).
241	IA ss.95(1), 102.
242	CA s.615A; B(Sc) Sch. 7 para. 20.
243	CA s.615B; B(Sc) Sch. 7 para. 20.
244	IA ss.95(1)(*a*), (*b*), 103.
245	IA ss.95(1)(*a*), (*b*), 104.
246	IA ss.95(1)(*a*), (*b*), (2), 105.
247	IA s.108(3) (part), (4).
248	IA s.108(3) (part).
249	IA s.108(5).
250	IA s.108(6).
251	IA s.108(3) (part).
252	IA s.112(1) (part), (3).
253	IA ss.110, 111(1), (2), (3) (part).
254	IA s.111(4), (5).
255	IA s.112(1) (part), (2), (4)–(7)(*a*).
256	IA s.113.
257	IA s.114(1) (part), (2), (3).
258	IA s.115(1)–(6), (9), (10).
259	IA s.115(7), (8).
260	IA s.116(1)–(3), (6), (7).
261	IA s.116(4), (5).
262	IA s.117.
263	IA s.118.
264	IA s.119(1).
265	IA s.119(2), (3).
266	IA s.119(4)–(7).
267	IA s.120(1), (2), (7)–(9).
268	IA s.120(3), (4).
269	IA s.120(5).
270	IA s.120(6).
271	IA s.121.
272	IA s.122.
273	IA s.123(1), (2), (8).
274	IA ss.111(3) (part), 112(1) (part), (7)(*b*), 114(1) (part), 123(3)–(5).
275	IA s.123(6), (7).
276	IA s.124.
277	IA s.125.
278	IA s.126(1).
279	IA s.126(2)–(5).
280	IA s.127.
281	IA s.128.
282	IA s.129.
283	IA s.130.
284	IA s.131.
285	IA s.132.
286	IA s.133.
287	IA s.134.
288	IA s.135.
289	IA s.136.
290	IA s.137.
291	IA s.138.

Provision	Derivation
292	IA s.139.
293	IA s.140.
294	IA s.141.
295	IA s.142.
296	IA s.143.
297	IA s.144.
298	IA s.145.
299	IA s.146.
300	IA s.147.
301	IA s.148.
302	IA s.149.
303	IA s.150.
304	IA s.151.
305	IA s.152.
306	IA s.153.
307	IA s.154(1)–(4), (7).
308	IA s.155(1), (2), (4), (5).
309	IA ss.154(5), (6), 155(3).
310	IA s.156.
311	IA s.157.
312	IA s.158.
313	IA s.159.
314	IA s.160.
315	IA s.161(1)–(4), (10).
316	IA s.161(5).
317	IA s.161(6), (7).
318	IA s.161(8).
319	IA s.161(9).
320	IA s.162(1)–(4), (9), (10).
321	IA s.162(5)–(8).
322	IA s.163.
323	IA s.164.
324	IA s.165(1)–(4).
325	IA s.165(5), (6).
326	IA s.165(7), (8).
327	IA s.165(9).
328	IA s.166(1)–(5), (7).
329	IA s.166(6).
330	IA s.167.
331	IA s.168(1), (2), (4).
332	IA s.168(3).
333	IA s.169.
334	IA s.170(1)–(3).
335	IA s.170(4)–(9).
336	IA s.171.
337	IA s.172.
338	IA s.173.
339	IA s.174(1) (part), (2).
340	IA s.174(1) (part), (3)–(6), (12) (part).
341	IA s.174(7)–(11), (12) (part).
342	IA s.175.
343	IA s.176.
344	IA s.177.
345	IA s.178.
346	IA s.179.
347	IA s.180.
348	IA s.181.
349	IA s.182.
350	IA ss.183(1)–(3), (5), (6), 192.

Provision	Derivation
351	IA ss.184(5), 187(3)(*a*).
352	IA s.183(4).
353	IA ss.183(4), 184(1).
354	IA ss.183(4), 184(2)–(4).
355	IA ss.183(4), 185.
356	IA ss.183(4), 186.
357	IA ss.183(4), 187(1)(3)(*b*).
358	IA ss.183(4), 187(2).
359	IA ss.183(4), 188.
360	IA s.189.
361	IA s.190.
362	IA s.191.
363	IA s.193.
364	IA s.194.
365	IA s.195.
366	IA s.196(1), (2).
367	IA s.196(3)–(6).
368	IA s.196(7).
369	IA s.197.
370	IA s.198.
371	IA s.199.
372	IA s.200.
373	IA s.201.
374	IA s.202.
375	IA s.203.
376	IA s.204.
377	IA s.205.
378	IA s.206.
379	IA s.210.
380	—
381	IA s.211(1) (part).
382	IA s.211(1) (part), (2), (3).
383	IA s.211(1) (part), (5)–(7).
384	IA ss.209(1) (part), 211(1) (part).
385	IA s.211(1) (part), (4).
386	CA ss.196(2), 475(1); IA ss.23(7), 89(1), 108(3), 115(9), 166(1), Sch. 4 para. 1(1), Sch. 6 para. 15(3).
387	CA ss.196(2)–(4), 475(3), (4); IA ss.23(8), 115(10), Sch. 4 Pt. II para.1(2), (3), Sch. 6 paras. 15(4), 20(3).
388	IA s.1(2)–(6).
389	IA s.1(1).
390	IA ss.2, 3(1).
391	IA s.3(2)–(5).
392	IA ss.4, 11 (part).
393	IA s.5.
394	IA s.6.
395	IA s.7.
396	IA ss.8(1), (2), (6), 11 (part).
397	IA s.8(3)–(5).
398	IA s.9.
399	IA s.222.
400	IA s.223.
401	IA s.224.
402	IA s.225.
403	INS 1970 s.1; INS 1976 s.3; IA Sch. 8 para. 28.
404	INS 1970 s.2.
405	INS 1970 s.3; INS 1976 Sch. 2 para. 5.
406	INS 1970 s.4; INS 1976 Sch. 2 para. 6; IA Sch. 8 para. 17.
407	INS 1970 s.5; INS 1976 Sch. 2 para. 7.
408	INS 1970 s.6; INS 1976 Sch. 2 para. 8.

Provision	Derivation
409	INS 1970 s.7; INS 1976 Sch. 2 para. 9.
410	INS 1970 s.9(3); INS 1976 s.14(6); IA s.236(3)(i).
411	IA s.106.
412	IA s.207.
413	IA s.226.
414	IA ss.106(5), 107.
415	IA ss.207(5), 208(1)–(3), (5).
416	CA s.664; IA Sch. 6 para. 49.
417	CA s.667(2) (part).
418	IA s.209(1) (part), (2), (3).
419	IA ss.10, 11 (part).
420	IA s.227.
421	IA s.228.
422	IA s.229.
423	IA s.212(1), (3), (7) (part).
424	IA s.212(2).
425	IA s.212(4)–(6), (7) (part).
426	IA s.213.
427	IA s.214.
428	IA s.217(1)–(3).
429	IA s.221(1), (3)–(5).
430	CA s.730; IA passim.
431	CA s.731; IA s.108(1).
432	IA s.230.
433	IA s.231.
434	IA s.234.
435	IA s.233.
436	IA s.232 (part).
437	—
438	—
439	—
440	IA s.236(3).
441	CA s.745; IA s.236(4).
442	IA s.236(5).
443	—
444	—
Sch. 1	IA Sch. 3.
Sch. 2	CA s.471(1); IA s.57.
Sch. 3	CA Sch. 16.
Sch. 4	
Pt. I	CA ss.539(1)(*d*)–(*f*), 598(1).
Pt. II	CA ss.539(1)(*a*), (*b*), 598(2).
Pt. III	CA ss.539(2), 598(2).
Sch. 5	
Pt. I	IA s.160(2).
Pt. II	IA s.160(1).
Pt. III	IA s.160(6).
Sch. 6	IA Sch. 4 Pt. I, Pt. II paras. 2–4.
Sch. 7	IA Sch. 1.
Sch. 8	IA Sch. 5.
Sch. 9	IA Sch. 7.
Sch. 10	CA and IA passim.
Sch. 11	
para. 1	IA Sch. 9 para. 6.
2	IA Sch. 9 para. 7.
3	IA Sch. 9 para. 8.
4	IA Sch. 9 para. 9(1).
5	IA Sch. 9 para. 9(2).
6	IA Sch. 9 para. 9(3)–(5), (8).

Provision	Derivation
Sch. 11	
para. 7	IA Sch. 9 para. 9(6).
8	IA Sch. 9 para. 9(7).
9	IA Sch. 9 para. 10.
10	IA Sch. 9 para. 11.
11	IA Sch. 9 para. 12.
12	IA Sch. 9 para. 13.
13	IA Sch. 9 para. 14.
14	IA Sch. 9 paras. 15, 16, 17.
15	IA Sch. 9 para. 18.
16	IA Sch. 9 para. 19.
17	IA Sch. 9 para. 20.
18	IA Sch. 9 para. 21.
19	IA Sch. 9 para. 22.
20	IA Sch. 9 para. 24.
21	IA Sch. 9 para. 1.
22–28	—
Schs. 12–14	—

TABLE OF DESTINATIONS

COMPANIES ACT 1985 (c.6)—*continued*

INSOLVENCY ACT 1985 (c.65)—*continued*

INDEX

References are to section and Schedule number

Index

[4]